The Castle Community

The Personnel of English and Welsh Castles, 1272–1422

JOHN RICKARD

THE BOYDELL PRESS

First published 2002
The Boydell Press, Woodbridge

ISBN 0 85115 913 3

The Boydell Press is an imprint of Boydell & Brewer Ltd
PO Box 9, Woodbridge, Suffolk IP12 3DF, UK
and of Boydell & Brewer Inc.
PO Box 41026, Rochester, NY 14604–4126, USA
website: www.boydell.co.uk

A catalogue record for this book is available
from the British Library

Library of Congress Cataloging-in-Publication Data applied for

Printed in Great Britain from camera-ready copy supplied by the author by
Antony Rowe Ltd, Chippenham, Wiltshire

Contents

Acknowledgements

Thanks must go to my supervisor, Dr Andrew Ayton, for his enthusiastic support and direction during the production of this study, to Dr John Palmer and Prof. Anthony Goodman for their invaluable suggestions, and to P&O North Sea Ferries for the use of a laser printer at essential moments.

List of Tables

Abbreviations

Ancient Deeds	*Catalogue of Ancient Deeds*, vols. 1–6, London, 1890–1915
Bates	J.C. Bates, 'The Border Holds of Northumberland, vol. 1', *Archaeologia Aeliana*, 14 (1891)
BL	British Library
C.&W.A.&A.S.	*Transactions of the Cumberland and Westmorland Antiquarian and Archaeological Society*
CACW	*Calendar of ancient correspondence concerning Wales*, ed. J.G. Edwards, Cardiff, 1935
CAPW	*Calendar of Ancient Petitions Relating to Wales*, ed. W. Rees, Glamorgan, 1975
CChR	*Calendar of Charter Rolls*
CChW	*Calendar of Chancery Warrants, 1244–1326*, London, 1927
CCR	*Calendar of Close Rolls*
CFR	*Calendar of Fine Rolls*
CMR	*Calendar of Memoranda Rolls (Exchequer), Michaelmas 1326–Michaelmas 1327*, London, 1968
CPR	*Calendar of Patent Rolls*
CSD	*Calendar of Documents relating to Scotland*, ed. J. Bain, 4 vols., 1881–88
CWR	'Calendar of Welsh Rolls, 1277–1294', in *Calendar of various Chancery Rolls*, London, 1912, pp. 157–382
Davies	J.C. Davies, 'The Despenser war in Glamorgan', *Transactions of the Royal Historical Society*, 3rd series, 9 (1915), pp. 21–64
Denholm-Young	N. Denholm-Young, *Seigniorial Administration in England*, London 1937, reprinted 1963
EHR	*English Historical Review*
Fry	P.S. Fry, *Castles of Britain and Ireland*, Newton Abbot, 1996
Fryde	N. Fryde, *List of Welsh Entries in the Memoranda Rolls 1282–1343*, Cardiff, 1975
GCH	*Glamorgan County History, vol. 3, The Middle Ages*, ed. T.B. Pugh, Cardiff, 1971
GEC	*The Complete Peerage*, ed. G.E. Cokayne, revised by V. Gibbs, H.A. Doubleday and Lord Haward de Waldon, 12 vols. in 13, London, 1910–57

HKW II	R.A. Brown, and H.M. Colvin, *The History of the King's Works volume II: The Middle Ages (Part 2)*, London, 1963
IMisc	*Calendar of Inquisitions Miscellaneous, Chancery*, vols. 1–7, London, 1916–68
IPM	*Calendar of Inquisitions Post Mortem*, vols. 2–20, London, 1906–95
Issue Roll	*Issue Roll of Thomas Brantingham, 1370*, ed. F. Devon, London, 1835
Jacob	E.F. Jacob, *The Fifteenth Century, 1399–1485*, Oxford, 1961
JGR 1372–1376	*'John of Gaunt's Register, 1372–1376'*, ed. S. Armitage-Smith, Camden Society, 3rd Series 20 (1911) and 21 (1911)
JGR 1379–1383	*'John of Gaunt's Register, 1379–1383'*, ed. E.C. Lodge and R. Somerville, Camden Society, 3rd series, 56 (1937) and 57 (1938)
McKisack	M. McKisack, *The Fourteenth Century, 1307–1399*, Oxford, 1959
Morris	J. Morris, *The Welsh Wars of Edward I*, Oxford, 1901
Nthumb Petitions	*Northumberland Petitions*, ed. C.M. Fraser, Surtees Society, 176 (1966)
Norwell	*Wardrobe Book of William de Norwell, 12 July 1338 to 27 May 1340*, ed. M. Lyon, B. Lyon, H.S. Lucas and J. de Sturler, Brussels, 1983
P.P.	Parliamentary Peer
Percy Chartulary	*Percy Chartulary*, ed. M.T. Martin, Surtees Society, 117 (1909)
Platt	C. Platt, *The Castle in England and Wales*, London, 1981
Pevsner	N. Pevsner, *The Buildings of England*, London, 1951–
RCH	*Royal Commission on Historical Monuments*
Scalacronica	*'The Scalacronica of Sir Thomas Gray'*, trans. H. Maxwell, Glasgow, 1907
Somerville	R. Somerville, *Duchy of Lancaster: Vol. 1, 1265–1603*, London, 1953
VCH	*Victoria County History*

County Abbreviations

Beds	Bedfordshire
Berks	Berkshire
Cambs	Cambridgeshire
Cumb	Cumberland
Glou	Gloucestershire
Herts	Hertfordshire
Lancs	Lancashire

Leics	Leicestershire
Lincs	Lincolnshire
Nhants	Northamptonshire
Notts	Nottinghamshire
Nthumb	Northumberland
Oxf	Oxfordshire
Shrops	Shropshire
Staffs	Staffordshire
Warks	Warwickshire
Worcs	Worcestershire
Yrks	Yorkshire

Those references in the county data entirely in italics indicate references that do not directly refer to the castle in question, most often the date of death of a castle owner.

FOR MY MOTHER

Introduction

> So that scarcely could they [the Scots] find anything to do upon these Marches, except at Norham, where a [certain] knight, Thomas de Gray, was in garrison with his kinsfolk. It would be too lengthy a matter to relate [all] the combats and deeds of arms and evils for default of provender, and sieges which happened to him during the eleven years that he remained [there] during such an evil and disastrous period for the English. It would be wearisome to tell the story of the less [important] of his combats in the said castle.[1]

If there was a castle community,[2] then the Grays of Heton were amongst its most enthusiastic members. Three generations of the family, including the chronicler, served as constable of Norham castle (Northumberland), while his descendants owned Heaton Coldstream castle and Wark on Tweed castle (both Northumberland), at one point actually exchanging the newly built Heaton for the older, exposed, frontier castle at Wark.[3] This introduction examines those people who were directly involved with the ownership or management of castles in the 150 years from the coronation of Edward I to the death of Henry V. It will examine the level and nature of involvement with castles and how these factors changed over time. The aim is to add the human element to the stone, earth and timber of traditional castle studies.

The period of this study has been carefully chosen. At the start of this period, the castle was an established part of the landscape. Great magnates were still constructing mighty fortresses, while Edward I was shortly to begin building his great castles in north Wales. By the end of this period, the castle has been seen as being in decline. Those new castles that were being built are seen as attempts by newly wealthy men to establish themselves, while the last new royal castle, Queenborough castle (Kent), was sixty years in the past. This period also saw several episodes of great turmoil, in particular during the reigns of Edward II and Richard II, and this study will attempt to examine how the castle featured in these crises. In addition, Glendower's revolt at the end of the period saw the great castles of north Wales put to the test for the first time. These moments of crisis and upheaval should help illuminate the changing status of the castle.

One of the principal themes of this study is the relationship between the castle community – whether owners or constables – and political power. In many parts

[1] *Scalacronica*, pp. 60–61.
[2] This term will be used to refer to all those people who were involved with castles whether as owners, constables or holders of wardships.
[3] Bates, p. 341.

of Europe, this relationship would be taken for granted, with local political power being linked directly to ownership of the local castle.[4] However, the absence of this concept in writings focusing on England and Wales may be explained by the absence of the actual phenomenon as opposed to historians' unawareness of it. Only on the Welsh Marches may such a relationship be seen. In England, the role played in continental Europe by the castellanies would appear to have been performed by the county castle and the sheriff, a post that remained firmly under the king's control in all but a few counties. Instead, a more subtle link between the castle community and political power will have to be found. It will be searched for in the appointment of constables to royal castles, and in grants of ownership of castles, royal or forfeited. It may be found in the building activity that was so common in this period, or in the marriage alliances that created many of the great castle owning estates.

* * *

Before proceeding further, we must define what we mean by a 'castle'. For the purposes of this study, a castle will be defined as a residential building with a complete circuit of fortifications. This excludes towers attached to an otherwise unfortified building. Fortifications can include natural defences such as cliffs, as at Dunstanburgh castle (Northumberland). Where man-made fortifications are involved, they must allow the defenders to return missile fire, excluding simple walled sites with no provision for the use of missile weapons from the walls. Thus at the lowest level of fortifications, the presence or absence of crenellation on the walls could be the deciding factor. The material from which the fortifications have been built is not important. Wooden constructions could still be found at some castles in 1272, while brick built castles were capable of resisting long sieges.

The standard definition of the castle is that it is a building where the military predominates over the domestic. This definition is almost impossible to use in practice as it requires some quite arbitrary value judgements. Contemporary terms for the various buildings under consideration in this study were many and varied. *Castrum, turris* and *fortalicium* were common,[5] while other terms occur less frequently. However, the usefulness of the original terms is somewhat limited. Two examples should suffice to demonstrate the various problems. First, the name used at the time did not always reflect the size of the building in question, as an examination of the *Turris nostre London'* should indicate.[6] While an extreme case, this demonstrates the tendency for names to reflect tradition as much as architecture. The second problem is that these contemporary terms were not used

[4] Erik Fügedi, *Castles and Society in Medieval Hungary (1000–1437)*, Budapest, 1986; Robert Hajdu, 'Castles, Castellans and the structure of politics in Poitou, 1152–1272', *Journal of Medieval Studies*, 4 (1978), pp. 27–53.

[5] All three terms can be found in the 1415 survey of Northumberland castles printed in Cadwallader John Bates, 'The Border Holds of Northumberland', *Archaeologia Aeliana*, 14 (1891).

[6] 6 November 1338, *Treaty Rolls, vol. 2: 1337–1339*, London, 1972, no. 628.

consistently, even within a single document. The 1415 survey of Northumberland contains several such examples, such as that of Blenkinsopp castle (Northumberland). In the text it was described as *castrum*, while in the margin it is called *fortalicium.*[7] With such imprecision within a single source, we must be wary of making judgements based only on contemporary terminology.

This definition includes the free standing towers of the northern border. Almost by definition, a tower has a complete fortified circuit. Where there is still room for uncertainty is when a tower was known to have been merely part of a larger building of unknown type. At least some of these towers may have been strong points within otherwise unfortified manor houses. However, unless archaeological evidence proves otherwise, these northern towers will be included in this study.

Table 1.i

Comparative numbers of castles in active use

Date	Source	Total
1154	Brown[1]	274
1214	Brown[2]	272
1272	this study	337
1300	this study	405
1350	this study	438
1400	this study	563
1422	this study	583

[1] R.A. Brown, 'A list of castles, 1154–1216', *English Historical Review*, 74 (1959), p. 249.
[2] *ibid.*

Regardless of how tightly we define the castle, it must be admitted that for many 'borderline' fortifications, no clear decision can be made. Where a building has disappeared, or been incorporated into a more recent structure, the evidence for deciding what structure had existed at the time of this study does not exist. Furthermore, even for intact or recreateable sites, there is, and can be, no clear criterion. A weak castle to one historian will be a fortified manor house to another. For this study, such borderline cases will be considered as castles. Another important point must be made. Castles must, whenever possible, be viewed as they were during the period of this study, not as they now appear. It is easy to forget those parts of a castle that have disappeared when discussing the strength of the building. A good example of this is Stokesay Castle (Shropshire). Because of the origins of the owner, Laurence of Ludlow, a wealthy financier, and the windows of the great hall this is frequently dismissed as not a serious fortification.[8] However, an examination of the castle would suggest otherwise.

[7] Bates, p. 15.
[8] Platt, p. 103.

According to Fry,[9] the place was surrounded by a curtain wall thirty feet high and a moat. To suggest that it was not a serious castle, despite these fortifications, on the evidence of three windows, seems somewhat unconvincing.

This study will make use of eight regions in order to provide a clearer view than can be provided by a county by county view (see table 2.i). These regions are not all of the same size, and it is readily admitted that they are largely arbitrary; however their usefulness will hopefully become clear during this work.

There were more extant castles during this period than in earlier centuries. This may, in part, reflect increased knowledge on our part; but despite this we can see a significant increase in the number of castles in use across the period of this study, rising by nearly three quarters between 1272 and 1422.

Table 1.ii

Number of castles by region

	1272	Increase	1350	Increase	1422	% increase
Northern Border	27 (6th)	50	77 (2nd)	92	169 (1st)	525%
North	34 (5th)	9	43 (5th)	11	54 (5th)	58%
Midlands	47 (3rd)	20	67 (3rd)	4	71 (3rd)	51%
East Anglia	19 (8th)	4	23 (8th)	2	25 (8th)	32%
South East	39 (4th)	2	41 (6th)	5	46 (6th)	28%
South West	27 (6th)	8	35 (7th)	6	41 (7th)	52%
Marches	56 (2nd)	0	56 (4th)	9	65 (4th)	16%
Wales	82 (1st)	14	96 (1st)	4	100 (2nd)	22%
Total	331	107	438	133	571	73%

An increase in the number of active castles does not reflect accurately the amount of castle building in an area. Kent alone saw seven new castles built, suggesting that it accounted for the entire increase in the south east. However, Kent saw two castles go out of use, resulting in a lower overall increase. Indeed, of the 647 castles in this study, only 278 were active both in 1272 and 1422.

The most dramatic increase in castle numbers was on the northern border, which accounted for well over half of the total change, with an increase of 142 active castles, compared to only 108 for the rest of England and Wales combined. Compared to this the north, with the second largest growth, looks almost static. This castle building was a direct response to a constant, localised, military threat. As can also be seen, the bulk of this building on the northern border took place after 1350.

* * *

The most important documentary materials for this volume are to be found among the Chancery records. The Patent and Fine Rolls contain the records of

[9] Fry, p. 182.

appointment of most constables of royal castles across this period and are thus the chief primary source for this study. The Close Rolls also provide much of interest, although rarely concerning appointments. The Inquisitions *Post Mortem* are the main source for private castle ownership,[10] and the printed calendars provide the information required for this study. However, there are limits to this source. Firstly, castles not held in chief are rarely referred to, and then only during minorities of the tenant in chief. This automatically slants our information on castle ownership towards the tenants in chief, and obscures those castles held below that level. Secondly, the inquisitions do not always include all castles in an individual estate, especially for the larger estates of the comital community. Indeed, some castles only appear in one or two inquisitions across the entire period.

While the Chancery records contain appointments, the Exchequer records shed light on the running of these castles. Perhaps the most useful exchequer class is King's Remembrancer, Accounts Various (E.101) which includes the particulars of account submitted by numerous castle constables. These accounts are an especially strong source for the study of garrisons, and contain pay rolls and muster lists. Furthermore, they are evenly distributed across this period. It should be noted that the date of some of these documents is unclear, and several can only be dated from comparison with the lists of constables assembled from the Chancery records.[11] Despite this problem, this class provides much information that can not be found elsewhere.

The most important secondary source for this study is D.J. Cathcart King's *Castellarium Anglicanum,*[12] with its encyclopaedic listing of the castles of England and Wales. Next in importance is the *Victoria County History*, which often contains ownership details not otherwise available in print, as is the case for the linked castles of Castleton and Danby (Yorkshire), where the only published information on ownership is the complete descent of the manor contained in the *VCH.*[13] Also of use is Emery's *Greater Medieval Houses,*[14] which provides similar information for many castles. The main works on the castle do not provide much information for this study. Castle owners are not dealt with in any depth in those volumes by Fry,[15] Platt,[16] Pounds,[17] and Thompson,[18] while only Pounds

[10] For a discussion of the problems involved in the use of the Inquisitions see R.F. Hunnisett, 'The Reliability of Inquisitions as Historical Evidence' in D.A. Bullough and R.L. Storey, eds., *The Study of Medieval Records*, Oxford, 1971.

[11] For an example see E.101/19/26, listed in the PRO catalogue as accounts of Welsh castles for 1335 (9 Edw. III). However, both John de Wells, accounting as constable of Criccieth castle (Caernarvon), and Vivian de Staundon, accounting as constable of Harlech castle (Caernarvon), were actually in post in 1316 (9 Edw. II) and had both been replaced long before 1335.

[12] D.J. Cathcart King, *Castellarium Anglicanum*, 2 vols., New York, 1983.

[13] *VCH Yorkshire, North Riding vol. 2*, pp. 334–6.

[14] Anthony Emery, *Greater Medieval Houses of England and Wales, 1300–1500*, 2 vols., Cambridge, 1996 and 1999.

[15] Plantagenet Somerset Fry, *Castles of Britain and Ireland*, Newton Abbot, 1996.

[16] C. Platt, *The Castle in Medieval England and Wales*, London, 1981.

Footnotes 17 and 18 appear on the following page

included a section on the constable. There are few works on the constable, the best being Shelagh Bond's 1967 article on the constables of Windsor castle,[19] and Andrew Ayton's 1989 article on Corfe castle (Dorset).[20]

Problems of identification are rarely difficult within the castle community. Those individuals who served at, or owned, more than one castle were a small group and where there was any chance of confusion at the time, identifiers were used, as with John de Beauchamp 'of Warwick' and 'of Somerset', both active in the 1350s, who are clearly identified in the records. One problem that does occur is that of distinguishing between a single long career, and the careers of father and son. This is most common at the county castles, where important local families could expect to serve over several generations. At York castle alone we find four examples of this. As a general rule, if more than thirty years elapse between two occurrences of a given name and no other relevant information is available, it will be assumed that two different individuals are involved, although no relationship between the two will be assumed. Thus, the John Bygod who served as constable of York castle in 1373 will be assumed to be a different man from the John Bygod who appears forty–five years later.

---

[17] N.J.G. Pounds, *The Medieval Castle in England and Wales, a social and political history*, Cambridge, 1990.

[18] M.W. Thompson, *The Decline of the Castle*, Cambridge, 1987; M.W. Thompson, *The Rise of the Castle*, Cambridge, 1990.

[19] Shelagh Bond, 'The Medieval Constables of Windsor Castle', *English Historical Review*, 82 (1967), pp. 225–249.

[20] Andrew Ayton, 'William de Thweyt, esquire, Deputy constable of Corfe Castle in the 1340s', *Somerset and Dorset Notes and Queries*, 32 (1989), pp. 731–738.

Castle Ownership

This period saw a change in the balance between the various groups of castle owners (see table 2.xxiii). The most obvious trend over time was that the number of castles owned at the lowest level of the castle owning community – knights or below – more than doubled during this period. Indeed, by 1350 this constituted the largest group of castles. However, the estates and castles involved were small. At the top stratum of society, we can see a changing balance between the king and the comital community. In 1300, Edward I controlled more castles than the comital community, but by 1350, the comital community had overtaken Edward III. Richard II had fallen further behind, and only his Lancastrian castles gave Henry IV a numerical advantage in 1400. However, we should not over-emphasize the numerical imbalance. While the king's estates were united, individual estates within the comital community never rose much above twenty castles, while the majority were much smaller. Only if the entire comital community was united could they equal the crown in the number of castles they controlled.

The king's castles

The royal castles represent the largest block of castles, with seventy-four long term royal castles,[21] and over two hundred that passed into royal ownership at least once during this period. Most of the core seventy-four were amongst the first rank of English and Welsh castles, including the great north Welsh castles of Edward I, and ending with Edward III's foundation, Queenborough castle on the Isle of Sheppey. They were relatively evenly spread throughout England and Wales, with the exception of the midlands, where they were almost completely absent, and Wiltshire, Hampshire and Kent, where they were present in large numbers.

Within the block of royal castles there were several clearly defined sub-groups. The status of individual royal castles could alter, and on occasion a castle could even leave royal ownership. Very few royal castles had a simple history during this period, with many passing through a variety of hands, some of whom were uncontroversial figures close to the king, like the queen, while others were controversial figures such as Piers Gaveston. The most important sub-groups were composed of castles linked to a sheriff; castles in direct royal control; castles held by the queen; and castles held by the heir to the throne.

The first group were the county castles. The constables of these castles were also the county sheriffs. The dual appointments were made as a single grant, normally recorded on the Fine Rolls, with the appointment as constable clearly coming second to that as sheriff. Twenty-five castles fall into this group at some time. Of those castles, eight – Appleby, Arundel, Gloucester, Guildford, Launceston, Lincoln and Nottingham – were linked temporarily, often after a

[21] Including those held by the heir to the throne and the queen.

forfeiture or during the wardship of a private castle. At most of the remaining seventeen county castles, there were some breaks in the connection between county and castle. Only at York castle, Canterbury castle (Kent) and Newcastle upon Tyne castle (Northumberland) was there no discontinuity in the link between the county and the castle.

These changes in status fall into two main categories. The first concerns castles that became independent royal castles for a limited period – Oxford from 1311–22, Norwich and Northampton from 1380–91. In each case constables were appointed for life, and only at Northampton did the split survive the death of the first such appointee. The second category consists of those castles that were permanently split from their county: Carlisle (1382), Cambridge (1399), Colchester (1376), Winchester (1385), Shrewsbury (1339), and Old Sarum castles (1382). In each case the newly independent constables can be traced for the rest of the period, and in every way resemble the more established independent royal castles. Finally, Sherborne castle (Dorset) became a private castle in 1331 when granted to William de Montague, and although sheriff-constables continued to be recorded for another two years, it remained in private hands for the rest of this period.

The second group of royal castles contains those that were independent of any of the other groups, under the King's direct control. Membership of this group was fluid, with large numbers of castles leaving it whenever there was a prince of Wales or to enter the queen's dower, but it was the largest group, and included a network of castles across most of the country. Only six castles remained in this group throughout the entire period – Windsor (Berkshire), Dover (Kent), the Tower of London, Bamborough (Northumberland), Scarborough (Yorkshire) and Rochester (Kent) – with another ten remaining in this group for over one hundred years during this period. Such independent royal castles were absent only from the marcher stronghold of south Wales, and the northern border, where Bamborough castle was the only representative.

The single largest source of newly aquired royal castles in this period were the twenty-eight Lancastrian castles that Henry Bolingbrook brought with him when he seized the throne, increasing the number of royal castles to over 100, from under eighty during the reign of Richard II. Under Henry IV and Henry V, this group of castles stayed almost entirely in royal hands. Only Brecon and Hay castles (both Brecknock), which went to Anne, lady Stafford in 1421 in a redistribution of the Bohun inheritance, and Grosmont castle (Monmouth), granted to Joan, widow of William de Beauchamp in 1413, left royal control.

The queen's castles

Fifty castles passed through the dowries of one or more of the nine queens of England who lived during this period.[22] Only Isabella of France (1396–1409) and

[22] See tables 2.xxxv to 2.xlii.

Catherine of Valois (1420–37), whose royal husbands died soon after their marriage, did not hold castles.

The number of castles involved remained remarkably consistent until the death of Queen Philippa. While Eleanor of Provence and Eleanor of Castile individually held fewer castles than their successors, their estates existed simultaneously and contained nineteen castles, while Queen Isabella never held more than seventeen castles at any one time. This level of allocation placed the queen above all but the greatest of the earls as castle owners. This may have been intended to secure the status of a widowed queen.

Table 1.iii

Castles held by the queens of England

Name	Marriage–Death	Husband	No of Castles[1]
Eleanor of Provence	1236–91	Henry III	9
Eleanor of Castile	1254–90	Edward I	10
Margaret	1299–1318	Edward I	17
Isabella of France	1308–58	Edward II	28
Philippa of Hainault	1328–69	Edward III	15
Anna	1382–94	Richard II	11
Joan of Navarre	1401–37	Henry IV	10

[1] Total number of different castles held rather than largest number held at any one time.

These estates were not static. Both Queen Margaret and Queen Isabella saw the resumption of their entire estates in the face of a threat from France,[23] while others saw minor changes such as Eleanor of Castile's loss of Tickhill and Stamford castles (Yorkshire) as part of a reorganisation of her estates. The extent of Queen Isabella's estates fluctuated frequently. She did not gain any castles until 1313, five years after her marriage and one year after the birth of the future Edward III, and had to wait until the death of Queen Margaret in 1318 to gain any of her castles. Of the castles that had been originally granted to Isabella, only Mere (Wiltshire) remained to her in 1358.

The castles held by the queen were concentrated in the same areas as the other royal castles. At the core of the queen's estates were eleven castles that were held by three or more queens. Due to the overlap between Queen Eleanor of Castile and Queen Eleanor of Provence no castles were held by all seven queens. However, only Odiham castle (Hampshire) was held by six queens, and only Devizes castle (Wiltshire) and Rockingham castle (Northamptonshire) by five.

The most obvious source for the queen's castles were the estates of her predecessor, although in four cases the king's mother was still alive when her son married. However, this made it more likely that the new queen would gain at least some of those castles at the death of the king's mother: after her death eleven of

[23] *Fœdera, conventiones, litteræ*, ed. Thomas Rymer, revised edn by A. Clarke, F. Holbrooke and J. Coley, ii, 1818, p. 569.

Queen Margaret's castles passed to Queen Isabella, while Queen Philippa gained seven of Isabella's castles after her fall in 1330. It was only when there was a period without a queen that this succession failed, with Queen Anne only gaining four castles from her predecessor.

Queen Isabella's infamous greed during her time in power was not reflected in the acquisition of castles. Only three previously private castles came into her hands during this period, and of those, Arundel (Sussex) and Hanley (Worcester) had both been forfeited castles. Pressure does appear to have been applied to Mary de St. Pol, widow of Aymer de Valence, who surrendered Hertford castle to Isabella in March 1327, but doubt is cast on this by the case of Haverford castle (Pembroke), also surrendered by Mary de St. Pol in 1327, but not acquired by Queen Isabella until 1331, after her fall from power, which suggests that Mary wished to be free of the castles.

One influence on the allocation of estates to the queen was their financial value, which had to match the value agreed before her marriage. This was sometimes explicit in the allocation of dower lands, as was the case for Queen Philippa in 1331.[24] Altogether these estates were valued at £4000, of which £2463 came from estates that included castles. However, the income from these estates came not from the castle, but from the associated honours, towns and manors.

Castles of the heir to the throne

The heirs to the throne were amongst the greatest castle owners in the country. Their castles were a part of their royal inheritance granted to them early. The significance of this split from the bulk of the king's estates varied considerably, depending on the age of the prince.

Edward of Caernarvon's time as heir to the throne saw the beginnings of the great estates of the later heirs. He was earl of Chester and prince of Wales, and although he never gained as many castles as the later princes of Wales, both Beaumaris castle (Anglesey) and Conway castle (Caernarvon) were to be found in his hands. In contrast, Edward III had very limited estates during his father's reign, owning only Carisbrooke castle (Hampshire), Chester castle, Rhuddlan castle (Flint) and Flint castles. Even at these castles, his impact must have been minimal, he was king before he came of age.

The most celebrated heir to the throne in this period was Edward, the Black Prince, with twenty-six castles, mostly connected to his titles as earl of Chester (1333), duke of Cornwall (1337) and prince of Wales (1343). This group of castles then remained intact for thirty-six years until his death. This made him a regional landowner, with very few castles outside Wales and the south-west. The forty years he spent as heir to the throne gave him time to have a real impact on his estates. In contrast, Richard II's time as heir can be seen as a coda to his father's.

24 1 January 1331, *CPR 1330–1334*, p. 55.

His council barely had time to confirm the Black Prince's appointments before the death of Edward III catapulted Richard to the throne.

Table 1.iv
Castles of the Black Prince

Source	Castles
Earl of Chester	Beeston (Cheshire), Chester (Cheshire), Flint (Flint), Rhuddlan (Flint)
Duke of Cornwall	Berkhamsted (Hertford), Launceston (Cornwall), Mere (Wiltshire), Restormel (Cornwall), Tintagel (Cornwall), Trematon (Cornwall), Wallingford (Berkshire) also Exeter (Devon) and Lydford (Devon) indirectly.
Prince of Wales	Beaumaris (Anglesey), Caernarvon (Caernarvon), Conway (Caernarvon), Criccieth (Caernarvon), Aberystwyth (Cardigan), Cardigan (Cardigan), Carmarthan (Carmarthan), Dryslwyn (Carmarthan), Dynevor (Carmarthan), Newcastle Emlyn (Carmarthan), Harlech (Merioneth)
Forfeited by Mortimer	Montgomery (Montgomery)
From Queen Isabella	Castle Rising (Norfolk), Haverford West (Pembroke)

In the aftermath of Henry Bolingbroke's victory in 1399, the titles and estates of the Black Prince were revived for Prince Henry after a twenty-two-year gap. However, before Prince Henry even came of age, the Glendower revolt began, and his estates changed from a source of prestige and income to a source of worry and endless financial drain. His correspondence with his father was filled with calls for more money, with all but three of his Welsh castles coming under attack by Glendower's men, and all but three of the attacked castles falling to the Welsh at least once.[25] While this constant strain cannot have endeared Wales to the Prince, it did provide him with his military training.

Privately Owned Castles

The majority of castles in England and Wales were the property of private landowners, ranging from the great castles of John of Gaunt down to the towers of the Scottish border, owned by the local gentry. As important as the individual was the family, and here we will examine both.

These castles were held by a variety of types of tenure.[26] The majority of privately owned castles were held in chief from the crown. In many parts of England, tenure in chief was entirely dominant. A small number of castles were held by mesne tenants, most commonly in Wales and the marches, more

[25] R.R. Davies, *The Revolt of Owain Glyn Dwr*, Oxford, 1995, pp. 229–262.
[26] Tenure at castles used the same legal mechanisms as all land holding in this period, for which see B. Lyon, *A Constitutional and Legal History of Medieval England*, New York, 1960.

infrequently elsewhere, as in Yorkshire, where only four out of fifty-six were held by mesne tenants.

Great efforts were made to avoid or alter standard inheritance laws. However, there was little consistency of action. Within a single estate, a wide range of tenures could occur. Of the four castles owned by Simon de Burley (d.1388), Newcastle Evelyn (Carmarthen) was held for life, Lyonshall (Hereford) and Llanstephan (Carmarthen) in fee simple and Leybourne (Kent) in tail male.

* * *

Table 1.v

'Level' of Castle Ownership by type of Owner

	Comital Community		Parliamentary Peers		Lesser Lay Landowners		Overall	
Castles	Men	Castles	Men	Castles	Men	Castles	Men	Castles
1	5	5	146	146	265	265	448	448
2	15	30	49	80	40	80	88	196
3	11	33	16	48	11	33	50	150
4	14	56	10	40	1	4	26	80
5	11	55	5	25			17	85
6	8	48	1	6			10	60
7	4	28	2	14			4	28
8	6	48	0	0			8	74
9	5	45	1	9			8	71
10	3	30	1	10			4	40
11	4	44	0	0			4	44
12	2	24	0	0			2	24
14	1	14	0	0			1	14
17	1	17	0	0			1	17
18	3	54	1	18			4	72
21	1	21					1	21
22	1	22					1	22
24	1	24					1	24
25	2	50					2	50
28	0	0					1	28
Total	98	648	223	396	317	382	681	1548

The distribution of castles among lay landowners, viewed in terms of the number of castles each person held, can be summarised in two ways: in terms of the number of owners holding a particular number of castles (or as we shall term it, holding at a particular 'level'); and the total number of castles held by owners at a particular 'level' of castle-holding. If we examine the owners of one castle from these two viewpoints, we see that from the first viewpoint, two thirds of castle owners across our period owned a single castle, making them the largest group of castle owners. However, from the second viewpoint, less that one third of castles across the period were in single castle estates.

The most important private castle owners were the comital community.[27] This group included some of the most powerful people in the country and this was reflected in both the number and type of castles they owned. The comital community in this period contained 112 individuals, whose estates have several elements in common, and that clearly distinguished most of them from other private estates.

The 112 members of the comital community owned a total of 648 castles: over one third of all private castles were in the hands of one sixth of the castle owners. Indeed, only two non-comital estates contained six or more castles, and none contained ten or more. Within the comital community, only fifteen individuals owned ten or more castles. Of these, five were the Mortimer earls of March and five the earls and dukes of Lancaster. The greatest of the remaining five was the last Clare earl of Gloucester, who owned twenty one castles. Towards the end of the period the eleven castles of Thomas Despenser, earl of Gloucester, included ten from the Clare estates. John Warenne, earl of Surrey (d.1347) and Richard fitzAlan, earl of Arundel (d.1397) were members of established comital families whose personal estates increased beyond their family inheritance, in Arundel's case by inheriting Warenne's castles. Finally, Edward, duke of York combined the seven castles he inherited from his father with four he had gained in his own right.

These comital castles were spread across much of England and Wales, and were only absent in the area around London (in 1300 there were none from Hampshire to Norfolk) and in Edward I's newly conquered principality of Wales. Individual families' estates were more concentrated, although the earls and duke of Lancaster had concentrations of castles in south Wales, the midlands, Lancashire and Lincolnshire. More typical were the estates of the earls of Warwick, with one concentration in the midlands and another in Glamorgan. All of the greatest castle owners had lands in the castle rich areas of Wales or the Marches.

The comital community, in keeping with their wealth and status, owned some of the greatest castles in the country. Even the Veres, amongst the poorest of the earls, owned Hedingham castle (Essex), containing one of the largest Norman great towers, as a constant reminder of their rank. At the top of society, the earls and dukes of Lancaster owned a group of great castles. Amongst the nineteen castles that were held by three or more members of the house of Lancaster, there were no weak links. They included Pontefract (Yorkshire) and Kenilworth (Warwickshire), two of the greatest castles in the country, both in military and residential terms. Even Whitecastle (Monmouth), renowned for its lack of comfort, was militarily powerful. In contrast, many of the newly created members of the comital community held lesser castles. Thomas Percy, earl of Worcester even had to rely on his own family, who granted him Warkworth castle (Northumberland) in 1400. There were a limited number of great castles in England and Wales, and only at a time of mass forfeitures were they available to the king to redistribute.

[27] Defined as those men of the rank of earl or higher.

The parliamentary peerage were less important as castle owners than the comital community, owning on average one third as many castles, although several families amongst them showed a remarkable level of stability. The Clifford family held the same group of five castles across eight generations, despite their forfeiture by Roger de Clifford in 1322,[28] the Audleys of Heighley held the same two castles from 1282 to 1391, while the Ros of Hamelak held Helmsley castle (Yorkshire) and Belvoir castle (Leicestershire) for this entire period. This level of stability was remarkable, and cannot be matched by any other noble family.

The knights and lesser gentry gained rapidly in importance as castle owners during the first half of this period. The number of castles they owned increased from fifty-one in 1300 to ninety-three in 1350, and to 114 in 1400, or one in five of the total. By 1430, there were probably no more than 200 knights in the country.[29] Although our period closes in 1422, we can still safely say that even in 1430 close to 100 of these knights were castle owners. Although they tended to own weak castles, and many of the towers, these were not all small or insignificant since they included such buildings as Bodiam castle (Sussex) and Dudley castle (Staffordshire). Members of this group owned one or at best two castles, which were almost invariably close together, for example Ralph Basset of Sapcote (d.1378), who owned Benefield castle in north-east Northamptonshire and Castle Bytham in south-west Lincolnshire, only fifteen miles apart.

Private castle ownership can be split into three rough geographical areas. The first is south Wales and the marches, where the bulk of castles were owned by the marcher lords, such as the Clare earls of Gloucester, Mortimer earls of March or the earls and dukes of Lancaster. The second area was the border facing Scotland, where few members of the comital community owned castles, the bulk being were in the hands of families of lower rank. Finally comes the rest of England, where there was a mix of castle owners, with all groups within the castle-owning community present in a similar ratio to the national figures.

Very few estates survived intact and in a single family across this period. However, over four hundred castles never came into the king's hands, suggesting that for two thirds of castles, the normal rules of inheritance did operate. Even when a family survived, there was often little stability. For the earls and dukes of Lancaster there were two breaks: first the forfeiture of Thomas of Lancaster, then the extinction of the male line following the death of Henry of Grosmont, after which it was only the death of his daughter Maud that preserved the family estates intact.

Normal inheritance rules account for the vast majority of changes of castle ownership. This could be a rapid process – at Swine castle (Yorkshire) only fourteen days elapsed between the death of Constance, widow of Peter de Mauley VI, and the grant of livery to her grandson, Peter de Mauley VIII. Only where the

[28] *GEC III*, p. 291.

[29] P. Coss, *The Knight in Medieval England, 1000–1400*, Stroud, 1993, p. 134.

heir was under-age was this process interrupted. Any attempt to interfere with direct male inheritance was controversial, as Richard II discovered in 1399.

The easiest way to gain large numbers of castles was by marriage. Although great heiresses were never common, a good marriage could greatly boost a family's fortunes. The best examples of this come from the earls and dukes of Lancaster. The fortunes of Thomas, earl of Lancaster, were greatly increased by his marriage to Alice de Lacy, as a result of which he gained eight castles on the death of her father. Eventually, the Lancastrian estates themselves passed to heiresses, and it was through his marriage to Philippa of Lancaster that John of Gaunt gained the majority of his castles, rising from earl of Richmond and owner of a single castle, Richmond (Yorkshire), to duke of Lancaster and one of the greatest castle owners in the country, well above all of his brothers other than the Black Prince.

Another major source of new castles was royal grant. However, very few castles were available for the crown to distribute without controversy. The grant of a royal castle to a private individual could take various forms. The most advantageous from the recipient's point of view was fee tail, the equivalent of most private ownership; then tale male, or descent through the male line only; and finally, ownership for life, with the level of rights over the castle made clear at the time of the grant.

The largest group of castles available for distribution by the king were those that had been forfeited. Forty-five castle owners, holding between them over 200 castles, forfeited their estates during this period (see table 2.xi). However, the majority of these forfeitures took place in two short periods. The first stretched from 1322 until 1330, and saw the single largest number of forfeitures. Fifty castles were forfeited in 1322 alone, as well as all but one of the forfeitures of Edward III's reign. The second started in 1388 and lasted until the rebellions of Richard II's supporters in 1400. Each of these periods saw over 100 castles forfeited. In contrast, the remaining 130 years of our period saw very few forfeitures. Moreover, most of these forfeited castles were eventually returned to the heirs of their original owner, often because the original beneficiary had himself forfeited. An example of this is Warwick castle, forfeited by Thomas Beauchamp, earl of Warwick in 1397, then granted to Thomas de Holland, earl of Kent, who himself forfeited in 1400 after which the castle returned to the Beauchamps.

Some castles changed hands after illegal actions against the then owner by a figure of national importance. The first such case was also the most blatant, and amounted to a private war between Thomas of Lancaster and John de Warenne. The hostilities were triggered by Warenne's kidnapping of Alice de Lacy, Lancaster's wife. The conflict reached such a level that Sandal castle (Yorkshire) was damaged during an armed attack,[30] and by 1319 Warenne had to admit defeat, handing four of his castles to Lancaster.[31] In comparison, the actions of the

[30] King, p. 524.

[31] Conisborough castle (Yorkshire), Dinas Bran castle (Denbigh), Caergwrle castle (Flint) and Sandal castle (Yorkshire), surrendered on 1 January 1319, *CPR 1317–1321*, p. 264.

younger Despenser were less public, although no less effective. First to suffer was Elizabeth de Comyn, an heiress of Aymer de Valence, earl of Pembroke, who was imprisoned until she transferred lands including Goodrich castle (Hereford) to Despenser in 1325. The same happened to John de Sutton, who was only freed after he had surrendered Dudley castle (Staffordshire) to Despenser in 1326.

Very few castle-owning families died out through lack of an heir. Even when the direct line ended, as with the death of John de Warenne, earl of Surrey, in 1347, his lands passed to his nephew, Richard fitzalan, earl of Arundel. Even when Roger Bigod, earl of Norfolk, died in 1306 leaving no heirs, his estates only returned to the king after the death of his widow Alice.

The least common method to gain a castle was by purchase. The best known example was that of Carisbrooke castle (Hampshire) by Edward I from Isabella de Forz, who sold him the reversion of the castle in 1276, and finally handed it over in 1296, just before her death. More straightforward was the sale of Broughton castle (Oxfordshire) bought by William de Wykeham, bishop of Winchester in 1377 when it had fallen into the hands of the husbands of heiresses.[32] At least six castles were leased during this period, and in each case debt appears to have been the motivation. Perhaps the most in debt was Robert de Neville. He owed £140 to Michael de la Pole, £2000 to Michael's father William,[33] and £1000 to Sir Robert de Swlyngton.[34] The lease of Hornby castle to Michael was part of a complex series of deals made to gain his release from Newgate prison, where he had been sent after defaulting on his debt to William de la Pole, and although he regained Hornby within months, it was only to grant the castle to Sir Robert de Swlyngton and his heirs.

* * *

One fifth of all private castle owners in this period were women (see table 1.vi). Although for many women this ownership was only short term, some held their castles for decades. Women generally acquired castles from three sources. First were those castles inherited from a blood relative and thus owned by the woman in her own right. Second were those castles that had been placed in jointure during marriage and which were held by the widow by virtue of that arrangement. Third were the widow's dower castles. The first and second groups are often visible in the records even during marriage, while the third group rarely appear until after the husband's death. Only in a very few cases is it possible to say whether there were set dower castles. The Mortimer family, with six widows across this period, is the best such case, and here Bridgewater castle (Somerset) appears to have been the main dower castle, held by four of the six widows, for a total of over fifty years, supported by a different group of castles for each widow. Where an heiress survived to become a widow, she almost invariably regained control of her

32 *VCH Oxfordshire vol. IX*, p. 89.
33 *CCR 1360–1364*, p. 390.
34 *CCR 1360–1364*, p. 403.

original castles. This can be seen with Eleanor de Bohun, who inherited Caldicot (Monmouth), Huntingdon (Hereford) and Pleshey (Essex), all back in her hands at her death in 1399, and with her daughter, Anne, who inherited the same group of castles, and once again regained them after the death of her husband, Edmund earl of Stafford, in 1403. It was common for a woman to hold castles by more than one method. A typical example of this was Elizabeth, widow of Nicholas de Audley. She held Llandovery castle (Carmarthen) and Newport castle (Pembroke) in jointure from July 1391 and Redcastle (Shropshire) from November of the same year, giving her three of her husband's four castles. The number of castles held could vary even in the same family. Philippa, widow of Roger de Mortimer (d.1360), held six of his twelve castles,[35] while Eleanor, widow of Roger de Mortimer (d.1398), held only three of his twenty-one castles.[36] In 'single castle' estates, the castle had often been placed in jointure, and so went to the widow, despite the presence of an heir, as at Wilton castle (Yrks), held by Agnes, widow of Ralph Bulmer after his death in 1406, keeping out their son. Few castles stayed in female hands for long, either because an heiress was betrothed before coming of age, or married before inheriting, while widows often remarried. However, there were exceptions, the greatest of whom was Mary de St. Pol, widow of Aymer de Valence, who retained control of Fotheringay castle (Northampton) from his death in 1324 until her own in 1377, fifty-three years later.

Table 1.vi
Castle ownership by women

No. of Castles	Women	Castles
1	106 (64.3%)	106 (34.%)
2	33 (21.2%)	66 (22.7%)
3	7 (4.2%)	21 (6.8%)
4	5 (3.0%)	20 (6.5%)
5	2 (0.6%)	10 (1.6%)
6	5 (3.0%)	30 (9.7%)
7	2 (1.2%)	14 (4.5%)
8	1 (0.6%)	8 (2.6%)
11	1 (0.6%)	11 (3.6%)
12	2 (1.2%)	24 (7.8%)
Total	**165**	**309**

Church-owned castles

The church was one of the greatest castle owners in this period, with nearly forty castles and towers, scattered across the entire country, from Saltwood castle (Kent) to Norham castle (Northumberland). However, the church was not a single

[35] *CCR 1360–1364*, pp. 46 and 81; *CPR 1370–1374*, p. 333; *IPM XV*, no. 564.
[36] 16 March 1399, *CCR 1396–1399*, p. 451.

unified body, and control of these castles was spread from the archbishop of Canterbury, down to local parish priests with their simple towers in Northumberland.

Table 1.vii

Church owned castles

Holder	Castles
Archbishop of Canterbury	Saltwood (Kent)
Archbishop of York	Hexham (Nthumb)
Bishop of Carlisle	La Rose (Cumb), Northallerton (Yrks)
Bishop of Chichester	Amberley (Sussex)
Bishop of Coventry and Lichfield	Eccleshall (Staffs)
Bishop of Durham	Bishop Auckland (Durham), Durham, Norham (Nthumb), Crayke (Yrks)
Bishop of Ely	Wisbech (Cambs)
Bishop of Hereford	Bishops Castle (Shrops)
Bishop of Lincoln	Sleaford (Lincs), Newark (Notts), Banbury (Oxf)
Bishop of London	Bishops Stortford (Herts)
Bishop of Salisbury	Sherborne (Dorset)
Bishop of Winchester	Wolvesey (Hampshire), Taunton (Somerset), Farnham (Surrey)
Furneys Abbey	Piel (Lancs)
The Rector	Elsdon no. 2 (Nthumb)
The Vicar	Chatton (Nthumb), Corbridge (Nthumb), Embleton (Nthumb), Ponteland (Nthumb), Stamfordham (Nthumb)
Tynemouth Priory	Coquet Island (Nthumb), Tynemouth (Nthumb), Whitley nr Tynemouth (Nthumb)
Windsor, canons of the free chapel	Deddington (Oxf)

Although nearly half of all church-owned castles were located on the northern border, the dominance of this region was not as clear cut as would first appear. All but five of the castles on the border were simple towers, whereas in the midlands and the south-west more significant castles were normal. This is also reflected in the ownership of these castles. The northern border saw a much wider range of church involvement in castle ownership, extending down to local priests. In contrast, the rest of the county saw bishops dominate.

By far the most important group of castles owned by the church were those of the bishops of Durham, which is not surprising when one considers the palatinate power of the prince-bishops and the threat from the Scots. This accounts for their ownership of Durham castle, an important castle that in other parts of the country would almost certainly have belonged to the crown, while Norham castle (Northumberland) was one of the most vulnerable in the country.

Only two abbeys owned castles during this period. Between them, Furness abbey (Lancs) and Tynemouth priory (Nthumb) owned four castles, although all but one were towers. All four of these castles were built during this period, although not all were built by the church. These castles were all close to their abbey. Piel castle (Lancashire) was on an island five miles from Furness abbey. Tynemouth castle (Lancs) is the most interesting, as the priory stood within the castle walls. The furthest away was that on Coquet Island (Nthumb), twenty miles north of Tynemouth. Finally, Whitley near Tynemouth was only two miles from the priory. It had been licensed to Gilbert de Whitley in 1345, but by 1415 was in the priory's hands, and was probably acquired due to its proximity to the priory.

Even at the lower levels of the church, some castle – or at least tower – building can be found. Six of the towers first mentioned in the 1415 survey of Northumberland were owned by the local priest. Of these, Corbridge (Nthumb) is the finest example. It is clearly a fortified residence, complete with a roof top crenellated parapet – truly a castle in miniature.

Many of these church-owned castles were relics from the reign of King Stephen: all three castles held by the bishops of Winchester were from this period, as were all three held by the bishops of Lincoln. While they had been maintained in the intervening years, very little castle building had been done by the church after that. More than any other group, church-owned castles appear to have been a reaction to crisis, and the increase in their number in this period can be seen to have been a reaction to the threat from Scotland.

Castle Builders

The period covered by this study started with the last and greatest spell of castle foundation by the kings of England, which witnessed the construction of the string of great castles in north Wales built by Edward I. From this high point, the castle has been seen as declining until castle building came to an end during the fifteenth century. While this is undoubtedly true for royal castles, the same may not be the case for those built privately.

At least 272 castles were built during our period. Northern England was dominant, with 147 new castles. Even excluding simple towers the north and the northern borders still account for one third of total castle building. The success of Edward I's conquest of Wales can be seen in the decline of castle building there. By the time of his death in 1307, twenty-eight castles had been built in Wales. In the remaining 115 years of this period, only seven more were constructed.

Table 1.viii
Castle building by region

Region	Total	Towers	Excluding Towers
Northern Border	125	88	37
The North	27	9	18
Midlands	31	2	29
South East	15	0	15
South West	18	5	13
East Anglia	9	0	9
The Marches	16	1	15
Wales	35	3	32
Total	276	108	168

Table 1.ix
Castle building by decade

Decade	Number	Percentage
1270	9	5.8%
1280	11	7.1%
1290	9	5.8%
1300	18	11.7%
1310	19	12.3%
1320	6	3.9%
1330	15	9.7%
1340	25	16.2%
1350	5	3.2%
1360	3	1.9%
1370	10	6.5%
1380	14	9.1%
1390	6	3.8%
1400	4	2.6%
Total	154	

As important as their location is the building date of these castles. Here there are two main problems. First, there are over 100 castles for which we do not have a clear building date. This includes fifty-nine castles first mentioned in the 1415 survey of Northumberland, many of which can be dated no more securely than to the period after 1346, when licences to crenellate finish in Northumberland. Second, we are reliant on the licence to crenellate for building dates for the majority of these castles. These provide us with an exact date at which building work was being considered, but do not tell us when the actual building took place. Accepting these limitations, 154 castles can be dated to a particular decade. Two-thirds of these castles were built during six decades: 1300–19, 1330–49 and 1370–89. This period saw as wide a range of new castles as any, from masterpieces such as Caernarvon castle or Harlech castle (Merioneth), down to the single towers of Northumberland.

Only eight true concentric castles were built from scratch during this period. By their very nature these castles were expensive to build, requiring two lines of fortification, and also to garrison effectively. It is notable that seven of the eight were built in Wales during the reign of Edward I, four by Edward himself, while the only concentric castle built in England was Queenborough castle (Kent), again a royal castle. While dramatic and powerful, they were thus in no way typical of castles built during this period.

The quadrangular castle was the most distinctive form of new private castle in this period. Although sometimes seen as a northern form, castles such as Hemyock (Devon), Chideock (Dorset) or Hever (Kent) demonstrate that quadrangular castles could be found across all of England, although none was built in Wales. Within England the distribution of quadrangular castles matches the overall concentration of new castles. However, the twenty-seven quadrangular castles represent only one-tenth of new castle building, and while more significant that concentric castles, were still not typical of the period.

Two thirds of the castles built on the northern border were simple towers, ranging in size from very small buildings such as the Vicar's Peel at Corbridge (Northumberland), up to substantial buildings such as Belsay castle (Northumberland). Northumberland was the home of over half of these towers, although many of them are only known to us through the 1415 survey of Northumberland and it is possible that many similar towers remain unknown in other counties.

The majority of castles, at least sixty in number, built in this period were enclosure castles, often of an irregular plan. Castles of this form can be found across the entire country, from Scotney castle (Kent), a two ward castle, to Etal castle (Northumberland), with an oblong ward.[37]

* * *

Who was building new castles? The crown and the comital community were not active builders of new castles in this period. Instead, gentry or lesser noble families such as the Dacres and the de la Beches provided the bulk of new castles in this period, each building as many castles as the most active magnate families.

Edward I was the only great royal founder of castles in this period, and his Welsh castles are well known. After the castles of Edward I, the only new royal castle in this period was Queenborough castle (Kent) on the Isle of Sheppey, built by Edward III and a favourite residence of his, also a fully concentric castle, resembling, if only in outline, a later artillery fort.[38] Queenborough also resembles the castles in north Wales in that it was associated with a new town, and can be

[37] *History of Northumberland*, vol. 11, London and Newcastle, 1922, pp. 464–470.

[38] Platt, *The Castle in Medieval England and Wales*, 1981, p. 1-09.

seen as the last example of a tradition dating back to the conquest. After Edward I, royal castle building was concentrated at existing castles.

Table 1.x

Castle builders by rank[1]

Builder	Castles
The King	9
Church	17
Comital Community	11
Parliamentary Peers	27
Knights	29
Esquires	1
Yeoman	1
Clerks	3
Unknown rank	39

[1]Where identity of builder is known.

The comital community were not great castle builders during this period. Of their ten newly built castles, only Caerphilly castle (Glamorgan) ranks amongst the greatest castles, and it was begun in 1268, although building continued on into this period. The remaining castles were middle ranking castles, although Thomas of Lancaster's original plans for Dunstanburgh castle (Nthumb) may have made it a first rank building. This lack of comital castle building can be explained in two ways. The first is suggested by the early date of most of these castles, with seven of the ten built by 1315 and of them five located in Wales. Once the threat from the Welsh was over, the main spur to the comital community building new castles was removed. Secondly, the easiest way to gain new castles was by marriage to a great heiress. While a new building could take years to complete and consume large amounts of money, for both construction and maintenance, marriage could bring a group of castles and the lands to maintain them.

Fifteen different elements of the church built castles during this period, led by the archbishops of York, who built three castles. Nationally, the bishops were responsible for another five castles, each built by a different diocese. Lower levels of the church hierarchy were only active as castle builders on the northern border, where both abbeys and local priests were to be found building castles and towers. This helps to account for the northern bias amongst these church owned castles, with twelve of the sixteen located in the northern counties. Once again it was the threat from the Scots that inspired the building of new castles.

The majority of new castles in this period were built by lesser lay landowners, dominated by the knightly community. They represent those families that had the lands and resources required to build and then maintain a castle, but who in all but eleven cases did not already own one. Typical of this group were builders of a single castle, such as Sir Edmund Bacon, who gained a licence to crenellate for

Gresham castle (Norfolk) in 1318, and John de Pulteneye, who gained a licence for Cheveley castle (Cambridge) in 1341. Very few of these families built more than a single castle. The main exception was in Northumberland, where several families built more than one castle, in particular the Ogle family, who during the course of this period built six castles, making them, at least numerically speaking, the greatest private castle builders of this period.

The thirteenth century was the last period to see major castle building by the native Welsh princes. Between 1282 and 1299 nine castles can be said to have built by them, and it was just such castle building, at Dolforwyn (Montgomery), that helped contribute to the start of the Welsh wars of Edward I. However, like many other Welsh castles most of these buildings were soon in English hands. It must also be remembered that many of the smaller, undocumented castles in the Welsh heartland must have been built by the Welsh. How long they stayed in use, or in Welsh hands, is unclear but their existence must be remembered. Powis castle (Montgomery) is unusual in that it remained in the hands of the descendants of its original Welsh builder across the entire period. In 1309 the castle had passed to Hawis de la Pole, sister and heir by English law of Griffith de la Pole.[39] She married John de Cherleton, and the castle was held by their direct descendants across the period, despite an attack on the castle by the heirs under Welsh custom in 1312.

Table 1.xi
Constable service by castle builders

Constable service	Individuals
0	49
1	26
2	11
3	3
4	3
5	1

Just under half of these castle builders served as constables in other castles, representing one third of the overlap between castle ownership and constable service. All ranks amongst castle builders can be found serving as a constable, from Henry de Lacy, earl of Lincoln, builder of Ruthin castle (Denbigh) and Denbigh castle, who served as constable of Corfe castle (Dorset) and Skipton castle (Yorkshire), in addition to his role as hereditary constable of Chester, to Roland de Vaus, builder of Triermain castle (Cumberland) and constable of Carlisle castle (Cumberland).

[39] *IPM V*, no. 147.

What were the motives behind this castle building? It is never going to be possible to give a definitive answer to such a question, but we can make some suggestions that may have some validity.

The most important factor in the founding of a new castle was a perceived military threat. This is shown most clearly by the dominance of the northern border as a location for new castles, and by the end of intense castle building in and around Wales after the Edwardian conquest. Even excluding the towers, the northern border still saw the largest number of new castles, followed closely by Wales. In contrast, on the south coast, where there was an intermittent danger of French raids, the impetus towards castle building was much reduced, and Kent, facing the French coast, saw eight of the thirteen castles constructed in the south east.

A second motivation for castle building was political uncertainty. The three main bursts of castle building – 1300 to 1319, the 1330s and early 1340s and finally 1370–89 – all match such periods. The first covers the old age of Edward I and most of the reign of Edward II, a period of uncertainty followed by crisis, followed by a gap in the 1320s when first the Despensers and then Mortimer had control of government and thus of the issuing of licences. The second covered the early years of Edward III. His problems in France in 1339, followed by the governmental crisis of 1340 and the very public dispute with Archbishop Stratford, would not have helped lay to rest the memories of his father's reign. Only after victory at Crécy did castle building die down. The final peak marks the old age and rapid decline of Edward III, the early, crisis-ridden years of Richard II and the change of fortunes in France.

One possible motive for castle building that can be dismissed is fear of civil unrest after the Peasants' Revolt of 1381. After a peak in 1380, castle building slowed across the decade. The best candidate for this is Cooling castle (Kent), not least on the strength of the unusual inscription on an enamel plaque on the outer gatehouse:

> Knoweth that beth and schul be
> That I am mad in help of the cuntrie
> In knowyng of whyche thyng
> Thys is chartre and wytnessyng.[40]

This message has been taken to be referring to either rebellious local peasants, or the French. Of these, the latter seems more likely. The locality of Cooling had been raided by the French in 1379,[41] providing a clear military motivation, while the licence to crenellate was issued on 10 February 1381, three months before the start of the revolt.

Some of these castles were built by newly wealthy men. The licence to crenellate and the resulting castle were only part of a series of grants gained by

[40] W.A.S. Robertson, 'Coulyng Castle', *Archaeologia Cantiana*, 9 (1877), p. 134.
[41] *Ibid.*, p. 130.

these men. Both Stephen de Pencestre, builder of Allington castle (Kent) in 1281, and Sir Edward Dalyngrugge, builder of Bodiam castle (Sussex), had gained a licence to hold a fair and a market and grants of free warren before building the castle. For some men it is possible to trace the increase in their estates that allowed their castle building. John de Pateshull, builder of Bletsoe castle (Bedfordshire), is one such case. Although he already held Beltsoe in 1313,[42] it was only after 1324, when he inherited the lands of Watler de Teye, that he gained a licence,[43] and built his castle.

There was undoubtedly a symbolic element to much castle building, particularly in areas without any realistic threat. Even buildings of undeniably military intent such as Caernarvon castle could contain such symbolism, in its resemblance to the walls of Constantinople, and a whole series of imperial connections. Indeed, Coulson has suggested that very few castles had anything but a symbolic nature.[44] However, one must not overplay this element. Even excluding towers, the northern border still saw more building work than any other area, and it is clear that a constant military threat was a more significant factor than any desire for ostentatious display for its own sake. In those areas where the military threat was not strong, new castles were rare.

We can draw some conclusions about this building. First is that there were massive regional differences in castle building in this period. This period saw the end of major castle building in Wales, after the great castles of Edward I and his supporters, and the success of Edward's conquest put an end to any major castle building in Wales across the rest of this period. In contrast, the failures of Edward I and Edward II in Scotland created a dangerous border area in the north of England, and that danger created a situation in which even minor landowners built themselves towers and minor castles. The pattern of building work here was thus different from that in Wales. Edward I had started to build great castles in Scotland on a par with those of Wales, but that was not the reaction on the northern border. Thus the size of the castles being built from scratch decreased during this period. However, it is not possible to say that the quality of castle building had also decreased. Although the greatest castles were concentrated in the first thirty years of this period, places such as Bodiam (Sussex) or Bolton (Northumberland) demonstrate that a high level of skill was still present across the period, and whatever their military potential, their quality as buildings cannot be denied.

[42] *IPM V*, no. 376.

[43] *IPM VI*, no. 533.

[44] C. Coulson, 'Structural Symbolism in Medieval Castle Architecture', *Journal of the British Archaeological Association*, 132 (1979), pp. 73–90.

Licences to crenellate

The licence to crenellate is one of the most important sources for both castle building and castle ownership in this period, often providing the only documented owner for many lesser castles. The vast majority of licences issued by the king were recorded on the Patent Rolls, with only four recorded on the Charter Rolls.[45] Unlike most areas covered by this work, licences to crenellate have been studied in some detail. Coulson's article in *Nottingham Medieval Studies* is the most recent, and best, work on this subject, and is both a discussion of the role of the licence and a guide to previous writing.[46]

Although not all licences resulted in castles, the unused licences also provide an insight into the desire for fortification and the value placed upon it. Here we will divide the licences into two groups – active and inactive. The active licences are those that resulted in the building of a new castle or were issued for an already existing castle, while the inactive licences are those for sites where no castle resulted. This does not imply that no building occurred at these sites, only that whatever was produced is not considered a castle. The inactive licences fall into several groups. Many did not result in any building work of any nature. Others can be linked to un-fortified buildings, while still others were gained for church buildings. Finally, a small group were gained for buildings within towns.

While the vast majority of these licences to crenellate were granted directly by the king, this was not always the case. The right to issue licences was one of the powers granted away by the king in the palatinate areas of the country. In effect this was limited to the bishop of Durham across the period, and the dukes of Lancaster when they held those powers. Although the same was true for the earls of Chester, that title was held either by the King or his heir during this period and thus remained attached to the crown.

Table 1.xii
Licences to crenellate by reign

	Total	Per Year	Used	Unused	% Used
Edward I	38	1.1	22	16	57.9
Edward II	57	2.9	30	27	52.6
Edward III to 1349	101	4.4	51	50	50.5
Edward III from 1350	17	0.6	13	4	76.5
Richard II	41	1.8	27	14	65.9
Henry IV	7	0.5	7	0	100.0
Henry V	1	0.1	1	0	100.0
Total	262	1.7	151	111	57.6

[45] Bampton (Devon), *CChR 1327–1341*, p. 353; Ogle (Northumberland), *CChR 1341–1417*, p. 4; Aston (Bucks), *CChR 1327–1341*, p. 353 and Boghton Malherbe (Kent), *CChR 1341–1417*, p. 1.
[46] C. Coulson, 'Freedom to Crenellate by Licence: An Historiographical Revision', *Nottingham Medieval Studies*, 38 (1994), pp. 86–137.

The number of licences to crenellate issued fell dramatically at the end of the 1340s. Until that point the number issued had been slowly increasing, reaching a rate of over four per year, a rate maintained until 1348. The following year, none were issued, and the rate of issue did not begin to recover until the 1370s. The most obvious cause of this dramatic fall in licensing (matching a fall in actual building) was the Black Death. No other explanation fits this date. Success in France had not stopped the licence seekers of 1347 or 1348, and the renewed campaigns of the 1350s likewise failed to rekindle interest. No such obvious cause can explain the lack of royal licences under Henry IV and Henry V. Of the eight licences issued during their reigns, the last two were issued by the bishop of Durham; Henry V issued no licences to crenellate. Here we may be seeing the first signs of the death of interest in castles, or an indication of the insecurity of the Lancastrian monarchs. A different situation appears to have prevailed in Northumberland. Of the twenty-three licences issued for Northumberland, only one was granted after 1346. The effective end of licences to crenellate in Northumberland coincides with the ravaging of the border by the Scots before their defeat at Neville's Cross, and it has been suggested that after this destruction Edward III decided to allow fortification without licence in the county.[47]

Of the 246 separate licences granted, ten were for two sites, and eight for three. Of these eighteen multiple licences, six produced no building work, while another nine only produced one castle. All together, these multiple licences account for twenty-eight licensed sites where no work was carried out, nearly one quarter of all such cases. Although such multiple licences can be found up until 1399, such licences were concentrated in the reign of Edward III, who granted ten between 1329 and 1343.

Table 1.xiii

Licences to crenellate by region

Region	Inactive	Active	% Active	Castles Built
Northern Border	2	46	95.8	125
The North	16	23	59.0	27
Midlands	27	28	50.9	31
East Anglia	8	4	33.3	9
South East	27	15	35.7	15
South West	19	15	44.1	18
Marches	10	15	60.0	16

Very similar numbers of licences were issued across most of England. However, it should be remembered that all but two of the twenty-five licences granted in Northumberland came before 1346, artificially lowering the number of licences in the northern border. The greatest differences came with the number of licences acted upon, which was most frequent in the northern border region, and

[47] Bates, p. 11.

dramatically lower the further south one goes, until it reached a low point in East Anglia and the south-east. The nature of a licence to crenellate thus varied across the country, from being a serious military grant in the north, to being a form of planning permission in London.

The Constables

The Royal Constable

The royal constables are the best documented and most numerous people in this study. It has proved possible to compile near complete lists of constables for many royal castles. The majority of these appointments were recorded on either the Patent Rolls (19 per cent, peaking under Richard II) or Fine Rolls (51 per cent, peaking under Edward II). The reign of Edward II saw by far the highest number of new appointments, mostly due to the large number of forfeitures during this period, with 1322 seeing twice as many recorded appointments as any other year, many to forfeited Mortimer and Lancaster estates, and another peak in 1326–7. The frequency of reference, and thus the completeness of our lists, varies from castle to castle, peaking at Dover, where we can be certain who was constable for all but 152 of the 1,800 months of our period. We are less well informed for sheriff-constables, where on average we lack information for forty-six of the 150 years of this period.

The basic form of appointment was a grant during pleasure. This was the standard form of appointment to county castles, where it was in effect a one year appointment. The method of appointment at county castles is well established. At a set date each year, November for much of Edward I's reign and October for Edward III's, the king in council appointed the new sheriff-constables.[48] Grants during pleasure were not limited to county castles and occur even at the greatest castles.

Grants for life only became common after 1350. At Dover castle (Kent), only one such grant was made before 1350, while after 1350, twelve of the eighteen appointments were for life. The same pattern can be seen at Windsor castle (Berkshire), with two appointments for life before 1350, and seven from thirteen afterwards, and similar patterns are to be seen at all of the independent royal castles.

Only Lincoln castle and Chester castle saw hereditary constables during this period, in both cases the earls of Lincoln. After the death of Henry de Lacy, control of Chester castle passed to the justice of Chester, while Lincoln castle passed to the house of Lancaster, and effectively became their personal property. While appearances would suggest that the Percys became hereditary constables of Berwick castle (Northumberland) between 1339 and 1402, this was not the case. In fact, the dominant role of the Percy family in the defence of the east march against Scotland led to their dominance at Berwick, and it does not appear in the inquisition either of the Henry Percy who died in 1352, nor in that of the Henry Percy who died in 1368.

The most common term used to describe these men was 'constabularius'.[49] A second, rarer, term was 'custos', translated variously as custodian, keeper or

[48] *PRO Lists and Indexes, vol. 9: List of Sheriffs for England and Wales*, London, 1898, p. iii.

[49] Thus Adam de Wells, constable of Rockingham castle (Northampton) in 1299, is referred to as 'constabar' Castri' on the original fine roll. *CFR 1272–1307*, p. 409; C.60/106 m.17.

warden.[50] The two terms were often used interchangeably, as can be seen in the six references to John de Wysham, constable of Knaresborough castle (Yorkshire) in 1318–19, who was referred to as constable four times and keeper twice. However, in some cases a keeper can be proven to have been the sub-constable. This was the case at Carisbrooke castle (Hampshire) in 1377, where John Griffyth was described as constable, and Hugh Tyrell as his keeper of the castle. Clearly, we must be wary of establishing any hierarchy based entirely on vocabulary.

A short-lived post associated with individual castles was that of superior custodian (see table 1.xiv).[51] This post appeared between 1312 and 1322 and was clearly separate from the post of constable, as can be seen at Carlisle, where the grant of superior custody to the bishop of Carlisle in 1314 specifically stated that Andrew de Harclay was to remain as constable. In another three cases superior custodian and constable were appointed within a day of each other. This post was probably an attempt by Edward II to make doubly sure of these castles, an idea supported by the disappearance of the post after his victories of 1322, reflecting his greater confidence after the defeat of his enemies.

Table 1.xiv

Occurrences of superior custody

Castle	Timespan
Carlisle (Cumberland)	1314–19
Scarborough (Yorkshire)	1311–12
St. Briavels (Gloucester)	1322–
Gloucester	1322–

Joint constables were appointed forty-eight times,[52] concentrated in the reigns of Edward II (19) and Richard II (17), and within those reigns concentrated further in periods of great crisis, with seven in 1321–22, three in 1326, and six in 1399. suggesting that these joint appointments were a panic measure caused by great upheaval. Only six times were three or more people appointed as joint constables, in each case as a reaction to crisis. Two occurred in late October 1326, when Isabella and Mortimer removed supporters of the deposed Edward II, in particular the younger Despenser, and replaced him by a group of three at Bristol castle (Gloucester). The remaining appointments all came under Richard II, first at Newcastle Emlyn (Carmarthen) after the execution of Simon de Burley, and the final three in 1399, when, faced with Bolingbroke's invasion, Richard appointed a combination of William le Scrope, John Bussy, Henry Grene and William Bagot,

[50] Thus Reynold de Grey, custodian of St. Briavels castle (Gloucestershire) in 1291, is referred to as 'custodiam castre'. *CFR 1272–1307*, p. 286; C.60/106 m.2.

[51] For the Latin terminology see the grant of superior custody of Carlisle castle (Cumberland) to the bishop of Carlisle; *CPR 1313–1317*, p. 103, calendared as 'De superiore custod' Castri de Carleol' in *Calendarium Rotularum Patentium in Turri Londinensi*, London, 1802.

[52] See table 2.xii (p. 60) for a complete list.

his most hated allies, at Wallingford castle (Berkshire), Rochester castle (Kent) and Leeds castle (Kent).

Father and son served together twice, brothers once. At Rochester castle (Kent), the joint appointment may have been intended as an act of kindness, intended tactfully to replace an elderly and loyal royal servant. Henry de Cobham had been constable of Rochester since 1303. In 1334, when aged seventy-four, he was joined by his son, John, who then went on to become the next constable in his own right. The remaining cases both occurred at Portchester castle (Hampshire). Possibly to bolster the defence of the castle, Roger Waldon, a king's clerk, constable of the castle since 1395, was joined in 1397 by his brother John, a king's esquire. In November 1399, Henry IV replaced them with Thomas Camoys and his son Richard. Thomas had been one of Bolingbroke's earliest supporters[53] and went on to play a part in Henry V's French wars, commanding one wing of the army at Agincourt.[54]

Three occasions saw husband and wife appointed together. First came Richard and Muriel Lovel at Corfe castle (Dorset) in 1315. This was the second of five appointments for Lovel, and the inclusion of Muriel here is inexplicable. In the second case, Alice de Lacy and her husband Ebulo le Strange were appointed joint constables of Builth castle (Brecknock) in February 1331, expanded to ownership in 1334, both for Alice's lifetime, and were clearly intended to honour her, although why Builth castle was chosen is unclear, it having no connection to either Alice's father or to Thomas of Lancaster, her first husband. The third case was clearly intended to endow a royal ally. Custody of Corfe castle (Dorset) was granted to Thomas Holland, earl of Kent (d.1397) and his wife Alesia in survivorship in 1391, a grant that was honoured by Henry IV in 1401, when the castle was restored to Alesia. Here the grant of joint custody was an alternative to a grant of outright ownership.

A small number of castles were almost invariably dealt with as a clearly defined stable group. The most consistent group were the three castles granted to the justiciar of Chester: Chester, Flint and Rhuddlan (Flint), linked together right up to 1341, only two years before the Black Prince was considered to have come of age. The various justiciars of Wales also gained groups of castles with their posts, although most of these posts were eventually subsumed within the principality of Wales, in existence for much of this period.

Very few constable appointments came without some other duties attached, whether it be control over a geographical area, as with Carisbrooke castle (Hampshire), linked to control over the Isle of Wight,[55] or an associated duty, as with Nottingham castle, where the constable had responsibility for the bridges over the Trent.[56] At the county castles, the post of constable was secondary to that of sheriff. At other castles the balance is not so clear, as at Dover castle (Kent),

[53] Jacob, p. 7.

[54] Jacob, p. 155.

[55] 18 April 1312, *CFR 1307–1319*, p. 130.

[56] 18 February 1363, *CPR 1361–1364*, p. 314.

where the constable was also warden of the Cinque Ports, an equally important post.

Many of these tied posts produced an income, making an appointment as constable a potential financial reward. However, in most cases the constable was expected to account for this income, which was often granted to a third party, such as Queen Eleanor, the King's Mother, who was granted £50 per year from the issues of Marlborough castle (Wiltshire) in 1273,[57] or Humphrey, duke of Gloucester, who was granted 500 marks per year from the king's Welsh castles in 1413.[58] On occasion, the constable benefited from such a grant. This was the case for William fitz Waryn, who had been granted custody of Montgomery castle for life, at a rent of 100 marks per year. In 1335 this grant was made rent free,[59] in effect a grant of 100 marks per year to fitz Waryn. Used in this way, appointment to a castle could be a valuable source of patronage for the king.

The wages received by the constable varied from castle to castle. At Dover, the £300 allocated to the constable was intended to pay for the constable and a list of specific staff, although even after their wages were paid, the constable cannot have been left with much less than £200 per year.[60] At Conway castle (Caernarvon) in 1378, the constable was allocated 100 marks, 60 for himself and 40 for his sub constable.[61] In 1382, this detail was hidden in a simple allocation of 100 marks to pay the wages of the constable,[62] and it is possible that other wage settlements hide details such as this. However, some constables' wages were too low for such a split to be possible. The constable of Beeston castle (Cheshire) was paid 3d. per day in 1299, less than many gatekeepers, and while Beeston was a relatively minor castle, the same cannot be said for Leeds castle (Kent), whose constables were no better paid in 1376[63] and 1382.[64]

A study of the rank of these constables poses two main problems. The first, and most serious, is that for much of this period, the rank of those individuals below the parliamentary peerage is rarely recorded. Fortunately, this changes after roughly 1375 and by the end of the period the rank of most constables is clear. The second problem is that rank was not static. Many knights first appear as esquires, while membership of the comital community could be very fluid. Here individuals will be considered at the highest rank they achieved during their lifetime.

The comital community did not play a significant role as constables. Only forty-five of its 113 members served (of 1,396 constables), thirty-two only after gaining their title, gaining 145 appointments (of 1,930). One third of all comital constable careers began under Richard II, most of which involved Richard's favourites and allies, such as William le Scrope, earl of Wiltshire.

57 16 December 1273, *CCR 1272–1279*, p. 10.
58 *CPR 1413–1416*, p. 146.
59 *CPR 1334–1338*, p. 84.
60 *CPR 1354–1358*, p. 512.
61 *CCR 1377–1381*, p. 530.
62 *CCR 1381–1385*, p. 166.
63 *CCR 1374–1377*, p. 396.
64 *CCR 1381–1385*, p. 55.

The spread of these comital appointments did not differ from the distribution of royal castles. Only five castles – Wallingford (Berkshire), Corfe (Dorset), Carlisle (Cumberland), Carmarthen and Dover (Kent) – saw any concentration of comital appointments, each with four or more. Of these castles, all but Carlisle castle (Cumberland) were independent royal castles, while Carlisle was the key to the defence of Cumberland, and its comital constables included Andrew Harclay, earl of Carlisle and Ralph de Neville, earl of Westmorland, key figures in the defence of the north.

As a clearly defined group, it is possible to say what proportion of the parliamentary peerage served as constables.[65] Members of this group did not serve consistently as constables, with only one in four ever receiving such an appointment, although those who were appointed received slightly more posts than was normal (8 per cent of individual constables, 11 per cent of all appointments). Thus, despite their relatively low involvement as a group, the parliamentary peerage account for one tenth of all constable appointments.

Table 1.xv

Constable service of parliamentary peers

Posts	Individuals	% overall[1]	% constable[2]	Castles
0	363	75.6%	–	0
1	65	13.5%	55.6%	65
2	29	6.0%	24.8%	58
3	9	1.9%	7.7%	27
4	7	1.5%	6.0%	28
5	2	0.5%	1.7%	10
6	3	0.6%	2.6%	18
8	1	0.2%	0.9%	8
13	1	0.2%	0.9%	13
Totals	480			227

[1] Percentage of all non-comital parliamentary peers.
[2] Percentage of those non-comital parliamentary peers serving as constables.

Sixty per cent of constable service by the parliamentary peerage occurred during the reign of Edward II (137 of 255 appointments). Within the reign there were four peaks. The first, in March 1308, was dominated by men who had been summoned to Parliament since at least 1299. The second came over the winter of 1311–12, when Edward was taking control of the great seal and chancery,[66] and show the importance he allocated to the royal castles. The third peak of 1317–18 was significant in that it included men such as Roger Damory, and the younger Despenser. Finally, the fourth peak (1321–2), although it included future rebels

[65] For the purposes of this discussion only the non-comital parliamentary peers will be considered.
[66] Edward had regained possession of the great seal by 28 December 1311; *CPR 1307–1313*, p. 411, the officers of chancery joined him on 20 January 1312.

such as Roger Mortimer of Chirk and Bartholomew Badlesmere, was dominated by the nine posts granted to the younger Despenser. These four peaks well demonstrate the increasingly limited circle of supporters that Edward came to depend on during his reign.

Only after 1375 can we make any comment on the involvement of knights and esquires as constables (see table 1.xvi). This improvement in the documentation of rank is sometimes considered to be a symptom of a decline in the number of knights. After 1375, only forty per cent of constables were knights. This ratio was lower at county castles, falling to a low of one in four at Canterbury castle (Kent), but higher at independent royal castles such as Bamborough castle (Northumberland), where nearly 65 per cent of constables after 1375 were knights. This pattern would fit with the idea of the knights as a military elite of declining numbers, used at the most sensitive posts, such as those facing the Scottish border.[67]

Table 1.xvi

Level of known knights and esquires

	Pre 1375		Post 1375			Overall
Castle	Knights	Total	Esquire	Knights	Total	Knights
Bamborough	1	19	1	7	11	8 of 30
Canterbury	2	49	0	7	31	9 of 80
Dover	5	17	0	5	11	10 of 28
Norwich	6	64	4	7	176	13 of 81
Scarborough	2	22	0	1	4	3 of 26
Shrewsbury	2	23	3	0	5	2 of 28
Tower of London	3	26	0	4	8	7 of 34
Winchester	2	33	2	7	12	9 of 45
Windsor	2	13	1	5	7	7 of 20
York	5	49	0	19	36	24 of 85

Esquires were not common as constables, and even when they do appear at a castle, they rarely account for more that one or two appointments. However, not all of these appointments were themselves insignificant or short term. Nicholas Gerard, constable of Shrewsbury castle (Shropshire) for life from 1407 until his replacement in 1413, was not untypical, and longer spans can be found. The type of castle does not appear to affect the appearance of esquires as constables and they are equally likely to be found serving at either county or independent castles.

The vast majority of constables were Englishmen. Only twenty clear cases of Welshmen serving have been found, and of these only two were outside Wales: Morgan Goch at Corfe castle (Dorset) and Sir Rhys ap Griffith at Wigmore castle (Hereford). Rhys was the most significant of these men, serving at twelve castles

[67] Coss suggests that the number of knights had declined from 1,250 in 1324 to a mere 200 by 1430; P. Coss, *The Knight in Medieval England, 1000–1400*, Stroud, 1993, pp. 84 and 134.

over twenty-one years from 1321 to 1342. He was an active supporter of Edward II, holding a military command in Wales in 1321, and after a brief eclipse under Isabella and Mortimer, he ended his life in the service of the Black Prince. Continental European constables were even rarer than Welshmen. Only Harlech castle (Merioneth), held by Master James of St. George (1290–93) and Sir Walter Mauny (1332–43), saw two overseas constables, while the majority of castles saw none.

Only on sixteen occasions did a woman serve as constable, and even then five were wives serving jointly with their husbands, two were widows of recently deceased constables, and another two may been incorrectly recorded wardships. Of the remaining cases, only the appointment of Isabel de Vescy at Bamborough castle (Northumberland) provoked any negative reaction, at the expense of Edward II, even though she had actually been appointed by his father.

Many constables did not serve in person for either part or all of their period in post. Some were on campaign with the king, or otherwise abroad, while others served at more than one castle simultaneously. A clear example of this was Richard le Vache, constable of the Tower of London from 26 January 1361, and of Windsor castle (Berkshire) from 22 May 1360, both held until his death in 1366. He must therefore have always been absent from at least one of these posts, and we also find him getting letters of protection for one year in 1363,[68] leaving both posts untended. However, we should not overemphasise this absenteeism. John Darcy was replaced as constable of the Tower of London in 1352 because he was unable to attend to the keeping of the castle.[69]

The vast majority of individuals only served as constable of a single castle during their career (see table 2.xv), while only 113 individuals served as the constable of three or more castles. These figures represent the number of castles served at as opposed to the number of periods of service. This does not affect many individuals, but for some of those men who served repeatedly at the same castle it does distort the figures slightly and they will be examined below. The 78 per cent of individuals who only served at a single castle represent only 55 per cent of constable appointments. At any one time, close to half of all constables serving were men who either had, or were going to gain, more experience. As will be seen below, many of the more experienced constables also served for longer periods at their castles than the single servers, increasing the level of experience represented by constables at any one time.

The patterns of service differed markedly between the two main types of royal castles (see table 1.xvii). At the county castles, most constables did not serve as constable of any other castle, as at Norwich castle where only four of sixty-three constables served elsewhere. In contrast, at the independent royal castles a greater level of experience was normal and men whose service was limited to one castle were in a minority. There were thus two separate groups of individuals serving as constables. There was very little overlap between these two groups. Of the fifty-

[68] *CPR 1361–1364*, p. 425.
[69] *CPR 1350–1354*, p. 241.

four men who served at four or more castles, only seven started their career at county castles.

Table 1.xvii
Relative level of experience of constables

Castle	Number of castles served at 1	2	3	4	5	6 or more	average service
Bamborough	30.8%	50.0%	7.7%	0%	3.8%	7.7%	2.54
Canterbury	96.0%	2.7%	0%	1.3%	0%	0%	1.18
Dover	26.7%	33.3%	16.7%	10.0%	3.3%	10.0%	2.83
Norwich	93.7%	4.8%	1.6%	0%	0%	0%	1.08
Scarborough	79.2%	8.3%	4.2%	0%	4.2%	4.2%	1.67
Shrewsbury	37.9%	34.5%	13.8%	6.9%	0%	6.9%	2.17
Tower	28.0%	48.0%	0%	0%	16.0%	8.0%	2.88
Winchester	75.5%	17.8%	0%	6.7%	0%	0%	1.36
Windsor	52.4%	28.6%	4.8%	9.5%	4.8%	0%	1.86
York	92.9%	7.1%	0%	0%	0%	0%	1.07
National	78%	14%	4%	1.7%	0.9%	1.4%	1.4

Table 1.xviii
Average length of service in months

Castle	Overall
Bamborough	69
Canterbury	11.8
Dover	69
Norwich	16
Scarborough	55
Shrewsbury	30
Tower of London	57
Winchester	30
Windsor	106
York	15

Repeat service at a single castle was most common at the county castles, where it served to overcome the one year limit on shrieval service by rotating the post amongst a small group of men.[70] This can be seen at its most extreme at York castle, where between October 1351 and September 1359 the post alternated between Peter de Nuttle, who held it three times, and Miles de Stapelton of Hathelseye who held it twice. Of the fifty-six men to hold this post, twelve held it

[70] This annual rotation can be seen in practice at most county castles, although there were always some breaks. For a good example see Norwich castle (Norfolk), where thirty-five constables served for a year or less.

twice and eight held it three times. Similar examples can be found at most county castles. This contrasts with the independent royal castles where such repeat appointments were rare (none at Windsor castle, four at the Tower of London). Here the king was free to appoint whoever he wanted, and no such workaround was required.

The average duration of appointments varied dramatically between the county castles and the independent castles (see table 1.xviii). At county castles it was under two years, reaching a low of 11.8 months at Canterbury (Kent). In contrast, the lowest average at the independent castles was the fifty-five months at Scarborough castle (Yorkshire), rising to nine years at Windsor castle (Berkshire). This is in part explained by some very long serving constables, such as Stephan de Penchester, constable of Dover for 32 years between 1267 and 1298, or Richard Tempest, constable of Scarborough castle (Yorkshire) for 26 years from 1350 to 1376.

The overall length of constable careers varied depending on the number of castles at which service was performed. Those who served at one castle were almost all sheriff-constables, and their careers at castles rarely lasted more that one year, other than when extended by repeat service at the same castle. The careers of those men who served at two or more castles were normally concentrated in a single decade: for example Sir Ralph Basset of Drayton, who was constable of Stafford castle from 1 November 1317, Northampton castle from 25 April 1321, and finally of Dover castle (Kent) from 15 December 1325. There were some exceptions, such as Andrew de Sakevill, constable of Old Sarum castle (Wiltshire) from 25 April 1345, and Guildford castle (Surrey) from 25 September 1367, a gap of twenty years, but such a long gap between appointments was very rare.[71] Even the constable career of William le Scrope, who served at more castles than any other individual, was concentrated into ten years.

Some appointments were ended by the death of the sitting constable. This was most common at independent castles such as Dover, where 11 of the 37 constables during this period died in post, or at the Tower of London (10 of 34); but even at county castles it was not unknown, with eight men dying in post at Canterbury, two at York and four at Norwich. This was most common amongst those men serving at four or more castles, with 28 per cent dying still in post, although it was often because, like William le Scrope, Roger de Mortimer or the younger Despenser, their careers ended in disgrace and execution.

The crises of 1321–2, 1326–7 and 1399 left a clear mark on the record of constable appointments. The most obvious element of the 1321–2 crisis was that from January to March 1322 Edward II made fifty-two appointments, both at the forfeited castles and at existing royal castles, by far the most concentrated burst of constable appointments in this period. In contrast, the 1326–7 crisis saw three separate peaks of appointments. The first came in October 1326, when Queen Isabella was pursuing Edward II. Two months later, after her successful seizure of power, thirteen appointments were made by Prince Edward and Queen Isabella.

[71] For the career of Sakevill see N. Saul, *Scenes from Provincial Life*, pp. 49–51.

Finally, in February 1327, twenty-five appointments were made, this time including many of the county castles, as Isabella and Mortimer tightened their grip on the country. The fall of Richard II provides the most clear cut case. His reaction to Bolingbroke's invasion was to appoint a small group of individuals as joint constable of several castles. William le Scrope, earl of Wiltshire, Henry Grene, William Bagot and John Bussy were appointed jointly as constable of Leeds castle (Kent), Rochester castle (Kent) and Wallingford castle (Berkshire) in July 1399, in an attempt to place the defence against Bolingbroke in trusted hands. In each of these crises, the royal castles were important both to the king and to his enemies, and the passage of seventy years had not reduced that importance.

As demonstrated above, the royal castles can be split into several groups. Of those groups, the county castles and the independent royal castles are of interest here. At county castles, the post of sheriff was more important than that of constable, and it was the requirements of that post that affected the pattern of constable service at those castles. Most sheriff-constables served for one-year spells, and only ever served at that one castle, although they often served there more than once. In contrast, the constables of independent castles served for much longer periods of time, and often served at several castles. It is amongst this group that we should look to see what motivated appointments as constables. To contrast these two groups, one need only look at the number of constables who served across this period. At Canterbury castle, linked to the shrievalty of Kent, there were one hundred and two constables during the period. In contrast, Windsor castle only saw twenty three and Dover castle only thirty-eight. This must have made a difference at the castles themselves. The constable as an ever changing man, with his own local lands and residences, as was the case for the county castles, must have had an impact on a castle very different from those who were long term residents, possibly from elsewhere in the county.

Forfeited castles formed a short lived group within the royal castles. The largest number of forfeitures occurred in 1322 and remained in the king's hands until 1327, allowing us to examine these castles over a significant period. Edward's reaction was to commit custody of the forfeited lands county by county to a group of fifteen men. These were all minor figures, such as Alan de Cubbelayk in Lincolnshire, for whom this was his only service as constable. The contrast in 1399 could not be more striking. Custody of the Lancastrian lands was shared between the dukes of Exeter, Surrey and Aumale, and the earls of Wiltshire and Salisbury. Richard was more willing to trust his closest allies with the custody of such great lands. This trust was not misplaced – by the end of 1400 all but Aumale had died resisting Henry IV.

The three most important royal castles – Dover (Kent), Windsor (Berkshire) and the Tower of London – appear in the records far more often than any other. They had an importance beyond that of any other castles, Dover controlling the shortest route to the continent, Windsor increasingly as a royal residence and then base for the Order of the Garter, and the Tower as armoury, mint and menagerie, all with more permanent staff than at any other royal castle. The role of constable at these castles was thus very different in nature from that of most independent royal castles.

Only four men served at more than one of these three castles (see table 1.xix), in each case with some overlap between the two appointments, short though it was for Burgherssh and Beauchamp, who both died soon after receiving their second appointment. Richard le Vache, who held two of these posts for five years, was eminently suited to them. He had a distinguished military career, rewarded by a granted of 100*l.* per year in 1356 for carrying the King's banner on campaign.[72] However, the same was true of Burley, whose career was ended by execution.

Table 1.xix

Overlap of constables at Dover, the Tower and Windsor

	Dover	Tower of London	Windsor
Bartholomew de Burgherssh	1326–30 and 1343–55	1355	
John de Beauchamp	1360	1352–5 and 1360	
Richard le Vache		1361–6	1360–6
Simon Burley	1385–8		1377–86

The constables of Dover and the Tower were significantly more experienced as constables than those of any other castle (see table 1.xvii), with over half of them having other constable experience, mostly at independent rather than county castles. For many, an appointment to Dover (10 of 29) or the Tower (13 of 30) was the last of their career. Clearly there was a consistent policy of appointing experienced men to fill these two posts that was absent at all other royal castles, even Windsor.

The royal household was more significant here than at other castles.[73] In the first twenty years of Edward III's reign, both constables of Dover and five of the seven constables of the Tower were members of Edward's household, while under Richard II and Henry IV, over half of the non-comital constables were at least king's knights when appointed. Nine members of the comital community were appointed to Dover and the Tower. Of these, seven were members of the wider royal family, appointed by either Richard II or Henry IV, showing the importance attached to these castles. Even so, comital constables were still in a minority. The lack of comital constables at Windsor castle (Berkshire) can probably be explained by its increasing role as the home of the monarch, meaning that the constable would often take direct orders from the King, something unlikely to appeal to the comital community.

[72] *CPR 1354–1358*, p. 360.

[73] Information on the early household of Edward III comes from Caroline Shenton, 'The English Court and the Restoration of Royal Prestige, 1327–1345', Oxford D.Phil thesis, 1995, pp. 254–263; that for Richard II and Henry IV from Chris Given-Wilson, *The Royal Household and the King's Affinity*, London, 1986, pp. 280–290.

There does not appear to have been a link between castle ownership and service as a constable. Only 193 of the 1,733 individual constables owned castles, representing just 10 per cent of constables, or 25 per cent of castle owners during this period. Unsurprisingly, the greatest number of castle-owning constables appear at Dover castle (Kent) with thirteen, and the Tower of London with ten. However, the corresponding figure for Windsor castle (Berkshire) was only one out of twenty-one, as low as at many county castles. This could suggest that the constables of Windsor were carefully selected so as not to detract from the royal family's presence at Windsor in any way.[74] Thus the longest serving constable of Windsor during this period was the relatively obscure Thomas de Foxle, who was in post from 1330 until his death in 1360, a period that saw the start of Edward III's ambitious building schemes at the castle.

The castles owned by these men were not always in the same region as their service, as at Scarborough castle (Yorkshire), where the castle-owning constables included John de Vescy, owner of Alnwick castle (Northumberland), and John de Mowbray, whose castles were located in Wales.

Sub-constables

Beneath the constables was a group of men who may have done much of the work at castles.[75] The sub-constable appears at many castles, either by name or in an order sent to the constable 'or whoever supplies his place'.[76] However, even at the best documented castles we have no more than a scattering of references to sub-constables for the entire period. At many castles, we only know the identity of one sub-constable. Even at Dover, we have information covering only thirty years while at the Tower of London that falls to thirteen years. In total we have the names of only eighty-seven sub-constables.

Unlike constables, the sub-constables were appointed not by the king, but by the sitting constable. Thus at Corfe castle (Dorset) in 1354 the newly appointed constable, Roger de Mortimer, selected John de Elmerugg as his deputy and had this recorded on the Patent Rolls;[77] and at the Tower of London, after the death of Robert Ruthyn, sub-constable for Alan de Buxhull, then overseas, the king appointed a temporary constable to cover until Buxhull's return rather than appoint a sub-constable himself.[78] This has the effect of massively reducing the amount of information we have about these men. The only exception to this method of appointment was at Conway in 1378, where when Edward de St. John was appointed constable it was with the proviso that there would be a permanent

[74] See S. Bond, 'The Medieval Constables of Windsor Castle', *English Historical Review*, 323 (1967), pp. 225–249 for a detailed account of the duties attached to this post.
[75] See table 2.xix.
[76] For example see *CCR 1346–1349*, p. 16.
[77] 3 November 1354, *CPR 1354–1358*, p. 134.
[78] 14 September 1371, *CCR 1369–1374*, p. 250.

lieutenant, nominated by the king, or at this date his council, and paid 40 marks per year, only 20 marks less than St. John himself.

A variety of terms were used to describe the sub-constable. The most common phrase was 'locum tenens',[79] followed by 'subconstabularius',[80] although other phrases can be found. These phrases were used interchangeably across this period. Thomas de Reynes, sub-constable of Dover castle (Kent), was described as lieutenant 10 July 1374 and deputy on 26 July, only sixteen days later.[81]

The role of the sub-constable is hard to pin down, and would have varied from appointment to appointment. However, when the constable was absent, the sub-constable would have performed his role. The sub-constables for the most senior constables must have performed day to day duties at all times. During the four years that Prince Henry was constable of Dover castle (Kent), we know of three sub-constables. On occasion the sub-constable was mistakenly referred to as constable, as at the Tower of London during the ten year tenure of Anthony Bek, bishop of Durham (1275–85), one of Edward I's inner circle and absent from London much of the time.[82] Two of his sub-constables – Giles de Audenard in 1276 and 1277 and Ranulph de Dacre in 1283 – were referred to as constable.[83] When Nicholas de la Beche replaced John de Cromwell as constable of the Tower of London in 1335, it was actually their respective sub-constables, Robert le Brut and William de Herlisonn, who performed the hand-over of goods contained in the castle.[84] Here the actual administration of the castle was being carried out by the sub-constables. The *Scalacronica* contains one of the few chronicle references to sub-constables. Thomas de Gray, the father of the chronicler, and constable of Norham castle (Northumberland), was forced to make a sortie from the castle to rescue part of his garrison, and handed control of the castle to his sadly unnamed sub-constable,

> 'I'll hand over to you this castle, albeit I have it in charge to hold in the King's cause, unless I actually drink of the same cup that my people over there have to drink.'[85]

Here both the constable and his deputy were present at the same time, and the sub-constable was trusted enough to be left in charge of this key border fortress.

Of the eighty-seven known sub-constables, fifteen went on to serve as constable in their own right. For some this was a purely temporary promotion, as at Dover in 1360–61 where Andrew de Guildford was appointed temporary

[79] E.101/36/6 m.1 for Corfe castle.

[80] E.101/19/26 m.1 for Beaumaris castle.

[81] *CPR 1370–1374*, pp. 460 and 492.

[82] In 1277 Bek helped negotiate a treaty with Llywelyn ap Gruffuyd at Conway, while in 1282 he was in Aragon negotiating for a marriage between Eleanor, daughter of Edward I and Alphonse, son and heir of Peter of Aragon; M. Prestwich, *Edward I*, London, 1988, pp. 180 and 321.

[83] *CCR 1272–1279*, pp. 270 and 370; *CPR 1281–1292*, p. 70.

[84] E.101/19/28.

[85] *Scalacronica*, p. 63.

constable 'until the king makes other arrangements',[86] but for most this was a permanent appointment, most often at a different castle, as for Roger Wigmore, sub-constable of Dover castle (Kent) in 1386–7 for Simon de Burley; or William Frodesham, sub-constable of Caernarvon castle in 1390, who in the following year appears as constable of Criccieth castle (Caernarvon). In other cases, the sub-constable had already had some contact with castles, as with Roger Wigmore, who had been granted the wardship of Montgomery castle and Dolforwyn castle (Montgomery) in 1383, before appearing as sub-constable of Dover castle (Kent) in 1386–7 for Simon de Burley, and finally returning to south Wales as constable of Carmarthen from 1390–5, demonstrating here the importance of Dover castle.

Constables for the queen

Queen Margaret, Queen Isabella and Queen Philippa all appointed constables in their own right. For each of these three queens, half of the constables known at their castles can be said to have been appointed by the queen, although only Queen Philippa can be proved to have appointed constables during the lifetime of her husband, such as Roger de Beauchamp, whose appointment as constable of Devizes castle (Wiltshire) in 1340 was confirmed on the Patent Rolls in a way that makes it clear that Queen Philippa had herself made the appointment.[87]

The queen's constables were unusually experienced as royal constables. Of the twenty-one known, twelve had also served for the king at other castles. This level of experience was the same under Queen Margaret, Queen Isabella and Queen Philippa and is also matched by the rank of this group. Of the nine men in this group whose rank was known, five were knights, a far higher proportion than amongst royal constables, although that may reflect a higher level of recording of rank for the queen's constables rather than a higher proportion of knights.

Constables for the heir to the throne

The constables that served the Black Prince are the best documented group of constables not directly appointed by the king. The Black Prince's Register, confirmations of his appointments issued by Prince Richard's council in 1377 and chance references in royal records provide us with the names of twenty-nine of his constables. Six of these twenty-nine served the Black Prince at more than one of his castles, each in a relatively small area. Typical of this was John de Skirbeck, constable of Launceston castle (Cornwall) and Tintagel castle (Cornwall). Sixteen of the twenty-nine were also appointed as royal constables. However, nine of those sixteen were men whose only royal service was to continue in place at the

[86] 5 December 1360, *CPR 1358–1361*, p. 509.

[87] *CPR 1340–1343*, p. 115, confirming his appointment the previous day by Queen Philippa.

same castle in which they had served the Black Prince. The remaining overlap consists of men who were constables for the Black Prince and Edward III at the same time, and men whose royal service began under Richard II but at castles that had not been held by the Black Prince. The nine men who were confirmed in their posts by Richard II give us an insight into the length of service at the Black Prince's castles. The longest serving was Henry de Berkhamsted, who had been constable of Berkhamsted castle (Hertfordshire) for thirty years, followed by Richard de la Bere, constable of Newcastle Emlyn castle (Carmarthen) for nineteen years. This would suggest a desire for stability at his castles on the part of the prince.

Constables of privately owned castles

The final, and least fully documented, group of men in this chapter are the private constables. Most of our knowledge of these men comes from chance references in royal documents. Only for the earls and dukes of Lancaster do we have more information, with John of Gaunt's registers providing the best picture of these private officials for a single landowner, especially when combined with confirmations in post issued by Richard II and Henry IV in 1399 and during the aftermath of Henry's seizure of the thrones.

Given the nature of our information, we can make only limited observations on the length of service of these private constables. Certainly, some of them stayed in post for very long periods. At Hertford castle Robert de Louth served for at least twenty-five years, first appearing as constable for Queen Isabella in 1358, and still in place under John of Gaunt in 1383. Indeed, John of Gaunt's estates provide most evidence for duration of private constable service. Amongst his constables the outstanding feature is a group of men who served for ten to twenty years. Louth at Hertford can be joined by John Deyncourt at Kenilworth castle (Warwickshire) from 1380 to 1391, and Oliver de Barton at Lincoln castle from 1375 to 1393.

Of the known private constables, only seven served as constable of royal castles. Of these, one was William le Scrope, who appeared as constable of Richmond castle (Yorkshire) for Edward, future duke of York in 1398. Of the six remaining, two continued in place at the same castle after the death of the owner, while the other four all served in the same area. This would suggest that the overlap between private and royal constables was not significant. The private constables formed yet another group within the castle community.

Wardships

At least 148 estates containing castles entered wardship during this period. These estates were a representative cross-section of castle-owning estates, with over half containing only a single castle. Here, where we can be certain of the age of our subjects, there is no pattern, with the heirs to these estates equally likely to be infants or almost of age when they inherited.

On average, ten estates containing castles entered wardship per decade across this period. The Black Death had no impact on the number of wardships involving castles. While two estates with castles fell into wardship during 1348, the same was true of both 1347 and 1349. Two more entered wardship in 1361, the second plague year, and only one in the third plague year, 1369. The key factor that influenced the numbers of castles in wardship would appear to have simply been the number of castles in existence. Before 1350, eight estates with castles fell into wardship each decade, compared to eleven per decade after 1350, an increase of only 40 per cent, actually lower than the increase in the number of castles.

Table 1.xx

Date estates containing castles fell into wardship

Decade	Male Heir	Female Heir	Total
1272–9	4	0	4
1280–9	1	1	2
1290–9	9	2	11
1300–9	7	4	11
1310–9	7	3	10
1320–9	7	0	7
1330–9	5	0	5
1340–9	10	0	10
1350–9	4	1	5
1360–9	12	5	17
1370–9	12	1	13
1380–9	6	2	8
1390–9	15	0	15
1400–9	14	1	15
1410–9	4	2	6
1420–2	3	0	3

The most common form of castle-related wardship grant involved individual castles, representing nearly three-quarters of all grants. For smaller estates, this could amount to a grant of the entire estate. At the start of our period, this was the norm, with very few examples of any other form of wardship. As our period proceeds, the number of appointments made in this way remained constant. However, the total number of wardships increased, and so the importance of this form of appointment slowly decreased.

Table 1.xxi

Types of wardship grant

Type	No. of cases
Grants of single named castle	156
Joint wardship of single castle	8
Entire estate to a single individual	23
Entire estate to a group	15
Estate split by region	11
Total	213

This type of wardship arrangement was similar in some ways to the institution of royal constables in that wardship appointments were often recorded as if they were for normal constables posts. This can been seen during the wardship of James Audley. Of the three references to the guardians of Llandovery castle (Carmarthen), one treated them as a constable. Two out of five references at Heighley castle (Staffordshire) did too while at Redcastle (Shropshire) all four references treated the guardian as a normal constable. This form of wardship was subject to change, as happened at Castle Barnard (Durham), held by seven different people during the twenty-year minority (1315–35) of Thomas de Beauchamp, earl of Warwick.

On five occasions late in the period, wardship of a single castle was granted to a group. Three of these occurred during the minority of Thomas Mowbray, earl Marshal, between his inheriting while under age in 1399 and his execution in 1405 for his part in Archbishop Scrope's rebellion. Nine men were involved, two of whom appear at all three castles, and another three at two of the three.

The final form of distribution of lands and castles in wardship was to grant an entire estate intact to one or more people (see table 1.xxii). If any subdivision of the estate was made between the various guardians, it was not specified. On a lesser scale, regions within an estate could be granted. However, this was far rarer than the granting of the entire estate.

Table 1.xxii

Wardship of entire estate by number of guardians and reign

Reign	1	2	3	4	5
Edward III	7	0	1	0	0
Richard II	4	2	1	0	1
Henry IV	6	2	3	0	0
Henry V	6	3	0	1	0
Total	23	7	5	1	1

In the majority of cases where wardship of an entire estate was granted, there was a single guardian. Just over half of these grants were made after 1400. The first such grant did not occur until 1330, when Roger de Mortimer, earl of March, was granted the wardship of Laurence de Hastings, then only eleven, in what would have been a valuable grant if Mortimer had survived to enjoy it. Such grants then disappeared, before reappearing under Richard II and peaking after 1400. As seen above, neither Henry IV nor Henry V were able to endow their supporters and families with large numbers of castles, and this use of wardship may have been intended to boost the income of figures such as Thomas and John Beaufort, Henry IV's half-brothers.

Like grants of a single castle to a single guardian, grants to multiple guardians were most common after 1400. The five cases to occur before that date all involved estates from the comital community, and may be explained as an attempt to ease the management of widely spread estates. After 1400 the majority of these estates were still from the comital community, but were joined by estates from the parliamentary peerage such as those of the Cliffords. Once again, Henry IV and Henry V appear to have been using these estates to endow their supporters.

Unlike most of the variations of wardship appointments, the eleven grants of wardship by region were evenly spread across the fourteenth century. It was most commonly used in Wales, especially in Glamorgan, which was clearly regarded as a single unit and was granted intact as a region on the three occasions it came into wardship during this period (1307, 1314 and 1375).

* * *

Having examined the mechanics of wardship, we will now move on to examine those people awarded wardships containing castles. This was a smaller group than either the castle owners or royal constables, involving 219 individuals. Many of the same questions that were asked about royal constables will also be relevant for those people granted wardships, but there are also questions specific to wardship to be considered.

Male relatives of the heir were granted wardship only six times during this period. Grants to the mother of the heir were more common, with nine across this period. However, three of these are accounted for by the Clifford family, all involving either the minority or the heirs of John de Clifford (1388–1422). First his grandmother, Maud, and after her death, his mother, Elizabeth, were awarded wardship of the Clifford estates. Finally, after the early death of John, the wardship of his young heir Thomas (born in 1414) was granted to his mother and grandmother (both Elizabeth). This was a major grant, for the Cliffords owned five castles and were amongst the most important non-comital castle owners, while the heir would not come of age for another thirteen years. This generosity to the widows was perhaps due to the nature of the death of John de Clifford, campaigning with Henry V at the siege of Meaux.[88]

[88] *GEC III*, p. 293.

During the first ten years of Richard II's reign, three heirs were granted full or joint wardship of their own lands. These involved the only three estates of the comital community to come into wardship during this period. In 1377, Edward Courtenay, earl of Devon, was granted wardship of his own lands, but he was already twenty when he inherited. In contrast, Roger de Mortimer, earl of March, was only seven when he inherited in 1381. Initially, his lands were parcelled out, but in 1383 he was granted joint custody with the earl of Warwick, earl of Northumberland and John Neville, an experienced group. Finally, Thomas, earl of Stafford, inherited in 1386, aged eighteen, and was immediately granted joint wardship with Warwick, Neville and William de Beauchamp.[89]

Wardships were granted to people from a wide range of social levels, from minor clerks through to the heir to the throne. However, the largest group amongst the guardians were knights, representing forty-two of the 108 guardians whose rank is known. They received control of all sizes of estate, from Sir William Beauchamp, who was granted joint wardship of the estates of the earls of Stafford in 1387,[90] through to Sir John Devereux, who was awarded wardship of the fitz Waryn castle of Whittington (Shropshire) in 1392.

Members of the comital community feature much more strongly as guardians than they do as constables, representing 12 per cent of all guardians (compared to only 2 per cent of constables). These twenty-eight men were granted a total of thirty-seven wardships, only thirteen of which were not of the lands of fellow members of the comital community, the majority of those being for the lands of the parliamentary peerage. At this level, guardians received wardship of lands from their own level of society.

The same was true of the twenty-six non-comital parliamentary peers granted wardships (10 per cent of the total), for these grants concentrated on estates from amongst the comital community and parliamentary peerage. Members of the royal household received a high proportion of wardships during the reigns of Richard II and Henry IV. Under Richard II, seventeen king's knights were granted wardships, and were involved in over three-quarters of castle wardships. The figure went down to less than half under Henry IV, with nine household knights gaining wardships. This is very different from the situation during the first twenty years of the reign of Edward III, where only three of forty-one household bannerets, and four of 119 household knights received wardships involving castles.

Only twenty individuals were awarded the wardship of castles from different families' estates, with no individual holding castles in wardship from more than three families. With only just over one such wardship available per year, this should not come as a surprise, and it is worth remembering that the number of castles involved could be very large, especially where the Mortimer estates were concerned. In keeping with the scarcity of these wardships, the rank of those people awarded them was significantly higher then normal, with the future Henry V, two queens, six earls and two dukes forming over half of this group.

[89] 25 Feb 1387, *CFR 1383–1391*, p. 173.
[90] *CFR 1383–1391*, p. 173.

Of these twenty individuals, eight were granted their wardships during the reign of Richard II and six during that of Henry IV. This is very much a phenomenon of their two reigns, and was very rare before 1377, with only three such people during the entire reign of Edward III. Excluding those grants made before Richard's declaration of full age in 1389, only one man, William le Scrope, earl of Wiltshire, was certainly awarded more than one wardship by Richard II, including the wardship of Knaresborough castle (Yorkshire), given within a fortnight of Bolingbroke's exile being extended for life (and this despite the castle already having been granted to Katherine Sywnford).

In most of these cases, the estates being granted were those of the comital community. Of the forty-three estates affected, only eleven were not, and of them, two were during the minority of Laurence Hastings, created earl of Pembroke in 1339 after he had come of age, while a further two came after the execution of Thomas Despenser, briefly earl of Gloucester. Not only were the people being awarded multiple wardships members of the comital community, so were the landowners whose estates they were being granted.

There was a significant level of overlap between guardians and constables; 39 per cent of guardians also served as constables. Within the overall group of guardians this overlap was evenly spread, including both major figures such as William le Scrope, and minor men such as John Smert, who was granted the wardship of Builth castle (Brecknock) in 1407.

Only just over one in four of the individuals granted wardships owned castles of their own. Amongst the fifty-three castle owners, the level of castle ownership was unusually high, with an average of six castles each, three times the norm, reflecting the presence amongst this group of men such as John of Gaunt, along with all five Mortimer earls of March. It is worthy of note that thirty-four of these castle owners also served as constables, giving them three separate forms of contact with castles.

From the above study it can be seen that wardship could present the king with a problem. The granting of wardship over great estates such as the Mortimer lands could substantially increase the wealth and thus power of the individual to whom they were granted. With this in mind, one can see why the kings of England during this period preferred to treat castles in wardship on an individual basis, with guardians resembling constables to the extent that they are sometimes indistinguishable in government records.

Conclusion

Returning to our original question, we can now see that the Grays of Heton were not typical of the castle community. The castle community can be split into four main groups, with very little overlap between those groups. The Grays were amongst the small group of men who fall into more than one of these groups. Indeed, as a family they fall into three.

The first group were the castle owners, containing 681 private individuals ranging from the greatest member of the comital community down to owners of a single castle, such as Roland de Thirlwall, owner of Thirwall castle (Northumberland) in 1415, as well as the church and the king. Second were the sheriff-constables, a group of 550 individuals that overlaps with any of the others the least: their service as sheriff-constable providing their only direct involvement with castles. Third were the constables of the independent royal castles, the largest of these groups, containing over 900 men, two thirds of whom only served once. This group includes all those men of national importance to serve as constables. Finally come the constables of private castles: only seventy-five are known, of whom only seven appear in any of the other groups. However this must represent only a tiny minority of the actual group.

* * *

The castle community can also be analysed in terms of rank and status, an approach that would have been meaningful to contemporaries. At the top comes the king. Despite the lack of royal castle building after Edward I, with only Queenborough castle (Kent) being built after his reign, the number of castles under direct royal control fluctuated repeatedly during this period. Very few royal castles remained in the king's control without interruption. Many were either linked to a county, held by the queen, or by the heir to the throne. Even Edward I's great new fortresses in north Wales were soon held by the Prince of Wales, and not the king. It is perhaps not a coincidence that the period of stability under Edward III coincided with the greatest concentration of castles in the hand of the royal family. The Black Prince and John of Gaunt each controlled over twenty-five castles, giving Edward III and his family control over an unprecedented number of castles.

The comital community changed dramatically during this period. In 1272, the earls were either members of the royal family, or representatives of long established families, and all were castle owners. This period saw an increase in the number of titles, while many of the men granted titles were less significant, such as Andrew Harclay, earl of Carlisle, or royal favourites. Not all of these men were ever castle owners. By the end of our period even some members of the royal family, such as Henry IV's half brothers, the Beauforts, did not become castle owners.

The non-comital parliamentary peerage also changed during our period, with summons to Parliament becoming hereditary. This may help explain the declining incidence of the non-comital parliamentary peerage serving as constables. The number of parliamentary peers appointed as constables halved, from one per year under Edward III, to one every two years after his reign. The son of a trusted member of parliament was not necessarily trusted himself.

Our period saw the rise of knights as castle owners. One-third of the castle builders whose rank we know were knights. At the same time, the number of knights was falling, reaching a suggested low of only 200 in 1430.[91] Although exact figures are impossible to calculate, it is clear that just over 100 knights were castle owners in 1422. They also retained their importance as constables. All eight sheriff-constables of York after 1400 were knights, as were four of the six constables of Bamborough castle (Northumberland), while similar ratios can be found at nearly every castle.

This was also the period that saw the 'rise' of esquires. By 1430, they outnumbered knights by close to six to one, and had been accepted as being of gentle birth.[92] Only one castle was definitely built by an esquire, Radcliff castle (Lancashire), licenced by James de Radcliffe, esquire, in 1403.[93] Very few castles were owned by esquires, even in 1422. Esquires also appear as constables, but not in great numbers. Only one constable of Bamborough castle was an esquire, two of Winchester castle (Hampshire) and none of Scarborough castle (Yorkshire). Whatever their social relationship to the knights, the esquires had not yet entered the castle community in 1422.

* * *

Castles played a different role in each of the major political crisis of this period. However, some features are common to most or all crises. Each crisis saw major changes in castle ownership, whether in the form of mass forfeitures, as in 1322 or 1397, or restorations, as after 1330 or 1399. Despite these upheavals, most castle-owning families were resilient enough to survive, and even the most notorious of forfeitures, those of the Despensers in 1326 and Roger de Mortimer in 1330, did not, in the end, damage their families. Indeed, while Roger de Mortimer, first earl of March, owned eighteen castles, his great-great-grandson, Roger de Mortimer, third earl of March, owned twenty-one castles at his death in 1398.[94]

However severe the shocks that impacted on the castle community, whether caused by the actions of the king, or of his greatest subjects, within a generation most or all of the same families can once again be found owning the same castles, or serving as constables. This tendency is represented at its most extreme by the Clifford family. The same five castles that were forfeited by Robert de Clifford in

[91] Coss, p. 134.
[92] *Ibid.*
[93] *CPR 1401–1405*, p. 255.
[94] *IPM XVII*, no. 1206.

1322[95] were owned by John de Clifford at his death in 1422, five generations and 100 years later.[96] Likewise, John Beaumont, constable of Dover castle in 1392–1396 for Richard II, was the great-grandson of Henry Beaumont, constable of Somerton castle (Lincolnshire) in 1311–22 for Edward II. Despite the changes that had occurred in English and Welsh society in the 150 years of our period, the castle community at its end was remarkably similar to that at its beginning.

95 Appleby castle, Brougham castle, Brough castle and Pendragon castle (all Westmorland), and Skipton castle (Yorkshire), forfeited on 8 February 1322; *CFR 1319–1327*, p. 94.
96 Dead by 27 May 1422; *CFR 1413–1422*, p. 433.

Tables

Table 2.i

Counties contained in each Regions

Region	Counties
Northern Border	Cumberland, Westmorland, Durham, Northumberland
The North	Lancashire & Yorkshire
Midlands	Derbyshire, Nottinghamshire, Lincolnshire, Staffordshire, Rutland, Leicestershire, Huntingdonshire, Bedfordshire, Buckinghamshire, Northamptonshire, Warwickshire, Worcestershire, Oxfordshire
South East	Berkshire, Hertfordshire, London, Surrey, Sussex, Hampshire, Kent
South West	Wilts, Dorset, Somerset, Devon, Cornwall
East Anglia	Norfolk, Suffolk, Essex, Cambridge
Marches	Gloucestershire, Herefordshire, Shropshire, Cheshire
Wales	all Welsh counties

Table 2.ii

Castles of the House of Lancaster

	No. of castles
Edmund, earl of 1267–1296	14
Thomas, earl of 1296–1322	25
Henry, earl of 1327–1345	17
Henry of Grosmont, duke of, 1345–1361	25
John of Gaunt, duke of, 1361–1399	24

Table 2.iii

Castles of the Mortimer Family

	No. of castles
Roger, –1330	18
Roger, 1328–1360	12
Edmund, 1352–1381	18
Roger, 1374–1398	21
Edmund, 1391–1425	18

Table 2.iv
Castles of the Barons and Earls of Stafford

	No. of castles
Ralph, 1301–72	5
Hugh, 1342–86	5
Thomas, 1368–92	4
Edmund, 1378–1403	7
Humphrey, 1402–60	4

Table 2.v
Castles of the Earls of Arundel

	No. of castles
Richard, –1302	4
Edmund, –1326	7
Richard, –1376	11
Richard, –1397	12
Thomas, –1415	2

Table 2.vi
Castles of the Bohun family

	No. of castles
Humphrey, –1275	4
Humphrey, –1298	6
Humphrey, –1322	4
John, –1336	5
Humphrey, –1361	6
Humphrey, –1373	9

Table 2.vii
Castles of the Earls of Warwick

	No. of castles
William, 1240–1298	3
Guy, 1273–1315	6
Thomas, 1314–1369	9
Thomas, 1349–1401	11
Richard, 1382–1439	6

Table 2.viii

Castles of the Despenser family

	No. of castles
Hugh, snr, 1261–1326	2
Hugh, yng, –1326	25
Hugh, 1308–1349	9
Edward, 1337–1385	10
Thomas, 1373–1400	11

Table 2.ix

Licences to Crenellate

Castle	Licensee	Date
Bletsoe (Beds)	John de Pateshull	23 June 1327
Aldworth (Berks)	Nicholas de la Beche	3 March 1338
Beaumyss (Berks)	Nicholas de la Beche	3 March 1338
Donnington (Berks)	Richard Abberbury	11 June 1386
Boarstall (Bucks)	John de Handlo	12 Sept 1312
Weston Turville (Bucks)	John de Molyns	23 Jan 1333
Cheveley (Cambs)	John de Pulteney	6 Oct 1341
Doddington (Cheshire)	John de Delves	1364
" " "	John de Delves	1403
Macclesfield (Cheshire)	John de Macclesfield	1398
" " "	John de Macclesfield	1410
Lanihorne (Corn)	John Larchdeacon	31 Jan 1335
Stratton (Corn)	Ralph de Whitchurch	30 Jan 1335
Dacre (Cumb)	William de Dacre	1307–13
Drumburgh (Cumb)	Robert le Brun	24 Aug 1307
Dunmalloght (Cumb)	William de Dacre	24 Aug 1307
Greystoke (Cumb)	William lord Greystoke	5 Oct 1353
Hay (Cumb)	Robert de Leybourne	13 March 1322
High Head (Cumb)	William Lengleys	6 Oct 1342
Millun (Cumb)	John de Hodleston	24 Aug 1335
Naworth (Cumb)	Ranulf de Dacre	27 July 1335
Penrith (Cumb)	William de Strickland	12 Feb 1397
" " "	William de Strickland	2 April 1399
Rose (Cumb)	John de Kirkby, bp of Carlisle	9 April 1336
" " "	Bishop of Carlisle	25 June 1355
Scaleby (Cumb)	Robert Tilliol	24 Aug 1307
Triermain (Cumb)	Roland de Vaux	4 Feb 1340
Wolsty (Cumb)	Holmcultram Abbey	13 Oct 1348
Workington (Cumb)	Gilbert de Culwen	4 March 1380
Wythope (Cumb)	Hugh Lowther	12 July 1318
Bretby (Derby)	John de Seagrave	19 March 1301
Melbourne (Derby)	Robert de Holland	17 June 1311
Bampton (Devon)	Richard Cogan	17 March 1336

Castle	Licensee	Date
Hemyock (Devon)	William Asthorp + wife	5 Nov 1380
Ilton (Devon)	John de Chevreston	10 Sept 1335
Kingswear (Devon)	John Corp	13 Oct 1402
Sampford Peverel (Devon)	Oliver de Denham	23 July 1337
Torrington (Devon)	Richard de Merton	29 Sept 1340
" " "	Richard de Merton	6 Jan 1347
Chideok (Dorset)	John de Chideock	9 Feb 1370
" " "	" " "	2 June 1380
Woodsford (Dorset)	William de Whitefield	8 Oct 1335
Ludworth (Durham)	?	1422
Lumley (Durham)	Ralph de Lumley	1389
" " "	Ralph de Lumley	24 Oct 1392
Raby (Durham)	?	1378
Witton le Wear (Durham)	Ralph Eure	23 Sept 1410
Ruardean (Glou)	Alexander Bicknore	1 June 1311
Ashperton (Hereford)	William de Grandison	3 May 1292
Eaton Tregoz (Hereford)	William de Grandison	14 Dec 1308
Moccas (Hereford)	Hugh de Frene	15 June 1293
Bp's Stortford (Herts)	Ralph de Stratford, bp London	12 March 1346
Allington (Kent)	Stephen de Pencestre	25 May 1281
Colbridge (Kent)	Sir Fulk Peyforer	19 July 1313
Cooling (Kent)	John Lord Cobham	10 Feb 1381
Hever (Kent)	Stephen de Pencestre	17 Jan 1271
" " "	John de Cobham	3 Nov 1383
Mereworth (Kent)	John de Mereworth	22 Oct 1332
Westhanger (Kent)	John de Kiriel	18 Aug 1343
Piel (Lancs)	Furness Abbey	26 Sept 1327
Radcliffe (Lancs)	James de Radcliffe	15 Aug 1403
Thurland (Lancs)	Thomas Tunstall	14 Oct 1402
Whitwick (Leics)	Henry de Beaumont	12 March 1321
Folkingham (Lincs)	Henry de Beaumont	26 April 1312
Somerton (Lincs)	Anthony Bek	23 May 1281
Claxton (Norfolk)	William de Kerdston	9 June 1340
" " "	William de Kerdston	4 Dec 1376
Great Hautboys (Norfolk)	Robert Baynard	7 Sept 1312
Gresham (Norfolk)	Edmund Bacon	4 Nov 1318
Marham (Norfolk)	William Belet	9 June 1271
North Elmham (Norfolk)	Henry Despenser, bp Norwich	29 Dec 1387
Barton Seagrave (Nhants)	Nicholas de Seagrave	3 Oct 1310
Braybrooke (Nhants)	Thomas de Latimer	30 Jan 1304
Castle Ashby (Nhants)	Walter Langton, bp Cov & Lich	16 Sept 1306
Maxey (Nhants)	William de Thorpe	5 May 1374
Moor End (Nhants)	Thomas de Ferrers	20 March 1347
Thorpe Waterville (Nhants)	Walter Langton, bp Cov & Lich	1 Jan 1301
Titchmarch (Nhants)	John Lovel	22 Nov 1304
Aydon (Nthumb)	Robert de Reymes	5 April 1305
Barmoor (Nthumb)	Thomas de Muschamps	17 May 1341
Blenkinsopp (Nthumb)	Thomas de Blenkinsop	4 Feb 1340

Castle	Licensee	Date
Blenkinsopp (Nthumb)	Thomas de Blenkinsop	11 May 1340
Bothal (Nthumb)	Robert Bertram	15 May 1343
Chillingham (Nthumb)	Thomas de Heton	27 Jan 1344
Crawley (Nthumb)	John Heron	20 Nov 1343
Dunstanburgh (Nthumb)	Thomas of Lancaster	28 Aug 1315
Eshot (Nthumb)	Robert Maudut	22 July 1310
Eslington (Nthumb)	Robert de Eslington	20 Feb 1335
Etal (Nthumb)	Robert de Manners	3 May 1341
Fenwick (Nthumb)	John de Fenwick	26 Nov 1378
Ford (Nthumb)	William Heron	16 July 1338
Haggerston (Nthumb)	Robert de Haggerston	4 June 1345
Horton near the Sea (Nthumb)	Guichard de Charrun	28 Dec 1292
Newlands in Warenton (Nthumb)	John de Middleton	22 July 1310
Ogle (Nthumb)	Robert de Ogle	11 May 1341
Shortflatt (Nthumb)	Robert de Reymes	5 April 1305
Swinburne, West (Nthumb)	Roger de Widdrington	10 May 1346
Tynemouth (Nthumb)	Tynemouth Priory	5 Sept 1296
Whitley nr Tynem. (Nthumb)	Gilbert de Whitley	9 April 1345
Widdrington (Nthumb)	Gerard de Widdrington	10 Sept 1341
Greasley (Notts)	Nicholas de Cantilupe	5 April 1340
Bampton (Oxf)	Aymer de Valence	3 May 1315
Broughton (Oxf)	Thomas Wykeham	19 March 1406
Rothersfield Greys (Oxf)	John de Grey	22 Feb 1348
Shirbourn (Oxf)	Warin de L'isle	5 March 1377
Watlington (Oxf)	Nicholas de la Beche	3 March 1338
Enor (Scilly)	Ralph de Albo Monasteri	12 March 1315
Apley (Shrops)	Alan de Charlton	10 July 1327
Cheney Longville (Shrops)	Hugh Cheney	1 Sept 1394
Dawley (Shrops)	William de Morton	17 Nov 1316
Myddle (Shrops)	John le Strange	1 April 1308
Stokesay (Shrops)	Laurence de Ludlow	19 Oct 1291
Tong (Shrops)	Fulk de Pembrugge	24 July 1381
Wrockwardine (Shrops)	John de Charlton	17 Nov 1316
Farleigh Hungerford (Somerset)	Thomas de Hungerford	26 Nov 1383
Nunney (Somerset)	John de la Mare	28 Nov 1373
Caverswall (Staffs)	William de Caverswell	7 Nov 1275
Stafford (Staffs)	Ralph, baron Stafford	6 Feb 1348
Bungay (Suffolk)	Roger le Bigod, e. Norfolk	20 April 1294
Mettingham (Suffolk)	John de Norwich	21 Aug 1343
Wingfield (Suffolk)	Michael de la Pole	27 April 1385
Betchworth (Surrey)	John Arundel, kn	26 July 1379
Sterborough (Surrey)	Reginald de Cobham	18 Oct 1341
Amberley (Sussex)	Bishop of Chichester	10 Dec 1377
Bodiam (Sussex)	Edward Dalyngrugge	21 Oct 1385
Beaudesert (Warks)	Walter Langton, bp Cov & Lich	16 Sept 1306
Caludon (Warks)	John de Seagrave	2 Feb 1305
Fillongley (Warks)	John de Hastings	2 Feb 1301
Maxstoke (Warks)	William de Clinton	12 Feb 1345

Castle	Licensee	Date
Ragley (Warks)	John Rous	8 Dec 1381
Broughton (Westmorland)	Robert de Clifford	1309
Hartley (Westmorland)	Thomas de Musgrave	4 Oct 1354
Pendragon (Westmorland)	Robert de Clifford	1309
Castle Eaton (Wilts)	Nicholas de Seymour	28 May 1311
Wardour (Wilts)	John 5th Lord Lovel	27 Feb 1393
Strensham (Worcs)	John Russel	12 Feb 1388
Bolton (Yrks)	Richard le Scrope	4 July 1379
Cottingham (Yrks)	Thomas Wake	6 March 1327
Elslack (Yrks)	Godfrey Dawtrey	24 Nov 1318
Flamborough (Yrks)	Marmaduke Constable	24 May 1351
" " "	" " "	11 Feb 1352
Harewood (Yrks)	William de Aldeburgh	27 Dec 1366
Hazlewood (Yrks)	William de Vavassour	28 Aug 1290
Killerby (Yrks)	Brian fitz Alan	20 Sept 1291
Kirkby Fleetham (Yrks)	Henry le Scrope	20 Sept 1314
Kirkby Sigston (Yrks)	John de Sigston	10 Feb 1336
Sheriff Hutton (Yrks)	John de Neville of Raby	26 April 1382
Slingsby (Yrks)	Ralph de Hastings	28 Jan 1344
Swine (Yrks)	John de Sutton	4 Feb 1352
Wilton (Bps Wilton (Yrks)	Ralph de Bulmer	12 May 1330

Table 2.x

Castles Built, 1272–1422

County	New Castles
Anglesey	Beaumaris
Bedfordshire	Bletsoe
Berkshire	Aldworth le Beche, Beaumyss, Donnington
Brecknock	Talgarth
Buckinghamshire	Boarstall, Weston Turville
Caernarvon	Caernarvon, Conway
Cambridgeshire	Cheveley
Cardigan	Aberystwyth
Carmarthen	Carreg Cennon, Roche Castle
Cheshire	Doddington, Macclesfield
Cornwall	Helston, Lanihorne, Stratton
Cumberland	Branthwaite, Dacre, Drumburgh, Dunmalloght, Greystoke, Hardrigg Hall, Hay, Hutton in forest, Irton Hall, Millom, Muncaster, Naworth, Penrith, Scaleby, Triermain, Wolsty, Workington, Wythop
Denbigh	Chirk, Denbigh, Ruthin
Derbyshire	Melbourne
Devon	Dartmouth, Gidleigh, Hemyock, Ilton, Kingswear, Plymouth Barbican, Powderham, Sampford Peverel
Dorset	Chideock, Woodsford
Durham	Bishop Auckland, Hylton, Lumley, Raby, Ravensworth

County	New Castles
Flint	Caergwrle, Flint, Rhuddlan
Glamorgan	Barry, Caerphilly, Candleston, Castel Coch, Llanblethian, Llandaff, Morlais, Penlle'r Castell, Penmark, St. Donats, Weobley
Gloucestershire	Ruardean, Yate Court
Hereford	Ashperton, Eaton Tregoz, Kentchurch, Moccas, Penyard
Kent	Allington, Colbridge, Cooling, Hever, Queensborough, Scotney, Westenhanger,
Lancashire	Broughton in Furness, Dalton in Furness, Gleaston, Piel, Radcliffe, Thurland
Leicestershire	Ashby de la Zouch, Whitwick
Lincs.	Folkingham, South Kyme, Somerton
Merioneth	Harlech
Monmouth	Cas Troggy, Llangibby, Penhow
Montgomery	Dolforwyn, Powis
Norfolk	Claxton, Great Hautboys, Gresham, Marham, North Elmham
Northamptonshire	Braybrooke, Castle Ashby, Maxey, Moor End, Northborough, Thorpe Waterville, Titchmarch, Woodcroft
Northumberland	Alnham, Aydon, Barmoor ,Bavington, Little Beaufont, Belford, Belsay, Berrington, Biddlestone Hall, Blenkinsopp, Bothal, Buckton, Capheaton (Hutton), Cartingham, Chatton, Chillingham, Chipchase, Coquet Island, Corbridge, Craster, Crawley, Detchant, Dunstanburgh, Edlingham, Elsdon no. 2, Elwick, Embleton, Eshot, Eslington, Etal, Farnham, Featherstone, Fenton, Fenwick, Flotterton, Ford, Haggerston, Halton, Haltwhistle no. 2, Harle, West, Harnham, Heaton Coldstream, Hepple, Hethpool, Hetton Hall, Hexham, Holburn, Hoppen, Horton in Glendale, Horton near Sea, Howick, Ilderton, Kirkley, Kyloe, Kirknewton, Lemmington, Lilburn, West, Meldon, Middleton by the Sea, Middleton, North, Morpeth, Nesbit in Glendale, Netherwitton, Newland in Warton, Newstead nr Bamb., Ogle, Ponteland, Preston by Alnwick, Shortflatt, Sremerston, Seaton Delaval, Seghill, Sewingshields, Shawden, Shilbottle, Simonburn, Stamfordham, Stanton, Trewitt, Nether, Thropton, Troughend, Twizel, Wallington, Weetslade, Whitfield, West Swinburne, Whitton nr Rothbury, Whitley nr Tyne, Whittingham, Widdrington
Nottinghamshire	Greasley
Oxfordshire	Bampton, Broughton, Rothersfield Greys, Shirburn, Watlington
Pembroke	Benton, Newton, Picton, Upton
Radnor	Aberedw
Shropshire	Apley, Cheney Longville, Dawley, Lea, Myddle, Stokesay, Wrockwardine
Somerset	Farleigh Hungerford, Nunney, Wells
Staffs	Cavershall, Stafford
Suffolk	Bungay, Mettingham, Wingfield
Surrey	Betchworth, Sterborough
Sussex	Amberley, Bodiam, Mountfield
Warwickshire	Caludon, Fillongley, Kingsbury, Maxstoke, Ragley

County	New Castles
Westmorland	Asby, Askham Hall, Beetham 2, Beetham Hall, Bewley, Hartley, Howgill, Kentmere, Lammerside, Sizergh, Strickland Roger, Yanwath
Wiltshire	Castle Eaton, Wardour
Worcestershire	Strensham
Yorkshire	Ayton, Bolton, Cawood, Cropton, Danby, Elslack, Flamborough, Gilling East, Harewood, Hazlewood, Killerby, Kirkby Fleetham, Kirkby Sigston, Leconfield, Markenfield, Sherburn in Elmet, Sheriff Hutton, Slingsby, Upsall, Wressle, Wilton

2.xi
Castles Forfeited, 1272–1422

	Forfeited	Restoration	No. of castles
Arundel, Edmund, earl of	1326	son in 1330	7
Arundel, Richard, earl of	1397	son in 1400	11
Audley, Hugh de, younger	1321	self	1
Audley, Hugh de, younger	1329	self in 1329	5
Balliol, John de	1294		2
Beauchamp, Thomas, earl of Warwick	1397	self in 1399	11
Bohun, Humphrey de, earl of Hereford	1322	son in 1326	4
Burley, Simon de	1388	no	4
Cary, John	1388	–	1
Clifford, Roger de	1322	brother in 1327	5
Cobham, John de	1398	self by 1408	1
Despenser, Thomas	1400		11
Despenser, Hugh, elder	1327		2
Despenser, Hugh, younger	1327		17
Ferrers, Thomas de	c.1276		1
Gaveston, Piers	1312		7
Giffard, John, of Brimpsfield,	1322		2
Gloucester, Thomas, duke of	1397		7
Grey, Thomas de, of Heton	1415		1
Hasting, John de, earl of Pembroke	1390		10
Holland, Robert de	1322		2
Holland, John de, duke of Exeter	1400		8
Holland, Thomas, earl of Kent	1400		5
Henry IV (Bolingbroke)	1399	took throne	5
Lancaster, Thomas de	1322	brother, slowly	24
Lumley, Ralph	1400		2
Lumley, Thomas	1400		1
Mautravers, John	1334		2
Montague, John de, earl of Salisbury	1400		5
Mortimer, Edmund,	1404		1
Mortimer, Roger de, of Chirk	1322	never restored	3
Mortimer, Roger de, earl of March	1322	soon restored	8

	Forfeited	Restoration	No. of castles
Mortimer, Roger de, earl of March	1330		17
Mowbray,. John	1322		4
Mowbray, Thomas, earl of Marshal	1405		6
Oldcastle, John	1414		2
Percy, Henry de, e. of Northumberland	1405		9
Percy, Thomas de, earl of Worcester	1403		1
Pole, Michael de la, e. Suffolk	1388	son in 1397	3
Scrope, William de, e. Wiltshire	1399		2
Strabolgi, David de	1329		3
Veer, Robert de, earl of Oxford	1388	uncle restored	3
Wake, Thomas	1329	restored 1329	3
Woodstock, Edmund, e. Kent	1330		4
Perrers, Alice	1377		1

2.xii

Joint Constables

Castle	Period
Barton Segrave (Nthants)	1406–8
Beaumaris (Anglesey)	1396–7
Brecon (Brecknock)	1403–4
Bridgewater (Somerset)	1322, 1326–
Bristol (Gloucestershire)	1321, 1326–8
Bronlyss (Brecknock)	1421–
Built (Brecknock)	1331–4
Caernarvon	1396–9
Carlisle (Cumberland)	1317–18, 1385–90
Carmarthen	1399–1402
Carreg Cennon (Carmarthen)	1322
Castel-y-Bere (Merioneth)	1292
Chester Castle	1341–, 1396–9
" "	1396–9
Chirk (Denbigh)	1331–3
Conisborough (Yrks)	1322
Conway (Caernarvon)	1394
Corfe (Dorset)	1299, 1315–18, 1391–7
Criccieth (Caernarvon)	1398–
Dryslwyn (Carmarthen)	1399–
Dunstanburgh (Nthumb)	1322–23
Eye (Suffolk)	1337
Flint	1341
Hanley (Worcester)	1321
Oakham (Rutland)	1327
Peak (Derbyshire)	1319

Castle	Period
Knaresborough (Yrks)	1318
Leeds (Kent)	1399
Lincoln	1327, 1331
Llanstephan (Carmarthen)	1326–
Neath (Glamorgan)	1321
Newcastle Emlyn (Carmarthen)	1388–9
Pontefract (Yrks)	1323
Portchester (Hampshire)	1397–1405
Rochester (Kent)	1334, 1399
Rockingham (Nthants)	1325
Rhuddlan (Flint)	1341
Scarborough (Yrks)	1324–1325
Somerton (Lincs)	1317
Tintagel (Cornwall)	1386–9
Tonbridge (Kent)	1321
Wallingford (Berks)	1399

2.xiii

Castle Ownership and Constable Totals

	Number of Constable Appointments													
Number of Castles Owned	0	1	2	3	4	5	6	7	8	9	12	13	14	**Totals**
0		1186	170	44	13	7	6	2	1	1	1	1	0	1432
1	496	56	23	4	5	2	1	1	0	0	0	0	0	587
2	107	16	8	3	1	0	2	0	0	0	0	0	1	138
3	42	9	6	0	0	2	1	0	0	0	0	0	0	60
4	27	5	1	2	1	0	0	1	0	0	0	0	0	37
5	16	3	2	1	1	0	0	0	0	0	0	0	0	23
6	11	1	1	0	1	0	0	0	0	0	0	0	0	14
7	3	1	1	0	1	0	1	0	0	0	0	0	0	7
8	2	0	1	4	0	0	0	0	1	0	0	0	0	8
9	6	1	2	0	0	0	0	0	0	0	0	0	0	9
10	3	3	0	0	0	0	0	0	0	0	0	0	0	6
11	3	1	0	2	0	0	0	0	0	0	1	0	0	7
12	2	0	1	0	0	0	0	0	0	0	0	0	0	3
14	2	0	0	0	0	0	0	0	0	0	0	0	0	2
16	1	0	0	0	0	0	0	0	0	0	0	0	0	1
17	0	0	0	0	1	0	0	0	0	0	0	0	0	1
18	2	0	0	0	0	0	1	0	0	0	0	0	0	3
21	1	0	0	0	0	0	0	0	0	0	0	0	0	1
22	1	0	0	0	0	0	0	0	0	0	0	0	0	1
24	0	1	0	0	0	0	0	0	0	0	0	0	0	1
25	1	0	1	0	0	0	0	0	0	0	0	0	0	2
28	0	0	1	0	0	0	0	0	0	0	0	0	0	1
31	1	0	0	0	0	0	0	0	0	0	0	0	0	1
Totals	1223	1283	218	60	24	11	12	4	2	1	2	1	1	2345

2.xiv
Castle ownership

Owned	Individuals	%	Castles	%
1	588	64.3	588	28.4
2	138	15.1	276	13.3
3	60	6.6	180	8.7
4	37	4.0	148	7.1
5	23	2.5	115	5.5
6	14	1.5	84	4.1
7	7	0.8	49	2.4
8	8	0.9	64	3.1
9	9	1.0	81	3.9
10	6	0.7	60	2.9
11	7	0.8	77	3.7
12	3	0.3	36	1.7
14	2	0.2	28	1.4
16	1	0.1	16	0.8
17	1	0.1	17	0.8
18	3	0.3	54	2.6
21	1	0.1	21	1.0
22	1	0.1	22	1.1
24	1	0.1	24	1.2
25	3	0.3	75	3.6
28	1	0.1	28	1.4
31	1	0.1	31	1.5
Total	915	100	2074	100

2.xv
Constable Service

Constables	Individuals	%	Castles	%
1	1283	76.4	1283	57.7
2	218	13.4	436	19.2
3	60	3.7	180	7.9
4	24	1.5	96	4.2
5	11	0.7	55	2.4
6	12	0.7	72	3.2
7	4	0.2	42	1.9
8	2	0.1	16	0.7
9	1	0.06	9	0.4
12	3	0.2	36	1.6
13	2	0.1	26	1.1
14	1	0.06	14	0/6
Total	1621	100.0	2265	100.0

2.xvi

Number of castles owned by constables

Castles Owned	Individuals
0	1433
1	92
2	31
3	18
4	10
5	7
6	3
7	4
8	6
9	3
10	3
11	4
12	1
17	1
18	1
24	1
25	2
28	1
Total	1621

2.xvii

No of castle owners serving as constables

Posts	Individuals
0	727
1	97
2	48
3	16
4	11
5	4
6	6
7	2
8	1
12	1
13	1
14	1
Total	915

2.xviii

People Serving as Constable of Four or More Castles

Name	Posts	Dates	Span	Counties
Audley, Hugh de, snr	4	1310–1318	8	3
Badelesmere, Bartholomew de	6	1307–1321	14	4
Bagot, William	5	1396–1399	3	4
Beauchamp, Giles	4	1318–1327	9	4
Beauchamp, William	6	1321–1341	10	4
Beaufort, John de, e. Somerset	5	1397–1410	13	5
Beche, John de la	4	1311–1322	11	3
Beche, Nicholas de la	5	1312–1340	28	5
Beler, Roger	4	1322–1323	1	3
Berkeley, Maurice de, of Brimpsfield	5	1328–1338	10	3
Bisshebury, Henry de	4	1320–1330	10	3
Burgherssh, Bartholomew de	5	1326–1355	29	4
Burley, Simon	4	1375–1388	13	3
Bussy, John	4	1394–1399	5	3
Chaundos, Roger	4	1312–1335	23	4
Cobham, Henry de	4	1313–1334	21	1
Cromwell, John de	5	1307–1335	28	5
Damory, Roger	4	1315–1321	6	3
Despenser, Hugh, elder	6	1294–1322	28	5
Despenser, Hugh, yng	13	1317–1326	9	7
Ercalowe, William de	6	1326–1331	5	4
Felton, John de	6	1316–1327	11	3
Felton, William de	5	1300–1344	44	3
Ferrers, Henry de	4	1333–1341	8	3
Gaveston, Piers	6	1308–1312	4	5
Golafre, John	5	1387–1397	10	4
Grey, Richard de, of Codnor	7	1402–1405	3	4
Griffeth, Res ap	12	1321–1342	21	8
Hathewy, William	5	1291–1292	2	2
Havering, John de	4	1274–1301	27	4
Holand, Robert de	4	1307–1312	5	2
Holand, John de, e. of Huntingdon	8	1389–1398	9	8
Inge, John	7	1321–1333	12	5
Ingham, Oliver de	6	1321–1328	7	5
Knovill, Bevis de	12	1274–1301	27	5
Lancaster, Henry earl of	4	1326–1342	16	4
Langley, Edmund, duke of York	4	1373–1400	27	4
L'isle, John de	4	1314–1330	16	4
Lucy, Anthony de	4	1318–1339	21	2
Mauduyt, Roger	4	1322–1334	12	1
Montague, William de, earl Salisbury	4	1330–1339	9	2
Mortimer, Roger de, e. of March	6	1310–1330	20	4
Mortimer, Roger de, of Chirk	6	1308–1321	13	4
Mosele, Richard de	4	1323–1326	3	1
Percy. Henry de, 'Hotspur'	6	1390–1400	10	4

Name	Posts	Dates	Span	Counties
Sandwich, Ralph de	9	1275–1308	33	7
Scrope, William le, e. of Wiltshire	14	1389–1399	10	12
Strange, Roger le, of Ellesmere	8	1273–1284	11	7
Talbot, Gilbert	6	1322–1346	24	3
Tybotet, Payn de	4	1307–1311	4	3
Tybotot, Robert de	7	1275–1298	23	3
Veer, Robert de, earl of Oxford	5	1384–1393	9	5
Waterton, Hugh	5	1387–1409	22	4
Woodstock, Edmund de, earl of Kent	7	1318–1328	10	6
York, Edward duke of	12	1390–1415	25	10

Span: total years from first to last appointment.

2.xix

Summary of known Sub-Constables

Castle	Individuals	Years Covered
Abergavenny (Monmouth)	1	1
Bamborough (Northumb.)	1	1
Bristol (Gloucester)	1	1
Caernarvon	2	2
Cardigan	1	1
Chepstow (Monmouth)	2	5
Chirk (Denb)	1	1
Conway (Caern.)	1	1
Corfe (Dorset)	4	11
Criccieth (Caern.)	1	1
Denbigh	1	1
Devizes (Wilts)	1	1
Dover (Kent)	21	30
Dynevor (Carm.)	1	1
Gloucester	2	2
Kenilworth (Warks.)	1	1
Knaresborough (Yorks.)	2	2
Melbourne (Derby)	1	2
Montgomery	3	4
Norwich	1	1
Nottingham	1	1
Oakham (Rutland)	1	1
Portchester (Hamps.)	2	2
Rochester (Kent)	4	4
Rockingham (Nhants)	2	2
St. Briavels (Glous.)	2	3
Sandal (Yorks.)	1	2
Scarborough (Yorks.)	1	2
Somerton (Lincs.)	1	1
Tower of London	14	13

Wallingford (Berks.)	2	2
Warwick	1	1
Windsor (Berks.)	6	15

2.xx

Castles in Wardship, 1272–1422: Male heirs

Name	Born	Inherited	Of Age[1]	Castles[2]
Albo Monasterio, John de	1338	1348	1359	1
Arundel, Richard fitzAlan, earl of	1267	1280	1288	4
Arundel, Edmund fitzAlan, earl of	1285	1302	1307	7
Audley, Thomas de	1289	1299	d.1308	2
Audley, Nicholas de	1289	1308	1310	3
Audley, James de	1313	1316	1334	3
Badlesmere, Giles de	1314	1328	1333[3]	2
Baskervill, Richard	1371	1374	1392	1
Beauchamp, Thomas de, earl of Warwick	1314	1315	1335	7
Beauchamp, Richard de, earl of Warwick	1382	1401	1403	6
Beaumont, John de	1361	1369	1383	1
Beaumont, Henry de	1380	1396	1401	1
Beaumont, John de	1409	1413	1430	1
Bere, Thomas	1401	1403	1422	1
Berkeley, Thomas de, of Brimpsfield	1333	1347	1354	1
Berkeley, Thomas de	1352	1368	1373	1
Brewosa, John	1302	1305	1323	1
Bohun, Humphrey de, earl of Hereford	1342	1361	1363	6
Botiller, William	1274	1290	1295	1
Carreu, Leonard de	1342	1362	1363	1
Cherleton, John de, of Powys	1360	1374	1381	2
Clare, Gilbert de, earl of Gloucester	1291	1295	1312	18
Clifford, Robert de	1274	1292	1295	5
Clifford, Roger de	1299	1314	1321	5
Clifford, Robert de	1328	1344	d.1345	3
Clifford, Roger de	1334	1345	1355	3
Clifford, John de	1388	1391	1409	4
Clifton, Adam	1307	1316	1328	1
Clifton, Constantine de	1372	1391	1393	1
Cobham, Thomas de, of Rundale	1343	1361	1363	1
Colbill, Robert de	1363	1367	d.1369	1
Cornwall, Brian	1355	1365	1376	1
Courtenay, Hugh de, earl of Devon	1275	1293	1296	1
Courtenay, Edward de, earl of Devon	1357	1377	1378	4
Courtenay, Thomas de, earl of Devon	1414	1422	1435	4
Dacre, Thomas	1387	1399	1408	1

[1] Or date of death if died before coming of age.
[2] Only includes those castles actually in wardship.
[3] While still underage.

Name	Born	Inherited	Of Age[1]	Castles[2]
Darcy, Philip	1352	1368	1373	1
Despenser, Edward	1337	1349	1358	5
Despenser, Thomas	1373	1375	1394	11
Despenser, Richard	–	1400	d.1416	3
Dyve, John de	1273	1275	1294	1
Faucomberge, Thomas de	1344	1362	1365	1
Felton, John de	1388	1396	d.1403	1
Freyville, Baldwin de	1368	1387	1389	1
Freyville, Baldwin de	1395	1400	1416	1
Fourivcal, Thomas de	1322	1339	1343	2
Giffard, John de, of Brymmesfeld	1287	1299	1308	2
Graystoke, Ralph, baron	1353	1359	1374	2
Grey, Richard de, of Wilton	1393	1396	1414	1
Harrington, John	1328	1347	1349	1
Harrington, Robert	1356	1363	1377	1
Hastings, John de, lord of Abergavenny	1262	1269	1283	2
Hastings, Laurence de, earl of Pembroke	1320	1325	1341	5
Hastings, John de, earl of Pembroke	1347	1348	1368	6
Hastings, John de, earl of Pembroke	1372	1375	d.1389	6
Hastings, Richard de	1381	1401	1402	1
Heton, William	1393	1399	d.1401	1
Holland, Thomas de, earl of Kent	1350	1360	1371	1
Holland, John de, earl of Huntingdon	1395	1400	1416	2
Latimer, Thomas de	1341	1361	1362	1
Lovel, John	1341	1347	d.1361	1
Lumley, Ralph de	1361	1374	1382	1
Lumley, John de	1384	1400	1404	1
Mauley, Peter, 8th	1378	1383	1399	1
Mohaut, Roger de	1262	1275	1283	1
Mohun, John de	1270	1279	1291	1
Montague, William de, earl of Salisbury	1329	1344	1350	6
Montfort, John de	1291	1296	1312	1
Mortimer, Roger de, earl of March	1288	1304	1309	5
Mortimer, Roger de, earl of March	1328	1332	1349	3
Mortimer, Edmund de, earl of March	1352	1360	1373	9
Mortimer, Roger de, earl of March	1374	1381	1395	19
Mortimer, Edmund de, earl of March	1391	1398	1412	19
Mowbray, Thomas, earl Marshal	1385	1399	d.1405	6
Mowbray, John	1392	1405	1414	5
Multon, John de	1308	1322	1329	1
Nevill, John de	1300	1319	1321	1
Norwico, John de	1352	1366	d.1372	1
Ogle, Robert de	1353	1362	1372	1
Pauncefot, Grymbald	1318	1332	1339	1
Percy, Henry de	1298	1314	1319	1
Pole, William de la, earl of Suffolk	1396	1415	1417	2
Pychard, Roger	1290	1306	1311	1
Restwold, Richard	1364	1374	1385	1

Name	Born	Inherited	Of Age[1]	Castles[2]
Roche, John de	1368	1376	1389	1
Ros, Thomas de, of Kendal	1306	1310	1327	1
Ros, William de, of Hamelak	1328	1343	1349	2
Ros, Thomas de, of Hamelak	1338	1353	1359	2
Ros, John de, of Hamelak	1263	1383	1384	2
Ros, John de, of Hamelak	1399	1414	1419	3
Ros, Thomas de, of Hamelak	1406	1421	1427	1
Scrope, Henry de, of Bolton	1418	1420	1439	1
Segrave, John de	1315	1325	1336	2
Somery, Roger	1255	1273	1278	1
Somery, John	1279	1291	1300	1
Stafford, Edmund, earl of	1378	1395	1399	4
Stafford, Humphrey, earl of	1402	1403	1423	4
Stafford, Thomas, earl of	1368	1386	1389	4
Stafford, William,	–	1392	d.1395	4
Strange, John le, of Blackmere	1309	1323	1330	1
Strabolgi, David de	1307	1327	1328	3
Strabolgi, David de	1334	1336	1355	1
Talbot, John, of Richard's Castle	1336	1355	1357	1
Talbot, John, of Richard's Castle	1374	1382	d.1388	1
Talbot, Gilbert de	1383	1396	1404	1
Tatershale, Robert de	1288	1303	d.1306	2
Tuchet, John, lord Audley	1371	1391	1392	2
Tuchet, James, lord Audley	1399	1409	1420	4
Ufford, Robert de	1279	1298	1300	1
Umfraville, Gilbert de, earl of Angus	1310	1325	1331	2
Umfraville, Gilbert de	1390	1391	1411	2
Veel, John	1408	1410	1429	1
Vere, John de, earl of Oxford	1312	1331	1333	2
Vere, Robert de, earl of Oxford	1362	1371	1383	3
Vere, Richard de, earl of Oxford	1385	1400	1406	2
Wake, Thomas	1298	1300	1319	2
Warenne, John de	1286	1286	1307	1
Waryn, Fulk fitz	1340	1349	1361	1
Waryn, Fulk fitz	1366	1372	1387	1
Waryn, Fulk fitz	1389	1391	d.1407	1
Waryn, Fulk fitz	1406	1407	1427	3
Waulter, Walter fitz	1344	1363	1365	1
Waulter, Humphrey fitz	1388	1406	1409	3
Wyderington, John de	1371	1372	1392	1

Castles in Wardship, 1272–1422: Female heiresses

	Born	Inherited	Castles
Bohun, Eleanor & Mary	1366 & 1370	1373	8
Brompton, Margaret & Elizabeth	1294 & 1295	1395	1
Brittania, Alice	1282	1285	2
Clare, Margaret & Isabel	1295 & 1296	1314	13
Clarence, Philippa	1352	1368	4
Faucomberge, Joan	1406	1407	1
Furnivalle, Joan de	1369	1383	1
Geneville, Joan, Beatrice & Maud	1286, 1287 & 1288	1292	1
Heton, Joan, Elizabeth & Margaret	1386, 1389, 1393	1401	1
Lerchedekene, Margery	1291	1307	1
Leyburne, Juliane de	1304	1307	1
Lovel, Joan	1312	1314	1
Lucy, Joan de	1366	1368	2
Malory, Elizabeth	1401	1412	2
Montague, Joan de	1349	1361	1
Mortimer, Joan & Margaret	1292, 1296	1305	2
Pole, Hawis la	1291	1309	1
Segrave, Elizabeth	1337	1353	2
Strabolgi, Elizabeth & Philippa	1362 & 1363	1369	1
Talbot, Eleanor, of Richard's Castle	1372	1388	1
Verdon, Elizabeth	1306	1316	1
Verdon, Joan		1316	1
Verdon, Margary		1316	1

Table 2.xxi

Royal Castles – List

County	Castles
Anglesey	Beaumaris
Berkshire	Wallingford, Windsor
Brecknock	Blaen Llyfni, Brecon, Bronlyss, Builth, Crickhowell, Dinas, Hay, Penkelly, Talgarth, Tretower
Caernarvon	Caernarvon, Conway, Criccieth, Degannwy, Dolwyddelan
Cambridge	Cambridge
Cardigan	Aberystwyth, Cardigan
Carmarthen	Carmarthen, Carreg Cennon, Dryslwyn, Dynevor, Llandovery, Llanstephan, Newcastle Emlyn
Cheshire	Beeston, Chester, Halton
Cornwall	Launceston, Mt. St. Michael, Restormel, Tintagel, Trematon
Cumberland	Carlisle, Cockermouth, High Head
Denbigh	Chirk, Denbigh, Dinas Bran, Holt
Derbyshire	Bolsover, Harestan, Melbourne, Peak
Devonshire	Barnstaple, Exeter, Lydford
Dorset	Corfe, Cranborne, Dorchester, Sherborne

County	Castles
Durham	Barnard Castle
Essex	Hadleigh, Ongar, Pleshey
Flint	Caergwrle, Flint, Hawarden, Rhuddlan
Glamorgan	Caerphilly, Neath, Swansea
Gloucester	Berkeley, Bristol, Gloucester, St. Briavels
Hampshire	Carisbrooke, Christchurch, Odiham, Portchester, Southampton, Winchester
Hereford	Eardisley, Hereford, Huntington, Lyonshall, Wigmore
Hertford	Berkhamstead, Hertford
Kent	Canterbury, Cooling, Dover, Leeds, Queenborough, Rochester, Sandwich
Lancashire	Clitheroe, Lancaster, Liverpool
Leicestershire	Castle Donnington, Leicester
Lincolnshire	Bolingbroke, Lincoln, Somerton, Stamford
London	The Tower
Merioneth	Castel-y-Bere, Harlech
Monmouth	Caldicot, Chepstow, Llangibby, Monmouth, Skenfrith
Montgomery	Dolforwyn, Montgomery, Powis
Norfolk	Castle Rising, Norwich
Northampton	Barton Seagrave, Fotheringay, Higham Ferrars, Moor End, Northampton, Rockingham
Northumberland	Alnham, Alnwick, Bamborough, Berwick, Dunstanburgh, Langley, Newcastle, Prudhoe, Staward, Wark on Tweed, Warkworth
Nottinghamshire	Nottingham
Oxfordshire	Oxford
Pembroke	Cilgerran, Haverford West, Narberth, Pembroke
Radnor	Cefnllys, New Radnor, Painscastle, Tinboeth
Rutland	Oakham
Shropshire	Bridgnorth, Clune, Dawley, Ludlow, Oswestry, Redcastle, Shrawardine, Shrewsbury, Whittington
Somerset	Bridgewater
Staffordshire	Chartley, Dudley, Tutbury
Suffolk	Clare, Eye, Framlingham, Orford
Surrey	Guildford, Reigate
Sussex	Arundel, Hastings, Lewes, Pevensey
Warwickshire	Kenilworth, Warwick
Westmorland	Appleby, Pendragon
Wiltshire	Devizes, Ludgershall, Marlborough, Mere, Old Sarum
Worcestershire	Elmley, Hanley
Yorkshire	Bowes, Burton-in-Lonsdale, Conisborough, Haverah Park, Knaresborough, Malton, Pickering, Pontefract, Richmond, Sandal, Scarborough, Skipton, Tickhill, Wakefield, Wressle, York

Table 2.xxii
Royal Castles – Summary

County	Total Royal Castles	Long Term[4]	Temporary[5]
Anglesey	1	1	0
Bedfordshire	0	0	0
Berkshire	2	2	0
Brecknock	10	1	5
Buckinghamshire	0	0	0
Caernarvon	5	3	0
Cambridge	2	1	0
Cardigan	2	2	0
Carmarthen	7	4	2
Cheshire	3	2	0
Cornwall	5	5	0
Cumberland	3	1	0
Denbigh	4	0	4
Derbyshire	4	3	1
Devonshire	3	2	1
Dorset	4	2	1
Durham	1	0	1
Essex	4	2	1
Flint	4	2	1
Glamorgan	4	0	4
Gloucester	4	3	1
Hampshire	6	5	0
Hereford	5	1	3
Hertford	2	1	0
Huntingdon	0	0	0
Kent	7	6	1
Lancashire	3	0	0
Leicester	2	0	0
Lincoln	4	1	1
London	1	1	0
Merioneth	2	1	0
Monmouth	4	0	1
Montgomery	3	1	2
Norfolk	2	1	0
Northampton	6	2	3
Northumberland	11	4	5
Nottingham	1	1	0
Oxford	1	1	0
Pembroke	4	1	0
Radnor	4	0	4
Rutland	1	0	0
Shropshire	9	2	7

[4] One fifty year span or 75 years in total including time with the heir to the throne and the Queen.
[5] Forfeited castles that remain in the kings hands for less than five year across the period.

County	Total Royal Castles	Long Term[4]	Temporary[5]
Somerset	1	0	1
Stafford	3	0	2
Suffolk	4	0	1
Surrey	2	1	1
Sussex	4	2	1
Warwick	2	0	1
Westmorland	2	0	2
Wiltshire	5	4	0
Worcester	2	0	2
Yorkshire	16	4	5
England	137	60	42
Wales	54	16	23
Total	191	76	65

Table 2.xxiii
Castle Ownership by type of owner

	c.1300	%	c.1350	%	c.1400	%
Crown	74	18.3	68	13.1	84	14.9
Female Owners	27	6.7	24	4.6	29	5.1
Church	18	4.4	23	4.4	29	5.1
Comital Community	56	13.8	82	15.7	80	14.2
Parliamentary Peers	53	13.1	57	10.9	36	6.4
Other Private	51	12.6	93	17.8	114	20.2
Unclear	126	31.1	174	33.4	191	33.9
Totals	405		521		563	

Table 2.xxiv
Crown Castles by region

Region	c.1300	c.1350	c.1400
Northern Border	4	4	5
North	5	5	8
Midlands	6	5	13
South East	20	17	16
South West	11	11	10
East Anglia	4	5	3
Marches	9	9	8
Wales	14	12	22
Totals	73	68	85

Table 2.xxv
Comital Castles by region

Region	c.1300	c.1350	c.1400
Northern Border	5	8	9
North	10	8	3
Midlands	10	13	10
South East	4	7	9
South West	4	5	7
East Anglia	7	10	12
Marches	6	10	9
Wales	14	25	23
Totals	60	86	82

Table 2.xxvi
Castle ownership by type of Owner – Northern Border

	c.1300	%	c.1350	%	c.1400	%
Crown	4	11.4	4	4.7	5	5.2
Female Owners	0	0	4	4.7	3	3.1
Church	4	11.4	6	7.1	8	8.2
Comital Community	5	14.3	8	9.4	9	9.3
Parliamentary Peers	6	17.1	9	10.6	7	7.2
Other Private	4	11.4	28	32.9	36	3.7
Unclear	12	34.3	26	30.6	29	29.9
Totals	35		85		97	

Table 2.xxvii
Castle ownership by type of Owner – North

	c.1300	%	c.1350	%	c.1400	%
Crown	5	13.5	5	10	8	16.4
Female Owners	0		2	4	3	5.5
Church	2	5.4	3	6	4	7.3
Comital Community	10	27.0	8	16	3	5.5
Parliamentary Peers	5	13.5	10	20	5	9.1
Other Private	4	10.8	7	14	12	21.8
Unclear	11	29.7	15	30	20	36.4
Totals	37		50		55	

Table 2.xxviii
Castle ownership by type of Owner – Midlands

	c.1300	%	c.1350	%	c.1400	%
Crown	7	14	5	7.4	11	14.9
Female Owners	0		3	4.4	3	4.1
Church	4	8	4	5.9	5	6.8
Comital Community	10	20	13	19.1	10	13.5
Parliamentary Peers	8	16	8	11.8	6	8.1
Other Private	8	16	12	17.7	14	18.9
Unclear	13	26	23	33.8	25	33.8
Totals	50		68		74	

Table 2.xxix
Castle ownership by type of Owner – South East

	c.1300	%	c.1350	%	c.1400	%
Crown	23	54.8	20	39.2	19	33.3
Female Owners	1	2.4	2	3.9	2	3.5
Church	3	7.1	4	7.8	4	7.0
Comital Community	4	9.5	7	13.8	9	15.8
Parliamentary Peers	1	2.4	2	3.9	6	10.5
Other Private	6	14.3	10	19.6	9	15.8
Unclear	4	9.5	6	11.8	8	14.0
Totals	42		51		57	

Table 2.xxx
Castle ownership by type of Owner – South West

	c.1300	%	c.1350	%	c.1400	%
Crown	7	26.9	7	21.2	5	12.5
Female Owners	2	7.7	0		2	5.0
Church	2	7.7	3	9.1	4	10.0
Comital Community	4	15.4	5	15.2	7	17.5
Parliamentary Peers	1	3.8	2	6.1	0	
Other Private	3	11.5	8	24.2	8	20.0
Unclear	7	26.9	8	24.2	14	35.0
Totals	26		33		40	

Table 2.xxxi
Castle ownership by type of Owner – East Anglia

	c.1300	%	c.1350	%	c.1400	%
Crown	4	13.8	5	13.2	5	12.5
Female Owners	1	3.4	1	2.6	3	7.5
Church	2	6.9	2	5.3	3	7.5
Comital Community	7	24.1	10	26.3	12	30.0
Parliamentary Peers	4	13.8	4	10.5	1	2.5
Other Private	1	3.4	5	13.2	2	5.0
Unclear	10	34.5	11	28.9	14	35.0
Totals	29		38		40	

Table 2.xxxii
Castle ownership by type of Owner – The Marches

	c.1300	%	c.1350	%	c.1400	%
Crown	9	13.7	9	12.3	8	10.8
Female Owners	3	4.5	3	4.1	4	5.4
Church	1	1.5	1	1.4	1	1.4
Comital Community	6	9.1	10	13.7	9	12.2
Parliamentary Peers	15	22.7	11	15.1	8	10.8
Other Private	14	21.2	12	16.4	13	17.6
Unclear	18	27.3	27	37.0	31	41.9
Totals	66		73		74	

Table 2.xxxiii
Castle ownership by type of Owner – Wales

	c.1300	%	c.1350	%	c.1400	%
Crown	15	12.5	13	10.6	23	18.3
Female Owners	20	16.7	9	7.3	9	7.1
Church						
Comital Community	14	11.7	25	20.3	23	18.3
Parliamentary Peers	11	9.2	10	8.1	5	4.0
Other Private	9	7.5	8	6.5	16	12.7
Unclear	51	42.5	58	47.2	50	39.7
Totals	120		123		126	

Table 2.xxxiv
Castle Ownership of the Comital Community

Name	Dates	Owner
Richard Fitzalan, earl of Arundel	1267–1302	4
Edmund Fitzalan, earl of Arundel	1285–1326	7
Richard Fitzalan, earl of Arundel	1313–1376	11
Richard Fitzalan, earl of Arundel	1346–1397	12
Thomas Fitzalan, earl of Arundel	1381–1415	2
John Fitzalan, earl of Arundel	1408–1435	?
Enguerrand de Coucy, earl of Bedford	1339–1397	1
John, duke of Bedford	1389–1435	3
Humphrey de Stafford, earl of Stafford, duke of Buckingham	1402–1460	4
Richard Langley, earl of Cambridge	1375–1415	0
Andrew Harclay, earl of Carlisle	–1323	0
Lionel, duke of Clarence	1338–1368	4
Thomas, duke of Clarence	1389–1421	3
Edmund, earl of Cornwall	1249–1300	10
Piers Gaveston, earl of Cornwall	1284–1312	7
John of Eltham, earl of Cornwall	1316–1336	9
Hugh Courtenay, earl of Devon	1262–1340	2
Hugh Courtenay, earl of Devon	1303–1377	2
Edward Courtenay, earl of Devon	1357–1422	4
Hugh Courtenay, earl of Devon	1389–1422	?
Thomas Courtenay, earl of Devon	1414–1458	4
John Holland, earl of Huntingdon, duke of Exeter	1350–1400	8
Thomas Beaufort, earl of Dorset, duke of Exeter	1396–1426	0
John Holland, earl of Huntingdon, duke of Exeter	1395–1447	2
Gilbert de Clare, earl of Gloucester	1243–1295	8
Gilbert de Clare, earl of Gloucester	1291–1314	22
Hugh de Audley, earl of Gloucester	–1347	6
Thomas of Woodstock, earl of Buckingham, d. of Gloucester	1355–1397	8
Thomas Despenser, earl of Gloucester	1373–1400	11
Humphrey, duke of Gloucester	1390–1447	5
Humphrey de Bohun, earl of Hereford	–1275	4
Humphrey de Bohun, earl of Hereford	1275–1298	6
Humphrey de Bohun, earl of Hereford	1276–1322	4
John de Bohun, earl of Hereford	1306–1336	5
Humphrey de Bohun, earl of Hereford	1309–1361	6
Humphrey de Bohun, earl of Hereford	1342–1373	9
Henry Bolingbroke, earl of Derby, duke of Hereford, King	1377–1413	5
William de Clinton, earl of Huntingdon	1337–1354	1
Guichard d'Angle, earl of Huntingdon	1323–1380	0
Edmund of Woodstock, earl of Kent	1301–1330	4
Edmund, earl of Kent	1326–1331	?
John, earl of Kent	1330–1352	2
Thomas Holland, earl of Kent	1310–1360	?
Thomas Holland, earl of Kent	1343–1397	5
Thomas Holland, earl of Kent, duke of Surrey	1370–1400	4

Name	Dates	Owner
Edmund Holland, earl of Kent	1383–1408	2
Edmund, earl of Lancaster	1245–1296	14
Thomas, earl of Lancaster	1278–1322	25
Henry, earl of Lancaster	1281–1345	17
Henry of Grosmont, e. Derby, e. Lincoln, d. Lancaster	1337–1361	25
John of Gaunt, duke of Lancaster	1340–1399	24
Henry de Lacy, earl of Lincoln	1251–1311	8
Roger Mortimer, earl of March	1288–1330	18
Roger Mortimer, earl of March	1328–1360	12
Edmund Mortimer, earl of March	1352–1381	18
Roger Mortimer, earl of March	1374–1398	21
Edmund Mortimer, earl of March	1391–1425	18
Roger Bigod, earl of Norfolk	1270–1306	4
Thomas of Brotherton, earl of Norfolk	1300–1338	4
Thomas Mowbray, e. Nottingham, duke of Norfolk	1366–1399	9
Thomas Mowbray, earl Marshal	1385–1405	6
John Mowbray, earl Marshal, duke of Norfolk	1392–1432	5
William de Bohun, earl of Northampton	1337–1360	2
Henry Percy, earl of Northumberland	1341–1408	8
Henry Percy, earl of Northumberland	1394–1455	5
John Mowbray, earl of Nottingham	1365–1383	1
Robert de Vere, earl of Oxford	1240–1296	3
Robert de Vere, earl of Oxford	1257–1331	2
John de Vere, earl of Oxford	1312–1360	3
Thomas de Vere, earl of Oxford	1336–1371	3
Robert de Vere, earl of Oxford, marq. Dublin, d. Ireland	1362–1392	3
Aubrey de Vere, earl of Oxford	1339–1400	3
Richard de Vere, earl of Oxford	1385–1417	3
John de Vere, earl of Oxford	1408–1462	3
Aymer de Valence, earl of Pembroke	1270–1324	8
Laurence de Hastings, earl of Pembroke	1320–1348	5
John de Hastings, earl of Pembroke	1347–1375	6
John de Hastings, earl of Pembroke	1372–1389	10
John, duke of Brittany, earl of Richmond	1239–1305	?
John, earl of Richmond	1266–1334	3
John, earl of Richmond	1286–1341	0
John de Montfort, d. Brittany, e. Richmond	1339–1399	1
William de Montague, earl of Salisbury	1302–1344	6
William de Montague, earl of Salisbury	1328–1397	10
John de Montague, earl of Salisbury	1350–1400	5
Thomas de Montague, earl of Salisbury	1388–1428	2
John Talbot, earl of Shrewsbury	1384–1453	2
John Beaufort, earl of Somerset	1371–1410	0
Henry Beaufort, earl of Somerset	1401–1418	0
Ralph Stafford, earl of Stafford	1301–1372	5
Hugh Stafford, earl of Stafford	1342–1386	5
Thomas Stafford, earl of Stafford	1368–1392	4
Edmund Stafford, earl of Stafford	1378–1403	7

Name	Dates	Owner
Robert de Ufford, earl of Suffolk	1298–1369	2
William de Ufford, earl of Suffolk	1330–1382	4
Michael de la Pole, earl of Suffolk	1330–1389	?
Michael de la Pole, earl of Suffolk	–1415	2
Michael de la Pole, earl of Suffolk	–1415	?
William de la Pole, earl of Suffolk	1396–1450	?
John de Warenne, earl of Surrey	1231–1304	4
John de Warenne, earl of Surrey	1286–1347	9
William Beauchamp, earl of Warwick	1240–1298	3
Guy Beauchamp, earl of Warwick	1273–1315	6
Thomas Beauchamp, earl of Warwick	1314–1369	9
Thomas Beauchamp, earl of Warwick	1339–1401	11
Richard Beauchamp, earl of Warwick	1382–1439	6
Ralph Neville, earl of Westmorland	1354–1425	5
William Scrope, earl of Wiltshire	1350–1399	2
Hugh Despenser the elder, earl of Winchester	1322–1326	2
Thomas Percy, earl of Worcester	1343–1403	1
Richard Beauchamp, lord Abergavenny, earl of Worcester	1397–1422	2
Edmund Langley, earl of Cambridge, duke of York	1341–1402	7
Edward, earl of Rutland, duke of Albemarle, duke of York	1373–1415	11

Table 2.xxxv

Castles held by Queen Eleanor of Provence (–1291)

Castle	Dates
Benefield (Nhants)	1275–
Gloucester	1236–1273–
Guildford (Surrey)	1272–1291
Hadleigh (Essex)	–1273–
Haverford (Pemb)	1291
Ludgershall (Wilts)	–1274–
Marlborough (Wilts)	–1273–1290–
Portchester (Hamps)	–1273–
Skipton (Yorks)	1286–

Table 2.xxxvi

Castles held by Queen Eleanor of Castile (–1290)

Castle	Dates
Bolsover(Derby)	1275–
Bristol (Glou)	1275–
Caergwle (Flint)	1283–
Harestan (Derby)	1275–
High Peak (Derby)	1254–, 1275–
Odiham (Hamps)	1275–
Orford (Suff)	1275–
Rockingham (Nhants)	1275–
Southampton (Hamps)	1276–1286
Stamford (Lincs)	1254–1275
Tickhill (Yorks)	1254–1275

Table 2.xxxvii

Castles held by Queen Margaret (1299–1318)

Castle	Dates
Berkhamstead (Herts)	1303–1317
Cambridge	1299–1318
Christchurch (Hamps)	1299–1310–
Devizes (Wilts)	1299–1310–
Gloucester	1299–1310–
Guildford (Surrey)	1299–1317
Hadleigh (Essex)	1299–1311–
Hertford	1299–, 1310–[6]
Leeds (Kent)	1299–1314–
Marlborough (Wilts)	1299–1310–
Mere (Wilts)	1304–1310–
Montgomery	1299–1301,1304–[7]
Odiham (Hamps)	1299–1311–
Oxford	poss. 1311
Pevensey (Sussex)	1299–1310–
Portchester (Hamps)	1299–1310–
Southampton (Hamps)	1299–1310–

[6] Out of her hands in 1309.
[7] Held by Prince Edward in 1301–1303.

Table 2.xxxviii
Castles held by Queen Isabella (1308–1358)

Castles	Dates	Notes
Arundel (Sussex)	1330–	Lost by 1331
Berkhamstead (Herts)	1318–1319–	Lost by December 1330
Built (Brecknock)	–1329–	–
Castle Rising (Norf)	–1337–1358	Location for her retirement
Christchurch (Hamps)	1318–1319–	Prob. lost by 1320
Clitheroe (Lancs)	1331–1345	Returned to Alice Lacy by 1348
Devizes (Wilts)	1318–1321–	–
Eye (Suff)	1319–1330	To John of Eltham, Dec. 1330
Gloucester	1330–	Lost by 1334
Guildford (Surrey)	1327–1330	–
Hadleigh (Essex)	1327–	Constables restart in 1334
Harestan (Derby)	–1330	Prob. gained after 1326
Haverford (Pemb)	1331–1358	–
Hanley (Worcs)	1330	Possible only
Hertford	1327–1358	Kept through her fall.
High Peak (Derby)	1313–1318, 1320–29–	To her children in the gap
Knaresborough (Yorks)	–1327–1328–	Lost 1330
Leeds (Kent)	1327–1355–	First granted the reversion in 1314
Marlborough (Wilts)	1318–1321–	Issues only from 1321
Mere (Wilts)	1318–1359, not 1331	Lost to John of Eltham 1331
Mold (Flint)	–1337–1338	Lost to Will. de Montagu
Montgomery	–1329–	Possible
Odiham (Hamps)	–1330–	Lost to Queen Philippa
Pontefract (Yorks)	–1328–1330	Her constable outlasted her tenure
Rockingham (Nhants)	–1327–	Prob. lost by 1331
Sandwich (Kent)	1327–	Constable for life
Southampton (Hamps)	1318–1319–	–
Tickhill (Yorks)	–1328–	Her constable rebelled by 1331
Wallingford	1317–1327	–

Table 2.xxxix
Castles held by Queen Philippa (1328–1369)

Castles	Dates
Bristol (Glou)	1331–1369
Caerphilly (Glam)	1330–
Devizes (Wilts)	1331–1350–
High Peak (Derby)	1331–1350–
Knaresborough (Yorks)	1331–1369
Marlborough (Wilts)	1331–1359
Neath (Glam)	1330–
Odiham (Hamps)	1331–1335–
Pevensey (Suss)	–1339–1364–
Pontefract (Yorks)	1330–1338–
Rockingham (Nhants)	1331–1347–
Southampton (Hamps)	1331–
Tickhill (Yorks)	1331–1369

Table 2.xl
Castles held by Queen Anne (1382–1394)

Castles	Dates
Bowes (Yorks)	–1388
Bristol (Glou)	1382–90–
Conway (Caernarvon)	1382–1392–
Devizes (Wilts)	–1382–1385–
Eye (Suff)	1382–1391–
Leeds (Kent)	1382–1394
Moor End (Nhants)	1382–1394
Nottingham	–1382–1390–
Odiham (Hamps)	1382–
Richmond (Yorks)	–1388
Rockingham (Northants)	1391–

Table 2.xli
Castles held by Queen Joan (1401–1437)

Castles	Dates
Barton Segrave (Nhants)	1405–
Bristol (Glou)	1403–
Carisbrooke (Hamps)	1405–
Devizes (Wilts)	1405–1437
Hertford	–1408–1413–
Leeds (Kent)	1403–1414–
Moor End (Nhants)	1408–
Nottingham	1403–1414–
Odiham (Hamps)	–1408–1419–
Rockingham (Nhants)	1403–

Table 2.xlii
County Distribution of the Castles of the Queen

County	Eleanor	Eleanor	Margaret	Isabella	Philippa	Anne	Joan
Berkshire				1		1	
Brecknock				1			
Caernarvon						1	
Cambridgeshire			1				
Derbyshire		3		2	1		
Essex	1		1	1			
Flint		1		1			
Glamorgan					2		
Gloucestershire	1	1	1	1	1	1	1
Hampshire	1	1	4	3	2	1	2
Hertfordshire			2	2			1
Kent			1	2		1	1
Lancashire				1			
Lincolnshire		1					
Montgomery			1	1			
Norfolk				1			
Northamptonshire	1	1		1	1	2	3
Nottingham						1	1
Oxford			1				
Pembroke	1			1			
Suffolk		1		1		1	
Surrey	1		1				
Sussex			1	1	1		
Wiltshire	2		3	3	2	1	1
Worcester				1			
Yorkshire	1	1		3	3	2	

Table 2.xliii
Number of Castles by County

County	1272	1350	1422	survived period	total in period	no date	Total in county
Anglesey	0	1	1	0	1	1	3
Bedfordshire	1	1	1	0	2	16	25
Berkshire	3	5	5	2	6	5	17
Brecknock	10	9	9	8	11	23	41
Buckingham	2	2	2	0	4	14	25
Caernarvon	3	4	3	1	5	8	16
Cambridge	5	4	4	3	6	2	15
Cardigan	1	2	2	1	2	15	31
Carmarthen	8	9	9	8	9	27	43
Cheshire	8	6	8	6	10	5	23
Cornwall	6	9	9	9	9	7	26
Cumberland	5	18	26	5	26	34	82
Denbigh	2	4	5	1	6	4	15
Derbyshire	4	6	6	4	6	8	16
Devonshire	5	14	17	4	18	20	43
Dorset	4	3	4	2	6	3	21
Durham	3	5	10	3	10	11	31
Essex	5	5	5	5	5	15	33
Flint	2	5	5	2	5	5	19
Glamorgan	17	24	27	15	29	35	78
Gloucester	6	6	6	5	7	16	33
Hampshire	9	8	8	8	9	8	35
Herefordshire	21	22	27	21	27	62	93
Hertfordshire	4	4	4	4	4	8	16
Huntingdonshire	1	1	1	1	1	2	7
Kent	13	16	18	11	21	16	50
Lancashire	4	10	12	4	12	9	35
Leicestershire	3	4	4	3	4	12	24
Lincolnshire	7	9	10	6	11	10	37
London	1	1	1	1	1	1	6
Merioneth	1	1	1	0	2	7	19
Monmouthshire	15	15	15	13	17	30	57
Montgomery	1	3	3	1	3	27	40
Norfolk	5	8	10	5	10	6	23
Northampton	4	12	13	4	13	13	35
Northumberland	14	41	117	12	119	21	233
Nottingham	3	4	3	2	4	4	12
Oxfordshire	3	7	7	2	8	5	21
Pembroke	13	14	14	11	16	24	53
Radnor	9	5	6	4	11	22	43
Rutland	1	1	1	1	1	5	6
Shropshire	21	22	24	16	29	63	112
Somerset	5	4	6	4	7	8	25
Staffordshire	8	9	9	7	10	2	16

County	1272	1350	1422	survived period	total in period	no date	Total in county
Suffolk	4	6	6	4	7	12	28
Surrey	3	3	4	2	5	5	12
Sussex	6	4	6	4	8	9	26
Warwickshire	6	7	9	3	12	7	31
Westmorland	5	13	16	5	16	11	34
Wiltshire	7	5	5	3	9	11	28
Worcestershire	4	4	5	4	5	4	15
Yorkshire	30	33	42	23	49	40	124
Totals	331	438	571	273	634	738	1932

Anglesey

BEAUMARIS

Owners

Built	1295–1306	King, p. 2
Crown for entire period		
Prince Edward (Edward II)		
from	7 February 1301	*CChR 1300–1326*, p. 6
from	7 February 1301	*CPR 1292–1301*, p. 576
Prince Edward, the Black Prince		
from	12 May 1343	*CChR 1341–1417*, p. 14
on	23 July 1351	*BPR III*, p. 39

Constables

William de Felton		
temp	1295–1302	*CACW*, XXVI.179
to	1 April 1300	*CFR 1272–1307*, p. 427
John de Havering, P.P.		
from	1 April 1300	*CFR 1272–1307*, p. 427
to	7 February 1301	*CPR 1292–1301*, p. 576
John de Medefeld		
to	11 August 1308	*CPR 1307–1313*, p. 93
Roger Mortimer of Chirk		
from	11 August 1308	*CPR 1307–1313*, p. 93
Simon de Montague, P.P.		
from	1 March 1309	*CPR 1307–1313*, p. 102
John de Sapy		
from	4 March 1312	*CFR 1307–1319*, p. 127
to	16 November 1321	*CPR 1321–1324*, p. 35
Giles de Beauchamp		
from	12 October 1321	*CFR 1319–1327*, p. 74
and from	25 March 1327	*CCR 1327–1330*, p. 67
Hugh Mortimer		
on	26 October 1327	*CCR 1327–1330*, p. 180
Gilbert de Ellesfeld		
for life from	29 April 1328	*CFR 1327–1337*, p. 88
on	8 May 1328	*CCR 1327–1330*, p. 279
Robert de Walkefare		
temp	July 1331–1333	*CAPW*, p. 253
for life on	8 June 1333	*CPR 1330–1334*, p. 465
William Trussel, king's yeoman		
for life from	18 November 1333	*CPR 1330–1334*, p. 480
to	12 May 1343	*CChR 1341–1417*, p. 14
David Cradok, king's knight		
from	6 April 1380	*CPR 1377–1381*, p. 454
not by	18 March 1382	*CPR 1381–1385*, p. 100
Gronov ap Tudor, king's esquire		
for life from	18 March 1382	*CPR 1381–1385*, p. 100

Baldwin de Radyngton, king's knight		
from	27 March 1382	*CPR 1381–1385*, p. 100
to	31 March 1385	*CPR 1381–1385*, p. 533 (R.I.P.)
Gilbert Trussel		
from	31 March 1385	*CPR 1381–1385*, p. 533
to	24 February 1394	*CPR 1391–1396*, p. 371
William le Scrope, earl of Wiltshire		
from	24 February 1394	*CPR 1391–1396*, p. 371
William le Scrope, earl of Wiltshire and William Warde		
for life from	8 July 1396	*CPR 1396–1399*, p. 16
William le Scrope, earl of Wiltshire		
for life from	22 February 1397	*CPR 1396–1399*, p. 82
William Newport, kn.		
to	5 November 1416	*CPR 1416–1422*, p. 46 (R.I.P.)
Edward Sprencheux		
from	5 November 1416	*CPR 1416–1422*, p. 46

Constable for Black Prince

John de St. Pere, kn.		
on	26 November 1359	*BPR III*, p. 378

Sub–Constables

'Urrici' de la Hay		
on	29 September 1315	E.101/19/26 m.1

Bedfordshire

BEDFORD (SITE ONLY)

Owners		
dismantled	1224	King, p. 5
Roger le Strange of Ellesmere, in right of his wife		
to	26 July 1311	*IPM V*, no. 351 (R.I.P.)
John de Mowbray, heir of wife of above		
from	26 July 1311	*IPM V*, no. 351
to	1322	McKisack, p. 73 (R.I.P.)
John de Mowbray of Axholme		
to	17 June 1368	*IPM XII*, no. 397 (R.I.P.)
John de Mowbray, son of above		
from	17 June 1368	*IPM XII*, no. 397
Thomas de Mowbray, duke of Norfolk		
on	14 October 1398	
to	22 September 1399	*IPM XVII*, no. 284 (R.I.P.)
Thomas de Mowbray, earl Marshal, son of above		
from	22 September 1399	*IPM XVII*, no. 284 (Age 14)
to	4 June 1405	*IPM XVIII*, no. 314 (R.I.P.)
John de Moubray, brother of above		
from	4 June 1405	*IPM XVIII*, no. 314
Constable for Mowbray		
John Woketon		
for life from	14 October 1398 (Keeper)	
confirmed	12 February 1400	*CPR 1399–1401*, p. 199 (Keeper)
on	4 June 1405	*IPM XVIII*, p. 314

BLETSOE

Owners		
John de Pateshull		
license to crenellate	23 June 1327	*CPR 1327–1330*, p. 130

YIELDEN

History		
mentioned	1173–4	King, p. 7
in decay	1360	King, p. 7

Berkshire

Unknown Licenses
STAUNTON HARECOURT for John Wyard, king's yeoman

	7 October 1327	*CPR 1327–1330*, p. 179

ALDWORTH (LA BECHE)

Owners

Nicholas de la Beche, kn.		
licence to crenellate	3 March 1338	*CPR 1338–1340*, p. 24

BEAUMYSS (BEAMS)

Owners

Nicholas de la Beche, kn.		
licence to crenellate	3 March 1338	*CPR 1338–1340*, p. 24

DONNINGTON

Owners

Richard Abberbury		
licence to crenellate	11 June 1386	*CPR 1385–1389*, p. 156
Alice, widow of John Phelipp, kn.		
from	28 November 1415	*CPR 1413–1416*, p. 234

WALLINGFORD

Owners

Richard, earl of Cornwall		
from	1231	*HKW II*, p. 850
to	1272	*HKW II*, p. 850 (R.I.P.)
Edmund, earl of Cornwall		
from	1272	*HKW II*, p. 850
to	1298	*IPM III*, no. 604 (R.I.P.)
The King, heir of above		
from	1298	*IPM III*, no. 605
Piers Gaveston		
from	5 August 1309	*CCR 1307–1313*, p. 225
on	16 January 1309	*CCR 1307–1313*, p. 190
Crown – Queen Isabella		
from	22 April 1317	*CPR 1313–1317*, p. 639
to	1327	*HKW II*, p. 850
John de Eltham, earl of Cornwall		
from	4 December 1330	*CChR 1327–1341*, p. 198
to	1336	*HKW II*, p. 851
Edward, the Black Prince		
from	1337	*HKW II*, p. 851
to	1376	*HKW II*, p. 851 (R.I.P.)

Joan, widow of the above		
from	13 October 1376	*CPR 1374–1377*, p. 374
to	1385	*HKW II*, p. 851 (R.I.P.)
Crown		
from	1385	
to	1399	
Prince Henry		
from	15 October 1399	*CCR 1399–1402*, p. 22
Constables		
Robert de la Mare		
on	1 June 1268	*CLibR 1267–1272*, no. 325
Walter de Aylesbury		
from	18 February 1301	*CFR 1272–1307*, p. 437
on	27 June 1305	*CCR 1302–1307*, p. 274
John de Clinton of Maxstoke		
from	17 June 1308	*CFR 1307–1319*, p. 24
to	5 August 1309	*CCR 1307–1319*, p. 171
Edmund Bacon, kn.		
from	10 December 1311	*CFR 1307–1319*, p. 118
to	10 February 1312	*CPR 1307–1313*, p. 429
Piers Gaveston		
from	10 February 1312	*CPR 1307–1313*, p. 429
Edmund Bacon, kn.		
and from	26 June 1312	*CFR 1307–1319*, p. 136
on	3 December 1318	*CCR 1318–1323*, p. 39
William le Marshall		
on	4 August 1326	*CFR 1319–1327*, p. 404
to	15 October 1326	*CPR 1324–1327*, p. 327
John le Stonore		
from	30 September 1326	*CFR 1319–1327*, p. 417
from	15 October 1326	*CPR 1324–1327*, p. 237
temp	1326	E.101/17/21
Miles de Beauchamp		
on	15 December 1326	*CFR 1319–1327*, p. 428
temp	1326–1328	E.101/17/28
William le Marshall		
to	1 December 1330	*CPR 1330–1334*, p. 51
Ralph de Restwold, king's yeoman		
from	26 September 1336	*CPR 1334–1338*, p. 321
from	13 January 1337	*CPR 1334–1338*, p. 348
Ralph de Ferrers		
to	12 December 1339	*CPR 1338–1340*, p. 401
John de Gadesdene		
from	12 December 1339	*CPR 1338–1340*, p. 401
Aubrey de Vere, kn.		
for life from	22 July 1375	
confirmed	22 March 1378	*CPR 1377–1381*, pp. 161, 239
to	12 April 1382	*CPR 1381–1385*, p. 120
Hugh de Segrave, king's kn.		
from	12 April 1382	*CPR 1381–1385*, p. 120
on	19 June 1383	*CCR 1381–1385*, p. 73

John Golafre		
for life from	14 February 1387	*CPR 1385–1389*, p. 275
to	20 November 1397	*CPR 1396–1399*, p. 271 (R.I.P.)
John Beaufort, earl of Somerset, marquess of Dorset		
for life from	20 November 1397	*CPR 1396–1399*, p. 271
on	30 August 1398	*CCR 1396–1399*, pp. 326, 332
William le Scrope, earl of Wiltshire, John Bussy, Henry Grene, William Bagot		
from	12 July 1399	*CPR 1396–1399*, p. 588
Thomas Chaucer		
for life from	14 October 1399	*CPR 1399–1401*, p. 13
on	15 November 1407	*CPR 1405–1408*, p. 374
Private Constables		
Sir Ralph Spigurnell		
on	8 August 1346	*BPR I*, p. 7
to	24 September 1351	*BPR IV*, p. 26
Sir Bartholomew de Burghersh, yng		
from	24 September 1351	*BPR IV*, p. 26
on	28 June 1355	*BPR IV*, p. 137
John de Alveton		
on	22 May 1360	*CPR 1358–1361*, p. 419
Sir Bartholomew de Burghersh, yng		
for life from	18 October 1363	*BPR IV*, p. 506
Private Under Constables		
Thomas Huberd		
on	8 August 1346	*BPR I*, p. 7
on	25 August 1346	*BPR I*, p. 12
on	5 November 1346	*BPR I*, p. 28
John de Anstey, prince's yeoman		
on	16 July 1351	*BPR IV*, p. 20
on	7 August 1351	*BPR IV*, p. 21
John de Alveton, prince's yeoman		
on	28 April 1352	*BPR IV*, p. 47
on	24 May 1352	*BPR IV*, p. 50
on	26 May 1352	*BPR IV*, p. 52
on	18 June 1352	*BPR IV*, p. 54
on	26 August 1352	*BPR IV*, p. 62
on	8 September 1352	*BPR IV*, p. 63
on	8 March 1353	*BPR IV*, p. 83
on	31 May 1353	*BPR IV*, p. 93
on	28 June 1354	*BPR IV*, p. 117
on	6 July 1355	*BPR IV*, p. 140
on	27 June 1361	*BPR IV*, p. 387
Under Constables		
Thomas de Hungerford		
on	1 March 1369	*CPR 1367–1370*, p. 227
Porters		
John Breton, yeoman		
for life from	16 September 1385	*CPR 1385–1389*, p. 12
Thomas Tylyn		
for life from	9 February 1400	*CPR 1399–1401*, p. 192

William Ferrour		
on	15 February 1416	*CPR 1413–1416*, p. 393
Private Chaplain		
Sir John Wendout		
on	8 March 1353	*BPR IV*, p. 83
Gatekeepers		
John Broun		
to	4 May 1365	*BPR IV*, p. 552
Simon de Lenguenhall		
for life from	4 May 1365	*BPR IV*, p. 552

WINDSOR

Constables		
Nicholas de Yatingden		
on	8 February 1269	*CLibR 1267–1272*, no. 598
on	25 May 1272	*CLibR 1267–1272*, no. 1937, 1953
Geoffrey de Picheford		
from	18 January 1272	*CPR 1272–1281*, p. 3
to	18 July 1298	*CPR 1292–1301*, p. 356 (R.I.P.)
John de London		
from	18 July 1298	*CPR 1292–1301*, p. 356
to	21 April 1305	*CFR 1272–1307*, p. 514
Roger le Sauvage		
from	21 April 1305	*CFR 1272–1307*, p. 514
to	12 December 1307	*CFR 1307–1319*, p. 10
Robert de Hausted		
from	12 December 1307	*CFR 1307–1319*, p. 10
to	13 July 1308	*CFR 1307–1319*, p. 26
Warin L'isle		
from	13 July 1308	*CFR 1307–1319*, p. 26
to	6 October 1319	*CFR 1319–1327*, p. 5
Oliver de Burdegala, king's yeoman		
from	6 October 1319	*CFR 1319–1327*, p. 5
to	22 February 1320	*CFR 1319–1327*, p. 18
Ralph de Camoys, P.P.		
from	22 February 1320	*CFR 1319–1327*, p. 18
on	30 September 1326	*CMR*, p. 9
Thomas de Huntercombe		
from	6 December 1326	*CFR 1319–1327*, p. 422
to	15 February 1327	*CFR 1327–1337*, p. 11
accounting	13 March 1327	*CMR*, no. 75
John L'isle		
from	15 February 1327	*CFR 1327–1337*, p. 11
for life from	30 November 1327	*CFR 1327–1337*, p. 71
on	21 October 1328	*CFR 1327–1337*, p. 105
Roger L'isle		
on	20 December 1328	*Ancient Deeds I*, C.1555
John L'isle		
on	16 March 1329	*CPR 1327–1330*, p. 376
to	21 December 1330	*CFR 1327–1337*, p. 209

Thomas de Foxle		
from	21 December 1330	*CFR 1327–1337*, p. 209
to	22 May 1360	*CFR 1358–1361*, p. 125 (R.I.P.)
Richard de la Vache		
from	22 May 1360	*CFR 1359–1361*, p. 125
to	18 January 1366	*CFR 1356–1368*, p. 321 (R.I.P.)
Thomas Cheyne		
for life from	18 January 1366	*CFR 1356–1368*, p. 321
to	19 February 1369	*CPR 1367–1370*, p. 214 (R.I.P.)
Helming Leget, king's esquire		
from	19 February 1369	*CPR 1367–1370*, p. 214
on	30 September 1375	*CPR 1374–1377*, p. 174
Simon de Burley, king's knight		
for life from	10 August 1377	*CPR 1377–1381*, p. 21
on	7 December 1386	*IMisc IV*, no. 379
Thomas Tyle		
on	5 March 1389	*CPR 1388–1392*, p. 22
on	22 May 1389	*CPR 1388–1392*, p. 36
Peter de Courtenay		
for life from	20 January 1390	*CPR 1388–1392*, p. 183
confirmed	2 October 1399	*CPR 1399–1401*, p. 40
not from	5 February 1405	*CPR 1401–1405*, p. 489
Hugh de Waterton, king's kn.		
for life from	4 February 1405	*CPR 1401–1405*, p. 489
to	3 July 1409	*CPR 1408–1413*, p. 90 (R.I.P.)
John Stanley		
for life from	3 July 1409	*CPR 1408–1413*, p. 90
to	28 January 1414	*CPR 1413–1416*, p. 155
John Waterton, esquire		
from	28 January 1414	*CPR 1413–1416*, p. 155
on	23 May 1414	*CPR 1413–1416*, p. 233
Walter de Hungerford, kn.		
on	28 May 1419	*CPR 1416–1422*, p. 236
Lieutenants		
James de Dorchester		
on	14 May 1351	*CPR 1350–1354*, p. 72
Robert de Hertley		
on	7 February 1374	*IMisc III*, no. 918
on	1 May 1381	*CPR 1377–1381*, p. 626
Thomas Tyle		
for life from	10 May 1384	
on	13 May 1384	*CPR 1381–1385*, p. 403
on	7 December 1386	*IMisc IV*, no. 379
Nicholas Loude		
on	12 June 1396	*CPR 1391–1396*, p. 732
John Horsey		
to	5 September 1413	*CPR 1413–1416*, p. 118
John Wyntershull		
from	5 September 1413	*CPR 1413–1416*, p. 118

Porter

Thomas Bastenthwayt		
from	20 March 1347	*CPR 1345–1348*, p. 273
Nicholas Lary		
for life from	25 February 1399	
confirmed	28 October 1399	*CPR 1399–1401*, p. 65
confirmed	14 June 1413	*CPR 1413–1416*, p. 48
John Parker, yeoman		
for life from	21 June 1408	*CPR 1405–1408*, p. 446

Gatekeepers

John Pollard and Philip de Wyz		
on	21 April 1272	*CLibR 1267–1272*, no. 1900
on	6 March 1275	*CCR 1272–1279*, p. 156
John Pollard		
to	2 August 1280	*CPR 1272–1281*, p. 392 (R.I.P.)
Hamo de la Chaumbre		
from	2 August 1280	*CPR 1272–1281*, p. 392
on	25 April 1287	*CCR 1279–1288*, p. 447
Edmund de Alegate (Bailiwick of the custody of the gate)		
from	29 October 1321	*CPR 1321–1324*, p. 30
John de Broughton		
on	5 March 1327	*CCR 1327–1330*, p. 14

Keeper of the tower gate of the castle

Roger Bulloc		
on	20 April 1269	*CLibR 1267–1272*, no. 692 (2d./day)
Philip de Wyz		
not by	23 January 1272	*CLibR 1267–1272*, no. 1776

Verger/ Usher to the order of the Garter

John Shefeld, esq.		
for life from	26 November 1410	*CPR 1408–1413*, p. 265
William Hargrove, esq.		
for life from	28 November 1415	*CPR 1413–1416*, p. 379

Usher of the Free Chapel

Walter Whithors, yeoman		
on	23 April 1361	*CPR 1361–1364*, p. 23

Kings Smith

Nicholas Smyth		
on	24 January 1368	*CPR 1367–1370*, p. 47

Chief Chaplain

Robert de Shutkingdon		
on	16 September 1318	*CCR 1318–1323*, p. 15

Canons of the Kings College

William Gyloth		
on	13 December 1410	*CPR 1408–1413*, p. 267

Chaplains

Richard de Welles, Adam de Bradeham, Laurence de London and Simon		
on	6 March 1269	*CLibR 1267–1272*, no. 629
Richard de Welles, Laurence Thome and Henry de la Grave		
on	16 June 1272	*CLibR 1267–1272*, no. 1989

Keeper of Beds and Armour
Giles Frensshe

on	12 January 1403	*CCR 1402–1405*, p. 13

Gardener
Fulk le Provincial, Edmund le Gardener

on	25 May 1272	*CLibR 1267–1272*, no. 1953 (5d./day)

Master Fulk

on	12 July 1272	*CLibR 1267–1272*, no. 2015 (2.5d./day)

Edmund

on	26 April 1287	*CCR 1279–1288*, p. 447

John de Windsor

from	20 January 1336	*CPR 1334–1338*, p. 194
for life from	24 February 1338	*CPR 1338–1340*, p. 18 (With herbage)

King's Serjeant of Windsor
Geoffrey de Squeler

on	4 July 1273	*CCR 1272–1279*, p. 19

Keeper of Forest
John Synagun

on	13 July 1270	*CLibR 1267–1272*, no. 1145

John Ingelard

on	27 January 1272	*CLibR 1267–1272*, no. 1787

Robert de Say (Chief forester)

on	4 March 1275	*CCR 1272–1279*, p. 155
on	26 April 1287	*CCR 1279–1288*, p. 447

Keeper of gate and buildings of the park
Robert Lightfoot

on	12 February 1271	*CLibR 1267–1272*, no. 1446
on	21 April 1272	*CLibR 1267–1272*, no. 1900
on	6 March 1275	*CCR 1272–1279*, p. 156
on	26 April 1287	*CCR 1279–1288*, p. 447

Carpenter
Master Gilbert

on	10 October 1273	*CCR 1272–1279*, p. 34
on	26 April 1287	*CCR 1279–1288*, p. 447

Parker of Kenington
John

on	26 April 1287	*CCR 1279–1288*, p. 447

Watchmen
Richard de Redyng and John de Cherleton

on	1 May 1364	*CPR 1361–1364*, p. 499

Parker of the old park
Thomas Cheyne

for life from	20 July 1365	*CPR 1364–1367*, p. 160

Keeper of the gates, doors and houses of the inner ward
Geoffrey de Denham

for life from	18 October 1365	*CPR 1364–1367*, p. 164

WOODHAY, WEST

History

in use	C13 or C14	King, p. 12

Brecknock

BLAEN LLYFNI (BLENLEVENY)

Reversions		
Henry de Ferrers		
on	8 July 1338	*CPR 1338–1340*, p. 110
Owners		
Sir Reginald fitz Peter		
before	Purification 1277	*IMisc I*, no. 1127
Sir John fitz Reynold, P.P.		
to	15 June 1310	*IPM V*, no. 205 (R.I.P.)
Roger Mortimer of Chirk, P.P.		
from	24 March 1316	*CChR 1300–1326*, p. 306
confiscated before	23 January 1322	*CFR 1319–1327*, p. 91
Hugh le Despenser yng, P.P.		
from	6 August 1324	*CChR 1300–1326*, p. 469
Roger Mortimer, earl of March		
to	26 November 1330	*IPM X*, no. 188
not by	24 April 1333	*CCR 1333–1337*, p. 36
Gilbert Talbot		
from	21 February 1346	*CPR 1345–1348*, p. 50
to	24 February 1346	*IPM VIII*, no. 714 (R.I.P.)
Richard Talbot, son of above		
heir on	24 February 1346	*IPM VIII*, no. 714
on	1 January 1347	*CPR 1345–1348*, p. 227
jointured	25 August 1347	*CPR 1345–1348*, p. 349
not by	27 June 1352	*CCR 1349–1354*, p. 490
Roger Mortimer, earl of March		
from	30 May 1354	*CPR 1354–1358*, p. 18
in	1355	*IPM X*, no. 188
died	*26 February 1360*	*IPM X*, no. 640
Edmund Mortimer, earl of March		
heir	*26 February 1360*	*IPM X*, no. 640
granted away	24 November 1374	*CPR 1374–1377*, p. 37
granted back	14 February 1380	*CCR 1377–1381*, p. 365
to	27 December 1381	*IPM XV*, no. 561 (R.I.P.)
Roger Mortimer, son of above		
from	27 December 1381	*IPM XV*, no. 561
John de Hastings and Philippa his wife		
for 8 years from	24 February 1388	*CPR 1385–1389*, p. 472
Roger Mortimer, earl of March		
to	20 July 1398	*IPM XVII*, no. 1206 (R.I.P.)
Edmund Mortimer, son of above		
from	20 July 1398	*IPM XVII*, no. 1206
Constables		
Ralph de Thedmershhe		
to	2 April 1308	*CPR 1307–1313*, p. 62

John fitz Reynold, P.P.		
from	2 April 1308	*CPR 1307–1313*, p. 62
on	1 October 1308	*CCR 1307–1313*, p. 77
to	25 February 1310	*CFR 1307–1319*, p. 58 (R.I.P.)
Roger Mortimer of Chirk, P.P.		
from	25 February 1310	*CFR 1307–1319*, p. 58
for life from	20 November 1310	*CPR 1307–1313*, p. 293
on	8 July 1316	*CCR 1313–1318*, p. 353
Griffin ap Rees		
from	23 January 1322	*CFR 1319–1327*, p. 91
John de Dene		
on	23 January 1322	*CCR 1318–1323*, p. 415
to	14 February 1322	*CFR 1319–1327*, p. 98
Robert Clement		
from	14 February 1322	*CFR 1319–1327*, p. 98
Hugh le Despenser yng, P.P.		
from	10 July 1322	*CFR 1319–1327*, p. 143
on	4 December 1322	*CCR 1318–1323*, p. 617
Robert de Harle		
to	30 December 1330	*CFR 1327–1337*, p. 220
Hugh Tyrel		
from	30 December 1330	*CFR 1327–1337*, p. 220
on	24 April 1333	*CCR 1333–1337*, p. 36
Gilbert Talbot		
for life from	2 October 1333	*CPR 1330–1334*, p. 476
on	24 March 1336	*CCR 1333–1337*, p. 550
Hugh Tyrel		
on	1 September 1337	*CCR 1337–1339*, p. 172
Gilbert Talbot		
on	23 April 1338	*CPR 1338–1340*, p. 52
to	21 February 1346	*CPR 1345–1348*, p. 50 (Becomes owner)

Wardships

Minority of Roger Mortimer, earl of March, 1381–1395

Thomas de Beauchamp, earl of Warwick, Roger Mortimer, earl of March, John lord Neville and Henry Percy, earl of Northumberland

from	16 December 1383	*CFR 1383–1391*, p. 22

Minority of Edmund Mortimer, earl of March, 1398–1412

John Holland, earl of Huntingdon, duke of Exeter		
from	11 August 1398	*CPR 1396–1399*, pp. 408, 514
Henry Percy, earl of Northumberland		
from	2 March 1400	*CFR 1399–1405*, p. 50

BRECON

Owners

Humphrey de Bohun, earl of Hereford and Essex		
on	13 September 1273	*CCR 1272–1279*, p. 56
died	*27 September 1275*	*IPM II*, no. 100
Humphrey de Bohun, earl of Hereford and Essex, grandson of above		
to	7 January 1299	*IPM III*, no. 552 (R.I.P.)

Humphrey de Bohun, earl of Hereford and Essex		
from	7 January 1299	*IPM III*, no. 552
confiscated before	23 January 1322	*CFR 1319–1327*, p. 91
John de Bohun, earl of Hereford and Essex		
to	26 January 1337	*IPM VIII*, no. 55 (R.I.P.)
Humphrey de Bohun, brother of above		
from	26 January 1337	*IPM VIII*, no. 55
to	15 October 1361	*IPM XI*, no. 485 (R.I.P.)
Humphrey de Bohun, earl of Hereford and Essex, son of above		
from	15 October 1361	*IPM XI*, no. 485
to	17 January 1373	*IPM XIII*, no. 167 (R.I.P.)
Bohun		
to	1380	*HKW II*, p. 575
Lancastrian		
from	1380	*HKW II*, p. 575
Henry of Lancaster and Mary his wife		
from	1380	*HKW II*, p. 575
livery	22 December 1384	*CCR 1381–1385*, p. 511
on	6 February 1397	*CPR 1396–1399*, p. 70
to	1399	*HKW II*, p. 575
Crown		
from	1399	*HKW II*, p. 575
to	1421	*HKW II*, p. 575
Anne, countess of Stafford		
from	12 July 1421	*CPR 1416–1422*, p. 381

Constables

Griffin ap Rees		
from	23 January 1322	*CFR 1319–1327*, p. 91
to	23 January 1322	*CFR 1319–1327*, p. 91
Robert de Morby		
from	23 January 1322	*CFR 1319–1327*, p. 91
on	23 January 1322	*CCR 1318–1323*, p. 415
Hugh le Despenser, yng, P.P.		
from	10 July 1322	*CFR 1319–1327*, p. 143
on	4 December 1322	*CCR 1318–1323*, p. 617
Richard, lord Grey, of Codnor		
from	26 September 1402	*CPR 1401–1405*, p. 122 (Keeper)
Richard de Beauchamp, earl of Warwick and John Tuchet, lord Audley, P.P.		
from	24 October 1403	
to	19 October 1404	*CPR 1401–1405*, p. 370
John Tuchet, lord Audley, P.P.		
from	14 October 1404	*CPR 1401–1405*, p. 504
from	19 October 1404	*CPR 1401–1405*, p. 370
Richard, lord Grey, of Codnor		
on	11 May 1405	*CPR 1405–1408*, p. 16 (Keeper)

Private Constables

Thomas son of Wendaubre for Humphrey de Bohun		
on	14 June 1282	*CACW*, XXII.155
Thomas fitz Walter		
on	4 November 1287	*CACW*, XXX.71

Hugh de Waterton, kn. for Henry Bolingbroke

from	26 June 1387	*CPR 1396–1399*, p. 70
confirmed	6 February 1397	*CPR 1396–1399*, p. 70

Wardships

Minority of Humphrey de Bohun, 1361–1363

Stephen atte Roche, William, abbot of Walden and Thomas de Walmesford

on	26 November 1361	*CPR 1361–1364*, p. 133

Minority of Eleanor and Mary de Bohun, 1373–

Thomas de Woodstock

from	24 May 1377	*CFR 1369–1377*, p. 403
confirmed	17 July 1377	*CPR 1377–1381*, p. 66

BRONLLYS

Owners

John Giffard of Brimpsfield, P.P.

to	5 June 1299	*IPM III*, no. 544 (R.I.P.)
to	23 October 1299	*CFR 1272–1307*, p. 421

Maud Giffard, daughter of above

from	23 October 1299	*CFR 1272–1307*, p. 421

Humphrey de Bohun, earl of Hereford and Essex

to	16 January 1373	*IPM XIII*, no. 85 (R.I.P.)

Joan, widow of above

on	11 February 1381	*CCR 1377–1381*, p. 440

Henry Bolingbroke, earl of Derby and Mary his wife, heir of above

from	10 March 1385	*CPR 1385–1389*, p. 56

1/3 Thomas Woodstock, duke of Gloucester

to	15 September 1397	*IPM XVII*, no. 1028 (R.I.P.)
not by	29 November 1397	*IMisc VI*, no. 226

1/3 Humphrey, son of above

from	15 September 1397	*IPM XVII*, no. 1028

1/3 Eleanor, wife of Thomas above

on	29 November 1397	*IMisc VI*, no. 226

Crown

from	1399	*HKW II*, p. 582
to	1421	*HKW II*, p. 582

Constables

Richard le Marshall

on	23 January 1322	*CCR 1318–1323*, p. 415

John Merbury and William Butiller

from	9 July 1421	*CFR 1413–1422*, p. 400

BUILTH

Reversions

Thomas de Bradeston

from	1 April 1340	*CPR 1338–1340*, p. 448

Owners

Roger Mortimer of Wigmore

before	1277	Morris, p. 147

Prince Edward

from	7 February 1301	*CPR 1296–1302*, p. 576

Queen Isabella

on	2 September 1329	*CFR 1327–1337*, p. 147

Ebulo le Strange, P.P. and Alice de Lacy, countess of Lincoln		
from	25 September 1334	*CPR 1333–1337*, p. 10 (Via Alice)
to	17 September 1335	*IPM VII*, no. 681 (R.I.P.)
Alice de Lacy, countess of Lincoln		
from	17 September 1335	*IPM VII*, no. 681
Hugh de Frene and Alice de Lacy, his wife		
on	12 March 1338	*CCR 1337–1339*, p. 353
Alice de Lacy, countess of Lincoln		
on	1 April 1340	*CPR 1338–1340*, p. 448
died	*1348*	
Roger Mortimer, earl of March		
on	25 May 1359	*CPR 1358–1361*, p. 202
to	26 February 1360	*IPM X*, no. 640 (R.I.P.)
Edmund Mortimer, earl of March and Ulster, son of above		
from	26 February 1360	*IPM X*, no. 640
to	27 December 1381	*IPM XV*, no. 560 (R.I.P.)
Roger Mortimer, earl of March, son of above		
from	27 December 1381	*IPM XV*, no. 560
to	20 July 1398	*IPM XVII*, no. 1206 (R.I.P.)
Eleanor, widow of Roger Mortimer (R.I.P.)		
from	16 March 1399	*CCR 1396–1399*, p. 451
to	6 October 1405	*IPM XVIII*, no. 49
Edmund Mortimer, earl of March		
on	28 September 1418	*CPR 1416–1422*, p. 180

Constables

Hoel son of Meuric		
from	7 January 1278	*CWR*, p. 162
on	12 March 1279	*CWR*, p. 178
Roger le Strange of Ellesmere, P.P.		
to	14 October 1282	*CWR*, p. 240
John Giffard of Brimpsfield, P.P.		
from	14 October 1282	*CWR*, p. 240
on	13 January 1292	*CCR 1288–1296*, p. 213
Philip ap Howel		
for 5 years from	23 June 1299	*CFR 1272–1307*, p. 423
to	26 February 1309	*CFR 1307–1319*, p. 58
Roger Mortimer of Wigmore		
from	26 February 1309	*CFR 1307–1319*, p. 58
to	12 December 1310	*CFR 1307–1319*, p. 76
Philip ap Howel		
from	12 December 1310	*CFR 1307–1319*, p. 76
to	25 January 1314	*CFR 1307–1319*, p. 188
John de Cherleton of Powis, P.P.		
from	25 January 1314	*CFR 1307–1319*, p. 188
on	8 September 1315	*CCR 1313–1318*, p. 248
John de Walewayn		
from	20 July 1318	*CFR 1307–1319*, p. 370
to	2 June 1319	*CPR 1317–1321*, p. 341
Roger Mortimer of Chirk, P.P.		
from	2 June 1319	*CPR 1317–1321*, p. 341
Humphrey de Bohun		
to	16 March 1321	*CFR 1319–1327*, p. 50

Griffin ap Rees		
from	23 January 1322	*CFR 1319–1327*, p. 91
on	8 December 1325	*CFR 1319–1327*, p. 368
Gilbert Talbot, P.P.		
from	12 December 1330	*CFR 1327–1337*, p. 205
Ebulo le Strange, P.P. and Alice de Lacy, his wife		
for her life from	16 February 1331	*CPR 1330–1334*, p. 74
Henry de Halton		
from	6 December 1335	*CFR 1327–1337*, p. 468

Wardship

minority of Roger Mortimer, earl of March, 1332–1342

William de Bohun and Elizabeth, his wife, widow of Edmund Mortimer		
from	6 September 1341	*CFR 1337–1341*, p. 239

minority of Edmund Mortimer, earl of March, 1360–1373

Edward, prince of Wales		
from	14 July 1360	*CPR 1358–1361*, p. 447

Minority of Roger Mortimer, earl of March, 1381–1395

William Jouet		
from	16 December 1382	*CPR 1381–1385*, p. 65
Walter Deverose		
from	8 February 1382	*CPR 1381–1385*, p. 96
Thomas de Beauchamp, earl of Warwick, Roger Mortimer, earl of March, John lord Neville and Henry Percy, earl of Northumberland		
from	16 December 1383	*CFR 1383–1391*, p. 22

Minority of Edmund Mortimer, earl of March, 1398–1412

John Holland, earl of Huntingdon, duke of Exeter		
from	11 August 1398	*CPR 1396–1399*, pp. 408, 514
Henry Percy, earl of Northumberland		
from	2 March 1400	*CFR 1399–1405*, p. 50
Richard, Lord Grey		
from	26 September 1402	*CPR 1401–1405*, p. 122 (Keeper)
John Smert, esq.		
from	15 March 1407	
on	6 May 1407	*CPR 1405–1408*, p. 326
from	9 May 1409	*CPR 1405–1408*, p. 75

Receiver

John Fayreford, clerk		
on	5 March 1403	*CPR 1401–1405*, p. 208

CRICKHOWELL

Tenant in Chief

Gilbert Talbot		
to	24 February 1346	*IPM IX*, no. 714 (R.I.P.)
Richard Talbot, son of above		
from	24 February 1346	*IPM IX*, no. 714

Owners

Confiscated		
before	23 January 1322	*CFR 1319–1327*, p. 91
Emery Pauncefoot		
to	15 December 1332	*IPM VII*, no. 449 (R.I.P.)

Grimbald, son of Emery de Pauncefoot		
from	15 December 1332	*IPM VII*, no. 449
from	23 January 1333	*CCR 1330–1333*, p. 523
John Pauncefoot		
on	8 September 1403	*CCR 1402–1405*, p. 111

Constables

Griffin ap Rees		
from	23 January 1322	*CFR 1319–1327*, p. 91
to	23 January 1322	*CFR 1319–1327*, p. 91
Edmund Gacelyn		
from	23 January 1322	*CFR 1319–1327*, p. 91
on	23 January 1322	*CCR 1318–1323*, p. 415

DINAS (BULKDINAS, BWLCH–Y–DDINAS)

Reversions

Henry de Ferrers		
on	8 July 1338	*CPR 1338–1340*, p. 110

Owners

William Gethin		
at	Purification 1277	*IMisc I*, no. 1127
John fitz Reynold, P.P., son of Peter		
to	26 November 1307	*CCR 1307–1313*, p. 46
Crown		
from	26 November 1307	*CCR 1307–1313*, p. 46
Roger Mortimer of Chirk, P.P.		
from	25 March 1316	*CChR 1300–1326*, p. 306
confiscated before	23 January 1322	*CFR 1319–1327*, p. 91
Hugh le Despenser yng, P.P.		
from	6 August 1324	*CChR 1300–1326*, p. 469
Gilbert Talbot		
on	8 July 1338	*CPR 1338–1340*, p. 110
from	21 February 1346	*CPR 1345–1348*, p. 50
to	24 February 1346	*IPM VIII*, no. 714 (R.I.P.)
Richard Talbot, son of above		
from	24 February 1346	*IPM VIII*, no. 714
jointured	25 August 1347	*CPR 1345–1348*, p. 349
not by	27 June 1352	*CCR 1349–1354*, p. 490
Roger Mortimer, earl of March		
from	30 May 1354	*CPR 1354–1358*, p. 18
Edmund Mortimer, earl of March and Ulster		
heir	*26 February 1360*	*IPM X, no. 640*
granted away	24 November 1374	*CPR 1374–1377*, p. 37
to	27 December 1381	*IPM XV*, no. 561 (R.I.P.)
Roger Mortimer, earl of March, son of above		
from	27 December 1381	*IPM XV*, no. 561
John de Hastings, earl of Pembroke, husband of Philippa, daughter of Edmund Mortimer above		
for 8 years from	24 February 1388	*CCR 1385–1389*, p. 472
Roger Mortimer, earl of March		
to	20 July 1398	*IPM XVII*, no. 1206 (R.I.P.)
Edmund Mortimer, son of above		
from	20 July 1398	*IPM XVII*, no. 1206

Constables

Ralph de Thedmersshe		
to	2 April 1308	*CPR 1307–1313*, p. 62
John fitz Reynold, P.P.		
from	2 April 1308	*CPR 1307–1313*, p. 62
on	1 October 1308	*CCR 1307–1313*, p. 77
to	25 February 1310	*CFR 1307–1319*, p. 58 (R.I.P.)
Roger Mortimer of Chirk, P.P.		
for life from	20 November 1310	*CPR 1307–1313*, p. 293
on	8 July 1316	*CCR 1313–1318*, p. 353
Griffin ap Rees		
from	23 January 1322	*CFR 1319–1327*, p. 91
John de Dene		
on	23 January 1322	*CCR 1318–1323*, p. 415
Robert de Harle		
to	30 December 1330	*CFR 1327–1330*, p. 220
Hugh Tyrel		
from	30 December 1330	*CFR 1327–1330*, p. 220
on	13 February 1332	*CCR 1330–1333*, p. 434
Gilbert Talbot		
for life from	2 October 1333	*CPR 1330–1334*, p. 476
Hugh Tyrel		
on	1 September 1337	*CCR 1337–1339*, p. 172
Gilbert Talbot		
on	20 February 1338	*IMisc II*, no. 1492, no. 1492
on	8 December 1340	*CCR 1339–1341*, p. 316
becomes owner on	21 February 1346	*CPR 1345–1348*, p. 50

Wardships

Minority of Roger Mortimer, earl of March, 1381–1395

Thomas de Beauchamp, earl of Warwick, Roger Mortimer, earl of March, John lord Neville and Henry Percy, earl of Northumberland

from	16 December 1383	*CFR 1383–1391*, p. 22

Minority of Edmund Mortimer, earl of March, 1398–1412

John Holland, earl of Huntingdon, duke of Exeter		
from	11 August 1398	*CPR 1396–1399*, pp. 408, 514
Henry Percy, earl of Northumberland		
from	2 March 1400	*CFR 1399–1405*, p. 50

HAY

Owners

Humphrey de Bohun, earl of Hereford and Essex, Maud his wife and their heirs		
restored	20 July 1275	*CChR 1257–1300*, p. 192
Humphrey de Bohun, earl of Essex and Hereford, grandson of above		
to	7 January 1299	*IPM III*, no. 552 (R.I.P.)
Humphrey de Bohun, earl of Essex and Hereford, son of above		
from	7 January 1299	*IPM III*, no. 552
confiscated before	23 January 1322	*CFR 1319–1327*, p. 91
John de Bohun, earl of Hereford and Essex (R.I.P.)		
to	26 January 1337	*IPM VIII*, no. 55
Humphrey de Bohun, earl of Essex and Hereford, brother of above		
from	26 January 1337	*IPM VIII*, no. 55
to	15 October 1361	*IPM XI*, no. 485 (R.I.P.)

Humphrey de Bohun, earl of Essex and Hereford, his son		
from	15 October 1361	*IPM XI*, no. 485
to	17 January 1373	*IPM XIII*, no. 167 (R.I.P.)
Henry Bolingbroke, earl of Derby and Mary de Bohun		
livery	22 December 1384	*CCR 1381–1385*, p. 511
on	6 February 1397	*CPR 1396–1399*, p. 70
Crown		
from	1399	*HKW II*, p. 671
to	1421	*HKW II*, p. 671
Anne, countess of Stafford		
from	12 July 1421	*CPR 1416–1422*, p. 381

Constables

Hugh de Dynneneton		
to	20 July 1275	*CPR 1272–1281*, p. 99
Griffin ap Rees		
from	23 January 1322	*CFR 1319–1327*, p. 91
to	23 January 1322	*CFR 1319–1327*, p. 91
John de Siggeston		
from	23 January 1322	*CFR 1319–1327*, p. 91
on	23 January 1322	*CCR 1318–1323*, p. 415
Hugh le Despenser yng, P.P.		
on	4 December 1322	*CCR 1318–1323*, p. 617
Thomas de Woodstock		
from	24 May 1377	
confirmed	17 July 1377	*CPR 1377–1381*, p. 66
James le Botiller, earl of Ormond (Bailiwick and keepership)		
for life to	6 November 1382	*IPM XV*, no. 701
Hugh de Waterton		
confirmed	6 February 1397	*CPR 1396–1399*, p. 70
Richard, lord Grey		
from	26 September 1402	*CPR 1401–1405*, p. 122 (Keeper)
Richard Arundel, kn.		
on	6 December 1404	*CPR 1401–1405*, p. 473 (Defending)
on	8 October 1405	*CPR 1405–1408*, p. 82

Private Constables

Hugh de Waterton, kn.		
from	26 June 1387	*CPR 1396–1399*, p. 70
confirmed	6 February 1397	*CPR 1396–1399*, p. 70

Wardships

Minority of Humphrey de Bohun, 1361–1363

Stephen atte Roche, William, abbot of Walden and Thomas de Walmesford		
on	26 November 1361	*CPR 1361–1364*, p. 133

Minority of Eleanor and Mary de Bohun, 1373–

Thomas de Woodstock		
from	24 May 1377	*CFR 1369–1377*, p. 403

PENKELLY

Owners

Confiscated		
before	23 January 1322	*CFR 1319–1327*, p. 91

Constables

Griffin ap Rees		
from	23 January 1322	*CFR 1319–1327*, p. 91
John de Dene		
on	23 January 1322	*CCR 1318–1323*, p. 415
on	21 February 1322	*CPR 1321–1324*, p. 74
Hugh le Despenser, yng. P.P.		
from	10 July 1322	*CFR 1319–1327*, p. 143
on	4 December 1322	*CCR 1318–1323*, p. 617

PENPONT (CASTELL EINION SAIS)

Owner

Einion		
temp	Henry III	King, p. 21

TALGARTH

Constables

Hugh le Despenser yng, P.P.		
from	10 July 1322	*CFR 1319–1327*, p. 143
on	4 December 1322	*CCR 1318–1323*, p. 617

TRETOWER (STRADDEWWY)

Owners

John Pycard		
to	16 May 1306	*IPM IV*, no. 352 (R.I.P.)
Roger Pycard, son of above		
from	16 May 1306	*IPM IV*, no. 352
Amicia Bluet		
restored	8 February 1322	*CPR 1321–1324*, p. 49
James Berkeley, kn.		
on	8 September 1403	*CCR 1402–1405*, p. 111

Constables

Edmund Gacelyn		
from	23 January 1322	*CFR 1319–1327*, p. 91
to	8 February 1322	*CPR 1321–1324*, p. 49

Buckinghamshire

Unknown Licenses

ASTON for John and Giles de Molyns

	18 March 1336	*CChR 1327–1341*, p. 353

DITTON and STOKE PUGEYS for John de Molyns, king's yeoman

	23 December 1331	*CPR 1330–1334*, p. 226

HAVERSHAM for James de la Plaunche

	9 June 1304	*CPR 1301–1307*, p. 233

BOARSTALL

Owners

John de Handlo		
licence to crenellate	12 September 1312	*CPR 1307–1313*, p. 493
de Handlo family		
to	1356	J.Timb and A. Gunn, *Abbeys, Castles and Ancient Halls of England and Wales, Midlands*, London, p. 87
de la Pole family		
from	1356	*ibid.*

BRADWELL

History

in use	C13–C14	King, p. 26

BUCKINGHAM

Owners

Giles de Brewosa from the earl of Gloucester (A capital messuage)

to	7 January 1305	*IPM IV*, no. 317 (R.I.P.)
John de Brewose, son of above		
from	7 January 1305	*IPM IV*, no. 317

WESTON TURVILLE

Owners

John de Molyns		
licence to crenellate	23 January 1333	*CPR 1330–1334*, p. 49

Caernarvon

CAERNARVON

Owners

Prince Edward		
from	12 May 1343	*CChR 1341–1417*, p. 14

Constables

Thomas de Maydenhach		
temp	1283–1284	*CACW*, XXX.152
John de Havering, P.P.		
from	21 October 1284	*CWR*, p. 291
Otto de Grandison, P.P.		
not by	8 May 1290	*CWR*, p. 325
Adam de Whetenhale		
just by	8 May 1290	*CWR*, p. 325
Roger Mortimer of Chirk, P.P.		
on	15 January 1308	*CPR 1307–1313*, p. 44
on	10 February 1315	*CCR 1313–1318*, p. 159
Richard Casteleyn		
on	12 February 1316	*CCR 1313–1318*, p. 267
Roger Mortimer of Chirk, P.P.		
on	8 March 1321	*CCR 1318–1323*, p. 290
Thomas de Kynnesbury		
to	12 December 1326	*CFR 1319–1327*, p. 427
William de Shaldeford		
from	12 December 1326	*CFR 1319–1327*, p. 427
on	24 March 1327	*CCR 1327–1330*, p. 47
Richard, earl of Arundel		
for life from	12 July 1339	*CFR 1337–1347*, p. 140
to	12 May 1343	*CChR 1341–1417*, p. 14
on	7 February 1352	*CPR 1350–1354*, p. 220
Robert de Fouleshurst		
on	8 May 1385	*CCR 1381–1385*, p. 549
William Bagot, kn.		
to	6 July 1396	*CPR 1396–1399*, p. 10
William le Scrope, earl of Wiltshire, and William de Audley, esq.		
for life from	6 July 1396	*CPR 1396–1399*, p. 10
Henry Percy, son of earl of Northumberland		
for life from	24 October 1399	*CPR 1399–1401*, p. 158
for life from	24 April 1400	*CPR 1399–1401*, p. 28
John Boolde, kn.		
from	9 October 1400	*CPR 1399–1401*, p. 555

Constable for Black Prince

Robert de Parys		
on	26 November 1359	*BPR III*, p. 378

Under constable

Robert de Malleye		
on	8 March 1321	*CCR 1318–1323*, p. 290
William Frodesham		
on	20 June 1390	*CPR 1388–1392*, p. 263
on	5 July 1390	*CCR 1389–1392*, p. 200
on	24 July 1390	*CCR 1389–1392*, p. 200

Gatekeepers

Simon Corbet and John de Dalington		
on	May 1290	*CACW*, XXIII.108
on	October 1292	*CACW*, XXIII.108

CONWAY

Owners

Crown – Prince Edward (Edward II)		
from	7 February 1301	*CChR 1300–1326*, p. 6
from	7 February 1301	*CPR 1292–1301*, p. 576
Crown – Prince Edward		
from	12 May 1343	*CChR 1341–1417*, p. 14
on	8 April 31 principate Edw.	
Crown – Queen Anne		
for life from	16 August 1382	*CCR 1381–1385*, p. 159
on	28 November 1392	*CPR 1385–1389*, p. 208

Constables

William de Cycons		
from	21 October 1284	*CWR*, p. 291
to	7 February 1301	*CPR 1292–1301*, p. 576
on	16 April 1310	*CCR 1307–1313*, p. 207
William Bagot		
for life from	18 May 1311	*CPR 1307–1313*, p. 350
on	13 February 1316	*CCR 1313–1318*, p. 266
Henry de Bisshebury		
from	2 January 1320	*CPR 1317–1321*, p. 407
to	30 January 1326	*CPR 1324–1327*, p. 215
Aline Burnell		
from	30 January 1326	*CPR 1324–1327*, p. 215
to	20 October 1326	*CFR 1319–1327*, p. 421
William de Arcalowe		
from	20 October 1326	*CFR 1319–1327*, p. 421
Roger Mortimer		
on	26 October 1327	*CCR 1327–1330*, p. 180
John le Strange of Mudele		
from	9 November 1330	*CFR 1327–1337*, p. 198
to	21 August 1337	*CPR 1334–1338*, p. 497
Edward de St. John		
from	21 August 1337	*CPR 1334–1338*, p. 497
to	12 May 1343	*CChR 1341–1417*, p. 15
Henry Mortimer, king's yeoman		
to	4 October 1354	*CPR 1354–1358*, p. 105

Edward de St. John, kn.		
confirmed	12 June 1376	*CPR 1374–1377*, p. 283
to	1 November 1382	*CCR 1381–1385*, p. 183
David Cradok, king's knight		
on	20 February 1380	*CCR 1377–1381*, p. 287
John de Beauchamp, kn.		
for life from	1 November 1382	*CCR 1381–1385*, p. 183
on	3 June 1386	*CPR 1385–1389*, p. 147
John Verdon, for Queen Anne		
from	20 May 1387	
for life	28 November 1392	*CPR 1391–1396*, p. 208
John Waltham, bishop of Salisbury and Thomas de Percy		
for 1 year	26 June 1394	*CPR 1391–1396*, p. 447
John Holland, earl of Huntingdon		
for life from	3 September 1394	*CPR 1391–1396*, p. 501
to	25 February 1398	*CPR 1396–1399*, p. 322
William le Scrope, earl of Wiltshire		
for life from	25 February 1398	*CPR 1396–1399*, p. 322
Henry Percy, son of earl of Northumberland		
for life from	24 October 1399	*CPR 1399–1401*, p. 158
for life from	24 April 1400	*CPR 1399–1401*, p. 28
John Bolde		
on	4 July 1422	*CPR 1416–1422*, p. 446

Private Constables

Thomas de Upton		
on	26 October 1347	*BPR. I*, p. 133
Edward de St. John, kn.		
on	24 June 1355	*BPR III*, p. 492
on	26 November 1358	*BPR III*, p. 377
for life from	8 April 31 principate Edward	

Deputy Constables

Henry Wildebore		
in	1377	*CAPW*, pp. 243–4
Robert Stratton		
on	12 November 1397	*CPR 1396–1399*, p. 183 (Lieutenant)

Master of the Works

Nicholas de Derneford		
on	12 May 1327	*CPR 1327–1330*, p. 103

Notes

Being held by William ap Tudor, a rebel		
on	13 April 1401	*CPR 1399–1401*, p. 470
pardoned	20 April 1401	*CPR 1399–1401*, p. 475

CRICCIETH

Owners

Prince Edward		
from	12 May 1343	*CChR 1341–1417*, p. 15

Constables

William de Leybourne, P.P.		
on	23 December 1284	*CWR*, p. 296

Richard Havering		
temp	1294–1295	E.101/5/23
William le Butiller		
to	30 October 1309	*CFR 1307–1319*, p. 51
William Trumwyn		
from	30 October 1309	*CFR 1307–1319*, p. 51
to	4 November 1316	*CPR 1313–1317*, p. 559
John de Welles		
on	29 September 1315	E.101/19/26 m.1
from	4 November 1316	*CPR 1313–1317*, p. 559
Oillard de Welles		
for life from	18 October 1317	*CPR 1317–1321*, p. 37
to	10 May 1321	*CFR 1319–1327*, p. 56
John de Swennerton		
from	10 May 1321	*CFR 1319–1327*, p. 56
Thomas Jay		
from	16 March 1322	*CFR 1319–1327*, p. 110
to	12 December 1326	*CFR 1319–1327*, p. 428
William de Shaldeford		
from	12 December 1326	*CFR 1319–1327*, p. 428
on	24 March 1327	*CCR 1327–1330*, p. 47
Richard de Munemuth		
on	26 October 1327	*CCR 1327–1330*, p. 180
Richard de Holland		
from	19 December 1330	*CCR 1330–1333*, p. 240
on	13 May 1331	*CCR 1330–1333*, p. 240
John de Allespath		
from	22 July 1333	*CFR 1327–1337*, p. 367
revoked	8 September 1333	*CPR 1330–1334*, p. 479
Richard de Holland		
restored	8 September 1333	*CPR 1330–1334*, p. 479
for life from	4 June 1335	*CPR 1334–1338*, p. 117
Robert de Hambury		
to	2 August 1338	*CPR 1338–1340*, p. 121
John le Strange of Muddle		
from	2 August 1338	*CPR 1338–1340*, p. 121
to	12 May 1343	*CChR 1307–1349*, p. 14
Thomas Beushef		
for life from	4 February 1381	*CPR 1377–1381*, p. 587
to	19 June 1391	*CPR 1388–1392*, p. 422
William Frodesham		
from	19 June 1391	*CPR 1388–1392*, p. 422
William Hugon		
for life from	19 September 1396	*CPR 1396–1399*, p. 29
to	6 April 1398	
John Gamull		
to	6 April 1398	*CPR 1396–1399*, p. 353
William Hugon and John Gamull, king's esquire		
for life from	6 April 1398	*CPR 1396–1399*, p. 353

Deputy constables

Henry Neuman		
on	22 December 1347	*BPR I*, p. 156

Jevan ap Wille Boy		
on	11 February 1399	*CPR 1396–1399*, p. 520

Constables for Black Prince

William de St. Omer		
on	22 December 1347	*BPR I*, p. 156
on	26 November 1359	*BPR III*, p. 378

DEGANNWY

Owners

Royal		
on	2 January 1278	*CPR 1272–1281*, p. 296

Notes

Total ruin by 1277.

DINAS EMRYS

History

built	C12 or C13	King, p. 34

DOLBARDARN

Owners

Welsh princely castle		
not by	1284	King, p. 34
Crown while being dismantled		
temp	1284	King, p. 34

DOLWYDDELAN

Owners

Llywellyn ap Griffith		
temp	1265–1273	M. Prestwich, *Edward I*, London, 1988, p. 173
David ap Griffith		
in	1281	
to	24 January 1283	Morris, p. 190
English		
from	1283	

Constables

Griffin son of Tudor		
from	24 January 1283	Morris, p. 190
on	7 February 1290	*CWR*, p. 325

Cambridgeshire

BASSINGBORN

History		
licensed	1266	King, p. 38

CAMBRIDGE

Owners		
Crown		
to	1299	
Crown – Queen Margaret		
from	10 September 1299	*CPR 1292–1301*, p. 451
to	1318	
Crown		
from	1318	
Constables		
William le Moigne		
to	25 October 1278	*CFR 1272–1307*, p. 103
Baldwin de St. George		
from	25 October 1278	*CFR 1272–1307*, p. 103
John de Swyneford		
to	29 November 1311	*CFR 1307–1319*, p. 119
John de Crek		
with county from	29 November 1311	*CFR 1307–1319*, p. 119
to	16 October 1314	*CFR 1307–1319*, p. 220
Thomas de Scalariis		
with county from	16 October 1314	*CFR 1307–1319*, p. 220
to	20 October 1315	*CFR 1307–1319*, p. 261
Ralph Giffard		
from	20 October 1315	*CFR 1307–1319*, p. 261
to	29 November 1318	*CFR 1307–1319*, p. 381
Matthew de Bassingbourn		
from	29 November 1318	*CFR 1307–1319*, p. 381
to	18 April 1319	*CFR 1307–1319*, p. 396
Ralph Giffard		
from	18 April 1319	*CFR 1307–1319*, p. 396
to	27 May 1319	*CFR 1307–1319*, p. 398
Matthew de Bassingburn		
from	27 May 1319	*CFR 1307–1319*, p. 398
to	17 October 1319	*CFR 1319–1327*, p. 6
John de Crek		
from	17 October 1319	*CFR 1319–1327*, p. 6
to	3 November 1320	*CFR 1319–1327*, p. 37
Amaury la Zusche		
from	3 November 1320	*CFR 1319–1327*, p. 37
to	24 April 1327	*CFR 1327–1337*, p. 37

Matthew de Bassingbourn		
from	24 April 1327	*CFR 1327–1337*, p. 37
to	11 August 1328	*CFR 1327–1337*, p. 99
William Howard		
from	11 August 1328	*CFR 1327–1337*, p. 99
to	22 September 1328	*CFR 1327–1337*, p. 104 (R.I.P.)
Amaury la Zusche		
from	22 September 1328	*CFR 1327–1337*, p. 104
to	5 December 1330	*CFR 1327–1337*, p. 200
William le Moigne		
from	5 December 1330	*CFR 1327–1337*, p. 200
to	6 February 1332	*CFR 1327–1337*, p. 298
Warin de Bassingbourn		
from	6 February 1332	*CFR 1327–1337*, p. 298
to	13 September 1332	*CFR 1327–1337*, p. 329
Richard de Baiocis		
from	13 September 1332	*CFR 1327–1337*, p. 329
to	10 November 1333	*CFR 1327–1337*, p. 378
William son of John Muchet		
from	10 November 1333	*CFR 1327–1337*, p. 378
to	5 May 1335	*CFR 1327–1337*, p. 441
John de Lymbury		
from	5 May 1335	*CFR 1327–1337*, p. 441
to	12 May 1336	*CFR 1327–1337*, p. 484
Thomas de Lacy		
from	12 May 1336	*CFR 1327–1337*, p. 484
to	20 October 1336	*CFR 1327–1337*, p. 499
William Muchet		
from	20 October 1336	*CFR 1327–1337*, p. 499
to	16 October 1338	*CFR 1337–1347*, p. 96
Warin de Bassingbourn		
from	16 October 1338	*CFR 1337–1347*, p. 96
to	10 November 1340	*CFR 1337–1347*, p. 196
John de Lascy		
from	10 November 1340	*CFR 1337–1347*, p. 196
John de Pappeworth		
to	4 December 1341	*CFR 1337–1347*, p. 250
Warin Bassyngbourn		
from	4 December 1341	*CFR 1337–1347*, p. 250
William, earl of Cambridge (Just castle)		
on	15 December 1341	*CCR 1341–1343*, p. 325
Warin Bassyngbourn		
and from	22 November 1343	*CFR 1337–1347*, p. 349
to	4 November 1345	*CFR 1337–1347*, p. 445
John Engayne of Teversham, P.P.		
from	4 November 1345	*CFR 1337–1347*, p. 445
to	13 November 1347	*CFR 1346–1356*, p. 67
Warin de Bassingbourn		
from	13 November 1347	*CFR 1346–1356*, p. 67
to	31 May 1349	*CFR 1346–1356*, p. 85 (R.I.P.)

Guy de Saint Cler		
from	13 May 1348	*CFR 1347–1356*, p. 83
and from	15 October 1350	*CFR 1347–1356*, p. 227
William Muschet		
on	24 September 1359	*CPR 1358–1361*, p. 286
on	22 May 1360	*CCR 1360–1364*, p. 113 (Keeper)
Nicholas de Styuecle		
from	17 February 1367	*CFR 1356–1368*, p. 348
William de Pappeworth		
from	5 November 1371	*CFR 1369–1377*, p. 146
Nicholas de Styuecle		
to	6 April 1372	*CFR 1369–1377*, p. 163
William de Pappeworth		
from	6 April 1372	*CFR 1369–1377*, p. 163
Roger de Harleston		
from	12 December 1372	*CFR 1369–1377*, p. 190
Thomas Sewall		
from	7 November 1373	*CFR 1369–1377*, p. 222
Thomas Torell		
from	12 December 1374	*CFR 1369–1377*, p. 272
Baldwin St. George		
from	4 October 1375	*CFR 1369–1377*, p. 297
John Dengayne		
from	26 October 1376	*CFR 1369–1377*, p. 369
and from	22 June 1377	*CFR 1377–1383*, p. 2
John Avenell		
from	26 November 1377	*CFR 1377–1383*, p. 34
William Moigne		
from	25 November 1378	*CFR 1377–1383*, p. 113
Ralph Wyke		
from	5 November 1379	*CFR 1377–1383*, p. 170
Henry Englyssh		
from	18 October 1380	*CFR 1377–1383*, p. 220
Thomas Sewale		
from	15 December 1381	*CFR 1377–1383*, p. 270
William Moigne		
from	24 November 1382	*CFR 1377–1383*, p. 327
Philip Tylney		
from	1 November 1383	*CFR 1383–1391*, p. 7
Henry Englyssh		
from	11 November 1385	*CFR 1383–1391*, p. 76
Roger Gate		
on	14 July 1391	*CPR 1388–1392*, p. 462 (And goal)
Thomas Hasilden		
from	22 August 1399	*CFR 1391–1399*, p. 308
Roger Gate		
to	5 November 1399	*CPR 1399–1401*, p. 78
William Clipston (Just castle)		
from	5 November 1399	*CPR 1399–1401*, p. 78
to	7 August 1405	*CPR 1405–1408*, p. 36 (R.I.P.)

John Banbury (Just castle)		
from	7 August 1405	*CPR 1405–1408*, p. 36
on	16 November 1408	*CPR 1408–1413*, p. 51
Ralph Passenham (Just castle)		
for life from	19 November 1415	*CPR 1413–1416*, p. 369 Vacated by surrender

Porter and Gaoler

John Windsor		
to	18 October 1381	*CPR 1381–1385*, p. 47 (R.I.P.)
John Dercy		
from	18 October 1381	*CPR 1381–1385*, p. 47

Gaoler

William Clipston		
on	20 October 1402	*CPR 1401–1405*, p. 161

CASTLE CAMPS

Owners

Aubrey de Vere		
from	temp William I	*VCH vol. II*, p. 21
Robert de Vere, earl of Oxford		
died	*1296*	
Robert de Vere, earl of Oxford, son of above		
from	*1296*	
died	*1331*	
John de Vere, earl of Oxford, nephew of above		
from	*1331*	
died	*1360*	
Thomas de Vere, earl of Oxford, son of above		
from	*1360*	
died	*1371*	
Robert de Vere, earl of Oxford, marquis of Dublin, duke of Ireland, son of above		
from	*1371*	
forfeited	*1388*	
Aubrey de Vere, earl of Oxford, uncle of above		
restored	*1393*	
died	*1400*	
Richard de Vere, earl of Oxford, son of above		
from	*1400*	
died	*1417*	
John de Vere, earl of Oxford, son of above		
from	*1417*	
executed	*1462*	
de Vere family		
to	1580	*VCH vol. II*, p. 21

Wardship

Minority Robert de Vere, earl of Oxford, heir of Thomas de Vere, earl of Oxford (1371–1383)

Thomas Tirell and John James		
from	*1 October 1377*	*CFR 1377–1383, p. 13*

Minority of Richard de Vere (1400–1406)

Alice, wife of Aubrey de Vere		
from	*11 May 1400*	*CFR 1399–1405*, p. 56
Gerard Braybrok, Thomas Ferriby and Joan de Bohun, countess of Hereford		
from	*9 May 1401*	*CFR 1399–1405*, p. 125

CHEVELEY

Owners

John de Pulteney		
licence to crenellate	6 October 1341	*CPR 1340–1343*, p. 331

KIRTLING

Owners

Robert de Tony		
to	28 November 1309	*IPM V*, no. 198 (R.I.P.)
Alice de Leybourne, sister of above, widow of Thomas de Leybourne		
from	28 November 1309	*IPM V*, no. 198

WISBECH

Owners

Thomas Lisle, bishop of Ely		
void by	24 October 1356	*CPR 1354–1358*, p. 462
void on	3 May 1358	*CPR 1358–1361*, p. 43
Thomas de Arundel, bishop of Ely		
on	26 February 1376	
John Fordham, bishop of Ely		
on	22 August 1401	*CPR 1399–1401*, p. 534

Constables during voidances

Thomas de Baa		
confirmed by King	24 October 1356	*CPR 1354–1358*, p. 462
to	3 May 1358	*CPR 1358–1361*, p. 43
John de Wesenham, custodian of all castles of bishop of Ely		
on	10 July 1357	*CCR 1354–60*, p. 413
John Herlyng		
from	3 May 1358	*CPR 1358–1361*, p. 43
possibly still in place	25 June 1364	*CPR 1361–1364*, p. 545

Constables for the Church

Thomas Lovet		
on	December 1346	J. Aberth, *Criminal Churchmen in the age of Edward III*, Pennsylvania, 1996, p. 57
on	8 June 1350	Aberth, p. 57
Thomas de Baa		
on	Easter 1355	Aberth, p. 57
to	3 May 1358	Aberth, p. 57
Ralph Danyell of Walsoken		
for life from	26 February 1376	*CPR 1385–1389*, p. 460
surrendered	September 1398	M. Aston, *Thomas Arundel, A Study of Church Life in the Reign of Richard II*, Oxford, 1967, p. 259

John de Rochefort, kn.		
from	17 August 1401	*CPR 1399–1401*, p. 534
inspected and confirmed	22 August 1401	*CPR 1399–1401*, p. 534

Porters for the Church

Thomas Canville		
in	1349	Aberth, p. 151
on	31 May 1352	Aberth, p. 154

Reeve of the castle for the Church

Thomas Bacon		
on	31 May 1352	Aberth, p. 154

Cardigan

ABERYSTWYTH

Owners		
Edward, the Black Prince		
on	23 October 1347	
Joan, princess of Wales		
on	30 June 1384	
Constables		
Roger de Molis		
from	8 March 1278	*CWR*, p. 166
to	5 January 1280	*CWR*, p. 182
Bogo de Knovill		
from	5 January 1280	*CWR*, p. 182
on	10 June 1280	*CCR 1279–1288*, p. 101
Robert de Tibotot		
from	8 June 1281	
on	12 November 1281	*CCR 1279–1288*, p. 105
John de Skydemore		
on	24 October 1300	*CPR 1292–1301*, p. 541
from	20 May 1309	*CPR 1307–1313*, p. 116
to	31 October 1326	*CFR 1319–1327*, p. 422
Res ap Griffith		
from	31 October 1326	*CFR 1319–1327*, p. 422
John de Skydemore		
on	27 February 1328	*CCR 1327–1330*, p. 258
John de Montgomery		
from	24 November 1328	
on	8 December 1330	*CCR 1330–1333*, p. 79
Owain de Montgomery		
on	25 July 1335	*CCR 1333–1337*, p. 432
on	29 September 1337	E101/20/23 m.5
John de Montgomery		
on	3 January 1340	*CCR 1339–1341*, p. 314
on	10 October 1340	*CCR 1339–1341*, p. 543
Thomas Peytevyn		
to	9 March 1384	*CPR 1381–1385*, p. 405
Joan, princess of Wales		
from	9 March 1384	*CPR 1381–1385*, p. 405
Richard Stury		
from	30 June 1384	
confirmed	26 July 1384	*CPR 1381–1385*, p. 453
dead by	27 March 1396	*CPR 1391–1396*, p. 670
Simon Felbrigg, king's knight		
for life from	27 March 1396	*CPR 1391–1396*, p. 670
John ap Henri		
for life from	27 October 1399	*CPR 1399–1401*, p. 38

Richard lord Grey		
from	26 September 1402	*CPR 1401–1405*, p. 122 (Keeper)

Constable for the Black Prince

John de Montgomery		
confirmed	4 October 1347	*BPR I*, p. 121
dead by	24 October 1347	*BPR I*, p. 131
Roger de Coteford		
for life from	24 October 1347	*BPR I*, p. 131
on	28 January 1348	*CPR 1348–1350*, p. 11
Robert de Stretton		
on	24 June 1355	*BPR III*, p. 492
on	26 November 1359	*BPR III*, p. 378

Sub–constables

Robert Clement for John de Montgomery		
to	24 October 1347	*BPR I*, p. 131
Robert de Holewell for Robert de Coteford		
to	9 January 1348	*BPR I*, p. 159
Robert Clement for Robert de Coteford		
from	9 January 1349	*BPR I*, p. 159

CARDIGAN

Owners

Edmund, earl of Lancaster		
from	1264	*HKW II*, p. 590
on	24 January 1277	*CPR 1272–1281*, p. 189
to	10 November 1279	*CChR 1257–1300*, p. 218
Crown		
from	10 November 1279	*CChR 1257–1300*, p. 218
Edward, the Black Prince		
on	21 September 1347	
Crown – Joan, mother of Richard II, wife of Edward, the Black Prince		
from	13 October 1376	*CPR 1374–1377*, p. 374
from	13 October 1376	*CCR 1374–1377*, p. 405
on	13 March 1378	

Constables

Bogo de Knovill		
from	5 January 1280	*CWR*, p. 182
Robert Tybetot		
from	8 June 1281	*CPR 1272–1281*, p. 443
on	27 April 1286	*CWR*, p. 305
Thomas de Chastiel		
from	5 January 1320	*CFR 1319–1327*, p. 14
to	17 April 1326	*CFR 1319–1327*, p. 385
William ap Eygnoun		
from	17 April 1326	*CFR 1319–1327*, p. 385
to	22 October 1327	*CFR 1327–1337*, p. 67
Geoffrey Beaufou		
from	22 October 1327	*CFR 1327–1337*, p. 67
on	18 December 1327	*CCR 1327–1330*, p. 193

William ap Eygnoun		
on	12 May 1328	*CCR 1327–1330*, p. 284
Geoffrey Beaufou		
to	18 December 1330	*CFR 1327–1337*, p. 277
Hugh de Frene		
from	18 December 1330	*CFR 1327–1337*, p. 227
dead by	9 February 1337	*CPR 1334–1338*, p. 380
to	9 February 1337	E.101/20/23 m.6
Gilbert de Turbervill, king's yeoman		
for life from	9 February 1337	*CPR 1334–1338*, p. 380
to	29 August 1347	*BPR I*, p. 116 (R.I.P.)
Thomas de Castle Goodrich		
from	29 August 1347	*BPR I*, p. 116
Lewis de Clifford, kn.		
from	13 March 1378	for Joan, the king's mother
confirmed	29 October 1382	*CPR 1381–1385*, p. 185
on	16 May 1387	*CPR 1385–1389*, p. 230
Richard lord Grey		
from	26 September 1402	*CPR 1401–1405*, p. 122
Hugh Mortimer		
to	7 June 1416	*CPR 1416–1422*, p. 32
John Burghope		
from	7 June 1416	*CPR 1416–1422*, p. 32

Private Constables

William de Bolevill		
to	24 January 1277	*CPR 1272–1281*, p. 189
John de Beauchamp		
from	24 January 1277	*CPR 1272–1281*, p. 189

Lieutenants

Andrew de Lynne		
on	19 July 1414	*CPR 1413–1416*, p. 89

Constables for Black Prince

Roland Daneys, yeoman		
from for life	21 September 1347	
on	20 January 1348	*BPR I*, p. 159
on	26 November 1359	*BPR III*, p. 378

LLANILAR

Owners

Maelgwn Fychan, grandson of the Lord Rhys		
temp	1242	King, p. 51 (n.40)

TREFILAN

Owners

Maelgwn, son of the Lord Rhys		
temp	1233	King, p. 52 (n.55)
Maelgwn Fychan, son of the above		
temp	after death of above	King, p. 52 (n.55)

Carmarthan

CARMARTHEN

Owners

Edward I, as Lord Edward		
from	1254	*HKW II*, p. 601
to	1264	*HKW II*, p. 601
Edmund, earl of Lancaster		
from	1264	*HKW II*, p. 601
on	24 January 1277	*CPR 1272–1281*, p. 189
to	1279	*HKW II*, p. 601
to	10 November 1279	*CChR 1257–1300*, p. 218
Crown		
from	1279	*HKW II*, p601
from	10 November 1279	*CChR 1257–1300*, p. 218
Prince Edward		
from	12 May 1343	*CChR 1307–1349*, p. 14
on	28 February 1376	*CCR 1374–1377*, p. 317

Constables

Bogo de Knovil		
from	5 January 1280	*CWR*, p. 182
on	10 June 1280	*CCR 1279–1288*, p. 101
Robert de Tibotot		
from	8 June 1281	*CPR 1272–1281*, p. 443
on	12 November 1281	*CCR 1279–1288*, p. 105
Walter de Pederton		
on	28 December 1284	*CWR*, p. 296
on	15 February 1286	*CCR 1279–1288*, p. 383
Robert de Tibotot		
on	27 April 1286	*CWR*, p. 305
Walter de Pederton		
on	21 November 1296	*CPR 1292–1301*, p. 210
Thomas Deyn		
not by	15 February 1327	*CPR 1327–1330*, p. 73; *CAPW*, p. 271
Richard de Pembrigge		
on	8 January 1329	*CCR 1327–1330*, p. 354
Gilbert Talbot, P.P.		
on	4 February 1340	*CCR 1339–1341*, p. 356
on	12 April 1340	*CCR 1339–1341*, p. 379
Res Ap Griffith		
to	17 February 1342	*CFR 1337–1347*, p. 263
Henry, earl of Lancaster		
for 10 years from	17 February 1342	*CFR 1337–1347*, p. 263
for 10 years from	2 May 1343	*CFR 1337–1347*, p. 335
Gilbert Talbot, P.P., to deliver to Prince Edward		
to	12 May 1343	*CChR 1307–1349*, p.15

Simon de Burley, king's knight		
for life from	26 September 1375	
confirmed	22 March 1378	*CPR 1377–1381*, p. 223
asks to be replaced	1385	*CAPW*, p. 413
to	20 February 1385	*CPR 1381–1385*, p. 534
Nicholas de Audley of Heighley, P.P.		
from	20 February 1385	*CPR 1381–1385*, p. 534
to	22 November 1390	*CPR 1388–1392*, p. 326
Roger Wigmore		
from	22 November 1390	*CPR 1399–1392*, p. 326
to	19 May 1399?	
William Walsall		
for life from	11 June 1395	*CPR 1391–1396*, p. 574
Roger Wigmore and William Asshe		
for life from	19 May 1399	*CPR 1399–1401*, p. 58
confirmed	6 October 1399	*CPR 1399–1401*, p. 12
Richard lord Grey		
from	26 September 1402	*CPR 1401–1405*, p. 122 (Keeper)
Edward, duke of York		
from	15 October 1403	*CPR 1401–1405*, p. 311 (For 1 year)
on	16 March 1404	*CPR 1401–1405*, p. 372
Thomas Beaufort, kn.		
on	29 April 1405	*CPR 1405–1408*, p. 16 (Keeper)
on	6 July 1405	*CPR 1405–1408*, p. 26

Private Constables

William de Bolevill		
to	24 January 1277	*CPR 1272–1281*, p. 189
John de Beauchamp		
from	24 January 1277	*CPR 1272–1281*, p. 189

Constables for the Black Prince

Reynold de Hope, kn.		
on	26 November 1354	*BPR III*, p. 378

Treasurer

John Morhay, clerk		
from	17 September 1403	*CPR 1401–1405*, p. 267

CARREG CENNON

Tenant In Chief

Edward, prince of Wales		
on	23 March 1361	*IPM XI*, no. 118 (R.I.P.)

Owners

Crown		
captured	April–May 1277	Morris, p. 125
on	5 June 1277	*CPR 1272–1281*, p. 212
John Giffard		
forfeited by	2 February 1323	*Ancient Deeds vol. III*, A.4886
Hugh le Despenser, yng, P.P.		
from	6 November 1322	*CPR 1321–1324*, p. 212 (Fee simple)
on	2 February 1323	*Ancient Deeds vol. III*, A.4886

John Giffard of Brimpsfield, P.P.		
to	12 February 1327	*IPM VII*, no. 78 (R.I.P.)
John de Caillewe		
to	19 May 1330	*CPR 1327–1330*, p. 527
John Mautravers, purchased from above		
from	19 May 1330	*CPR 1327–1330*, p. 527
foot of fine	6 October 1330	*Feet of fines relating to Wiltshire* Wiltshire Record Society 29 (1973), no. 65
Ralph de Wylyngton		
to	20 June 1340	*CPR 1338–1340*, p. 549
Henry, earl of Lancaster		
from	20 June 1340	*CPR 1338–1340*, p. 549
Henry, duke of Lancaster		
to	23 March 1361	*IPM XI*, no. 118 (R.I.P.)
Maud, his daughter, late the wife of William duke of Bavaria		
to	10 April 1362	*IPM XI*, no. 299 (R.I.P.)
John of Gaunt, duke of Lancaster		
from	10 April 1362	*IPM XI*, no. 299
on	14 November 1371	*JGR 1372–1376*, no. 882
to	1380	
Crown		
from	1399	

Constables

John Penrhys		
from	April–May 1277	Morris, p. 125
Payn de Cadurcis		
from	5 June 1277	*CPR 1272–1281*, p. 212
Bogo de Knovill		
from	5 January 1280	*CWR*, p. 182
on	10 June 1280	*CCR 1279–1288*, p. 101
Robert de Tibotot		
from	8 June 1281	
on	12 November 1281	*CCR 1279–1288*, p. 105
Richard Wroth and William de Beauchamp		
to	6 November 1322	*CPR 1321–1324*, p. 222
Roger Bauent, P.P.		
from	20 February 1327	*CFR 1327–1337*, p. 18
to	29 November 1328	*CFR 1327–1337*, p. 113
Edward, duke of York		
from	15 October 1403	*CPR 1401–1405*, p. 311
Rhys ap Thomas		
temp	*1414–1421*	*HKW II*, p. 602

Private Constable for Hugh Despenser

Sir John Inge		
from	6 December 1322	*Ancient Deeds vol. III*, A.4887

Private Constable for John of Gaunt

John Wrenche		
from	14 November 1371	*JGR 1372–1376*, no. 882

DRYSLWYN (DROSLAN, DRUSSELAN)

Owners

Rhys ap Maredudd		
on	11 April 1277	Morris, p. 124
to	August 1287	Morris, p. 213; *HKW II*, p. 641
forfeited as a rebel by	24 September 1287	*CWR*, p. 311
Crown		
from	1287	*HKW II*, p. 642
to	1317	*HKW II*, p. 642
Hugh Despenser, yng, P.P.		
restored	7 May 1322	*CPR 1321–1324*, p. 115
to	20 May 1318	*Ancient Deeds vol. III*, A.4878
Rhys ap Griffith, leased from above		
for 7 years from	20 May 1318	*Ancient Deeds vol. III*, A.4878
Hugh Despenser, yng, P.P.		
to	1326	*HKW II*, p. 642
Crown		
from	1326	*HKW II*, p. 642
to	1343	*HKW II*, p. 642
Crown – Black Prince		
from	12 May 1343	*CChR 1307–1349*, p. 15
not by	1353	*HKW II*, p. 642
on	21 September 1356	*IPM X*, no. 324
Crown – Henry, Prince of Wales		
on	2 March 1402	
on	17 March 1402	*CPR 1401–1405*, p. 57

Constables

Alan de Plogenet, P.P.		
from	24 September 1287	*CWR*, p. 31
on	18 August 1289	*CPR 1281–1292*, p. 320
John le Ussher		
for life from	17 February 1302	*CPR 1301–1307*, p. 15
John Giffard of Brimpsfield, king's yeoman, P.P.		
from	5 July 1309	*CPR 1307–1313*, p. 163
to	22 February 1312	*CFR 1307–1319*, p. 126
Thomas le Blount, P.P.		
on	20 May 1312	*CFR 1307–1319*, p. 133
on	30 Auy 1312	*CCR 1307–1313*, p. 476
Thomas de Hewish		
from	16 April 1314	*CFR 1307–1319*, p. 193
Thomas le Blount, P.P.		
on	1 August 1315	*CCR 1313–1318*, p. 240
to	18 November 1317	*CPR 1317–1321*, p. 56
Hugh le Despenser yng, P.P.		
for life from	18 November 1317	*CPR 1317–1321*, p. 56
Walter Box		
from	4 July 1318	*CFR 1307–1319*, p. 364
Giles de Beauchamp		
from	14 September 1318	*CFR 1307–1319*, p. 375
to	21 November 1318	*CPR 1317–1321*, p. 248

Hugh le Despenser yng, P.P.		
from	21 November 1318	*CPR 1317–1321*, p. 248
for life from	21 November 1318	*CPR 1317–1321*, p. 255
Res ap Griffith		
to	30 September 1321	*CFR 1319–1327*, p. 72
Walter de Beauchamp		
from	30 September 1321	*CFR 1319–1327*, p. 72
from	24 October 1321	*CPR 1321–1324*, p. 30
William de Beauchamp		
to	7 May 1322	*CPR 1321–1324*, p. 115
Hugh Despenser yng		
to	7 November 1326	*CFR 1319–1327*, p. 422
Llewellyn du ap Griffith		
from	7 November 1326	*CFR 1319–1327*, p. 422
Roger Pycard		
on	20 June 1327	*CFR 1327–1337*, p. 50
Richard de Pembrigge		
from	8 November 1328	*CFR 1327–1337*, p. 111
Rees ap Griffin (ap Howel)		
from	6 August 1333	*CFR 1327–1337*, p. 370
for life from	13 February 1335	*CFR 1327–1337*, p. 431
on	12 May 1339	*CCR 1339–1341*, p. 127
for life from	1353	*HKW II*, p. 642
to	1356	*HKW II*, p. 642 (R.I.P.)
on	26 November 1359	*BPR III*, p. 378
William de Houton		
for life from	5 June 1380	*CPR 1377–1381*, p. 498
on	8 May 1385	*CCR 1381–1385*, p. 549
William de Houton and William Bredewardye, king's esquire		
for life from	11 February 1399	*CPR 1396–1399*, p. 471
Rees ap Griff, esquire		
from	2 March 1402	
confirmed	17 March 1402	*CPR 1401–1405*, p. 57
Rhys ap Gruffydd		
on	1403	*HKW II*, p. 642

DYNEVOR

Tenant in Chief

Sir John son of Reginald		
on	16 May 1306	*IPM IV*, no. 352

Owners

Rhys ap Mareddud		
to	11 April 1277	Morris, p. 124
requests compensation	1284–1287	*CAPW*, p. 97–8
Taken into King's hands by Payn de Cadurcis		
on	5 June 1277	*CPR 1272–1281*, p. 212
Hugh Despenser, yng.		
restored	7 May 1322	*CPR 1321–1324*, p. 115
to	20 May 1318	*Ancient Deeds vol. III*, A.4878
Rhys ap Griffith, leased from above		
for 7 years from	20 May 1318	*Ancient Deeds vol. III*, A.4878

Hugh Despenser, yng.		
to	1326	*HKW II*, p. 643
Crown		
from	1326	*HKW II*, p. 644
to	1343	*HKW II*, p. 644
Crown – Black Prince		
from	12 May 1343	*CChR 1307–1349*, p. 15
Constables		
John Penrhys		
from	April–May 1277	Morris, p. 125
Payn de Cadurcis		
from	12 June 1277	*CPR 1272–1281*, p. 212
Bogo de Knovill		
from	5 January 1280	*CWR*, p. 182
on	10 June 1280	*CCR 1279–1288*, p. 101
Robert de Tibotot		
from	8 June 1281	
on	12 November 1281	*CCR 1279–1288*, p. 105
John Giffard of Brimpsfield, P.P.		
from	8 February 1290	*CPR 1281–1292*, p. 341 (Corpus)
for life from	8 February 1290	*CPR 1281–1292*, p. 341 (Corpus)
to	29 July 1297	*CPR 1292–1301*, p. 296
Robert de Tibotot		
from	29 July 1297	*CPR 1292–1301*, p. 296
William de Langeton		
from	31 July 1310	*CFR 1307–1319*, p. 67
Edmund Hakelut		
for life from	4 December 1310	*CPR 1307–1313*, p. 291
to	3 April 1318	*CPR 1317–1321*, p. 130
Hugh le Despenser, yng, P.P.		
from	3 April 1318	*CPR 1317–1321*, p. 130
Edmund Hakelut		
from	11 July 1318	*CCR 1318–1323*, p. 1
on	12 July 1318	*IMisc II*, no. 343
Hugh le Despenser, yng, P.P.		
for life from	21 November 1318	*CPR 1317–1321*, p. 255
Griffin ap Rees		
from	23 January 1322	*CFR 1319–1327*, p. 91
to	23 January 1322	*CFR 1319–1327*, p. 91
William de Beauchamp		
to	7 May 1322	*CPR 1321–1324*, p. 115
Edmund Gracelyn		
from	23 January 1322	*CFR 1319–1327*, p. 91
Hugh le Despenser yng		
to	7 November 1326	*CFR 1319–1327*, p. 422
Llewellyn du ap Griffith		
from	7 November 1326	*CFR 1319–1327*, p. 422
to	2 December 1326	*CPR 1319–1327*, p. 422 (Res ap Griffith)
Edmund Hakelut		
from	2 December 1326	*CPR 1319–1327*, p. 341
for life on	2 June 1327	*CCR 1327–1330*, p. 129
on	27 April 1329	*CCR 1327–1330*, p. 447

Edmund Hakelut ynr		
for life from	7 July 1329	*CFR 1327–1337*, p. 140
to	1360	*HKW II*, p. 644 (R.I.P.)
Edmund de Bradeston		
on	13 May 1385	*CCR 1381–1385*, p. 549
Richard Mawardyn, esquire		
for life from	1 December 1388	*CPR 1388–1392*, p. 1
Edmund Bradston		
to	28 June 1397	*CPR 1396–1399*, p. 197
William Walsall		
for life from	28 June 1397	*CPR 1396–1399*, p. 197
John Hauard, esquire		
for life from	3 November 1399	*CPR 1399–1401*, p. 49
William Walsall		
confirmed	14 November 1399	*CPR 1399–1401*, p. 120

Deputies

Walter de Pederton		
on	29 July 1297	*CPR 1292–1301*, p. 296

Porter

Richard Mauardyn, esquire		
for life from	1 December 1388	*CPR 1388–1392*, p. 1

KIDWELLY

Tenant in Chief

Edward black prince		
on	23 March 1361	*IPM XI*, no. 118 (R.I.P.)

Owners

Payn de Chaworth		
c.	mid 1270s	Platt p. 85
Henry, earl of Lancaster, through his wife Matilda de Chaworth, niece of above		
from	1298	Platt p. 85
to	1333	DL.27/192
Henry, duke of Lancaster		
from	1333	DL.27/192
to	23 March 1361	*IPM XI*, no. 118 (R.I.P.)
dead by	16 July 1361	*CFR 1356–1368*, p. 165
Maud, his daughter, wife of William duke of Bavaria		
from	16 July 1361	*CFR 1356–1368*, p. 165
to	10 April 1362	*IPM XI*, no. 299 (R.I.P.)
John of Gaunt, duke of Lancaster, through Blanche his wife, sister of above		
from	10 April 1362	*IPM XI*, no. 299
on	1 March 1373	*JGR 1372–1376*, no. 565
Crown		
from	1399	

Private Constables

Richard de Burley for John of Gaunt		
for life from	1 March 1373	*JGR 1372–1376*, no. 565

LAUGHARNE

Owners		
Guy de Brian		
to	26 July 1307	*IPM V*, no. 64 (R.I.P.)
Guy de Brian, son of above		
from	26 July 1307	*IPM V*, no. 64
Hugh le Despenser, yng and Eleanor his wife		
from	9 July 1322	*CChR 1300–1326*, p. 448
Guy de Brian, kn., snr, in chief		
to	29 October 1349	*CCR 1349–1354*, p. 120
to	17 June 1349	*IPM IX*, no. 333 (R.I.P.)
Guy de Brian, kn., jnr, son of above, in chief, P.P.		
from	17 June 1349	*IPM IX*, no. 333
on	16 August 1386	*CChR 1341–1417*, p. 306
Henry le Scrope, kn.		
on	8 September 1403	*CCR 1402–1405*, p. 111

LLANDOVERY

Owners		
Res Grege		Morris, p. 125
Res Mychyll, bastard son		Morris, p. 125
Res Vachan, son		Morris, p. 125
Res Wyndot and LLeweyn ap Res, sons		Morris, p. 125
Captured by English		
temp	April–May 1277	Morris, p. 125
John Giffard of Brimpsfield, invader, P.P.		
seisen on	2 June 1282	*CWR*, no. 222
to	5 June 1299	*IPM III*, no. 544 (R.I.P.)
Katherine de Audley, daughter and heir of above		
from	23 October 1299	*CFR 1272–1307*, p. 421
to	24 November 1312	*CPR 1307–1313*, p. 512
James de Peres and Ela, daughter of above		
from	24 November 1312	*CPR 1307–1313*, p. 512
confirmed	7 October 1313	*CCR 1307–1313*, p. 75
Nicholas de Audley of Heighley, unclear title, P.P.		
to	6 December 1316	*IPM VI*, no. 56 (R.I.P.)
James de Audley, of Heighley, son of above, P.P.		
from	6 December 1316	*IPM VI*, no. 56
under age	20 May 1319	*CCR 1318–1323*, p. 72
died	*1 April 1386*	*GEC I, p. 339*
Nicholas de Audley of Heighley, son of above, P.P.		
confirmed	12 May 1368	*CPR 1367–1370*, p. 111 (Probably)
to	22 July 1391	*IPM XVI*, no. 1064 (R.I.P.)
forfeited by	5 August 1391	*IMisc V*, no. 325
Crown		
in	1391	*CPR 1388–1392*, p. 519
Elizabeth, widow of Nicholas de Audley		
from	22 July 1391	*IPM XVI*, no. 1064 (Jointure)
on	16 November 1391	*CCR 1389–1392*, p. 400

One third to John Tuchet, lord Audley, P.P.		
on	8 September 1403	*CCR 1402–1405*, p. 111
to	19 December 1409	*IPM XIX*, no. 594 (R.I.P.) (1/3)
One third to James Tuchet, lord Audley, son of above, P.P.		
from	19 December 1409	*IPM XIX*, no. 594 (1/3)
One third to Fulk Fitz Waryn		
to	31 October 1407	*IPM XIX*, no. 429 (R.I.P.)
One third to Fulk Fitz Waryn, son of above		
from	31 October 1407	*IPM XIX*, no. 429

Constables

Taken into King's hands by Payn de Cadurcis		
on	5 June 1277	*CPR 1272–1281*, p. 212
Bogo de Knovill		
on	10 June 1280	*CWR*, p. 186
Robert de Tibotot		
from	8 June 1281	
on	12 November 1281	*CCR 1279–1288*, p. 105
Gilbert de Clare, earl of Gloucester (d.1295)		
to	9 April 1282	*CPR 1281–1292*, p. 15
to	14 April 1282	*CWR*, p. 213
John Giffard of Brimpsfield, P.P.		
from	9 April 1282	*CPR 1281–1292*, p. 15
from	14 April 1282	*CWR*, p. 213
to	2 June 1282	*CWR*, p. 222 (Becomes owner)

Wardships

Minority of James de Audley, 1316–1334, heir of Nicholas de Audley

John Giffard of Brimpsfield		
on	14 March 1317	*CPR 1313–1317*, p. 634 (Wardship)
on	20 May 1319	*CCR 1318–1323*, p. 72 (Wardship)
Griffin ap Res		
from	14 February 1322	*CFR 1319–1327*, p. 98 (Custody)

LLANSTEPHAN

Tenant in Chief

Edward, the Black Prince, Prince of Wales		
on	11 March 1357	*IPM X*, no. 407

Owners

Camville family		
temp	13th century	R.R.Davies, *Lordship and society in the March of Wales, 1282–1400*, Oxford, 1978, p. 74
Geoffrey de Camville		
died	*1308*	*GEC III, p. 3*
William de Camville		
from	*1308*	*GEC III, p. 3*
to	*1338*	*GEC III, p. 3*
Richard de Penres, from Eleanor, his wife		
to	11 March 1357	*IPM X*, no. 407 (R.I.P.)

Robert Penres		
from	11 March 1357	*IPM X*, no. 407
on	20 June 1367	*CPR 1364–1367*, p. 413
Simon de Burley, king's knight		
fee simple from	16 June 1377	
confirmed	26 June 1378	*CPR 1377–1381*, p. 262
to	11 Rich II (1387/8)	
Robert de Penres		
fee simple from	27 July 1391	*CPR 1388–1392*, p. 473
Humphrey duke of Gloucester, temporary grant to clear debts		
to	1 July 1418	*CPR 1416–1422*, p. 129

Constables

David ap Meuric and Howel Seys and Griffith ap Yevan		
from	30 October 1326	*CPR 1324–1327*, p. 335
John Penres		
for life from	24 September 1403	*CPR 1401–1405*, p. 295
to	19 December 1403	*CPR 1401–1405*, p. 311
David Houwell, esquire		
from	19 December 1403	*CPR 1401–1405*, p. 331
on	5 August 1404	*CPR 1401–1405*, p. 411

NEWCASTLE EMLYN /EMELYN

Reversions

Henry de Ferrars		
on	8 July 1338	*CPR 1327–1330*, p. 110

Owners

Maredudd ap Rhys		
temp	1240	*HKW II*, p. 646
Rhys ap Maredudd		
in	March 1277	*CACW*, XVI.24
to	August 1287	Morris, p. 214
Crown		
from	1288	*HKW II* p. 646
to	1349	*HKW II* p. 647
Gilbert Talbot		
on	8 July 1338	*CPR 1338–1340*, p. 110
Edward, prince of Wales		
from	1343	
on	4 July 1346	
to	1349	
Richard de la Bere, chamberlain of above		
for life from	1349	*HKW II*, p. 647
Simon de Burley, king's knight		
on	16 February 1383	*CCR 1381–1385*, p. 196
before	6 October 1388	*CFR 1383–1391*, p. 254

Constables

Robert de Tibotot		
from	January 1287	Morris, p. 218

David Vaghan		
from	1294/5	
on	14 September 1309	*IMisc II*, no. 68
Richard Wrothe		
from	4 March 1311	*CPR 1307–1313*, p. 330
Robert de Acton		
to	29 July 1314	*CFR 1307–1319*, p. 203
John de Welles		
from	29 July 1314	*CFR 1307–1319*, p. 203
Robert de Acton		
from	20 September 1314	*CFR 1307–1319*, p. 210
dead by	7 February 1316	*CCR 1313–1318*, p. 263
William Martyn, P.P.		
on	3 August 1315	*CCR 1313–1318*, p. 241
Geoffrey de Bella Fago		
from	8 August 1316	*CFR 1307–1319*, p. 293
on	13 February 1317	*CCR 1313–1318*, p. 392
to	28 May 1319	*CPR 1317–1321*, p. 338
William de Knovill		
from	28 May 1319	*CPR 1317–1321*, p. 338
on	19 April 1322	*CCR 1318–1323*, p. 438
Hugh de Turpyngton		
from	29 November 1327	*CPR 1324–1327*, p. 238
Thomas de Blaunkfrount		
from	24 October 1331	*CFR 1327–1337*, p. 285
Gilbert Talbot		
on	29 May 1331	*CCR 1330–1333*, p. 243
for life from	2 October 1333	*CPR 1330–1334*, p. 476
on	23 April 1338	*CPR 1338–1340*, p. 52
Simon de Burley, king's knight		
for life from	14 March 1382	*CPR 1381–1385*, p. 107
for life from	2 May 1382	*CPR 1381–1385*, p. 118
John de Hastings, John Trailly, John Prat, Robert Poley		
from	6 October 1388	*CFR 1383–1391*, p. 254
Thomas Paytevyn		
from	26 January 1389	*CFR 1393–1391*, p. 331
Thomas de Percy		
for life from	20 December 1390	*CPR 1388–1392*, p. 354
for life from	15 May 1391	*CPR 1388–1392*, p. 413
John Ayschell, esquire		
for life from	11 November 1399	*CPR 1399–1401*, p. 68

Private Constables

Richard de la Bere, kn.		
from	4 July 1346	
on	8 February 1347	*BPR I*, p. 44
on	8 March 1347	*BPR I*, p. 53
on	9 March 1347	*BPR I*, p. 53
on	29 April 1347	*BPR I*, p. 73
on	16 October 1347	*BPR I*, p. 126
on	8 November 1347	*BPR I*, p. 142
for life from	4 February 1348	*CPR 1348–1350*, p. 9
on	26 November 1359	*BPR III*, p. 378

confirmed	27 May 1379	*CPR 1377–1381*, p. 349
not by	14 March 1382	*CPR 1381–1385*, p. 107

ST. CLEARS

History

built	pre. 1153	King, p. 59
in use	temp. Glendower	King, p. 59

Cheshire

Unknown Licenses

ST. WERBURGHS ABBEY for Abbot and Convent		
	28 March 1377	*CPR 1374–1377*, p. 442

ALDFORD

Owners

Sir Peter de Ardern		
on	24 February 1276	*IPM II*, no. 181
on	10 June 1290	*IPM II*, no. 749

BEESTON

Owners

Royal earls of Chester		
from	1254	*HKW II*, p. 560
Edward of Caernarvon		
on	14 October 1301	*CPR 1292–1301*, p. 616
in	1303–4	*HKW II*, p. 559
Edward, the Black Prince		
from	19 March 1333	*CChR 1327–1341*, p. 300
in	1353–1360	J.H.Hewitt, *Medieval Cheshire*, Chetham Society New Series, 88 (1929), p. 96

Constables

Robert de Crevequer		
for life from	8 November 1289	*CPR 1281–1292*, p. 328
on	16 August 1302	*CCR 1296–1302*, p. 549
to	grant to Edward II as prince of Wales	
Robert de Pulford or Payn Tybotot		
to	30 January 1312	*CFR 1307–1319*, p. 124
Robert de Holland, P.P.		
from	30 January 1312	*CFR 1307–1319*, p. 124
to	27 July 1312	*CPR 1307–1313*, p. 482
Ralph de Vernoun, yng		
from	27 July 1312	*CPR 1307–1313*, p. 482
Robert de Huxlegh		
on	29 May 1329	E.101/18/17 m.1
John de Wlyde, king's archer		
for life from	27 February 1389	*CPR 1388–1392*, p. 23
Henry Champneys		
for life from	17 February 1396	*CPR 1391–1396*, p. 670

Constables for the Black Prince

Richard de Chastel		
on	7 July 1346	*BPR I*, p. 54
Robert de Houghton		
from	23 November 1358	*BPR III*, p. 455

Alan Cheyne		
for life from	24 April 1363	*BPR III*, p. 455

CHESTER

Owners

Earls of Chester		
to	1237	*HKW II*, p. 608
Crown		
from	1237	*HKW II*, p. 608
to	1254	*HKW II*, p. 608
Crown – earls of Chester		
from	1254	*HKW II*, p. 608
Edward, earl of Chester		
on	1 November 1317	*CCR 1313–1318*, p. 505
Crown – Edward the Black Prince		
from	18 March 1333	*CChR 1327–1341*, p. 300
on	4 March 1351	*BPR III*, p. 2
in	1353–1360	H.J.Hewitt, *Medieval Cheshire*, Chetham Society New Series, 88 (1929), p. 96

Constables

Reynold de Grey of Wilton and Ruthin, P.P.		
to deliver to below	16 October 1274	*CFR 1272–1307*, p. 31
Guncelin de Badelesmere		
from	16 October 1274	*CFR 1272–1307*, p. 31
on	16 October 1274	*CPR 1272–1281*, p. 60
Robert de Ufford		
on	20 October 1276	*CCR 1272–1279*, p. 314 (Justice)
Guncelin de Badelesmere		
on	4 August 1279	*CCR 1272–1279*, p. 536 (Justice)
to	14 November 1281	*CFR 1272–1307*, p. 155
Henry de Lacy, earl of Lincoln		
on	26 May 1278	*CChR 1257–1300*, p. 207 (Constable)
on	28 October 1294	*CChR 1257–1300*, p. 455 (Constable)
Reynold de Grey of Wilton and Ruthin, P.P.		
from	14 November 1281	*CFR 1272–1307*, p. 155
on	20 August 1295	*CCR 1288–1296*, p. 423 (Reginald)
Richard de Mascy		
from	7 June 1300	*CFR 1272–1307*, p. 428
William de Ormesby		
to	1 October 1307	*CFR 1307–1319*, p. 5
Robert de Holland, P.P.		
from	1 October 1307	*CFR 1307–1319*, p. 5
to	24 October 1309	*CFR 1307–1319*, p. 50
Payn Tybotot, P.P.		
from	24 October 1309	*CFR 1307–1319*, p. 50
on	19 December 1311	*CFR 1307–1319*, p. 121
not by	30 January 1312	*CCR 1307–1313*, p. 396
Robert de Holland, P.P.		
from	19 December 1311	*CFR 1307–1319*, p. 121
on	30 January 1312	*CCR 1307–1313*, p. 396

Oliver de Ingham, P.P., kn.		
from	19 February 1322	*CPR 1321–1324*, p. 72
Joan de Lacy, widow of Henry de Lacy		
to	15 July 1322	*CPR 1321–1324*, p. 194
Hugh le Despenser, yng, P.P.		
from	15 July 1322	*CPR 1321–1324*, p. 194
confirmed	28 July 1322	*CPR 1321–1324*, p. 194
Thomas de Warwick		
for life on	16 May 1328	*CPR 1327–1330*, p. 271
Oliver de Ingham, P.P., kn.		
from	29 November 1328	*CFR 1327–1337*, p. 113
Prince Edward		
on	24 September 1334	*CCR 1333–1337*, p. 254
Edmund de Langley, duke of York		
on	20 March 1387	*CPR 1385–1389*, p. 288 (Justice)
Roger Crophull		
for life from	31 October 1388	*CPR 1385–1389*, p. 518
to	25 April 1396	*CPR 1391–1396*, p. 694
William de Venables and Roger Crophull		
from	25 April 1396	*CPR 1391–1396*, p. 694
Henry Percy, son of earl of Northumberland		
for life from	24 October 1399	*CPR 1399–1401*, p. 158
for life from	24 April 1400	*CPR 1399–1401*, p. 28
William de Venables of Kynderton		
on	18 August 1413	*CPR 1413–1416*, p. 93

Deputy Justices

Thomas Illeston		
from	20 March 1387	*CPR 1385–1389*, p. 288

Maker of Engines of War

Thomas le Attiliour		
for life from	6 July 1329	*CPR 1327–1330*, p. 411

Constables for Black Prince

Henry de Ferrers, P.P.		
to	14 February 1341	*CFR 1337–1347*, p. 214
William de Beauchamp and Hugh de Berwick		
from	14 February 1341	*CFR 1337–1347*, p. 214
John de Byntre		
not by	4 March 1351	*BPR III*, p. 2
Richard Doun		
to	16 August 1353	*BPR III*, p. 2
Thomas de Warwick		
on	26 June 1355	*BPR III*, p. 205
on	22 July 1362	*BPR III*, p. 449
Thomas Chaundeller		
from	4 April 1365	*BPR III*, p. 477

DODDINGTON

Owners

Sir John Delves		
poss. license	1364	Pevsner, p. 198; King, p. 67

John Delves		
poss. license	1403	Pevsner, p. 198; King, p. 67

DODLESTON

Owners		
John Boydel		
in	6 February 1277	*IPM II*, no. 213
in	24 February 1283	*IPM II*, no. 493

DUNHAM MASSEY

History		
in use	1173	King, p. 67
mentioned	1323	King, p. 67

FRODSHAM

Owners		
David ap Gruffydd		
to	1282	D. Sylvester, *A History of Chester*, Henley on Thames, 1971, p. 32

HALTON

Owners		
Henry de Lacy, earl of Lincoln		
on	25 August 1294	*CFR 1272–1307*, p. 343
to	6 February 1311	*IPM V*, no. 279 (R.I.P.)
Thomas of Lancaster and Alice de Lacy his wife, daughter of above		
from	6 February 1311	*IPM V*, no. 279
Ebulo le Strange, P.P.		
to	21 December 1324	*CPR 1324–1327*, p. 63
Crown		
on	23 June 1349	*CPR 1345–1348*, p. 329
on	5 October 1349	*CCR 1349–1354*, p. 113
Henry, duke of Lancaster		
on	28 February 1359	*BPR IV*, p. 280
John of Gaunt, duke of Lancaster		
from	6 March 1361	*BPR II*, p. 4
on	8 January 1375	*JGR 1372–1376*, no. 696
on	1379/80	Somerville p. 370
Private Constables		
William de Wambelle		
in	September 1296	*Two Compoti of the Lancashire and Cheshire Manors of Henry de Lacy, earl of Lincoln*, trans. Rev. P. A. Lyons, Chetham Society, 112 (1884)
Robert de Pylkyngton		
for life from	8 January 1375	*JGR 1372–1376*, no. 696
on	1379/80	Somerville p. 370

Constable

John Travers		
to	6 April 1322	*CFR 1319–1327*, p. 116
Gilbert de Sengelton		
from	6 April 1322	*CFR 1319–1327*, p. 116
John Travers		
from	24 March 1322	*CFR 1319–1327*, p. 118
Gilbert de Sengelton		
to	12 July 1322	*CPR 1321–1324*, p. 181
Alice de Lacy		
for life from	12 July 1322	*CPR 1321–1324*, p. 181
Gilbert de Sengelton		
on	25 September 1323	*CCR 1323–1327*, p. 140
William de Clinton		
from	18 September 1327	*CPR 1327–1330*, p. 170
on	12 March 1337	*CCR 1337–1339*, p. 21
not by	24 October 1348	*CPR 1348–1350*, p. 195
not by	5 October 1349	*CCR 1349–1354*, p. 113
to	28 October 1348	*CCR 1346–1349*, p. 571
Henry, duke of Lancaster		
from	28 October 1348	*CCR 1346–1349*, p. 571

MACCLESFIELD

Owners

John de Macclesfield, clerk, snr.		
licence to crenellate	30 August 1398	G. Ormerod, *History of the County Palatine and City of Chester*. 2nd edn London 1882, vol. 3, part 2, p. 747
licence to crenellate	1410	*ibid.*
died	1422	*ibid.*
John de Macclesfield, ynr. probable son of above		
from	1422	*ibid.*

MALPAS

Owners

John son of Richard de Sutton		
on	12 April 1327	*CPR 1327–1330*, p. 97
to	10 May 1328	*CPR 1327–1330*, p. 273
John de Charlton, give by previous, P.P.		
for life from	10 May 1328	*CPR 1327–1330*, p. 273
to	28 February 1354	*BPR III*, p. 149 (R.I.P.)
John de Sutton, son of two above, and Isabel, daughter of John de Cherleton above, his wife		
from	5 May 1354	*BPR III*, p. 156
to	23 January 1360	*BPR III*, p. 379
Isabel, above, widow of John de Sutton		
from	23 January 1360	*BPR III*, p. 379

NEWHALL

Owners

Henry de Audley of Heighley		
to	22 April 1276	*IPM II*, no. 196 (R.I.P.)

William de Audley of Heighley, brother of above		
from	22 April 1276	*IPM II*, no. 196 (R.I.P.)

NORTHWICH

Owners

John de Baunville		
on	14 January 1278	*IMisc I*, no. 1128
Hugh de Venables		
to	February 1382	*IPM XV*, no. 160 (R.I.P.)
Richard de Venables, son of above		
from	February 1382	*IPM XV*, no. 160
on	1385	

Subtenent

William de Brerton, kn.		
on	February 1382	*IPM XV*, no. 160

PULFORD

History

mentioned	late C12	King, p. 68
in use	temp. Glendower	King, p. 68

SHOCKLACK

Owners

Beatrice, widow of Roderick son of Griffin		
to	10 June 1290	*IPM II*, no. 749 (R.I.P.)
Isabel, wife of Richard de Sutton		
from	10 June 1290	*IPM II*, no. 749

SHOTWICK

Owners

Edward, the Black Prince		
in	1353–1360	H.J.Hewitt, *Medieval Cheshire*, Chetham Society New Series, 88 (1929), p. 96

Cornwall

Unknown Licenses		
ENTHIDY for William Basset		
	23 July 1330	*CPR 1327–1330*, p. 541
SHEVYOK for John Dauney, kn		
	19 March 1336	*CPR 1334–1338*, p. 230
TREGEWELL for Ralph de Bloiou		
	1 February 1335	*CPR 1334–1338*, p. 77

HELSTON

History		
built	temp. Edward I	King, p. 77
destroyed	by 1478	King, p. 77

LANIHORNE

Owners		
John Larchdeacon		
licence to crenellate	31 January 1335	*CPR 1334–1338*, p. 79

LAUNCESTON

Owners		
Edmund, earl of Cornwall		
to	1298	*IPM III*, no. 604 (R.I.P.)
The King, his heir		
from	1298	*IPM III*, no. 605
Piers Gaveston		
on	1307/8	*IPM V*, no. 101
John of Eltham, earl of Cornwall		
from	10 October 1331	*CChR 1327–1341*, p. 233
Crown – Black Prince		
on	12 December 1346	*BPR I*, p. 37
on	11 June 1351	*BPR II*, p. 9
Crown – Prince Henry		
from	15 October 1399	*CCR 1399–1402*, p. 22
on	17 January 1407	*IPM VII*, no. 185
Constables		
Peter Burdet, king's yeoman		
for life from	18 February 1301	*CPR 1292–1301*, p. 573
on	16 April 1309	*CPR 1307–1313*, p. 107
William de Botereaux		
from	27 July 1312	*CFR 1307–1319*, p. 141
on	20 March 1312	*CCR 1307–1313*, p. 453
Henry de Wylington		
from	15 April 1316	*CFR 1307–1319*, p. 278

Peter Burdet		
on	26 July 1313	*CCR 1313–1318*, p. 4
on	8 April 1331	*CCR 1330–1333*, p. 224
William de Beauchamp		
to	18 January 1331	*CFR 1327–1337*, p. 222
Robert de Bilkemore		
from	18 January 1331	*CFR 1327–1337*, p. 222
to	10 February 1331	*CFR 1327–1337*, p. 232
William de Botreaux		
from	10 February 1331	*CFR 1327–1337*, p. 232
to	23 June 1333	*CFR 1327–1337*, p. 364
Henry Trethewy		
from	23 June 1333	*CFR 1327–1337*, p. 364
to	28 October 1334	*CFR 1327–1337*, p. 422
John le Petit		
from	28 October 1334	*CFR 1327–1337*, p. 422
to	8 November 1336	*CFR 1327–1337*, p. 500
Oliver de Carmynou		
from	8 November 1336	*CFR 1327–1337*, p. 500
John le Petit		
to	1 February 1337	*CFR 1337–1347*, p. 2
John Hamely		
from	1 February 1337	*CFR 1337–1347*, p. 2
William Corby, king's esquire		
from	1 February 1377	*CCR 1396–1399*, p. 444
on	9 February 1401	*CPR 1399–1401*, p. 407

Constables for the Black Prince

John de Moveroun		
on	12 December 1346	*BPR I*, p. 37
on	1 August 1347	*BPR I*, p. 106
on	8 August 1347	*BPR I*, p. 110
on	27 August 1347	*BPR I*, p. 114
on	9 September 1347	*BPR I*, p. 121
John de Skirbek		
on	11 June 1351	*BPR II*, p. 9
on	1 October 1354	*BPR II*, p. 71
on	13 February 1358	*BPR II*, p. 134
on	1 October 1359	*BPR II*, p. 164
on	21 November 1359	*BPR II*, p. 166

Wardships

John of Gaunt, duke of Lancaster		
from	25 March 1361	*CFR 1356–1368*, p. 157

Clerk

Bartholomew, son of Gilbert de Aqua		
on	Late December 1286	*Ancient Deeds I*, B.172

MOUNT ST. MICHAEL

Constables

Ralph de Bloyou		
to	16 July 1339	*CFR 1337–1347*, p. 141

Edward, the Black Prince		
from	16 July 1339	*CFR 1337–1347*, p. 141

RESTORMEL

Owners

Edmund, earl of Cornwall		
to	1298	*IPM III*, no. 604 (R.I.P.)
The King, his heir		
from	1298	*IPM III*, no. 605
John of Eltham, earl of Cornwall		
from	10 October 1331	*CChR 1327–1341*, p. 233
on	25 February 1335	
dead by	12 February 1337	*CPR 1334–1338*, p. 383
Edward the Black Prince		
on	11 June 1351	*BPR II*, p. 9
on	24 January 1373	
Richard II as Prince		
on	25 February 1377	
John, de Holland, earl of Huntingdon or his adherents		
forfeited by	February 1400	*IMisc VII*, no. 90
Crown – Prince Henry		
from	15 October 1399	*CCR 1399–1402*, p. 22

Private Constables

William Waldessef for Edmund of Cornwall		
in	*1296–1297*	L.M. Midgley, *Ministers Accounts of the earldom of Cornwall 1296–1297, vol. II*, Camden Society, 3rd Series, 68 (1945), p. 250
John de Kendale		
temp	John of Eltham	*BPR II*, p. 186
for life from	12 February 1337	*CPR 1334–1338*, p. 383
on	7 December 1361	*BPR II*, p. 186

Constables

Thomas de la Hyde		
on	20 March 1312	*CCR 1307–1312*, p. 455
Reynold de Barber		
from	8 October 1312	*CFR 1307–1319*, p. 148
Henry de Wylington		
from	15 April 1316	*CFR 1307–1319*, p. 278
John de Carminou		
from	26 April 1331	*CPR 1330–1334*, p. 106
on	27 April 1331	*CCR 1330–1333*, p. 228
Rotelin de Ostry (Dostry, Dostriche)		
from	24 January 1373	
confirmed	25 February 1377	
confirmed	22 March 1378	*CPR 1377–1381*, p. 228
to	8 December 1398	*CPR 1396–1399*, p. 458
Robert Thorley, king's esquire		
for life from	8 December 1398	*CPR 1396–1399*, p. 458

STRATTON

Owners

Ranulph de Whitchurch (Blankmonster)		
license to crenellate	30 January 1335	*CPR 1334–1338*, p. 75 (Biename)

TINTAGEL

Owners

Edmund, earl of Cornwall		
to	1298	*IPM III*, no. 604 (R.I.P.)
The King, his heir		
from	1298	*IPM III*, no. 605
John of Eltham, earl of Cornwall		
from	10 October 1331	*CChR 1327–1341*, p. 233
Crown – Black Prince		
on	11 June 1351	*BPR II*, p. 9
John Holland, earl of Huntingdon or his adherents		
forfeited by	February 1400	*IMisc VII*, no. 90
Crown – Prince Henry		
from	15 October 1399	*CCR 1399–1402*, p. 22

Constables

Thomas de Ercedekne		
on	20 March 1312	*CCR 1307–1313*, p. 455
from	26 July 1312	*CFR 1307–1319*, p. 141
Peter de Trevalvarth		
from	3 August 1314	*CPR 1313–1317*, p. 163
to	15 April 1316	*CFR 1307–1319*, p. 278
Henry de Wylingham		
from	15 April 1316	*CFR 1307–1319*, p. 278
William de Botereux		
from	17 December 1325	*CPR 1324–1327*, p. 202
Walter Stapleton, bishop of Exeter		
for life from	23 July 1326	*CFR 1319–1327*, p. 401
for life from	23 July 1326	*CCR 1323–1327*, p. 591
Robert de Bilkemore		
to	13 April 1331	*CFR 1327–1337*, p. 247
Richard Hampton		
for life from	15 February 1377	
confirmed	22 March 1378	*CPR 1377–1381*, p. 169
to	5 January 1386	*CPR 1377–1381*, p. 618
Richard Hampton and John Slegh, king's esquire		
for life from	5 January 1386	*CPR 1385–1389*, p. 97
to	6 January 1389	*CPR 1385–1389*, p. 537 (R.I.P.)
John de Holland, earl of Huntingdon, duke of Exeter		
for life from	6 January 1389	*CPR 1385–1389*, p. 537
on	5 November 1397	*CCR 1396–1399*, p. 161
John Lewes, clerk		
on	1 December 1397	*CPR 1396–1399*, p. 267

Constable for the Black Prince

John Dabernoun		
on	11 June 1351	*BPR II*, p. 9

John de Skirbek		
from	22 July 1351	*BPR II*, p. 14
on	14 July 1364	*BPR II*, p. 207

TREGONY

History

built	temp. Richard I	King, p. 76
standing	1478	King, p. 76

TREMATON

Owners

Edmund, earl of Cornwall		
to	1298	*IPM III*, no. 605 (R.I.P.)
The King, his heir		
from	1298	*IPM III*, no. 605
John of Eltham, earl of Cornwall		
on	25 February 1335	*CPR 1334–1338*, p. 392
dead by	12 February 1337	*CPR 1334–1338*, p. 383
Crown		
on	12 February 1337	*CPR 1334–1338*, p. 383
on	10 March 1337	*CPR 1334–1338*, p. 392
Edward, the Black Prince		
on	11 June 1351	*BPR II*, no. 9
Crown – Prince Henry		
from	15 October 1399	*CCR 1399–1402*, p. 22
John de Holland, earl of Huntingdon and Elizabeth his wife		
from	temp. Rich II	*CCR 1413–1419*, p. 467
to death	1400	*CCR 1413–1419*, p. 467
forfeited by	February 1400	*IMisc VII*, no. 90
Robert de Holland, earl of Huntingdon, son of above		
from death of above	1400	*CCR 1413–1419*, p. 467
to	7 January 1403	*CCR 1413–1419*, p. 467 (R.I.P.)
John de Cornwall and Elizabeth, countess of Huntingdon, his wife, two above		
from	7 January 1403	*CCR 1413–1419*, p. 467
on	6 May 1408	*IPM vol. XIX*, no. 354
John de Holland, earl of Huntingdon, duke of Exeter, second son of John de Holland above		
under age	7 March 1418	*CFR 1413–1422*, p. 235
prob on	14 June 1418	*CCR 1413–1419*, p. 467

Constables

Odo le Ercedekne		
on	20 March 1312	*CCR 1307–1313*, p. 455
from	27 July 1312	*CFR 1307–1319*, p. 141
Thomas de Genely		
from	11 June 1315	*CFR 1307–1319*, p. 251
to	15 April 1316	*CFR 1307–1319*, p. 278
Henry de Wylington		
from	15 April 1316	*CFR 1307–1319*, p. 278
Odo le Ercedekne		
on	1 November 1318	*CPR 1317–1321*, p. 291
Robert de Bilkemore		
to	13 April 1331	*CFR 1327–1337*, p. 247

John de Carminou		
from	26 April 1331	*CPR 1330–1334*, p. 106
on	10 March 1337	*CPR 1334–1338*, p. 392
John Dabernoun		
on	11 June 1351	*BPR II*, p. 9
Neel le Lohereyn		
for life from	29 January 1372	*CPR 1377–1381*, p. 209
confirmed	22 March 1378	*CPR 1377–1381*, p. 209
John Bevyll		
from	7 April 1380	*CPR 1377–1381*, p. 462
on	8 April 1380	*CPR 1377–1381*, p. 455
Henry Kirkestede		
for life from	6 September 1380	*CPR 1377–1381*, p. 545
on	15 June 1402	*CCR 1399–1402*, p. 535

Private Constables

Henry de Erth		
from	25 February 1335	(For John of Cornwall)
on	12 February 1337	*CPR 1334–1338*, p. 383

Wardships

minority of John de Holand, earl of Huntingdon, duke of Exeter, 1400–1416

Robert Kendal and Robert Clynton		
from	7 March 1418	*CFR 1413–1422*, p. 235

TRURO

History

ruined by	1478	King, p. 77

Cumberland

BEWCASTLE

Owners

John de Strivelyn, kn., P.P.		
to	15 August 1378	*IPM Vol. XV*, no. 143 (R.I.P.)
dead by	4 November 1378	*CFR 1377–1383*, p. 116
Jacoba, his widow		
on	4 November 1378	*CFR 1377–1383*, p. 116

BRANTHWAITE HALL

History

built	late C14	King, p. 83

CARLISLE

Owners

Crown		
on	6 April 1308	*CCR 1307–1313*, p. 29
Anthony de Lucy and heirs		
from	4 June 1323	*CChR 1300–1326*, p. 452

Superior Custodian

John Halton, bishop of Carlisle		
from	6 April 1314	*CPR 1313–1317*, p. 103
Andrew de Harclay		
from	8 April 1319	*CPR 1317–1321*, p. 325

Constables

Roger de Leybrun		
not by	20 April 1268	*CLibR 1267–1272*, no. 257
Eustace de Balliolo		
not by	30 May 1269	*CLibR 1267–1272*, no. 738
Ranulph de Dacre		
not by	8 May 1272	*CLibR 1267–1272*, no. 1919
Richard de Crepping		
to	17 Oct 1274	*CFR 1272–1307*, p. 31
Robert de Hampton		
from	17 Oct 1274	*CFR 1272–1307*, p. 31
Thomas de Normanvill		
to	27 Oct 1277	*CFR 1272–1307*, p. 84
John de Swynburn		
from	27 Oct 1277	*CFR 1272–1307*, p. 84
to	25 Oct 1278	*CFR 1272–1307*, p. 103
Gilbert de Corewen		
from	25 Oct 1278	*CFR 1272–1307*, p. 103
to	14 April 1282	*CFR 1272–1307*, p. 160

William de Boyvill		
on	10 April 1282	*CCR 1279–1288*, p. 151
from	14 April 1282	*CFR 1272–1307*, p. 160
to	2 May 1283	*CFR 1272–1307*, p. 183
Robert de Bruce		
from	2 May 1283	*CFR 1272–1307*, p. 183
to	28 July 1285	*CPR 1281–1292*, p. 186
Michael de Harclay		
from	28 July 1285	*CPR 1281–1292*, p. 186
to	6 October 1295	*CPR 1292–1301*, p. 151
Robert de Bruce, lord of Annandale		
from	6 October 1295	*CFR 1272–1307*, p. 361
to	30 September 1296	*CPR 1292–1301*, p. 204
Michael de Harclay		
from	30 September 1296	*CPR 1292–1301*, p. 204
Robert de Bruce		
to	13 October 1297	*CFR 1272–1307*, p. 392
John de Halton, bishop of Carlisle		
from	13 October 1297	*CFR 1272–1307*, p. 392
to	1303	*HKW II*, p. 597
William de Mulcastre		
to	26 March 1307	*CFR 1272–1307*, p. 552
Alexander de Bastenthwayt		
from	26 March 1307	*CFR 1272–1307*, p. 552
to	10 April 1310	*CFR 1307–1319*, p. 60
John de Castre		
from	10 April 1310	*CFR 1307–1319*, p. 60
to	15 October 1311	*CFR 1307–1319*, p. 118
Andrew de Harclay		
from	15 October 1311	*CFR 1307–1319*, p. 118
to	15 December 1311	*CFR 1307–1319*, p. 120
John de Castre		
from	15 December 1311	*CFR 1307–1319*, p. 120
to	25 January 1312	*CFR 1307–1319*, p. 123
Andrew de Harclay		
from	25 January 1312	*CFR 1307–1319*, p. 123
John de Castre		
to	11 March 1312	*CFR 1307–1319*, p. 128
John de Weston		
from	11 March 1312	*CFR 1307–1319*, p. 128
to	13 March 1312	*CFR 1307–1319*, p. 129
Piers Gaveston		
from	13 March 1312	*CFR 1307–1319*, p. 129
John de Weston		
on	15 March 1312	*CCR 1307–1313*, p. 411
to	12 March 1313	*CFR 1307–1319*, p. 164
Andrew de Harclay		
from	12 March 1313	*CFR 1307–1319*, p. 164
on	20 November 1314	*CCR 1313–1318*, p. 126
Robert de Leybourne		
on	12 February 1316	*CPR 1313–1317*, p. 389

John de Castre		
on	22 January 1316	*CCR 1313–1318*, p. 261
on	30 July 1316	*CCR 1313–1318*, p. 356
John de Castre and William de Dacre		
from	1 November 1317	*CFR 1307–1319*, p. 344
to	8 June 1318	*CFR 1307–1319*, p. 363
then to	20 July 1318	*CFR 1307–1319*, p. 369
Andrew de Harclay (Perhaps never taken up?)		
from	8 June 1318	*CFR 1307–1319*, p. 363
revoked	10 July 1318	*CCR 1318–1323*, p. 1
Anthony de Lucy, P.P.		
from	20 July 1318	*CFR 1307–1319*, p. 369
to	8 April 1319	*CFR 1307–1319*, p. 395
Richard de Lymesy		
from	8 April 1319	*CFR 1307–1319*, p. 395
Andrew de Harclay		
on	24 January 1320	*CPR 1317–1321*, p. 416
to	11 February 1323	*CFR 1319–1327*, p. 196
Anthony de Lucy, P.P.		
from	11 February 1323	*CFR 1319–1327*, p. 196
on	20 December 1328	*CCR 1327–1330*, p. 351
Peter Tilliol		
to	10 December 1330	*CFR 1327–1337*, p. 203
Randolf de Dacre, P.P.		
from	10 December 1330	*CFR 1327–1337*, p. 203
to	30 November 1335	*CFR 1327–1337*, p. 469
John de Glanton		
for life from	30 November 1335	*CFR 1327–1337*, p. 469
on	12 March 1338	*CCR 1337–1339*, p. 319
dead by	20 May 1338	*CCR 1337–1339*, p. 369
Roland de Vaux		
to	12 May 1338	*CFR 1337–1347*, p. 78
Anthony de Lucy, P.P.		
from	12 May 1338	*CFR 1337–1347*, p. 78
to	20 June 1339	*CFR 1337–1347*, p. 140
John, bishop of Carlisle		
from	20 June 1339	*CFR 1337–1347*, p. 140
Anthony de Lucy, P.P.		
on	19 November 1341	*CCR 1339–1341*, p. 316
to	25 June 1343	*CFR 1337–1347*, p. 334
John, bishop of Carlisle		
from	25 June 1343	*CFR 1337–1347*, p. 334
temp	1345	C.49/46/16
Hugh de Moriceby		
from	8 September 1345	*CFR 1337–1347*, p. 438
to	18 October 1345	*CFR 1337–1347*, p. 441
Thomas de Lucy, P.P.		
from	18 October 1345	*CFR 1337–1347*, p. 441
to	16 April 1350	*CFR 1347–1356*, p. 229
Richard de Denton		
from	16 April 1350	*CFR 1347–1356*, p. 229
to	3 November 1351	*CFR 1347–1356*, p. 307

Hugh de Louthre		
from	3 November 1351	*CFR 1347–1356*, p. 307
to	4 March 1354	*CFR 1347–1356*, p. 408
William de Lye		
from	4 March 1354	*CFR 1347–1356*, p. 408
to	15 March 1354	*CFR 1347–1356*, p. 408
Hugh de Louthre		
from	15 March 1354	*CFR 1347–1356*, p. 408
William de Threlkeld		
from	16 January 1355	*CFR 1347–1356*, p. 419
to 23 Jan	7 January 1357	*CFR 1356–1368*, p. 25
Thomas de Lucy		
keeper on	20 May 1356	*CCR 1354–1360*, p. 259
on	7 December 1357	*CPR 1354–1358*, p. 380
William de Lancastre		
from	3 November 1358	*CFR 1356–1368*, p. 80
Matthew de Redman		
from	1 Oct 1359	*CFR 1356–1368*, p. 102
to	24 March 1360	*CFR 1356–1368*, p. 121 (R.I.P.)
Christopher de Moriceby		
from	24 March 1360	*CFR 1356–1368*, p. 121
Robert Tilliol		
from	10 December 1361	*CFR 1356–1368*, p. 154
Christopher de Moriceby		
from	20 November 1362	*CFR 1356–1368*, p. 236
and from	17 November 1365	*CFR 1356–1368*, p. 315
Robert Tillioll		
from	16 November 1366	*CFR 1356–1368*, p. 328
to	20 May 1367	*CFR 1356–1368*, p. 347 (R.I.P.)
William de Windsor, P.P.		
from	20 May 1367	*CFR 1356–1368*, p. 347
to	27 November 1368	*CFR 1356–1368*, p. 391
Adam Parvyng		
from	27 November 1368	*CFR 1356–1368*, p. 391
and from	28 March 1370	*CFR 1369–1377*, p. 98
John de Denton		
from	5 November 1371	*CFR 1369–1377*, p. 146
Robert de Mowbray, kn.		
from	12 December 1372	*CFR 1369–1377*, p. 190
John de Derwentwater		
from	7 November 1373	*CFR 1369–1377*, p. 222
John de Denton		
from	12 December 1374	*CFR 1369–1377*, p. 272
to	4 Oct 1375	*CFR 1369–1377*, p. 297
John de Derwentwater		
from	4 Oct 1375	*CFR 1369–1377*, p. 297
John Bruyn		
from	26 Oct 1376	*CFR 1369–1377*, p. 369
to	9 March 1377	*CFR 1369–1377*, p. 386
Roger de Clifford, P.P.		
from	9 March 1377	*CFR 1369–1377*, p. 386
from	24 June 1377	*CFR 1377–1383*, p. 6

John de Derwentwater		
from	26 November 1377	*CFR 1377–1383*, p. 34
William Stapelton		
from	25 November 1378	*CFR 1377–1383*, p. 113
Gilbert de Culwen		
from	5 November 1379	*CFR 1377–1383*, p. 170
John de Derwentwater		
from	18 Oct 1380	*CFR 1377–1383*, p. 220
Richard le Scrope		
keeper	18 February 1381	*CPR 1377–1381*, p. 604
temp	1381	E.101/39/16
Amand Mounceux		
from	1 November 1381	*CFR 1377–1383*, p. 269
Roger de Clifford		
from	29 May 1382	*CPR 1381–1385*, p. 122
Robert Parvyng		
from	24 November 1382	*CFR 1377–1383*, p. 327
Roger de Clifford, P.P.		
from	29 May 1382	*CCR 1381–1385*, p. 275
on	26 May 1383	*CCR 1381–1385*, p. 275
to	29 May 1383	
John Neville of Raby		
on	26 January 1385	*CPR 1381–1385*, p. 518
on	28 July 1385	*CPR 1385–1389*, p. 10
Ralph son of Lord Neville and Thomas son of Lord Clifford		
from	26 October 1385	*CPR 1385–1389*, p. 42
Ralph de Neville and John de Ros		
on	8 November 1389	*CCR 1389–1392*, p. 36
John de Beaumont, P.P.		
on	1 March 1390	*CCR 1389–1392*, p. 124
Henry Percy 'le fitz'		
warden	16 October 1390	*CPR 1388–1392*, p. 305
temp	1390–1396	E.101/41/19
John Holland, earl of Huntingdon, the king's brother		
on	28 February 1397	*CPR 1396–1399*, p. 86
Henry Percy, earl of Northumberland		
on	24 December 1400	*CPR 1399–1401*, p. 406 (Warden)
on	15 April 1402	*CPR 1401–1405*, p. 61
Ralph Neville, earl of Westmorland		
on	7 July 1404	*CPR 1401–1405*, p. 408
on	17 February 1408	*CPR 1405–1408*, p. 410 (Warden)

Gatekeepers

John de Ispania, elder		
on	5 June 1319	*CCR 1318–1323*, p. 86
Peter de Routhe		
for life from	13 March 1343	*CPR 1343–1345*, p. 19
Robert de Strangeways		
for life from	14 February 1408	*CPR 1405–1408*, p. 386
confirmed	13 June 1413	*CPR 1413–1416*, p. 50

Porters

John de Dene		
to	2 May 1392	*CPR 1391–1396*, p. 73 (R.I.P.)
Robert Bele		
for life from	2 May 1392	*CPR 1391–1396*, p. 73
William Ferrour		
for life from	12 April 1402	*CPR 1401–1405*, p. 61
Robert Blacburne of Bywell		
for life from	13 August 1403	*CPR 1401–1405*, p. 253
Robert de Strangways		
for life from	17 October 1405	*CPR 1405–1408*, p. 85
vacated	9 Henry IV	

Janitors

Robert Strangways		
on	4 October 1405	*CCR 1405–1409*, p. 1 (For life)

COCKERMOUTH

Owners

Isabella de Forz, countess of Aumale		
temp	late 13th century	Powicke, p. 364
died	*1293*	
Piers Gaveston		
from	7 June 1308	*CChR 1300–1326*, p. 111
to	5 August 1309	*CChR 1300–1326*, p. 131
to	5 August 1309	*CCR 1307–1313*, p. 225
Anthony de Lucy, P.P.		
from	4 June 1323	*CChR 1300–1326*, p. 452
on	20 April 1327	*CMR*, no. 31
to death	*10 June 1343*	*GEC VIII, p. 250*
Thomas de Lucy, son of above, P.P.		
inherited	*1343*	*GEC VIII, p. 250*
to	4 December 1365	*IPM XII*, no. 17 (R.I.P.)
Anthony de Lucy, son of above		
from	4 December 1365	*IPM XII*, no. 17
to	20 May 1368	*IPM XII*, no. 233 (R.I.P.)
Joan, daughter and heir to Anthony de Lucy		
from	20 May 1368	*IPM XII*, no. 233
to	30 September 1369	*IPM XII*, no. 374 (R.I.P.)
Gilbert de Umfraville, earl of Angus, P.P., from Maud his wife, sister and heir of Anthony de Lucy		
from	30 September 1369	*IPM XII*, no. 374
to	6 January 1381	*IPM XV*, no. 433 (R.I.P.)
Maud, widow of above		
from	6 January 1381	*IPM XV*, no. 433
on	8 February 1381	*CCR 1377–1381*, p. 434 (Her own right)
Maud, wife of Henry earl of Northumberland and heir to Lucy		
claimed	2 September 1393	*IMisc I*, no. 50
on	28 June 1397	*CPR 1396–1399*, p. 164
dead by	1 April 1398	*CCR 1396–1399*, p. 255
to	18 December 1398	*IPM XVII*, no. 1247 (R.I.P.)

Henry Percy		
from	18 December 1398	*IPM XVII*, no. 1247
livery	1 April 1399	*CCR 1396–1399*, p. 482
on	15 April 1402	*CPR 1401–1405*, p. 61
not by	27 June 1405	*CPR 1405–1408*, p. 40
Ralph Neville, earl of Westmorland		
on	27 June 1405	*CPR 1405–1408*, p. 40

Private Constables

John Sampson		
from	November 1266	Denholm–Young, p. 39
to	August 1267	Denholm–Young, p. 39
Thomas de Weston		
in	1280–1283	Denholm–Young, p. 36

Constables

John de St. John		
for life from	26 September 1300	*CPR 1292–1301*, p. 537
dead by	20 October 1303	*CPR 1301–1307*, p. 160
John de Kirkeby		
on	20 October 1303	*CPR 1301–1307*, p. 160
Gilbert de Culevenn		
on	26 November 1309	*CCR 1307–1313*, p. 189 (Keeper)
Robert de Leybourne		
on	20 July 1311	*CPR 1307–1313*, p. 377
to	7 April 1314	*CPR 1313–1317*, p. 102
Edmund de Mauley		
for life from	7 April 1314	*CPR 1313–1317*, p. 102
on	28 February 1315	*CCR 1313–1318*, p. 157
Robert de Clitheroe		
on	3 August 1316	*CCR 1313–1318*, p. 350
Robert de Leybourne		
on	10 November 1316	*CCR 1313–1318*, p. 374
to	10 December 1318	*CFR 1307–1319*, p. 386
Anthony de Lucy, P.P.		
from	10 December 1318	*CFR 1307–1319*, p. 386
to	8 April 1318	*CFR 1307–1319*, p. 395
Andrew de Harclay		
from	8 April 1318	*CFR 1307–1319*, p. 395
on	26 May 1321	*CPR 1317–1321*, p. 608
Ralph Neville, earl of Westmorland		
from	15 June 1405	*CPR 1405–1408*, p. 69 (Keeper)

DACRE

History

mentioned	1354	King, p. 84

DRUMBURGH

Owners

Robert le Brun		
licence to crenellate	24 August 1307	*CPR 1307–1313*, p. 11

DUNMALLOGHT

Owners

William de Dacre		
licence to crenellate	24 August 1307	*CPR 1307–1313*, p. 11; *CSD III*, p. 6

EGREMONT

Owners

Thomas de Multon, P.P.		
on	15 May 1318	*CPR 1317–1321*, p. 143
to	8 February 1322	*IPM VI*, no. 331 (R.I.P.)
John de Multon, P.P., son of above		
from	8 February 1322	*IPM VI*, no. 331
to	23 November 1334	*IPM VII*, no. 628 (R.I.P.)
Joan, widow of Robert fitz Walter, daughter of above		
from	23 November 1334	*IPM VII*, no. 628
to	20 June 1363	*IPM XI*, no. 499 (R.I.P.)
Walter fitz Walter, her grandson		
from	20 June 1363	*IPM XI*, no. 499
to	4 November 1375	*CCR 1374–1377*, p. 274
Edmund Lorence, Thomas Thelewall, clerk, and John Bretby, clerk.		
from	4 November 1375	*CCR 1374–1377*, p. 274
Walter fitz Walter, above		
to	26 September 1386	*IPM XVI*, no. 385 (R.I.P.)
Walter fitz Walter, kn., son of above		
from	26 September 1386	*IPM.XVI*, no. 385
from	15 August 1386	*CPR 1385–1389*, p. 204
died	*1406*	
Humphrey fitz Walter, son of above		
inherited	*1406*	

Wardships

John de Multon, 1322–1329

Robert Leybourne		
to	10 June 1323	*CFR 1319–1327*, p. 212
Anthony de Lucy		
from	10 June 1323	*CFR 1319–1327*, p. 212

GREYSTOKE

Owners

William lord Greystoke, P.P.		
licence to crenellate	5 October 1353	*CPR 1350–1354*, p. 495
died	*1359*	*GEC VI, p. 192*
Ralph lord Greystoke, son of above, P.P.		
from	*1359*	*GEC VI, p. 195*
died	*1418*	*GEC VI, p. 195*

John de Greystoke, son of above, P.P.		
from	*1418*	*GEC VI, p. 196*
on	10 September 1431	*Bishop Langley's Register, vol. 4*, Surtees Society 170, no. 1229
on	16 October 1436	*Wills and Inventories, part 1*, Surtees Society 2 (1835), p. 85
died	*1436*	*GEC VI, p. 196*

HARDRIG HALL

History

built	late C14 or early C15	King, p. 86

HAY (HAYESCASTLE, AYKHURST)

Owners

Robert de Leybourne		
licence to crenellate	13 March 1322	*CPR 1321–1324*, p. 82

HIGH HEAD

Owners

John de Harclay		
to	16 November 1322	*IMisc II*, no. 1072 (R.I.P.)
Ermeiarde, wife of above (from Andrew de Harcla)		
1/3 on	22 November 1322	*IPM VI*, no. 378
William Lenglis, king's yoeman		
licence to crenellate	6 October 1342	*CPR 1340–1343*, p. 536
William, son of Ralph Restwold		
to	October 1374	*IPM XIV*, no. 49 (R.I.P.)
Richard, his son		
from	October 1374	*IPM XIV*, no. 49 (Age 10+)

Constables

Thomas de Featherstonehalgh		
on	18 March 1324	*CCR 1324–1327*, p. 82
to	29 November 1326	*CFR 1319–1327*, p. 426
Randolf de Dacre, P.P.		
from	29 November 1326	*CFR 1319–1327*, p. 426
for 10 years from	3 February 1327	*CFR 1327–1337*, p. 16
taken back by	27 Oct 1328	*CFR 1327–1337*, p. 111
John de Cromwell, P.P.		
from	6 August 1328	*CCR 1327–1330*, p. 307
to	16 November 1328	*CCR 1327–1330*, p. 342
William Lenglis, king's yeoman		
from	16 November 1328	*CCR 1327–1330*, p. 342
Thomas del Clogh		
for life on	28 February 1351	*CPR 1350–1354*, p. 43

HUTTON–IN–FOREST

Owners

Thomas de Hoton		
to	1362	Pevsner, p. 140 (R.I.P.)

IRTON HALL

History		
built	C14	King, p. 87

KIRKOSWALD

History		
licensed	1201	King, p. 87
modified	C14	King, p. 87
modified	pre 1485?	King, p. 87

LANERCOST NO 2

History		
built	C13	King, p. 88

LIDDEL

Owners		
Baldwin Wake		
extent	18 March 1282	*IPM II*, no. 439
John Wake, P.P.		
to	10 April 1300	*IPM III*, no. 597 (R.I.P.)
Thomas Wake of Liddel, son of above, P.P.		
from	10 April 1300	*IPM III*, no. 597
to	31 May 1349	*IPM IX*, no. 219 (R.I.P.)
Blanch, widow of Thomas Wake		
from	31 May 1349	*IPM IX*, no. 210 (Jointure)
on	1 July 1349	*CCR 1349–1354*, p. 42
on	20 May 1357	
Reversion to John of Gaunt, duke of Lancaster		
	20 May 1357	
Blanche, widow of Thomas Wake		
on	10 June 1357	*CPR 1354–1358*, p. 562
Constables		
Walter de Selby		
before	October 1346	*Historical Papers and Letters from the Northern Registers*, Rolls Series 61 (1873), item CCXLIII

MELMERBY

Owner		
John de Denum		
temp	Edward II	*VCH vol. II*, p. 255

MILLUM

Owners		
John de Hodleston		
licence to crenellate	24 August 1335	*CPR 1334–1338*, p. 167

MUNCASTER

Owners

Pennington family		
temp	'ancient residence of'	S.Lewis, *A Topographical Dictionary of England,* London, 1862, p. 319

NAWORTH

Owners

Randolf de Dacre, P.P.		
licence to crenellate	27 July 1335	*CPR 1334–1338*, p. 168
died	*20 April 1339*	*GEC IV, p. 1*
Margaret de Dacre, widow of Randolph de Dacre		
to	10 December 1362	*IPM XI*, no. 317 (R.I.P.)
Randolf de Dacre, fourth son of above, P.P.		
from	8 March 1362	*CCR 1360–1364*, p. 323
dead by	12 November 1375	*CFR 1369–1377*, p. 305
Hugh de Dacre, brother of above, P.P.		
to	24 December 1383	*IPM XV*, no. 972 (R.I.P.)
William de Dacre, kn, son of above, P.P.		
from	24 December 1383	*IPM XV*, no. 972
to	20 July 1399	*IPM XVII*, no. 1324 (R.I.P.)
Thomas de Dacre, son of above, P.P.		
from	20 July 1399	*IPM XVII*, no. 1324
died	*5 January 1457/8*	*GEC IV, p. 7*

Constables

Roger Lord Clifford		
from	12 November 1375	*CFR 1369–1377*, p. 305

Wardships

Minority of Thomas Dacre, 1399–1408

Ralph Neville, earl of Westmorland		
from	19 October 1399	*CCR, 1399–1402*, p. 122

PENRITH

Owners

William de Strickland, future bishop of Carlisle, archbishop of Canterbury		
licence to crenellate	12 February 1397	*CPR 1396–1399*, p. 66
licence to crenellate	2 April 1399	*CPR 1396–1399*, p. 524

ROSE

Owners

John Halton, bishop of Carlisle		
licence to crenellate	9 April 1336	*CPR 1334–1338*, p. 245
Gilbert, bishop of Carlisle		
licence to crenellate	25 June 1355	*CPR 1354–1358*, p. 252
William, bishop of Carlisle		
on	20 November 1408	*CPR 1408–1413*, p. 28
on	4 June 1414	

Constables for the Church

John de Dokwra, esquire		
for life from	1 December 1404	*CPR 1408–1413*, p. 28
on	20 November 1408	*CPR 1408–1413*, p. 28
William Louthre, son of Sir Robert de Louthre		
for life from	4 June 1414	*CPR 1413–1416*, p. 202
confirmed	30 June 1414	*CPR 1413–1416*, p. 202

SCALEBY

Owners

Robert Tilliol		
licence to crenellate	24 August 1307	*CPR 1307–1313*, p. 8
Robert Tilliol, kn.		
to	7 April 1367	*IPM XII*, no. 170 (R.I.P.)
Peter Tilliol, son of above		
from	7 April 1367	*IPM XII*, no. 170

TRIERMAIN

Owners

Roland de Vaux		
licence to crenellate	4 February 1340	*CPR 1338–1340*, p. 471

WOLSTY

Owners

Holmcultram Abbey		
licence to crenellate	13 October 1348	*CPR 1348–1350*, p. 194

WORKINGTON

Owners

Gilbert de Culwen, kn.		
licence to crenellate	4 March 1380	*CPR 1377–1381*, p. 447

WYTHOPE

Owners

Hugh Lowther		
licence to crenellate	12 July 1318	*CPR 1317–1321*, p. 189

Denbigh

CHIRK

Owners

Roger Mortimer of Chirk, P.P.		
built	soon after 1282	King, p. 102
imprisoned	22 January 1322	*GEC IX, p. 251*
not by	25 March 1322	*CChR 1300–1326*, p. 441
Edmund, earl of Arundel		
from	25 March 1322	*CChR 1300–1326*, p. 441
executed	17 November 1326	McKisack, p. 86
Roger Mortimer, earl of March		
forfeited by	29 March 1332	*IMisc II*, no. 1314
Richard, earl of Arundel		
from	22 September 1334 (Fee simple)	
confirmed	28 August 1337	*CPR 1334–1338*, p. 519
Roger Mortimer		
not by	12 May 1354	*CPR 1354–1358*, p. 69
granted to below	March 1354	
Richard earl of Arundel		
from	March 1354	
by	12 May 1354	*CPR 1354–1358*, p. 69
on	28 September 1359	*CPR 1358–1361*, p. 274
Richard, earl of Arundel		
on	6 November 1386	
on	20 January 1388	*CPR 1385–1389*, p. 462
on	18 July 1396	*IMisc VI*, no. 233

Constables

Griffin ap Res		
to	22 January 1322	*CFR 1319–1327*, p. 90
Peter Giffard		
from	22 January 1322	*CFR 1319–1327*, p. 90
to	22 April 1323	*CFR 1319–1327*, p. 205 (R.I.P.)
William de Ercalewe		
to	4 February 1331	*CFR 1327–1337*, p. 230
Thomas de Cloune		
from	4 February 1331	*CFR 1327–1337*, p. 230
John Inge and Thomas de Wynnesbury, yng		
from	2 December 1331	*CFR 1327–1337*, p. 290
to	13 September 1333	*CFR 1327–1337*, p. 373
Richard earl of Arundel		
for life from	13 September 1333	*CFR 1327–1337*, p. 373
John Whethales		
not by	6 November 1397	*IMisc VI*, no. 233
Peter ap Dutton		
on	6 November 1397	*IMisc VI*, no. 233

John Over		
on	21 February 1420	*CPR 1416–1422*, p. 68
Deputies		
John ap William		
temp.	John Whethales	
on	6 November 1397	*IMisc VI*, no. 233

DENBIGH

Tenant in Chief		
Prince of Wales		
on	20 February 1335	*IPM VII*, no. 710
Owners		
David ap Griffin		
from	November 1277	Morris, p. 142
Crown		
to	7 October 1282	*CWR*, p. 240
Henry de Lacy, earl of Lincoln		
from	16 October 1281	Morris, p. 178
on	25 August 1294	*CFR 1272–1307*, p. 343
to	6 February 1311	*IPM V*, no. 279 (R.I.P.)
Thomas de Lancaster and Alice de Lacy his wife, daughter of above		
from	6 February 1311	*IPM V*, no. 279
from	1 June 1311	*CCR 1307–1313*, p. 314
Edmund, earl of Kent, king's brother		
from	30 March 1322	*CChR 1300–1326*, p. 442
Hugh le Despenser, snr		
from	9 July 1322	*CChR 1300–1326*, p. 448
on	8 August 1322	*CPR 1321–1324*, p. 203
before	13 September 1327	*CPR 1324–1327*, p. 328
Roger Mortimer		
from	13 September 1327	*CPR 1324–1327*, p. 328
from	13 September 1327	*CChR 1327–1341*, p. 55
William de Montague, earl of Salisbury		
from	18 January 1331	*CChR 1327–1341*, p. 210
to	30 January 1344	*IPM VIII*, no. 532 (R.I.P.)
William de Montague, son of above		
heir on	30 January 1344	*IPM VIII*, no. 532
from	30 April 1344	*CCR 1343–1346*, p. 306
to	Trinity Term 1354	
Roger Mortimer, earl of March		
recovered	Trinity Term 1354	
from just before	20 January 1355	*CPR 1354–1358*, p. 159
to	23 May 1360	*CPR 1358–1361*, p. 32
Edmund Mortimer, son of above		
from	23 May 1360	*CPR 1358–1361*, p. 32 (Minor)
Philippa, widow of Roger, in dower		
on	12 August 1373	*CPR 1370–1374*, p. 333
not by	16 December 1382	*CPR 1381–1385*, p. 65
Roger Mortimer, earl of March		
under age	16 December 1382	*CPR 1381–1385*, p. 65
to	20 July 1398	*IPM XVII*, no. 1197 (R.I.P.)

Edmund Mortimer, son of above		
from	20 July 1398	*IPM XVII*, no. 1197
under age	17 May 1400	*IMisc VII*, no. 1
Receivers of Issues while in royal hands		
Walter de Burncestre		
from	29 April 1322	*CFR 1319–1327*, p. 125
Constables		
Roger Mortimer of Chirk, P.P.		
from	24 April 1311	*CCR 1307–1313*, p. 309
to	1 June 1311	*CCR 1307–1313*, p. 314
Giles de Beauchamp		
on	26 March 1322	*IMisc II*, no. 507
Hugh le Despenser, earl of Winchester		
on	4 August 1322	*CPR 1321–1324*, p. 195
Richard Damory, P.P.		
to	15 December 1326	*CFR 1319–1327*, p. 428
Roger Mortimer of Wigmore		
from	15 December 1326	*CFR 1319–1327*, p. 428
on	23 June 1328	*CCR 1327–1330*, p. 300
Sir William de Erkalwe		
on	9 February 1331	*IMisc II*, no. 1135
Henry Percy		
on	6 November 1399	*CFR 1399–1405*, p. 38
on	14 December 1401	*CCR 1399–1402*, p. 437 (Jnr)
Deputies		
Sir Robert de Pievlesdon		
on	9 February 1331	*IMisc II*, no. 1135
Wardships		
Minority of Edmund Mortimer, earl of March, 1360–1373		
Edward, prince of Wales		
from	23 May 1360	*CPR 1358–1361*, p. 32
Thomas de Stathum, appointed by above		
from	5 June 1360	*BPR III*, p. 383
on	27 May 1362	*BPR III*, p. 446
Minority of Roger Mortimer, earl of March (1381–1395)		
Philip Holgoyt		
from	16 December 1382	*CPR 1381–1385*, p. 65 (Steward)
Henry de Kirkested		
for life from	3 February 1382	*CPR 1381–1385*, pp. 92, 100
on	22 March 1383	*CPR 1381–1385*, p. 261
Thomas de Beauchamp, earl of Warwick, Roger Mortimer, earl of March, John lord Neville and Henry Percy, earl of Northumberland		
from	16 December 1383	*CFR 1383–1391*, p. 22
Minority of Edmund Mortimer, earl of March (1398–1412)		
William le Scrope, earl of Wiltshire		
from	11 August 1398	*CPR 1396–1399*, p. 408
Henry Percy, earl of Northumberland		
from	2 March 1400	*CFR 1399–1405*, p. 50
Henry Percy, son of the earl of Northumberland		
from	17 May 1400	*IMisc VII*, no. 1

DINAS BRAN

Owners

Gruffydd ap Madog Gfychan		
lost by	1282	King, p. 106
John de Warenne, earl of Surrey		
from	7 October 1282	*CWR*, p. 240
from	7 October 1282	Morris, p. 178
to	5 August 1284	
William de Warenne, gift from above		
from	5 August 1284	
to	21 December 1286	*IPM I*, no. 633 (R.I.P.)
John de Warenne, earl of Surrey, son of above		
from	21 December 1286	*IPM I*, no. 633
to king and back	1 July 1316	*CPR 1313–1317*, p. 485
to	1 January 1319	*CPR 1317–1321*, p. 264
Thomas, earl of Lancaster		
from	1 January 1319	*CPR 1317–1321*, p. 264
John de Warenne, earl of Surrey, as two above		
on	12 December 1346	*CPR 1345–1348*, p. 221
dead by	6 July 1347	*CFR 1347–1356*, p. 39
Joan de Bars, countess of Surrey		
jointured	24 August 1347	*CCR 1346–1349*, p. 314
enfeofed away	1 December 1347	*CPR 1345–1348*, p. 434
Richard earl of Arundel		
granted reversion	12 December 1346	*CPR 1345–1348*, p. 221
enfeofed with	1 December 1347	*CPR 1345–1348*, p. 434
on	23 January 1366	*CPR 1364–1367*, p. 198 (Granted out..)
on	12 April 1366	*CPR 1364–1367*, p. 237 (..and back)

Constables

Roger le Strange of Ellesmere, P.P.		
on	18 July 1277	*CCR 1272–1279*, p. 398 (Keeper?)
on	27 July 1279	*CWR*, 178

GLYN

Owners

John de Warenne, earl of Surrey		
in	1282	King, p. 107 n.32a

HOLT (CASTLE LIONS)

Owners

John de Warenne, earl of Surrey		
built	1280s	J.R.Kenyon, *Medieval Fortifications*, London, 1990, p. 81
died	*1304*	
John de Warenne, earl of Surrey		
to king and back	1 July 1316	*CPR 1313–1317*, p. 485
to	1 January 1319	*CPR 1317–1321*, p. 264
Thomas, earl of Lancaster		
from	1 January 1319	*CPR 1317–1321*, p. 264
not by	13 May 1322	*CPR 1321–1324*, p. 119

John de Warenne, earl of Surrey, as two above		
requests its return	1318–1322	*CAPW*, p. 293
from	13 May 1322	*CPR 1321–1324*, p. 119
to	4 July 1347	*BPR I*, p. 93
dead by	6 July 1347	*CFR 1347–1356*, p. 39
Joan de Bars, countess of Surrey		
jointure	24 August 1347	*CCR 1346–1349*, p. 314
enfeofed away	1 December 1347	*CPR 1345–1348*, p. 434
Richard earl of Arundel		
granted reversion	12 December 1346	*CPR 1345–1348*, p. 221
enfeofed with	1 December 1347	*CPR 1345–1348*, p. 434
on	12 April 1366	*CPR 1364–1367*, p. 237
Roger Mortimer, earl of March		
to	27 December 1381	*IPM XV*, no. 558 (R.I.P.)
Richard, earl of Arundel		
forfeited by	3 November 1397	*IMisc VI*, no. 229

Constables

Bartholomew de Badelesmere, P.P.		
to	5 December 1314	*CCR 1313–1318*, p. 132
Roger de Peuelesdon		
on	6 March 1322	*CCR 1318–1323*, p. 426
Oliver de Ingham, P.P., kn.		
to	27 May 1322	*CPR 1321–1324*, p. 122
David de Eyton		
on	5 March 1389	*CPR 1388–1392*, p. 19
William Bagot, king's kn.		
for life from	22 October 1397	*CPR 1396–1399*, p. 210
to	29 May 1398	*CPR 1396–1399*, p. 347
William le Scrope, earl of Wiltshire		
for life from	29 May 1398	*CPR 1396–1399*, p. 347
Roger Corbet		
on	4 July 1422	*CPR 1416–1422*, p. 446

LLANSILIN

Owners

Owen Glendower		
to	1403	King, p. 104

RUTHIN

Owners

Wentheliana de Lascy		
not by	23 October 1282	*CChR 1257–1300*, p. 262
Reynold de Grey of Ruthin and Wilton, P.P.		
from	23 October 1282	*CChR 1257–1300*, p. 262
to	5 April 1308	*IPM V*, no. 53 (R.I.P.)
John de Grey, son of above, of Wilton, P.P.		
from	5 April 1308	*IPM V*, no. 53
to	27 December 1323	*IPM VI*, no. 517 (R.I.P.)
Henry de Grey, son of above, P.P.		
from	27 December 1323	*IPM VI*, no. 517

Roger de Grey of Ruthin, son of John and brother of Henry above, P.P.		
from	June/August 1328	*CCR 1327–1330*, p. 398
to	6 March 1353	*IPM X*, no. 107
dead by	1 October 1353	*CFR 1347–1356*, p. 379
Reynold de Grey, son of above, P.P.		
from	1 October 1353	*CFR 1347–1356*, p. 379
to	4 August 1388	*IPM XVI*, no. 696 (R.I.P.)
Reynold de Grey, son of above, P.P.		
from	4 August 1388	*IPM XVI*, no. 696
died	*1440*	*GEC VI, p. 155*

Wardships

John de Grey, son of Reginald, already of age (1308–)

Richard le Jouene		
from	14 April 1308	*CPR 1307–1313*, p. 64

Sir Roger, son of John

Roger de Grey		
on	11 March 1324	*CCR 1323–1327*, p. 77 (Probably)

Derbyshire

Unknown Licenses

PLESELE to Thomas, Bishop of St. Davids		
	1 January 1285	*CPR 1281–1292*, p. 150

BOLSOVER

Owners

Crown		
from	temp. Richard I	*HKW II*, p. 573
Queen Eleanor of Castile, wife of Edward I		
from	22 October 1275	*CChR 1257–1300*, p. 192
died	*28 November 1290*	

Constables

Walter de la Grave		
from	12 November 1290	*CFR 1272–1307*, p. 285
from	12 November 1290	*CPR 1281–1292*, p. 394
Master John de Everdon		
to	8 June 1310	*CPR 1307–1313*, p. 230
Robert de Mauley		
for life from	8 June 1310	*CPR 1307–1313*, p. 230
on	3 June 1314	*CCR 1313–1318*, p. 65
for life from	13 May 1330	*CFR 1327–1337*, p. 177
in	April 1333	E.404/497
Richard de la Vache		
for life from	12 May 1358	*CPR 1358–1361*, p. 42
on	10 May 1359	*CPR 1358–1361*, p. 209
Richard Stury, kn.		
for life to	12 September 1395	*IPM XVII*, no. 677 (R.I.P.)
Nicholas de Clifton		
for life from	19 January 1396	*CPR 1391–1396*, p. 662
on	20 June 1396	*IMisc VI*, no. 126
Thomas Colevill, kn.		
for life from	14 October 1399	*CPR 1399–1401*, p. 23
Robert Litton		
for life from	4 December 1399	*CPR 1399–1401*, p. 141 (A moiety)

BRETBY

Owners

John de Segrave, P.P.		
licence to crenellate	19 March 1301	*CPR 1292–1301*, p. 580
died	*4 October 1325*	*GEC XI, p. 605*
Stephen de Segrave, son of above		
to	12 December 1325	*IPM VI*, no. 700 (R.I.P.)
John Segrave, son of above		
from	12 December 1325	*IPM VI*, no. 700
to	1 April 1353	*IPM X*, no. 116 (R.I.P.)

Margaret, widow of John de Segrave		
from	1 April 1353	*IPM X*, no. 116 (Jointure)
on	30 May 1354	*CPR 1354–1358*, p. 24
Thomas de Mowbray, duke of Norfolk		
to	22 September 1399	*IPM XVII*, no. 282 (R.I.P.)
Margaret, duchess of Norfolk		
to	24 March 1399	*IPM XVII*, no. 241
Thomas de Mowbray, earl Marshal, great grandson of above		
from	24 March 1399	*IPM XVII*, no. 241 (Age 14)
Elizabeth, widow of Thomas, duke of Norfolk.		
from	27 November 1400	*CPR 1399–1401*, p. 399
confiscated because she married Robert Goushill without permission		
on	19 August 1401	*CFR 1399–1405*, p. 130
Robert Goushill, kn., husband of above		
on	26 September 1401	*CCR 1399–1402*, p. 381
to	20 July 1403	*IPM XVIII*, no. 910 (R.I.P.)
Elizabeth, widow of Norfolk and Goushill		
from	20 July 1403	*IPM XVIII*, no. 910
livery	12 November 1403	*CCR 1402–1405*, p. 209

CODNOR

Owners

Henry de Grey, P.P.		
to	16 September 1308	*IPM V*, no. 116 (R.I.P.)
Richard de Grey, P.P.		
from	16 September 1308	*IPM V*, no. 116
to	10 March 1335	*IPM VII*, no. 683 (R.I.P.)
John de Grey, son of above, P.P.		
from	10 March 1335	*IPM VII*, no. 683
died	*14 December 1392*	*GEC VI, p. 125*
Richard de Grey, grandson of above, P.P.		
inherited	*14 December 1392*	*GEC VI, p. 127*
died	*1 August 1418*	*GEC VI, p. 127*
John de Grey, son of above, P.P.		
inherited	*1 August 1418*	*GEC VI, p. 129*
died	*14 September 1430*	*GEC VI, p. 129*

HARESTAN (HORESTON)

Owners

Queen Eleanor of Castile		
from	22 October 1275	*CCR 1272–1279*, p. 192
died	*28 November 1290*	
Jordan Foliot		
to	2 May 1299	*IPM III*, no. 538 (R.I.P.)
Richard Foliot, son of above		
from	2 May 1299	*IPM III*, no. 538
Queen Isabella		
on	20 April 1327	*CMR*, no. 35
from	3 April 1330	*CPR 1327–1330*, p. 519
Henry, earl of Lancaster		
from	10 November 1347	*CChR 1341–1417*, p. 70 (And heirs)

Edward de Twyford, kn.		
to writ	27 November 1375	*IPM XIV*, no. 210 (R.I.P.) (For life)
John Holland, earl of Huntingdon, duke of Exeter (Owned site)		
forfeited	1400	*IMisc VII*, no. 32

Constables

Hugh de Habington		
to	27 April 1275	*CFR 1272–1307*, p. 44
Walter de Stirkesle		
from	27 April 1275	*CFR 1272–1307*, p. 44
Thomas de Normanvill		
to	27 January 1282	*CPR 1281–1292*, p. 31
William Bagot		
from	27 January 1282	*CPR 1281–1292*, p. 31
Richard Foliot		
for life from	27 October 1290	*CPR 1281–1292*, p. 391
on	7 November 1290	*CPR 1281–1292*, p. 108
Ralph de Shirle		
on	23 June 1301	*CCR 1396–1302*, p. 452
Hugh de Nottingham		
on	10 October 1304	*CCR 1302–1307*, p. 176
Robert de Mauley		
on	6 May 1311	*CCR 1307–1313*, p. 311
to	15 March 1322	*CFR 1319–1327*, p. 109
Roald de Richmond		
from	15 March 1322	*CFR 1319–1327*, p. 109
to	13 May 1322	*CPR 1321–1324*, p. 119
Robert de Mauley		
from	13 May 1322	*CPR 1321–1324*, p. 119
John de Denham		
on	25 March 1326	*CCR 1323–1327*, p. 457
Edward de Chaundos		
from	11 January 1331	*CFR 1327–1337*, p. 216
Robert Chaundos		
for life from	23 October 1345	*CFR 1337–1347*, p. 444
Robert de Swllyngton		
for life from	1 December 1376	*CPR 1374–1377*, p. 394
to	11 July 1391	*IPM XVI*, no. 122 (R.I.P.)
Roger Crophull, king's esquire		
for life from	11 July 1391	*CPR 1388–1392*, p. 460
to	29 September 1391	*CPR 1388–1392*, p. 483
John Holland, earl of Huntingdon, duke of Exeter		
for life from	29 September 1391	*CPR 1388–1392*, p. 483
John Curson, esquire		
for life from	18 January 1400	*CPR 1399–1401*, p. 179
to	6 June 1405	*CPR 1405–1408*, p. 20
Richard Lord Grey		
for life from	6 June 1405	*CPR 1405–1408*, p. 20
Philip Leche, kn.		
to	2 August 1420	*CPR 1416–1422*, p. 333 (R.I.P.)
Richard Hastings, kn.		
for life from	2 August 1420	*CPR 1416–1422*, p. 333

MELBOURNE

Owners

Robert de Holland, P.P.		
licence to crenellate	17 June 1311	*CPR 1307–1313*, p. 358
confiscated before	12 March 1322	*CFR 1319–1327*, p. 106
Thomas, earl of Lancaster		
not by	7 July 1322	*CCR 1318–1323*, p. 475
writ	5 February 1327	*IPM VII*, no. 92
Henry, earl of Lancaster		
heir on	5 February 1327	*IPM VII*, no. 82
Henry, duke of Lancaster		
to	18 March 1347	*Descriptive Catalogue of Derbyshire Charters*, London, 1906, p. 210
Matilda of Lancaster, countess of Ulster		
from	18 March 1347	*ibid.*
Henry, duke of Lancaster		
to	23 March 1361	*IPM XI*, no. 118 (R.I.P.)
John of Gaunt, duke of Lancaster		
on	11 October 1375	*JGR 1372–1376*, no. 1693
on	10 March 1380	*JGR 1379–1383*, no. 223

Constables

John de Hardedeshull		
to	12 March 1322	*CFR 1319–1327*, p. 106
Ralph Basset of Drayton		
from	12 March 1322	*CFR 1319–1327*, p. 106
Roger Beler		
on	7 July 1322	*CCR 1318–1323*, p. 475
to	4 July 1323	*CFR 1319–1327*, p. 220
Robert Tochet		
from	4 July 1323	*CFR 1319–1327*, p. 220
on	25 September 1323	*CCR 1318–1323*, p. 140
Ingram Fauconer		
on	11 October 1375	*JGR 1372–1376*, no. 1693
Peter de Melbourne, esquire		
on	*1379–1380*	Somerville, p. 377
on	10 March 1380	*JGR 1379–1383*, no. 223

Deputies

John Halswayn		
on	*1379–80*	Somerville, p. 377

PEAK (HIGH PEAK)

Owners

Queen Eleanor of Castile		
from	22 October 1275	*CCR 1272–1279*, p. 192
Piers Gaveston		
from	7 June 1308	*CChR 1300–1326*, p. 111
to	5 August 1309	*CCR 1307–1313*, p. 225
John de Warenne, earl of Surrey		
for life from	7 September 1310	*CFR 1307–1319*, p. 71
to	12 November 1313	*CFR 1307–1319*, p. 182

Crown		
from	12 November 1313	*CFR 1307–1319*, p. 183
Queen Isabella		
from	14 November 1313	*CPR 1313–1317*, p. 38
Crown		
to	1314	*CFR 1307–1319*, p. 244
John de Warenne, earl of Surrey		
from	1314	*CFR 1307–1319*, p. 244
Queen Isabella		
from	28 April 1315	*CPR 1313–1317*, p. 276
to	30 October 1318	*CPR 1317–1321*, p. 223
John and Eleanor, the king's children		
from	31 October 1318	*CPR 1317–1321*, p. 222
on	27 May 1319	*CPR 1317–1321*, p. 335
Queen Isabella		
from	1 May 1320	*CPR 1317–1321*, p. 453
on	20 June 1329	*CPR 1317–1321*, p. 399
Queen Philipa		
from	1 January 1331	*CPR 1330–1334*, p. 55
on	20 July 1335	*CPR 1334–1338*, p. 206
John de Warenne, earl of Surrey		
from	1345	*Descriptive Catalogue of Derbyshire Charters*, London, 1906, p. 231
fully for life by	1345	*Ancient Deeds vol. I*, A.210
John of Gaunt, duke of Lancaster		
from	25 June 1366	
on	18 February 1370	Somerville p. 383
on	11 February 1397	*CPR 1396–1399*, p. 76
Katherine, widow of John of Gaunt		
from	9 March 1398	*CCR 1396–1399*, p. 365
from	9 March 1399	*CPR 1396–1399*, p. 516

Constables

Roger le Strange of Ellesmere, P.P.		
on	3 May 1274	*CPR 1272–1279*, p. 49
on	12 September 1275	*CCR 1272–1279*, p. 210
Robert Bozoun		
from	17 March 1283	*CFR 1272–1307*, p. 182
for 5 years from	17 April 1283	*CPR 1281–1292*, p. 61
Piers Gavaston		
to	27 July 1309	*CFR 1307–1319*, p. 47
John de Warenne, earl of Surrey		
from	15 June 1310	*CFR 1307–1319*, p. 63
becomes owner	7 September 1310	*CFR 1307–1319*, p. 71
Robert de Clitheroe		
to	28 April 1315	*CPR 1313–1317*, p. 276
Richard Damory, P.P. and Robert de Mauley		
from	16 January 1319	*CFR 1307–1319*, p. 389
Ralph de Ispannia		
from	3 December 1330	*CFR 1327–1337*, p. 202
John Chaundos		
to	18 February 1370	*CPR 1367–1370*, p. 374 (R.I.P.)

John de Ipre, kn.		
from	18 February 1370	*CPR 1367–1370*, p. 374
to	28 October 1371	*CPR 1370–1374*, p. 152
Robert de Morton		
from	28 October 1371	*CPR 1370–1374*, p. 152
Sir Godfrey Foljaumbe		
for 3 years from	6 November 1371	*CFR 1369–1377*, p. 139
John de Legh, king's esquire		
from	5 March 1399	*CPR 1396–1399*, p. 489
on	26 April 1399	*CPR 1396–1399*, p. 538

Devonshire

Unknown Licenses

BEER FERERES for John de Ferrers
 2 October 1340 *CPR 1340–1343*, p. 51

BUKLOND ABBEY for Abbot and Convent
 2 October 1337 *CPR 1334–1338*, p. 529

BYR for Matilda, widow of William de Ferrers, kn.
 2 August 1337 *CPR 1334–1338*, p. 558

CHUDELE for Thomas Brantingham, bishop of Exeter
 30 July 1379 *CPR 1377–1381*, p. 377

EXETER, CLOSE and BISHOPS HOUSE for Walter Stapledon, bishop of Exeter
 23 June 1322 *CPR 1321–1324*, p. 140

EXETER, A HOUSE IN for Peter Quivel, bishop of Exeter
 30 October 1290 *CPR 1281–1292*, p. 393

HOLDICH for Thomas Brook, kn.
 20 February 1397 *CPR 1396–1399*, p. 85

MEDEBURY for Richard de Chaumbernoun
 1 June 1334 *CPR 1330–1334*, p. 554

TAMER for John Ocle
 7 September 1335 *CPR 1334–1338*, p. 166

BAMPTON

Owners

Richard Cogan
 licence to crenellate 17 March 1336 *CChR 1327–1341*, p. 353

BARNSTAPLE

Owners

Robert de Vere, duke of Ireland
 on 1 October 1386 *IMisc IV*, no. 113

John Holland, earl of Huntingdon
 lost by 6 March 1400 *IMisc VII*, no. 77

John, heir of above
 on 12 December 1406 *IPM XIX*, no. 298
 on 26 November 1407 *IPM XIX*, no. 358

Constables

James de Audley of Heighley
 on 12 October 1385 *CPR 1385–1389*, p. 115 (For life)

BERRY POMEROY

History

mentioned 1497 King, p. 115
modifed temp. Tudors King, p. 115

DARTMOUTH

History		
built	C14	King, p. 115

EXETER

Owners		
Piers Gaveston		
from	5 August 1309	*CCR 1307–1313*, p. 225
Edward, the Black Prince		
on	4 February 1352	*BPR I*, p. 28
Constables		
Thomas de Pyno		
to	15 October 1274	*CFR 1272–1307*, p. 30
John Wyger		
from	15 October 1274	*CFR 1272–1307*, p. 30
on	15 December 1274	*IMisc I*, no. 1005
not by	20 April 1277	*CPR 1272–1281*, p. 198 (R.I.P.)
Matthew de Egglesheyl		
on	20 April 1277	*CPR 1272–1281*, p. 198
to	18 January 1278	*CFR 1272–1307*, p. 92
Thomas de Pyn		
from	18 January 1278	*CFR 1272–1307*, p. 92
to	25 October 1278	*CFR 1272–1307*, p. 104
Warin de Sechevill		
from	25 October 1278	*CFR 1272–1307*, p. 104
Ralph de Sandwich		
to	17 May 1287	*CFR 1272–1307*, p. 236
Matthew son of John		
from	17 May 1287	*CFR 1272–1307*, p. 236
for life from	12 February 1288	*CPR 1282–1292*, p. 291
Matthew de Furneux		
to	16 January 1315	*CFR 1307–1319*, p. 221
Robert de Horton		
from	16 January 1315	*CFR 1307–1319*, p. 221
Matthew de Clyvedon		
from	8 October 1316	*CFR 1307–1319*, p. 301
to	15 May 1318	*CFR 1307–1319*, p. 360
Robert Bendyn		
from	15 May 1318	*CFR 1307–1319*, p. 360
to	29 November 1318	*CFR 1307–1319*, p. 381
John Bikkebury		
from	29 November 1318	*CFR 1307–1319*, p. 381
to	12 October 1319	*CFR 1319–1327*, p. 5
Robert Beudyn		
from	12 October 1319	*CFR 1319–1327*, p. 5
to	16 June 1321	*CFR 1319–1327*, p. 61
Nicholas de Cheigny		
from	16 June 1321	*CFR 1319–1327*, p. 61
to	30 November 1321	*CFR 1319–1327*, p. 73

John Inge		
from	30 November 1321	*CFR 1319–1327*, p. 73
to	30 May 1322	*CFR 1319–1327*, p. 130
Matthew. de Crauthorn		
from	30 May 1322	*CFR 1319–1327*, p. 130
to	4 October 1325	*CFR 1319–1327*, p. 363
James de Cokyngton		
from	4 October 1325	*CFR 1319–1327*, p. 363
to	15 February 1327	*CFR 1327–1337*, p. 17
Roger Rodde		
from	15 February 1327	*CFR 1327–1337*, p. 17
James de Cokyngton		
from	2 March 1327	*CFR 1327–1337*, p. 21
Roger Rodde		
to	19 February 1328	*CFR 1327–1337*, p. 81
William de Chevereston		
from	19 February 1328	*CFR 1327–1337*, p. 81
to	5 November 1328	*CFR 1327–1337*, p. 109
William de Faucomberge		
from	5 November 1328	*CFR 1327–1337*, p. 109
to	5 December 1330	*CFR 1327–1337*, p. 200
Matthew de Crauthorn		
from	5 December 1330	*CFR 1327–1337*, p. 200
to	20 September 1332	*CFR 1327–1337*, p. 327
Reynold de Montfort		
from	20 September 1332	*CFR 1327–1337*, p. 327
to	7 November 1333	*CFR 1327–1337*, p. 378
William de Albamarle		
from	7 November 1333	*CFR 1327–1337*, p. 378
to	7 October 1335	*CFR 1327–1337*, p. 460 (R.I.P.)
John de Chiddeleigh		
from	7 October 1335	*CFR 1327–1337*, p. 460
to	3 November 1335	*CFR 1327–1337*, p. 463
Hildebrand de London		
from	3 November 1335	*CFR 1327–1337*, p. 463
to	11 December 1335	*CPR 1334–1338*, p. 185
John de Chiddeleigh		
from	11 December 1335	*CFR 1327–1337*, p. 467
to	9 April 1336	*CFR 1327–1337*, p. 479
Peter de Veel		
from	9 April 1336	*CFR 1327–1337*, p. 479
to	25 September 1337	*CFR 1337–1347*, p. 44
John de Raleigh of Beaudeport		
from	25 September 1337	*CFR 1337–1347*, p. 44
to	28 January 1340	*CFR 1337–1347*, p. 157
John de Rale of Charles		
from	28 January 1340	*CFR 1337–1347*, p. 157
to	16 March 1341	*CFR 1337–1347*, p. 216
Roger de Prydeaux		
from	16 March 1341	*CFR 1337–1347*, p. 216
to	2 May 1341	*CFR 1337–1347*, p. 221

Hervey Tyrel		
from	2 May 1341	*CFR 1337–1347*, p. 221
to	10 February 1342	*CFR 1337–1347*, p. 262
John de Raleigh of Beaudeport		
from	10 February 1342	*CFR 1337–1347*, p. 262
to	27 March 1342	*CFR 1337–1347*, p. 262
William Pipard		
from	27 March 1342	*CFR 1337–1347*, p. 262
to	29 July 1343	*CFR 1337–1347*, p. 320
William Chambernoun		
from	29 July 1342	*CFR 1337–1347*, p. 320
William Pipard		
to	1 September 1343	*CFR 1337–1347*, p. 320
John de la Ryvere		
from	1 September 1343	*CFR 1337–1347*, p. 320
to	16 October 1343	*CFR 1337–1347*, p. 320
Walter de Horton		
from	16 October 1343	*CFR 1337–1347*, p. 320
to	4 November 1344	*CFR 1337–1347*, p. 397
James de Cokyngton		
from	4 November 1344	*CFR 1337–1347*, p. 397
Walter de Horton		
to	9 November 1344	*CFR 1337–1347*, p. 397
John de Chivereston		
from	9 November 1344	*CFR 1337–1347*, p. 397
to	26 November 1345	*CFR 1337–1347*, p. 445
Walter de Horton		
from	26 November 1345	*CFR 1337–1347*, p. 445
Hervey Tyrel		
from	30 December 1345	*CFR 1337–1347*, p. 445
Robert de Beudele		
to	10 July 1346	*CCR 1346–1349*, p. 96
Hervey Tyrel		
from	10 July 1346	*CCR 1346–1349*, p. 96
to	16 January 1347	*CFR 1337–1347*, p. 463
Thomas de Raleigh		
from	16 January 1347	*CFR 1337–1347*, p. 463
or to	20 March 1347	*CFR 1347–1356*, p. 22 (R.I.P.)
Richard Cogan		
from	22 February 1347	*CFR 1347–1356*, p. 22
Ralph Beaupel		
from	20 March 1347	*CFR 1347–1356*, p. 22
to	28 April 1347	*CFR 1347–1356*, p. 22
Ralph Byrt		
from	28 April 1347	*CFR 1347–1356*, p. 22
to	7 February 1348	*CFR 1347–1356*, p. 66
Amaury fitz Waryn		
from	7 February 1348	*CFR 1347–1356*, p. 66
Sheriff of Devon		
to	10 April 1348	*CPR 1347–1356*, p. 47
Edward, prince of Wales		
from	10 April 1348	*CPR 1347–1356*, p. 47

Constable for the Black Prince

John Dabernoun		
on	4 February 1352	*BPR II*, p. 28
on	28 October 1353	*BPR II*, p. 53

Gatekeeper

John de Badderby		
from	19 June 1328	*CFR 1327–1337*, p. 301
John de Cheveleston		
from	28 October 1353	*BPR II*, p. 53
William Hampstead		
for life from	28 February 1408	
confirmed on	12 June 1413	*CPR 1413–1416*, p. 39

Porters

Richard de Paulesholte		
in	c.1288	*State Trials of the Reign of Edward the First, 1298–1293*, Camden Society, 3rd series, 9 (1906), p. 52
Robert Person		
to	22 March 1386	*CPR 1385–1389*, p. 124 (R.I.P.)
Robert Wycheley		
from	22 March 1386	*CPR 1385–1389*, p. 124 (For Life)
confirmed	27 October 1399	*CPR 1399–1401*, p. 38
to	8 July 1406	
William Parl		
for life from	15 November 1399	*CPR 1399–1401*, p. 130 (Gaoler)
William Hampstead		
for life from	8 July 1406	*CPR 1405–1408*, p. 204
for life from	28 February 1408	*CPR 1405–1408*, p. 409

HEMYOCK

Owners

William Asthorp and Margaret his wife		
licence to crenellate	5 November 1380	*CPR 1377–1381*, p. 552

ILTON

Owners

John de Chevreston		
licence to crenellate	10 September 1335	*CPR 1334–1338*, p. 167

KINGSWEAR

Owners

John Corp		
licence to crenellate	13 October 1402	*CPR 1401–1405*, p. 219

LYDFORD

Owners

Edmund 'of Alamaine', earl of Cornwall		
to	1300	King, p. 123 (n.18)

Piers Gaveston		
from	5 August 1309	*CChR 1300–1326*, p. 131
on	5 August 1309	*CPR 1307–1313*, p. 186
Margaret, countess of Cornwall, wife of Hugh de Audley, earl of Gloucester		
from	20 July 1319	*CPR 1317–1321*, p. 386
to	22 February 1320	*CPR 1317–1321*, p. 424
Tavystok convent		
from	22 February 1320	*CPR 1317–1321*, p. 424 (For 5 years)
Hugh de Audley, earl of Gloucester and Margaret, his wife		
from	20 July 1326	
livery	1 July 1329	*CCR 1327–1330*, p. 472
confirmed	18 April 1334	*CPR 1330–1334*, p. 540
Edward, the Black Prince		
from	22 July 1342	*CCR 1341–1343*, p. 463

Constables

Thomas le Ercedekne		
on	27 March 1313	*CFR 1307–1319*, p. 166
Richard Sergeaux		
from	12 July 1376	*CFR 1369–1377*, p. 353

OKEHAMPTON

Owners

John de Courtenay		
to	11 May 1274	*IPM II*, no. 71 (R.I.P.)
Hugh de Courtenay, earl of Devon, son of above		
from	11 May 1274	*IPM II*, no. 71
to	3 January 1341	*IPM VIII*, no. 273 (R.I.P.)
Hugh de Courtenay, earl of Devon, son of above		
heir on	3 January 1341	*IPM VIII*, no. 273
from	20 January 1341	*CCR 1339–1341*, p. 606
to	2 May 1377	*IPM XIV*, no. 325 (R.I.P.)
Edward de Courtenay, earl of Devon, grandson of above		
from	2 May 1377	*IPM XIV*, no. 325

Wardships

Minority of Edward de Courtenay, earl of Devon, 1377–1378

Edward de Courtenay, earl of Devon and William Latimer		
from	21 August 1377	*CFR 1377–1383*, p. 8

Minority of Thomas de Courtenay, earl of Devon, 1422–1435

Walter Colles and John Copleston of Devon		
from	3 July 1422	*CFR 1377–1383*, p. 438

PLYMOUTH (BARBICAN)

History

built	1404	King, p. 118
siege	1549	King, p. 118

PLYMPTON

Owners

Isabel de Forz, countess of Aumale		
to	13 November 1293	*IPM III*, no. 156 (R.I.P.)

Hugh de Courtenay, earl of Devon

from	13 November 1293	*IPM III*, no. 156
to	3 January 1341	*IPM VIII*, no. 273 (R.I.P.)

Hugh de Courtenay, earl of Devon, son of above

heir on	3 January 1341	*IPM VIII*, no. 273
from	20 January 1341	*CCR 1339–1341*, p. 606
to	2 May 1377	*IPM XIV*, no. 325 (R.I.P.)

Edward de Courtenay, grandson of above

from	2 May 1377	*IPM XIV*, no. 325

Wardships

Minority of Edward de Courtenay, earl of Devon, 1377–1378

Edward de Courtenay, earl of Devon and William Latimer

from	21 August 1377	*CFR 1377–1383*, p. 8

Minority of Thomas de Courtenay, earl of Devon, 1422–1435

Walter Colles and John Copleston of Devon

from	3 July 1422	*CFR 1413–1422*, p. 438

Notes

Right to dwell in the castle granted to William de Gorges

from	6 July 1294	*CPR 1292–1301*, p. 79

POWDERHAM

Owners

Courtenay Earls of Devon

temp	period	

Wardships

Minority of Edward de Courtenay, earl of Devon, 1377–1378

Edward de Courtenay, earl of Devon and William Latimer

from	21 August 1377	*CFR 1377–1383*, p. 8

Minority of Thomas de Courtenay, earl of Devon, 1422–1435

Walter Colles and John Copleston of Devon

from	3 July 1422	*CFR 1413–1422*, p. 438

SAMPFORD PEVEREL

Owners

Oliver de Denham

licence to crenellate	23 July 1337	*CPR 1334–1338*, p. 473

TIVERTON

Owners

Courtenay earls of Devon

temp	period	

Wardships

Minority of Edward de Courtenay, earl of Devon, 1377–1378

Edward de Courtenay, earl of Devon and William Latimer

from	21 August 1377	*CFR 1377–1383*, p. 8

Minority of Thomas de Courtenay, earl of Devon, 1422–1435

Walter Colles and John Copleston of Devon

from	3 July 1422	*CFR 1413–1422*, p. 438

TORRINGTON

Owners

Richard de Merton		
licence to crenellate	29 September 1340	*CPR 1340–1343*, p. 39
to	25 September 1370	*IPM XIII*, no. 42 (R.I.P.)
Four daughters		
from	25 September 1370	*IPM XIII*, no. 42
To be split four ways		
after	14 June 1371	*CFR 1369–1377*, p. 130
Peter Veel and Eleanor his wife, oldest daughter of Richard de Merton		
to	30 May 1386	*CPR 1385–1389*, p. 143
John Cary, kn. and Thomas Cary		
from	30 May 1386	*CPR 1385–1389*, p. 143
John Cary, kn.		
forfeited by	17 April 1388	*IMisc V*, no. 61
forfeited by	26 November 1388	*CPR 1385–1389*, p. 555

Notes

Peter Veel and Eleanor granted the castle to the Cary's to clear their debts of 550 marks, with 4 years to pay it back.

TOTNES

Owners

William de Cauntelo		
to	25 April 1273	*CPR 1272–1281*, p. 8 (R.I.P.)
George de Cauntelo		
from	25 April 1273	*CPR 1272–1281*, p. 8
to	4 November 1273	*IPM II*, no. 17 (R.I.P.)
Eudo de Zouche, brother in law of above		
from	1 March 1274	*CFR 1272–1307*, p. 17
Ralph le Zouche of Harringworth		
away and back	26 March 1326	*CPR 1324–1327*, p. 254
William la Zouche of Harringworth, P.P.		
on	30 April 1326	*CCR 1323–1327*, p. 476
died	*1351/2*	*GEC VII (ii), p. 938*
William la Zouche of Harringworth, grandson of above, P.P.		
to	23 April 1382	*IPM XV*, no. 630 (R.I.P.)
William la Zouche, kn., son of above		
from	23 April 1382	*IPM XV*, no. 630
to	13 May 1396	*IPM XVII*, no. 720 (R.I.P.)
William Lord la Zouche, son of above		
from	13 May 1396	*IPM XVII*, no. 720
on	30 December 1415	*CPR 1413–1416*, p. 386

Wardships

Minority of George de Cauntelo		
Ralph le Ussher		
from	5 November 1273	*CFR 1272–1307*, p. 13

Stewards

Walter de Kancia		
to	25 April 1273	*CPR 1272–1281*, p. 8

Constables for le Zouche

John Isham son of Robert Isham

on	30 December 1415	*CPR 1413–1416*, p. 386

Dorset

Unknown Licenses

COLEWEHEYS for Ralph de Bloiou		
	1 February 1335	*CPR 1334–1338*, p. 77
HOKE for Robert Sifrewast		
	12 December 1344	*CPR 1343–1345*, p. 384

CHIDEOCK

Owners

John de Chideock, kn.		
licence to crenellate	9 February 1370	*CPR 1367–1370*, p. 371
confirmed	2 June 1380	*CPR 1377–1381*, p. 491

CORFE

Owners

Crown		
from	temp William I	*HKW II*, p. 616
to	temp Charles I	*HKW II*, p. 616
Thomas de Holland, earl of Kent		
to	25 April 1397	*IPM XVII*, no. 822 (R.I.P.)
Thomas, son of above		
from	25 April 1397	*IPM XVII*, no. 822
Alice de Holland, countess of Kent		
livery	16 August 1401	*CCR 1399–1402*, p. 370

Constables

Hugh Paynel		
on	17 October 1240	*CLibR 1267–1272*, no. 2275
Matthias de la Mare		
on	4 January 1261	
on	10 June 1261	
paid	26 June 1262	*CLibR 1267–1272*, no. 2331
Alan de Plogenet, P.P. and Henry de Alemannia, king's nephew		
on	2 April 1270	*CLibR 1267–1272*, no. 1059
Alan de Plogenet, P.P.		
not by	27 June 1273	*CCR 1272–1279*, p. 17
Elias de Rabayn		
on	6 November 1272	*CLibR 1267–1272*, no. 2134
on	24 April 1278	*CPR 1272–1281*, p. 289
?Nicholas de Stapelton		
?on	22 June 1278	*CCR 1272–1279*, p. 464
?Peter de Mauley		
?on	15 November 1279	*CChR 1257–1300*, p. 217
Richard de Bosco		
from	25 February 1280	*CFR 1272–1307*, p. 123
to	4 March 1280	*CPR 1272–1281*, p. 365

John de Cormailles		
from	4 March 1280	*CPR 1272–1281*, p. 365
to	4 March 1280	*CPR 1272–1281*, p. 365
Richard de Bosco		
from	4 March 1280	*CPR 1272–1281*, p. 365
to	16 September 1299	*CPR 1292–1301*, p. 436
Richard de Bosco and Simon de Montague, P.P.		
from	16 September 1299	*CPR 1292–1301*, p. 436
Simon de Montague, P.P.		
to	1 February 1301	*CPR 1292–1301*, p. 564
Henry de Lacy, earl of Lincoln		
from	1 February 1301	*CPR 1292–1301*, p. 564
to	20 March 1305	*CFR 1272–1307*, p. 511
Robert fitz Payn, P.P.		
from	20 March 1305	*CFR 1272–1307*, p. 511
on	15 March 1312	*CCR 1307–1313*, p. 414
Richard Lovel and Muriel his wife		
from	1 September 1315	*CFR 1307–1319*, p. 258
Richard Lovel		
from	1 November 1317	*CFR 1307–1319*, p. 344
to	20 February 1318	*CFR 1307–1319*, p. 353
Roger Damory, P.P.		
from	20 February 1318	*CFR 1307–1319*, p. 353
to	8 May 1321	*CFR 1319–1327*, p. 55
John de Ryther		
from	8 May 1321	*CFR 1319–1327*, p. 55
on	11 May 1321	*CCR 1318–1323*, p. 299
Roger Damory		
to	3 December 1321	*CFR 1319–1327*, p. 81
John le Latimer		
from	3 December 1321	*CFR 1319–1327*, p. 81
to	16 December 1325	*CPR 1324–1327*, p. 202
John Pecche, P.P.		
from	16 December 1325	*CPR 1324–1327*, p. 202
on	15 December 1325	*CPR 1324–1327*, p. 236
John Mautravers		
on	26 August 1329	*CCR 1327–1330*, p. 487
from	24 September 1329	*CFR 1327–1337*, p. 149
William de Montague		
from	28 December 1330	*CFR 1327–1337*, p. 211
keeper (garrison?)	15 March 1339	*CCR 1339–1341*, p. 56
not by	15 May 1340	*CPR 1338–1340*, p. 521
Walter de Wydecombe		
on	15 March 1339	*CCR 1339–1341*, p. 56
on	20 October 1339	*CCR 1337–1339*, p. 605
Thomas Cary		
from	15 May 1340	*CPR 1338–1340*, p. 521
to	28 October 1341	*CFR 1337–1347*, p. 245
Ralph de Ufford		
for life from	28 October 1341	*CFR 1337–1347*, p. 245
to	13 January 1344	*CFR 1337–1347*, p. 404

Philip de Weston		
from	13 January 1344	*CFR 1337–1347*, p. 404
to	28 October 1346	E.101/36/6 m.1
John de Grey of Ruthin		
from	28 October 1346	E.101/36/6 m.1
Ralph de Bagley		
on	14 March 1351	*CPR 1350–1354*, p. 82
Roger Mortimer, earl of March		
from	3 November 1354	*CPR 1354–1358*, p. 134
on	26 May 1359	*CPR 1358–1361*, p. 204
Ralph Bagley		
on	20 November 1361	*CPR 1361–1364*, p. 142
John de Elmerugg		
on	22 February 1363	*CPR 1361–1364*, p. 362
on	29 January 1376	*CCR 1374–1377*, p. 290
Bernard Brocas		
from	9 September 1376	*CPR 1374–1377*, p. 339
for life from	16 October 1376	*CPR 1374–1377*, p. 358
to	14 May 1377	*CPR 1374–1377*, p. 463
John de Arundel, P.P.		
from	14 May 1377	*CPR 1374–1377*, p. 463
Philip Walwayn		
for life from	3 February 1380	*CPR 1377–1381*, p. 436
to	8 July 1388	*CPR 1385–1389*, p. 484 (R.I.P.)
Morgan Gogh		
requests appointment	before 8 July 1388	*CAPW*, p. 376
for life from	8 July 1388	*CPR 1385–1389*, p. 484
to	1 May 1391	*CPR 1388–1392*, p. 402
Thomas de Holland, earl of Kent and Alesia his wife		
for life from	1 May 1391	*CPR 1388–1392*, p. 402
to	25 April 1397	*IPM XVII*, no. 822 (R.I.P.)
Alesia, widow of earl of Kent		
to	19 January 1400	*CPR 1399–1401*, p. 182
John Lord Lovell, P.P.		
for life from	19 January 1400	*CPR 1399–1401*, p. 182
died	*10 September 1408*	*GEC VIII, p. 219*
John de Beaufort, earl of Somerset		
for life from	7 May 1407	*CPR 1405–1408*, p. 335
to	16 March 1410	*IPM XIX*, no. 773.
Henry de Beaufort, son of above		
under age	20 April 1410	*CPR 1408–1413*, p. 198
2/3 Margaret widow of above		
on	1 October 1413	*CPR 1413–1416*, p. 39

Deputy Constables

William de Thwayt		
to	13 January 1344	*CFR 1337–1347*, p. 404; C.60/144 m.7
Walter de Turpeton for Philip de Weston		
to	14 April 1346	E.101/36/6 m.2
Thomas de Bridport for Philip de Weston		
from	14 April 1346	E.101/36/6 m.2
on	18 September 1346	*CCR 1346–1349*, p. 160
to	28 October 1346	E.101/36/6 m.1

Ralph de Bagley for John de Grey of Ruthin		
from	28 October 1346	E.101/36/6 m.1
John de Elmerugg		
from	3 November 1354	*CPR 1354–1358*, p. 134
on	26 May 1359	*CPR 1358–1361*, p. 204
John de Moulham for John de Elmerugg		
on	November 1363	C.258/13 m.34
William Tybenham, esq.		
from	19 September 1408	(For earl of Somerset)

Wardships

minority of Henry, son and heir of John, earl of Somerset

William Tybenham, esq.		
from	20 April 1410	*CPR 1408–1413*, p. 198
Margaret, John's widow and Thomas duke of Clarence her husband		
from	16 July 1412	*CPR 1408–1413*, p. 422

CRANBORNE

Constables

John de Botiller of Lanultit		
from	22 February 1322	*CFR 1319–1327*, p. 101

DORCHESTER

Owners

Crown		
to	1290	*HKW II*, p. 629
John Gervase of Bridport		
from	1290	*HKW II*, p. 629
To Franciscan friars		
	?	*HKW II*, p. 629

SHERBORNE (SHIRBORNE)

Owners

Crown		
from	1183	*HKW II*, p. 832
to	1331	*CChR 1327–1341*, p. 210
William de Montague, earl of Salisbury		
from	18 January 1331	*CChR 1327–1341*, p. 210
to	30 January 1344	*IPM VIII*, no. 532 (R.I.P.)
dead by	15 April 1344	*CCR 1343–1346*, p. 323
Katherine, widow of William de Montague		
from	30 January 1344	*IPM VIII*, no. 532 (Jointure)
to	23 April 1349	*IPM IX*, no. 310 (R.I.P.)
Roger, son of above		
from	23 April 1349	*IPM IX*, no. 310
Bishop of Salisbury		
decision to claim	11 April 1342	*Hemingby's Register*, Wiltshire Record Society, 18 (1962), p. 112
poss. from	7 February 1355	
by	12 February 1355	*CCR 1354–1360*, p. 180

Robert bishop of Salisbury		
on	3 February 1363	*CPR 1361–1364*, p. 358
Constables		
Matthias de la Mare		
on	4 January 1261	*CLibR 1267–1272*, no. 2331
paid	26 June 1262	*CLibR 1267–1272*, no. 2331
John de St. Valery, with Dorset and Somerset		
from	6 May 1273	*CFR 1272–1307*, p. 5
to	7 November 1274	*CFR 1272–1307*, p. 35
Richard de Coleshull, with Dorset and Somerset		
from	7 November 1274	*CFR 1272–1307*, p. 35
to	19 January 1278	*CPR 1272–1281*, p. 253 (Just castle)
Archbishop of Canterbury		
from	19 January 1278	*CPR 1272–1281*, p. 253
John de Somerset		
on	30 December 1279	*CPR 1272–1281*, p. 356
to	5 April 1282	*CPR 1281–1292*, p. 14 (Keeper)
John de Cormaillies		
to	17 August 1282	*CPR 1281–1292*, p. 34
Elias de Rabayn		
from	17 August 1282	*CPR 1281–1292*, p. 34
William Favelore		
to	18 February 1283	*CPR 1281–1292*, p. 57
John de St. Laudo		
from	18 February 1283	*CPR 1281–1292*, p. 57
Walter de Skydemor		
from	16 March 1308	*CFR 1307–1319*, p. 18
to	14 January 1313	*CFR 1307–1319*, p. 160
John de Chideock		
from	14 January 1313	*CFR 1307–1319*, p. 160
to	20 November 1314	*CFR 1307–1319*, p. 221
John de Erle		
from	20 November 1314	*CFR 1307–1319*, p. 221
to	20 October 1315	*CFR 1307–1319*, p. 262
Matthew de Furneux		
from	20 October 1315	*CFR 1307–1319*, p. 262
to	12 June 1316	*CFR 1307–1319*, p. 282 (R.I.P.)
John de Kyngeston		
from	12 June 1316	*CFR 1307–1319*, p. 282
to	1 December 1318	*CFR 1307–1319*, p. 382
Nicholas de Cheigny		
from	1 December 1318	*CFR 1307–1319*, p. 382
to	4 January 1319	*CFR 1319–1327*, p. 13
Thomas de Marlborough		
from	4 January 1319	*CFR 1319–1327*, p. 13
to	18 June 1326	*CFR 1319–1327*, p. 391
John de Erle		
from	18 June 1326	*CFR 1319–1327*, p. 391
to	15 October 1326	*CFR 1319–1327*, p. 420
Thomas de Marlborough		
from	15 October 1326	*CFR 1319–1327*, p. 420

John de Erle		
to	4 February 1327	*CFR 1327–1337*, p. 15
William de Whitfeld		
from	4 February 1327	*CFR 1327–1337*, p. 15
William de Montague		
for life from	27 May 1330	*CPR 1327–1330*, p. 528
on	27 May 1330	*CPR 1327–1330*, p. 563
William de Whitfeld		
to	5 December 1330	*CFR 1327–1337*, p. 200
Hugh de Langelonde		
from	5 December 1330	*CFR 1327–1337*, p. 200
to	28 January 1332	*CFR 1327–1337*, p. 296
John de Wroxhale		
from	28 January 1332	*CFR 1327–1337*, p. 296
to	7 November 1333	*CFR 1327–1337*, p. 378
Hildebrand of London		
from	7 November 1333	*CFR 1327–1337*, p. 378

Constable for archbishop of Canterbury

William de Shomershete		
from	7 January 1281	*Registrum Epistolarum J. Peckham Arch. Cant. vol.3*, Rolls Series 77 (1885), p. 1086

WOODSFORD

Owners

Belet family		
to	early C14	*RCH*, p. 397
William de Whitefield		
licence to crenellate	8 October 1335	*CPR 1334–1338*, p. 221
Guy de Brian		
from	1367	*RCH*, p. 397

Durham

BARNARD CASTLE

Owners

John Balliol		
doing homage	1279	*CCR 1272–1279*, p. 579
forfeited in	1295	D. Austin, 'Barnard Castle co. Durham, 2nd Interim Report: Excavations in the Town Ward 1974–6', *Journal of the British Archaeological Association* 132 (1979), p. 54
forfeited by	2 February 1307	*CChR 1300–1326*, p. 79
Bishop of Durham		
from	1295	Austin, p. 54
to	1306	Austin, p. 54
Crown		
from	1306	Austin, p. 54
to	2 February 1307	*CChR 1300–1327*, p. 79
Guy de Beauchamp, earl of Warwick		
from	2 February 1307	*CChR 1300–1326*, p. 79
to	16 August 1315	*IPM V*, no. 615 (R.I.P.)
Thomas de Beauchamp, earl of Warwick, son of above		
from	16 August 1315	*IPM V*, no. 615
of age	*1335*	
Bishop of Durham		
on	9 December 1321	*CPR 1321–1324*, p. 39
Thomas de Beauchamp, earl of Warwick		
jointured	24 April 1344	*CPR 1343–1345*, p. 251
to	13 November 1369	*IPM XII*, no. 326 (R.I.P.)
Thomas de Beauchamp, earl of Warwick, son of above		
from	13 November 1369	*IPM XII*, no. 326
to	1397	
William le Scrope, earl of Wiltshire		
tail male from	29 September 1397	*CPR 1396–1399*, pp. 200, 267
Thomas de Beauchamp, earl of Warwick		
enfeofed away	18 December 1399	*CPR 1399–1401*, p. 163
Richard de Beauchamp, son of above		
enfeofed with	18 December 1399	*CPR 1399–1401*, p. 163

Wardships

Minority of Thomas de Beauchamp (1315–1335)

John de Castre		
on	3 December 1315	*CCR 1313–1318*, p. 256
to	18 December 1315	*CFR 1307–1319*, p. 267
Henry fitz Hugh, P.P.		
from	18 December 1315	*CFR 1307–1319*, p. 267
to	27 September 1319	*CFR 1319–1327*, p. 4

William Rydel		
from	27 September 1319	*CFR 1319–1327*, p. 4
to	6 July 1323	*CFR 1319–1327*, p. 219 (Wardship)
Richard de Bernyngham		
from	6 July 1323	*CFR 1319–1327*, p. 219
on	26 July 1323	*CFR 1319–1327*, p. 10
Ivo de Aldeburgh		
on	7 December 1326	*CCR 1323–1327*, p. 622
to	9 June 1327	*CFR 1327–1337*, p. 46
Roger Mortimer of Wigmore		
from	9 June 1327	*CFR 1327–1337*, p. 46
to	15 July 1327	*CCR 1327–1330*, p. 144
Bishop of Durham		
from	15 July 1327	*CCR 1327–1330*, p. 144

Wardships

Minority of Richard Beauchamp, Earl of Warwick (1401–1403)

Thomas de Aldebury and William Beauchamp of Abergavenny and John Owdeby		
from	12 May 1401	*CFR 1399–1405*, p. 135

Private Constables

Thomas Chancellor		
temp	Balliol	Austin, p. 54
temp	Bishop of Durham	Austin, p. 54

Constables

William Rydel		
on	22 May 1321	*CCR 1318–1323*, p. 304
on	13 February 1322	*CCR 1318–1323*, p. 418
John Ros		
on	13 November 1387	*IMisc IV*, no. 346 (For Beauchamp)
William le Scrope, earl of Wiltshire		
from	4 August 1397	*CPR 1396–1399*, p. 176
to	29 September 1397	*CPR 1396–1399*, p. 200

BISHOP AUCKLAND

Owners

Bishop's of Durham		
from	12th Century	Pevsner p. 101
Bishop Anthony Bek of Durham		
temp.	1283–1310	King p. 140

BRANCEPETH

Owners

Neville family, eventual earls of Westmorland		
from	c.1216	Pevsner, p. 101
to	1569	Pevsner, p. 101
Randolf Neville of Raby		
to	*1331*	*GEC IX, p. 487 (R.I.P.)*
Ralph Neville of Raby, son of above		
from	*1331*	*GEC IX, p. 487*
to	*5 August 1367*	*IPM XII, no. 160 (R.I.P.)*

John Neville, lord Neville of Raby, son of above		
from	*5 August 1367*	*IPM XII, no. 160*
to	*17 October 1388*	*IPM XVI, no. 734 (R.I.P.)*
Ralph Neville, earl of Westmorland, son of above		
from	*17 October 1388*	*IPM XVI, no. 734*
died	*1425*	

DURHAM

Owners
Bishops of Durham

Constables for the bishop's of Durhan

Philip Darcy		
on	22 June 1301	*Records of Anthony Bek, Bishop and Patriarch, 1283–1311*, Surtees Society, 162 (1953), p. 82

Constables while void

Robert de Sapy		
to	20 November 1316	*CPR 1313–1317*, p. 563
Henry de Beaumont		
from	20 November 1316	*CPR 1313–1317*, p. 563
to	4 May 1317	*CPR 1313–1317*, p. 644
William Chaunceller, esq.		
from	7 May 1406	*CPR 1405–1408*, p. 175

HYLTON

Owners

William de Hylton, kn., probable builder		
inherited	1376	B. Morley, 'Hylton Castle', *The Archaeological Journal* 133 (1976), p. 119
died	1435	*ibid.*

LUDWORTH

History

licence to crenellate	1422	W. Hutchinson, *History of the County Palatine of Durham, vol. I*, Durham, 1823, p. 408

LUMLEY

Owners

Sir Ralph de Lumley, P.P.		
licence to crenellate.	24 October 1392	*CPR 1391–1396*, p. 188

Royal Constables

John de Beaufort, earl of Somerset		
from	22 January 1400	*CPR 1399–1401*, p. 173

RABY

History

licensed	1378 by Bishop of Durham	King, p. 141 n.16
siege	1648	King, p. 137

Owners

Ralph de Neville, earl of Westmorland		
on	10 April 1404	*Ancient Deeds vol. III*, D.1163
on	18 October 1424	*Wills and Inventories, part 1*, Surtees Society 2 (1835), p. 73

RAVENSWORTH

Owners

Henry fitz Hugh, kn.		
on	6 April 1391	*CPR 1388–1392*, p. 395

STANHOPE

History

mentioned as place	1283–1310	King, p. 138

WITTON LE WEAR

Owned

Sir Ralph de Eure		
license to crenellate.	23 September 1410	W. Hutchinson, *The History of the County Palatine of Durham, vol. 3*, Durham, 1823, pp. 304–6

Essex

COLCHESTER

Owners
Crown – entire period

Constables

John de Burgo		
for life from	18 December 1273	*CPR 1272–1281*, p. 41
before	20 November 1274	*CFR 1272–1307*, p. 36 (R.I.P.)
Thomas de Sandwich		
from	20 November 1274	*CFR 1272–1307*, p. 36
to	7 November 1275	*CFR 1272–1307*, p. 57
Laurence de Scaccario		
from	7 November 1275	*CFR 1272–1307*, p. 57
to	17 May 1276	*CPR 1272–1281*, p. 141
Richard de Holebrok		
from	17 May 1276	*CPR 1272–1281*, p. 141
Simon de Bradenham		
to	22 October 1299	*CFR 1272–1307*, p. 419
John de la Lee		
from	22 October 1299	*CFR 1272–1307*, p. 419
on	14 April 1300	*CCR 1296–1302*, p. 349
John de Hoo		
to	8 October 1314	*CFR 1307–1319*, p. 220
Richard de Perers		
from	8 October 1314	*CFR 1307–1319*, p. 220
to	29 November 1318	*CFR 1307–1319*, p. 381
John de Dover		
from	29 November 1318	*CFR 1307–1319*, p. 381
to	27 May 1319	*CFR 1307–1319*, p. 397
Ralph Giffard		
from	27 May 1319	*CFR 1307–1319*, p. 397
to	25 October 1320	*CFR 1319–1327*, p. 36
John de Dover		
from	25 October 1320	*CFR 1319–1327*, p. 36
to	24 October 1321	*CFR 1319–1327*, p. 73
Nicholas Engaigne		
from	24 October 1321	*CFR 1319–1327*, p. 73
to	15 January 1323	*CFR 1319–1327*, p. 192 (R.I.P.)
Thomas Gobioun		
from	15 January 1323	*CFR 1319–1327*, p. 192
to	24 November 1324	*CFR 1319–1327*, p. 321
Richard de Perers		
from	24 November 1324	*CFR 1319–1327*, p. 321
and from	4 February 1327	*CFR 1327–1337*, p. 16
to	26 September 1327	*CFR 1327–1337*, p. 64

William de Baud		
from	26 September 1327	*CFR 1327–1337*, p. 64
to	26 October 1328	*CFR 1327–1337*, p. 107
Richard de Perers		
from	26 October 1328	*CFR 1327–1337*, p. 107
to	5 December 1330	*CFR 1327–1337*, p. 200
John de Wauton		
from	5 December 1330	*CFR 1327–1337*, p. 200
to	5 May 1332	*CFR 1327–1337*, p. 311
John de la Haye		
from	5 May 1332	*CFR 1327–1337*, p. 311
to	9 June 1333	*CFR 1327–1337*, p. 362
Adam le Bloy		
from	9 June 1333	*CFR 1327–1337*, p. 362
to	8 March 1334	*CFR 1327–1337*, p. 392
William Baud		
from	8 March 1334	*CFR 1327–1337*, p. 392
to	15 November 1334	*CFR 1327–1337*, p. 425
John de Cogeshale		
from	15 November 1334	*CFR 1327–1337*, p. 425
to	28 September 1339	*CFR 1327–1337*, p. 144
William Wauton		
from	28 September 1339	*CFR 1337–1347*, p. 144
to	6 May 1340	*CFR 1337–1347*, p. 172
John de Cogeshale		
from	6 May 1340	*CFR 1337–1347*, p. 172
to	8 January 1341	*CFR 1337–1347*, p. 199
William de la More		
from	8 January 1341	*CFR 1337–1347*, p. 199
to	4 December 1341	*CFR 1337–1347*, p. 250
Richard de Monte Caniso		
from	4 December 1341	*CFR 1337–1347*, p. 250
to	29 July 1342	*CFR 1337–1347*, p. 263 (R.I.P.)
Henry Gernet		
from	29 July 1342	*CFR 1337–1347*, p. 263
to	22 November 1343	*CFR 1337–1347*, p. 349
John Cogeshale		
from	22 November 1343	*CFR 1337–1347*, p. 349
to	12 May 1348	*CFR 1347–1356*, p. 83
Peter de Boxstede		
from	12 May 1348	*CFR 1347–1356*, p. 84
to	12 November 1348	*CFR 1347–1356*, p. 84
William Bret		
from	12 November 1348	*CFR 1347–1356*, p. 84
to	7 July 1349	*CFR 1347–1356*, p. 130 (R.I.P.)
Humphrey de Walden		
from	7 July 1349	*CFR 1347–1356*, pp. 130, 170
to	12 December 1349	*CFR 1347–1356*, p. 171
Peter de Boxstede		
from	12 December 1349	*CFR 1347–1356*, p. 171

Robert de Benhale		
from	5 April 1350	*CFR 1347–1356*, p. 235
to	16 June 1364	*IPM XI*, no. 622 (R.I.P.)
John de Hevenyngham		
from	5 November 1369	*CFR 1369–1377*, p. 36
William Wauton		
from	6 December 1369	*CFR 1369–1377*, p. 36
Roger Keterich		
from	22 January 1370	*CFR 1369–1377*, p. 37
William Baud, elder		
from	28 March 1370	*CFR 1369–1377*, p. 98
Thomas de Bassingbourn		
from	16 December 1370	*CFR 1369–1377*, p. 99
William Baud		
from	5 November 1371	*CFR 1369–1377*, p. 146
John Bataille		
from	18 November 1371	*CFR 1369–1377*, p. 141
George Felbrigg		
from	6 October 1376	*CPR 1374–1377*, p. 368
to	17 July 1384	
Robert de Vere, earl of Oxford		
from	17 July 1384	*CPR 1381–1385*, p. 442
on	18 July 1384	*CPR 1381–1385*, p. 440
on	1 October 1386	
Walter atte Lee, kn.		
for life from	23 March 1388	*CPR 1385–1389*, p. 424
to	22 June 1396	*CPR 1396–1399*, p. 1 (R.I.P.)
John Littelbury		
for life from	26 July 1395	*CPR 1391–1396*, p. 609
Robert Teye		
for life from	22 June 1396	*CPR 1396–1399*, p. 1
on	14 December 1403	*CPR 1401–1405*, p. 189
Humphrey duke of Gloucester, temporary grant to clear debts		
to	1 July 1418	*CPR 1416–1422*, p. 129
on	Annunciation 1419	

HADLEIGH

Owners

Queen Eleanor of Provence		
on	23 August 1273	*CPR 1272–1281*, p. 27
Queen Margaret		
from	10 September 1299	*CPR 1292–1301*, p. 451
on	28 September 1311	*CCR 1307–1313*, p. 375
Queen Isabella		
for life from	1 February 1327	*CPR 1327–1330*, p. 66
to	December 1330	*HKW II*, p. 662
Reversion to Edmund de Langley, duke of York		
on	9 February 1391	*CPR 1388–1392*, p. 375
Joan, countess of Hereford		
not by	27 January 1400	*CCR 1399–1402*, p. 43

Aubrey de Vere, earl of Oxford		
livery	27 January 1400	*CCR 1399–1402*, p. 43
to	23 April 1400	*IPM vol. XVIII*, no. 196 (R.I.P.)
Richard de Vere, earl of Oxford, son and heir		
under age	23 April 1400	*IPM vol. XVIII*, no. 196
Edmund de Langley, duke of York		
for life from	17 July 1400	*CPR 1399–1401*, p. 354
to	1 August 1402	*IPM vol. XVIII*, no. 639 (R.I.P.)
Humphrey duke of Gloucester (temporary grant to clear debts)		
to	1 July 1418	*CPR 1416–1422*, p. 129

Constables

Robert fitz Walter, P.P.		
on	10 July 1293	*CFR 1272–1307*, p. 325
Roger Filiol		
from	29 September 1311	*CFR 1307–1319*, p. 103
on	4 February 1312	*CCR 1307–1313*, p. 394
Alan de Clavering		
from	23 June 1321	*CPR 1317–1321*, p. 599
to	22 July 1321	*CFR 1319–1327*, p. 66
Roger de Blakesale		
from	22 July 1321	*CFR 1319–1327*, p. 66
Roger de Wodeham		
on	22 February 1327	*CCR 1327–1330*, p. 49
Henry Swan		
to	28 August 1334	*CFR 1327–1337*, p. 415 (R.I.P.)
John Stormy		
for life from	28 August 1334	*CFR 1327–1337*, p. 415
for life on	14 January 1337	*CPR 1334–1338*, pp. 350, 385
Roger de Wodham		
from	25 July 1343	*CFR 1337–1347*, p. 335
to	26 August 1354	*CFR 1347–1356*, p. 405 (R.I.P.)
Walter Whithors, yeoman		
for life from	26 August 1354	*CFR 1347–1356*, p. 405
and again from	30 September 1374	*CFR 1369–1377*, p. 262
on	4 January 1375	*CPR 1374–1377*, p. 63 (Keeper)
George Felbrigg		
from	15 July 1376	*CFR 1369–1377*, p. 357
to	10 November 1376	*CPR 1374–1377*, p. 397
Walter Whithors, yeoman		
for life from	10 November 1376	*CPR 1374–1377*, p. 397
confirmed	17 March 1378	*CPR 1377–1381*, p. 170
not by	2 February 1378	*CPR 1377–1381*, p. 193
Aubrey de Vere, earl of Oxford		
on	2 February 1378	*CPR 1377–1381*, p. 193
for life from	1 February 1378	*CPR 1377–1381*, p. 112
on	9 February 1391	*CPR 1388–1392*, p. 375

King's Stewards

Humphrey de Walden		
from	26 April 1320	*CFR 1319–1327*, p. 20

Humphrey de Walden and Richard de Ikene		
from	8 March 1324	*CFR 1319–1327*, p. 259
Richard de Wynferthyng and Richard de Ikene		
from	20 August 1324	*CFR 1319–1327*, p. 295

HEDINGHAM (HENGHAM)

Owners

Robert de Vere, earl of Oxford		
to	7 September 1296	*IPM III*, no. 367 (R.I.P.)
Robert de Vere, earl of Oxford, son of above		
from	7 September 1296	*IPM III*, no. 367
dead by	19 April 1331	*IPM VII*, no. 379 (R.I.P.)
John de Vere, earl of Oxford, nephew of above		
from	19 April 1331	*IPM VII*, no. 379
to	23 January 1360	*IPM X*, no. 638 (R.I.P.)
Thomas de Vere, earl of Oxford, son of above		
from	23 January 1360	*IPM X*, no. 638
died	*1371*	
Robert de Vere, earl of Oxford, son of above		
inherited	*1371*	
of age	*c.1383*	
granted away	10 June 1385	*CPR 1381–1385*, p. 557
forfeited by	1 July 1388	*CFR 1383–1391*, p. 242
Maud de Vere, countess of Oxford		
for 20 years from	1 July 1388	*CFR 1383–1391*, p. 242
Aubrey de Vere, earl of Oxford		
from	10 February 1393	*CCR 1392–1396*, p. 41 (Fee simple)
to	23 April 1400	*IPM XVIII*, no. 196 (R.I.P.)
Richard de Vere, earl of Oxford, son and heir		
from	23 April 1400	*IPM XVIII*, no. 196 (Age 14)
died	*1417*	

Wardships

Minority of Robert de Vere, earl of Oxford, heir of Thomas de Vere, earl of Oxford (1371–1383)

Thomas Tirell and John James		
from	1 October 1377	*CFR 1377–1383*, p. 13

Minority of Richard de Vere (1400–1406)

Alice, wife of Aubrey de Vere		
from	11 May 1400	*CFR 1399–1405*, p. 56
Gerard Braybrok, Thomas Ferriby and Joan de Bohun, countess of Hereford		
from	9 May 1401	*CFR 1399–1405*, p. 125

ONGAR

Owners

Hugh de Audley, younger, earl of Gloucester		
before	14 May 1321	*CFR 1319–1327*, p. 57
Ralph, earl Stafford		
to	31 August 1372	*IPM XIII*, no. 210
Hugh, earl of Stafford		
from	31 August 1372	*IPM XIII*, no. 210

Constables

Sheriff of Essex		
to	14 May 1321	*CFR 1319–1327*, p. 57
Henry atte Ree		
from	14 May 1321	*CFR 1319–1327*, p. 57
on	27 March 1322	*CCR 1318–1323*, p. 434
to	13 May 1322	*CFR 1319–1327*, p. 128
John le Porter of Stebbyng		
from	13 May 1322	*CFR 1319–1327*, p. 128

PLESHEY

Owners

John de Bohun, earl of Hereford and Essex		
on	28 March 1330	*CPR 1327–1330*, p. 558
to	26 January 1337	*IPM VIII*, no. 55 (R.I.P.)
Humphrey de Bohun, earl of Hereford and Essex, brother of above		
from	26 January 1337	*IPM VIII*, no. 55
to	15 October 1361	*IPM X*, no. 485 (R.I.P.)
Humphrey de Bohun, earl of Hereford and Essex, son of above		
from	15 October 1361	*IPM X*, no. 485
to	17 January 1373	*IPM XIII*, no. 167 (R.I.P.)
Thomas earl of Buckingham, duke of Gloucester and Eleanor his wife		
livery	22 June 1380	*CCR 1377–1381*, p. 390
to	15 September 1397	*IPM XVII*, no. 1032 (R.I.P.)
Eleanor, duchess of Gloucester		
from	30 November 1397	*CCR 1396–1399*, p. 182
to	3 October 1399	*IPM VII*, no. 127 (R.I.P.)
Anne, daughter of Eleanor		
from	12 June 1400	*CFR 1399–1405*, p. 72
Edmund, earl of Stafford, husband of Anne.		
to	21 July 1403	*IPM XVIII*, no. 816 (R.I.P.)
Anne, widow of above		
livery	21 October 1403	*CCR 1402–1405*, p. 226
Crown		
from	6 May 1421	W. Hardy, *Charters of the Duchy of Lancaster*, London, 1845, p. 175

Constables

Nicholas de la Beche, kn.		
from	30 December 1321	*CFR 1319–1327*, p. 84
to	13 May 1322	*CFR 1319–1327*, p. 128
John de Porter of Stebbyng		
from	13 May 1322	*CFR 1319–1327*, p. 128
John L'isle		
to	26 September 1326	*CPR 1319–1327*, p. 322
Stephen de Abyngdon		
from	26 September 1326	*CPR 1319–1327*, p. 322

Wardships

Minority of Humphrey de Bohun, 1361–1363

Stephen atte Roche, William, abbot of Walden and Thomas de Walmesford		
on	26 November 1361	*CPR 1361–1364*, p. 133

Minority of Eleanor and Mary de Bohun, 1373–

Thomas Maundevill		
from	20 February 1374	*CFR 1369–1377*, p. 245
on	22 February 1374	*CPR 1370–1374*, p. 476
Thomas Woodstock		
from	6 October 1376	
confirmed	17 July 1377	*CPR 1377–1381*, p. 66
from	6 October 1377	*CPR 1374–1377*, p. 407

Chantry of the Chapel

John Dirland		
from	28 October 1374	*CPR 1374–1377*, p. 19

Flint

CAERGWRLE (HOPE)

Tenant in Chief		
Prince Edward (II)		
from	7 February 1301	*CPR 1292–1301*, p. 576
Owners		
David ap Griffin		
from	November 1277	Morris, p. 142
to	16 June 1282	Morris, p. 161
forfeited by	24 February 1283	*CWR*, p. 265 (A rebel)
English		
from	1282	
Crown		
on	7 October 1282	*CWR*, p. 240
Queen Eleanor		
by	24 February 1283	*CWR*, p. 265
John de Warenne, earl of Surrey		
on	7 February 1301	*CPR 1292–1301*, p. 576 (For life)
on	7 February 1301	*CChR 1300–1326*, p. 6 (From Prince Edward)
John de Warenne, earl of Surrey		
to king on	1 July 1316	*CPR 1307–1319*, p. 483
and back	6 July 1316	*CPR 1307–1319*, p. 484
to Lancaster	1 January 1319	*CPR 1317–1321*, p. 264
Thomas of Lancaster		
from	1 January 1319	*CPR 1317–1321*, p. 264
John de Warenne, earl of Surrey, as two above		
on	12 December 1346	*CPR 1345–1348*, p. 221
dead by	July 1347	*CFR 1347–1356*, p. 39
Reversions		
Prince Edward		
from	24 November 1312	*CChR 1300–1326*, p. 202
Constables		
Hugh de Pulford		
from	16 June 1282	Morris, p. 161
John de Cromwell, P.P.		
for life from	29 June 1308	*CPR 1307–1313*, p. 76 (Hope)

DYSERTH

Owners		
Crown		
from	1241	*HKW II*, p. 645
to	1254	*HKW II*, p. 645

Crown – Lord Edward		
from	1254	*HKW II*, p. 645
to	1263	*HKW II*, p. 645

Notes
Destroyed by Llwelyn ap Gruffydd, very thoroughly.

FLINT

Owners

Royal		
on	2 January 1278	*CPR 1272–1281*, p. 296
Prince Edward		
from	24 November 1312	*CChR 1300–1326*, p. 202
Crown – Edward the Black Prince		
from	18 March 1333	*CChR 1327–1341*, p. 300
on	30 September 1351	*BPR III*, p. 43

Constables

Gerard de St. Laurence		
to	14 November 1281	*CFR 1272–1307*, p. 146
William de Perton		
on	1282	*CCR 1279–1288*, p. 172
Reynold de Grey of Ruthin and Wilton, P.P.		
from	14 November 1281	*CFR 1272–1307*, p. 146
on	8 October 1283	*CPR 1281–1292*, p. 82
William de la Leye		
on	11 April 1288	*CACW*, XXV.100[1]
Reynold de Grey of Ruthin and Wilton, P.P.		
on	30 June 1290	*CFR 1272–1307*, p. 280
on	20 August 1295	*CCR 1288–1296*, p. 423
Richard de Mascy		
from	7 June 1300	*CFR 1272–1307*, p. 428
William de Ormesby		
to	1 October 1307	*CFR 1307–1319*, p. 5
Robert de Holland, P.P.		
from	1 October 1307	*CFR 1307–1319*, p. 5
to	24 October 1309	*CFR 1307–1319*, p. 50
Payn Tybotot, P.P.		
from	24 October 1309	*CFR 1307–1319*, p. 50
on	19 December 1311	*CPR 1307–1313*, p. 121
not by	30 January 1312	*CCR 1307–1313*, p. 396
Robert de Holland, P.P.		
from	26 December 1311	*CFR 1307–1319*, p. 122
on	30 January 1312	*CCR 1307–1313*, p. 396
Oliver de Ingham, P.P., kn.		
from	19 February 1322	*CPR 1321–1324*, p. 72
from	29 November 1328	*CFR 1327–1337*, p. 113
Henry de Ferrers, P.P.		
to	14 February 1341	*CFR 1337–1347*, p. 214

[1] Confirmed by Reginald de Grey.

Roger Coughill		
on	8 May 1385	*CCR 1381–1385*, p. 549
on	26 September 1386	*CPR 1385–1389*, p. 210
John Golafre		
for life from	30 July 1390	*CPR 1388–1392*, p. 297
to	19 December 1396	*CPR 1396–1399*, p. 49 (R.I.P.)
Nicholas Hauberk, kn.		
from	19 December 1396	*CPR 1396–1399*, p. 49
Henry Percy, son of earl of Northumberland		
for life from	24 October 1399	*CPR 1396–1399*, p. 158
for life from	24 April 1400	*CPR 1399–1401*, p. 28
Nicholas Hauberk, kn.		
on	15 August 1404	*CPR 1401–1405*, p. 411 (Captain)

Gatekeepers

Ralph de Broghton		
on	9 June 1281	*CWR*, p. 189

Surveyor of the Works

Thomas de Holden		
for life from	28 July 1414	*CPR 1413–1416*, p. 232

Constable for the Black Prince

William de Beauchamp and Hugh de Berewyk		
from	14 February 1341	*CFR 1337–1347*, p. 214
Ithel ap Cynfrig Sais		
on	30 September 1351	*BPR III*, p. 43
on	15 April 1357	*BPR III*, p. 272
David de Backarn		
on	2 June 1364	*BPR III*, p. 469

HAWARDEN

Owners

Roger de Clifford		
in	1282	Powicke, p. 419
Robert de Mohaut, P.P.		
died	*26 December 1329*	*GEC IX, p. 15*
dead by	1 January 1330	*CCR 1327–1330*, p. 512
Emma, widow of above		
from	1 January 1330	*CCR 1327–1330*, p. 512 (Livery)
Queen Isabella		
from	23 November 1331	*CPR 1330–1334*, p. 218
to	12 July 1338	*CPR 1338–1340*, p. 114
William de Montague, earl of Salisbury		
from	12 July 1338	*CPR 1338–1340*, p. 114
dead by	30 January 1344	*IPM VIII*, no. 532 (R.I.P.)
William de Montague, earl of Salisbury and Elizabeth his wife		
on	11 September 1358	*BPR III*, p. 311
to	3 June 1398	*IPM* XVII, no. 865 (R.I.P.)
Elizabeth, widow of above		
from	27 November 1397	*CPR 1396–1399*, p. 265 (Jointure)
from	6 November 1399	*IMisc VII*, no. 7

John de Montague, earl of Salisbury (d.1400)		
forfeited before	27 April 1415	*CPR 1413–1416*, p. 306
Elizabeth widow of William de Montague		
restored to	6 November 1399	*CPR 1399–1401*, p. 124
dead by	27 April 1415	*CPR 1413–1416*, p. 306
Thomas duke of Clarence		
reversion granted	2 February 1412	*CPR 1408–1413*, p. 407
from	27 April 1415	*CPR 1413–1416*, p. 306

MOLD

Owners

Robert de Mohaut, P.P.		
on	8 April 1327	*CPR 1327–1330*, p. 96
dead by	1 January 1330	*CCR 1327–1330*, p. 512
Emma, widow of above		
from	1 January 1330	*CCR 1327–1330*, p. 512 (Livery)
Queen Isabella		
on	1 October 1337	*CChR 1327–1341*, p. 431
to	12 July 1338	*CPR 1338–1340*, p. 114
William de Montague, earl of Salisbury		
granted reversion	1 October 1337	*Ancient Deeds vol. III,* A.5572
from	12 July 1338	*CPR 1338–1340*, p. 114
to	10 February 1341	*CPR 1340–1343*, p. 145
William de Montague, earl of Salisbury		
from	10 February 1341	*CPR 1340–1343*, p. 145
jointured	5 February 1363	*BPR IV*, p. 487
to	3 June 1398	*IPM VI*, no. 865 (R.I.P.)
Elizabeth, wife of above		
livery on	8 November 1397	*CCR 1396–1399*, p. 159
from	6 November 1399	*IMisc VII*, no. 7 (Jointure)
John de Montague, earl of Salisbury (d.1400)		
forfeited before	27 April 1415	*CPR 1413–1416*, p. 306
Elizabeth widow of William de Montague		
restored	6 November 1399	*IMisc VII*, no. 7
dead by	27 April 1415	*CPR 1413–1416*, p. 306
Thomas duke of Clarence		
from	27 April 1415	*CPR 1413–1416*, p. 306

OVERTON

History

mentioned	1138,1201	King, p. 155

RHUDDLAN (ROTHELAN?)

Owners

Royal		
on	2 January 1278	*CPR 1272–1281*, p. 296
Prince Edward		
from	24 November 1312	*CChR 1300–1326*, p. 202
Crown – Edward the Black Prince		
from	18 March 1333	*CChR 1327–1341*, p. 300
on	1 December 1377	*CPR 1377–1381*, p. 613

Constables

Reynold de Grey of Ruthin and Wilton, P.P.		
on	30 June 1290	*CPR 1281–1292*, p. 369
on	20 August 1295	*CCR 1288–1296*, p. 423
Robert de Holland, P.P.		
from	1 October 1307	*CFR 1307–1319*, p. 5
to	24 October 1309	*CFR 1307–1319*, p. 50
Payn Tybotot, P.P.		
from	24 October 1309	*CFR 1307–1319*, p. 50
on	19 December 1311	*CPR 1307–1313*, p. 411
not by	30 January 1312	*CCR 1307–1313*, p. 396
Robert de Holland, P.P.		
from	26 December 1311	*CFR 1307–1319*, p. 122
on	30 January 1312	*CCR 1307–1313*, p. 396
Oliver de Ingham		
from	19 February 1322	*CPR 1321–1324*, p. 72
from	29 November 1328	*CFR 1327–1337*, p. 113
Richard de Pembrugg		
to	20 December 1330	*CFR 1327–1337*, p. 209
Res ap Griffith		
from	20 December 1330	*CFR 1327–1337*, p. 209
on	6 October 1331	*CCR 1327–1337*, p. 268
Henry de Ferrers, P.P.		
to	14 February 1341	*CFR 1337–1347*, p. 214
William de Beauchamp and Hugh de Berewyk		
from	14 February 1341	*CFR 1337–1347*, p. 214
Alan Cheyne		
on	15 February 1377	
on	18 March 1381	*CPR 1377–1381*, p. 613
on	8 June 1385	*CPR 1381–1385*, p. 576
Henry Conway, kn.		
reversion	8 June 1385	*CPR 1385–1389*, p. 576
to	28 June 1385	*CPR 1385–1389*, p. 9
William de Drayton, kn.		
from	28 June 1385	*CPR 1385–1389*, p. 9
on	16 June 1387	*CCR 1385–1389*, p. 239
Henry de Conway, kn .		
for life from	17 November 1397	*CPR 1396–1399*, p. 282
confirmed	3 November 1399	*CPR 1399–1401*, p. 47
on	7 February 1406	*CPR 1405–1408*, p. 285

Constables for Edward III while Prince of Wales

Hugh de Sprotton		
on	July–December 1319	*CAPW*, pp. 512–13

Constables for the Black Prince

William de Shaldeford		
for life from	3 July 1346	*BPR I*, p. 3
on	17 September 1346	*BPR I*, p. 17
John de Byntre, kn.		
on	2 September 1352	*BPR III*, p. 77
on	3 October 1362	*BPR III*, p. 452

Surveyor of the Works

Thomas de Holden		
for life from	28 July 1414	*CPR 1413–1416*, p. 232

Glamorgan

BARRY

History

built	early C14	King, p. 160

CAERPHILLY

Owners

Gilbert de Clare		
to	14 December 1295	*IPM III*, no. 371 (R.I.P.)
Joan, widow of Gilbert Clare		
to	1 May 1307	*IPM IV*, no. 435 (R.I.P.)
Gilbert de Clare, son of above		
from	1 May 1307	*IPM IV*, no. 435
to	10 July 1314	*IPM V*, no. 538 (R.I.P.)
Hugh le Despenser, younger, through Eleanor, sister of above		
from	15 November 1317	Davies, p. 24
Taken into king's hands		
on	15 February 1327	*CPR 1327–1330*, p. 13
Queen Philippa		
from	18 April 1330	*CPR 1327–1330*, p. 512
Hugh le Despenser , P.P.		
to	8 February 1349	*IPM IX*, no. 428 (R.I.P.)
Edward le Despenser, kn., son of brother of above, P.P.		
from	8 February 1349	*IPM IX*, no. 428
to	12 November 1375	*IPM XIV*, no. 209 (R.I.P.)
Elizabeth, widow of above		
from	22 February 1376	*CCR 1374–1377*, p. 305
at death		*IMisc. VII*, no. 492
Constance, Dame Despenser		
on	8 September 1403	*CCR 1402–1405*, p. 111

Wardships

Minority of Gilbert Clare, 1307–1312

William son of Richard le Flemmyng		
to	24 June 1307	*CPR 1301–1307*, p. 534
Ralph de Montemer, earl of Gloucester		
from	24 June 1307	*CPR 1301–1307*, p. 534

After death of Gilbert de Clare, 1314

John Giffard		
from	20 April 1316	*CFR 1307–1319*, p. 270

Constables

Richard de Chyverton, king's serjeant		
on	22 November 1271	*CLibR 1267–1272*, 1770 (12d./day)
Roger de Chaundos, P.P.		
from	30 December 1326	*CFR 1319–1327*, p. 430
John de Felton		
to	15 February 1327	*CFR 1327–1337*, p. 120

William la Zouche Mortimer, P.P.		
from	15 February 1327	*CPR 1327–1330*, p. 13
William de Aune		
from	12 March 1329	*CFR 1327–1337*, p. 122
to	5 February 1330	*CFR 1327–1337*, p. 162
Roger Chaundos		
from	5 February 1330	*CFR 1327–1337*, p. 162
to	4 March 1330	*CFR 1327–1337*, p. 163
William de Aune		
from	4 March 1330	*CFR 1327–1337*, p. 163
to	5 April 1330	*CFR 1327–1337*, p. 171
Peter de Veel		
from	5 April 1330	*CFR 1327–1337*, p. 171
to	18 April 1330	*CPR 1327–1337*, p. 512
on	6 June 1330	*CCR 1327–1337*, p. 38

CANDLESTON

History

built	C14	King, p. 162

CARDIFF

Owners

Gilbert de Clare		
to	14 December 1295	*IPM III*, no. 371 (R.I.P.)
Joan, widow of Gilbert Clare		
to	1 May 1307	*IPM IV*, no. 435 (R.I.P.)
Gilbert de Clare, son of above		
from	1 May 1307	*IPM IV*, no. 435
to	10 July 1314	*IPM V*, no. 538 (R.I.P.)
Hugh le Despenser, yng. P.P.		
on	28 October 1326	*CPR 1324–1327*, p. 336
Hugh le Despenser, P.P.		
to	8 February 1349	*IPM IX*, no. 428 (R.I.P.)
Edward le Despenser, Kn., son of brother of above, P.P.		
from	8 February 1349	*IPM IX*, no. 428
to	12 November 1375	*IPM XIV*, no. 209 (R.I.P.)
Thomas le Despenser, son of above		
from	12 November 1375	*IPM XIV*, no. 209
forfeited	5 January 1400	*IMisc VII*, no. 492

Wardships

Minority of Gilbert Clare, 1307–1312

Henry de Lancarvan		
to	24 June 1307	*CPR 1301–1307*, p. 534
Ralph de Montemer, earl of Gloucester		
from	24 June 1307	*CPR 1301–1307*, p. 534

After death of Gilbert de Clare, 1314–

Payn de Turbervill		
to reside in the castle	1 December 1315	*CACW*, XXXI.154

John Giffard		
from	10 February 1316	*CPR 1313–1317*, p. 433
from	20 April 1316	*CFR 1307–1319*, p. 270

Minority of Thomas Despenser, 1375–1394

Richard Storey		
from	19 March 1376	*CPR 1374–1377*, p. 251
from	22 June 1377	*CPR 1377–1381*, p. 6

Constables

Henry de Pembrigg		
to	14 July 1297	*CPR 1292–1301*, p. 292
Richard Talbot		
from	14 July 1297	*CPR 1292–1301*, p. 292
Payn Turbervill		
on	1 December 1315	*CPR 1313–1317*, p. 370
to	10 February 1316	*CPR 1313–1317*, p. 433
John Giffard of Brimpsfield		
from	10 February 1316	*CPR 1313–1317*, p. 433
William Wye		
in	c.1403	C. Given Wilson, *The Chronicle of Adam Usk, 1377–1421*, Oxford, 1997, p. 173

Private Constables

Roger Graunt		
on	28 October 1326	*CPR 1324–1327*, p. 336

CASTELL COCH

History

built	early C13?	King, p. 162
built	late C13 or early C14	King, p. 162
rebuilt	C19	King, p. 162

CHERITON

History

mentioned	1396	King, p. 171

COYTY

Tenant in Chief

Gilbert de Clare–		
to	10 July 1314	*IPM V*, no. 538 (R.I.P.)
Hugh le Despenser		
to	8 February 1349	*IPM IX*, no. 428
Edward le Despenser, nephew of above		
from	8 February 1349	*IPM IX*, no. 428
Richard le Despenser		
on	18 October 1411	*IPM XIX*, no. 989

Owners

Payn Turbervill		
on	10 July 1314	*IPM V*, no. 538
Richard de Turbervill		
on	8 February 1349	*IPM IX*, no. 428

Alexander Berkkerolles		
on	13 November 1404	*CCR 1402–1405*, p. 479
Laurence Berkkerolles, kn.		
to	18 October 1411	*CFR 1405–1413*, p. 226
to	18 October 1411	*IPM XIX*, no. 989
William Gamage and Sarah his wife, fourth sister of Turbervill		
from	18 October 1411	*IPM XIX*, no. 990
writ	16 January 1412	*IPM XIX*, no. 990

DINAS POWIS

Owners

Joan, widow of Gilbert Clare		
to	1 May 1307	*IPM IV*, no. 435 (R.I.P.)
Gilbert de Clare, son of above–		
from	1 May 1307	*IPM IV*, no. 435
Isabel, widow of John de Sutton		
to	10 April 1397	*IPM XVIII*, no. 432 (R.I.P.)
John de Sutton of Dudley, her great grand son		
from	10 April 1397	*IPM XVIII*, no. 432 (Age 21)
on	4 March 1400	*CCR 1399–1402*, p. 251

FONMON

History

built	early C13	King, p. 163
modified	C13–C14	King, p. 164

KENFIG

Owners

Gilbert de Clare		
to	14 December 1295	*IPM III*, no. 371 (R.I.P.)
Joan, widow of Gilbert Clare		
to	1 May 1307	*IPM IV*, no. 435 (R.I.P.)
Gilbert de Clare, son of above–		
from	1 May 1307	*IPM IV*, no. 435
to	10 July 1314	*IPM V*, no. 538 (R.I.P.)
Hugh le Despenser, younger, through Eleanor, sister of above		
from	15 November 1317	Davies, p. 24
Hugh de Despenser, P.P.		
to	8 February 1349	*IPM IX*, no. 428 (R.I.P.)
Elizabeth, widow of Hugh Despenser (and Giles de Badelesmere), from above		
from	8 February 1349	*IPM IX*, no. 428
to	30 May 1359	*IPM X*, no. 523 (R.I.P.) (Dower)
Edward le Despenser, kn., nephew of Hugh above, P.P.		
from	30 May 1359	*IPM X*, no. 523
to	12 November 1375	*IPM XIV*, no. 209 (R.I.P.)
Thomas le Despenser, son of above		
from	12 November 1375	*IPM XIV*, no. 209
forfeited	5 January 1400	*IMisc VII*, no. 492
dead by	6 April 1405	*CPR 1405–1408*, p. 4

Richard le Despenser		
under age on	6 April 1405	*CPR 1405–1408*, p. 4
Constance, widow of Thomas Lord Despenser		
from	8 December 1415	*CPR 1413–1416*, p. 246

Constables for Despensers

Thomas Sprotley		
for life from	21 October 1395	
confirmed	16 September 1400	*CPR 1399–1401*, p. 336

Wardships

Minority of Gilbert Clare, 1307–1312–

Roger de Lyt		
to	24 June 1307	*CPR 1301–1307*, p. 534
Ralph de Montemer, earl of Gloucester		
from	24 June 1307	*CPR 1301–1307*, p. 534

After death of Gilbert de Clare, 1314—

John Giffard		
from	20 April 1316	*CFR 1307–1319*, p. 270

Minority of Thomas Despenser, 1375–1394

Richard Storey		
from	19 March 1376	*CPR 1374–1377*, p. 251
from	22 June 1377	*CPR 1377–1381*, p. 6

Minority of Richard Despenser, 1400–

Constance, widow of Thomas le Despenser, mother of Richard		
from	20 February 1400	*CFR 1399–1405*, p. 48
Edward, duke of York		
from	17 May 1403	*CPR 1401–1405*, p. 235
Queen Joan		
from	6 April 1405	*CPR 1405–1408*, p. 4

LLANBLETHIAN

Owners

Gilbert de Clare		
to	10 July 1314	*IPM V*, no. 538 (R.I.P.)
Hugh le Despenser, younger, through Eleanor, sister of above		
from	15 November 1317	Davies, p. 24
Hugh de Despenser, P.P.		
to	8 February 1349	*IPM IX*, no. 428 (R.I.P.)
Elizabeth, widow of Hugh Despenser (and Giles de Badelesmere) from above		
from	8 February 1349	*IPM IX*, no. 428
to	30 May 1359	*IPM X*, no. 523 (R.I.P.) (Dower)
Edward le Despenser, kn., nephew of Hugh above, P.P.		
heir on	30 May 1359	*IPM X*, no. 523
to	12 November 1375	*IPM XIV*, no. 209 (R.I.P.)
Elizabeth, widow of above		
from	22 February 1376	*CCR 1374–1377*, p. 305
to	death	*IMisc VII*, no. 492

Wardships

After death of Gilbert de Clare, 1314—

John Giffard		
from	20 April 1316	*CFR 1307–1319*, p. 270

Minority of Thomas Despenser, 1375–1394

Richard Storey		
from	19 March 1376	*CPR 1374–1377*, p. 251
from	22 June 1377	*CPR 1377–1381*, p. 6

LLANDAFF

History

built	c.1300	King, p. 164
siege	temp. Glendower	King, p. 164

LLANEILO TALYBONT

History

mentioned	1215,1396	King, p. 165

LLANGYNWYD

Owners

Gilbert de Clare		
to	14 December 1295	*IPM III*, no. 371 (R.I.P.)
Gilbert de Clare, son of above–		
from	14 December 1295	*IPM III*, no. 371
Joan, widow of Gilbert de Clare		
to	1 May 1307	*IPM IV*, no. 435 (R.I.P.) (Langunyth)
Gilbert de Clare, son of above–		
from	1 May 1307	*IPM IV*, no. 435 (Langunyth)

LLANTRISANT

Owners

Joan, widow of Gilbert Clare		
to	1 May 1307	*IPM IV*, no. 435 (R.I.P.)
Gilbert de Clare		
to	10 July 1314	*IPM V*, no. 538 (R.I.P.)
Hugh le Despenser, younger, through Eleanor, sister of above		
from	15 November 1317	Davies, p. 24
Hugh de Despenser, P.P.		
to	8 February 1349	*IPM IX*, no. 428 (R.I.P.)
Edward le Despenser, kn., nephew of above, P.P.		
from	8 February 1349	*IPM IX*, no. 428
on	Midsummer 1374	
to	12 November 1375	*IPM XIV*, no. 209 (R.I.P.)
Thomas le Despenser, son of above		
from	12 November 1375	*IPM XIV*, no. 209
forfeited	5 January 1400	*IMisc VII*, no. 492
dead by	6 April 1405	*CPR 1405–1408*, p. 4
Richard le Despenser		
minor on	6 April 1405	*CPR 1405–1408*, p. 4
Constance, widow of Thomas Lord Despenser		
from	8 December 1415	*CPR 1413–1416*, p. 246

Constables

William de Flemmyng		
from	20 May 1316	*CCR 1313–1318*, p. 289
from	6 June 1316	*CFR 1307–1319*, p. 283

Private Constables

William Davyntre, esq., for Despensers		
from	Midsummer 1374	
confirmed	15 April 1391	*CPR 1388–1392*, p. 398

Wardships

Minority of Gilbert Clare, 1307–1312–

Robert le Seer		
to	24 June 1307	*CPR 1301–1307*, p. 534
Ralph de Montemer, earl of Gloucester		
from	24 June 1307	*CPR 1301–1307*, p. 534

After death of Gilbert de Clare, 1314—

John Giffard		
from	20 April 1316	*CFR 1307–1319*, p. 270
William de Flemmyng		
from	20 May 1316	*CCR 1313–1318*, p. 289
from	6 June 1316	*CFR 1307–1319*, p. 283

Minority of Thomas Despenser, 1375–1394

Richard Storey		
from	19 March 1376	*CPR 1374–1377*, p. 251
from	22 June 1377	*CPR 1377–1381*, p. 6

Wardship of Richard Despenser, 1400–

Constance, widow of Thomas le Despenser, mother of Richard		
from	20 February 1400	*CFR 1399–1405*, p. 48
Edward, duke of York		
from	17 May 1403	*CPR 1401–1405*, p. 235
Queen Joan		
from	6 April 1405	*CPR 1405–1408*, p. 4

LOUGHOR

Owners

John de Mowbray, P.P.		
to	1322	McKisack, p. 73
lost by	9 July 1322	*CChR 1300–1326*, p. 448
Hugh le Despenser, yng, P.P. and Eleanor his wife (Loghern)		
from	May 1322	McKisack, p. 73
to	10 July 1322	*CPR 1321–1324*, p. 176
Elizabeth, widow of John de Burgo (Loghern)		
from	10 July 1322	*CPR 1321–1324*, p. 176
William de Brewose		
to	22 June 1324	*Ancient Deeds vol. III*, A.4876
Hugh Despenser, earl of Winchester		
from	22 June 1324	*Ancient Deeds vol. III*, A.4876

MORLAIS

Owners

Gilbert de Clare		
temp	1287–1290	*GCH III*, p. 431
to	1295	*GCH III*, p. 431 (R.I.P.)

NEATH

Owners

Gilbert de Clare		
to	14 December 1295	*IPM III*, no. 371 (R.I.P.)
Joan, widow of Gilbert Clare		
to	1 May 1307	*IPM IV*, no. 435 (R.I.P.)
Gilbert de Clare, son of above		
from	1 May 1307	*IPM IV*, no. 435
to	10 July 1314	*IPM V*, no. 538 (R.I.P.)
Hugh le Despenser, younger, through Eleanor, sister of above		
from	15 November 1317	Davies, p. 24
Queen Philippa		
from	12 February 1330	
on	20 May 1330	*CCR 1330–1333*, p. 37
Hugh de Despenser, P.P.		
to	8 February 1349	*IPM IX*, no. 428 (R.I.P.)
Elizabeth, widow of Hugh Despenser and Giles de Badelesmere		
from	8 February 1349	*IPM IX*, no. 428
to	30 May 1359	*IPM X*, no. 523 (R.I.P.) (Dower)
Edward le Despenser, kn., P.P.		
from	30 May 1359	*IPM X*, no. 523
to	12 November 1375	*IPM XIV*, no. 209 (R.I.P.)
Thomas le Despenser, son of above		
from	12 November 1375	*IPM XIV*, no. 209
forfeited	5 January 1400	*IMisc VII*, no. 492
Constance, widow of Thomas Lord Despenser		
from	8 December 1415	*CPR 1413–1416*, p. 246

Wardships

Minority of Gilbert Clare, 1307–1312

John de Wynton		
to	24 June 1307	*CPR 1302–1307*, p. 534
Ralph de Montemer, earl of Gloucester		
from	24 June 1307	*CPR 1302–1307*, p. 534

After death of Gilbert de Clare, 1314–

John Giffard		
from	20 April 1316	*CFR 1307–1319*, p. 270

Minority of Thomas Despenser, 1375–1394

Richard Storey		
from	19 March 1376	*CPR 1374–1377*, p. 251
from	22 June 1377	*CPR 1377–1381*, p. 6

Constables

Peter de Straddeleye		
to	14 July 1297	*CPR 1292–1301*, p. 292
Walter Hakelute		
from	14 July 1297	*CPR 1292–1301*, p. 292

Robert le Norreis		
on	26 October 1298	*Ancient Deeds I*, B.2731
Nicholas de Kyngeston and John Iweyn		
from	16 May 1321	*CPR 1317–1321*, p. 584
Hugh Hakelut		
from	24 February 1330	*CFR 1327–1337*, p. 166

OGMORE

Tenant in Chief

Edward le Despenser		
on	23 March 1361	*IPM XI*, no. 118

Owners

Henry, earl of Lancaster		
on	31 October 1327	Somerville, p. 357
to	1333	DL.27/192
Henry, duke of Lancaster		
from	1333	DL.27/192
to	23 March 1361	*IPM XI*, no. 118 (R.I.P.)
Maud, his daughter, late the wife of William, duke of Bavaria		
to	10 April 1362	*IPM XI*, no. 299 (R.I.P.)
John of Gaunt		
from	10 April 1362	*IPM XI*, no. 299
on	6 August 1372	*JGR 1372–1376*, no. 110

Private Constables

David ap Llewellyn		
on	31 October 1327	Somerville, p. 357
John Wrenche		
from	14 November 1371	*JGR 1372–1376*, no. 882
on	6 August 1372	*JGR 1372–1376*, no. 110

OXWICH

History

mentioned	1396	King, p. 167

Owners

Manor held by de la Mare family		
	C13–C14	*GCH I*, p. 210

OYSTERMOUTH

Owners

John de Mowbray, P.P.		
to	1322	
Hugh le Despenser, yng., P.P. and Eleanor his wife		
from	May 1322	McKisack, p. 73
from	9 July 1322	*CChR 1300–1326*, p. 448
to	10 July 1322	*CPR 1318–1323*, p. 176
Elizabeth, widow of John de Burgo		
from	10 July 1322	*CPR 1318–1323*, p. 176
William de Brewose		
to	22 June 1324	*Ancient Deeds vol. III*, A.4876

Hugh Despenser, earl of Winchester		
from	22 June 1324	*Ancient Deeds vol. III*, A.4876
Thomas de Beauchamp, earl of Warwick		
to	13 November 1369	*IPM XII*, no. 326 (R.I.P.)
Thomas de Beauchamp, earl of Warwick, son of above		
from	13 November 1369	*IPM XII*, no. 326
from	7 February 1370	*CCR 1369–1374*, p. 123
forfeited	1397	
Richard de Beauchamp, earl of Warwick		
on	12 May 1401	*CFR 1399–1405*, p. 135

Wardships

Minority of Richard Beauchamp, earl of Warwick (aged 19 in 1401)

Thomas de Aldebury		
from	12 May 1401	*CFR 1399–1405*, p. 135

PENARD

Owners

William de Brewose, lord of Gower		
on	1317	*RCH*, p. 288
John de Mowbray, P.P.		
to	1322	McKisack, p. 73
Hugh Despenser, lord of Glamorgan, yng., P.P. and Eleanor his wife		
from	May 1322	McKisack, p. 73
from	9 July 1322	*CChR 1300–1326*, p. 448
from	1322	*RCH*, p. 289
Lords of Gower		
soon after	1322	*RCH*, p. 289
Hugh le Despenser and Eleanor his wife		
to	10 July 1322	*CPR 1321–1324*, p. 176
Elizabeth, widow of John de Burgo		
from	10 July 1322	*CPR 1321–1324*, p. 176
William de Brewose		
to	22 June 1324	*Ancient Deeds vol. III*, A.4876
Hugh Despenser, earl of Winchester		
from	22 June 1324	*Ancient Deeds vol. III*, A.4876

PENLLE'R CASTELL

Owners

William de Brewose		
	late C13	*GCH III*, p. 226
John lord Mowbray		
to	1354	*GCH III*, p. 226
Thomas Beauchamp, earl of Warwick		
from	1354	*GCH III*, p. 226
to	1369	*GCH III*, p. 226 (R.I.P.)

PENMARK

History

built	C14	King, p. 168
mentioned	1362	King, p. 168

PENRICE

Owners

Robert de Penres		
to	1283	*GCH III*, p. 434 (R.I.P.)
Robert de Penres		
on	20 June 1367	*CPR 1364–1367*, p. 413

PORT EYNON

History

mentioned	1396	King, p. 172

Notes

possibly a thirteenth century fortified house?	*G.C.H. III*, p. 444

ST. DONAT'S

Owners

Thomas de Havey		
before	1298	C.J. Spurgeon, 'St. Donat's Castle', *The Archaeological Journal*, 150 (1993), p. 502
Peter de Stradling, husband of Joan, daughter of above		
marriage	1297	Spurgeon, p. 502

ST. FAGANS

Tenant in Chief

Richard Lord Despenser		
on	14 January 1411	*IPM XIX*, no. 1055

Owners

Peter de Veel and Henry de Percehay quitclaim their right to Henry Waryner of Charfeld and John Russel of Segre

on	20 February 1376	*CPR 1374–1377*, p. 247
John Veel, esquire.		
to	14 January 1411	*IPM XIX*, no. 1055 (R.I.P.)
John Veel, son of above		
from	14 January 1411	*IPM XIX*, no. 1055

SWANSEA

Owners

William de Brewose II		
from	1241	*GCH III*, p. 225
to	1290	*GCH III*, p. 225
William de Brewose III		
from	1290	*GCH III*, p. 231
John de Mowbray, P.P.		
to	1322	McKisack, p. 73
Hugh le Despenser, yng, P.P. and Eleanor his wife		
from	May 1322	McKisack, p. 73
from	9 July 1322	*CChR 1300–1326*, p. 448
to	10 July 1322	*CPR 1321–1324*, p. 176

Elizabeth, widow of John de Burgo		
from	10 July 1322	*CPR 1321–1324*, p. 176
William de Brewose		
to	22 June 1324	*Ancient Deeds vol. III*, A.4876
Hugh Despenser, earl of Winchester		
from	22 June 1324	*Ancient Deeds vol. III*, A.4876
John, lord Mowbray		
from	1331	*GCH III*, p. 247
to	1354	*GCH III*, p. 247
Thomas de Beauchamp, earl of Warwick		
from	1354	*GCH III*, p. 249
to	13 November 1369	*IPM XII*, no. 326 (R.I.P.)
Thomas de Beauchamp, earl of Warwick, son of above		
from	13 November 1369	*IPM XII*, no. 326
from	7 February 1370	*CCR 1369–1374*, p. 123
quitclaimed away	2 June 1397	*CCR 1396–1399*, p. 123
William de Beauchamp, lord of Abergavenny		
quitclaimed away	17 May 1397	*CCR 1396–1399*, p. 125
Thomas de Mowbray, duke of Norfolk		
quitclaimed to	2 June 1397	*CCR 1396–1399*, p. 123
quitclaimed to	17 May 1397	*CCR 1396–1399*, p. 125
to	22 September 1399	*IPM XVII*, no. 265 (R.I.P.)
Thomas de Mowbray, earl Marshall, son of above		
from	22 September 1399	*IPM XVII*, no. 265 (Age 14)
1/3 held by Elizabeth, widow of duke of Norfolk and Robert Gousil (R.I.P.)		
to	20 July 1403	*IPM XVIII*, no. 925 (R.I.P.)
livery	12 November 1403	*CCR 1402–1405*, p. 209
Thomas de Mowbray, earl Marshall		
by	29 August 1405	*CPR 1405–1409*, p. 44
to	4 June 1405	*IPM XVIII*, no. 316 (R.I.P.)
John de Mowbray, brother of above		
heir on	4 June 1405	*IPM XVIII*, no. 316
gained possession	1413	*GCH III*, p. 256

Private Constables

Bernard Pee de Fer for Brewose		
to	1321	Davies, p. 58
requests to be reinstalled	1322–1324	*CAPW*, p. 226

Constable

Richard Beauchamp, earl of Warwick		
for life from	29 August 1405	*CPR 1405–1409*, p. 44

Steward and receiver during wardship

Hugh de Waterton, kn.		
from	6 December 1399	*CPR 1399–1401*, p. 265
on	6 May 1401	*CPR 1399–1401*, p. 478

Wardship

minority of Thomas de Mowbray, earl Marshall, 1399–1405

John de Lancaster, John Lewes, Richard fitz Nicholl, John de St. John		
from	30 May 1403	*CFR 1399–1405*, p. 213

TALAVAN

Owners

Joan, widow of Gilbert de Clare		
to	1 May 1307	*IPM IV*, no. 435 (R.I.P.)
Gilbert de Clare, son of above–		
from	1 May 1307	*IPM IV*, no. 435
to	10 July 1314	*IPM V*, no. 538 (R.I.P.)
Hugh le Despenser, younger, through Eleanor, sister of above		
from	15 November 1317	Davies, p. 24
Hugh de Despenser, P.P.		
to	8 February 1349	*IPM IX*, no. 428
Elizabeth, widow of Hugh Despenser and Giles de Badelesmere		
from	8 February 1349	*IPM IX*, no. 428
to	30 May 1359	*IPM X*, no. 523 (R.I.P.)
Edward le Despenser, kn., P.P.		
from	30 May 1359	*IPM X*, no. 581
to	12 November 1375	*IPM XIV*, no. 209 (R.I.P.)
Elizabeth, mother of Thomas le Despenser, widow of above		
to death		*IMisc VII*, no. 492

Wardships

After death of Gilbert de Clare, 1314—

John Giffard		
from	20 April 1316	*CFR 1307–1319*, p. 270

WEOBLEY (LEYSHANSTON)

History

built	late C13	King, p. 170
modified	early C14	King, p. 170
mentioned	1396,1409	King, p. 170
in use to	mid C16	King, p. 170

WHITCHURCH (RHIWBINA)

Owners

Gilbert de Clare		
to	10 July 1314	*IPM V*, no. 538 (R.I.P.)
Hugh le Despenser, younger, through Eleanor, sister of above		
from	15 November 1317	Davies, p. 24
Hugh le Despenser, P.P.		
to	8 February 1349	*IPM IX*, no. 428 (R.I.P.)
Edward le Despenser, son of brother of above, P.P.		
from	8 February 1349	*IPM IX*, no. 428
Elizabeth, mother of Thomas le Despenser		
to death		*IMisc VII*, no. 492

Gloucestershire

Unknown Licenses

CRUMHALE for William de Wauton		
	9 February 1311	*CPR 1307–1313*, p. 346
CULVERDEN for Henry de Wylington		
	9 May 1318	*CPR 1317–1321*, p. 141
STANLEY POUNDELARGE for John le Rous of Ragley		
	19 December 1391	*CPR 1388–1392*, p. 46
LITTLE CUMPTON for John Romeyn, archbishop of York		
	11 November 1291	*CPR 1281–1292*, p. 451

BERKELEY

Owners

Thomas de Berkeley, P.P.		
to	3 August 1321	*IPM VI*, no. 332 (R.I.P.)
Maurice de Berkeley, P.P. son of above		
from	3 August 1321	*IPM VI*, no. 332
forfeited	7 February 1322	*CFR 1319–1327*, p. 91 (R.I.P.)
Thomas Berkeley, son of above, P.P.		
from	1327	*IPM VII*, no. 97
to	1362	*IPM XI*, no. 121 (R.I.P.)
Maurice Berkeley, son of above, P.P.		
from	10 November 1361	*CCR 1360–1364*, p. 236
to	8 June 1368	*IPM XII*, no. 217 (R.I.P.)
Thomas Berkeley, son of above, P.P.		
from	8 June 1368	*IPM XII*, no. 217
died	*1417*	*GEC II*, p. 130
Thomas Berkeley, grandson of above		
from	1 December 1417	*CFR 1413–1422*, p. 212

Constables

Simon de Driby		
from	13 February 1322	*CFR 1319–1327*, p. 96
to	2 August 1322	*CFR 1319–1327*, p. 175 (R.I.P.)
James de Broughton		
from	2 August 1322	*CFR 1319–1327*, p. 175
Robert de Mucheldeure		
to	3 March 1324	*CFR 1319–1327*, p. 260
John Frelond		
from	3 March 1324	*CFR 1319–1327*, p. 257
to	15 October 1326	*CPR 1319–1327*, p. 327
Thomas de Bradeston, P.P.		
from	15 October 1326	*CPR 1319–1327*, p. 327

Receivers

James de Broughton, king's Clerk		
on	20 May 1322	*CFR 1319–1327*, p. 131

Wardships

Minority of Thomas de Berkeley (1417–)

John Harewell, John Barton and John Baysham		
from	21 July 1417	*CFR 1413–1422*, p. 207
to	1 December 1417	*CFR 1413–1422*, p. 212

BEVERSTONE

Owners

Thomas ap Adam		
on	12 January 1326	*CPR 1324–1327*, p. 237
to	11 April 1330	*CPR 1327–1330*, p. 507
Thomas de Berkeley, P.P.		
from	11 April 1330	*CPR 1327–1330*, p. 607
on	20 June 1352	*CPR 1350–1354*, p. 294
Thomas de Berkeley, P.P. , Katherine, his second wife and their heirs male		
from	13 April 1354	NRA 21647 A1/12/01/007/00/00
to	1362	*IPM XI*, no. 121 (R.I.P.)
Katherine, widow and second wife of Thomas Berkeley		
on	30 November 1361	*CCR 1360–1364*, p. 236
to	13 March 1386	*IPM XVI*, no. 217
John de Berkeley, kn., son of above		
from	13 March 1386	*IPM XVI*, no. 217

Private constables for Thomas ap Adam

William Thurmond		
quitclaimed rights on	23 June 1330	NRA 21647 A1/12/03/001/01/00

BRIMPSFIELD

Owners

John Giffard of Brimpsfield, P.P.		
to	12 February 1327	*IPM VII*, no. 78
Aveline, widow of above		
from	17 March 1327	*CCR 1327–1330*, p. 58
John de Caillewe		
to	19 May 1330	*CPR 1327–1330*, p. 527
John Mautravers		
from	19 May 1330	*CPR 1327–1330*, p. 527
forfeited by	8 April 1340	*CPR 1338–1340*, p. 446
Maurice de Berkeley		
from	8 April 1340	*CPR 1338–1340*, p. 446 (in fee)
on	1 March 1342	*CCR 1341–1343*, p. 391
to	12 February 1347	*IPM IX*, no. 46 (R.I.P.)
Thomas de Berkeley, son of above		
from	12 February 1347	*IPM IX*, no. 46

Constables

Maurice de Berkeley		
for life	15 May 1338	*CCR 1337–1339*, p. 370
on	12 October 1338	*CCR 1337–1339*, p. 549

BRISTOL

Owners		
Queen Eleanor of Castile		
from	22 October 1275	*CChR 1257–1300*, p. 192
Crown		
on	6 April 1308	*CCR 1307–1313*, p. 29
Crown – Queen Isabella		
from	1327	*HKW II*, p. 580
to	1330	*HKW II*, p. 580
Crown – Queen Philippa		
from	1 January 1331	*CPR 1330–1334*, p. 55
to	1369	*HKW II*, p. 581 (R.I.P.)
Crown – Queen Anne		
for life from	24 May 1382	*CPR 1381–1385*, p. 125
to	1394	*HKW II*, p. 581 (R.I.P.)
Crown – Queen Joan		
from	1403	*HKW II*, p. 581
to	1437	*HKW II*, p. 581
Constables		
Robert de Muscegros		
on	27 February 1274	*CCR 1272–1279*, p. 71
to	12 July 1275	*CFR 1272–1307*, p. 53
Bartholomew le Juvene		
from	12 July 1275	*CFR 1272–1307*, p. 53
to	16 October 1277	*CFR 1272–1307*, p. 82 (R.I.P.)
Peter de la Mare		
from	16 October 1277	*CFR 1272–1307*, p. 82
to	26 October 1291	*CPR 1281–1292*, p. 448 (R.I.P.)
Ralph de Mercato		
from	26 October 1291	*CFR 1272–1307*, p. 297
from	26 October 1291	*CPR 1282–1292*, p. 448
Nicholas Fermbald		
on	2 January 1293	*CPR 1292–1301*, p. 59
to	21 August 1307	*CFR 1307–1319*, p. 2
Bartholomew de Badelesmere, P.P.		
from	21 August 1307	*CFR 1307–1319*, p. 2
to	30 January 1312	*CFR 1307–1319*, p. 122
Edmund de Mauley		
on	24 January 1312	*CCR 1307–1313*, p. 400
on	20 April 1312	*CPR 1307–1313*, p. 452
Bartholomew de Badelesmere, P.P.		
on	30 July 1312	*CPR 1307–1313*, p. 483
to	1 October 1320	*CFR 1319–1327*, p. 33
Hugh le Despenser, yng, P.P.		
from	1 October 1320	*CFR 1319–1327*, p. 33
to	10 May 1321	*CFR 1319–1327*, p. 56
Matthew and John de Clyvedon		
from	10 May 1321	*CFR 1319–1327*, p. 56
tó	15 May 1321	*CFR 1319–1327*, p. 56

Richard Lovel		
from	15 May 1321	*CFR 1319–1327*, p. 56
to	3 May 1322	*CFR 1319–1327*, p. 126
Hugh le Despenser yng, P.P.		
from	3 May 1322	*CFR 1319–1327*, p. 126
on	3 July 1322	*CCR 1318–1323*, p. 469
Richard de Rodeneye		
on	16 August 1322	*CCR 1318–1323*, p. 595
Hugh le Despenser yng, P.P.		
on	17 April 1323	*CCR 1318–1323*, p. 637
to	21 October 1326	*CFR 1319–1327*, p. 421
Gilbert de Clenkerny and Robert Fleming and Burgesius de Tyle		
from	21 October 1326	*CFR 1319–1327*, p. 421
Thomas de Gournay		
on	15 December 1328	*CCR 1327–1330*, p. 352
Roger Mortimer, earl of March		
for life from	16 August 1330	*CFR 1327–1337*, p. 187
Maurice de Berkeley		
to	22 January 1331	*CPR 1330–1334*, p. 47
Almaric la Zousch		
from	22 January 1331	*CPR 1330–1334*, p. 47
John de Hegham		
confirmed	12 June 1335	*CPR 1334–1338*, p. 123 (For Queen)
John la Ryvere		
during	1338	E.101/21/20
from	2 August 1338	E.101/21/34
to	14 February 1342	E.101/21/34
Robert Flambard		
on	12 September 1347	*CCR 1346–1349*, p. 319
Edmund Flambard for the Queen		
on	25 August 1347	*CCR 1346–1349*, p. 390
on	17 March 1360	*CCR 1358–1361*, p. 15
Robert de Fouleshurst (for Queen)		
on	17 March 1361	*CPR 1358–1361*, p. 570 (For life)
to	2 April 1369	
Hugh de Segrave, queen's esquire		
from	2 April 1369 (For Queen)	
confirmed	20 August 1369	*CPR 1367–1370*, p. 335
to	15 July 1373	*CPR 1370–1374*, p. 327 (Kn.)
John de Thorpe		
from	15 July 1373	*CPR 1370–1374*, p. 327 (Knight)
on	13 January 1386	*CPR 1385–1389*, p. 79 (For life)
Queen Anne		
on	26 February 1389	*CPR 1388–1392*, p. 23
Thomas Beaupyne		
for life from	3 November 1399	*CPR 1399–1401*, p. 45

Underconstables

Peter de la Mare		
to	16 October 1277	*CFR 1272–1307*, p. 82

Porters

John Dave		
to	13 September 1394	*CPR 1391–1396*, p. 480
Richard Marets		
for life from	13 September 1394	*CPR 1391–1396*, p. 480

GLOUCESTER

Owners

Queen Eleanor of Provence		
from	17 September 1273	*CPR 1272–1281*, p. 31
to	1291	*HK.W. II*, p. 654
Crown		
from	1291	*HK.W. II*, p. 654
on	6 April 1308	*CCR 1307–1313*, p. 29
Queen Margaret		
from	10 September 1299	*CPR 1292–1301*, p. 451
confirmed	19 March 1310	*CPR 1307–1313*, p. 216
Crown – Queen Isabella		
on	20 April 1327	*CMR*, no. 40
from	29 September 1330	
not by	4 July 1334	*CCR 1333–1337*, p. 234
Seized by King		
on	20 July 1397	*CFR 1391–1399*, p. 219

Superior Custody

Hugh le Despenser, yng		
from	2 November 1322	*CPR 1321–1324*, p. 214

Constables

Matthew Becill		
on	9 July 1252	*IMisc I*, no. 154
not by	25 April 1270	*CLibR 1267–1272*, no. 1059
Peter de Chaumpvent		
on	6 Feb 1269	*CLibR 1267–1272*, no. 591
to	17 September 1273	*CCR 1272–1279*, p. 31
Imbert de Monte Ferrandi		
on	28 December 1278	*CCR 1272–1279*, p. 434
Walter de Beauchamp		
on	23 October 1291	*CCR 1288–1296*, p. 181
on	6 May 1299	*CCR 1296–1302*, p. 247
John Botetourt		
on	16 July 1299	*CCR 1296–1302*, p. 258
Walter de Beauchamp		
on	14 April 1300	*CCR 1296–1302*, p. 349
on	26 September 1300	*CCR 1296–1302*, p. 367
Alice, widow of Walter de Beauchamp		
from	18 February 1303	*CFR 1272–1307*, p. 469
Walter de Gloucester		
on	22 July 1305	*CCR 1302–1307*, p. 282
to	12 March 1308	*CPR 1307–1313*, p. 58
Nicholas de Kyngeston		
from	12 March 1308	*CPR 1307–1313*, p. 58
to	2 December 1308	*CPR 1307–1313*, p. 96

Roger Damory, P.P.		
from	24 October 1317	*CPR 1317–1321*, p. 38
to	1 November 1317	*CPR 1317–1321*, p. 46
Richard de la Ryvere		
from	1 November 1317	*CPR 1317–1321*, p. 46
Edmund de Woodstock, earl of Kent		
for life from	16 February 1318	*CPR 1317–1321*, p. 105
to	24 April 1320	*CFR 1319–1327*, p. 20
Richard Lovel		
from	24 April 1320	*CFR 1319–1327*, p. 20
to	12 May 1321	*CPR 1317–1321*, p. 578
Edmund de Woodstock, earl of Kent		
from	12 May 1321	*CPR 1317–1321*, p. 578
Simon de Driby		
temp	1322	E.101/531/6
from	13 February 1322	*CFR 1319–1327*, p. 96
to	2 August 1322	*CFR 1319–1327*, p. 175 (R.I.P.)
James de Broughton		
from	2 August 1322	*CFR 1319–1327*, p. 175
to	1 November 1322	*CFR 1319–1327*, p. 182
Gilbert Talbot, P.P.		
from	1 November 1322	*CFR 1319–1327*, p. 182
on	6 October 1326	*CFR 1319–1327*, p. 420
Maurice de Berkeley		
from	26 December 1328	*CPR 1327–1330*, p. 345
Thomas de Bradeston, P.P.		
on	14 February 1331	*CCR 1330–1333*, p. 205
for life from	25 February 1331	*CFR 1327–1337*, p. 238
on	2 October 1331	*CCR 1330–1333*, p. 265
Gilbert Talbot		
on	12 October 1331	*CCR 1330–1333*, p. 268
Thomas de Bradeston, P.P.		
on	6 January 1332	*CCR 1330–1333*, p. 520
for life from	23 February 1334	*CFR 1327–1337*, p. 407
on	22 September 1345	*CPR 1343–1345*, p. 551
not by	12 October 1348	*CPR 1345–1348*, p. 225
Simon Basset		
from	12 November 1346	*CFR 1337–1347*, p. 462
Thomas de Bradeston, P.P.		
on	1 February 1350	*CPR 1348–1350*, p. 461
to	25 August 1360	*IPM* X, no. 614 (R.I.P.)
James de Audley		
for life from	14 September 1360	*CPR 1358–1361*, p. 458
to	23 August 1369	*IPM* XII, no. 157 (R.I.P.)
Peter de Veel		
for life from	17 February 1370	*CPR 1367–1370*, p. 377
on	28 May 1373	*CPR 1370–1374*, p. 293
not by	3 November 1376	*CPR 1374–1377*, p. 368
John de Beauchamp of Powyk		
for life from	3 November 1376	*CPR 1374–1377*, p. 368
on	8 May 1386	*CPR 1385–1389*, p. 151 (Of Powyk)

Thomas duke of Gloucester		
for life from	14 February 1384	*CPR 1385–1389*, p. 7
on	9 December 1392	*CPR 1389–1392*, p. 200
William Beauchamp of Powyk, king's knight		
from	28 June 1393	
on	2 January 1400	*CPR 1399–1401*, p. 477
Thomas lord le Despenser		
from	20 July 1397	*CFR 1391–1399*, p. 219
for life from	28 September 1397	*CPR 1396–1399*, p. 219
William Beauchamp of Powyk, as above		
on	10 July 1405	*CPR 1405–1408*, p. 63
on	30 January 1406	*CPR 1405–1408*, p. 156

Deputies

Robert Aston		
from	23 August 1369	*IPM XII*, no. 157

Deputies for Thomas duke of Gloucester

William Beauchamp		
from	9 December 1392	*CPR 1391–1396*, p. 200

Fermours

Thomas de Bardstone		
on	11 January 1334	*CCR 1333–1337*, p. 172
on	11 March 1336	*CCR 1333–1337*, p. 553

Receivers

James de Broughton		
on	20 May 1322	*CFR 1319–1327*, p. 131

Surveyors and Controllers

William Heybere and John Hede		
from	14 July 1377	*CPR 1377–1381*, p. 12

RUARDEAN

Owners

Alexander Bicknore, king's clerk		
license to crenellate.	1 June 1311	*CPR 1307–1313*, p. 355

ST. BRIAVELS

Owners

Period Crown		
Queen Isabella		
from	1327	*HKW II*, p. 823
to	1331	*HKW II*, p. 823
Thomas duke of Gloucester		
from	26 July 1390	*CPR 1388–1392*, p. 360
to	1397	*HKW II*, p. 823
John de Aure and his heirs		
from	16 December 1399	*CCR 1402–1405*, p. 9
on	10 October 1402	*CCR 1402–1405*, p. 9

Superior Custody

Hugh le Despenser, yng		
from	2 November 1322	*CPR 1321–1324*, p. 214

Constables

Grimbald Pauncefoot		
on	2 February 1282	*CCR 1279–1288*, p. 146
on	7 June 1285	*CPR 1281–1292*, p. 170
William Hathewy		
to	3 January 1291	*CFR 1272–1307*, p. 286
Reynold de Grey		
from	3 January 1291	*CFR 1272–1307*, p. 286
John Botetourt, P.P.		
from	4 January 1291	*CPR 1281–1292*, p. 412
to	12 March 1308	*CFR 1307–1319*, p. 18
John de Handlo		
from	12 March 1308	*CFR 1307–1319*, p. 18
on	28 August 1309	*CCR 1307–1313*, p. 170
John de Wysham		
from	25 December 1310	*CFR 1307–1319*, p. 76
on	25 December 1310	*CPR 1307–1313*, p. 316
John de Annesleye		
to	30 October 1311	*CFR 1307–1319*, p. 109
John de Wysham		
on	1 May 1311	*CCR 1307–1313*, p. 309
for life from	1 June 1311	*CPR 1307–1313*, p. 355
on	28 January 1312	*CCR 1307–1313*, p. 402
John de Handlo		
on	30 April 1313	*CPR 1307–1313*, p. 570
John de Wysset		
on	20 November 1314	*CCR 1313–1318*, p. 126
John de Wysham		
on	9 February 1316	*CCR 1313–1318*, p. 265
to	4 June 1318	*CFR 1307–1319*, p. 363
Roger Damory, P.P.		
from	4 June 1318	*CFR 1307–1319*, p. 363
on	22 June 1320	*CCR 1318–1323*, p. 199
William de Beauchamp		
from	11 April 1321	*CFR 1319–1327*, p. 51
on	21 April 1321	*CPR 1317–1321*, p. 576
Simon de Driby		
from	13 February 1322	*CFR 1319–1327*, p. 96
to	2 August 1322	*CFR 1319–1327*, p. 175 (R.I.P.)
James de Broughton		
from	20 May 1322	*CFR 1319–1327*, p. 131
to	1 November 1322	*CFR 1319–1327*, p. 182
Robert de Sapy		
from	1 November 1322	*CFR 1319–1327*, p. 182
to	16 February 1325	*CFR 1319–1327*, p. 331
John de Myners		
from	16 February 1325	*CFR 1319–1327*, p. 331
accounting	30 September 1326	*CMR*, no. 11
John de Hardredeshull		
from	1 December 1326	*CFR 1319–1327*, p. 424
William Deveross		
to	21 December 1330	*CFR 1327–1337*, p. 211

Robert de Sapy		
from	21 December 1330	*CFR 1327–1337*, p. 211
to	17 October 1335	*CFR 1327–1337*, p. 461
Guy Brian, II, king's yeoman		
from	17 October 1335	*CFR 1327–1337*, p. 461
for life from	7 October 1341	*CFR 1337–1347*, p. 243
on	30 April 1345	*CPR 1343–1345*, p. 466
Guy de Brian, III, P.P.		
for life on	20 November 1349	*CCR 1349–1354*, p. 112
on	29 January 1352	*CPR 1350–1354*, p. 255
John Joce		
on	10 March 1356	*CPR 1354–1358*, p. 394
Walter Vaghan		
on	18 July 1356	*CPR 1354–1358*, p. 449
Guy de Brian, P.P.		
on	29 January 1364	*IPM XI*, no. 609
to	13 November 1384	*CPR 1385–1389*, p. 52
John Greindour, appointed by above		
from	13 November 1384	*CPR 1385–1389*, p. 52
Guy de Brian, P.P.		
on	12 June 1385	*CPR 1381–1385*, p. 579
Thomas de Woodstock, future duke of Gloucester		
reversion	12 June 1385	*CPR 1381–1385*, p. 579
John Greindour		
on	8 November 1385	*CPR 1385–1389*, p. 52
Guy de Briane, P.P.		
on	13 August 1387	*CPR 1385–1389*, p. 343
Thomas de Woodstock, duke of Gloucester		
for life from	26 July 1390	*CPR 1389–1392*, p. 297
on	8 August 1394	*CPR 1391–1396*, p. 504
Henry Moton		
to	4 November 1399	*CFR 1399–1405*, p. 14
Thomas lord le Despenser		
from	20 July 1397	*CFR 1391–1399*, p. 219
for life from	28 September 1397	*CPR 1396–1399*, p. 224
Hugh de Waterton, kn.		
from	4 November 1399	*CFR 1399–1405*, p. 14

Deputies

John Lyoun		
on	24 May 1317	*CPR 1313–1317*, p. 697 (Deputy)

Constables for Gloucester

Guy de Brian		
for life on	26 July 1390	*CPR 1388–1392*, p. 297
on	30 July 1391	*CPR 1388–1392*, p. 406

Porters

John Cosyn		
for life from	17 January 1394	
confirmed	12 November 1399	*CPR 1399–1401*, p. 127

Receivers

James de Broughton on	20 May 1322	*CFR 1319–1327*, p. 131

Hampshire

Unknown Licenses

FRESHWATER for Giles de Beauchamp		
	23 March 1342	*CPR 1340–1343*, p. 396
WESTBURY for Robert Lewer		
	22 January 1322	*CPR 1321–1324*, p. 52

ASHLEY (CHURCH CLOSE; GAIN'S CASTLE)

History

licenced	1200?	King, p. 189

BASING

History

mentioned	mid C12	King, p. 189
licenced	1261	King, p. 189
abandoned by	1347–9	King, p. 189
licensed	1531	King, p. 189
siege	1643, 1644–5	King, p. 189

CARISBROOKE

Owners

Isabella da Forz, countess of Aumale		
record of sale	1276	*CCR, 1272–9,* p. 347, to Edward I with Isle of Wight
to	1293	*HKW II*, p. 591 (R.I.P.)
Crown		
from	1293	*HKW II*, p. 591
to	7 June 1308	*CChR 1300–1326*, p. 111
Piers Gaveston		
from	7 June 1308	*CChR 1300–1326*, p. 111
to	5 August 1309	*CCR 1307–1313*, p. 225
Crown		
from	1309	
to	1312	
Crown – Prince Edward		
from	2 December 1312	*CChR 1300–1326*, p. 202
on	28 October 1324	*CCR 1323–1327*, p. 232
to	1327	
Crown		
from	*1327–1355*	
Isabella, daughter of Edward II and Enguerrand de Coucy, earl of Bedford, her husband		
from	29 November 1355	*CPR 1354–1358*, p. 317
to	1377	*HKW II*, p. 593
Crown		
from	1377	*HKW II*, p. 593
to	1385	*HKW II*, p. 593

William de Montague, earl of Salisbury		
for life from	1385	*HKW II*, p. 593
to	3 June 1397	*IPM vol. XVII*, no. 858
Edward, earl of Rutland, future duke of York		
for life from	4 June 1397	*CPR 1396–1399*, p. 150
on	26 October 1400	*CPR 1399–1401*, p. 366
Queen Joan		
for life from	5 April 1405	*CPR 1401–1405*, p. 501
Edward, duke of York		
on	5 December 1409	*CPR 1408–1413*, p. 152
Farmed out to Philippa, duchess of York, not Constable		
reversion	26 October 1400	*CPR 1399–1401*, p. 366
from	10 December 1415	*CPR 1413–1416*, p. 398

Constables

John son of Thomas		
from	15 November 1293	*CFR 1272–1307*, p. 331
Humphrey de Donesterr		
on	20 June 1297	*IMisc I*, no. 1759
on	8 July 1297	*CPR 1292–1301*, p. 43
William Russel		
on	21 February 1306	*IMisc II*, no. 1994
to	3 September 1307	*CFR 1307–1319*, p. 3
Nicholas de Bosco		
from	3 September 1307	*CFR 1307–1319*, p. 3
Piers Gaveston		
to	26 August 1309	*CFR 1307–1319*, p. 48
Nicholas de Bosco		
from	10 September 1309	*CFR 1307–1319*, p. 49
Nicholas du Boys		
on	28 January 1312	*CCR 1307–1313*, p. 402
Nicholas de la Beche, kn.		
with Isle of Wight from	18 April 1312	*CFR 1307–1319*, p. 130
to	2 October 1312	*CFR 1307–1319*, p. 147
John de la Beche		
with Isle of Wight from	2 October 1312	*CFR 1307–1310*, p. 147
to	2 December 1312	*CChR 1300–1326*, p. 202
Roger de Clotherum		
to	20 February 1313	*CPR 1307–1313*, p. 553
Richard de Byflet		
from	20 February 1313	*CPR 1307–1313*, p. 553
John de la Hoese		
on	10 December 1325	*CCR 1323–1327*, p. 432
on	2 May 1331	*CCR 1330–1333*, p. 241
Gilbert de Wygeton		
to	5 September 1331	*CFR 1327–1337*, p. 272
John de la Hoese		
from	5 September 1331	*CFR 1327–1337*, p. 272
Gilbert de Wygeton		
on	24 November 1331	*CFR 1327–1337*, p. 290
to	3 December 1334	*CFR 1327–1337*, p. 426
John de Wygeton		
from	3 December 1334	*CFR 1327–1337*, p. 426

John de Langeford		
on	19 August 1335	*CCR 1333–1337*, p. 435
to	8 March 1341	*CFR 1337–1347*, p. 212
Richard de Lymboteseye		
from	8 March 1341	*CFR 1337–1347*, p. 212
to	15 April 1342	*CFR 1337–1347*, p. 277
Philip de Weston		
from	15 April 1342	*CFR 1337–1347*, p. 277
to	20 August 1342	*CFR 1337–1347*, p. 277
John de Weston		
from	20 August 1342	*CFR 1337–1347*, p. 277
to	25 April 1343	*CFR 1337–1347*, p. 326
Philip de Weston		
from	25 April 1343	*CPR 1343–1345*, p. 34
to	20 November 1343	*CFR 1337–1347*, p. 340
William de la Dale		
from	20 November 1343	*CFR 1337–1347*, p. 340
to	24 April 1344	*CPR 1343–1345*, p. 242
Henry Romyn		
from	24 April 1344	*CPR 1343–1345*, p. 242
William de la Dale		
on	20 April 1345	*IMisc II*, no. 1939
on	23 April 1345	*CPR 1343–1345*, p. 503
Henry Romyn		
from	6 June 1346	*CFR 1337–1347*, p. 471
to	10 November 1347	*CPR 1345–1348*, p. 423
William de Dale		
from	10 November 1347	*CPR 1345–1348*, p. 423
to	29 November 1355	*CPR 1354–1358*, p. 317
John fitz Eustace		
on	23 January 1369	*CPR 1367–1370*, pp. 189, 205
John Griffyth		
on	30 May 1377	*CCR 1374–1377*, p. 496
Laurence de St. Martin, kn.		
governor	22 April 1380	*CPR 1377–1381*, p. 510
William de Montague, earl of Salisbury		
from	30 March 1382	*CPR 1381–1385*, p. 103
on	28 February 1384	*CCR 1381–1385*, p. 358
for life from	19 August 1385	*CPR 1385–1389*, p. 16
on	12 May 1396	*CCR 1392–1396*, p. 457
Edward, duke of York		
on	2 March 1405	*CPR 1401–1405*, p. 497
John Laurence		
for life from	30 January 1416	*CPR 1413–1416*, p. 391

Private Constables

John de Pagrave (For Isabella de Forz)		
temp	Isabella da Forz	Denholm-Young, p. 29

Keepers

Hugh Tyrel		
on	30 May 1377	*CCR 1374–1377*, p. 496

Gatekeepers

William de Bewyk		
for life from	2 March 1327	*CFR 1327–1337*, p. 26
Robert de Driffeld		
for life from	14 April 1343	*CPR 1343–1345*, p. 21

Porter

Roger de Braibury		
for life from	8 February 1338	*CPR 1338–1340*, p. 5
John Hemyngburgh		
from	16 March 1405	*CPR 1405–1408*, p. 5

CHRISTCHURCH (TWYNHAM)

Owners

Queen Margaret		
from	10 September 1299	*CPR 1292–1301*, p. 451
confirmed	19 March 1310	*CPR 1307–1313*, p. 216
Queen Isabella		
from	5 March 1318	*CPR 1317–1321*, p. 115
from	10 July 1319	*CCR 1318–1323*. p. 149
William de Montague, earl of Salisbury		
from	18 January 1331	*CChR 1327–1341*, p. 210
to	30 January 1344	*IPM VIII*, no. 532 (R.I.P.)
Katherine, widow of above		
from	30 January 1344	*IPM VIII*, no. 532 (Jointure)
to	23 April 1349	*IPM IX*, no. 310 (R.I.P.)
William de Montague, earl of Salisbury, son of above		
from	23 April 1349	*IPM IX*, no. 310
to	3 June 1398	*IPM XVII*, no. 858 (R.I.P.)
John de Montague, son of above		
from	3 June 1398	*IPM XVII*, no. 858
Thomas son of John de Montague, earl of Salisbury		
from	14 June 1409	*CCR 1405–1409*, p. 443

Constables

John de Mere		
to	12 December 1330	*CFR 1327–1337*, p. 205
Thomas West		
from	12 December 1330	*CFR 1327–1337*, p. 205
on	23 January 1331	*CPR 1327–1337*, p. 54

ODIHAM

Owners

Queen Eleanor of Castile		
from	22 October 1275	*CChR 1257–1300*, p. 192
Queen Margaret		
from	10 September 1299	*CPR 1292–1301*, p. 451
on	28 September 1311	*CCR 1307–1313*, p. 375
Queen Isabella		
on	20 April 1327	*CMR*, no. 50
on	27 April 1330	*CFR 1327–1337*, p. 173

Queen Philippa		
from	20 July 1331	*CPR 1330–1334*, p. 161
dead by	17 August 1369	*CFR 1369–1377*, p. 27
Queen Anne		
for life from	24 May 1382	*CPR 1381–1385*, p. 125
Queen Joan		
to	16 November 1408	*CPR 1408–1413*, p. 31
Henry Lord Beaumont, from above		
from her life	16 November 1408	*CPR 1408–1413*, p. 31
Queen Joan		
on	16 February 1419	*CFR 1413–1422*, p. 268
Constables		
Robert L'isle		
on	1 August 1273	*CCR 1272–1279*, p. 25
to	21 July 1275	*CFR 1272–1307*, p. 53
John de London		
from	21 July 1275	*CFR 1272–1307*, p. 53
Philip de Pirye		
on	26 July 1278	*CCR 1272–1279*, p. 470
Ralph de Sandwich		
to	8 June 1282	*CFR 1272–1307*, p. 164
and	7 June 1282	*CPR 1281–1292*, p. 25
Nicholas le Gras		
from	8 June 1282	*CFR 1272–1307*, p. 164
and	7 June 1282	*CPR 1281–1292*, p. 25
Simon de Wyntonia		
to	12 June 1294	*CFR 1272–1307*, p. 339
Hugh le Despenser, yng. P.P.		
from	12 June 1294	*CFR 1272–1307*, p. 339
Robert le Ewer		
from	29 September 1311	*CFR 1307–1313*, p. 103
on	28 September 1311	*CCR 1307–1313*, p. 375
John de Luke		
to	23 July 1312	*CPR 1307–1313*, p. 481
Robert le Ewer, king's yeoman		
from	23 July 1312	*CPR 1307–1313*, p. 481
Hugh le Despenser elder		
from	1 November 1317	*CPR 1317–1321*, p. 46
Robert le Ewer		
from	10 December 1318	*CFR 1307–1319*, p. 386
to	22 February 1320	*CFR 1319–1327*, p. 15
Hugh le Despenser yng		
from	22 February 1320	*CFR 1319–1327*, p. 15
to	21 June 1321	*CPR 1317–1321*, p. 595
Robert Lewer		
from	9 July 1321	*CFR 1319–1327*, p. 64
to	19 September 1322	*CFR 1319–1327*, p. 178
John de St. John of Basing, P.P.		
from	19 September 1322	*CFR 1319–1327*, p. 178
to	27 April 1323	*CFR 1319–1327*, p. 206

John de Aulton		
from	27 April 1323	*CFR 1319–1327*, p. 206
to	29 March 1324	*CPR 1321–1324*, p. 403
Bertrand de la More		
from	29 March 1324	*CPR 1321–1324*, p. 403
accounting	13 March 1327	*CMR*, no. 76
John de Aulton		
on	30 September 1326	*CMR*, no. 7
Roger Wodelok		
from	28 December 1330	*CFR 1327–1337*, p. 212
and from	15 January 1331	*CFR 1327–1337*, p. 220
William Trussel of Cublesdon		
on	6 June 1339	*CCR 1339–1341*, p. 138
on	18 September 1362	*CPR 1361–1364*, p. 247
Walter Walssh		
for life from	17 August 1369	*CFR 1369–1377*, p. 27
to	7 May 1377	*CPR 1374–1377*, p. 461
Bernard Brocas, kn.		
from	7 May 1377	*CPR 1374–1377*, p. 461
on	13 September 1386	*CPR 1385–1389*, p. 260
John de Leventhorpe		
for life from	8 October 1399	*CPR 1396–1399*, p. 266
repeated	26 February 1402	
on	27 February 1402	*CCR 1399–1402*, p. 463
William Pomeray, esq.		
from	16 September 1421	*CPR 1416–1422*, p. 396

Keeper and Farmer (Not Constables)

Bernard Brocas		
`on	13 July 1381	*CPR 1381–1385*, p. 30

Queens Constables

Nicholas de la Beche, kn. for Queen Isabella		
for life on	27 April 1330	*CFR 1327–1337*, p. 173
Walter Walssh		
before	16 February 1369	*CFR 1369–1377*, p. 27

Clerks of the Works

William Dionys, clerk		
on	1 October 1399	*CPR 1399–1401*, p. 58

Keeper of victuals and stores

William de Kyngeston, clerk		
from	10 July 1321	*CPR 1321–1324*, p. 1

PORTCHESTER

Owners

Queen Eleanor of Provence		
on	23 August 1273	*CPR 1272–1281*, p. 27
on	27 October 1274	*CPR 1272–1281*, p. 71
Queen Margaret		
from	10 September 1299	*CPR 1292–1301*, p. 451
confirmed	19 March 1310	*CPR 1307–1313*, p. 216

Queen Isabella		
on	20 April 1327	*CMR*, no. 50
Constables		
Henry Husee, P.P., kn.		
on	17 May 1289	*CPR 1281–1292*, p. 10
Robert le Ewer		
to	22 August 1320	*CFR 1319–1327*, p. 32
Hugh le Despenser, yng, P.P.		
from	22 August 1320	*CFR 1319–1327*, p. 32
William de Weston		
from	12 October 1321	*CPR 1321–1324*, p. 28
to	1324	*IMisc II*, no. 986
Hugh le Despenser		
to	17 July 1324	*CFR 1319–1327*, p. 290 (Ynr.)
Thomas de Saunford		
from	17 July 1324	*CFR 1319–1327*, p. 290
on	8 December 1325	*CPR 1324–1327*, p. 197
accounting	30 September 1326	*CMR*, no. 7
Robert de Hausted		
on	10 March 1326	*CCR 1323–1327*, p. 551
John de Bassynges		
from	8 February 1327	*CFR 1327–1337*, p. 11
John Randulf		
from	14 December 1330	*CFR 1327–1337*, p. 215
to	13 May 1331	*CPR 1330–1334*, p. 120
William de Weston, king's yeoman		
from	13 May 1331	*CPR 1330–1334*, p. 120
to	30 March 1335	*CFR 1327–1337*, p. 437
Richard earl of Arundel		
from	6 February 1335	*CFR 1327–1337*, p. 431
for life from	30 March 1335	*CFR 1327–1337*, p. 437
on	22 September 1337	*CCR 1337–1339*, p. 184
John Haket		
on	3 August 1338	*CCR 1337–1339*, p. 446
Richard earl of Arundel		
on	10 November 1338	*CCR 1337–1339*, p. 564
on	1 July 1342	*CCR 1341–1343*, p. 452
John Haket		
on	8 January 1346	*CCR 1343–1346*, p. 632
Richard earl of Arundel		
on	5 June 1346	*CCR 1346–1349*, p. 31
on	20 January 1358	*CPR 1354–1358*, p. 378
to	14 May 1357	
William Daunvers		
for life from	14 May 1357	
confirmed	20 October 1357	*CPR 1354–1358*, p. 629
Richard earl of Arundel		
to	7 February 1361	*CPR 1358–1361*, p. 539
John de Edyndon		
from	7 February 1361	*CPR 1358–1361*, p. 539
on	20 January 1362	*CPR 1361–1364*, p. 141
not by	14 October 1367	*CPR 1367–1370*, p. 51 (R.I.P.), keeper

Thomas atte More		
on	26 February 1369	*CPR 1367–1370*, p. 221
Richard earl of Arundel		
on	29 September 1369	*CPR 1367–1370*, p. 348
not by	15 February 1376	*CPR 1374–1377*, p. 250
Thomas atte More		
on	23 April 1370	*Issue Roll*, p. 5
on	22 January 1371	*Issue Roll*, p. 424
Robert de Assheton		
for life from	15 February 1376	*CPR 1374–1377*, p. 250
to	1 February 1381	*CPR 1377–1381*, p. 589
Edmund de Langley, future duke of York		
possibly	1 February 1381	*CPR 1377–1381*, p. 589
Robert Bardolf, esq.		
for life from	4 February 1381	*CPR 1377–1381*, p. 594
on	26 April 1386	*CPR 1385–1389*, p. 134
not by	12 May 1395	*CPR 1391–1396*, p. 568
Roger Walden		
for life from	12 May 1395	*CPR 1391–1396*, p. 569
Roger and John Waldon, brothers		
for life from	1 February 1397	*CPR 1396–1399*, p. 64
to	3 November 1399	*CPR 1399–1401*, p. 46
Thomas de Camoys, P.P. and Richard de Camoys, his son		
from	3 November 1399	*CPR 1399–1401*, p. 46
on	12 February 1405	*CCR 1402–1405*, p. 409
Thomas, duke of Clarence		
for life from	17 September 1410	*CPR 1408–1413*, p. 215
Thomas de Camoys, above, P.P.		
on	14 January 1411	*CCR 1409–1413*, p. 135

Keeper of the Tower

Robert de Hausted		
from	8 December 1325	*CPR 1324–1327*, p. 197

Captains

Roger de Elmerigg		
from	15 August 1369	*CPR 1367–1370*, p. 304

Deputies

Thomas del More		
on	29 September 1369	*CPR 1367–1370*, p. 348
John Cook		
on	1 May 1390	*CPR 1388–1392*, p. 251

Porters

John Hayward		
from	18 June 1422	*CPR 1416–1422*, p. 435

Janitors

Nicholas de Havering		
for life from	18 October 1358	*CPR 1358–1361*, p. 107
not by	26 April 1374	*CCR 1374–1377*, p. 15 (R.I.P.)
John Portchester		
on	26 April 1374	*CCR 1374–1377*, p. 15

Gatekeepers

Alexander Campyoun		
from	6 July 1324	*CPR 1323–1327*, p. 3

ROWLAND'S CASTLE

History

place mentioned	temp. Edward II	King, p. 193

SOUTHAMPTON

Owners

Queen Eleanor of Castile		
from	1276	J.C. Parsons, *Eleanor of Castile, Queen and Society in Thirteenth-Century England*, London, 1994, p. 38
on	1286	*ibid.*
Queen Margaret		
from	10 September 1299	*CPR 1292–1301*, p. 451
confirmed	19 March 1310	*CPR 1307–1313*, p. 216
Queen Isabella		
from	5 March 1318	*CPR 1317–1321*, p. 115
from	10 July 1319	*CCR 1318–1323*, p. 149
Crown – Queen Philippa		
from	1 January 1331	*CPR 1330–1334*, p. 55
not by	26 June 1359	*CPR 1358–1361*, p. 237

Constables

William de Beauchamp		
to	12 December 1330	*CFR 1327–1337*, p. 205
Thomas West		
from	12 December 1330	*CFR 1327–1337*, p. 205
on	8 October 1331	*CFR 1327–1337*, p. 275
John de Beauchamp of Warwick		
from	28 November 1343	*CPR 1343–1345*, p. 142 (Lease)
John de Palton		
from	10 November 1355	*CFR 1347–1356*, p. 444
John de Beauchamp of Warwick (Had held from the queen earlier), P.P.		
for life from	16 July 1359	*CPR 1358–1361*, p. 246
John de Foxle		
from	30 January 1372	*CFR 1369–1377*, p. 155
for life from	7 October 1376	*CPR 1374–1377*, p. 350
confirmed	23 March 1378	*CPR 1377–1381*, p. 190
Thomas de Holland, earl of Kent		
on	24 January 1384	*CCR 1381–1385*, p. 502
for life from	16 June 1397	*CPR 1396–1399*, p. 151
Richard Mawardyn, esq.		
from	30 January 1400	*CPR 1399–1401*, p. 185 (Keeper)
John Popham		
from	23 March 1404	*CPR 1401–1405*, p. 385
from	9 March 1414	*CPR 1413–1416*, p. 168

Chaplain		
Simon		
on	18 December 1271	*CLibR 1267–1272*, no. 1781 (50s./year)

WINCHESTER

Constables		
William de Wyntreshull		
on	27 November 1270	*CLibR 1267–1272*, no. 1308
to	28 October 1273	*CFR 1272–1307*, p. 13
Henry de Shotbroc		
from	28 October 1273	*CFR 1272–1307*, p. 13
to	22 October 1274	*CFR 1272–1307*, p. 32
John de Havering, P.P.		
with county from	22 October 1274	*CFR 1272–1307*, p. 32
to	25 October 1278	*CFR 1272–1307*, p. 103
William de Brayboef		
from	25 October 1278	*CFR 1272–1307*, p. 103
to	8 July 1280	*CFR 1272–1307*, p. 131
John de Bottele		
from	8 July 1280	*CFR 1272–1307*, p. 131
Philip de Heyvill		
on	10 April 1282	*CCR 1279–1288*, p. 150
Richard de Aston		
on	14 April 1292	*CCR 1288–1296*, p. 226
Thomas Warblyngton		
to	16 March 1308	*CFR 1307–1319*, p. 18
Robert fitz Payn, P.P.		
from	16 March 1308	*CFR 1307–1319*, p. 18
to	15 May 1314	*CFR 1307–1319*, p. 196
John de la Beche		
castle from	15 May 1314	*CFR 1307–1319*, p. 196
to	1 November 1314	*CFR 1307–1319*, p. 220
John L'isle		
from	1 November 1314	*CFR 1307–1319*, p. 220
to	1 October 1315	*CFR 1307–1319*, p. 259
John de la Beche		
with county from	1 October 1315	*CFR 1307–1319*, p. 259
to	5 April 1317	*CFR 1307–1319*, p. 322
Richard de Byflet		
from	5 April 1317	*CFR 1307–1319*, p. 322
to	29 November 1318	*CFR 1307–1319*, p. 382
James de Norton		
from	29 November 1318	*CFR 1307–1319*, p. 382
to	20 October 1320	*CFR 1319–1327*, p. 35
John de Ticheburn		
from	20 October 1320	*CFR 1319–1327*, p. 35
to	8 October 1321	*CFR 1319–1327*, p. 73
John de Scures		
from	8 October 1321	*CFR 1319–1327*, p. 73
and from	6 March 1327	*CFR 1327–1337*, p. 25
to	10 November 1338	*CPR 1338–1340*, p. 161

Robert Daundely		
from	10 November 1338	*CPR 1338–1340*, p. 161
on	25 March 1339	*CCR 1339–1341*, p. 109
Robert de Popham		
from	28 April 1340	*CPR 1338–1340*, p. 508
to	26 January 1341	*CFR 1337–1347*, p. 203
John de Palton		
from	26 January 1341	*CFR 1337–1347*, p. 203
to	6 April 1342	*CFR 1337–1347*, p. 262
Thomas de Chisenhale		
from	6 April 1342	*CFR 1337–1347*, p. 262
to	22 November 1343	*CFR 1337–1347*, p. 349
Thomas Aspale		
from	22 November 1343	*CFR 1337–1347*, p. 349
to	13 November 1347	*CFR 1347–1356*, p. 57
Henry de Sturmy		
from	13 November 1347	*CFR 1347–1356*, p. 57
to	18 March 1351	*CFR 1347–1356*, p. 280
John de Wynton		
from	18 March 1351	*CFR 1347–1356*, p. 280
William de Overton		
from	28 December 1354	*CFR 1347–1356*, p. 409
Walter Haywood		
from	10 November 1356	*CFR 1356–1368*, p. 19
and from	1 October 1359	*CFR 1356–1368*, p. 103
John de Potenhale		
from	21 November 1360	*CFR 1356–1368*, p. 121
to	10 August 1361	*CFR 1356–1368*, p. 154 (R.I.P.)
Thomas de Hampton		
from	10 August 1361	*CFR 1356–1368*, p. 154
and from	20 November 1363	*CFR 1356–1368*, p. 268
Nicholas Wodelok		
from	17 November 1365	*CFR 1356–1368*, p. 315
to	1 May 1366	*CFR 1356–1368*, p. 328
Roger Colrithe		
from	1 May 1366	*CFR 1356–1368*, p. 328
Peter de Brugg		
from	16 May 1366	*CFR 1356–1368*, p. 328
and from	27 November 1368	*CFR 1356–1368*, p. 392
John Botiller		
from	5 November 1369	*CFR 1369–1377*, p. 36
and from	28 March 1370	*CFR 1369–1377*, p. 98
Thomas Warner		
from	5 November 1371	*CFR 1369–1377*, p. 146
Philip de Popham		
from	12 December 1372	*CFR 1369–1377*, p. 189
to	7 November 1373	*CFR 1369–1377*, p. 221
Laurence de St. Martin		
from	7 November 1373	*CFR 1369–1377*, p. 221
Richard Pauncefoot		
from	12 December 1374	*CFR 1369–1377*, p. 272

Theobald Gorge		
from	4 October 1375	*CFR 1369–1377*, p. 297
Thomas Bokelond		
from	26 October 1376	*CFR 1369–1377*, p. 369
and from	22 June 1377	*CFR 1377–1383*, p. 3
Ralph de Norton		
from	26 November 1377	*CFR 1377–1383*, p. 34
John Buttesthorn		
from	25 November 1378	*CFR 1377–1383*, p. 113
Walter Romseye		
from	5 November 1379	*CFR 1377–1383*, p. 171
William Ryngebourne		
from	18 October 1380	*CFR 1377–1383*, p. 220
Hugh Creaan		
from	1 November 1381	*CFR 1377–1383*, p. 269
John de Sandes		
from	24 November 1382	*CFR 1377–1383*, p. 327
to	1 November 1383	*CFR 1383–1391*, p. 7
John Shone		
from	1 November 1383	*CFR 1383–1391*, p. 7
Robert Chalmeley, esq.		
for life from	2 December 1383	*CPR 1381–1385*, p. 363 (Custody)
on	12 November 1385	*CCR 1385–1389*, p. 12 (Keeper)
John la Zouche		
from	11 November 1385	*CFR 1383–1391*, p. 76
Robert Chalmeley		
on	17 June 1387	*CPR 1385–1389*, p. 311
on	24 June 1392	*CPR 1391–1396*, p. 98
dead by	4 December 1404	*CPR 1401–1405*, p. 455
William le Marshall, king's knight		
for life from	4 December 1404	*CPR 1401–1405*, p. 455
on	14 January 1411	*CCR 1409–1413*, p. 136

Gatekeeper

William de Sibesdon		
on	8 June 1317	*IMisc II*, no. 261

Chaplain

Nicholas, 40s./year		
on	1 November 1267	*CLibR 1267–1272*, no. 6
John de St. Andrea, 50s./year		
on	10 October 1275	*CCR 1272–1279*, p. 212

WOLVESEY

Owners

Bishop of Winchester		
on	29 January 1269	*CLibR 1267–1272*, no. 579
void	6 August 1323	*CCR 1323–1327*, p. 132

Herefordshire

Unknown Licenses

ATTE WALLE for William le Galeys

	25 January 1329	*CPR 1327–1330*, p. 388

ASHPERTON

Owners

William de Grandison, P.P.		
license to crenellate	3 May 1292	*CPR 1281–1292*, p. 490
died	*27 June 1335*	*GEC VI, p. 60*
Piers de Grandison, son of above, P.P.		
inherited	*27 June 1335*	*GEC VI, p. 62*
died	*10 August 1358*	*GEC VI, p. 62*
John de Grandison, bishop of Exeter, brother of above		
inherited	*10 August 1358*	*GEC VI, p. 64*
died	*16 July 1369*	*GEC VI, p. 64*

BRAMPTON BRYAN

Owners

Bryan de Brampton		
to	1309	*RCH*, p. 20
Harley Family		
from	1309	*RCH*, p. 20
Brian de Brampton		
on	8 September 1403	*CCR 1402–1405*, p. 111

BREDWARDINE

Owners

John Baskervill ('a place called Castle Toft')		
to death	1374	King, p. 215 (n.7)

CLIFFORD CASTLE

Owners

Clifford family		
temp	thirteenth century	*RCH,* p. 39
John Giffard of Brimpsfield, P.P. from Maud Lungespete, his wife		
to	5 June 1299	*IPM III*, no. 544 (R.I.P.)
to	23 October 1299	*CFR 1272–1307*, p. 421 (R.I.P.)
Henry de Lacy, earl of Lincoln		
from	23 October 1299	*CFR 1272–1307*, p. 421 (from wife)
to	6 February 1311	*IPM V*, no. 279 (R.I.P.)
Thomas of Lancaster and Alice de Lacy, his wife, daughter of above		
from	6 February 1311	*IPM V*, no. 279
Alice de Lacy		
for life from	12 July 1322	*CPR 1321–1324*, p. 179

Ebulo le Strange, P.P. and Alice de Lacy his wife		
away and back	10 February 1325	*CPR 1324–1327*, p. 103
to	17 September 1335	*IPM VII*, no. 716 (R.I.P.)
Alice de Lacy		
from	17 September 1335	*IPM VII*, no. 716
Alice de Lacy, wife of Nicholas de Cauntelo		
on	26 June 1337	*CPR 1334–1338*, p. 463
Alice de Lacy		
on	9 October 1335	*CCR 1333–1337*, p. 444
Roger Mortimer		
to	24 January 1356	*CPR 1354–1358*, p. 328
Ralph Spigurnell, kn, from Roger Mortimer		
for life from	24 January 1356	*CPR 1354–1358*, p. 328
to	1372	*IPM XIII*, no. 201 (R.I.P.)
Edmund Mortimer, earl of March and Ulster		
from	1372	*IPM XIII*, no. 201
to	27 December 1381	*IPM XV*, no. 560 (R.I.P.)
Roger Mortimer, earl of March, son of above		
from	27 December 1381	*IPM XV*, no. 560
to	20 July 1398	*IPM XVII*, no. 1206 (R.I.P.)
Edmund Mortimer, earl of March, son of above		
from	20 July 1398	*IPM XVII*, no. 1206
under age	14 February 1404	*CPR 1401–1405*, p. 354

Private Constables

William Ravlyns		
for life from	12 October 1397	
confirmed	19 February 1400	*CPR 1399–1401*, p. 200
on	22 February 1400	*CCR 1399–1402*, p. 48

Wardships

minority of Roger Mortimer, earl of March, 1381–1395

William de Burley		
from	8 February 1382	*CPR 1381–1385*, p. 121
on	21 April 1383	*CCR 1381–1385*, p. 269
John de Bromwich		
from	26 May 1382	*CFR 1377–1383*, p. 295
Thomas de Beauchamp, earl of Warwick, Roger Mortimer, earl of March, John lord Neville and Henry Percy, earl of Northumberland		
from	16 December 1383	*CFR 1383–1391*, p. 22
John de Bromwich		
confirmed	1394	*CCR 1392–1396*, p. 268

Minority of Edmund Mortimer, earl of March, 1398–1412

Edward, duke of York		
from	11 August 1398	*CPR 1396–1399*, p. 408
Henry Percy, earl of Northumberland		
from	2 March 1400	*CFR 1399–1405*, p. 50
Robert Whiteney		
from	14 February 1404	*CPR 1401–1405*, p. 354

DORSTONE

Owners

Richard de Burley, kn.		
to	7 June 1387	*IPM XVI*, no. 515
Beatrice, widow of above.		
not yet	1 August 1388	*CPR 1385–1389*, p. 525
from	20 November 1388	*CPR 1385–1389*, p. 543
not by	22 November 1388	*CPR 1385–1389*, p. 554
Walter fitz Walter, kn.		
on	8 September 1403	*CCR 1402–1405*, p. 111
to	16 May 1406	*IPM XIX*, no. 275 (R.I.P.)
Joan, widow of above		
from	16 May 1406	*IPM XIX*, no. 275
to	10 May 1409	*IPM XIX*, no. 571 (R.I.P.)
Humphrey fitz Wauter, son of above		
from	10 May 1409	*IPM XIX*, no. 571

EARDISLEY

Tenant in Chief

Henry de Ferrers		
on	15 November 1374	*CPR 1374–1377*, p. 57

Owners

Roger de Clifford, held from Walter de Baskervill and his heirs		
forfeited	29 September 1276	*CPR 1272–1281*, p. 162
restored	29 October 1276	*CPR 1272–1281*, p. 163
granted to King	24 June 1278	*CCR 1272–1279*, p. 466
restored	25 June 1278	*CPR 1272–1281*, p. 272
Richard de Baskervill		
from	6 February 1290	*CPR 1281–1292*, p. 340
on	25 June 1309	*CPR 1307–1313*, p. 173
Richard Baskervill, kn		
to	March 1374	*IPM XIV*, no. 13 (R.I.P.)
Richard Baskervill, his son		
from	March 1374	*IPM XIV*, no. 13 (Age 2.5)
Nicholas Montgomery, kn		
on	8 September 1403	*CCR 1402–1405*, p. 111

Constables

John de Geyton		
from	29 September 1276	*CPR 1272–1281*, p. 162
to	15 October 1276	*CPR 1272–1281*, p. 163
Sheriff of Herefordshire		
from	24 June 1278	*CPR 1272–1281*, p. 466

Private Constables

Peter le Taillur		
on	25 June 1309	*CPR 1307–1313*, p. 173

EATON TREGOZ

Owners

William de Grandison, P.P.		
license to crenellate	14 December 1308	*CPR 1307–1313*, p. 203
died	*27 June 1335*	*GEC VI, p. 60*
Piers de Grandison, son of above, P.P. .		
from	*27 June 1335*	*GEC VI, p. 60*
died	*10 August 1358*	*GEC VI, p. 62*
John de Grandison, brother of above, Bishop of Exeter,		
from	*10 August 1358*	*GEC VI, p. 62*
died	*16 July 1369*	*GEC VI, p. 64*
Elizabeth, widow of John de Penbrugge		
to	23 August 1400	*IPM* XVIII, no. 58
Alice, sister of John de Penbrugge		
from	23 August 1400	*IPM* XVIII, no. 58

EWYAS HAROLD

Owners

John Tregoz of Ewyas Harold, P.P.		
to	6 September 1300	*IPM III*, no. 603 (R.I.P.)
to	26 November 1300	*CFR 1272–1307*, p. 435 (R.I.P.)
John la Ware, grandson of above, P.P.		
from	26 November 1300	*CFR 1272–1307*, p. 435
died	*9 May 1347*	*GEC IV, p. 141*
Roger le Warre, kn., P.P.		
inherited	*9 May 1347*	*GEC IV, p. 141*
to	27 August 1370	*IPM XIII*, no. 57 (R.I.P.)
John la Warre, kn, his son, P.P.		
from	27 August 1370	*IPM XIII*, no. 57
to	12 February 1373	*CPR 1370–1374*, p. 246
Lewis de Clifford		
from	12 February 1373	*CPR 1370–1374*, p. 246 (for life)
granted away	20 February 1393	*CPR 1391–1396*, p. 227
William de Beauchamp, lord of Abergavenny, P.P.		
on	20 February 1400	*CCR 1399–1402*, p. 116
to	1411	*IPM XIX*, no. 854 (R.I.P.)
Joan, widow of above		
from	6 July 1411	*CCR 1409–1413*, p. 144
on	23 March 1413	*CCR 1413–1419*, p. 11

GOODRICH

Owners

William de Valence		
on	8 July 1280	*CPR 1272–1281*, p. 26
on	4 June 1292	*CCR 1288–1296*, p. 286
Joan de Valence, countess of Pembroke		
to	20 September 1307	*IPM V*, no. 56 (R.I.P.)
Aymer de Valence, earl of Pembroke, son of above		
from	20 September 1307	*IPM V*, no. 56
to	26 June 1324	*IPM VI*, no. 518 (R.I.P.)

Crown		
from	15 November 1324	*CFR 1319–1327*, p. 319
Elizabeth Comyn, heir of Aymer de Valence		
from	22 March 1325	*CFR 1319–1327*, p. 338
to	6 April 1325	*CPR 1324–1327*, p. 116
Hugh Despenser, yng, P.P.		
from	6 April 1325	*CPR 1324–1327*, p. 116
Richard Talbot		
jointured on	12 March 1337	*CPR 1334–1338*, p. 395
to	23 October 1356	*IPM X*, no. 326 (R.I.P.)
Elizabeth, widow of Richard Talbot above		
from	23 October 1356	*IPM X*, no. 326 (Jointure)
to	20 November 1372	*IPM XIII*, no. 213 (R.I.P.)
Gilbert Talbot, son of above, P.P.		
from	20 November 1372	*IPM XIII*, no. 213
died	*24 April 1387*	*GEC XII(I), p. 614*
Richard Lord de Talbot, P.P., from Talbots of Richard's Castle		
dead by	20 September 1396	*CPR 1396–1399*, p. 28
Gilbert, Talbot, son of above, P.P.		
under age	20 September 1396	*CPR 1396–1399*, p. 28
under age	9 July 1399	*CCR 1336–1399*, p. 506
Thomas Neville, Lord Furnivall, kn		
on	8 September 1403	*CCR 1402–1405*, p. 111
Elizabeth, widow of Warin Lerchedeken, kn		
to	1 August 1407	*IPM XIX*, no. 219 (R.I.P.)
Gilbert Talbot, above, P.P.		
on	1411	*IPM XIX*, no. 892

Constables

John de Hampton		
from	15 November 1324	*CFR 1319–1327*, p. 319
Philip de la More		
from	1 February 1397	
confirmed	5 December 1400	*CPR 1399–1401*, p. 392

Constables for owner

Robert Cokerel		
on	8 July 1280	*CPR 1272–1281*, p. 26

Wardship

Minority of Gilbert, son and heir of Richard Talbot, 1396–1404

John Skydemore, esq		
from	20 September 1396	*CPR 1396–1399*, p. 28
Thomas de Mowbray, earl of Nottingham		
from	20 May 1397	*CFR 1391–1399*, p. 211
John Skydemore of Kentchurch		
from	22 February 1398	*CFR 1391–1399*, p. 249
on	8 May 1398	*CCR 1396–1399*, p. 264
Hugh de Waterton, kn.		
from	4 June 1402	*CFR 1399–1405*, p. 161

HEREFORD

Owners

Queen Eleanor		
on	23 February 1285	*CCR 1279–1288*, p. 314

Constables

Bartholomew de Sulye		
to	5 November 1274	*CFR 1272–1307*, p. 34
John le Ware		
from	5 November 1274	*CFR 1272–1307*, p. 34
to	12 November 1275	*CFR 1272–1307*, p. 58
Giles de Berkeley		
from	12 November 1275	*CFR 1272–1307*, p. 58
John de Swynburn		
to	25 October 1278	*CFR 1272–1307*, p. 103
Roger de Boruhill		
from	25 October 1278	*CFR 1272–1307*, p. 103
John de Sapy		
to	25 October 1311	*CFR 1307–1319*, p. 119
Richard de Baskervill		
from	25 October 1311	*CFR 1307–1319*, p. 119
to	24 January 1312	*CFR 1307–1319*, p. 120
Ralph de Chaundos, P.P.		
from	24 January 1312	*CFR 1307–1319*, p. 120
to	20 November 1314	*CFR 1307–1319*, p. 221
Roger de Baskervill		
from	20 November 1314	*CFR 1307–1319*, p. 221
to	20 October 1315	*CFR 1307–1319*, p. 261
Richard de Baskervill		
from	20 October 1315	*CFR 1307–1319*, p. 261
to	8 December 1316	*CFR 1307–1319*, p. 302
Hugh Hakelut		
from	8 December 1316	*CFR 1307–1319*, p. 302
to	23 December 1318	*CFR 1307–1319*, p. 376
Richard de Baskervill		
from	23 December 1318	*CFR 1307–1319*, p. 376
to	29 November 1318	*CFR 1307–1319*, p. 381
Roger de Elmerigg		
from	29 November 1318	*CFR 1307–1319*, p. 381
to	5 January 1322	*CFR 1319–1327*, p. 87
Roger Chaundos, P.P.		
from	5 January 1322	*CFR 1319–1327*, p. 87
to	23 October 1327	*CFR 1327–1337*, p. 67
Roger Pycard		
from	23 October 1327	*CFR 1327–1337*, p. 67
to	6 October 1328	*CFR 1327–1337*, p. 104
Roger Chaundos, P.P.		
from	6 October 1328	*CFR 1327–1337*, p. 104
to	30 January 1332	*CFR 1327–1337*, p. 297
Roger Pycard		
from	30 January 1332	*CFR 1327–1337*, p. 297
to	7 May 1332	*CFR 1327–1337*, p. 312

John le Rous		
from	7 May 1332	*CFR 1327–1337*, p. 312
to	23 July 1334	*CFR 1327–1337*, p. 411
Roger Chaundos, P.P.		
from	8 March 1334	*CFR 1327–1337*, p. 392
to	4 February 1335	*CFR 1327–1337*, p. 430
John Mauger		
from	4 February 1335	*CFR 1327–1337*, p. 430
to	20 January 1335	*CFR 1327–1337*, p. 469
Richard Wawayn		
from	20 January 1335	*CFR 1327–1337*, p. 469
Richard de Danseye		
to	22 October 1350	*CFR 1347–1356*, p. 227
Thomas de Aston		
from	22 October 1350	*CFR 1347–1356*, p. 227
to	29 May 1352	*CFR 1347–1356*, p. 349
Richard de Brugge		
from	29 May 1352	*CFR 1347–1356*, p. 349
and from	22 November 1352	*CFR 1347–1356*, p. 349
Richard de la Bere		
from	10 November 1354	*CFR 1347–1356*, p. 409
Thomas att Barre		
from	8 December 1355	*CFR 1347–1356*, p. 444
Walter Hurtesleye		
from	6 June 1356	*CFR 1356–1368*, p. 19
to	18 June 1356	*CFR 1356–1368*, p. 7
Thomas atte Bare		
from	18 June 1356	*CFR 1356–1368*, p. 7
Edmund Hakelut of Crokbarwe		
from	10 November 1356	*CFR 1356–1368*, p. 19
and from	3 November 1358	*CFR 1356–1368*, p. 80
Thomas Chaundos		
from	1 October 1359	*CFR 1356–1368*, p. 102
Richard de la Bere		
from	21 November 1360	*CFR 1356–1368*, p. 121

Gatekeepers

Philip de Leministre		
on	8 February 1265	*IMisc I*, no. 289

Clerk of the Works

Richard Kyngeston, archdeacon of Hereford		
from	8 May 1402	*CPR 1401–1405*, p. 91

HUNTINGTON

Owners

Humphrey de Bohun, earl of Hereford and Essex		
to	7 January 1299	*IPM III*, no. 552 (R.I.P.)
Humphrey de Bohun, earl of Hereford and Essex, son of above		
from	7 January 1299	*IPM III*, no. 552
confiscated before	23 January 1322	*CFR 1319–1327*, p. 91
John de Bohun, earl of Hereford and Essex		
to	26 January 1337	*IPM VIII*, no. 55 (R.I.P.)

Humphrey de Bohun, earl of Hereford and Essex, brother of above		
from	26 January 1337	*IPM VIII*, no. 55
to	15 October 1361	*IPM X*, no. 485 (R.I.P.)
Humphrey de Bohun, earl of Hereford and Essex, his son		
from	15 October 1361	*IPM X*, no. 485
to	17 January 1373	*IPM XIII*, no. 167 (R.I.P.)
Thomas, earl of Buckingham, duke of Gloucester and Eleanor his wife, from the Bohuns		
livery	22 June 1380	*CCR 1377–1381*, p. 390
to	15 September 1397	*IPM XVII*, no. 1028 (R.I.P.)
not by	29 November 1397	*IMisc VI*, no. 226
Eleanor, duchess of Gloucester		
from	15 September 1397	*IPM XVII*, no. 1028
to	3 October 1399	*IPM XVIII*, no. 132 (R.I.P.)
Isabel, daughter of Eleanor, widow of Thomas		
a minor on	2 July 1400	*CFR 1399–1405*, p. 65
entered a nunnery	23 April 1402	*IPM XVIII*, no. 172
Edmund, earl of Stafford, through Anne, his wife, sister of above		
from	23 April 1402	*IPM XVIII*, no. 172
to	21 July 1403	*IPM XVIII*, no. 805 (R.I.P.)
Anne, countess of Stafford, widow of Edmund		
on	8 September 1403	*CCR 1402–1405*, p. 111
from	12 July 1421	*CPR 1416–1422*, p. 381

Constables

Griffin ap Rees		
from	23 January 1322	*CFR 1319–1327*, p. 91
to	23 January 1322	*CFR 1319–1327*, p. 91
John de Siggeston		
from	23 January 1322	*CFR 1319–1327*, p. 91
on	23 January 1322	*CCR 1318–1323*, p. 415
Hugh le Despenser, yng., P.P.		
on	4 December 1322	*CCR 1318–1323*, p. 617
Roger Carles		
to	16 April 1324	*CFR 1319–1327*, p. 274
John de Barewe		
from	16 April 1324	*CFR 1319–1327*, p. 274
Thomas de Woodstock		
from	24 May 1377	
confirmed	17 July 1377	*CPR 1377–1381*, p. 66
John Draper of Gamelyngeye		
from	23 October 1405	*CPR 1413–1416*, p. 244
John Smert		
on	21 January 1406	*CCR 1405–1409*, p. 27
Robert Pek		
from	30 May 1414	
to	24 October 1414	*CPR 1413–1416*, p. 244
John Draper of Gamelyngeye		
from	24 October 1414	*CPR 1413–1416*, p. 244
Robert Pek		
from	5 November 1414	
to	18 October 1415	*CPR 1413–1416*, p. 363

Wardships

Minority of Humphrey de Bohun, 1361–1363

Stephen atte Roche, William, abbot of Walden and Thomas de Walmesford

on	26 November 1361	*CPR 1361–1364*, p. 133

Minority of Eleanor and Mary de Bohun, 1373–c.1380

Thomas de Woodstock

from	24 May 1377	*CFR 1369–1377*, p. 403

KILPECK

Tenant in Chief

Robert Walraund		
on	25 December 1298	*IPM III*, no. 543
Richard Talbot, kn.		
to	7 September 1396	*IPM XVII*, no. 915
Gilbert Talbot, son of above		
from	7 September 1396	*IPM XVII*, no. 915

Owners

Robert Waleraund		
to	Easter 1273	*IPM II*, no. 6 (R.I.P.)
Alan de Plogenet, P.P.		
from	Easter 1273	*IPM II*, no. 6
to	25 December 1298	*IPM III*, no. 543 (R.I.P.)
Alan de Plogenet, son of above, P.P.		
from	25 December 1298	*IPM III*, no. 543
Owned by Bohuns		
on	10 October 1327	*CPR 1327–1330*, p. 181
Eleanor, widow of James le Botiller, earl of Ormond		
to	7 October 1363	*IPM XI*, no. 483 (R.I.P.)
James le Botiller, earl of Ormond, her son		
from	7 October 1363	*IPM XI*, no. 483
to	6 November 1382	*IPM XV*, no. 701 (R.I.P.)
James le Botiller, son of above		
heir on	6 November 1382	*IPM XV*, no. 710
Elizabeth, widow of James le Botiller, earl of Ormond		
livery	30 March 1384	*CCR 1381–1385*, p. 372
James le Botiller, earl of Ormond, two above		
on	7 September 1396	*IPM XVII*, no. 915 (From Talbot)

LONGTON (EWYAS LACY)

Owners

Theobald de Verdon, P.P.		
on	12 November 1279	*CPR 1272–1281*, p. 350
to	28 August 1309	*IPM V*, no. 187 (R.I.P.)
Theobald de Verdon, P.P. son of above		
from	28 August 1309	*IPM V*, no. 187
to	30 July 1316	*IPM VI*, no. 54 (R.I.P.)
Elizabeth daughter of above and Bartholomew de Burghersh, P.P.		
livery	16 October 1328	*CCR 1327–1330*, p. 327
on	January 1332	*IPM VII*, no. 389
Bartholomew de Burghersh, snr., P.P.		
jointured	1 May 1335	*CPR 1334–1338*, p. 112

Elizabeth, wife of Bartholomew Burghersh
to 1 May 1360 *IPM X*, no. 603 (R.I.P.)
Sir Bartholomew de Burghersh yng
from 1 May 1360 *IPM X*, no. 603
to 5 April 1369 *IPM XII*, no. 322 (R.I.P.)
Elizabeth, daughter. of above, (= Edward le Despenser)
heir on 5 April 1369 *IPM XII*, no. 322
Margaret, widow of two above
from 5 April 1369 *IPM XII*, no. 322 (Jointure)
on 15 June 1369 *CCR 1369–1374*, p. 41
Edward le Despenser, kn., P.P., from his wife
to 12 November 1375 *IPM XIV*, no. 209 (R.I.P.)
Elizabeth le Despenser, widow of above
from 12 November 1375 *IPM XIV*, no. 209
on 24 October 1405 *CCR 1405–1409*, p. 7
Constance, dame Despenser
on 8 September 1403 *CCR 1402–1405*, p. 111
Edmund, son of Roger earl of March
on 11 March 1406 *CFR 1405–1413*, p. 29
Richard de Beauchamp of Abergavenny, P.P. and Isabel his wife, heir of Despenser
from 13 December 1415 *CPR 1413–1416*, p. 242

Wardships
minority of Elizabeth, daughter and heir of Theobald de Verdon (1316–1328)
Roger Damory
from 24 January 1317 *CFR 1307–1319*, p. 316
Bartholomew de Burghersh, snr., P.P.
from 20 October 1327 *CPR 1327–1330*, p. 183
minority of Edmund Mortimer, earl of March, 1398–1412
Edward, duke of York
from 11 August 1398 *CPR 1399–1405*, p. 408
Henry Percy, earl of Northumberland
from 2 March 1400 *CFR 1399–1405*, p. 50
on 11 March 1406 *CFR 1405–1413*, p. 29

LYONSHALL

Tenant in Chief
Joan Mortimer, countess of March
on 16 July 1338 *IPM VIII*, no. 185
Roger Mortimer
on 23 January 1360 *IPM X*, no. 638
Edmund Mortimer, earl of March
on 12 September 1371 *IPM XIII*, no. 125

Owners
Giles de Badelesmere, P.P.
to 16 July 1338 *IPM VIII*, no. 185 (R.I.P.)
Maud, sister of Giles de Badelesmere, wife of John de Vere
on 30 March 1360 *CCR 1360–1364*, p. 18
John de Vere, earl of Oxford
to 23 January 1360 *IPM X*, no. 638 (R.I.P.)

Maud, widow of John de Vere		
from	23 January 1360	*IPM X*, no. 638 (In her own right)
to	24 May 1366	*IPM XII*, no. 81 (R.I.P.)
Thomas de Vere, earl of Oxford, son of above		
from	24 May 1366	*IPM XII*, no. 81
to	12 September 1371	*IPM XIII*, no. 125 (R.I.P.)
Robert, earl of Oxford, son of above		
from	12 September 1371	*IPM XIII*, no. 125
to	c.1381/2 (fee simple)	
Simon de Burley, king's knight		
from	c.1381/2 (fee simple)	
confirmed	3 August 1384	*CPR 1381–1385*, p. 447 (Fee simple)
to	c.1387/8 (fee simple)	
John Devereux, kn, P.P.		
from	9 December 1390	*CPR 1388–1392*, p. 361 (Fee simple)
died	*22 February 1392/3*	*GEC IV, p. 296*
Walter fitz Walter, kn, P.P.		
on	8 September 1403	*CCR 1402–1405*, p. 111
to	16 May 1406	*IPM XIX*, no. 275 (R.I.P.)
Joan, widow of above		
from	16 May 1406	*IPM XIX*, no. 275
to	10 May 1409	*IPM XIX*, no. 571 (R.I.P.)
Humphrey fitz Walter, son of above, died underage		
from	10 May 1409	*IPM XIX*, no. 571
Being held against king		
on	24 May 1409	*CFR 1405–1413*, p. 150 (LYNALX)

Constables

Stephen Dunheved		
from	18 February 1322	*CFR 1319–1327*, p. 95 (LENHALES)
Richard Wawayn		
from	12 July 1322	*CFR 1319–1327*, p. 144 (LENHALES)

Wardships

Minority Robert de Vere, earl of Oxford, heir of Thomas de Vere, earl of Oxford (1371–1383)

John de Burley		
from	1 April 1373	*CFR 1369–1377*, p. 209
Thomas Tirell and John James		
from	1 October 1377	*CFR 1377–1383*, p. 13

MOCCAS

History

licenced	15 June 1293	*CPR 1292–1301*, p. 23

Owned

Hugh de Frene, P.P.		
licence to crenellate	15 June 1293	*CPR 1292–1301*, p. 23

PEMBRIDGE (NEAR MONMOUTH)

Owners

Wake family		
temp	fourteenth century	*RCH*, p. 250

Mortimer family		
temp	fourteenth century	*RCH*, p. 250
temp	fifteenth century	*RCH*, p. 250

PENYARD

Building

Built first half of C14. Of considerable extent. Replaced C17 when ruined.
RCH, p. 166

RICHARDS CASTLE

Owners

Hugh Mortimer of Richards Castle		
to	28 November 1274	*IPM II*, no. 144 (R.I.P.)
Robert Mortimer of Richards Castle, son of above		
from	28 November 1274	*IPM II*, no. 144
Hugh Mortimer of Richards Castle, P.P.		
to	5 August 1304	*IPM IV*, no. 221 (R.I.P.)
dead by	12 August 1305	*CCR 1302–1307*, p. 285
John Talbot of Richard's Castle		
to	3 October 1355	*IPM X*, no. 251 (R.I.P.)
Juliana, widow of John Talbot above		
from	3 October 1355	*IPM X*, no. 251 (Jointure)
on	23 November 1355	*CCR 1354–1360*, p. 168
John Talbot of Richard's Castle, kn.		
to	18 February 1375	*IPM XIV*, no. 213 (R.I.P.)
Richard Talbot, son of above.		
from	18 February 1375	*IPM XIV*, no. 213
to	13 September 1382	*IPM XV*, no. 862 (R.I.P.)
John Talbot, son of John Talbot.		
from	13 September 1382	*IPM XV*, no. 862
to	3 July 1388	*IPM XVI*, no. 774 (R.I.P.)
Richard Talbot, kn.		
to	7 September 1396	*IPM XVII*, no. 915 (R.I.P.)
Gilbert Talbot, his son.		
from	7 September 1396	*IPM XVII*, no. 915
under age	26 March 1397	*CPR 1396–1399*, p. 145

Wardships

Joan and Margaret, heirs of Hugh Mortimer (d.1305)

Thomas de Bykenore		
from	12 August 1305	*CCR 1302–1307*, p. 285

SNODHILL

Owners

Roger de Chaundos, kn., P.P.		
to	24 September 1353	*IPM X*, no. 131 (R.I.P.)
Thomas Chandos, kn., son of above		
from	24 September 1354	*IPM X*, no. 131
to	6 October 1375	*IPM XIV*, no. 106 (R.I.P.)

John Chaundos, son of above		
from	6 October 1375	*IPM XIV*, no. 106
away and back	16 March 1421	*CPR 1416–1422*, p. 131

STAPLETON (STEPPELTON)

Owners

Hugh Mortimer of Richards Castles, P.P.		
to	5 August 1304	*IPM IV*, no. 221 (R.I.P.)
Richard de Cornwall		
dead by	24 April 1346	*CFR 1337–1347*, p. 468
Geoffrey de Cornwall, son of Richard		
from	24 April 1346	*CFR 1337–1347*, p. 468 (Under Age)
to	18 May 1365	*IPM XII*, no. 12 (R.I.P.)
Brian de Cornwall, kn., son of above		
from	18 May 1365	*IPM XII*, no. 12
to	17 January 1400	*IPM XVIII*, no. 61
Richard, his brother		
from	17 January 1400	*IPM XVIII*, no. 61
John Bryan, Baron Burford		
on	8 September 1403	*CCR 1402–1405*, p. 111

Wardships
minority of Geoffrey de Cornwall

John Talbot of Richards Castle		
from	24 April 1346	*CFR 1337–1347*, p. 468

WEOBLEY

Owners

Theobald de Verdon, P.P.		
to	28 August 1309	*IPM V*, no. 187 (R.I.P.)
Theobald de Verdon II, P.P. son of above		
from	28 August 1309	*IPM V*, no. 187
to	30 July 1316	*IPM VI*, no. 54
William le Blount, P.P. and Margery his wife, da. of Thomas? de Verdon		
livery	30 October 1328	*CCR 1327–1330*, p. 328
to	3 October 1337	*IPM VIII*, no. 115 (R.I.P.)
Margery le Blount		
from	3 October 1337	*IPM VIII*, no. 115
to	16 February 1338	*CPR 1338–1340*, p. 9
John le Blount		
for life from	16 February 1338	*CPR 1338–1340*, p. 9
Hugh Burnell, kn.		
away and back	22 May 1386	*CPR 1385–1389*, p. 149
from	10 May 1407	*CCR 1405–1409*, p. 204

WIGMORE

Owners

Edmund Mortimer of Wigmore, P.P.		
in	1283	*CACW*, no. XVIII.162
to	25 July 1304	*IPM IV*, no. 235 (R.I.P.)

Roger Mortimer of Wigmore, son of above		
heir on	25 July 1304	*IPM IV*, no. 235
on	24 June 1316	*CPR 1313–1317*, p. 491
Crown		
from	23 January 1322	*CFR 1319–1327*, p. 9
on	30 October 1324	*CPR 1324–1327*, p. 72
Edmund Mortimer II , son of Roger, earl of March		
from	12 October 1331	*CCR 1330–1333*, p. 345
to	21 January 1332	*IPM VII*, no. 387 (R.I.P.)
Roger Mortimer, earl of March, son of above		
from	21 January 1332	*IPM VII*, no. 387
to	26 February 1360	*IPM X*, no. 640 (R.I.P.)
Edmund Mortimer, earl of March and Ulster, son of above		
from	26 February 1360	*IPM X*, no. 640
to	27 December 1381	*IPM XV*, no. 560 (R.I.P.)
Roger Mortimer, earl of March, son of above		
from	27 December 1381	*IPM XV*, no. 560
to	20 July 1398	*IPM XVII*, no. 1206 (R.I.P.)
Edmund Mortimer, earl of March, son of above		
from	20 July 1398	*IPM XVII*, no. 1206
on	7 May 1411	*CCR 1409–1413*, p. 207

Constables

Alan de Cherleton		
on	23 January 1322	*CCR 1318–1323*, p. 415
on	1 November 1322	*CPR 1321–1324*, p. 215
Roger Carles		
to	16 April 1324	*CFR 1319–1327*, p. 274
John de Barewe		
from	16 April 1324	*CFR 1319–1327*, p. 274
Alan de Cherleton		
on	17 June 1324	*CCR 1323–1327*, p. 122
William atte Wode (de la)		
to	10 October 1324	*CFR 1319–1327*, p. 306
John Inge		
from	10 October 1324	*CFR 1319–1327*, p. 306
Res ap Griffith		
on	26 October 1326	*CFR 1319–1327*, p. 421
Henry Burghersh, Bishop of Lincoln		
from	3 February 1333	*CFR 1327–1337*, p. 345
Richard Botirell		
from	18 February 1382	*CCR 1381–1385*, p. 144
on	26 June 1382	*CCR 1381–1385*, p. 144

Wardships

minority of heir of Roger Mortimer the elder

Roger Springehoese		
from	29 October 1282	*CPR 1281–1292*, p. 39

minority of Roger Mortimer, earl of March, 1332–1342

Robert de Middleton, King's yeoman		
from	28 March 1332	*CPR 1330–1334*, p. 264
on	18 April 1332	*CCR 1330–1333*, p. 455

Henry Burghersh, bishop of Lincoln		
from	3 February 1333	
on	20 June 1333	*IMisc II*, no. 1382
on	15 October 1333	*CCR 1333–1337*, p. 143
William de Bohun, earl of Northampton		
from	23 September 1336	*CFR 1327–1337*, p. 495
Minority of Roger Mortimer, earl of March, 1381–1395		
Thomas de Beauchamp, earl of Warwick, Roger Mortimer, earl of March, John lord Neville and Henry Percy, earl of Northumberland		
from	16 December 1383	*CFR 1383–1391*, p. 22
minority Edmund Mortimer, earl of March, 1398–1412		
Edward, duke of York		
from	11 August 1398	*CPR 1396–1399*, p. 408
Henry Percy, earl of Northumberland		
from	2 March 1400	*CFR 1399–1405*, p. 50
Edmund Mortimer, kn.		
from	4 December 1401	*CFR 1399–1405*, p. 150
Richard Boterell		
to	29 July 1402	*CPR 1401–1405*, p. 112
John Burford, esq.		
from	29 July 1402	*CPR 1401–1405*, p. 112
Thomas Beaufort, king's brother.		
from	28 September 1406	*CPR 1405–1408*, p. 219

Porter during wardship

William de Mamelshire		
from	16 August 1360	*CPR 1358–1361*, p. 454

WILTON

Tenant in Chief

John de Bromwich and Elizabeth his wife		
on	4 June 1370	*IPM XIII*, no. 30

Owners

Reynold de Grey, of Ruthin and Wilton, P.P.		
to	5 April 1308	*IPM V*, no. 53 (R.I.P.)
John de Grey, son of above, P.P.		
from	5 April 1308	*IPM V*, no. 53
to	27 December 1323	*IPM VI*. no. 517 (R.I.P.)
Henry de Grey, son of above, P.P.		
from	27 December 1323	*IPM VI*, no. 517
to	20 December 1342	*IPM VIII*, no. 391 (R.I.P.)
dead by	1 February 1343	*CCR 1343–1346*, p. 8
Reynold de Grey of Wilton, son of above, P.P.		
heir on	20 December 1342	*IPM VIII*, no. 391
to	4 June 1370	*IPM XIII*, no. 30 (R.I.P.)
Henry Grey, kn., son of above, P.P.		
from	4 June 1370	*IPM XIII*, no. 30
to	22 April 1396	*IPM XVII*, no. 648 (R.I.P.)
Elizabeth, wife of above		
from	22 April 1396	*IPM XVII*, no. 648 (Jointure)

Hertfordshire

Unknown Licenses

BYGRAVE for John de Thornbury, kn.		
	31 October 1386	*CPR 1385–1389*, p. 235

ANSTEY

Owners

Mary de St. Pol, countess of Pembroke		
on	8 October 1376	*CPR 1374–1377*, p. 354
to	16 March 1377	*IPM XIV*, no. 339 (R.I.P.)
Edmund de Langley, duke of York and Isabel his wife		
from	25 May 1377	*CPR 1374–1377*, p. 469 (tail male)
to	1 August 1402	*IPM XVIII*, no. 637 (R.I.P.)
Edward, duke of York, son of above		
from	1 August 1402	*IPM XVIII*, no. 637

BERKHAMSTED

Owners

Richard, earl of Cornwall		
from	1227	*HKW II*, p. 561
to	1272	*HKW II*, p. 561 (R.I.P.)
Edmund, earl of Cornwall		
from	1272	*HKW II*. P. 561
on	16 May 1296	*CCR 1288–1296*, p. 484
The King, his heir		
from	1298	*IPM III*, no. 605
from	1300	*HKW II*, p. 561
Crown – Queen Margaret		
from	20 February 1303	*CPR 1301–1307*, p. 118
to	16 March 1308	*CFR 1307–1319*, p. 18
Piers Gaveston		
from	16 March 1308	*CFR 1307–1319*, p. 18
Crown – Queen Margaret		
confirmed	19 March 1310	*CPR 1307–1313*, p. 216
to	1317	*HKW II*, p. 562
Crown – Queen Isabella		
from	1317	*HKW II*, p. 562
to	1328	*HKW II*, p. 561
John of Eltham, earl of Cornwall, king's brother		
from	1329	*HKW II*, p. 562
to	1336	*HKW II*, p. 562
Edward, the Black Prince, as duke of Cornwall		
from	1337	*HKW II*, p. 562
on	18 May 1375	*CPR 1374–1377*, p. 106
Richard II as Prince		
on	25 February 1377	

Robert de Vere, duke of Ireland		
for one year	1 November 1387	*CPR 1281–1292*, p. 366
Crown – Prince Henry		
from	15 October 1399	*CCR 1399–1402*, p. 22

Constables

William Merre		
on	13 October 1301	*CCR 1296–1302*, p. 468
Hugh de Beaurepair		
to	29 September 1311	*CFR 1307–1319*, p. 103
William de Montague		
from	29 September 1311	*CFR 1307–1319*, p. 103
on	28 September 1311	*CCR 1307–1313*, p. 375
Henry Norman		
on	8 December 1321	*CCR 1318–1323*, p. 412
to	1 October 1326	*CFR 1319–1327*, p. 418
John de la Haye		
from	1 October 1326	*CFR 1319–1327*, p. 418
John de Shobangre		
to	1 December 1330	*CPR 1330–1334*, p. 51
Bartholomew de Burghersh, snr., P.P.		
for 2 years from	26 September 1336	*CFR 1327–1337*, p. 493
Henry de Berkhamsted		
from	16 November 1357	*CPR 1377–1381*, p. 223
on	16 May 1381	*CCR 1377–1381*, p. 450
John de Holland, earl of Huntingdon		
for life from	24 January 1391	*CPR 1388–1392*, p. 369 (At no rent.)
William Cresshill, esq.		
for life from	24 March 1397	
confirmed	30 January 1398	*CPR 1396–1399*, p. 276
Robert Corbet, kn.		
from	14 October 1399	*CPR 1399–1401*, p. 13
on	21 September 1404	*CPR 1401–1405*, p. 416
Wincelaus Dorsteynour, kn.		
on	8 June 1421	*CPR 1416–1422*, p. 365

Private Constables

William de Hampton		
in	*1296–1297*	*Ministers' Accounts of the Earldom of Cornwall*, Surtees Society, Third Series 66 (1942), p. 21
Roger le Graunt, prince's yeoman		
on	14 September 1346	*BPR I*, p. 12
on	23 March 1352	*BPR IV*, p. 42
not by	19 December 1352	*BPR IV*, p. 79
Robert de Eleford		
from	21 December 1352	*BPR IV*, p. 79
on	8 August 1355	*BPR IV*, p. 145
Henry de Berkhamsted		
for life from	27 November 1356	*BPR IV*, p. 27
confirmed	25 February 1377	*CPR 1377–1381*, p. 223

Private Porters		
Henry de Berkhamsted		
from	5 November 1347	*BPR I*, p. 141
on	8 July 1365	*BPR IV*, p. 559
Private Chaplain		
Sir John		
on	22 August 1352	*BPR IV*, p. 61
Receivers		
Thomas Terry		
from	20 November 1386	*CFR 1383–1391*, p. 155
Hugh Stanley		
from	18 July 1414	*CPR 1413–1416*, p. 229
John Purchas		
from	11 February 1417	*CPR 1416–1422*, p. 65
Porters		
Roger Bygg (R.I.P.)		
to	14 July 1414	*CPR 1413–1416*, p. 231
John Asshall		
from	14 July 1414	*CPR 1413–1416*, p. 231

Notes

Hugh de Waterton, kn. to dwell here and govern the king's children John and Philippa and the earl of March and his brother, until the King returned from wales

	5 July 1402	*CPR 1401–1405*, p. 108

BISHOP'S STORTFORD

Owners		
Bishop of London		
licence to crenellate	12 March 1346	*CPR 1345–1348*, p. 61
Robert, bishop of London		
on	5 April 1392	*CPR 1391–1396*, p. 45
on	20 May 1401	*CPR 1399–1401*, p. 501

HERTFORD

Owners		
William de Valence, half brother of Henry III		
to	1296	*HKW II*, p. 678
Crown		
from	1296	*HKW II*, p. 678
to	10 September 1299	CPR *1292–1301*, p. 451
Queen Margaret		
from	10 September 1299	*CPR 1292–1301*, p. 451
not by	4 March 1309	*CPR 1307–1313*, p. 153
but confirmed	19 March 1310	*CPR 1307–1313*, p. 216
Aymer de Valence, earl of Pembroke		
by	4 March 1309	*CPR 1307–1313*, p. 153
to	26 June 1324	*IPM VI*, no. 518 (R.I.P.)
Mary de St. Pol, widow of Aymer de Valence		
released by	13 March 1327	*CPR 1327–1330*, p. 37
released by	13 March 1327	*CCR 1327–1330*, p. 109

Queen Isabella		
for life from	1 February 1327	*CPR 1327–1330*, p. 66
on	13 March 1345	*CPR 1343–1345*, p. 447
dead by	1358	*CPR 1358–1361*, p. 97 (R.I.P.)
John of Gaunt		
from	20 May 1360	*CPR 1358–1361*, p. 428
on	14 June 1397	*CPR 1396–1399*, p. 148
Queen Joan		
on	28 May 1408	
on	14 November 1414	*CPR 1413–1416*, p. 256

Constables

John de Blomvill		
to	9 December 1326	*CFR 1319–1327*, p. 424
Thomas Wake, P.P.		
from	9 December 1326	*CFR 1319–1327*, p. 424
again	4 February 1327	*CFR 1327–1337*, p. 4
John Hotham, bishop of Ely		
from	14 December 1330	*CFR 1327–1337*, p. 214
Robert de Louth		
for life from	19 July 1358 (For Queen)	
for life from	24 August 1358	*CPR 1358–1361*, p. 97 (For King)
Edward Beauchamp		
confirmed	3 April 1399	*CPR 1396–1399*, p. 537

Private Constables

Robert de Louth		
on	1383	*JGR 1379–1383*, no. 814
Edward Beauchamp (For Lancaster)		
for life from	6 February 1394	
on	1395–7	Somerville p. 370
confirmed	3 April 1399	*CPR 1396–1399*, p. 537

Head Carpenter

William de Wyntringham		
on	28 April 1380	*JGR 1379–1383*, no. 276
on	12 May 1381	*JGR 1379–1383*, no. 521

Bailiff

Richard del Newyn		
on	31 March 1382	*JGR 1379–1383*, no. 707

Porter

Walter de Multon		
for life from	20 January 1359	*CPR 1358–1361*, p. 148

Huntingdon

HUNTINGDON

Owners

Mary de St. Pol, countess of Pembroke		
for life	to death	*CFR 1377–1383*, p. 89
died	*16 March 1377*	
John de Hastings, earl of Pembroke, heir of John above		
underage	12 May 1378	*CFR 1377–1383*, p. 89
underage	21 July 1380	*CFR 1377–1383*, p. 211
died	*1389*	

Wardships

minority of John de Hastings, 1375–1389

John de Wykes		
from	12 May 1378	*CFR 1377–1383*, p. 89
from	21 July 1380	*CFR 1377–1383*, p. 211

after death of John de Hastings, 1389–

John de Wykes		
for ten years from	4 July 1390	*CFR 1383–1391*, p. 328
John Bekeley and William Routh		
from	5 November 1414	*CFR 1413–1422*, p. 79

Justices of Goal Delivery

Roger de Kirketon and John de Holt		
on	2 February 1375	*CPR 1374–1377*, p. 74
on	28 February 1376	*CPR 1374–1377*, p. 288

KIMBOLTON

Owners

Humphrey de Bohun, earl of Essex and Hereford		
to	27 September 1275	*IPM II*, no. 100 (R.I.P.)
Humphrey de Bohun, earl of Hereford and Essex, grandson of above		
from	27 September 1275	*IPM II*, no. 100
to	29 January 1299	*IPM XII*, no. 454
Maud, widow of John de Bohun, earl of Hereford and Essex		
from	16 April 1336	*CCR 1333–1337*, p. 568
Humphrey de Bohun, earl of Hereford and Essex		
to	15 October 1361	*IPM XI*, no. 485 (R.I.P.)
Humphrey de Bohun, earl of Hereford and Essex, his son		
from	15 October 1361	*IPM XI*, no. 485
to	17 January 1373	*IPM XIII*, no. 167 (R.I.P.)
Joan, widow of above		
from	29 March 1373	*CCR 1369–1374*, p. 495

Constables

William de Risceby		
from	19 February 1373	*CFR 1369–1377*, p. 206

Wardships

Minority of Humphrey de Bohun, ***1361–1363***

Stephen atte Roche, William, abbot of Walden and Thomas de Walmesford
on 26 November 1361 *CPR 1361–1364*, p. 133

Kent

Unknown Licenses

BOCTONE ALUPH BY WY for Thomas de Aledon		
	12 May 1339	*CPR 1338–1340*, p. 253
BOGHTON MALHERBE for Robert de Corby, king's yeoman		
	6 January 1363	*CChR 1341–1417*, p. 174
BROMLE for William de Bliburghe, king's clerk		
	26 August 1310	*CPR 1307–1313*, p. 278
CHERITON, A CHAMBER for John de Mereworth		
	22 October 1332	*CPR 1330–1334*, p. 365
ORKESDENE for Reginald de Cobham		
	18 October 1341	*CPR 1340–1343*, p. 304
PENSHURST for John de Pulteney		
	6 October 1341	*CPR 1340–1343*, p. 331
PENSHURST for John Devereux, P.P.		
	21 September 1392	*CPR 1391–1396*, p. 164
SHOFORD (MAIDSTONE PARISH) for William de Topclyve		
	18 June 1382	*CPR 1381–1385*, p. 132
STANSTEDE for Robert Burghcher (Possibly in Essex)		
	3 June 1341	*CPR 1340–1343*, p. 225

ALLINGTON

Tenant in Chief

heir of Roger de Kirkby		
minor on	14 June 1340	*IPM VIII*, no. 272

Owners

Stephen de Penchestre		
license to crenellate	25 May 1281	*CPR 1272–1281*, p. 437
Margaret, widow of Stephen de Penchestre		
to	1308	*IPM V*, no. 134 (R.I.P.)
Avice, widow of Stephen de Cobham		
to	14 June 1340	*IPM VIII*, no. 272 (R.I.P.)
John de Cobham of Rundale		
to	14 September 1361	*IPM XI*, no. 240 (R.I.P.)
Thomas de Cobham, son of above		
from	14 September 1361	*IPM XI*, no. 240
to	8 February 1394	*IPM XVII*, no. 308 (R.I.P.)
Reynold de Cobham, son of above		
from	8 February 1394	*IPM* XVII, no. 308

CANTERBURY

Constables

Henry Malemeyns		
to	20 March 1273	*CPR 1272–1281*, p. 7
William de Heure		
from	20 March 1273	*CPR 1272–1281*, p. 7

Simon de Graye		
to	17 October 1274	*CFR 1272–1307*, p. 31
William de Valoynes		
from	17 October 1274	*CFR 1272–1307*, p. 31
to	3 February 1278	*CFR 1272–1307*, p. 92
Ralph de Sandwich		
from	3 February 1278	*CFR 1272–1307*, p. 92
to	11 February 1278	*CFR 1272–1307*, p. 92
Henry Pyrot		
from	11 February 1278	*CFR 1272–1307*, p. 92
to	25 October 1278	*CFR 1272–1307*, p. 103
Robert de Scothou		
from	25 October 1278	*CFR 1272–1307*, p. 103
Peter de Huntingfield		
with county from	12 January 1283	*CFR 1272–1307*, p. 178
John de Blund		
from	25 October 1311	*CFR 1307–1319*, p. 118
Edward de Blund		
from	18 February 1313	*CFR 1307–1319*, p. 163
to	2 April 1313	*CFR 1307–1319*, p. 167
John son of John de Haudlo		
from	2 April 1313	*CFR 1307–1319*, p. 167
to	7 June 1314	*CFR 1307–1319*, p. 198
Henry de Cobham (elder)		
from	7 June 1314	*CFR 1307–1319*, p. 198
to	1 November 1314	*CFR 1307–1319*, p. 221
William de Basing		
from	1 November 1314	*CFR 1307–1319*, p. 221
to	20 October 1315	*CFR 1307–1319*, p. 262
Henry de Cobham (yng)		
from	20 October 1315	*CFR 1307–1319*, p. 262
to	18 May 1316	*CFR 1307–1319*, p. 279
William de Basing		
from	18 May 1316	*CFR 1307–1319*, p. 279
to	24 June 1316	*CFR 1307–1319*, p. 288
John Malemayns		
from	24 June 1316	*CFR 1307–1319*, p. 288
John de Frenyngham		
to	29 November 1318	*CFR 1307–1319*, p. 383
Henry de Sarden		
from	29 November 1318	*CFR 1307–1319*, p. 383
to	18 April 1320	*CFR 1319–1327*, p. 20
William de Setvans		
from	18 April 1320	*CFR 1319–1327*, p. 20
to	16 July 1321	*CFR 1319–1327*, p. 65
Ralph le Sauvage		
from	16 July 1321	*CFR 1319–1327*, p. 65
to	2 November 1322	*CFR 1319–1327*, p. 182
John de Shelvyng		
from	2 November 1322	*CFR 1319–1327*, p. 182
to	2 July 1324	*CFR 1319–1327*, p. 289

John son of Ralph de Frenyng		
from	2 July 1324	*CFR 1319–1327*, p. 289
to	20 June 1326	*CFR 1319–1327*, p. 400
Ralph de St. Laurencio		
from	20 June 1326	*CFR 1319–1327*, p. 400
and from	4 March 1327	*CFR 1327–1337*, p. 24
to	24 March 1327	*CFR 1327–1337*, p. 31
William de Orlaston		
from	24 March 1327	*CFR 1327–1337*, p. 31
Adam de Limbergh		
to	24 March 1328	*CFR 1327–1337*, p. 86
Richard de Grofhurst		
from	24 March 1328	*CFR 1327–1337*, p. 86
William de Orlaston		
from	12 April 1328	*CFR 1327–1337*, p. 87
to	16 May 1329	*CFR 1327–1337*, p. 133
John Shelvyng		
from	16 May 1329	*CFR 1327–1337*, p. 133
to	12 January 1330	*CFR 1327–1337*, p. 159 (R.I.P.)
John de Bourn		
from	12 January 1330	*CFR 1327–1337*, p. 159
to	5 December 1330	*CFR 1327–1337*, p. 199
Roger de Reyham		
from	5 December 1330	*CFR 1327–1337*, p. 199
Ralph de St. Laurencio		
from	3 March 1331	*CFR 1327–1337*, p. 239
to	5 February 1332	*CFR 1327–1337*, p. 297
John de Frenyngham		
from	5 February 1332	*CFR 1327–1337*, p. 297
Thomas de Brokhill		
from	28 March 1332	*CFR 1327–1337*, p. 306
to	7 December 1333	*CFR 1327–1337*, p. 380
John de Frenyngham		
from	7 December 1333	*CFR 1327–1337*, p. 380
to	17 June 1335	*CFR 1327–1337*, p. 448
Stephen de Cobham		
from	17 June 1335	*CFR 1327–1337*, p. 448
to	25 March 1336	*CFR 1327–1337*, p. 475
Henry de Valoynes		
from	25 March 1336	*CFR 1327–1337*, p. 475
to	6 May 1336	*CFR 1327–1337*, p. 483
Thomas de Brokhill		
from	6 May 1336	*CFR 1327–1337*, p. 483
to	26 September 1337	*CFR 1337–1347*, p. 44
William Moraunt		
from	26 September 1337	*CFR 1337–1347*, p. 44
Henry de Valoynes		
from	25 October 1339	*CFR 1337–1347*, p. 147
to	6 February 1341	*CFR 1337–1347*, p. 205
Thomas de Merworth		
from	6 February 1341	*CFR 1337–1347*, p. 205
to	8 December 1341	*CFR 1337–1347*, p. 250

John de Vieleston		
from	8 December 1341	*CFR 1337–1347*, p. 250
to	29 October 1345	*CFR 1337–1347*, p. 445
William de Langeleye		
from	29 October 1345	*CFR 1337–1347*, p. 445
to	27 November 1346	*CFR 1337–1347*, p. 463
John de Frenyngham		
from	27 November 1346	*CFR 1337–1347*, p. 463
to	26 September 1348	*CFR 1347–1356*, p. 83
Arnald Sauvage		
from	26 September 1348	*CFR 1347–1356*, p. 83
to	22 January 1349	*CFR 1347–1356*, p. 84
William de Langley		
from	22 January 1349	*CFR 1347–1356*, p. 84
to	7 December 1351	*CFR 1347–1356*, p. 280
James Lapyn		
from	7 December 1351	*CFR 1347–1356*, p. 280
William de Apulderfeld		
from	18 April 1353	*CFR 1347–1356*, p. 355
Reynold atte Pyk		
from	10 November 1354	*CFR 1347–1356*, p. 409
Gilbert de Helles		
from	10 November 1355	*CFR 1347–1356*, p. 444
William de Apulderfeld		
from	10 November 1356	*CFR 1356–1368*, p. 19
to	20 November 1357	*CFR 1356–1368*, p. 52
Ralph de Frenyngham		
from	20 November 1357	*CFR 1356–1368*, p. 52
William Makenade		
from	3 November 1358	*CFR 1356–1368*, p. 80
and from	1 October 1359	*CFR 1356–1368*, p. 103
William de Apulderfeld		
from	27 November 1359	*CFR 1356–1368*, p. 103
William de Pympe		
from	20 November 1362	*CFR 1356–1368*, p. 236
to	20 November 1363	*CFR 1356–1368*, p. 268
William de Apulderfeld		
from	20 November 1363	*CFR 1356–1368*, p. 268
to	10 November 1364	*CFR 1356–1368*, p. 283
Geoffrey Colpeper		
from	10 November 1364	*CFR 1356–1368*, p. 283
to	17 November 1365	*CFR 1356–1368*, p. 315
John Colpeper, elder		
from	17 November 1365	*CFR 1356–1368*, p. 315
Richard atte Lese		
from	16 November 1366	*CFR 1356–1368*, p. 328
John de Brokhull		
from	26 November 1367	*CFR 1356–1368*, p. 359
John Colpeper		
from	26 November 1367	*CFR 1356–1368*, p. 359
William de Apulderfeld		
from	5 November 1369	*CFR 1369–1377*, p. 36

William de Pympe		
from	28 March 1370	*CFR 1369–1377*, p. 98
to	5 November 1371	*CFR 1369–1377*, p. 146
John Barry		
from	5 November 1371	*CFR 1369–1377*, p. 146
to	12 December 1372	*CFR 1369–1377*, p. 189
Geoffrey Colpeper		
from	12 December 1372	*CFR 1369–1377*, p. 189
Robert de Nottingham		
from	7 November 1373	*CFR 1369–1377*, p. 221
to	16 October 1374	*CFR 1369–1377*, p. 259
William Pympe		
from	16 October 1374	*CFR 1369–1377*, p. 259
to	21 September 1375	*CFR 1369–1377*, p. 298 (R.I.P.)
Nicholas atte Crouche		
from	21 September 1375	*CFR 1369–1377*, p. 298
Henry Appuldrefeld		
from	26 October 1376	*CFR 1369–1377*, p. 369
and from	22 June 1377	*CFR 1377–1383*, p. 2
Thomas de Cobeham		
from	26 November 1377	*CFR 1377–1383*, p. 34
John de Frenyngham		
from	25 November 1378	*CFR 1377–1383*, p. 113
John de Pekham		
from	5 November 1379	*CFR 1377–1383*, p. 170
William Sevaunce		
from	18 October 1380	*CFR 1377–1383*, p. 220
Arnald Savage		
from	23 November 1381	*CFR 1377–1383*, p. 269
John de Brokhull		
from	24 November 1382	*CFR 1377–1383*, p. 327
to	19 May 1383	*CFR 1377–1383*, p. 366 (R.I.P.)
William Chivaler		
from	19 May 1383	*CFR 1377–1383*, p. 366
Thomas Brokhull		
from	26 May 1383	*CFR 1377–1383*, p. 366
Robert de Corby		
from	11 November 1385	*CFR 1383–1391*, p. 76
Arnald Savage		
from	20 October 1385	*CFR 1383–1391*, p. 107
Ralph de St. Leger		
from	18 November 1386	*CFR 1383–1391*, p. 152
William Guildford		
from	18 November 1387	*CFR 1383–1391*, p. 208
James de Pekham		
from	1 December 1388	*CFR 1383–1391*, p. 248
to	15 November 1389	*CFR 1383–1391*, p. 306
William Burcestre		
from	15 November 1389	*CFR 1383–1391*, p. 306
Richard de Berham		
from	7 November 1390	*CFR 1383–1391*, p. 341

Thomas Chicche		
from	21 October 1391	*CFR 1391–1399*, p. 7
to	19 September 1392	*CFR 1391–1399*, p. 55 (R.I.P.)
Roger Gate		
on	15 November 1391	*CCR 1389–1392*, p. 403
Richard atte Lese		
from	19 September 1392	*CFR 1391–1399*, p. 55
William Barry		
from	27 September 1392	*CFR 1391–1399*, p. 56
to	7 November 1393	*CFR 1391–1399*, p. 95
John de Frenyngham		
from	7 November 1393	*CFR 1391–1399*, p. 95
to	11 November 1394	*CFR 1391–1399*, p. 131
Thomas Colepeper		
from	11 November 1394	*CFR 1391–1399*, p. 131
to	9 November 1395	*CFR 1391–1399*, p. 166
Nicholas Haut		
from	9 November 1395	*CFR 1391–1399*, p. 166
Thomas St. Leger		
from	1 December 1396	*CFR 1391–1399*, p. 197
Nicholas Potyn		
from	3 November 1397	*CFR 1391–1399*, p. 240
to	17 July 1398	*CFR 1391–1399*, p. 277 (R.I.P.)
John Dyg		
from	17 July 1398	*CFR 1391–1399*, p. 277
John Botiller		
from	17 November 1398	*CFR 1391–1399*, p. 277
to	22 August 1399	*CFR 1391–1399*, p. 308
Robert de Clifford		
from	22 August 1399	*CFR 1391–1399*, p. 308
Thomas Ludlow		
to	8 November 1401	*CFR 1399–1405*, p. 143
John Digge		
from	8 November 1401	*CFR 1399–1405*, p. 143
to	29 November 1402	*CFR 1399–1405*, p. 181
Thomas Chicche of Balverlegh		
from	29 November 1402	*CFR 1399–1405*, p. 181
to	5 November 1403	*CFR 1399–1405*, p. 231
Richard Clitheroe		
from	5 November 1403	*CFR 1399–1405*, p. 231
Valentine Baret		
to	22 November 1406	*CFR 1405–1413*, p. 53
Henry Horne		
from	22 November 1406	*CFR 1405–1413*, p. 53
Edmund of Haute		
to	2 October 1408	*CFR 1405–1413*, p. 126 (R.I.P.)
William Snayth		
from	2 October 1408	*CFR 1405–1413*, p. 126

Gatekeepers

Geoffrey Gilmyn of Canterbury		
from	30 May 1327	*CPR 1327–1330*, p. 105

CHILEHAM

Owners

Alexander de Balliol of Chileham, P.P.		
dead by	*June 1311*	*GEC I, p. 386*
not by	6 October 1314	*CPR 1313–1317*, p. 191
Bartholomew de Badelesmere, P.P.		
on	16 March 1310	*CCR 1307–1313*, p. 252
on	6 October 1314	*CPR 1327–1330*, p. 554
David de Strabolgi, earl of Athol		
from	28 November 1321	*CPR 1321–1324*, p. 33 (Fee simple)
to	8 January 1327	*IPM* VI, no. 759 (R.I.P.)
David de Strabolgi, son of above		
from	8 January 1327	*IPM* VI, no. 759
Giles de Badelesmere, P.P.		
to	16 July 1338	*IPM* VIII, no. 185 (R.I.P.)
William de Ros of Helmsley, P.P. and Margary his wife, sister of above		
from	20 November 1338	*CPR 1388–1392*, p. 320
to	16 February 1343	*IPM VIII*, no. 474 (R.I.P.)
Thomas de Arundel, kn.		
on	28 October 1351	*CPR 1350–1354*, p. 172
jointured	26 November 1351	*Feet of fines relating to Wiltshire* Wiltshire Record Society 29 (1973), no. 394
William de Ros of Helmsley		
holds reversion	28 October 1351	*CPR 1350–1354*, p. 172
Margary, widow of William de Ros and Thomas de Arundel		
to	18 October 1363	*IPM XI*, no. 528 (R.I.P.)
Thomas de Ros of Helmsley, kn., her son		
from	18 October 1363	*IPM XI*, no. 528
to	21 May 1383	*IPM XVI*, no. 41
Beatrice, widow of above		
livery	24 October 1384	*CCR 1381–1385*, p. 487 (Jointure)
Richard de Burley, kn.		
on	4 November 1385	*CPR 1385–1389*, p. 57
jointured	16 April 1386	*CPR 1385–1389*, p. 148
William de Ros of Helmsley, P.P.		
inherited	*6 August 1393*	*GEC XI, p. 101*
died	*1 September 1414*	*G.E.C XI, p. 102*
John de Ros, kn., son of above,		
inherited	*1 September 1414*	*GEC XI, p. 102*
not by	22 November 1421	*CPR 1416–1422*, p. 187
Margery, wife of above		
from	22 November 1421	*CPR 1416–1422*, p. 187 (Dower)

Wardships

Minority of John de Ros (1414–1419)

Thomas Beaufort, earl of Dorset, duke of Exeter.		
from	22 September 1414	*CPR 1413–1416*, p. 235
to	8 July 1419	*CPR 1416–1422*, p. 263

COLBRIDGE

Owners

Sir Fulk Peyforer		
licence to crenellate	19 July 1313	*CPR 1313–1317*, p. 10

COOLING

Owners

John, lord de Cobham, P.P.		
licence to crenellate	10 February 1381	*CPR 1377–1381*, p. 596
to	10 January 1408	*IPM XIX*, no. 365 (R.I.P.)
Nicholas Hauberk through Joan de Cobham, his wife		
from	10 January 1408	*IPM XIX*, no. 365
John de Oldcastle, P.P. in the right of Joan, Lady Cobham		
forfeited by	12 July 1418	*IMisc VII*, no. 561
Joan, Lady Cobham		
from	22 November 1418	*CPR 1416–1422*, p. 488

Constables while in King's Hands

Reynold Braybrooke		
from	11 May 1398	*CFR 1391–1399*, p. 257

DOVER

Owners

Crown		
on	6 April 1308	*CCR 1307–1313*, p. 29

Constables

Stephen de Penchester		
from	1267	*HKW II*, p. 638
on	11 September 1297	*CPR 1292–1301*, p. 308
dead by	25 April 1298	*CPR 1292–1301*, p. 347 (R.I.P.)
Robert de Burghersh, P.P.		
short term from	25 April 1298	*CPR 1292–1301*, p. 347
during pleasure	20 July 1299	*CPR 1292–1301*, p. 427
to	16 October 1306	*CFR 1272–1307*, p. 542 (R.I.P.)
Henry de Cobham		
from	16 October 1306	*CFR 1272–1307*, p. 542
to	16 September 1307	*CFR 1307–1319*, p. 4
Robert de Kendal		
from	16 September 1307	*CFR 1307–1319*, p. 4
to	19 February 1315	*CFR 1307–1319*, p. 231
Henry de Cobham yng.		
from	19 February 1315	*CFR 1307–1319*, p. 231
to	15 March 1315	*CFR 1307–1319*, p. 235
Robert de Kendal		
from	15 March 1315	*CFR 1307–1319*, p. 235
to	30 October 1320	*CFR 1319–1327*, p. 38
Bartholomew de Badelesmere, P.P.		
from	30 October 1320	*CFR 1319–1327*, p. 38
to	16 June 1321	*CFR 1319–1327*, p. 62

Edmund de Woodstock, earl of Kent		
from	16 June 1321	*CFR 1319–1327*, p. 62
to	17 November 1323	*CFR 1319–1327*, p. 242
John Pecche, P.P.		
from	17 November 1323	*CFR 1319–1327*, p. 242
to	21 May 1324	*CFR 1319–1327*, p. 277
Robert de Kendal		
from	21 May 1324	*CFR 1319–1327*, p. 277
to	15 December 1325	*CFR 1319–1327*, p. 370
Ralph Basset of Drayton, P.P.		
from	15 December 1325	*CFR 1319–1327*, p. 370
on	29 September 1326	*CMR*, no. 806
Bartholomew de Burghersh, snr., P.P.		
from	1 December 1326	*CFR 1319–1327*, p. 425
to	14 December 1330	*CFR 1327–1337*, p. 204
William de Clinton		
from	14 December 1330	*CFR 1327–1337*, p. 204
to	3 December 1343	*CPR 1340–1343*, p. 152
Bartholomew de Burghersh, P.P.		
from	3 December 1343	*CPR 1343–1345*, p. 152
to	5 August 1355	*CPR 1354–1358*, p. 273
Otto de Grandison		
from	5 August 1355	*CPR 1354–1358*, p. 273
to	8 August 1355	*CFR 1347–1356*, p. 433
Roger Mortimer, earl of March		
for life from	8 August 1355	*CFR 1347–1356*, p. 433
on	16 November 1359	*CPR 1358–1361*, p. 324
dead by	1 March 1360	*CPR 1358–1361*, p. 328
Guy de Seintcer		
to	1 March 1360	*CPR 1358–1361*, p. 328 (Keeper)
John de Beauchamp of Warwick, P.P.		
for life from	1 March 1360	*CPR 1358–1361*, p. 328
on	20 November 1360	*CPR 1358–1361*, p. 147
dead by	5 December 1360	*CPR 1358–1361*, p. 509
Andrew de Guildford		
from	5 December 1360	*CPR 1358–1361*, p. 509
Robert de Herle		
for life from	26 January 1361	*CPR 1358–1361*, p. 519
to	7 September 1364	*CPR 1361–1364*, p. 520 (R.I.P.)
Ralph Spigurnell		
for life from	7 September 1364	*CPR 1361–1364*, p. 520
to	18 June 1370	*CCR 1369–1374*, p. 187
Richard de Pembrugge		
for life from	21 June 1370	*CPR 1367–1370*, p. 434
to	18 November 1371	*CFR 1370–1374*, p. 140
Andrew de Guildford		
from	18 November 1371	*CFR 1370–1374*, p. 140
William Latimer, P.P.		
on	3 November 1372	*CPR 1370–1374*, p. 210
to	12 June 1376	*CPR 1374–1377*, p. 278

Edmund de Langley, earl of York		
from	12 June 1376	*CPR 1374–1377*, p. 278
to	1 February 1381	*CPR 1377–1381*, p. 589
Robert de Assheton		
for life from	1 February 1381	*CPR 1377–1381*, p. 589
to	5 January 1384	*CPR 1381–1385*, p. 366 (R.I.P.)
Simon de Burley, king's knight		
for life from	5 January 1384	*CPR 1381–1385*, p. 366
to	3 January 1388	*CPR 1385–1389*, p. 381
John Devereux, P.P.		
from	3 January 1388	*CPR 1385–1389*, p. 381
for life from	12 March 1388	*CPR 1385–1389*, p. 415
on	11 December 1392	*CPR 1391–1396*, p. 199
died	*22 February 1393*	*GEC IV, p. 296*
John de Beaumont, P.P.		
granted reversion	11 December 1392	*CPR 1391–1396*, p. 199
on	20 February 1393	*IMisc VI*, no. 20
for life from	5 March 1393	*CPR 1391–1396*, p. 242
on	30 June 1396	*CCR 1396–1399*, p. 3
Edward, earl of Rutland		
on	15 November 1396	*CCR 1396–1399*, p. 32
on	22 July 1397	*CPR 1396–1399*, p. 228
John Beaufort, earl of Somerset		
from	5 February 1398	*CPR 1396–1399*, p. 289
to	21 August 1399	*CPR 1396–1399*, p. 592
Thomas Erpyngham, kn.		
for life from	21 August 1399	*CPR 1396–1399*, p. 592
to	28 February 1409	*CPR 1408–1413*, p. 57
Henry, prince of Wales		
from	28 February 1409	*CPR 1408–1413*, p. 57
to	1413	*HKW II*, p. 640
Thomas, earl of Arundel		
for life from	22 March 1413	*CPR 1413–1416*, p. 1
to	13 October 1415	*CPR 1416–1422*, p. 34
Humphrey, duke of Gloucester		
from	27 November 1415	*CPR 1413–1416*, p. 374
to	1447	*HKW II*, p. 640

Deputies

William de Bernefeld		
on	15 June 1316	*CCR 1313–1318*, p. 294
Henry de Cobham and Nicholas Criel, supplying place of the above		
on	29 July 1323	*CPR 1321–1324*, p. 318
Nicholas Criel		
on	26 September 1323	*CPR 1321–1324*, p. 375
Alexander Hurtyn		
in	1335	E.101/695/11
Thomas Spygournel		
on	14 August 1346	*CCR 1346–1349*, pp. 102, 149
on	24 August 1346	*IMisc II*, no. 2000
William Barry		
on	2 December 1350	*CPR 1348–1350*, p. 277

John James		
on	3 May 1359	*IMisc III*, no. 372
Andrew de Guildford for Beauchamp		
to	5 December 1360	*CPR 1358–1361*, p. 509
on	18 October 1361	*IMisc III*, no. 490
Thomas de Reynes		
lieutenant	18 March 1373	*CCR 1369–1374*, p. 498
temp	1374	E.101/33/8
lieutenant	10 July 1374	*CPR 1370–1374*, p. 460
deputy	26 July 1374	*CPR 1370–1374*, p. 492
Thomas de Reynes		
deputy	6 August 1374	*CPR 1370–1374*, p. 494
on	12 October 1374	*CPR 1370–1374*, p. 474
on	1 December 1374	*CPR 1374–1377*, p. 62
lieutenant	3 December 1374	*CPR 1374–1377*, p. 60
lieutenant	16 February 1375	*CPR 1374–1377*, p. 141
on	3 April 1375	*CPR 1374–1377*, p. 148
lieutenant	3 May 1375	*CPR 1374–1377*, p. 149
from	7 July 1375	*CFR 1369–1377*, p. 294
deputy	18 July 1375	*CPR 1374–1377*, p. 155
lieutenant	24 September 1375	*IMisc III*, no. 980
Roger de Wylasham		
on	20 June 1378	*CPR 1377–1381*, p. 253
on	28 September 1379	*CCR 1377–1381*, p. 267
Ralph Cheyne		
on	10 April 1381	*CPR 1377–1381*, p. 632
Walter Clopton		
on	22 May 1381	*CPR 1377–1381*, p. 581
Hugh Fastolf		
on	15 April 1385	*CPR 1381–1385*, p. 589
on	26 February 1386	*CPR 1385–1389*, p. 173
Roger Wigmore		
on	30 May 1386	*CPR 1385–1389*, p. 178
on	12 December 1386	*CCR 1385–1389*, p. 278
on	27 November 1387	*IMisc IV*, no. 415
Robert de Berneye, kn.		
on	24 July 1400	*CCR 1399–1402*, p. 170
on	1 December 1401	*CPR 1401–1405*, p. 23
on	28 May 1404	*IMisc VII*, no. 276
Simon Blakeburn		
on	2 March 1408	*CPR 1405–1408*, p. 420 (Lieut.)
on	31 May 1408	*CPR 1405–1408*, p. 453 (Lieut.)
Robert and Thomas Oxbrigge		
on	6 May 1409	*CPR 1408–1413*, p. 108 (Possibly)
Andrew Boteler, kn.		
on	12 July 1410	*CPR 1408–1413*, p. 212
Richard Weyvile		
on	16 August 1414	*IMisc VII*, no. 494
Geoffrey Louther		
on	19 June 1421	*CPR 1416–1422*, p. 390

Bedels of Dover		
Richard de Dover		
from	16 February 1327	*CPR 1327–1330*, p. 11
Gatekeepers of Dover		
Richard Lyoun		
from	16 February 1327	*CPR 1327–1330*, p. 11
Bailif of the Ward		
Richard de Dover		
from	12 October 1327	*CPR 1327–1330*, p. 212
Keeper of Victuals		
Richard Haket		
from	18 January 1337	*CFR 1327–1337*, p. 507
William de Tatlyngbury		
from	7 July 1375	*CFR 1369–1377*, p. 294
Andrew Wodehull		
on	9 July 1377	*CPR 1377–1381*, p. 6
Simon de Earth and Andrew Wodeshull		
from	25 August 1385	*CPR 1385–1389*, p. 8
Seman de Tonge		
from	12 November 1399	*CPR 1399–1401*, p. 65
Reginald Curtoys, esq.		
from	2 March 1402	*CPR 1401–1405*, p. 46
Keeper of Victuals and Armour		
William de Langley		
from	5 August 1355	*CFR 1347–1356*, p. 433
Serjeant to the Constable		
John de Beywik		
on	10 June 1273	*CPR 1272–1281*, p. 10
on	4 May 1275	*CPR 1272–1281*, p. 85
Alan de Hucham		
on	14 January 1276	*CPR 1272–1281*, p. 128
Robert Hert and James Plommer		
on	20 December 1418	*CPR 1416–1422*, p. 177
Chaplains		
Robert son of John de Sutton		
for life from	4 November 1302	*CPR 1301–1307*, p. 68
William de Lychesfeld, chaplain		
on	16 March 1345	*CPR 1343–1345*, p. 445
Artiller		
John Musket		
on	16 October 1358	*CPR 1358–1361*, p. 104

EYNESFORD

Tenant in Chief		
Archbishop of Canterbury		
on	19 September 1303	*IPM I*, no. 162

Owners

Nicholas Criel		
to	19 September 1303	*IPM I*, no. 162 (R.I.P.)
Nicholas Criel, son of above		
from	19 September 1303	*IPM I*, no. 162
Nicholas Criel		
to	17 October 1388	*IPM XV*, no. 245 (R.I.P.)
William Criel, son of above		
from	17 October 1388	*IPM XV*, no. 245 (Underage)
William son of Nicholas Oryel, kn		
on	16 July 1403	*IPM VII*, no. 768

FOLKSTONE

Owners

John de Clinton, P.P.		
on	9 July 1377	*CCR 1377–1381*, p. 6
died	*6 September 1398*	*GEC III, p. 314*
William de Clinton, grandson of above, P.P.		
inherited	*6 September 1398*	*GEC III, p. 314*
died	*July or August 1431*	*GEC III, p. 314*

HEVER

Owners

Stephen de Penchester		
licenced	17 January 1271	*CPR 1266–1272*, p. 507
Sir John de Cobham		
licence to crenellate	3 November 1383	*CPR 1381–1385*, p. 326

LEEDS

Owners

Queen Margaret		
from	10 September 1299	*CPR 1292–1301*, p. 451
on	11 April 1314	*Ancient Deeds vol. III*, A.5298
Bartholomew de Badelesmere and his heirs, P.P.		
from	20 March 1318	*CCR 1313–1318*, p. 607
Queen Isabella		
granted reversion	11 April 1314	*CPR 1313–1317*, p. 111
for life from	1 February 1327	*CPR 1327–1330*, p. 66
on	13 March 1345	*CPR 1343–1345*, p. 447
Queen Anne		
on	24 May 1382	*CPR 1381–1385*, p. 125
to	her death	
Joan Mohun, granted by above		
on	21 February 1399	*CPR 1396–1399*, p. 526
for life from	19 May 1399	*CPR 1396–1399*, p. 562
not by	5 July 1401	*CPR 1399–1401*, p. 509
Joan countess of Hereford		
from	4 June 1403	*CPR 1401–1405*, p. 234
for life from	10 March 1414	*CPR 1413–1416*, p. 168
Thomas, archbishop of Canterbury		
for Queen's life	7 December 1412	*CPR 1308–1314*, p. 453

Constables

John Bacun		
from	20 January 1291	*CFR 1272–1307*, p. 288
John de Northwode, P.P.		
on	24 March 1300	*CCR 1296–1302*, p. 340
Bartholomew de Badelesmere, P.P., for Queen Margaret		
from	29 September 1311	*CFR 1307–1319*, p. 103
on	28 September 1311	*CCR 1307–1313*, p. 375
Thomas de Cottingham, for Queen Margaret		
from	26 May 1314	*CPR 1313–1317*, p. 117
Bartholomew de Badelesmere, P.P., for Queen Margaret		
from	1 November 1317	*CPR 1317–1321*, p. 46
on	20 March 1318	*CPR 1317–1321*, p. 128
Robert de Grovehurst		
on	13 March 1327	*CMR*, no. 73
Owan Corder		
from	4 June 1331	*CPR 1330–1334*, p. 123
Archbishop of Canterbury		
from	26 July 1337	
confirmed	26 July 1337	*CPR 1334–1338*, p. 474 (For Queen)
to	12 December 1340	*CFR 1337–1347*, p. 197
Reynold de Cobham of Sterborough, P.P.		
from	12 December 1340	*CFR 1337–1347*, p. 197
to	6 January 1340	*CPR 1340–1343*, p. 79
to	6 January 1341	*CCR 1339–1341*, p. 593
Walter de Chesthunte for Queen Isabella		
from	6 January 1340	*CPR 1340–1343*, p. 79
Robert de Corby, yeoman, for Queen Isabella		
from	11 December 1354	
on	3 March 1355	*CPR 1354–1358*, p. 188
John de Beverley, king's esquire		
for life from	8 August 1365	*CPR 1364–1367*, p. 162
on	26 October 1372	*CPR 1370–1374*, p. 207
on	14 November 1376	*CCR 1374–1377*, p. 396
John Devereux, P.P.		
from	1 March 1378	*CPR 1377–1381*, p. 137
for life from	13 March 1378	*CPR 1377–1381*, p. 141
on	16 September 1380	*CPR 1377–1381*, p. 546
on	1 May 1382	*CCR 1381–1385*, p. 55
died	*22 February 1392/3*	*GEC IV, p. 296*
Hugh Luterell, kn.		
from	20 June 1394	
confirmed	28 October 1397	*CCR 1396–1399*, p. 154
William le Scrope, earl of Wiltshire, John Bussy, Henry Grene, Walter Bagot		
from	12 July 1399	*CPR 1396–1399*, p. 588
John Norbury, esquire		
for life from	31 August 1399	*CPR 1396–1399*, p. 595

Gatekeepers

Geoffrey Yonge		
from	27 October 1420	*CPR 1416–1422*, p. 300
and from	7 June 1421	*CPR 1416–1422*, p. 400

Porter and Keeper of the Park

John Germeyn		
for life from	28 December 1358	*CPR 1358–1361*, p. 131

Clerk of the Works

John Edward		
from	18 December 1367	*CPR 1367–1370*, p. 46
William Dionys, clerk		
on	1 October 1399	*CPR 1399–1401*, p. 58

Controllers and Surveyors

Thomas, Prior of Leeds		
from	18 December 1367	*CPR 1367–1370*, p. 46

LEYBOURNE

Tenant in Chief

William de Leybourne		
on	30 May 1307	*IPM IV*, no. 410

Owners

Thomas de Leybourne		
to	17 March 1308	*CCR 1307–1313*, p. 26
to	30 May 1308	*IPM IV*, no. 410 (R.I.P.)
Alice, widow of Thomas de Leybourne		
from	17 March 1308	*CCR 1307–1313*, p. 26
from	30 May 1308	*IPM IV*, no. 410
Crown		
on	21 June 1377	*CPR 1381–1385*, p. 423
Simon de Burley, king's knight		
from	28 January 1384	*CPR 1381–1385*, p. 367 (Tail male)
on	12 December 1385	*CPR 1385–1389*, p. 96

MAIDSTONE

Owners

Walter de Maidstone		
license to crenellate	16 July 1310	*CPR 1307–1313*, p. 271

MEREWORTH

Owners

John de Mereworth		
licence to crenellate	22 October 1332	*CPR 1330–1334*, p. 365

QUEENBOROUGH

Constables

John de Foxle		
for life from	1 October 1365	*CPR 1364–1367*, p. 186
on	1 July 1377	*CPR 1377–1381*, p. 2
Thomas atte Lee		
for life from	28 October 1384	*CPR 1381–1385*, p. 467 (Custody)
on	17 January 1385	*CPR 1381–1385*, p. 517
Robert de Vere, earl of Oxford		
for life from	13 March 1385	*CPR 1381–1385*, p. 542

Degary Seys		
on	27 December 1387	*CPR 1385–1389*, p. 381
on	13 January 1388	*CPR 1385–1389*, p. 392
William le Scrope, earl of Wiltshire		
from	1 May 1389	*CPR 1388–1392*, p. 25
Arnald Savage		
for life from	4 January 1393	*CPR 1391–1396*, p. 206
to	15 June 1397	*CPR 1396–1399*, p. 153
William le Scrope, earl of Wiltshire		
from	5 June 1396	*CPR 1391–1396*, p. 715
on	15 June 1399	*CPR 1396–1399*, p. 578
Hugh de Waterton, kn.		
for life from	18 October 1399	*CPR 1399–1401*, p. 15
to	14 October 1402	*CPR 1399–1401*, p. 15
Thomas, archbishop of Canterbury		
for life from	10 March 1409	*CPR 1408–1413*, p. 59
to	21 March 1413	*CPR 1413–1416*, p. 10
Gilbert Umfraville		
for life from	21 March 1413	*CPR 1413–1416*, p. 10
on	16 November 1413	*CPR 1413–1416*, p. 133

Sub–constables

John de Welton		
temp	1376	E.101/531/28

Clerk of the Works

Bernard Cok		
from	8 January 1368	*CPR 1367–1370*, p. 43

Comptroller of the Works

John Barler		
on	8 January 1368	*CPR 1367–1370*, p. 43

Surveyors of the Works

John Barry, Fulk Payforer, Thomas Harcherigge, William Symme		
on	8 January 1368	*CPR 1367–1370*, p. 43

Organiser of the Works

Richard de Thwayt, mason		
from	21 June 1361	*CPR 1361–1364*, p. 38

ROCHESTER

Owners

Crown		
on	6 April 1308	*CCR 1307–1313*, p. 29

Constables

Roger de Leybourne		
not by	28 March 1268	*CLibR 1267–1272*, no. 211
Simon de Kraye		
on	20 January 1272	*IMisc I*, no. 405
to	17 October 1274	*CFR 1272–1307*, p. 31
William de Valoynes		
from	17 October 1274	*CFR 1272–1307*, p. 31

Ralph de Sandwich		
to	4 June 1280	*CPR 1272–1281*, p. 376
John de Cobham		
from	4 June 1280	*CPR 1272–1281*, p. 376
for life	21 April 1281	*CPR 1272–1281*, p. 430
on	15 April 1282	*CCR 1279–1288*, p. 152
William Scarlet		
on	14 June 1297	*CPR 1292–1301*, p. 36
John de Cobham		
to	28 March 1300	*CFR 1272–1307*, p. 426
R. bishop of London		
from	28 March 1300	*CFR 1272–1307*, p. 426
Henry de Cobham		
for life from	14 January 1303	*CFR 1272–1307*, p. 486
on	6 May 1331	*CFR 1327–1337*, p. 254
Henry de Cobham and John his son, P.P.		
from	24 September 1334	*CFR 1327–1337*, p. 416
John de Cobham, P.P.		
on	12 March 1347	*CCR 1346–1349*, p. 252
on	7 September 1347	*CCR 1346–1349*, p. 384
William de Clinton, earl of Huntingdon		
for life from	15 March 1354	*CPR 1354–1358*, p. 22
Geoffrey de Say IV		
for life from	1 September 1354	*CFR 1347–1356*, p. 401
to	1 July 1359	*CFR 1356–1368*, p. 97 (R.I.P.)
John de Grey of Codnor, P.P.		
from	1 July 1359	*CFR 1356–1368*, p. 97
to	14 April 1370	*CPR 1367–1370*, p. 394
Simon de Burgh		
from	14 April 1370	*CPR 1367–1370*, p. 394 (King's esq.)
to	25 October 1379	*CPR 1377–1381*, p. 395
John de Newenton, kn.		
for life from	25 October 1379	*CPR 1377–1381*, p. 395
on	7 October 1393	*CPR 1391–1396*, p. 194
William de Arundel		
on	22 April 1394	*CCR 1392–1396*, p. 344
on	28 July 1395	*CPR 1391–1396*, p. 609
William le Scrope, earl of Wiltshire, John Bussy, Henry Grene		
from	7 July 1399	*CPR 1396–1399*, p. 588
Richard Arundel, kn.		
for life from	4 September 1400	*CPR 1399–1401*, pp. 357, 389
from	23 August 1412	*CPR 1408–1413*, p. 425
on	12 July 1413	*CPR 1413–1416*, p. 77

Deputies

Roger de Say		
temp	Geoffrey de Say (1353–60)	*IMisc III*, no. 743
Nicholas Heryng		
temp	John de Grey (1360–9)	*IMisc III*, no. 743
William Godefray		
temp	John de Grey (1360–9)	*IMisc III*, no. 743
Thomas White		
lately	29 January 1384	*CPR 1381–1385*, p. 372

Chaplains
Geoffrey Norman

on	7 August 1271	*CLibR 1267–1272,* no. 1634
from	27 June 1273	*CCR 1272–1279*, p. 17

Chief master of the Works
John Prior of Rochester

from	11 January 1368	*CPR 1367–1370*, p. 43

Controllers and Surveyers of the Works
William de Bassing and Gilbert Goldewyn

on	11 January 1368	*CPR 1367–1370*, p. 43

Farmers
Henry de Cobham

on	22 March 1331	*CPR 1330–1334*, p. 86

SALTWOOD

Owners

Archbishop of Canterbury		
on	25 July 1271	*CLibR 1267–1272,* no. 1576
on	6 September 1343	*CPR 1343–1345*, p. 169
Church		
on	8 March 1383	*CPR 1381–1385*, p. 233
Archbishop of Canterbury		
on	October 1397	*IMisc VI*, no. 321
on	19 September 1407	*CCR 1405–1409*, p. 291

Constables
Wages 14d/day

on	25 July 1271	*CLibR 1267–1272,* no. 1576

Constables for the Church
John Charney alias Cherney, esquire

for life from	Annunciation 1382	*CPR 1381–1385*, p. 233
inspected and confirmed	8 March 1383	*CPR 1381–1385*, p. 233
Roger Honyton		
not by	19 September 1407	*CCR 1405–1409*, p. 291

SANDWICH

Owners
Queen Isabella

from	1 February 1327	*CCR 1327–1330*, p. 66

Constables

Peter Barde		
to	13 March 1315	*CFR 1307–1319*, p. 236
Nicholas le Archer		
from	13 April 1314	*CPR 1313–1317*, p. 106
from	13 March 1315	*CFR 1307–1319*, p. 236
Queen Isabella		
for life from	1 February 1327	*CPR 1327–1330*, p. 66
Peter Barde		
from	20 March 1332	*CFR 1327–1337*, p. 305

Thomas More		
to	2 March 1397	*CPR 1396–1399*, p. 87 (Keeper)
Thomas Dongeselee alias Mewe		
from	2 March 1397	*CPR 1396–1399*, p. 97 (Keeper)
John Whitney		
in	1403–1404	E.101/43/27

Verger

John Whitney		
from	6 July 1401	*CFR 1413–1422*, p. 25
confirmed	12 June 1413	*CFR 1413–1422*, p. 25

Keeper of the Gaol

John Fige of Almain		
on	8 May 1358	*CPR 1358–1361*, p. 48

SCOTNEY

History

built	late 14th century	King, p. 234

SHOREHAM (LULLINGSTONE)

Owners

John Poyntz, kn.		
to	28 February 1371	*CCR 1369–1374*, p. 286
Nicholas Bonde, leased from above		
from	28 February 1371	*CCR 1369–1374*, p. 286
Alan Seint Joust		
on	16 July 1403	*IPM XVIII*, no. 768
Philip Seynclere, kn.		
to	1408	*IPM XIX*, no. 461 (R.I.P.)

TONBRIDGE

Tenant in Chief

Archbishop of Canterbury		
on	14 December 1295	*IPM III*, no. 371
on	6 April 1395	*IPM XVII*, no. 1273

Owners

Gilbert de Clare, earl of Gloucester		
to	14 December 1295	*IPM III*, no. 371 (R.I.P.)
Joan, widow of above		
on	16 May 1296	*CCR 1288–1296*, p. 484
Ralph de Montemer, earl of Gloucester and Joan his wife		
livery	16 November 1301	*CCR 1296–1302*, p. 473
Joan, widow of Gilbert Clare		
to	1 May 1307	*IPM IV*, no. 435 (R.I.P.)
Gilbert de Clare, earl of Gloucester, son of above		
from	1 May 1307	*IPM IV*, no. 435
to	10 July 1314	*IPM V*, no. 538 (R.I.P.)
Taken into Royal hands		
on	23 May 1315	*CFR 1307–1319*, p. 248

Hugh de Audley, earl of Gloucester		
forfeited by	22 May 1321	*CPR 1317–1321*, p. 587
restored	6 February 1329	*CCR 1327–1330*, p. 434
to	11 November 1347	*IPM IX*, no. 56 (R.I.P.)
Margaret, daughter of above and Ralph, Baron Stafford, her husband		
from	11 November 1347	*IPM IX*, no. 56
John of Gaunt, duke of Lancaster		
on	18 October 1366	*CPR 1364–1367*, p. 327
Ralph, earl of Stafford		
to	August 1372	*IPM XIII*, no. 210 (R.I.P.)
Hugh, son of above		
from	August 1372	*IPM XIII*, no. 210
William de Montague, earl of Salisbury		
on	14 November 1381	*CCR 1381–1385*, p. 25
Hugh, earl of Stafford		
to	16 October 1386	*IPM XVI*, no. 439 (R.I.P.)
Thomas, earl of Stafford		
from	16 October 1386	*IPM XVI*, no. 439
to	4 July 1392	*IPM XVII*, no. 209 (R.I.P.)
One third to Anne, widow of above		
from	8 February 1393	*CCR 1392–1396*, p. 38
William, earl of Stafford, brother of Thomas above		
to	6 April 1395	*IPM XVII*, no. 1273 (R.I.P.)
Edmund, earl of Stafford, brother of above		
from	6 April 1395	*IPM XVII*, no. 1273
on	8 March 1397	*CPR 1396–1399*, p. 92
to	21 July 1402	*IPM XVIII*, no. 823 (R.I.P.)
Humphrey, son of above		
from	21 July 1402	*IPM XVIII*, no. 823
on	18 May 1408	*IPM XIX*, no. 461

Constable

John de Luke		
from	14 August 1315	*CPR 1313–1317*, p. 341
to	1 November 1315	*CPR 1313–1317*, p. 364
Thomas de Cottingham		
from	1 November 1315	*CPR 1313–1317*, p. 364
from	30 May 1316	*CPR 1313–1317*, p. 468
Sheriff of Kent		
to	13 April 1321	*CFR 1319–1327*, p. 51
Robert de Steyngrave		
from	13 April 1321	*CFR 1319–1327*, p. 51
Bartholomew de Badelesmere, P.P., delivered by Sheriff of Kent (Later held illegally)		
from	17 May 1321	*CFR 1319–1327*, p. 57
to	26 September 1321	*CFR 1319–1327*, p. 71
Edmund de Woodstock, earl of Kent		
from	26 September 1321	*CFR 1319–1327*, p. 71
Nicholas de la Beche, kn. and Richard de Grofhirst, as Badelesmere had refused to hand it to Woodstock		
from	3 November 1321	*CPR 1321–1324*, p. 31
to	5 November 1321	*CFR 1319–1327*, p. 76

Alexander de Mowbray		
from	5 November 1321	*CFR 1319–1327*, p. 76
to	3 July 1322	*CFR 1319–1327*, p. 137
Henry Cobham		
from	3 July 1322	*CFR 1319–1327*, p. 137
to	8 June 1326	*CPR 1324–1327*, p. 275
John de Pabenham		
from	8 June 1326	*CPR 1324–1327*, p. 275
on	28 June 1326	*CCR 1323–1327*, p. 486
on	13 March 1327	*CMR*, no. 74
Bartholomew de Burghersh, snr., P.P.		
from	16 January 1329	*CPR 1327–1330*, p. 357
to	6 February 1329	*CCR 1327–1330*, p. 434
John de Montague		
from	22 March 1399	*CFR 1391–1399*, p. 296

TONGE

Owners

Giles de Badelesmere, P.P.		
to	7 June 1338	*IPM VIII*, no. 185
Edmund Mortimer, earl of March and Ulster		
to	27 December 1381	*IPM XV*, no. 550 (R.I.P.)
Roger Mortimer, son of above		
from	27 December 1381	*IPM XV*, no. 550

WESTHANGER

Owners

John de Kiriel		
license to crenellate	18 August 1343	*CPR 1343–1345*, p. 106
Lettice, widow of John de Kiriel, kn.		
on	11 February 1382	*CPR 1381–1385*, p. 133
on	22 September 1383	*CPR 1381–1385*, p. 319

Lancashire

Unknown Licenses

HOLLAND for Robert de Holland		
	24 March 1308	*CPR 1307–1313*, p. 57
NEWTON IN MAKERFELD for Robert de Langeton		
	18 October 1341	*CPR 1340–1343*, p. 304

BORWICK HALL

History

built	C14	King, p. 244

BROUGHTON IN FURNESS

Owners

Nicholas de Broughton		
by	1299	*VCH vol. 8*, p. 402–4
Christiana, wife of above		
alive	1340	*ibid.*
dead by	1346	*ibid.*
Christopher de Broughton		
inherited by	1346	*ibid.*
Christopher II de Broughton		
inherited by	1378	*ibid.*
alive	1404–1405	*ibid.*

CLITHEROE

Tenant in Chief

Thomas of Lancaster		
to	6 February 1311	*IPM V*, no. 279

Owners

Henry de Lacy, earl of Lincoln		
on	25 August 1294	*CFR 1272–1307*, p. 343
to	6 February 1311	*IPM V*, no. 279 (R.I.P.)
Thomas of Lancaster and Alice de Lacy, his wife, da. of above		
from	6 February 1311	*IPM V*, no. 279
confiscated on	13 March 1322	*CFR 1319–1327*, p. 105
Queen Isabella		
on	20 April 1327	*CMR*, no. 57
on	13 March 1345	*CPR 1343–1345*, p. 447
Alice de Lacy, countess of Lincoln		
to	2 October 1348	*IPM IX*, no. 107 (R.I.P.)
Henry duke of Lancaster		
from	2 October 1348	*IPM IX*, no. 107
to	23 March 1361	*IPM XI*, no. 118 (R.I.P.)
Earls of Lancaster		
to	1399	

Crown		
from	1399	
Constables		
While confiscated 1322–		
John Travers		
to	15 July 1323	*CFR 1319–1327*, p. 222
William de Tatham		
from	15 July 1323	*CFR 1319–1327*, p. 222
on	26 April 1331	*CPR 1330–1334*, p. 104
Serjeant bailiff		
Henry le Barber		
from	28 December 1330	*CPR 1330–1334*, p. 32

DALTON IN FURNESS

Owners		
Furness Abbey		
temp	from building C14	*VCH vol. 8*, pp. 308–9

GLEASTON

Owners		
Harrington family		
temp	entire period	*VCH vol. 8*, p. 321
John de Harrington, P.P.		
died	*2 July 1347*	*GEC VI, p. 314*
John de Harrington, P.P., grandson of above		
from	*2 July 1347*	*GEC VI, p. 314*
died	*28 May 1363*	*GEC VI, p. 316*
Robert de Harrington, P.P., son of above		
from	*28 May 1363*	*GEC VI, p. 316*
died	*21 May 1406*	*GEC VI, p. 316*
John de Harrington, P.P., son of above		
from	*21 May 1406*	*GEC VI, p. 316*
died	*11 February 1418*	*GEC VI, p. 317*
William de Harrington, P.P., son of above		
from	*11 February 1418*	*GEC VI, p. 317*
died	*March 1458*	*GEC VI, p. 318*

HORNBY

Tenant in Chief		
Thomas of Lancaster		
on	20 February 1319	*IPM VI*, no. 175
Henry of Lancaster		
on	1 December 1335	*IPM VII*, no. 682
Owners		
Margaret de Neville		
to	20 February 1319	*IPM VI*, no. 175 (R.I.P.)
John de Neville		
from	20 February 1319	*IPM VI*, no. 175
to	1 December 1335	*IPM VII*, no. 682 (R.I.P.)

Robert de Neville, grandson of above		
from	1 December 1335	*IPM VII*, no. 682
to	6 July 1351	*CCR 1349–1354*, p. 372
Henry, duke of Lancaster		
for life from	6 July 1351	*CCR 1349–1354*, p. 372
to	23 March 1361	*IPM XI*, no. 118 (R.I.P.)
Robert de Neville, as two above		
from	23 March 1361	*IPM XI*, no. 118
Michael de la Pole to hold for 3 years unless Neville clears his debts		
from	20 May 1362	*CCR 1360–1364*, p. 390
Robert de Neville, as four above		
to	23 October 1362	*CCR 1360–1364*, p. 427
Sir Robert de Swylyngton, kn.		
from	23 October 1362	*CCR 1360–1364*, p. 427

LANCASTER

Owned

Edmund, earl of Lancaster, the king's brother		
from	18 August 1268	
on	12 May 1277	*CPR 1272–1281*, p. 208
confiscated on	13 March 1322	*CFR 1319–1327*, p. 105
Thomas, earl of Lancaster		
writ on	5 February 1327	*IPM VII*, no. 82
Henry, earl of Lancaster		
heir on	5 February 1327	*IPM VII*, no. 82
on	23 April 1327	*CCR 1327–1330*, p. 78
Henry, duke of Lancaster		
to	23 March 1361	*IPM XI*, no. 118 (R.I.P.)

Constables

Henry, earl of Lancaster		
from	7 December 1326	*CFR 1319–1327*, p. 424
William Rygmayden		
on	1 September 1401	PL.1/3/60

LIVERPOOL

Owners

Lancastrian		
from	1280–1399	*VCH vol. 4*, p. 5
Thomas, earl of Lancaster		
forfeited	13 March 1322	*CFR 1319–1327*, p. 105
writ	5 February 1327	*IPM VII*, no. 82
Henry, earl of Lancaster		
heir on	5 February 1327	*IPM VII*, no. 82
Henry, duke of Lancaster		
on	6 July 1351	Somerville, p. 361
to	23 March 1361	*IPM XI*, no. 118 (R.I.P.)
John of Gaunt, duke of Lancaster		
on	16 March 1372	*JGR 1372–1376*, no. 225
on	10 December 1374	*JGR 1372–1376*, no. 347
Crown		
from	1399	*VCH, vol. 4*, p. 11

Private Constables

John Baret		
for life from	6 July 1351	Somerville, p. 361
on	20 September 1361	*CCR 1360–1364*, p. 212
William de Bradshagh		
for life from	16 March 1372	*JGR 1372–1376*, no. 225
Thomas de Heselden		
from	8 April 1374	*JGR 1372–1376*, no. 724
John Botiller, kn.		
for life from	10 December 1374	*JGR 1372–1376*, no. 347

MELLING WITH WRAYTON

Owners

Ralph de Neville, kn.		
to	6 July 1351	*CCR 1349–1354*, p. 372
Henry, duke of Lancaster		
for life from	6 July 1351	*CCR 1349–1354*, p. 372

PIEL

Owners

Furness Abbey		
licence to crenellate	26 September 1327	*CPR 1327–1330*, p. 169
temp	entire period	

RADCLIFFE

Owners

James de Radcliffe, esq.		
license to cren.	15 August 1403	*CPR 1401–1405*, p. 255

THURLAND

Owners

Tunstall family		
temp	entire period	*VCH vol. 8*, p. 232
Sir Thomas Tunstall, kn.		
licence to crenellate	14 October 1402	*CPR 1401–1405*, p. 164

WEST DERBY

Owners

Edmund, earl of Lancaster		
not by	3 July 1297	*IPM III*, no. 423 (R.I.P.)

Leicestershire

Unknown Licenses

BAGGEWORTH for Robert de Holland, P. P

	15 July 1318	*CPR 1317–1321*, p. 189

BELVOIR

Owners

Isabel de Ros		
to	23 June 1301	*IPM IV*, no. 25 (R.I.P.)
William de Ros of Helmsley, son of above, P.P.		
from	23 June 1301	*IPM IV*, no. 25
died	*May–August 1316*	*GEC XI, p. 96*
William de Ros of Helmsley, son of above, P.P.		
inherited	*May–August 1316*	*GEC XI, p. 96*
to	16 February 1343	*IPM VIII*, no. 474 (R.I.P.)
William de Ros, son of above, P.P.		
from	16 February 1343	*IPM VIII*, no. 474
to	29 September 1352	*IPM X*, no. 45 (R.I.P.)
Thomas de Ros of Helmsley, kn., brother of above		
from	29 September 1352	*IPM X*, no. 45
to	21 May 1383	*IPM XVI*, no. 50 (R.I.P.)
John de Ros of Helmsley, kn., son of above, P.P.		
from	21 May 1383	*IPM XVI*, no. 50
to	6 August 1394	*IPM XVII*, no. 413 (R.I.P.)
William de Ros of Helmsley, kn., brother of above, P.P.		
from	6 August 1394	*IPM XVII*, no. 413
died	*1* September *1414*	*GEC XI, p. 102*
John de Ros of Helmsley, son of above		
inherited	*1* September *1414*	*GEC XI, p. 103*
died	*22 March 1420/1*	*GEC XI, p. 103*
Thomas de Ros of Helmsley, brother of above, P.P.		
inherited	*26* September *1406*	*GEC XI, p. 104*
died	*18* August *1430*	*GEC XI, p. 104*

Private Constables

Richard Shropshire		
confirmed	5 May 1388	*CPR 1385–1388*, p. 434 (For life)

Wardships

Minority of William de Ros (1343–1349)

Ralph de Neville		
from	15 May 1343	*CFR 1337–1347*, p. 330

Minority of Thomas, brother of William de Ros (1353–1359)

Simon de Thorneleye		
from	20 January 1353	*CFR 1347–1356*, p. 352
Robert Sauvage		
from	3 July 1354	*CFR 1347–1356*, p. 399

Roger Mortimer, earl of March		
from	15 July 1355	*CPR 1354–1358*, p. 271
to	8 November 1356	*CPR 1354–1358*, p. 475

Minority of John de Ros (1414–1419)

Thomas Beaufort, earl of Dorset, duke of Exeter		
from	22 September 1414	*CPR 1413–1416*, p. 235
to	8 July 1419	*CPR 1416–1422*, p. 263

Minority of Thomas de Ros (1421–1427)

William Heton		
from	17 May 1421	*CPR 1416–1422*, p. 341 (As steward)

CASTLE DONNINGTON

Owners

Henry de Lacy, earl of Lincoln		
to	6 February 1311	*IPM V*, no. 279 (R.I.P.)
Thomas, earl of Lancaster and Alice de Lacy, his wife, da. of above		
from	6 February 1311	*IPM V*, no. 279
forfeited by	12 March 1322	*CFR 1319–1327*, p. 106
Hugh le Despenser, yng, P.P.		
from	16 July 1322	*CChR 1300–1326*, p. 449
on	16 March 1323	*CPR 1321–1324*, p. 262
Alice de Lacy, countess of Lincoln		
before	11 February 1325	*CPR 1324–1327*, p. 102
Hugh le Despenser, earl of Gloucester		
from	11 February 1325	*CPR 1324–1327*, p. 102 (In fee)
Edmund de Woodstock, earl of Kent		
from	27 February 1327	*CChR 1327–1341*, p. 4
forfeited by	25 April 1330	*CChR 1327–1341*, p. 176
dead by	20 December 1330	*IPM VII*, no. 300 (R.I.P.)
Geoffrey Mortimer		
from	25 April 1330	*CChR 1327–1341*, p. 176
Edmund, earl of Kent, son of Edmund of Woodstock		
underage	21 May 1331	*CFR 1327–1337*, p. 252
John, earl of Kent, son of above		
to	27 December 1352	*IPM X*, no. 46 (R.I.P.)
Thomas de Holland, earl of Kent, brother in law of above		
to	26 December 1360	*IPM X*, no. 657 (R.I.P.)
Thomas de Holland, son of above		
from	26 December 1360	*IPM X*, no. 657
Joan, princess of Wales		
to	8 July 1385	*IPM XVI*, no. 325
Thomas de Holland, earl of Kent		
from	8 July 1385	*IPM XVI*, no. 325
to	25 April 1397	*IPM XVII*, no. 812 (R.I.P.)
forfeited		*IMisc VII*, no. 32
Thomas de Holland, earl of Kent, duke of Surrey		
from	25 April 1397	*IPM XVII*, no. 812
to	7 January 1400	*IPM XVIII*, no. 974 (R.I.P.)
forfeited	20 February 1400	*CCR 1399–1402*, p. 59
Edmund de Holland, earl of Kent, brother of above		
from	7 January 1400	*IPM XVIII*, no. 974

Crown		
from	20 November 1400	*CPR 1399–1401*, p. 426
Private Constables		
Roger de Pickering		
in	August 1315	J.R.Maddicott, *Thomas of Lancaster*, Oxford, 1970, p. 339
Constables		
Nicholas de Grey		
to	12 March 1322	*CFR 1319–1327*, p. 106
Ralph Basset of Drayton		
from	12 March 1322	*CFR 1319–1327*, p. 106
Roger Beler		
on	7 July 1322	*CCR 1318–1323*, p. 475
Edmund de Woodstock, earl of Kent		
on	2 December 1326	*CCR 1323–1327*, p. 622
Hugh Shirley		
on	11 January 1400	*IMisc VII*, no. 44
Steward		
Thomas Barse, esq.		
on	11 January 1400	*IMisc VII*, no. 44
Wardships		
minority of Edmund, earl of Kent, 1330–1331		
Margaret, countess of Kent, mother of above		
from	21 May 1331	*CFR 1327–1337*, p. 252

LEICESTER

Owners		
Simon de Montfort		
in	13 November 1278	*CPR 1272–1281*, p. 486
Edmund, earl of Lancaster, Brother of Edward I		
on	5 May 1277	*CPR 1272–1281*, p. 202
on	13 November 1278	*CPR 1272–1281*, p. 486
dead by	1297	
Thomas, earl of Lancaster		
writ	5 February 1327	*IPM VII*, no. 82
Henry, earl of Lancaster		
restored	29 March 1324	*CFR 1319–1327*, p. 268
on	5 December 1330	*CChR 1327–1341*, p. 196
died	1345	
Henry of Grosmont, duke of Lancaster		
to	23 March 1361	*IPM XI*, no. 118 (R.I.P.)
dead by	16 July 1361	*CFR 1356–1368* p. 165
Maud, his daughter, wife of duke of Bavaria (R.I.P.)		
from	16 July 1361	*CFR 1356–1368*, p. 165
to	10 April 1362	*IPM XI*, no. 299 (R.I.P.)
John of Gaunt, duke of Lancaster		
from	10 April 1362	*IPM XI*, no. 299

Constables while in Royal hands

Robert Beler		
to	4 July 1323	*CFR 1319–1327*, p. 220
Roger de Belgrave		
from	4 July 1323	*CFR 1319–1327*, p. 220
to	29 March 1324	*CFR 1319–1327*, p. 268
Thomas Walsshe		
on	10 April 1394	*CCR 1392–1396*, p. 212
Edward, future duke of York		
from	20 March 1399	*CFR 1391–1399*, p. 297

WHITWICK

Owners

Henry de Beaumont		
licence to crenellate	12 March 1321	*CPR 1318–1323*, p. 571

Lincolnshire

Unknown Licenses

ERESBY for John Beke, P.P.		
	6 August 1276	*CPR 1272–1281*, p. 158
FRISKENEYE for Ranulph de Friskeneye		
	30 January 1303	*CPR 1301–1307*, p. 103
LA BRUERE MANOR for the Knight's Templers		
	10 September 1306	*CPR 1301–1307*, p. 462
LEE for John de Brehous		
	22 October 1330	*CPR 1330–1334*, p. 17
NETTLEHAM for Henry Burghersh, bishop of Lincoln		
	16 November 1336	*CPR 1334–1338*, p. 330
ST. MARY'S LINCOLN for bishop of Lincoln		
	6 December 1318	*CPR 1317–1321*, p. 257
STOW ST. MARY for Henry Burghersh, bishop of Lincoln		
	16 November 1336	*CPR 1334–1338*, p. 330

BOLINGBROKE

Owners

Henry de Lacy, earl of Lincoln		
to	6 February 1311	*IPM V*, no. 279 (R.I.P.)
Thomas, earl of Lancaster, and Alice de Lacy, his wife, daughter of above		
from	6 February 1311	*IPM V*, no. 279
from	27 May 1311	*CPR 1307–1313*, p. 350
forfeited by	12 March 1322	*CFR 1319–1327*, p. 106
Alice de Lacy		
for life from	12 July 1322	*CPR 1321–1324*, p. 179
Ebulo le Strange, P.P. and Alice de Lacy his wife		
on	14 March 1325	*CCR 1323–1327*, p. 270
to	17 September 1335	*IPM VII*, no. 681 (R.I.P.)
Alice de Lacy, countess of Lincoln		
from	17 September 1335	*IPM VII*, no. 681
to	2 October 1348	*IPM IX*, no. 107 (R.I.P.)
Henry, duke of Lancaster		
from	2 October 1348	*IPM IX*, no. 107
on	16 March 1361	*CPR 1358–1361*, p. 575
dead by	4 December 1364	*CPR 1364–1367*, p. 50
John of Gaunt, duke of Lancaster		
from	1361	DL.27/242
from	18 November 1361	*CPR 1361–1364*, p. 118
from	4 December 1364	*CPR 1364–1367*, p. 50

Royal Stewards

Sheriff of Lincoln		
from	12 March 1322	*CFR 1319–1327*, p. 106

Constables

Philip de Kyme, P.P.		
to	27 May 1311	*CPR 1307–1313*, p. 350
Alan de Cubbeldyk		
from	24 March 1322	*CFR 1319–1327*, p. 119
Edward, future duke of York		
from	20 March 1399	*CFR 1396–1399*, p. 308

Private Constables for Thomas, earl of Lancaster

Geoffrey de Villers for Thomas, earl of Lancaster		
on	9 June 1318	Somerville, p. 350

BOURNE

Owners

Thomas Wake of Liddel, P.P.		
to	31 May 1349	*IPM IX*, no. 219 (R.I.P.)
Blanche, widow of Thomas Wake		
from	31 May 1349	*IPM IX*, no. 219
to	3 July 1380	*IPM XV*, no. 445 (R.I.P.)
Joan, princess of Wales		
from	3 July 1380	*IPM XV*, no. 445
to	8 July 1385	*IPM XVI*, no. 328 (R.I.P.)
Thomas Holland, earl of Kent		
from	8 July 1385	*IPM XVI*, no. 328
died	*1397*	
Thomas Holland, earl of Kent, son of above		
to	7 January 1400	*IPM XVIII*, no. 977 (R.I.P.)
forfeited by	Purification 1 Henry IV	
Edmund Holland, brother of above		
from	7 January 1400	*IPM XVIII*, no. 977

BYTHAM

Tenant in Chief

Enguerrand de Coucy, earl of Bedford and Isabel his wife		
on	27 January 1368	*IPM XII*, no. 218

Owners

Robert de Coleville of Bytham, P.P.		
on	2 July 1351	*CPR 1350–1354*, p. 116
to	27 January 1368	*IPM XII*, no. 218 (R.I.P.)
Cicely, widow of Robert de Coleville		
from	27 January 1368	*IPM XII*, no. 218 (Jointly)
on	6 May 1368	*CCR 1364–1368*, p. 427
Ralph Basset of Sapcote, Kn.		
from	1369	GEC II, p. 7
to	July 1378	*IPM XV*, no. 86 (R.I.P.)
Alice, widow of Ralph Bassat		
livery	27 September 1378	*CCR 1377–1381*, p. 159 (Jointure)
to	12 October 1412	*IPM XIX*, no. 1035 (R.I.P.)
Elizabeth, granddaughter of above		
from	12 October 1412	*IPM XIX*, no. 1035

Elizabeth, widow Richard lord Grey of Codnor		
from	10 November 1418	*CPR 1416–1422*, p. 473

Chaplain

Gerard de Wenge		
from	13 June 1291	*Registrum Antiquissimum of the Cathedral Church of Lincoln, vol. I,* Lincoln Record Society, 27 (1931), no. 134

Private Constables for Sir Robert Coleville

William de Corby		
on	1 October 1366	*Records of some Sessions of the Peace in Lincolnshire, 1360–75,* Lincoln Record Society, 30 (1933), pp. 167–8

CAISTOR

Owners

Joan, princess of Wales		
to	8 July 1385	*IPM XVI*, no. 328
Thomas de Holland, earl of Kent		
from	8 July 1385	*IPM XVI*, no. 328
to	25 April 1397	*IPM XVII*, no. 821 (R.I.P.)
Thomas de Holland, son of above, earl of Kent, duke of Surrey		
from	25 April 1397	*IPM XVII*, no. 821
Edmund de Holland, earl of Kent, brother of above		
from	1403	*CPR 1401–1405*, p. 260

CAYTHORPE

Owners

Elizabeth de Burgo		
on	25 September 1340	*CCR 1339–1341*, p. 532
William Bardolf of Wermgay, kn.		
on	23 November 1383	*CPR 1381–1385*, p. 337
dead by	18 July 1385	*IMisc IV*, no. 351
not by	26 October 1386	*CPR 1385–1389*, p. 179 (R.I.P.)

FOLKINGHAM

Owners

Gilbert de Gaunt, P.P.		
temp.	Henry III	*IMisc III*, no. 608
died	5 January *1273/4*	*GEC V, p. 625*
Gilbert de Gaunt, P.P.		
inherited	*1273/4*	*GEC V, p. 626*
died	*17 March 1297/8*	*GEC V, p. 626*
Henry de Beaumont		
licence to crenellate	26 April 1312	*CPR 1307–1313*, p. 457
Isabel de Vescy		
to	1332	
Peruzzi of Florence		
from	1332 (Four year lease)	*IPM VII*, no. 622
on	1 November 1334	*IPM VII*, no. 622
to	*1336*	

Henry de Beaumont, earl of Bogham		
heir on	1 November 1334	*IPM VII*, no. 622
to	16 April 1340	*IPM VIII*, no. 271 (R.I.P.)
John de Beaumont, son of above, P.P.		
from	16 April 1340	*IPM VIII*, no. 271
died	*May 1342*	*GEC II, p. 60*
Richard earl of Arundel and Eleanor his wife, mother of below (from Eleanor)		
granted away	12 November 1367	*CPR 1367–1370*, p. 31
Henry de Beaumont, son of Eleanor and John above, P.P.		
from	12 November 1367	*CPR 1367–1370*, p. 31
died	*17 June 1369*	*GEC II, p. 61*
Eleanor, countess of Arundel, mother of above		
to	12 January 1373	*IPM XIII*, no. 239 (R.I.P.)
John de Beaumont, kn., P.P.		
from	12 January 1373	*IPM XIII*, no. 239
to	25 December 1396	*IPM XVII*, no. 763 (R.I.P.)
Henry lord of Beaumont, son of above, P.P.		
from	25 December 1396	*IPM XVII*, no. 763
died	*June 1413*	*GEC II, p. 61*
John de Beaumont, son of above, P.P.		
from	*June 1413*	*GEC II, p. 61*
died	*10 July 1460*	*GEC II, p. 61*

Wardships

Minority of John de Beaumont, 1413–1430

Henry, bishop of Winchester		
from	6 November 1413	*CFR 1413–1422*, p. 42

GRIMSTHORPE

History

probably	C13	King, p. 261

KYME, SOUTH

History

built	C14	King, p. 261

LINCOLN

Owners

Henry de Lacy, earl of Lincoln		
to	6 February 1311	*IPM V*, no. 279 (R.I.P.)
Thomas de Lancaster and Alice de Lacy, his wife, da. of above		
from	6 February 1311	*IPM V*, no. 279
confiscated on	24 February 1322	*CFR 1319–1327*, p. 98
Alice de Lacy, countess of Lincoln		
from	20 September 1322	*CCR 1318–1323*, p. 596
Ebulo le Strange, P.P. and Alice de Lacy, countess of Lincoln		
on	25 September 1327	*CCR 1327–1330*, p. 169
to	17 September 1335	*IPM VII*, no. 681 (R.I.P.)
Alice de Lacy, countess of Lincoln		
from	17 September 1335	*IPM VII*, no. 681
to	2 October 1348	*IPM IX*, no. 107 (R.I.P.)

Henry, duke of Lancaster		
from	2 October 1348	*IPM IX*, no. 107
on	24 October 1348	*CFR 1347–1356*, p. 97
John of Gaunt, duke of Lancaster		
on	3 March 1372	*JGR 1372–1376*, no. 226
on	1392–3	Somerville p. 377
Judged to be a Royal Castle		
on	13 November 1408	*CPR 1408–1413*, p. 79
Constables		
Thomas de Wyberton		
in	1295	*Registrum Antiquissimum of the Cathedral Church of Lincoln, vol. II*, Lincoln Record Society, 28 (1933), no. 466
Alan de Cubbeldyk		
from	24 March 1322	*CFR 1319–1327*, p. 119
William de Paunton		
to	20 September 1322	*CCR 1318–1323*, p. 596
Alice de Lacy		
from	20 September 1322	*CCR 1318–1323*, p. 596
Reynold de Donnington		
to	5 February 1327	*CFR 1327–1337*, p. 12
Ebulo and Alesia le Strange		
from	4 February 1327	*CCR 1327–1330*, p. 28
from	16 February 1331	
William Fraunk		
from	5 February 1327	*CFR 1327–1337*, p. 12
John de Boys		
from	20 November 1362	*CFR 1356–1368*, p. 236
William de Hauley the elder		
from	20 November 1363	*CFR 1356–1368*, p. 268
and from	17 November 1365	*CFR 1356–1368*, p. 315
Thomas de Fulnetby		
from	27 November 1368	*CFR 1356–1368*, p. 392
and from	28 March 1370	*CFR 1369–1377*, p. 98
Oliver de Barton		
on	28 October 1375	*CCR 1374–1377*, p. 261
on	1392–1393	Somerville p. 377
John Stafford		
on	11 November 1397	*CPR 1396–1399*, p. 183
Edward, future duke of York		
from	20 March 1399	*CFR 1391–1399*, p. 297
John Stafford		
on	20 June 1403	*CCR 1402–1405*, p. 73
John Rocheford		
from	13 February 1410	*CFR 1405–1413*, p. 172
John Stafford, king's esquire		
on	13 October 1410	*CCR 1409–1413*, p. 127
on	1416	*IMisc VII*, no. 578
Thomas Chaworth		
from	16 February 1419	*CFR 1413–1422*, p. 267

Private Constables

John de Beek for Lancaster		
for life from	28 May 1319	*CPR 1317–1321*, p. 340
William de Hamsterleye		
on	11 March 1339	*1341 Royal Inquest in Lincolnshire*, ed. B.W. McLane, Lincoln Record Society 78 (1987), no. 342
Hugh de Muskham		
on	31 December 1340	*ibid.*, no. 494
Oliver de Barton for John of Gaunt		
from	3 March 1372	*JGR 1372–1376*, no. 226
on	1392–3	Somerville p. 377

SLEAFORD (LAFFORD)

Owners

Bishop of Lincoln		
on	13 April 1149	Registrum Antiquissimum of the Cathedral Church of Lincoln, vol. I, *Lincoln Record Society*, 27 (1931), no. 250
to	30 January 1322	*CFR 1319–1327*, p. 91
void	1 March 1322	*CPR 1321–1324*, p. 76
on	13 March 1322	*CCR 1318–1323*, p. 427
restored	27 March 1324	*CCR 1323–1327*, p. 85
on	20 April 1327	*CPR 1327–1330*, p. 148
on	25 September 1340	*CCR 1339–1341*, p. 531
on	14 July 1398	
on	6 September 1404	

Constables during voidances

Sheriff of Lincoln		
to	8 February 1322	*CFR 1319–1327*, p. 93
Robert de Darcy		
from	8 February 1322	*CFR 1319–1327*, p. 93
to	27 March 1324	*CCR 1323–1327*, p. 85

Constables for the Church

John de Cotesmor		
on	30 September 1338	*1341 Royal Inquest in Lincolnshire*, ed. B.W.Mclane, Lincoln Record Society 78 (1987), no. 102
Reginald Courtoys		
for life from	14 July 1398	*CPR 1401–1405*, p. 462
confirmed by sub–dean	6 September 1404	*CPR 1401–1405*, p. 462
inspected and confirmed	18 October 1404	*CPR 1401–1405*, p. 462

SOMERTON

Events

Attacked by Walter de Eboraco of Lincoln and other		
before	6 July 1325	*CPR 1324–1327*, p. 146

Owners

Anthony Bek, bishop of Durham		
licence to crenellate	23 May 1281	*CPR 1272–1281*, p. 440
to	3 March 1311	*IPM V*, no. 274 (R.I.P.) for life only
George de Dunbar, earl of the March of Scotland, Cristiana his wife, and their male heirs		
from	28 June 1401	*CPR 1399–1401*, p. 529

Constable/Wardship?

Henry de Beaumont		
on	28 January 1312	*CCR 1307–1313*, p. 402
on	18 January 1316	*CCR 1313–1318*, p. 260
William de Ferrers, P.P. and Robert de Staundon		
from	1 November 1317	*CFR 1307–1319*, p. 344
Henry de Beaumont		
to	16 March 1322	*CFR 1319–1327*, p. 112
William Bacoun		
from	16 March 1322	*CFR 1319–1327*, p. 112
to	30 June 1322	*CPR 1321–1324*, p. 143
Thomas de Grey		
from	4 June 1322	*CFR 1319–1327*, p. 133
from	30 June 1322	*CPR 1321–1324*, p. 143
Henry de Beaumont		
to	3 June 1323	*CFR 1319–1327*, p. 210
Henry de Barynton		
from	3 June 1323	*CFR 1319–1327*, p. 210
John de Baryngton		
on	17 August 1323	*CCR 1323–1327*, p. 12
Henry de Baryngton		
on	13 March 1327	*CMR*, no. 78
John de Ros		
on	26 June 1328	*CCR 1327–1330*, p. 297
to	24 June 1334	*CFR 1327–1337*, p. 407
John Crabbe		
from	24 June 1334	*CFR 1327–1337*, p. 407
on	20 August 1347	*CCR 1346–1349*, p. 372
Simon de Spense		
not by	28 February 1348	*CPR 1348–1350*, p. 73
John Crabbe		
from	28 February 1348	*CPR 1348–1350*, p. 73
William de Brantyngham, king's yeoman		
from	7 December 1369	*CPR 1367–1370*, p. 336
to	18 November 1377	*CPR 1377–1381*, p. 61
John Auncel, kn.		
from	18 November 1377	*CPR 1377–1381*, p. 61
on	1 August 1379	*CPR 1377–1381*, p. 377
Adam de Ramsey, esq.		
for life from	23 November 1380	*CPR 1377–1381*, p. 560
to	15 February 1390	*CPR 1388–1392*, p. 191
Anketil Mallory, kn.		
from	15 February 1390	*CPR 1388–1392*, p. 191
John Buscy		
for life from	6 December 1390	*CFR 1383–1391*, p. 346

Anthony Mallory.		
to	22 February 1394	*CPR 1391–1396*, p. 380 (R.I.P.)
John Bussy		
for life from	22 February 1394	*CPR 1391–1396*, p. 380
Thomas de Swynford, kn.		
for life from	31 October 1399	*CPR 1399–1401*, p. 42
George de Dunbar, earl of the March of Scotland		
for life from	7 March 1402	*CPR 1401–1405*, p. 53
on	22 March 1402	*CCR 1399–1402*, p. 467
Ralph Rocheford, kn.		
for life from	3 July 1408	*CPR 1405–1408*, p. 433
to	15 May 1415	*CPR 1413–1416*, p. 327
Thomas duke of Clarence		
from	15 May 1415	*CPR 1413–1416*, p. 327

Deputies

Nicholas Beek		
on	9 June 1377	*CCR 1374–1377*, p. 553 (Lieutenant)

Porters

John Golde		
from	30 September 1410	
on	14 November 1411	*CPR 1408–1413*, p. 350

Maker of the Crossbows

Gerard le Artiller		
on	10 March 1337	*CCR 1337–1339*, p. 28

STAMFORD

Owners

Queen Eleanor of Castile		
on	10 June 1280	*CPR 1272–1281*, p. 380
John de Warenne, earl of Surrey (For life)		
on	20 June 1338	*CPR 1338–1340*, p. 100
to	30 June 1347	*IPM IX*, no. 54 (R.I.P.)
William de Bohun, earl of Northampton		
reversion	20 June 1338	*CPR 1337–1339*, p. 100
from	30 June 1347	*IPM IX*, no. 54
to	16 September 1360	*IPM X*, no. 639 (R.I.P.)
Humphrey de Bohun, , earl of Hereford and Essex, son of above		
from	16 September 1360	*IPM X*, no. 639
Edmund de Langley, duke of York		
from	8 May 1363	*CChR 1341–1417*, p. 178
to	1 August 1402	*IPM XVIII*, no. 634 (R.I.P.)
Edward, duke of York, son of above		
from	1 August 1402	*IPM XVIII*, no. 634

Constables

Philip de Stanburn		
possibly	19 July 1276	*CCR 1272–1279*, p. 303

TATTERSHALL

Owners

Robert de Tattershall		
licence to crenellate	1231	
to	August 1273	*IPM II*, no. 4 (R.I.P.)
Robert de Tattershall, son of above, P.P.		
from	August 1273	*IPM II*, no. 4
to	8 September 1298	*IPM III*, no. 476 (R.I.P.)
Robert de Tattershall, son of above, P.P.		
from	8 September 1298	*IPM III*, no. 476
to	28 July 1303	*IPM IV*, no. 163 (R.I.P.)
Robert de Tattershall jnr., son of above		
from	28 July 1303	*IPM IV*, no. 163
to	30 January 1306	*IPM IV*, no. 391 (R.I.P.)
Joan de Driby		
from	30 January 1306	*IPM IV*, no. 391
to	15 October 1329	*IPM VII*, no. 241 (R.I.P.)
John de Driby, son of above		
from	15 October 1329	*IPM VII*, no. 241
not by	24 June 1334	*CPR 1330–1334*, p. 554
John de Kirketon, P.P.		
by	24 June 1334	*CPR 1330–1334*, p. 554
to	20 February 1367	*IPM XII*, no. 150 (R.I.P.)
Ralph Cromwell, P.P.		
from	20 February 1367	*IPM XII*, no. 150 (With Maud, his wife)
to	27 August 1398	*IPM XVII*, no. 1133 (R.I.P.)
Maud, wife of above		
from	27 August 1398	*IPM XVII*, no. 1133
from	18 November 1398	*CCR 1396–1399*, p. 361 (Jointure)

Wardship of Robert de Tattershall (1303–1306)

Queen Margaret		
to	30 December 1303	*CPR 1301–1307*, p. 206
Henry Percy and John de Neville		
from	30 December 1303	*CPR 1301–1307*, p. 206

London and Middlesex

City Licenses

CHAMBER IN BRADESTRERE for John de Wengrave, citizen of London

	22 May 1314	*CPR 1313–1317*, p. 118

DWELLING IN CASTLE BAYNARD for John de Molyns

	6 May 1338	*CPR 1338–1340*, p. 62

FLETSTRETE for Robert Wyville, bishop of Salisbury

	30 August 1337	*CPR 1334–1338*, p. 498

HOUSE IN LONDON for John de Pulteney

	6 October 1341	*CPR 1340–1343*, p. 331

HOUSE IN ST. MARY ATTE STRONDE for Walton Langton, bishop of Coventry and Lichfield

	19 June 1305	*CPR 1301–1307*, p. 367

HOUSE IN WEST CHEPE for Robert de Keleseye

	28 May 1315	*CPR 1313–1317*, p. 292

HOUSES IN SILVERSTRETE and DISTAFLANE for John de Pelham, king's clerk

	2 November 1311	*CPR 1307–1313*, p. 398

HOUSE ON CORNHILL for John de Coloygne, king's yeoman

	12 August 1337	*CPR 1334–1338*, p. 505

ROSEMONT AT EYE near WESTMINSTER for John de Benstede

	11 March 1308	*CPR 1307–1313*, p. 61

TURRET IN LONDON for William Servat

	3 October 1305	*CPR 1301–1307*, p. 379

THE TOWER OF LONDON

Constables

Walter Gray, archbishop of York		
on	13 November 1271	*CLibR 1267–1272*, no. 1768
on	8 November 1272	*CLibR 1267–1272*, no. 2135, 2145
John de Burgo the Elder		
for life from	18 December 1273	*CPR 1272–1281*, p. 41
Anselm de Gyse		
to	21 January 1275	*CFR 1272–1307*, p. 39
Anthony Bek, future bishop of Durham		
from	21 January 1275	*CFR 1272–1307*, p. 39
on	2 June 1275	*CPR 1272–1281*, p. 92
Giles de Audenard		
on	10 February 1276	*CCR 1272–1279*, p. 270
Anthony Bek, future bishop of Durham		
on	13 November 1276	*CPR 1272–1281*, p. 168
Giles de Audenard		
on	7 February 1277	*CCR 1272–1279*, p. 370
Anthony Bek, future bishop of Durham		
on	6 May 1277	*CPR 1272–1281*, p. 203
on	27 April 1279	*CPR 1272–1281*, p. 310
Ranulph de Dacre		
on	20 July 1283	*CPR 1281–1292*, p. 70

Anthony Bek, future bishop of Durham		
to	10 September 1285	*CFR 1272–1307*, p. 220
Ralph de Sandwich		
from	10 September 1285	*CFR 1272–1307*, p. 220
to	26 January 1289	*CPR 1281–1292*, p. 311
Ralph de Berners		
from	26 January 1289	*CFR 1272–1307*, p. 244
to	22 July 1289	*CPR 1282–1292*, p. 317
Ralph de Sandwich		
from	22 July 1289	*CFR 1272–1307*, p. 263
to	12 March 1308	*CFR 1307–1319*, p. 18
John de Cromwell, P.P.		
from	12 March 1308	*CFR 1307–1319*, p. 18
on	10 April 1315	*CPR 1313–1318*, p. 314
Guy Ferre		
from	2 July 1321	*CFR 1319–1327*, p. 63
to	30 August 1321	*CFR 1319–1327*, p. 70
Roger de Swynnerton, P.P.		
from	30 August 1321	*CFR 1319–1327*, p. 70 (Constable)
on	26 February 1322	*CPR 1321–1324*, p. 75 (Keeper)
Stephen de Segrave		
from	4 February 1323	*CFR 1319–1327*, p. 196
to	6 August 1323	*CCR 1323–1327*, p. 13
Walter Stapledon, bishop of Exeter		
from	6 August 1323	*CCR 1323–1327*, p. 13
on	17 November 1323	*CFR 1319–1327*, p. 244
John de Weston		
from	17 November 1323	*CFR 1319–1327*, p. 244
on	14 October 1326	*CMR*, no. 198
John de Gisors		
petition for wages	1327	C.49/6/7
Thomas Wake, P.P.		
from	9 December 1326	*CFR 1319–1327*, p. 424
to	16 April 1328	*CFR 1327–1337*, p. 87
Maurice de Berkeley		
from	16 April 1328	*CFR 1327–1337*, p. 87
William la Zouche Mortimer, P.P.		
temp	1328–1329	E.101/18/14
to	31 January 1329	*CFR 1327–1337*, p. 118
John de Cromwell, P.P.		
for life from	31 January 1329	*CFR 1327–1337*, p. 118
to	15 October 1335	*CPR 1334–1338*, p. 171
Nicholas de la Beche, kn.		
from	15 October 1335	*CPR 1334–1338*, p. 171
on	22 June 1340	*CPR 1340–1343*, p. 1
William Lenglis		
to	8 March 1341	*CFR 1337–1347*, p. 212
Robert de Dalton		
from	8 March 1341	*CFR 1337–1347*, p. 212
to	12 March 1346	*CPR 1345–1348*, p. 54

John Darcy, the father, P.P.		
from	12 March 1346	*CPR 1345–1348*, p. 54
to	7 June 1347	*CPR 1345–1348*, p. 536 (R.I.P.)
John Darcy, the son, P.P.		
from	7 June 1347	*CPR 1345–1348*, p. 536
on	24 February 1351	*CPR 1350–1354*, p. 79
John de Beauchamp of Warwick, P.P.		
on	15 March 1352	*CPR 1350–1354*, p. 241
on	30 January 1355	*CPR 1354–1358*, p. 229
Bartholomew de Burghersh, snr., P.P.		
for life from	27 June 1355	*CPR 1354–1358*, p. 248
on	3 July 1355	*CCR 1354–1360*, p. 135
Robert de Morley, P.P.		
from	8 August 1355	*CPR 1354–1358*, p. 275 (Keeper)
to	25 January 1360	*CCR 1354–1360*, p. 328 (R.I.P.)
John de Beauchamp of Warwick, P.P.		
for life from	25 January 1360	*CPR 1358–1361*, p. 328
Richard de la Vache		
for life from	26 January 1361	*CPR 1358–1361*, p. 531
to	18 January 1366	*CFR 1356–1368*, p. 321 (R.I.P.)
Alan de Buxhull		
for life from	18 January 1366	*CFR 1356–1368*, p. 321
on	20 July 1381	*CCR 1381–1385*, p. 6
not by	20 November 1381	*CCR 1381–1385*, p. 6 (R.I.P.)
Thomas Morieux		
for life from	8 December 1381	*CPR 1381–1385*, p. 64
for life from	26 May 1382	*CPR 1381–1385*, p. 124
on	15 January 1387	*CPR 1385–1389*, p. 216
Thomas de Holland, earl of Kent		
for life from	9 May 1387	*CPR 1385–1389*, p. 301
on	27 January 1392	*CPR 1391–1396*, p. 16
Edward, future duke of York, earl of Rutland, granted reversion on death of above		
on	27 January 1392	*CPR 1391–1396*, p. 16
Thomas de Holland, earl of Kent		
on	14 April 1395	*CPR 1391–1396*, p. 560
Ralph de Neville of Raby		
from	21 September 1397	*CPR 1396–1399*, p. 194
Edward, future duke of York, earl of Rutland		
for life from	30 October 1397	*CPR 1396–1399*, p. 250
to	31 August 1399	*CPR 1396–1399*, p. 593
Thomas de Rempston, king's kn.		
for life from	31 August 1399	*CPR 1396–1399*, p. 593
on	6 January 1406	*CCR 1405–1409*, p. 20
Edward, duke of York		
on	21 October 1409	*CCR 1409–1413*, p. 7
to	26 November 1415	*CPR 1413–1416*, p. 375 (R.I.P.)
William Burghchier, kn.		
from	26 November 1415	*CPR 1413–1416*, p. 375
on	15 November 1418	*CPR 1416–1422*, p. 473
Roger Aston, kn.		
from	26 June 1420	*CPR 1416–1422*, p. 294

Lieutenants / Sub–constables

Giles de Audenard		
on	20 May 1276	*CCR 1272–1279*, p. 289 (Subconstable)
on	20 July 1276	*CPR 1272–1281*, p. 152
on	29 January 1278	*CPR 1272–1282*, p. 255
on	22 January 1279	*CPR 1272–1281*, p. 298
Richard de Waldegrave		
on	8 June 1280	*CCR 1272–1281*, p. 22
on	1 May 1282	*CWR*, p. 217
Ranulph de Dacre		
on	24 December 1284	*CPR 1281–1292*, p. 148 (Constable)
on	27 December 1284	*CPR 1281–1292*, p. 147 (Sub–constable)
William de Herlisonn		
temp	c.1335	E.101/19/28
Robert le Brut		
temp	c.1335	E.101/19/28
Walter de Harewell		
temp	c.1338	E.101/19/28
John de Wynewyk		
on	27 November 1342	*CPR 1340–1343*, p. 566 (Lieutenant)
on	7 December 1342	E.403/327 m.15
Thomas Rous		
temp	1347–1348	E.101/25/29
on	7 June 1348	E.403/341 m.13
Walter de Birton		
on/to	25 January 1360	*CPR 1358–1361*, p. 328 (For Morlee)
Thomas de la Vache		
on	23 November 1365	*CCR 1364–1368*, p. 152
Robert Ruthyn		
dead by	14 September 1371	*CCR 1369–1374*, p. 250
Walter de Chippenham		
from	14 September 1371	*CCR 1369–1374*, p. 250
Robert Neuton		
on	20 November 1381	*CCR 1381–1385*, p. 26 (For Buxhull)
William de Lye		
on	14 April 1395	*CPR 1391–1396*, p. 560
Robert Thorle, esq.		
on	9 January 1400	*CCR 1399–1402*, p. 34
Robert German		
on	8 August 1400	*CCR 1399–1402*, p. 171
Henry Mulsho		
to	4 August 1411	*CPR 1408–1413*, p. 303
Simon Kampe		
from	4 August 1411	*CPR 1408–1413*, p. 303
not by	24 May 1414	*CPR 1413–1416*, p. 191
Robert de Morley		
from	8 July 1413	*CPR 1413–1416*, p. 68
on	13 July 1413	*CPR 1413–1416*, p. 24 (Warden)
John Dabrichecourt, kn.		
from	28 October 1413	*CPR 1413–1416*, p. 103
on	16 November 1413	*CCR 1413–1419*, p. 40 (Warden)

Clerk and Keeper of the privy wardrobe in the Tower

William de Rothewell, king's clerk		
from	24 March 1359	*CPR 1358–1361*, p. 221
on	15 November 1359	*CPR 1358–1361*, p. 323

Master of the Works

Master Robert de Beverlaco		
on	14 February 1278	*CCR 1272–1279*, p. 444
Brother John of the Order of St. Thomas of Acre		
on	14 February 1278	*CCR 1272–1279*, p. 444

Viewers of the Works

Philip de Otington		
from	9 July 1267	
on	26 January 1270	*CLibR 1267–1272*, no. 994
on	20 July 1270	*CLibR 1267–1272*, no. 1193
on	6 November 1271	*CLibR 1267–1272*, no. 1714
on	7 November 1271	*CLibR 1267–1272*, no. 1748 (8d./day)

Keeper of the Works

Giles de Audenard		
on	14 February 1278	*CCR 1272–1279*, p. 444
on	26 Jube 1278	*CPR 1272–1281*, p. 273
John de Ditton		
from	20 February 1320	*CFR 1319–1327*, p. 18
Richard de Kenebrok		
from	13 March 1327	*CFR 1327–1337*, p. 26

Clerk of the Works

Walter de Weston		
on	18 March 1337	*CCR 1337–1339*, p. 41
Peter de Brugge		
from	8 October 1347	*CPR 1345–1348*, p. 413 (and Surveyor)
Thomas de Stapelford		
from	21 September 1354	*CPR 1354–1358*, p. 104 (and Surveyor)
Richard de Normanton		
from	24 April 1361	*CPR 1361–1364*, p. 2
Thomas Chamberleyn		
from	26 April 1361	*CPR 1361–1364*, p. 2
Arnald Brocas		
from	3 May 1381	*CPR 1381–1385*, p. 6
John Bernard, clerk		
from	16 December 1396	*CPR 1396–1399*, p. 48
John Strange		
on	7 April 1413	*CPR 1413–1416*, p. 11
John Skipton		
from	18 July 1413	*CPR 1413–1416*, p. 59
William Purveour		
from	18 July 1413	*CPR 1413–1416*, p. 59

Organiser of the Works

John de Alkeshull		
from	5 May 1361	*CPR 1361–1364*, p. 17

Deputy Clerk of the Works		
Thomas de Stapelford		
on	18 March 1337	*CCR 1337–1339*, p. 41
Hugh Swayne		
from	3 May 1381	*CPR 1381–1385*, p. 19
Keeper of Accounts		
William de Hanney		
from	3 May 1381	*CPR 1381–1385*, p. 19
Purveyor of the Works		
John Pritwell		
from	18 March 1401	
to	23 October 1409	*CPR 1408–1413*, p. 143
John Seyntclere		
for life from	23 October 1409	*CPR 1408–1413*, p. 143
Keeper of the Lions		
Peter Fabre of Montpeller		
on	26 July 1313	*CCR 1313–1318*, p. 4
on	24 June 1314	*CCR 1313–1318*, p. 60
on	3 November 1314	*CCR 1313–1318*, p. 124
on	1 October 1315	*CCR 1313–1318*, p. 249
Berenger de Aragon		
on	18 June 1335	*CCR 1333–1337*, p. 412
on	3 October 1336	*CCR 1333–1337*, p. 611
on	7 June 1337	*CCR 1337–1339*, p. 67
on	9 August 1338	*CCR 1337–1339*, p. 458
not by	16 October 1341	*CPR 1340–1343*, p. 301
Robert le Bowyer of Doncaster		
from	16 October 1341	*CPR 1340–1343*, p. 301
on	29 March 1346	*CCR 1346–1349*, p. 61
not by	5 August 1349	*CPR 1348–1350*, p. 255 (R.I.P.)
John Styrop		
from	5 August 1349	*CPR 1348–1350*, p. 255
to	6 March 1369	*CPR 1367–1370*, p. 226 (R.I.P.)
William de le Garderobe		
from	6 March 1369	*CPR 1367–1370*, p. 226
on	12 October 1370	*Issue Rolls*, p. 298
on	5 March 1378	*CPR 1377–1381*, p. 139
on	4 June 1380	*CCR 1377–1381*, p. 313
to	7 November 1381	*CPR 1381–1385*, p. 50 (R.I.P.)
John de Evesham		
from	7 November 1381	*CPR 1381–1385*, p. 50
for life from	6 October 1382	*CPR 1381–1385*, p. 170
Nicholas de Wenlyng		
for life from	28 October 1399	*CPR 1399–1401*, p. 28
to	24 October 1404	*CPR 1401–1405*, p. 468
Nicholas de Wenlyng and John Wolde		
for life from	24 October 1404	*CPR 1401–1405*, p. 468
John de Riche		
for life from	5 February 1410	*CPR 1408–1413*, p. 157
William Kerby		
from	26 March 1413	*CFR 1413–1422*, p. 10

The Lions

1 Lion		
on	3 November 1314	*CCR 1313–1318*, p. 124
1 Leopard		
on	1 October 1315	*CCR 1313–1318*, p. 249
on	23 November 1320	*CCR 1318–1323*, p. 281
2 Lions, 2 Leopards		
on	18 June 1335	*CCR 1333–1337*, p. 412
on	3 October 1336	*CCR 1333–1337*, p. 611
1 Lion, 1 Lioness, 1 Leopard and 2 whelps of the Lioness		
on	16 October 1341	*CPR 1340–1343*, p. 301
5 Lions, 2 young		
on	12 October 1370	*Issue Roll*, p. 298

Chaplains

Brothers Reyner and Richard		
on	6 February 1272	*CLibR 1267–1272*, no. 1792
Peter Parker		
from	23 January 1414	*CPR 1413–1416*, p. 156

Chief Smith

Master Andrew le Feure		
for life from	9 June 1354	*CPR 1354–1358*, p. 72

Carpenter of the Works

John Dobson of London		
for life from	12 April 1402	*CPR 1401–1405*, p. 83

Keeper of the Jewels

John de Flete		
on	3 November 1343	*CCR 1343–1346*, p. 246
on	1 February 1344	*CCR 1343–1346*, p. 271
on	4 February 1344	*CCR 1343–1346*, p. 338
on	10 May 1344	*CCR 1343–1346*, p. 367
Robert de Mildenhale		
on	16 October 1344	*CCR 1343–1346*, p. 422

Keeper of the Exchange

John de Flete		
on	10 February 1344	*CCR 1343–1346*, p. 274
on	25 October 1344	*CCR 1343–1346*, p. 424

Keeper of the King's Arms in the Tower

John de London, yeoman		
on	24 February 1354	*CPR 1354–1358*, p. 11
William de le Garderobe		
to	7 November 1381	*CPR 1381–1385*, p. 50 (R.I.P.)
John de Evesham		
from	7 November 1381	*CPR 1381–1385*, p. 50
Robert Penford, yeoman		
from	17 April 1409	*CPR 1408–1413*, p. 77 (For life)

Keeper of the King's Bed in the Tower

Adam atte Wode		
to	22 August 1409	*CPR 1408–1413*, p. 104 (R.I.P.)

William Hert, king's yeoman		
from	22 August 1409	*CPR 1408–1413*, p. 104

Keeper of the Bows

Adam Bowyer		
to	20 November 1396	*CPR 1396–1399*, p. 35 (R.I.P.)
Robert Bridford		
from	20 November 1396	*CPR 1396–1399*, p. 35
Thomas Coton of London		
from	19 November 1399	*CPR 1396–1399*, p. 98

Artiller

John Alblaster		
from	2 April 1406	*CPR 1405–1408*, p. 165

Artiller of the King's Crossbows

Master Conrad		
on	10 July 1269	*CLibR 1267–1272*, no. 788
on	27 November 1270	*CLibR 1267–1272*, no. 1296
Master Thomas de St. Sepulcro		
on	11 November 1272	*CLibR 1267–1272*, no. 2136

Artiller of the King's Quarrels

Richard de Hereford, smith		
on	6 November 1272	*CLibR 1267–1272*, no. 2130

Yeoman of the King's Armour

William de la Garderobe		
on	6 March 1369	*CPR 1367–1370*, p. 226

King's Serjeants at Arms

William Bygod		
on	1 April 1266	*CLibR 1267–1272*, no. 2386
on	16 July 1267	*CLibR 1267–1272*, no. 2393
Robert de Clopton		
on	16 July 1267	*CLibR 1267–1272*, no. 2393

Merioneth

CARNDOCHAN

History

built	C13	King, p. 275

CASTEL–Y–BERE

Owners

Llywelyn ap Griffin		
temp	1267–75	
to	25 April 1283	Morris, p. 193
English		
from	25 April 1283	Morris, p. 193; *CACW*, XXXI.35

Constables

Roger le Strange, of Ellesmere, P.P.		
to	20 March 1284	*CWR*, p. 284
Walter de Huntercumbe, P.P., kn.		
from	20 March 1284	*CWR*, p. 284
to	5 October 1285	*CWR*, p. 302
Hugh de Turbervill		
from	5 October 1285	*CWR*, p. 302
on	20 June 1290	*CWR*, p. 326
dead by	28 November 1292	*CWR*, p. 352
Joan de Turbervill and Roger de Verduno		
custody to	28 November 1292	*CWR*, p. 352
Robert de Staundon		
custody from	28 November 1292	*CWR*, p. 352
Robert fitz Walter, P.P.		
from	28 June 1292	*CWR*, p. 352
from	28 June 1293	*CPR 1292–1301*, p. 28
Roger le Strange		
on	18 October 1293	*CWR*, p. 360

CYM PRYSOR

History

mentioned	1284	King, p. 276

HARLECH

Owners

Prince Edward		
from	12 May 1343	*CChR 1341–1417*, p. 14
Joan, widow of Prince Edward		
from	13 October 1376	*CPR 1374–1377*, p. 374
on	13 October 1376	*CCR 1374–1377*, p. 405

Constables

Hugh de Wlonkeslowe		
from	21 October 1284	*CWR*, p. 291
to	5 October 1285	*CWR*, p. 302
John de Benelare		
from	5 October 1285	*CWR*, p. 302
to	3 July 1290	*CWR*, p. 326 (R.I.P.)
Master James de St. George		
from	3 July 1290	*CWR*, p. 326
to	28 December 1293	*CWR*, p. 353
Robert de Staundon		
from	28 December 1293	*CWR*, p. 353
Richard Havering		
temp	1294–1295	E.101/5/23
John de Colier		
from	12 February 1316	*CFR 1307–1319*, p. 271
Vivian de Staundon		
on	c.1316	E/101/19/26 m.1
to	21 April 1321	*CFR 1319–1327*, p. 54
Roger de Swynnerton, P.P.		
from	21 April 1321	*CFR 1319–1327*, p. 54
on	21 April 1321	*CCR 1318–1323*, p. 296
Oillard de Welles		
from	30 March 1323	*CPR 1321–1324*, p. 269
on	25 May 1331	*CCR 1330–1333*, p. 235
Walter de Mauny, P.P.		
from	29 December 1332	*CCR 1339–1341*, p. 75
to	12 May 1343	*CChR 1341–1417*, p. 15
Richard Massey, esquire		
on	8 May 1385	*CCR 1381–1385*, p. 549
confirmed	16 May 1391	*CPR 1388–1392*, p. 419

Constables for the Black Prince

Walter de Mauny, kn.		
on	24 June 1355	*BPR III*, p. 492
on	26 November 1359	*BPR III*, p. 378
Richard Massey, esquire		
from	8 October 33 principate Edward (1377)	

Constables of Prince Richard

Richard Massey, esquire		
confirmed	20 February 1 principate Richard	

Master of the Works

Nicholas de Derneford		
on	12 May 1327	*CPR 1327–1330*, p. 103

LLANEGRYN

History

mentioned	1274	King, p. 277

Monmouthshire

ABERGAVENNY

Owners

George de Cauntelo		
dead by	28 October 1273	*CFR 1272–1307*, p. 12
not by	1274	*CCR 1272–1279*, p. 114
John de Hastings the elder , son of Joan, sister of George, P.P.		
from	1274	*CCR 1272–1279*, p. 114
to	28 February 1313	*IPM V*, no. 412 (R.I.P.)
John de Hastings, son of above, P.P.		
from	28 February 1313	*IPM V*, no. 412
to	27 January 1325	*IPM VI*, no. 612 (R.I.P.)
Laurence de Hastings, earl of Pembroke, son of above		
from	27 January 1325	*IPM VI*, no. 612
to	28 August 1348	*IPM IX*, no. 118 (R.I.P.)
John de Hastings, son of above		
from	28 August 1348	*IPM IX*, no. 118
Agnes, widow of Laurence Hastings		
from	28 April 1349	*CCR 1349–1354*, p. 17
to	25 July 1368	*IPM XII*, no. 226 (R.I.P.)
John Hastings earl of Pembroke		
from	25 July 1368	*IPM XII*, no. 226
to	16 April 1375	*IPM XIV*, no. 148 (R.I.P.)
Anne, countess of Pembroke		
from	16 April 1375	*IPM XIV*, no. 148 (Jointure)
to	3 April 1384	*IPM XVI*, no. 13 (R.I.P.)
John de Hastings, son of John de Hastings, earl of Pembroke		
from	3 April 1384	*IPM XVI*, no. 13
to	30 December 1389	*IPM XVI*, no. 889 (R.I.P.)
Reynold de Grey of Ruthin, P.P.		
from	30 December 1389	*IPM XVI*, no. 889
away and back	2 December 1391	*CPR 1388–1392*, p. 514
Six Men		
to	26 April 1396	*CPR 1391–1396*, p. 697
Another Six Men		
from	26 April 1396	*CPR 1391–1396*, p. 697
Richard, earl of Arundel (1/3)		
to	21 September 1396	*IPM XVII*, no. 986
dead by	5 December 1397	*CCR 1396–1399*, p. 181
forfeited by	29 November 1397	*IMisc VI*, no. 227
Philippa, widow of above (1/3)		
from	5 December 1397	*CCR 1396–1399*, p. 181
William de Beauchamp, lord of Abergavenny, P.P.		
2/3 from	24 November 1399	*CPR 1396–1399*, p. 265
to	8 May 1411	*IPM XIX*, no. 846, (R.I.P.)

Joan, widow of above		
from	6 July 1411	*CCR 1409–1413*, p. 144
on	23 March 1413	*CCR 1413–1419*, p. 11
Constables		
William de Aune		
from	4 February 1331	*CFR 1327–1337*, p. 230
Roger Chaundos, P.P.		
to	16 March 1331	*CFR 1327–1337*, p. 243
William de Aune		
from	16 March 1331	*CFR 1327–1337*, p. 243
Roger de Grey		
on	12 April 1333	*IMisc II*, no. 1334
on	22 January 1334	*CCR 1333–1337*, p. 172
Subconstables		
William de Brome, kn.		
on	12 April 1333	*I Misc II*, no. 1334 (Supplying place)
Wardships		
Minority of John de Hastings, 1273–1283		
Henry de Bray		
from	28 October 1273	*CFR 1272–1307*, p. 12
to	3 March 1281	*CCR 1279–1288*, p. 116
William de Valence		
from	26 February 1281	*CPR 1272–1281*, p. 426
from	3 March 1281	*CCR 1279–1288*, p. 116
Minority of Laurence, son and heir of John de Hastings, 1325–1341		
Roger Mortimer, earl of March		
from	29 July 1330	*CPR 1327–1330*, p. 546
Roger de Chaundos,		
from	18 February 1331	*CFR 1327–1337*, p. 235
Roger de Grey, lord of Deffrencloyt		
from	6 May 1331	*CFR 1327–1337*, p. 253
on	3 February 1333	*CPR 1330–1334*, p. 440
Henry, earl of Lancaster		
from	1 May 1334	*CFR 1327–1337*, p. 401
from	10 December 1336	*CPR 1334–1338*, p. 349
Minority of John de Hastings, earl of Pembroke, 1348–1368		
Jevan ap Rees		
from	6 November 1348	*CFR 1347–1356*, p. 101

CAERLEON

Owners		
Gilbert de Clare		
to	14 December 1295	*IPM III*, no. 371 (R.I.P.)
Joan, widow of Gilbert Clare		
to	1308 (R.I.P.)	
Gilbert de Clare		
to	10 July 1314	*IPM V*, no. 538 (R.I.P.)
Matilda, widow of above		
from	5 December 1314	*CCR 1313–1318*, p. 132

Elizabeth, widow of John de Burgo		
to	10 July 1322	*CPR 1321–1324*, p. 176
Hugh le Despenser yng., P.P. and Eleanor his wife		
from	9 July 1322	*CChR 1300–1326*, p. 449
from	10 July 1322	*CPR 1321–1324*, p. 176
Elizabeth, widow of John de Burgo and William her son		
from	25 July 1322	*CCR 1318–1323*, p. 578
on	21 October 1333	*CPR 1330–1334*, p. 476
Lionel, duke of Clarence		
to	17 October 1368	*IPM XII*, no. 332 (R.I.P.)
Philippa, daughter of above		
from	17 October 1368	*IPM XII*, no. 322
Edmund Mortimer, earl of March and Ulster		
to	27 December 1381	*IPM XV*, no. 558 (R.I.P.)
Roger Mortimer, earl of March, son of above		
from	27 December 1381	*IPM XV*, no. 558
to	20 July 1398	*IPM XVII*, no. 1207 (R.I.P.)
Eleanor, widow of above		
from	16 March 1399	*CCR 1396–1399*, p. 451 (Tower)
Edward Charlton of Powis, husband of Eleanor, above, in dower right		
by	18 October 1401	*Records of some Sessions of the Peace in Lincolnshire, 1360–75,* Lincoln Record Society 30 (1933), p. 147
on	8 September 1403	*CCR 1402–1405*, p. 111

Wardships

Minority of Gilbert Clare

John de Turbervill		
to	24 June 1307	*CPR 1301–1307*, p. 534
Ralph de Montemer, earl of Gloucester		
from	24 June 1307	*CPR 1301–1307*, p. 534

Minority of Roger Mortimer, earl of March, 1381–1395

John Reynald		
from	8 February 1382	*CPR 1381–1385*, p. 100
Thomas de Beauchamp, earl of Warwick, Roger Mortimer, earl of March, John lord Neville and Henry Percy, earl of Northumberland		
from	16 December 1383	*CFR 1383–1391*, p. 22

Minority of Edmund Mortimer, earl of March, 1398–1412

John Holland, earl of Huntingdon, duke of Exeter		
from	11 August 1398	*CPR 1396–1399*, pp. 408, 514
Henry Percy, earl of Northumberland		
from	2 March 1400	*CFR 1399–1405*, p. 50
Henry Prince of Wales		
from	3 March 1407	*CFR 1405–1413*, p. 66

Constables while in Royal hands

Bartholomew de Badelesmere		
to	5 December 1314	*CCR 1313–1318*, p. 132
John Inge		
from	10 July 1322	*CFR 1319–1327*, p. 142

CALDICOT

Owners

Humphrey de Bohun, earl of Hereford and Essex
to 7 January 1299 *IPM III*, no. 552 (R.I.P.)
Humphrey de Bohun, earl of Hereford and Essex, son of above
from 7 January 1299 *IPM III*, no. 552
John de Bohun, earl of Hereford and Essex
to 26 January 1337 *IPM VIII*, no. 55 (R.I.P.)
Humphrey de Bohun, earl of Hereford and Essex, brother of above
from 26 January 1337 *IPM VIII*, no. 55
to 15 October 1361 *IPM X*, no. 485 (R.I.P.)
Humphrey de Bohun, earl of Hereford and Essex, son of above
from 15 October 1361 *IPM X*, no. 485
to 17 January 1373 *IPM XIII*, no. 167 (R.I.P.)
Thomas Woodstock, earl of Buckingham, duke of Gloucester and Eleanor his wife
livery 22 June 1380 *CCR 1377–1381*, p. 390
to 15 September 1397 *IPM XVII*, no. 1029 (R.I.P.)
Eleanor, duchess of Gloucester
to 3 October 1399 *IPM XVIII*, no. 134 (R.I.P.)
Joan daughter of Eleanor
to 16 August 1400 *IPM XVIII*, no. 154 (R.I.P.)
Isabel, daughter of Eleanor
entered a nunnery 23 April 1402 *IPM XVIII*, no. 170
Edmund, earl of Stafford, from Anne his wife, sister of above
from 23 April 1402 *IPM XVIII*, no. 170
to 21 July 1403 *IPM XVIII*, no. 815 (R.I.P.)
Anne, widow of above
livery 21 October 1403 *CCR 1402–1405*, p. 226
The Crown
from 6 May 1421 W. Hardy, *Charters of the Duchy of Lancaster*, London, 1845, p. 178

Constables

Thomas de Woodstock, earl of Buckingham, duke of Gloucester
from 24 May 1377
confirmed 17 July 1377 *CPR 1377–1381*, p. 66
James Clifford, king's esq.
on 8 August 1403 *CPR 1401–1405*, p. 438

Private constables

John Clopton
for life from 3 December 1396 *CPR 1399–1401*, p. 545
on 28 June 1401 *CCR 1399–1402*, p. 383

Wardships

Minority of Humphrey de Bohun, 1361–1363
Stephen atte Roche, William, abbot of Walden and Thomas de Walmesford
on 26 November 1361 *CPR 1361–1364*, p. 133
Minority of heir of Humphrey de Bohun, 1373–
Thomas de Woodstock, earl of Buckingham, duke of Gloucester
from 24 May 1377 *CFR 1369–1377*, p. 403

CAS TROGGY (TORROGY)

Owners

Roger le Bygod, earl of Norfolk and Marshal		
to	6 December 1306	*IPM IV*, no. 434 (R.I.P.)
Crown, as has no heir		
from	6 December 1306	*IPM IV*, no. 434
Thomas de Brotherton, earl of Norfolk		
from	16 December 1312	*CChR 1300–1326*, p. 205

CHEPSTOW(STRUGOILL)

Owners

Roger le Bygod, earl of Norfolk and Marshal		
to	6 December 1306	*IPM IV*, no. 434 (R.I.P.)
Crown, as has no heir		
from	6 December 1306	*IPM IV*, no. 434
on	6 April 1308	*CCR 1307–1313*, p. 29
Thomas of Brotherton, earl of Norfolk		
from	16 December 1312	*CChR 1300–1326*, p. 205
to	17 August 1323	*CCR 1323–1327*, p. 168
Hugh le Despenser, lord of Glamorgan, yng., from above P.P.		
for life from	17 August 1323	*CCR 1323–1327*, p. 168
confirmed	31 August 1323	*CPR 1321–1324*, p. 341
Thomas of Brotherton, earl of Norfolk and Mary his wife		
jointured	1 October 1336	*CPR 1334–1338*, p. 327
restored to them	22 June 1338	*CPR 1338–1340*, p. 93
Mary, countess Marshal, king's aunt, widow of above		
from	16 December 1338	*CCR 1337–1339*, p. 582
to	9 June 1362	*IPM XI*, no. 397 (R.I.P.)
Walter de Mauny, P.P. and Margaret, his wife, daughter of Thomas		
from	1 August 1362	*CFR 1356–1368*, p. 218
to	8 January 1371	*IPM XIII*, no. 148 (R.I.P.)
Margaret, wife of above		
from	8 January 1371	*IPM XIII*, no. 148
on	5 June 1375	*CCR 1369–1374*, p. 135
John de Hastings earl of Pembroke, jointly with Anne, his wife, who survives		
to	16 April 1375	*IPM XIV*, no. 148
John de Hastings, son of above		
from	16 April 1375	*IPM XIV*, no. 148
Margaret, duchess of Norfolk		
to	24 March 1399	*IPM XVII*, no. 260
Thomas de Mowbray, earl Marshal, great grandson of above		
from	24 March 1399	*IPM XVII*, no. 260 (Age 14)
to	4 June 1405	*IPM XVIII*, no. 316 (R.I.P.)
John de Mowbray, brother of above		
from	4 June 1405	*IPM XVIII*, no. 316

Constables

Ellis Puger		
to	21 August 1307	*CFR 1307–1319*, p. 3
John de Cromwell, P.P.		
from	21 August 1307	*CFR 1307–1319*, p. 3
to	12 March 1308	*CFR 1307–1319*, p. 17

Hugh le Despenser		
from	12 March 1308	*CFR 1307–1319*, p. 17
to	18 July 1310	*CPR 1307–1313*, p. 272
Robert de Darcy		
from	17 July 1310	*CFR 1307–1319*, p. 67
on	10 October 1310	*CCR 1307–1313*, p. 288
John de Pateshull		
on	7 March 1311	*CPR 1307–1313*, p. 331 (Keeper)
Robert de Darcy		
from	10 April 1311	*CPR 1307–1313*, p. 332
on	17 May 1313	*CPR 1307–1313*, p. 599
John Greyndor, kn.		
from	11 June 1405	*CPR 1405–1408*, p. 25
Robert Giffard		
on	24 August 1405	*CCR 1405–1408*, p. 460

Deputy constables

John de Tany		
on	10 May 1308	*CPR 1307–1313*, p. 68
John de Pateshull		
on	10 October 1310	*CCR 1307–1313*, p. 288
on	17 May 1313	*CPR 1307–1313*, p. 599

Porters

Robert Atkyns		
for life from	27 July 1405	*CPR 1405–1408*, p. 35

DINHAM

History

built	C13	King, p. 283

GROSMONT

Owned

Edmund, earl of Lancaster		
on	12 May 1277	*CPR 1272–1281*, p. 208
to	28 April 1292	*CPR 1281–1292*, p. 487
from	28 August 1292	*CChR 1257–1300*, p. 423
Henry, earl of Lancaster		
confiscated	10 October 1326	*CFR 1319–1327*, p. 418
to	1333	DL.27/192
Henry of Grosmont, duke of Lancaster		
from	1333	DL.27/192
to	23 March 1361	*IPM XI*, no. 118 (R.I.P.)
dead by	16 July 1361	*CFR 1356–1368*, p. 165
Maud, his daughter, wife of William duke of Bavaria		
from	16 July 1361	*CFR 1356–1368*, p. 165
to	10 April 1362	*IPM XI*, no. 299 (R.I.P.)
John of Gaunt, duke of Lancaster		
from	10 April 1362	*IPM XI*, no. 299 (R.I.P.)
on	24 July 1387	*JGR 1379–1383*, no. 1240
William de Beauchamp, lord of Abergavenny, P.P.		
to	8 May 1411	*IPM XIX*, no. 846 (R.I.P.)

Joan, widow of William de Beauchamp		
for life on	23 March 1413	*CCR 1413–1419*, p. 11

Constables

William Hathewy		
from	28 April 1292	*CPR 1281–1292*, p. 487

Private Constables

Nicholas de Upton		
for life from	28 April 1353	*JGR 1372–1376*, no. 736
confirmed	8 May 1372	*JGR 1372–1376*, no. 736
William atte Hall		
on	1384–5	Somerville p. 383
Sir William de Lucy		
for life from	24 July 1387	*JGR 1379–1383*, no. 1240

LLANGIBBY (TREGRUK)

Owners

Joan, widow of Gilbert Clare		
to	1 May 1307	*IPM IV*, no. 1308 (R.I.P.)
Gilbert de Clare		
to	10 July 1314	*IPM V*, no. 538 (R.I.P.)
Matilda, widow of above		
from	5 December 1314	*CCR 1313–1318*, p. 132
Elizabeth, widow of John de Burgo		
to	10 July 1322	*CPR 1321–1324*, p. 176
Hugh le Despenser yng., P.P. and Eleanor his wife		
from	9 July 1322	*CChR 1300–1326*, p. 449
from	10 July 1322	*CPR 1321–1324*, p. 176
Elizabeth, widow of John de Burgo and William her son, in fee simple for ever		
from	25 July 1322	*CCR 1318–1323*, p. 578
from	26 February 1327	*CPR 1327–1330*, p. 32
Lionel, duke of Clarence		
to	17 October 1368	*IPM XII*, no. 332 (R.I.P.)
Philippa, daughter. of above		
from	17 October 1368	*IPM XII*, no. 332
Edmund Mortimer, earl of March and Ulster		
to	27 December 1381	*IPM XV*, no. 558 (R.I.P.)
Roger Mortimer, earl of March, son of above		
from	27 December 1381	*IPM XV*, no. 558
to	20 July 1398	*IPM XVII*, no. 1207 (R.I.P.)
Edmund Mortimer, son of above		
from	20 July 1398	*IPM XVII*, no. 1207

Constables

Bartholomew de Badelesmere, P.P.		
to	5 December 1314	*CCR 1313–1318*, p. 132
John Inge		
from	10 July 1322	*CFR 1319–1327*, p. 142

Wardships
Minority of Roger Mortimer, earl of March, 1381–1395
Thomas de Beauchamp, earl of Warwick, Roger Mortimer, earl of March, John lord Neville and Henry Percy, earl of Northumberland

from	16 December 1383	*CFR 1383–1391*, p. 22

Minority of Edmund Mortimer, earl of March, 1398–1412
John Holland, earl of Huntingdon, duke of Exeter

from	11 August 1398	*CPR 1396–1399*, pp. 408, 514

Henry Percy, earl of Northumberland

from	2 March 1400	*CFR 1399–1405*, p. 50

MACHEN

Owners
Gilbert de Clare, earl of Gloucester and Hertford

to	10 July 1314	*IPM V*, no. 538 (R.I.P.)

MONMOUTH

Owners
John de Monmouth

On	13 November 1278	*CCR 1272–1279*, p. 486

Edmund, earl of Lancaster, the king's brother

on	1 March 1270	*CLibR 1267–1272*, no. 1012
to	28 April 1292	*CPR 1281–1292*, p. 487

Confiscated from Henry, earl of Lancaster

on	10 October 1326	*CFR 1319–1327*, p. 418

Henry, duke of Lancaster

to	23 March 1361	*IPM XI*, no. 118 (R.I.P.)
dead by	16 July 1361	*CFR 1356–1368*, p. 165

Maud, his daughter

from	16 July 1361	*CFR 1356–1368*, p. 165

John of Gaunt, duke of Lancaster

on	18 February 1375	*JGR 1372–1376*, no. 358
on	1384–5	Somerville p. 384

Constables
William Hathewy

from	28 April 1292	*CPR 1281–1292*, p. 487

Private Constables
Sir Thomas de Hungerford

for life from	18 February 1375	*JGR 1372–1376*, no. 358

Sir Richard de Burley

in	1381	A. Goodman, *John of Gaunt*, Harlow, 1992
in	1384–5	Somerville p. 384

William atte Hall

on	1384–5	Somerville p. 384

Private sub–constables
John Serjeant

in	1381	A. Goodman, *John of Gaunt*, Harlow, 1992

Porter

Robert de Blakewell, esq.		
restored	25 June 1382	*JGR 1379–1383*, no. 718

NEWPORT

Owners

Joan, widow of Gilbert Clare		
to	1 May 1307	*IPM IV*, no. 435 (R.I.P.)
Gilbert de Clare, son of above		
from	1 May 1307	*IPM IV*, no. 435
to	10 July 1314	*IPM V*, no. 538 (R.I.P.)
Hugh de Audley, earl of Gloucester		
to	28 December 1318	*CPR 1317–1321*, p. 257
Hugh le Despenser, yng., P.P., and Margaret, his wife, and her heirs		
from	28 December 1318	*CPR 1317–1321*, p. 257
from	10 January 1320	*CPR 1317–1321*, p. 415
Ralph, earl of Stafford, husband of Margaret, daughter of above		
to	August 1372	*IPM XIII*, no. 210 (R.I.P.)
Hugh, earl of Stafford		
from	August 1372	*IPM XIII*, no. 210 (R.I.P.)
died	*1386*	
Thomas, earl of Stafford, son of above		
inherited	*1386*	
to	4 July 1392	*IPM XVI*, no. 208 (R.I.P.)
William, earl of Stafford, brother of Thomas earl of Stafford		
from	4 July 1392	*IPM XVI*, no. 208
to	6 April 1395	*IPM XVII*, no. 1277 (R.I.P.)
Edmund, earl of Stafford, brother of above		
from	6 April 1395	*IPM XVII*, no. 1278
to	21 July 1403	*IPM XVIII*, no. 815 (R.I.P.)
Humphrey, earl of Stafford, son of above		
heir	21 July 1403	*IPM XVIII*, no. 815
Anne, countess of Stafford, owned 1/3		
from	16 November 1403	*CCR 1402–1405*, p. 212

Wardships

Minority of Gilbert Clare

John de Turbervill		
to	24 June 1307	*CPR 1301–1307*, p. 534
Ralph de Montemer, earl of Gloucester		
from	24 June 1307	*CPR 1301–1307*, p. 534

Minority of Clare sisters

John de Sapy		
from	30 January 1318	*CPR 1317–1321*, p. 103
to	14 March 1318	*CPR 1317–1321*, p. 120
John de Walewayn, king's clerk		
from	14 March 1318	*CPR 1317–1321*, p. 120

Minority of Thomas, earl of Stafford (1386–1389)

Thomas de Beauchamp, earl of Warwick and William Beauchamp and John lord Neville		
from	25 February 1387	*CFR 1383–1391*, p. 173

Minority of William, Brother of Thomas earl of Stafford (1392–1395)		
Roger le Strange, kn.		
from	18 July 1392	*CPR 1391–1396*, p. 119
Thomas Woodstock, duke of Gloucester		
from	24 July 1392	*CFR 1391–1399*, p. 54 (All lands)
Minority of Edmund, earl of Stafford (1395–1399)		
Thomas Woodstock, duke of Gloucester		
to	23 July 1397	*CFR 1391–1399*, p. 219
Edward, earl of Rutland, future earl of York		
from	23 July 1397	*CFR 1391–1399*, p. 219
Minority of Humphrey de Stafford (1402–1423)		
Anne, countess of Stafford, his mother		
two thirds from	20 July 1421	*CFR 1413–1422*, p. 389

PENHOW

History		
built	middle or late C13	King, p. 286
modified	C15	King, p. 286

PENROS

Tenant in Chief		
George de Cauntelo		
to	3 November 1273	*CFR 1272–1307*, p. 13 (R.I.P.)
Constable		
Henry de Bray		
from	3 November 1273	*CFR 1272–1307*, p. 13

SKENFRITH

Owned		
Edmund, earl of Lancaster, the king's brother		
on	12 May 1277	*CPR 1272–1281*, p. 208
to	28 April 1292	*CPR 1281–1292*, p. 487
from	28 August 1292	*CChR 1257–1300*, p. 423
Henry, earl of Lancaster		
confiscated	10 October 1326	*CFR 1319–1327*, p. 418
to	1333	DL.27/192
Henry of Grosmont, duke of Lancaster		
from	1333	DL.27/192
to	23 March 1361	*IPM XI*, no. 118 (R.I.P.)
dead by	16 July 1361	*CFR 1356–1369*, p. 165
Maud, late the wife of William, duke of Bavaria, daughter of above		
from	16 July 1361	*CFR 1356–1369*, p. 165
to	10 April 1362	*IPM XI*, no. 299 (R.I.P.)
John of Gaunt, duke of Lancaster		
from	10 April 1362	*IPM XI*, no. 299
on	24 July 1387	*JGR 1379–1383*, no. 1240
Constables		
William Hathewy		
from	28 April 1292	*CPR 1281–1292*, p. 487

Private Constables

Raulyn Greindore, elder		
from	19 June 1381	*JGR 1379–1383*, no. 531 (Guardian)
Sir William de Lucy		
for life from	24 July 1387	*JGR 1379–1383*, no. 1240

TRELLECK (TRILLECH)

Owners

Joan, widow of Gilbert de Clare		
to	1 May 1307	*IPM IV*, no. 435 (R.I.P.)
Gilbert de Clare, son of above		
from	1 May 1307	*IPM IV*, no. 435
Roger Mortimer, earl of March		
on	22 February 1398	*CCR 1396–1399*, p. 278
to	20 July 1398	*IPM XVII*, no. 1207 (R.I.P.)
Edmund Mortimer, son of above		
from	20 July 1398	*IPM XVII*, no. 1207

Wardships

Minority of Roger Mortimer, earl of March, 1381–1395

Thomas de Beauchamp, earl of Warwick, Roger Mortimer, earl of March, John lord Neville and Henry Percy, earl of Northumberland

from	16 December 1383	*CFR 1383–1391*, p. 22

Minority of Edmund Mortimer, earl of March, 1398–1412

John Holland, earl of Huntingdon, duke of Exeter		
from	11 August 1398	*CPR 1396–1399*, pp. 408, 514
Henry Percy, earl of Northumberland		
from	2 March 1400	*CFR 1399–1405*, p. 50

USK

Owners

Joan, widow of Gilbert Clare		
to	1 May 1307	*IPM IV*, no. 435 (R.I.P.)
Gilbert de Clare, son of above		
from	1 May 1307	*IPM IV*, no. 435
to	10 July 1314	*IPM V*, no. 538 (R.I.P.)
Matilda, widow of above		
from	5 December 1314	*CCR 1313–1318*, p. 132
Roger Damory, husband of sister of Gilbert de Clare above		
from	15 November 1317	Davies, p. 25
Elizabeth, widow of John de Burgo		
to	10 July 1322	*CPR 1321–1324*, p. 176
Hugh le Despenser yng., P.P. and Eleanor his wife		
from	9 July 1322	*CChR 1300–1326*, p. 449
from	10 July 1322	*CPR 1317–1321*, p. 176
Elizabeth, widow of John de Burgo and William her son		
from	25 July 1322	*CCR 1318–1323*, p. 578
on	21 October 1333	*CPR 1330–1334*, p. 476
Lionel, duke of Clarence		
to	17 October 1368	*IPM XII*, no. 332 (R.I.P.)
Philippa, daughter of above		
from	17 October 1368	*IPM XII*, no. 332

Edmund Mortimer, earl of March and Ulster		
to	27 December 1381	*IPM XV*, no. 558 (R.I.P.)
Roger Mortimer, earl of March , son of above		
from	27 December 1381	*IPM XV*, no. 558
on	24 July 1397	
on	22 February 1398	*CCR 1396–1399*, p. 278
to	20 July 1398	*IPM XVII*, no. 1207 (R.I.P.)
Eleanor, widow of above		
from	16 March 1399	*CCR 1396–1399*, p. 451
Edward Cherlton of Powis, husband of Eleanor, above, in dower right		
by	18 October 1401	*Records of some Sessions of the Peace in Lincolnshire, 1360–75,* Lincoln Record Society 30 (1933), p. 147
on	8 September 1403	*CCR 1402–1405*, p. 111

Wardships

Minority of Gilbert Clare, 1295–1312

Ralph Hathewy		
to	24 June 1307	*CPR 1302–1307*, p. 534
Ralph de Montemer, earl of Gloucester		
from	24 June 1307	*CPR 1302–1307*, p. 534

Minority of Roger Mortimer, earl of March, 1381–1395

Thomas de Beauchamp, earl of Warwick, Roger Mortimer, earl of March, John lord Neville and Henry Percy, earl of Northumberland		
from	16 December 1383	*CFR 1383–1391*, p. 22

Minority of Edmund Mortimer, earl of March, 1398–1412

John Holland, earl of Huntingdon, duke of Exeter		
from	11 August 1398	*CPR 1396–1399*, pp. 408, 514
Henry Percy, earl of Northumberland		
from	2 March 1400	*CFR 1399–1405*, p. 50
Henry Prince of Wales		
from	3 March 1407	*CFR 1405–1413*, p. 66

Constables while in Royal hands

Bartholomew de Badelesmere, P.P.		
to	5 December 1314	*CCR 1313–1318*, p. 132
John Inge		
from	10 July 1322	*CFR 1319–1327*, p. 142

Private Constable

John Lassales		
on	25 December 1325	*Ancient Deeds vol. III*, A.4881

WHITECASTLE

Owned

Edmund, earl of Lancaster king's brother		
on	12 May 1277	*CPR 1272–1281*, p. 208
to	28 April 1292	*CPR 1281–1292*, p. 487
from	28 August 1292	*CChR 1257–1300*, p. 423
Henry, earl of Lancaster		
on	26 October 1320	*CPR 1317–1321*, p. 512
confiscated	10 October 1326	*CFR 1319–1327*, p. 418

Henry, duke of Lancaster		
to	23 March 1361	*IPM XI*, no. 118 (R.I.P.)
dead by	16 July 1361	*CFR 1356–1368*, p. 165
Maud, his daughter, wife of William duke of Bavaria		
from	16 July 1361	*CFR 1356–1368*, p. 165
to	10 April 1362	*IPM XI*, no. 299 (R.I.P.)
John of Gaunt, duke of Lancaster		
from	10 April 1362	*IPM XI*, no. 299
on	24 July 1384	*JGR 1379–1383*, no. 1240

Constables

William Hathewy		
from	28 April 1292	*CPR 1281–1292*, p. 487

Private Constables

Sir William de Lucy		
for life from	4 July 1384	*JGR 1379–1383*, no. 1240

Montgomery

CHURCHSTOKE (SNETH, SNEAD or SIMOND'S CASTLE)

Constables

Philip de Middleton		
inquiry into terms	16 December 1336	Fryde, no. 887

DOLFORWYN

Owners

Llewelyn ap Griffin		
forbidden to build	23 June 1273	*CCR 1272–1279*, p. 51
in	March 1274	Edwards, XI.47
to	Feb–May 1277	Morris, p. 121
Roger Mortimer of Wigmore		
from	7 January 1278	*CFR 1272–1307*, p. 106
in	1280	Morris, p. 147
Roger Mortimer of Wigmore, earl of March		
on	24 June 1316	*CPR 1313–1317*, p. 491
not by	25 March 1322	*CChR 1300–1326*, p. 441
Edmund, earl of Arundel		
from	25 March 1322	*CChR 1300–1326*, p. 441
Edmund Mortimer of Wigmore, P.P., son of Roger, earl of March		
from	12 October 1331	*CCR 1330–1334*, p. 345
by	21 October 1331	*CPR 1330–1334*, p. 193
Joan, wife of Roger Mortimer		
to	19 October 1356	*IPM X*, no. 307 (R.I.P.)
Roger Mortimer, earl of March		
from	19 October 1356	*IPM X*, no. 307
to	26 February 1360	*IPM X*, no. 640
Philippa, wife of above		
on	3 July 1360	*CCR 1360–1364*, p. 46
Edmund Mortimer, earl of March and Ulster		
heir on	26 February 1360	*IPM X*, no. 640
to	27 December 1381	*IPM XV*, no. 556 (R.I.P.)
Roger Mortimer, earl of March, son of above		
from	27 December 1381	*IPM XV*, no. 556
to	20 July 1398	*IPM XVII*, no. 1197 (R.I.P.)
Edmund Mortimer, son of above		
from	20 July 1398	*IPM XVII*, no. 1197

Constables

Griffin son of Wenunwen		
soon after	8 April 1277	*CACW*, IV.91
to	8 July 1277	*CFR 1272–1307*, p. 80
Adam de Montgomery		
from	8 July 1277	*CFR 1272–1307*, p. 80
to	16 July 1277	*CFR 1272–1307*, p. 81

Lewis son of Griffin		
from	16 July 1277	*CFR 1272–1307*, p. 81
to	16 June 1278	*CFR 1272–1307*, p. 98
Bevis de Knovill		
from	16 June 1278	*CFR 1272–1307*, p. 98
confiscated on	7 January 1278	*CFR 1272–1307*, p. 106
Griffin ap Tuder		
for life from	21 August 1284	*CChW 1244–1326*, p. 21
Griffin ap Rees		
from	23 January 1322	*CFR 1319–1327*, p. 91
to	23 January 1322	*CFR 1319–1327*, p. 91
William de la Beche		
from	23 January 1322	*CFR 1319–1327*, p. 91
temp	1322	E.101/15/38
John de la Beche		
to	25 March 1322	*CChR 1300–1326*, p. 441
Roger Tremelowe		
from	23 January 1331	*CPR 1330–1334*, p. 50
William de Ercalewe		
to	4 February 1331	*CFR 1327–1337*, p. 230
Thomas de Cloune		
from	4 February 1331	*CFR 1328–1337*, p. 230

Captain of the garrison

Roger le Strange for Gruffyd ap Gwenwynwyn		
soon after	8 April 1277	*CACW*, IV.91

Wardships

Minority of Roger Mortimer, earl of March, 1381–1395

Roger Wigmore		
from	9 September 1383	*CPR 1381–1385*, p. 309
Thomas de Beauchamp, earl of Warwick, Roger Mortimer, earl of March, John lord Neville and Henry Percy, earl of Northumberland		
from	16 December 1383	*CFR 1383–1391*, p. 22

minority Edmund Mortimer, earl of March, 1398–1412

William le Scrope, earl of Wiltshire		
from	11 August 1398	*CPR 1396–1399*, p. 408
Henry Percy, earl of Northumberland		
from	2 March 1400	*CFR 1399–1405*, p. 50
Hugh Burnell, kn.		
from	24 November 1401	*CPR 1401–1405*, p. 22
from	9 March 1402	*CFR 1401–1405*, p. 155

MONTGOMERY

Owners

Queen Margaret		
from	10 September 1299	*CPR 1292–1301*, p. 451
to	10 May 1301	*CChR 1300–1326*, p. 9
Edward, Prince of Wales		
from	12 May 1301	*CPR 1292–1301*, p. 592
on	20 February 1303	*CPR 1301–1307*, p. 118

Queen Margaret		
from	21 June 1304	*CPR 1301–1307*, p. 240
Crown		
from	10 April 1321	*CPR 1317–1321*, p. 575
Queen Isabella		
on	20 April 1327	*CMR*, no. 37
on	2 September 1329	*CFR 1327–1337*, p. 147
Roger Mortimer, earl of March		
to	26 November 1330	*IPM X*, no. 188 (R.I.P.)
Edward, the Black Prince		
on	1351	*BPR III*, p. 18
Roger Mortimer, earl of March		
recovered by	15 July 1355	*CPR 1354–1358*, p. 267
to	26 February 1360	*IPM X*, no. 640 (R.I.P.)
Philippa, wife of above		
on	3 July 1360	*CCR 1360–1364*, p. 46
Edmund Mortimer, earl of March and Ulster		
on	22 November 1360	*CCR 1360–1364*, p. 80
to	27 December 1381	*IPM XV*, no. 556 (R.I.P.)
Roger Mortimer, earl of March, son of above		
from	27 December 1381	*IPM XV*, no. 556
to	20 July 1398	*IPM XVII*, no. 1197 (R.I.P.)
Edmund Mortimer, earl of March, son of above		
from	20 July 1398	*IPM XVII*, no. 1197
under age on	7 August 1405	*CPR 1405–1408*, p. 36
Constables		
Bevis de Knovill		
from	10 December 1274	*CFR 1272–1307*, p. 39
to	12 May 1301	*CPR 1292–1301*, p. 592
William de Leybourne, P.P.		
to	18 March 1310	*CPR 1307–1313*, p. 215 (R.I.P.)
Hugh de Audley of Stratton Audley, senior, P.P.		
from	18 March 1310	*CPR 1307–1313*, p. 215
for life from	28 May 1310	*CPR 1307–1313*, p. 229
on	25 June 1315	*CCR 1313–1318*, p. 187
William de Leybourne		
to	28 March 1315	*CFR 1307–1319*, p. 240 (R.I.P.)
Hugh de Audley of Stratton Audley, senior, P.P.		
on	10 March 1315	*CPR 1313–1317*, p. 315
temp	1318–1319	*CAPW*, p. 343
Edmund, earl of Arundel		
from	26 May 1321	*CACW*, XIII.150
to	2 June 1321	*CFR 1319–1327*, p. 60
Alan de Cherleton		
from	2 June 1321	*CFR 1319–1327*, p. 60
on	5 June 1321	*CCR 1318–1323*, p. 312
Philip de Middleton		
from	29 June 1321	*CFR 1319–1327*, p. 62
to	30 November 1321	*CFR 1319–1327*, p. 81
Nicholas de la Beche, kn.		
from	30 November 1321	*CFR 1319–1327*, p. 81
on	16 February 1322	*CCR 1318–1323*, p. 524

Philip de Middleton		
on	22 January 1322	*CPR 1321–1324*, p. 51
to	13 February 1326	*CFR 1319–1327*, p. 375
Alan de Cherleton		
from	13 February 1326	*CFR 1319–1327*, p. 375
William de Ercalewe		
to	20 December 1330	*CFR 1327–1337*, p. 209
William fitz Waryn		
from	20 December 1330	*CFR 1327–1337*, p. 209
for life from	17 June 1332	*CFR 1327–1337*, p. 316
to	30 October 1339	*CPR 1338–1340*, p. 344
William Gunneys		
from	30 October 1339	*CPR 1338–1340*, p. 344
William fitz Waryn		
on	13 July 1341	*CPR 1340–1343*, p. 312
to	15 July 1355	*CPR 1354–1358*, p. 267
John de Burnell, kn.		
for three months from	31 July 1402	*CPR 1401–1405*, p. 140
to	2 January 1403	*CPR 1401–1405*, p. 184
Thomas Talbot, kn.		
from	2 January 1403	*CPR 1401–1405*, p. 184
to	20 April 1403	*CCR 1402–1405*, p. 88
Henry, prince of Wales		
from	20 April 1403	*CCR 1402–1405*, p. 88

Private Constables

William fitz Waryn		
falsely reported dead	8 November 1347	*BPR I*, p. 142

Deputies

Philip de Middleton		
on	8 June 1314	*CPR 1313–1317*, p. 151
not by	10 March 1315	*CPR 1313–1317*, p. 315
William de Chauldon		
on	8 August 1318	*IMisc II*, no. 386
William Gunneys		
on	26 June 1334	*CCR 1333–1337*, p. 228

Wardships

minority of Edmund, son of Roger Mortimer, 1360–1373

Edward, prince of Wales		
from	22 November 1360	*CCR 1360–1364*, p. 80

Minority of Roger Mortimer, earl of March, 1381–1395

Roger Wigmore		
from	9 September 1383	*CPR 1381–1385*, p. 309

Thomas de Beauchamp, earl of Warwick, Roger Mortimer, earl of March, John lord Neville and Henry Percy, earl of Northumberland

from	16 December 1383	*CFR 1383–1391*, p. 22

minority Edmund Mortimer, earl of March, 1398–1412

William le Scrope, earl of Wiltshire		
from	11 August 1398	*CPR 1396–1399*, p. 408
Henry Percy, earl of Northumberland		
from	2 March 1400	*CFR 1399–1405*, p. 50

Hugh Burnell, kn.		
from	24 November 1401	*CPR 1401–1405*, p. 22
from	9 March 1402	*CFR 1399–1405*, p. 155
Thomas Talbot, kn.		
from	2 January 1403	*CPR 1401–1405*, p. 184
temp	1402–1403	E.101/43/20
to	7 August 1405	*CPR 1405–1408*, p. 36
Thomas Neville, Lord Furnivall, kn.		
from	7 August 1405	*CPR 1405–1408*, p. 36
John Talbot, earl of Salisbury, esq.		
from	25 April 1407	*CPR 1405–1408*, p. 315

Viewers of the works

William Baudewyne and Alexander de Montgomery		
from	28 July 1279	*CPR 1272–1281*, p. 322

Captain of the Garrison

Roger Mortimer of Wigmore		
on	13 July 1282	*CWR*, p. 231

POWIS (CASTELL COCH; POOL; TRALLWNG)

Owners

Llewelyn ap Griffin		
holding	c.1274	Morris, p. 111
Gruffyd ap Gwenwynwyn		
restored	February–May 1277	Morris, p. 123
Owen de la Pole *alias* Owen ap Gruffyd		
not by	28 September 1294	*CPR 1292–1301*, p. 88
Hawisia de la Pole		
on	1 April 1299	*CPR 1292–1301*, p. 464
on	1 April 1299	*CCR 1296–1302*, p. 238
Griffith de la Pole, son of Owen		
to	25 June 1309	*IPM* V, no. 147 (R.I.P.)
Hawis, sister of above		
from	25 June 1309	*IPM V*, no. 147
John de Cherleton of Powis, P.P.		
on	12 April 1312	*CCR 1307–1313*, p. 417 (Jointly)
to	1354	*IPM X*, no. 117 (R.I.P.)
John de Cherleton II, P.P.		
from	20 January 1354	*CCR 1349–1354*, p. 576
to	30 August 1360	*IPM X*, no. 632 (R.I.P.)
John de Cherleton, kn. , son of above, P.P.		
from	30 August 1360	*IPM X*, no. 632
to	July 1374	*IPM XIV*, no. 19 (R.I.P.)
John de Cherleton, his son, P.P.		
from	July 1374	*IPM XIV*, no. 19 (Age 14)
to	19 October 1401	*IPM XVIII*, no. 650 (R.I.P.)
Edward de Cherleton, kn., brother of above, P.P.		
from	19 October 1401	*IPM XVIII*, no. 650
to garrison for 3 months	23 July 1402	*CPR 1401–1405*, p. 139
died	*14 March 1421*	*GEC III, p. 161*

Constables

Robert Sapy		
from	19 January 1322	*CFR 1319–1327*, p. 89
on	18 February 1322	*CCR 1318–1323*, p. 422
Res ap Griffith		
on	26 October 1326	*CFR 1319–1327*, p. 421
John Gomound		
on	29 September 1375	*Ancient Deeds I*, B.2928
Edward Cherlton of Powys		
for three months from	31 July 1402	*CPR 1401–1405*, p. 139
Hugh Say		
on	3 April 1411	*CPR 1408–1413*, p. 284
on	16 July 1411	*CPR 1408–1413*, p. 303

Wardships

Minority of heir of Owen de la Pole

Roger le Strange of Ellesmere		
from	28 September 1294	*CPR 1292–1301*, p. 88

Norfolk

Unknown Licenses

BLAKWORTH and LYNG for John de Norwich, P.P.

	21 August 1343	*CPR 1343–1345*, p. 106

EDGEFIELD for Thomas Rocelyn

	18 May 1334	E.156/28/6; *CPR 1334–1338*, p. 10

GAYWODE for Henry, bishop of Norwich

	29 December 1387	*CPR 1385–1389*, p. 381

SCULTON for Constantine Mortimer

	16 October 1319	*CPR 1317–1321*, p. 395

BUCKENHAM, NEW

Owners

Robert de Tattershall

to	August 1273	*IPM II*, no. 4 (R.I.P.)

Robert de Tattershall, son of above, P.P.

from	August 1273	*IPM II*, no. 4
died	*8 September 1298*	*GEC XII(I), p. 650*

Robert de Tattershall, son of above, P.P.

to	28 July 1303	*IPM IV*, no. 163 (R.I.P.)

Robert de Tattershall, jnr., son of above

from	28 July 1303	*IPM IV*, no. 163
to	25 November 1306	*CFR 1272–1307*, p. 547 (R.I.P.)

Thomas de Cailly, P.P.

from	30 January 1306	*IPM IV*, no. 391
to	30 July 1316	*IPM VI*, no. 48

Adam de Clifton, the elder, kn., nephew and one heir of above

from	30 July 1316	*IPM VI*, no. 48, (one heir)
to	27 January 1367	*IPM XII*, no. 128 (R.I.P.)

John de Clifton, kinsman of above, P.P.

from	27 January 1367	*IPM XII*, no. 128
to	10 August 1388	*IPM XVI*, no. 678 (R.I.P.)

Elizabeth, widow of John de Clifton, kn.

from	29 January 1389	*CPR 1385–1389*, p. 562 (Jointure)
to	24 September 1391	*IPM XVI*, no. 319 (R.I.P.)

Constantine de Clifton, P.P. son of John de Clifton above

from	24 September 1392	*IPM XVI*, no. 319
on	28 May 1392	*CCR 1389–1392*, p. 467
died	*1395*	*GEC III, p. 308*

Edmund, duke of York

from	2 October 1397	*CPR 1396–1399*, p. 213 (Tail male) vacated by surrender

1/3 Gilbert Talbot

to	6 February 1399	*IPM XVII*, no. 1289 (R.I.P.)

1/3 Richard Talbot, son of above

from	6 February 1399	*IPM XVII*, no. 1289

Wardship
Minority of Adam de Clifton, heir of Thomas de Cailly (1316–1328)

Walter de Norwich		
from	4 August 1316	*CFR 1307–1319*, p. 297

Minority of Constantine de Clifton (1391–1393)

Thomas Alnewyk, king's butler		
from	15 December 1391	*CPR 1391–1396*, p. 11
on	28 May 1392	*CCR 1389–1392*, p. 467
Robert Bucton		
from	8 February 1392	*CFR 1391–1399*, p. 35
to	28 May 1392	*CFR 1391–1399*, p. 41
Ralph Cromwell		
from	28 May 1392	*CFR 1391–1399*, p. 41

Constables

Adam de Clifton		
not by	1 May 1358	*CPR 1358–1361*, p. 46
John de Merle		
before	1 May 1358	*CPR 1358–1361*, p. 46
confirmed for life	1 May 1358	*CPR 1358–1361*, p. 46
dead by	17 December 1391	*IMisc V*, no. 350

Private Constables
For Adam de Clifton

John de Merle		
on	27 January 1367	*IPM XII*, no. 128

Constables Wages

104s./year	27 January 1367	*IPM XII*, no. 128

CASTLE ACRE

Owners

John de Warenne, earl of Surrey		
not by	27 December 1316	*CPR 1313–1317*, p. 607
Aymer de Valence, earl of Pembroke		
by	27 December 1316	*CPR 1313–1317*, p. 607
to	26 June 1324	*IPM VI*, no. 518 (R.I.P.)
David de Strabolgi, earl of Athol		
on	8 February 1326	*CCR 1323–1327*, p. 446
to	8 January 1327	*IPM VI*, no. 759 (R.I.P.)
David de Strabolgi, son of above		
from	8 January 1327	*IPM VI*, no. 759
John de Warenne, earl of Surrey		
for life from Arundel on	10 June 1347	*Feet of fines relating to Wiltshire*, Wiltshire Record Society 29 (1973), no. 334
to	30 June 1347	*IPM IX*, no. 54 (R.I.P.)
dead by	6 July 1347	*CFR 1347–1356*, p. 39
Richard fitzAlan, earl of Arundel		
jointured	1 March 1347	*CPR 1345–1348*, p. 328
foot of fine	2 November 1354	*Feet of fines relating to Wiltshire*, Wiltshire Record Society 29 (1973), no. 421

John, duke of Brittany		
from	14 September 1378	*CPR 1377–1381*, p. 284
to	St. Peter and Paul 1396/7	*IMisc VI*, no. 265
Thomas de Woodstock, duke of Gloucester		
reversion	26 October 1397	*IMisc VI*, no. 265
Thomas de Mowbray, earl Marshal, earl of Nottingham		
from	28 September 1397	*CPR 1396–1399*, p. 220 (Tail male)

Constables

Thomas Beaufort		
for life from	24 September 1398	*CPR 1396–1399*, p. 414

CASTLE RISING

Owners

Robert de Mohaut, P.P.		
to	16 September 1276	*IPM II*, no. 128
Roger de Mohaut, son of above, P.P. .		
from	16 September 1276	*IPM II*, no. 128 (Age 13)
on	25 June 1294	N.R.A. 12614, MTD/A2/3
died	*2 December 1296*	*GEC IX, p. 14*
Robert de Mohaut, brother of above, P.P. .		
inherited	*2 December 1296*	*GEC IX, p. 14*
died	*26 December 1329*	*GEC IX, p. 14*
dead by	1 June 1330	*CCR 1327–1330*, p. 512
Emma, widow of above.		
livery	1 June 1330	*CCR 1327–1330*, p. 512
Queen Isabella		
from	23 November 1331	*CPR 1330–1334*, p. 218
to	22 August 1358	*IPM X*, no. 447 (R.I.P.)
Edward, prince of Wales		
on	21 July 1352	
after	20 February 1359	*CPR 1358–1361*, p. 549
on	21 July 1353	
King Richard as Prince		
on	25 February 1377	
John de Montfort, duke of Brittany		
on	26 January 1379	*CPR 1377–1381*, p. 315
on	17 May 1386	*CPR 1385–1389*, p. 147
Thomas, duke of Gloucester		
on	9 June 1391	*CChR 1341–1417*, p. 323
John de Montfort, duke of Brittany		
on	23 June 1393	*CCR 1392–1396*, p. 155
Edmund de Langley, duke of York		
from	8 August 1398	*CPR 1396–1399*, p. 404 (Tail Male)
to	1 August 1402	*IPM XVIII*, no. 636 (R.I.P.)
Edward, duke of York		
from	1 August 1402	*IPM XVIII*, no. 636
Prince Henry		
from	6 February 1403	*CCR 1402–1405*, p. 30

Reversion granted

Thomas Woodstock, duke of Gloucester		
from	17 May 1386	*CPR 1385–1389*, p. 147 (Fee simple)

Receiver of Issues

John Talman		
from	20 October 1377	*CFR 1377–1381*, p. 84

Royal Constables

Thomas de Stirston (Possibly)		
for life on	20 February 1359	*CPR 1358–1361*, p. 549
John Herlyng		
confirmed	15 June 1376	*CPR 1374–1377*, p. 284
confirmed	1 June 1378	*CPR 1377–1381*, p. 234
not by	26 January 1379	*CPR 1377–1381*, p. 315

Private Constables

John Herlyng, wages 12d./day		
from	6 November 1352	*BPR IV*, p. 98; for Queen Isabella
surrendered	21 September 1359	*BPR IV*, p. 314
Roger de Saham, prince's yeoman		
for life from	1 October 1359	*BPR IV*, p. 317
on	8 July 1365	*BPR IV*, p. 559
John Austin		
to	15 May 1378	*CPR 1381–1385*, p. 402
Richard Fotheringay, for Brittany		
from	15 May 1378	
confirmed	18 May 1384	*CPR 1381–1385*, p. 402
on	14 September 1386	*CPR 1385–1389*, p. 259

Receivers

John de Pynchun		
on	26 July 1377	*CCR 1377–1381*, p. 8

Stewards

Richard de Wythermerssh		
from	3 November 1377	*CPR 1377–1381*, p. 56

CLAXTON

Owners

William de Kerdston, P.P.		
licence to crenellate	9 June 1340	*CPR 1338–1340*, p. 529
died	*14 August 1361*	*GEC VII, p. 191*
Sir William de Kerdston, son of above		
inherited	*14 August 1361*	*GEC VII, p. 191*
licence to crenellate	4 December 1376	*CPR 1374–1377*, p. 395

GREAT HAUTBOYS

Owners

Robert Baynard of Hautboys, P.P.		
licence to crenellate	7 September 1312	*CPR 1307–1313*, p. 492

GRESHAM

Owners

Edmund Bacon, kn.		
licence to crenellate	4 November 1318	*CPR 1317–1321*, p. 224

MARHAM

Owners

William Belet		
licence to crenellate	9 June 1271	*CPR 1266–1272*, p. 540

NORTH ELMHAM

Owners

Henry Despenser, bishop of Norwich		
licence to crenellate.	29 December 1387	*CPR 1385–1389*, p. 381

NORWICH

Constables

William Giffard		
to	25 October 1274	*CFR 1272–1307*, p. 33
debts	15 May 1275	*CCR 1272–1279*, p. 166
Robert son of John		
from	25 October 1274	*CFR 1272–1307*, p. 33
to	11 November 1275	*CFR 1272–1307*, p. 58
Walter de Shelfhengre		
from	11 November 1275	*CFR 1272–1307*, p. 58
to	8 April 1277	*CFR 1272–1307*, p. 78
Walter de Grauncurt		
from	8 April 1277	*CFR 1272–1307*, p. 78
John de Breton		
to	15 December 1278	*CFR 1272–1307*, p. 105
William de Redham		
from	15 December 1278	*CFR 1272–1307*, p. 105
to	16 November 1281	*CFR 1272–1307*, p. 156
William de Roynges		
from	16 November 1281	*CFR 1272–1307*, p. 156
William de Sutton		
to	24 March 1301	*CFR 1272–1307*, p. 439
Robert Hereward		
from	24 March 1301	*CFR 1272–1307*, p. 439
Robert Baynard		
from	29 November 1311	*CFR 1307–1319*, p. 119
to	6 February 1312	*CFR 1307–1319*, p. 125
Alexander de Clavering		
from	6 February 1312	*CFR 1307–1319*, p. 125
to	10 October 1312	*CFR 1307–1319*, p. 148
Robert Baynard of Hautboys, P.P.		
from	10 October 1312	*CFR 1307–1319*, p. 148
to	27 October 1312	*CFR 1307–1319*, p. 148
Alexander de Clavering		
from	27 October 1312	*CFR 1307–1319*, p. 148
to	16 October 1314	*CFR 1307–1319*, p. 220
Roger de Refham		
from	16 October 1314	*CFR 1307–1319*, p. 220
to	2 May 1316	*CFR 1307–1319*, p. 276

Alexander de Clavering		
from	2 May 1316	*CFR 1307–1319*, p. 276
to	6 August 1316	*CFR 1307–1319*, p. 294 (R.I.P.)
John de Fitton		
from	6 August 1316	*CFR 1307–1319*, p. 294
to	22 April 1317	*CFR 1307–1319*, p. 324
William de Rungeton		
from	22 April 1317	*CFR 1307–1319*, p. 324
to	8 October 1317	*CFR 1307–1319*, p. 342
John Haward		
from	8 October 1317	*CFR 1307–1319*, p. 342
to	1 February 1319	*CFR 1307–1319*, p. 391
John Sefoul		
from	1 February 1319	*CFR 1307–1319*, p. 391
to	16 October 1319	*CFR 1319–1327*, p. 6
John Haward		
from	16 October 1319	*CFR 1319–1327*, p. 6
to	7 June 1320	*CFR 1319–1327*, p. 24
John de Thorpe, P.P.		
from	7 June 1320	*CFR 1319–1327*, p. 24
to	16 July 1320	*CFR 1319–1327*, p. 30
Edmund de Hemegrave		
from	16 July 1320	*CFR 1319–1327*, p. 30
to	1 June 1321	*CFR 1319–1327*, p. 58
John Haward		
from	1 June 1321	*CFR 1319–1327*, p. 58
to	12 June 1323	*CFR 1319–1327*, p. 212
Giles de Wachesham		
from	12 June 1323	*CFR 1319–1327*, p. 212
to	4 February 1327	*CFR 1327–1337*, p. 17
Thomas de Hyndringham		
from	4 February 1327	*CFR 1327–1337*, p. 17
to	19 June 1327	*CFR 1327–1337*, p. 49
Robert de Walkefare		
from	19 June 1327	*CFR 1327–1337*, p. 49
to	2 February 1328	*CFR 1327–1337*, p. 78
John de Loudham		
from	2 February 1328	*CFR 1327–1337*, p. 78
John de Preston		
to	28 March 1328	*CCR 1327–1330*, p. 269 (For Murder)
John de Loudham		
for life from	26 October 1328	*CPR 1327–1330*, p. 329
to	5 December 1330	*CFR 1327–1337*, p. 199
Thomas de Hyndringham		
from	5 December 1330	*CFR 1327–1337*, p. 199
Simon Costyn		
to	10 June 1331	*CFR 1327–1337*, p. 262
Roger de Kerdeston, P.P.		
from	10 June 1331	*CFR 1327–1337*, p. 262
to	27 January 1332	*CFR 1327–1337*, p. 295

Roger de Bourne		
from	27 January 1332	*CFR 1327–1337*, p. 295
to	21 September 1332	*CFR 1327–1337*, p. 330
Edmund de Baconesthorp		
from	21 September 1332	*CFR 1327–1337*, p. 330
to	9 April 1333	*CFR 1327–1337*, p. 356
Roger de Bourne		
from	9 April 1333	*CFR 1327–1337*, p. 356
to	4 November 1333	*CFR 1327–1337*, p. 378
John de Cailly		
from	4 November 1333	*CFR 1327–1337*, p. 378
to	6 October 1335	*CFR 1327–1337*, p. 460
Robert de Causton		
from	18 February 1335	*CPR 1334–1338*, p. 76
from	6 October 1335	*CFR 1327–1337*, p. 460
to	25 June 1337	*CFR 1337–1347*, p. 22
John de Harsyk		
from	25 June 1337	*CFR 1337–1347*, p. 22
to	8 July 1338	*CFR 1337–1347*, p. 86
John de Ormesby		
from	8 July 1338	*CFR 1337–1347*, p. 86
to	29 July 1338	*CFR 1337–1347*, p. 89
John de Harsyk		
from	29 July 1338	*CFR 1337–1347*, p. 89
to	7 February 1339	*CFR 1337–1347*, p. 115
Robert de Causton		
from	7 February 1339	*CFR 1337–1347*, p. 115
to	20 February 1341	*CFR 1337–1347*, p. 213
Thomas de Batesford		
from	20 February 1341	*CFR 1337–1347*, p. 213
to	3 December 1341	*CFR 1337–1347*, p. 250
Edward de Cretyng		
from	3 December 1341	*CFR 1337–1347*, p. 250
and from	22 November 1343	*CFR 1337–1347*, p. 349
to	18 October 1344	*CFR 1337–1347*, p. 397
John Haward		
from	18 October 1344	*CFR 1337–1347*, p. 397
to	24 October 1345	*CFR 1337–1347*, p. 444
William de Middelton		
from	24 October 1345	*CFR 1337–1347*, p. 444
to	26 July 1349	*CFR 1347–1356*, p. 131
John de Colby		
from	26 July 1349	*CFR 1347–1356*, p. 131
to	24 October 1350	*CFR 1347–1356*, p. 227
William de Middelton		
from	24 October 1350	*CFR 1347–1356*, p. 227
John de Colby		
in	1352	*IMisc III*, no. 378
William de Middelton		
and from	22 November 1352	*CFR 1347–1356*, p. 349
in	1353	*IMisc III*, no. 378
to	1 August 1353	*CFR 1347–1356*, p. 355

Edward de Cretyng		
from	1 August 1353	*CFR 1347–1356*, p. 355
in	1354	*IMisc III*, no. 378
Thomas de Moryeaux		
from	10 November 1354	*CFR 1347–1356*, p. 409
Guy de Seyntcler		
from	1 December 1355	*CFR 1347–1356*, p. 444
John de Ratlesden		
from	3 December 1358	*CFR 1356–1368*, p. 80
and from	1 October 1359	*CFR 1356–1368*, p. 102
Thomas de St Omer		
from	21 November 1360	*CFR 1356–1368*, p. 121
to	24 August 1364	*CFR 1356–1368*, p. 280 (R.I.P.)
William de St Omer		
from	24 August 1364	*CFR 1356–1368*, p. 280
Edmund de Thorpe		
from	10 November 1364	*CFR 1356–1368*, p. 283
William de Clere		
from	17 November 1365	*CFR 1356–1368*, p. 316
Thomas Morieux		
from	16 November 1366	*CFR 1356–1368*, p. 328
Richard Holdych		
from	27 November 1368	*CFR 1356–1368*, p. 391
Edmund de Thorpe		
from	5 November 1369	*CFR 1369–1377*, p. 36
and from	28 March 1370	*CFR 1369–1377*, p. 98
Robert Bacon		
from	5 November 1371	*CFR 1369–1377*, p. 146
John Holbrok		
from	12 December 1372	*CFR 1369–1377*, p. 190
John de Mauteby		
from	7 November 1373	*CFR 1369–1377*, p. 222
to	9 September 1374	*CFR 1369–1377*, p. 271
William de Kerdston, kn.		
from	9 September 1374	*CFR 1369–1377*, p. 271
Oliver de Calthorp		
from	4 October 1375	*CFR 1369–1377*, p. 297
John de Brewes		
from	26 October 1376	*CFR 1369–1377*, p. 369
and from	22 June 1377	*CFR 1377–1383*, p. 3
John Harsyk		
from	26 November 1377	*CFR 1377–1383*, p. 34
Stephen de Hales		
from	25 November 1378	*CFR 1377–1383*, p. 113
John de Mauteby		
from	5 November 1379	*CFR 1377–1383*, p. 171
William Wynter of Bernyngham		
from	18 October 1380	*CFR 1377–1383*, p. 220
John Cray		
from	6 February 1381	*CPR 1377–1381*, p. 594
for life from	4 September 1381	*CPR 1381–1385*, p. 45
on	20 June 1383	*CPR 1381–1385*, p. 287

John Grey, king's esquire		
on	7 January 1386	*CPR 1385–1389*, p. 95
William Wynter		
from	19 March 1392	*CFR 1391–1399*, p. 56
Thomas Gyney		
from	18 October 1392	*CFR 1391–1399*, p. 56
William Argentem, kn.		
from	1 December 1393	*CFR 1391–1399*, p. 95
Thomas Courson		
from	9 November 1395	*CFR 1391–1399*, p. 166
Robert Asshefeld		
from	1 December 1396	*CFR 1391–1399*, p. 197
William Rees		
from	15 May 1397	*CFR 1391–1399*, p. 197
and from	3 November 1397	*CFR 1391–1399*, p. 240
from	17 November 1398	*CFR 1391–1399*, p. 277
John Payn, esq.		
from	14 September 1399	*CPR 1396–1399*, p. 595
from	10 February 1400	*CPR 1399–1401*, p. 199
John Reymes, esq.		
for life from	8 November 1402	*CPR 1401–1405*, p. 172
to	8 March 1411	*CPR 1408–1413*, p. 278 (R.I.P.)
William Phelyp, P.P.		
for life from	8 March 1411	*CPR 1408–1413*, p. 278

Under constables

John de Middleton		
on	12 July 1390	*CPR 1388–1392*, p. 341
on	12 July 1390	*IMisc V*, no. 315

Gatekeepers

John Griffoun		
from	27 August 1317	*CPR 1317–1321*, p. 21
John Maille		
from	10 February 1327	*CFR 1327–1337*, p. 17

YARMOUTH, GREAT

History

mentioned	1399	King, p. 310
destroyed	1620	King, p. 310

Northamptonshire

Unknown Licenses
DRAYTON for Simon de Drayton

	16 September 1328	*CPR 1327–1330*, p. 319

BARTON SEAGRAVE

Owners
Nicholas de Segrave of Barton Segrave, P.P.

licence to crenellate	3 October 1310	*CPR 1307–1313*, p. 303
to	28 November 1321	*IPM VI*, no. 322 (R.I.P.)

Maud, da. of above and Edmund de Bohun, her husband

from	28 November 1321	*IPM VI*, no. 322

John Segrave

to	1 April 1353	*IPM X*, no. 116 (R.I.P.)

Margaret, widow of John Segrave

on	30 May 1354	*CPR 1354–1358*, p. 24

Thomas de Mowbray, duke of Norfolk

granted away	1394	*IMisc VI*, no. 392

Thomas de Mowbray, earl Marshal, son of above

under age	24 April 1401	*IMisc VII*, no. 173
before	5 April 1406	*CFR 1405–1413*, p. 30
to	*1405 (R.I.P.)*	

Queen Joan's dower

from	10 August 1405	

Constables
Richard de Colfox and Arnold Hulker

from	5 April 1406	*CFR 1405–1413*, p. 30
to	2 March 1408	*CPR 1405–1408*, p. 412

Wardship
Minority of Thomas de Mowbray, earl Marshal (1399–1405)
Henry Lyvermere, esq.

to	30 June 1402	*CPR 1401–1405*, p. 113

Thomas Beston and Richard Burgh, Richard fitz Nicholl, John Rome, John Lancaster, of two thirds of the castle

from	7 July 1402	*CFR 1399–1405*, p. 162

After death of Thomas de Mowbray, earl Marshal (1405–)
Richard Colfox and Arnuld Hulker

from	5 April 1406	*CFR 1405–1413*, p. 30
to	2 March 1408	*CPR 1405–1408*, p. 412

BENEFIELD

Owners
Humphrey de Bassingbourn

to	13 January 1273	*CCR 1272–1279*, p. 112

Queen Eleanor of Provence, from above for clearing his debts with a Jew		
for 25 years from	13 January 1273	*CCR 1272–1279*, p. 112
Humphrey de Bassingbourn		
to	22 February 1298	*IPM III*, no. 468 (R.I.P.)
Humphrey de Bassingbourn, son of above		
from	22 February 1298	*IPM III*, no. 468 (age 23+)
to	22 January 1349	*IPM IX*, no. 114 (R.I.P.)
Margaret, daughter of above and Walter de Coleville, her husband		
from	22 January 1349	*IPM IX*, no. 114
from	6 February 1349	*CCR 1348–1350*, p. 2
Walter de Coleville, kn.		
to	10 October 1367	*IPM XII*, no. 129 (R.I.P.)
Robert de Coleville, son of above		
from	10 October 1367	*IPM XII*, no. 129
to	14 July 1369	*IPM XII*, no. 334 (R.I.P.)
dead by	16 October 1369	*CFR 1369–1377*, p. 47
Ralph Basset of Sapcote, kn., P.P.		
to	July 1378	*IPM XV*, no. 87 (R.I.P.)
Alice, widow of Ralph		
to	12 October 1412	*IPM XIX*, no. 1034 (R.I.P.)
Elizabeth, her Granddaughter		
from	12 October 1412	*IPM XIX*, no. 1034

BRAYBROOKE

Owners

Thomas de Latimer, P.P.		
licence to crenellate	30 January 1304	*CPR 1301–1307*, p. 209
castellan	28 July 1326	*CCR 1323–1327*, p. 638
dead shortly before	*2 February 1334*	*GEC VII, p. 2*
John Latimer 'Bochard'		
to	3 May 1361	*BPR IV*, p. 383 (R.I.P.)
Katherine Latimer		
from	28 June 1361	*BPR IV*, p. 387
to	10 August 1361	*IPM XI*, no. 109 (R.I.P.)
Thomas Latimer, kn., son of above and Anne, his wife		
from	10 August 1361	*IPM XI*, no. 109
to	14 September 1401	*IPM XVIII*, no. 439 (R.I.P.)
Anne, widow of Thomas Latimer Bochard		
livery	22 October 1401	*CCR 1399–1402*, p. 432
to	17 July 1402	*IPM XVIII*, no. 610 (R.I.P.)
Edward Latimer Bochard		
from	17 July 1402	*IPM XVIII*, no. 610
to	31 January 1411	*IPM XIX*, no. 808
Margaret, wife of above, in jointure		
from	31 January 1411	*IPM XIX*, no. 808
Nicholas Merbury and Margaret his wife		
dead by	26 May 1422	*CCR 1419–1422*, p. 244
Their feofees		
on	26 May 1422	*CCR 1419–1422*, p. 244

CASTLE ASHBY

Owners

Walter de Langton, bishop of Coventry and Lichfield		
licence to crenellate	16 September 1306	*CPR 1301–1307*, p. 462
Robert Peverel and Alice his wife, from above		
after above		*VCH vol. 4*, p. 232
John de Oldcastle, P.P. kn., via his wife		
forfeited by	20 May 1392	*IMisc V*, no. 559
Gerard de Braybrooke, kn.		
from	1392	*VCH vol. 4*, p. 232
to	1 February 1403	*IPM XVIII*, no. 728 (R.I.P.)
Gerard de Braybrooke, kn, son of above		
from	1 February 1403	*IPM XVIII*, no. 728
Reynold de Braybrooke and Joan his wife		
on	8 April 1403	*CCR 1402–1405*, p. 58

FOTHERINGAY

Owners

John Balliol as king of Scotland		
to	1294	*HKW II*, p. 649
Crown		
from	1294	*HKW II*, p. 649
John de Brittany, Earl of Richmond		
from	temp. Edward I	
on	18 October 1295	*CCR 1392–1396*, p. 283
to	1 February 1333	*CPR 1330–1334*, p. 404
Mary de St. Pol, countess of Pembroke, widow of Aymer de Valence		
from	5 May 1331	*CPR 1330–1334*, p. 124
to	16 March 1377	*IPM XIV*, no. 339 (R.I.P.)
Edmund, de Langley, duke of York and Isabel his wife		
from	25 May 1377	*CPR 1374–1377*, p. 474 (tail male)
to	1 August 1402	*IPM XVIII*, no. 630 (R.I.P.)
Edward, duke of York		
from	1 August 1402	*IPM XVIII*, no. 630

Reversions

William de Bohun		
on	20 June 1338	*CPR 1338–1340*, p. 100

Constables

Walter de Gloucester		
on	22 April 1299	*CCR 1296–1302*, p. 245
John Asphull		
for life from	20 May 1377	*CPR 1374–1377*, p. 469
Thomas Burton		
on	27 August 1419	*CCR 1413–1419*, p. 16 (Warden)

HIGHAM FERRARS

Owners

Thomas earl of Lancaster		
not by	15 March 1322	*CPR 1321–1324*, p. 87

Aymer de Valence, earl of Pembroke and Mary his wife		
from	15 March 1322	*CPR 1321–1324*, p. 87 (Fee tail)
John of Gaunt, duke of Lancaster		
on	19 July 1374	*JGR 1372–1376*, no. 1447

Constable

Edward, duke of Aumale, future duke of York		
from	20 March 1399	*CFR 1391–1399*, p. 297

Private Constable

Nicholas Grene for John of Gaunt		
on	19 July 1374	*JGR 1372–1376*, no. 1447

MAXEY

Owners

William de Thorpe, P.P.		
licence to crenellate	5 May 1374	*CPR 1370–1374*, p. 434

MOOR END

Owners

Thomas de Ferrers (Ferrariis)		
licence to crenellate	20 March 1347	*CPR 1345–1348*, p. 270
Thomas le Despenser		
to	30 June 1363	*Ancient Deeds vol. III*, A.4795
to	30 September 1363	*CPR 1361–1364*, pp. 395, 409
Crown		
from	30 June 1363	*Ancient Deeds vol. III*, A.4795
from	30 September 1363	*CPR 1361–1364*, pp. 395, 409
Alice Perrers		
on	6 June 1377	*CPR 1374–1377*, p. 477
to	29 May 1378	*IMisc III*, no. 12
Queen Anne		
for life from	24 May 1382	*CPR 1381–1385*, p. 125
on	October 1389	*IMisc V*, no. 248
dead by	24 May 1394	*CPR 1391–1396*, p. 420
Queen Joan		
from	20 May 1408	*CPR 1405–1408*, p. 438

Notes

Thomas de Ferrers quitclaims all his rights to the King		
on	16 November 1363	*CCR 1360–1364*, p. 551

Constables

John de Newenham		
from	30 September 1363	*CPR 1361–1364*, p. 395 (Attorney)
John de Ipre		
for life from	28 June 1369	*CFR 1369–1377*, p. 10
on	30 September 1376	*CCR 1374–1377*, p. 418
not by	6 June 1377	*CPR 1374–1377*, p. 477
Richard Waldegrave		
for life from	6 December 1377	*CPR 1377–1381*, p. 74
from	1 February 1378	*CFR 1377–1383*, p. 68
on	20 August 1378	*CCR 1377–1381*, p. 152

Philippa de Coucy, duchess of Ireland		
confirmed	19 May 1399	
confirmed	22 November 1399	*CPR 1396–1399*, p. 273
on	9 March 1400	*CPR 1399–1401*, p. 258 (For life)

King's Farmer

John de Ipre		
on	16 July 1376	*IMisc III*, no. 1008

Stewards

Richard Wydevile		
on	13 December 1377	*CFR 1377–1383*, p. 50

Porters

William Dygeley		
from	1 January 1394	
for life from	24 May 1394	*CPR 1391–1396*, p. 420
John Cope, esq.		
for life from	28 January 1409	*CPR 1408–1413*, p. 48

NORTHAMPTON

Constables

William de Boyvill		
to	29 November 1272	*CFR 1272–1307*, p. 1
Roger de Seyton		
from	29 November 1272	*CFR 1272–1307*, p. 1
to	15 October 1274	*CFR 1272–1307*, p. 30
Gilbert de Kirkeby		
from	15 October 1274	*CFR 1272–1307*, p. 30
to	25 October 1278	*CFR 1272–1307*, p. 103
Thomas de Ardern		
from	25 October 1278	*CFR 1272–1307*, p. 103
to	13 November 1279	*CFR 1272–1307*, p. 119
Robert le Baud		
from	13 November 1279	*CFR 1272–1307*, p. 119
John de Asshton		
to	20 August 1307	*CFR 1307–1319*, p. 2
Payn Tybotet, P.P.		
from	20 August 1307	*CFR 1307–1319*, p. 2
to	12 March 1308	*CFR 1307–1319*, p. 17
Nicholas de Segrave of Barton Segrave, P.P.		
from	12 March 1308	*CFR 1307–1319*, p. 17
to	22 August 1315	*CFR 1307–1319*, p. 258
Eustace de Burneby		
from	22 August 1315	*CFR 1307–1319*, p. 258
to	20 October 1315	*CFR 1307–1319*, p. 261
John de Asshton		
from	20 October 1315	*CFR 1307–1319*, p. 261
to	23 October 1316	*CFR 1307–1319*, p. 301
John de Houby		
from	23 October 1316	*CFR 1307–1319*, p. 301
to	26 September 1317	*CMR*, no. 867

Robert de Ardern		
from	26 September 1317	*CFR 1307–1319*, p. 341
to	2 April 1319	*CFR 1307–1319*, p. 395
Richard de Lymesy		
from	2 April 1319	*CFR 1307–1319*, p. 395
to	5 May 1320	*CFR 1319–1327*, p. 21
John de Whytelbury		
from	5 May 1320	*CFR 1319–1327*, p. 21
to	25 April 1321	*CFR 1319–1327*, p. 54
Ralph Basset of Drayton, P.P.		
from	25 April 1321	*CFR 1319–1327*, p. 54
Humphrey de Bassingbourn		
from	1 June 1321	*CFR 1319–1327*, p. 59
to	9 July 1322	*CFR 1319–1327*, p. 142
John de St. Mauro		
from	9 July 1322	*CFR 1319–1327*, p. 142
to	19 May 1324	*CFR 1319–1327*, p. 276
John Daundelyn		
from	19 May 1324	*CFR 1319–1327*, p. 276
to	2 March 1327	*CFR 1327–1337*, p. 21
William de Samor of Hanyngton		
from	2 March 1327	*CFR 1327–1337*, p. 21
William de Pilarton		
from	22 August 1327	*CPR 1327–1330*, p. 15
grant on	29 September 1327	*CFR 1327–1337*, p. 64
William de Semor of Hanyngton		
to	16 November 1328	*CFR 1327–1337*, p. 110
Eustace de Brunneby		
from	16 November 1328	*CFR 1327–1337*, p. 110
William de Pillarton		
on	19 August 1329	*CCR 1327–1330*, p. 484
to	20 November 1330?	E.101/18/16
Thomas Wake of Bliseworth		
from	16 November 1329	*CFR 1327–1337*, p. 154
to	5 December 1330	*CFR 1327–1337*, p. 199
Thomas de Bucton		
from	5 December 1330	*CFR 1327–1337*, p. 199
to	26 October 1332	*CFR 1327–1337*, p. 333
William Lovel		
from	26 October 1332	*CFR 1327–1337*, p. 333
to	8 March 1333	*CFR 1327–1337*, p. 392
Thomas de Bucton		
from	8 March 1333	*CFR 1327–1337*, p. 392
to	12 October 1335	*CFR 1327–1337*, p. 460
Thomas Wake of Alisworth		
from	12 October 1335	*CFR 1327–1337*, p. 460
to	19 November 1341	*CFR 1337–1347*, p. 250
Thomas de Pabenham		
from	19 November 1341	*CFR 1337–1347*, p. 250
to	12 November 1342	*CFR 1337–1347*, p. 300

Thomas de Bukton		
from	12 November 1342	*CFR 1337–1347*, p. 300
to	22 November 1343	*CFR 1337–1347*, p. 349
Robert de Pavely		
from	22 November 1343	*CFR 1337–1347*, p. 349
to	5 November 1346	*CFR 1337–1347*, p. 462
Walter Parles		
from	5 November 1346	*CFR 1337–1347*, p. 462
to	11 November 1348	*CFR 1347–1356*, p. 84
Richard Blundel		
from	11 November 1348	*CFR 1347–1356*, p. 84
to	3 March 1351	*CFR 1347–1356*, p. 280
Peter Mallory		
from	3 March 1351	*CFR 1347–1356*, p. 280
Walter Parles		
to	7 October 1351	*CFR 1347–1356*, p. 307
Peter Mallory		
from	7 October 1351	*CFR 1347–1356*, p. 307
to	10 October 1351	*CFR 1347–1356*, p. 280
Walter Parles		
from	10 October 1351	*CFR 1347–1356*, p. 280
Peter Mallory		
to	22 January 1352	*CFR 1347–1356*, p. 307
Walter Parles		
from	22 January 1352	*CFR 1347–1356*, p. 307
and from	22 January 1354	*CFR 1347–1356*, p. 388
John Keynes		
from	10 November 1354	*CFR 1347–1356*, p. 409
to	10 November 1355	*CFR 1347–1356*, p. 444
Walter Parles		
from	10 November 1355	*CFR 1347–1356*, p. 444
and from	20 November 1357	*CFR 1356–1368*, p. 52
Andrew Landwath		
from	13 November 1358	*CFR 1356–1368*, p. 80
Walter Parles		
from	1 October 1359	*CFR 1356–1368*, p. 102
Richard de Wydevill		
from	20 November 1362	*CFR 1356–1368*, p. 236
and from	17 November 1365	*CFR 1356–1368*, p. 316
Thomas de Preston		
from	27 November 1368	*CFR 1356–1368*, p. 392
and from	5 November 1369	*CFR 1369–1377*, p. 36
Richard de Wydevill		
from	28 March 1370	*CFR 1369–1377*, p. 98
Robert Hutot		
from	5 November 1371	*CFR 1369–1377*, p. 146
Simon Warde		
from	12 December 1372	*CFR 1369–1377*, p. 190
John Karnell		
from	7 November 1373	*CFR 1369–1377*, p. 222
Thomas de Preston		
from	12 December 1374	*CFR 1369–1377*, p. 271

Robert Botevileyn		
from	4 October 1375	*CFR 1369–1377*, p. 297
to	26 October 1376	*CFR 1369–1377*, p. 369
John Carnell		
from	26 October 1376	*CFR 1369–1377*, p. 369
and from	22 June 1377	*CFR 1377–1383*, p. 2
William de Murrers, kn.		
from	7 October 1377	*CPR 1374–1377*, p. 247
Thomas de Preston		
from	26 November 1377	*CFR 1377–1383*, p. 34
William de Murrers		
from	7 October 1378	*CPR 1377–1381*, p. 277
John Lyons		
from	25 November 1378	*CFR 1377–1383*, p. 113
John Pavely		
from	5 November 1379	*CFR 1377–1383*, p. 171
John Widevyll		
from	18 October 1380	*CFR 1377–1383*, p. 220
William de Murrers, kn.		
for life from	7 April 1380	*CPR 1377–1381*, p. 480
to	5 February 1387	*CPR 1385–1389*, p. 276
Nicholas de Exton		
from	5 February 1387	*CPR 1385–1389*, p. 276
to	23 March 1388	*CPR 1385–1389*, p. 414
Matthew Swetenham		
for life	23 March 1388	*CPR 1385–1389*, p. 414
temp	1388–1390	E.101/41/9
John Tyndale		
from	21 October 1391	*CFR 1391–1399*, p. 7
John Mallory		
from	18 October 1392	*CFR 1391–1399*, p. 56
John Mulsho		
from	7 November 1393	*CFR 1391–1399*, p. 95
John Harwedon		
from	11 November 1394	*CFR 1391–1399*, p. 132
John Mulsho		
from	9 November 1395	*CFR 1391–1399*, p. 166
to	1 December 1396	*CFR 1391–1399*, p. 197
John Warrewyk		
from	1 December 1396	*CFR 1391–1399*, p. 197
John Mulsho		
from	3 November 1397	*CFR 1391–1399*, p. 240
and from	17 November 1398	*CFR 1391–1399*, p. 277
William Trussel		
to	30 October 1399	*CPR 1399–1401*, p. 43
Sheriff of Northants		
from	30 October 1399	*CPR 1399–1401*, p. 43
John Warwick		
to	24 November 1400	*CFR 1399–1405*, p. 93
John Cope		
from	24 November 1400	*CFR 1399–1405*, p. 93

John Chitewode, kn.		
from	8 November 1401	*CFR 1399–1405*, p. 143
Warin Lucian, kn.		
to	29 October 1404	*CFR 1399–1405*, p. 271
Ralph Greve		
from	29 October 1404	*CFR 1399–1405*, p. 271
to	22 November 1405	*CFR 1405–1413*, p. 18
Richard Wodevylle		
from	22 November 1405	*CFR 1405–1413*, p. 18
Ralph Grene		
from	23 November 1407	*CFR 1405–1413*, p. 87
Ralph Parles		
to	4 November 1410	*CFR 1405–1413*, p. 167
Thomas Mulsho		
from	4 November 1410	*CFR 1405–1413*, p. 167
to	29 November 1410	*CFR 1405–1413*, p. 204
Thomas Wydeville		
from	29 November 1410	*CFR 1405–1413*, p. 204

Chaplain

Geoffrey de Melbur		
on	5 November 1271	*CLibR 1267–1272*, no. 1736 (50s./year)

ROCKINGHAM

Owners

Queen Eleanor of Castile		
from	22 October 1275	*CChR 1257–1300*, p. 192
Queen Isabella		
on (for life)	20 April 1327	*CMR*, no. 42
on (for life)	16 August 1327	*CPR 1327–1330*, p. 146
Queen Philippa		
from	1 January 1331	*CPR 1330–1334*, p. 55
on	20 August 1347	*CCR 1346–1349*, p. 372
Queen Anne		
from	26 April 1391	*CPR 1388–1392*, p. 413
Queen Joan		
from	4 June 1403	*CPR 1401–1405*, p. 234

Constables

Richard de Holebrok		
on	22 February 1284	*CCR 1279–1288*, p. 255
to	10 March 1291	*CPR 1281–1292*, p. 424 (R.I.P.)
Ellis de Hauvill		
from	10 March 1291	*CFR 1272–1307*, p. 290
to	19 August 1294	*CPR 1292–1301*, p. 84
Thomas de Hauvill		
from	19 August 1294	*CFR 1272–1307*, p. 343
from	19 August 1294	*CPR 1292–1301*, p. 84
to	16 July 1297	*CFR 1272–1307*, p. 388
William de Beauchamp, earl of Warwick		
from	16 July 1297	*CFR 1272–1307*, p. 388
to	19 July 1298	*CPR 1292–1301*, p. 356

John Drvel		
from	19 July 1298	*CFR 1272–1307*, p. 402
to	17 January 1299	*CFR 1272–1307*, p. 409
Adam de Welle, P.P.		
from	17 January 1299	*CFR 1272–1307*, p. 409
to	20 August 1307	*CFR 1307–1319*, p. 1
Baldwin de Maneriss		
from	20 August 1307	*CFR 1307–1319*, p. 1
to	12 March 1308	*CFR 1307–1319*, p. 18
William de Latimer, P.P.		
from	12 March 1308	*CFR 1307–1319*, p. 18
to	1 August 1309	*CFR 1307–1319*, p. 46
Baldwin de Manerii		
from	1 August 1309	*CFR 1307–1319*, p. 46
to	3 February 1312	*CFR 1307–1319*, p. 124
Alan la Zouche, P.P.		
from	3 February 1312	*CFR 1307–1319*, p. 124
to	18 February 1314	*CPR 1313–1317*, p. 85
Aymer de Valence, earl of Pembroke		
from	18 February 1314	*CPR 1313–1317*, p. 85
on	25 May 1321	*CCR 1318–1323*, p. 302
Amaury la Zouche		
on	17 November 1323	*CCR 1323–1327*, p. 43
on	20 December 1324	*CFR 1319–1327*, p. 323
Amaury la Zouche and John de Miners		
to	12 February 1325	*CFR 1319–1327*, p. 329
John de Morteyn		
from	12 February 1325	*CFR 1319–1327*, p. 329
to	10 October 1326	*CFR 1319–1327*, p. 419
Douenald de Mar		
from	10 October 1326	*CFR 1319–1327*, p. 419
Robert de Veer		
on	13 October 1331	*CCR 1330–1333*, p. 347
John de Verdon, P.P. for Queen Philippa		
on	4 December 1336	*CCR 1333–1337*, p. 730
on	20 August 1354	*CPR 1354–1358*, p. 97
Amauri de St. Amand, P.P.		
from	8 June 1373	*CFR 1369–1377*, p. 216
William de Thorpe, P.P.		
from	22 September 1378	*CFR 1377–1383*, p. 109
not by	26 April 1391	*CPR 1388–1392*, p. 413 (R.I.P.)
dead by	26 April 1391	*CCR 1389–1392*, p. 257
John de Holland, earl of Exeter		
for life from	19 April 1391	*CPR 1388–1392*, p. 394

Deputies

Almaric la Zousche		
on	25 May 1321	*CCR 1318–1323*, p. 302
Thomas de Stone		
on	20 August 1347	*CCR 1346–1349*, p. 372

Porters

John Cokeram		
for life from	4 September 1414	*CPR 1413–1416*, p. 235

Clerk of the Works

William Dionys, clerk		
on	1 October 1399	*CPR 1399–1401*, p. 58

THORPE WATERVILLE

Owners

Walter Langton, bishop of Coventry and Lichfield		
licence to crenellate.	1 January 1301	*CPR 1292–1301*, p. 561
Thomas, earl of Lancaster		
on	20 November 1313	Somerville, p. 353
on	3 October 1314	*CChR 1300–1326*, p. 242
not by	15 March 1322	*CPR 1321–1324*, p. 87
Robert de Holland, P.P., ally of Thomas of Lancaster		
forfeited before	14 March 1322	*CCR 1323–1327*, p. 206
Aymer de Valence, earl of Pembroke and Mary his wife		
from	15 March 1322	*CPR 1321–1324*, p. 87
Mary de St. Pol, widow of above		
livery	4 August 1324	*CCR 1323–1327*, p. 206

Notes

Aymer de Valence quitclaims all of his rights		
on	3 October 1314	*CCR 1313–1318*, p. 242

Private Constable

John de Barrinton for Thomas, earl of Lancaster		
from	20 November 1313	Somerville, p. 353
John Bentley		
after	1313	J.R.Maddicott, *Thomas of Lancaster*, Oxford, 1970, p. 339

TITCHMARCH

T. in C.

Walter de Langton, bishop of Chester		
on	18 July 1314	*IPM V*, no. 520

Owners

John Lovel of Titchmarch, P.P.		
license to crenellate	22 November 1304	*CPR 1301–1307*, p. 290
died	*1 October 1310*	*GEC VIII, p. 215*
John Lovel, son of above, P.P.		
inherited	*1 October 1310*	*GEC VIII, p. 215*
to	18 July 1314	*IPM V*, no. 520 (R.I.P.)
Joan, da. of above		
from	18 July 1314	*IPM V*, no. 520
John Lovel		
to	3 November 1347	*IPM IX*, no. 44 (R.I.P.)
John Lovel II, son of above		
from	3 November 1347	*IPM IX*, no. 44
to	18 June 1361	*IPM XI*, no. 358 (R.I.P.)

John Lovel?		
from	18 June 1361	*IPM XI*, no. 358
Sir Thomas Wriothesley		
in	1363	

WOODCRAFT

History		
built	c.1280	King, p. 318

Northumberland

Unknown Licenses

BOUTLON HOSPITAL for Thomas de Bamborough

	3 June 1336	*CPR 1334–1338*, p. 279

ALNHAM (EARL'S TOWER)

History

first mentioned	1405	King, p. 325

Owners

Henry Percy, earl of Northumberland		
in	1405	King, p. 325
Henry Percy, earl of Northumberland, grandson of above		
on	1415	Bates, p. 17

ALNWICK

Owners

John de Vescy		
to	2 April 1289	*IPM II*, no. 723 (R.I.P.)
William de Vescy, P.P. brother of above		
from	2 April 1289	*IPM II*, no. 723
died	*19 July 1297*	*GEC XII (ii), p. 281*
Anthony Bek, bishop of Durham		
to	13 October 1309	*CPR 1307–1313*, p. 197
Henry Percy, P.P.		
from	13 October 1309	*CPR 1307–1313*, p. 197
to	10 October 1314	*IPM V*, no. 536 (R.I.P.)
Henry Percy, son of above		
from	10 October 1314	*IPM V*, no. 536
to	26 February 1352	*IPM X*, no. 43 (R.I.P.)
Henry Percy, son of above		
from	26 February 1352	*IPM X*, no. 43
to	18 May 1368	*IPM XII*, no. 242 (R.I.P.)
Henry Percy, earl of Northumberland, son of above		
from	18 May 1368	*IPM XII*, no. 242
on	6 August 1374	*CPR 1374–1377*, p. 111
not by	27 June 1405	*CPR 1405–1408*, p. 40
John, duke of Bedford, son of Henry IV		
from	27 June 1405	*CPR 1405–1408*, p. 40
Henry Percy, earl of Northumberland, grandson of two above		
on	1415	Bates, p. 14

Wardships
Minority of Henry Percy, 1314–1318

John de Felton		
from	26 November 1314	*CFR 1319–1327*, p. 219
captured	27 November 1317	*CPR 1317–1321*, p. 61
on	4 February 1318	*CCR 1313–1318*, p. 524
returned to Henry Percy even though a minor		
on	13 November 1318	*CFR 1319–1327*, p. 378

Constables

William de Faucomberge, kn.		
on	20 February 1411	*CCR 1409–1413*, p. 253

Chaplains

John de Crayk		
on	12 December 1334	Percy Chartulary, p. 301

AYDON

Owners

Robert de Reymes		
licence to crenellate.	5 April 1305	*CPR 1301–1307*, p. 328
Robert Reymes		
on	1415	Bates, p. 15

BAMBOROUGH

Owners

Scots		
to	1157	
Crown		
from	1157	*HKW II*, p. 554
to	temp James I	*HKW II*, p. 554

Constables

Robert de Neville		
on	3 May 1264	
on	27 January 1268	*CLibR 1267–1272*, no. 111
to	7 June 1276	*CFR 1272–1307*, p. 70
Thomas de Normanvill		
from	7 June 1276	*CFR 1272–1307*, p. 70
Walter de Camhou, kn.		
in	1288	Bates, p. 242
on	6 February 1290	*IMisc I*, no. 1523
to	10 August 1293	*CFR 1272–1307*, p. 327
Hugh Gobioun		
to	6 October 1295	*CFR 1272–1307*, p. 361
John de Warenne, earl of Surrey		
from	6 October 1295	*CFR 1272–1307*, p. 361
on	23 August 1301	*CPR 1292–1301*, p. 605
Isabel de Vescy, widow of John de Vescy		
for life from	8 October 1305	*CFR 1272–1307*, p. 528
to	18 December 1311	*CFR 1307–1319*, p. 121
Henry Percy, P.P.		
from	18 December 1311	*CFR 1307–1319*, p. 121

Isabel de Vescy		
from	28 January 1312	*CPR 1307–1313*, p. 427
to	28 May 1312	*CFR 1307–1319*, p. 133
John de Eslington		
from	28 May 1312	*CFR 1307–1319*, p. 133
on	25 November 1313	*CCR 1313–1318*, p. 31
Roger de Horsley		
on	4 December 1315	*CCR 1313–1318*, p. 256
to	20 December 1315	*CFR 1307–1319*, p. 267
William de Felton		
from	20 December 1315	*CFR 1307–1319*, p. 267
to	5 December 1316	*CFR 1307–1319*, p. 313
Roger Heron		
from	5 December 1316	*CFR 1307–1319*, p. 313
and from	1 November 1317	*CFR 1307–1319*, p. 344
John de Fenwick		
on	20 March 1318	*CCR 1313–1318*, p. 532
to	6 February 1318	*CPR 1317–1321*, p. 76
Roger de Horsley		
from	6 February 1318	*CPR 1317–1321*, p. 76
to	8 February 1327	*CFR 1327–1337*, p. 5
Robert de Hornclyf		
from	8 February 1327	*CFR 1327–1337*, p. 5
to	28 January 1332	*CFR 1327–1337*, p. 296
John de Kyngeston		
from	28 January 1332	*CFR 1327–1337*, p. 296
to	23 September 1334	*CFR 1327–1337*, p. 417 (R.I.P.)
Walter de Creyk		
from	23 September 1334	*CFR 1327–1337*, p. 417
on	29 August 1335	*CPR 1334–1338*, p. 166
Ralph de Neville of Raby, P.P.		
for life from	29 August 1335	*CPR 1334–1338*, p. 174
to	15 August 1367	*CPR 1367–1370*, p. 2 (R.I.P.)
Richard de Pembrugg		
for life from	15 August 1367	*CPR 1367–1370*, p. 2
removed by	10 March 1372	*CCR 1364–1368*, p. 420
Richard Stury		
on	6 October 1376	*CPR 1374–1377*, p. 347
to	10 December 1377	*CPR 1377–1381*, p. 80 (Kn.)
John de Neville of Raby		
from	10 December 1377	*CPR 1377–1381*, p. 80
to	17 October 1388	*IPM XVI*, no. 734 (R.I.P.)
William le Scrope, earl of Wiltshire		
for life from	14 February 1389	*CPR 1388–1392*, p. 13
to	12 October 1397	*CPR 1396–1399*, p. 251
Stephen le Scrope of Masham, P.P.		
from	12 October 1397	*CPR 1396–1399*, p. 251
Henry Percy the son		
for life from	24 October 1399	*CPR 1399–1401*, p. 31
on	24 October 1399	*CCR 1399–1401*, p. 51
Richard Arundel, kn., custody and supervision.		
for life from	15 August 1403	*CPR 1401–1405*, p. 249

John Coppill, esq.		
for life from	26 July 1403	*CPR 1401–1405*, p. 252 (Constable)
on	23 January 1404	Bates, p. 252
Ralph Neville, earl of Westmorland		
purchased post before	6 August 1404	*Ancient Deeds I*, B.3515
Thomas Grey of Wark, kn., granted by above		
by	6 August 1404	*Ancient Deeds I*, B.3515
for life from	29 August 1404	*CPR 1401–1405*, p. 412
to	31 May 1408	*CPR 1405–1408*, p. 453
Richard Arundel		
for life from	10 Nov 1404	*CPR 1401–1405*, p. 471
to	23 May 1415	
Alexander de Lounde, kn.		
from	29 May 1415	*CPR 1413–1416*, p. 328
on	12 June 1416	*CPR 1416–1422*, p. 76
Sir William de Elmeden		
from	1419	*HKW II*, p. 557
Deputies		
Alan de Heton		
temp	c.1367–1372	Bates, p. 249
John de Fenwick		
temp	c.1367–1372	Bates,.p. 249
John Heron		
temp	c.1376–1377	*IMisc III*, no. 979
Stewards		
William Scra		
temp	c.1367–1372	Bates, p. 249
Gatekeepers		
Robert de Bamborough		
from	16 February 1327	*CFR 1327–1337*, p. 19
Porters		
Robert le Porter of Bamborough		
to	15 April 1288	*IPM II*, no. 655 (R.I.P.)
mention when dead	10 February 1327	*IMisc II*, no. 963 (Gatekeeper)
Robert Porter of Bamborough		
to	15 February 1342	*IPM VIII*, no. 393 (R.I.P.)
Alexander de Bamborough		
from	15 February 1342	*IPM VIII*, no. 393
William de Hadham, king's yeoman		
for life from	22 April 1344	*CPR 1343–1345*, p. 236
dead by	16 November 1362	*CPR 1361–1364*, p. 267
Thomas de Hadham, king's yeoman		
for life from	16 November 1362	*CPR 1361–1364*, p. 267
Thomas Frost, esq.		
to	4 December 1388	*CPR 1385–1389*, p. 66
Robert Kerkenny		
for life from	4 December 1388	*CPR 1385–1389*, p. 66
Robert Fynkell		
from	19 October 1418	*CPR 1416–1422*, p. 171

Receiver Generals

William de Elmeden, kn.		
from	15 November 1419	*CPR 1416–1422*, p. 247

Master of the Works

Nicholas de Derneford		
on	12 November 1318	*CCR 1318–1323*, p. 27

BARMOOR

Owners

Thomas de Muschamps		
licence to crenellate	17 May 1341	*CPR 1340–1343*, p. 221
John Preston		
on	1415	Bates, p. 17

BAVINGTON, LITTLE

Owners

Robert Langwath		
on	1415	Bates, p. 16

BEAUFRONT

Owners

John de Widdrington		
on	1415	Bates, p. 17

BELFORD

Owners

Thomas de Dacre		
on	1415	Bates, p. 15

BELLINGHAM

Owners

Bellingham family across period		
temp	entire period	C.H. Hunter Blair, 'The Early Castles of Northumberland', *Arch. Ael.* 4th series, 22 (1944), p. 162

BELSAY

Owners

John de Middleton		
in	1415	Bates, p. 18

BERRINGTON

Owners

Robert Manners		
in	1415	Bates, p. 17

BERWICK

Owners		
Scottish		
to	1296	*HKW II*, p. 563
Crown		
from	1296	*HKW II*, p. 564
to	1318	*HKW II*, p. 564
Scottish		
from	1318	*HKW II*, p. 564
to	20 July 1333	*HKW II*, p. 566
Crown		
from	20 July 1333	*HKW II*, p. 566
Henry Percy		
on	3 February 1363	*CPR 1361–1364*, p. 304
Henry Percy, earl of Northumberland		
on	28 March 1385	*CPR 1381–1385*, p. 550
in fee	10 August 1394	*CPR 1391–1396*, p. 492
Ralph Percy, his son		
in tail male from	10 August 1394	*CPR 1391–1396*, p. 492
John, duke of Bedford, son of Henry IV		
from	28 January 1408	*CPR 1405–1408*, p. 388
to	16 February 1427	
Captains		
Ralph de Lumley		
captain	18 November 1387	*CPR 1385–1389*, p. 370
Constables		
John Burdon		
temp	1297–1299	E.101/7/6
on	15 July 1299	*CCR 1296–1302*, p. 260
on	16 November 1299	*CPR 1292–1301* (Bindon)
temp	1299–1300	E.101/8/25
William le Latimer		
in	1301	BL Cotton MS, Vesp. F VII, 1
John de Segrave, P.P.		
to	26 October 1305	*CFR 1272–1307*, p. 529
John de Sandal		
from	26 October 1305	*CFR 1272–1307*, p. 529
Edmund de Hastings, P.P.		
on	28 April 1313	*CCR 1307–1313*, p. 529
Roger de Horsley		
on	26 June 1327	*CMR*, no. 166
Henry Percy		
on	1 August 1333	Percy Chartulary, p. 448–9
on	1 March 1334	*IMisc II*, no. 1425
Richard Talbot		
on	16 October 1338	*CCR 1337–1339*, p. 506
Henry Percy		
on	15 February 1339	*CCR 1339–1341*, p. 14
Richard Talbot		
on	13 October 1339	*CCR 1338–1340*, p. 201
to	20 March 1341	E.101/22/21 m.2

Henry Percy		
on	6 November 1342	E.403/327 m.8
James de Audley		
temp	1342	E.101/23/24
Henry Percy		
on	24 April 1345	*CCR 1343–1346*, p. 516
Henry Percy		
to	1368	E.101/29/27 (R.I.P.)
Henry Percy, earl of Northumberland		
temp	1368–1371	E.101/29/27
custody	17 February 1385	*CPR 1381–1385*, p. 526
keeper	17 November 1394	*CPR 1391–1396*, p. 513
Henry Percy, 'Hotspur'		
on	12 May 1397	*CPR 1396–1399*, p. 121
Henry Percy, earl of Northumberland		
on	14 March 1400	*CPR 1399–1401*, p. 228
on	12 June 1400	*CPR 1399–1401*, p. 316
Henry Percy, 'Hotspur'		
on	10 April 1401	*CPR 1399–1401*, p. 469, keeper
on	18 July 1401	*CPR 1399–1401*, p. 523, keeper
Henry Percy, earl of Northumberland		
on	1 November 1402	*CPR 1401–1405*, p. 169
John, duke of Bedford, son of Henry IV		
on	6 October 1403	*CCR 1402–1405*, p. 194
on	16 July 1413	*CPR 1413–1419*, p. 27 (For life)

BIDDLESTONE HALL

Owners

John Selby		
in	1415	Bates, p. 19

BLENKINSOPP

Owners

Thomas de Blenkinsopp		
licence to crenellate	4 February 1340	*CPR 1338–1340*, p. 417
licence to crenellate	11 May 1340	*CPR 1338–1340*, p. 524
John Blenkinsopp		
in	1415	Bates, p. 15

BOTHAL

Owners

Robert Bertram		
licence to crenellate	15 May 1343	*CPR 1343–1345*, p. 30
to	November 1363	*IPM XI*, no. 487
Robert and John, parsons		
from	November 1363	*IPM XI*, no. 487
on	1364	
Blanche, widow of Robert Bertram		
to	12 July 1366	*CPR 1364–1367*, p. 255
Ellen and John de Hatfield of London, for Bertram's life		
granted by above	12 July 1366	*CPR 1364–1367*, p. 255

Blanche, widow of Robert Bertram		
to	28 June 1377	*CPR 1377–1381*, p. 1
Elena and David de Holgrave, for Bertram's life at 80l./year		
granted by above	28 June 1377	*CPR 1377–1381*, p. 1
on	18 May 1403	*CPR 1401–1405*, p. 230
David Holgrave		
to	13 June 1405	*IPM XVIII*, no. 1032 (R.I.P.)
Robert de Ogle, son and heir of Helen wife of David Holgrave		
from	13 June 1405	*IPM XVIII*, no. 1032
on	17 February 1406	*CPR 1405–1408*, p. 141 (Elder)
not on	1 November 1409	*IPM XIX*, no. 734
John Bertram, kn.		
in	1415	Bates, p. 15

BUCKTON

Owners

William Atkinson		
in	1415	Bates, p. 19

CALLALY

Owners

John de Clavering, kn.		
in	1415	Bates, p. 14

CAPHEATON (HUTTUN)

History

mentioned	1415	King, p. 346

CARTINGTON

Owners

John Cartington, kn.		
in	1415	Bates, p. 17

CHATTON

Owners

The Vicar		
in	1415	Bates, p. 19

CHILLINGHAM

Tenant in Chief

Henry Percy		
to	18 May 1368	*IPM XII*, no. 242 (R.I.P.)
Henry Percy, earl of Northumberland		
from	18 May 1368	*IPM XII*, no. 242
on	12 June 1388	*CPR 1385–1389*, p. 391
on	27 September 1401	*IPM XVIII*, no. 896

Owners

Thomas de Heton		
licence to crenellate	27 January 1344	*CPR 1343–1345*, p. 191

Alan de Heton, kn.		
on	18 May 1368	*IPM XII*, no. 242
on	28 February 1387	*CPR 1385–1389*, p. 321
Henry de Heton, held from Percys		
from	12 June 1388	*CPR 1385–1389*, p. 391 (Chevelyngham)
to	25 October 1399	*IPM XVIII*, no. 5
William de Heton, held from Percys		
from	25 October 1399	*IPM XVIII*, no. 5 (Age 6)
to	27 September 1401	*IPM XVIII*, no. 896 (R.I.P.)
Three sisters of above (Joan, Elizabeth, Margaret)		
from	27 September 1401	*IPM XVIII*, no. 896
Heirs of Alan Heton		
on	1415	Bates, p. 14

CHIPCHASE

Owners

Alexander Heron		
in	1415	Bates, p. 18

COQUET ISLAND

Owners

Tynemouth Priory		
in	1415	Bates, p. 19

CORBRIDGE

Owners

The Vicar		
in	1415	Bates, p. 18

CORNHILL

Owners

William Swinhowe		
in	1415	Bates, p. 17

CRASTER

Owners

Edmund Craster		
in	1415	Bates, p. 19

CRAWLEY

Owners

John Heron		
licence to crenellate	20 Nov 1343	*CPR 1343–1345*, p. 143
John Heron		
on	1415	Bates, p. 17

DALLEY (DALA)

History		
built	1237?	King, p. 331
modified	C14 and C15	King, p. 331

DETCHANT

Owners		
Richard Lilleburn		
in	1415	Bates, p. 15

DUNSTANBURGH

Owners		
Thomas, earl of Lancaster		
licence to crenellate	28 August 1315	*CPR 1313–1317*, p. 344
confiscated before	12 March 1322	*CFR 1321–1324*, p. 106
Henry, earl of Lancaster		
from	1324	Bates, p. 172
on	29 April 1326	*CCR 1324–1327*, p. 476
Henry, duke of Lancaster		
to	23 March 1361	*IPM XI*, no. 118 (R.I.P.)
dead by	16 July 1361	*CFR 1356–1368*, p. 165
John of Gaunt, duke of Lancaster		
from	16 July 1361	*CFR 1356–1368*, p. 165
on	11 May 1380	*JGR 1379–1383*, no. 303
after	1381	Somerville, p. 370
Crown		
from	1399	
in	1415	Bates, p. 14
Royal Stewards		
Roger de Horsley		
from	12 March 1322	*CFR 1319–1327*, p. 106
Constables		
John de Lilleburn and Roger Mauduyt		
on	15 September 1322	*CPR 1321–1324*, p. 205
to	2 January 1323	*CPR 1321–1324*, p. 233
John de Lilleburn		
from	2 January 1323	*CPR 1321–1324*, p. 233
to	6 July 1323	*CFR 1319–1327*, p. 219
Roger Heron		
from	6 July 1323	*CFR 1319–1327*, p. 219
on	19 August 1323	*CCR 1323–1327*, p. 12
Richard de Emeldon		
on	12 March 1325	*CCR 1323–1327*, p. 269
Sir John Fenwick		
after	1381	Somerville p. 370
Stephen le Scrope of Masham, P.P.		
from	20 March 1399	*CFR 1391–1399*, p. 295
Robert Harbottle		
Temp.	1399–1401	E.101/42/38

Ralph de Eure, kn.		
on	22 September 1402	*CCR 1399–1402*, p. 552
Robert de Harbottle		
on	14 February 1404	*CPR 1401–1405*, p. 365
from	13 June 1409	Bates, p. 175
to	c.1420–1421	Bates, p. 175
John de Harbottle, brother of above		
from	c.1420–1421	Bates, p. 175
Henry Lound		
from	February 1421	Bates, p. 175

Private Constables

Robert de Bincestre		
from	20 March 1319	J.R.Maddicott, *Thomas of Lancaster*, Oxford, 1970, p. 339
John de Lilleburn		
in	1326	Bates, p. 172
Robert Bertram, kn.		
for life to	23 March 1361	*IPM XI*, no. 118
William Querneby for John of Gaunt		
on	20 November 1372	*JGR 1372–1376*, no. 1106
Sir Thomas Ildreton		
from	29 July 1379	Bates, p. 174
on	17 April 1380	*JGR 1379–1383*, no. 264
on	11 May 1380	*JGR 1379–1383*, no. 303 (Ildreton)

EDLINGHAM

Owners

William de Felton		
builder	c.1340	Fairclough, p. 46
to	1358	Fairclough, p. 49
William de Felton		
from	1358	Fairclough, p. 49
to	1368	Fairclough, p. 49
John de Felton, kn., half brother of above		
from	1368	Fairclough, p. 49
to	31 March 1396	*IPM XVII*, no. 632 (R.I.P.)
John de Felton, kn., son of above		
from	31 March 1396	*IPM XVII*, no. 632
to	31 January 1403	*IPM XVIII*, no. 756 (R.I.P.)
John Faucomberge, cousin of above		
from	31 January 1403	*IPM XVIII*, no. 756
Edmund Hastings of Roxby, Yorkshire, by marriage to half sister of John de Felton (d.1403)		
in	1415	Bates, p. 14

ELSDON NO. 2

Owners

The Rector		
in	1415	Bates, p. 19

ELWICK NO. 1

Owners

Thomas Bradford		
in	1415	Bates, p. 17

ELWICK NO. 2

Owners

Thomas de Elwick		
in	1415	Bates, p. 17

EMBLETON

Owners

The Vicar		
in	1415	Bates, p. 19

ESHOT

Owners

Robert Maudut		
licence to crenellate	22 July 1310	*CPR 1307–1313*, p. 272 (Mauduit)
John Heron		
in	1415	Bates, p. 14

ESLINGTON

Owners

Robert de Eslington		
licence to crenellate	20 February 1335	*CPR 1334–1338*, p. 78
Thomas de Hessilrige		
in	1415	Bates, p. 17

ETAL

Owners

Sir Robert de Manners		
licence to crenellate	3 May 1341	*CPR 1340–1343*, p. 179
dead by	10 October 1355	*CPR 1354–1358*, p. 283
Heir of Robert de Manner		
under age	10 October 1355	*CPR 1354–1358*, p. 283
under age	24 May 1368	*CPR 1367–1370*, p. 119
John Manners, kn.		
dead by	10 August 1408	*CFR 1405–1413*, p. 113
Robert Manners		
in	1415	Bates, p. 14

Wardships

minority of heir of Sir Robert de Manners (–1355–1368–)

Edward de Letham		
from	10 October 1355	*CPR 1354–1358*, p. 283
Joan, widow of Edward de Letham		
on	24 May 1368	*CPR 1367–1370*, p. 119

minority of the heir of John Manners (–1408–)

John Manners.		
on	10 August 1408	*CFR 1405–1413*, p. 113

FARNHAM

Owners

Robert Horsley		
in	1415	Bates, p. 18

FEATHERSTONE

Owners

Featherstonehaugh family		
temp	entire period	J. Gibson, 'Featherston Castle', *Archealogia Aeliena*, 4th series, 2 (1926), p. 125–131

FENTON

Owners

Ralph Grey		
in	1415	Bates, p. 19

FENWICK

Owners

John de Fenwick		
licence to crenellate	26 November 1378	*CPR 1377–1381*, p. 290
Henry Fenwick		
in	1415	Bates, p. 18

FLOTTERTON

Owners

Robert Ogle		
on	1415	Bates, p. 18

FORD

Owners

William Heron, P.P.		
licence to crenellate	16 July 1338	*CPR 1338–1340*, p. 114
owned	21 April 1340	*CChR 1337–1347*, p. 468
William Heron		
in	1415	Bates, p. 14

HAGGERSTON

Owners

Robert de Haggerston		
licence to crenellate	4 June 1345	*CPR 1343–1345*, p. 479
Thomas de Haggerston		
in	1415	Bates, p. 17

HALTON

Owners

William Carnaby		
on	1415	Bates, p. 18

HALTWHISTLE (CASTLE HILL)

History

abandoned by	1415	King, p. 334

HARBOTTLE

Owners

Robert de Umfraville, earl of Angus, P.P.		
on	20 February 1316	*CPR 1313–1317*, p. 400
to	12 April 1325	*IPM VI*, no. 607 (R.I.P.)
Gilbert de Umfraville, earl of Angus, son of above, P.P.		
from	12 April 1325	*IPM VI*, no. 607
to	6 January 1381	*IPM XV*, no. 434 (R.I.P.)
Thomas de Umfraville		
to	21 May 1387	*IPM XVI*, no. 470 (R.I.P.)
Thomas de Umfraville II, son of above		
from	21 May 1387	*IPM XVI*, no. 470
to	12 February 1391	*IPM XVI*, no. 1043 (R.I.P.)
Gilbert de Umfraville, son of above		
from	12 February 1391	*IPM XVI*, no. 1043 (Age 28 weeks)
inherited	10 January 1409	*CPR 1408–1413*, p. 156 (Underage)
of age	28 January 1415	*IPM XIX*, no. 1005
Joan de Umfraville		
not by	24 November 1421	*CPR 1416–1422*, p. 183
Robert de Umfraville, son of above		
from	24 November 1421	*CPR 1416–1422*, p. 183

Constables

John de Penereth		
on	25 August 1321	*CPR 1321–1324*, p. 21

HARLE, WEST

Owners

John Harley		
in	1415	Bates, p. 16

HARNHAM

Owners

Robert Swinburn		
in	1415	Bates, p. 16

HAUGHTON

Owners

Roger de Widdrington		
to	13 April 1372	*IPM* XIII, no. 215

John de Widdrington, son of above

from	13 April 1372	*IPM* XIII, no. 215
in	1415	Bates, p. 15

HEATON COLDSTREAM

Owners

Thomas de Grey of Heton and Wark

on	1415	Bates, p. 14

HEATON NEAR NEWCASTLE

Owners

Adam of Jesmond

in	1267	King, p. 335

HEPPLE

Owners

Robert Ogle

in	1415	Bates, p. 18

HETHPOOL

Owners

Robert Manners

in	1415	Bates, p. 17

HEXHAM

Owners

Archbishop of York

in	1415	Bates, p. 18

HOLBURN

History

mentioned	1415	King, p. 349

HOPPEN

Owners

Robert Hoppen

in	1415	Bates, p. 16

HORTON IN GLENDALE

Owners

Thomas Grey

in	1415	Bates, p. 15

HORTON NEAR THE SEA

Owners

Guichard de Charrun, kn.

licence to crenellate	28 December 1292	*CPR 1291–1301*, p. 2

Allies of Gilbert de Middleton		
to	April 1318	Nthumb Petitions, p. 135
Henry Delaval		
dead by	1402	Bates, p. 14
William de Wychester, from Alice, his mother, sister of above		
to	1410	Bates, p. 14

HOWICK

Owners

Emeric Hering		
in	1415	Bates, p. 16

ILDERTON

Owners

Thomas de Ilderton, kn.		
in	1415	Bates, p. 17

KIRKLEY

Owners

Sir William Eure		
in	1415	Bates, p. 16

KIRKNEWTON

Owners

Thomas Strother		
in	1415	Bates, p. 19

KYLOE

Owners

David Grey		
in	1415	Bates, p. 19

LANGLEY

Owners

Thomas de Lucy, kn., P.P.		
to	4 December 1365	*IPM XII*, no. 17 (R.I.P.)
Anthony de Lucy, son of above		
from	4 December 1365	*IPM XII*, no. 17
to	20 May 1368	*IPM XII*, no. 233 (R.I.P.)
Joan, wife of above		
from	9 July 1369	*CCR 1369–1374*, p. 30
Joan, daughter and heir to Anthony de Lucy		
heir on	20 May 1368	*IPM XII*, no. 233
to	30 September 1369	*IPM XII*, no. 374 (R.I.P.)
Maud, sister of Anthony, wife of Gilbert de Umfraville		
from	30 September 1369	*IPM XII*, no. 374
Umfraville family		
to	1381	Bates, pp. 38–56
Percy family		
from	1381	Bates, pp. 38–56

Maud, wife of Henry earl of Northumberland		
to	18 December 1398	*IPM XVII*, no. 1246 (R.I.P.)
Henry Percy		
from	18 December 1398	*IPM XVII*, no. 1246
forfeited by	7 August 1405	*CPR 1405–1408*, p. 50
Henry Percy, earl of Northumberland, grandson of above		
in	1415	Bates, p. 15

Constables

Alexander Featherstonehaugh		
to	20 July 1405	*CPR 1405–1408*, p. 74
Robert Umfraville, kn.		
for life on	27 June 1405	*CPR 1405–1408*, p. 40
from	20 July 1405	*CPR 1405–1408*, p. 74
for life from	7 August 1405	*CPR 1405–1408*, p. 50

LANGTON

Owners

Henry Strother		
in	1415	Bates, p. 17

LEMMINGTON

Owners

William Bednell		
in	1415	Bates, p. 19

LILBURN, WEST

Owners

John Carr		
in	1415	Bates, p. 19

LOWICK

Owners

Philip, lord Darcy		
in	1415	Bates, p. 17

MELDON

Owners

Nicholas Heron		
in	1415	Bates, p. 16

MIDDLETON BY THE SEA

Owners

William Muschamp		
in	1415	Bates, p. 19

MIDDLETON, NORTH

Owners

Robert Ogle		
in	1415	Bates, p. 16

MITFORD

Owners

Roger Bertram of Mitford		
on	7 June 1267	*CPR 1301–1307*, p. 363
before	7 November 1274	*CFR 1272–1307*, p. 34 (R.I.P.)
Alexander de Balliol and Eleanor, his wife		
from	22 July 1270 or 1271	A.H.Thompson, ed., *Northumbrian Pleas from the De Banco Rolls 1–19*, Surtees Society 158 (1943), no. 205
in	Easter 1275	*ibid.*
Robert de Stuteville via Eleanor, his wife		
to	14 April 1306	*IPM IV*, no. 369 (R.I.P.)
Elizabeth, widow of Robert de Stuteville		
from	1 November 1306	*CCR 1302–1307*, p. 420
Eleanor, widow of Robert de Stuteville		
to	27 September 1310	*IPM V*, no. 237 (R.I.P.)
John de Stuteville, their son		
from	27 September 1310	*IPM V*, no. 237
to	16 February 1315	*CPR 1313–1317*, p. 254
Aymer de Valence, earl of Pembroke		
from	16 February 1315	*CPR 1313–1317*, p. 254
to	26 June 1324	*IPM VI*, no. 518 (R.I.P.)
David de Strabolgi, earl of Athol		
on	8 February 1326	*CCR 1323–1327*, p. 446
to	8 January 1327	*IPM VI*, no. 759 (R.I.P.)
David de Strabolgi, son of above		
heir on	8 January 1327	*IPM VI*, no. 759
David de Strabolgi, from his grandmother		
from	29 March 1332	*CCR 1330–1333*, p. 455
to	1334	*IPM VIII*, no. 677
Thomas Grey of Heton, kn.		
from	1334 (Five year loan)	*IPM VIII*, no. 677
on	8 January 1336	*IPM VIII*, no. 677
David de Strabolgi, earl of Athol		
heir on	8 January 1336	*IPM VIII*, no. 677
to	10 October 1369	*IPM XII*, no. 327 (R.I.P.)
Elizabeth countess of Athol, widow of John Malewayn		
to	23 October 1375	*IPM XIV*, no. 86 (R.I.P.)
Philippa, widow of Ralph de Percy, daughter of Strabolgi and above		
from	23 October 1375	*IPM XIV*, no. 86
from	6 May 1377	*CCR 1374–1377*, p. 506
Elizabeth, widow of Thomas de Percy, ynr		
on	21 May 1388	*CPR 1385–1389*, p. 421
Henry Percy de Athol		
on	1415	Bates, p. 14
on	6/8 July 1418	*CPR 1416–1422*, p. 505

Guarding the castle

John de Eure		
in	1316	E.101/68/2 m.36

Private Constables for earl of Pembroke

John de Lilleburn		
on	20 February 1316	*CPR 1313–1317*, p. 396

Wardships

2 Parts, for minority of Elizabeth and Philippa, daughters of David de Strabolgi, earl of Athol

Henry, Lord Percy		
from	8 July 1373	*CPR 1370–1374*, p. 330

MORPETH

Owners

William, Baron Greystoke, P.P.		
from	1342	
to	10 July 1359	*IPM X*, no. 524 (R.I.P.)
Joan, widow of William, Baron Greystoke.		
from	8 October 1359	*CCR 1354–1360*, p. 598
to	1 September 1403	*IPM XVIII*, no. 902 (R.I.P.)
Ralph de Greystoke, son of above, P.P.		
from	1 September 1403	*IPM XVIII*, no. 902
on	1415	Bates, p. 13
died	*1418*	*GEC VI, p. 195*
John de Greystoke, son of above, P.P. .		
inherited	*1418*	*GEC VI, p. 195*
on	10 September 1431	*Bishop Langley's Register, vol. IV*, Surtees Society 170 (1955), no. 1229
on	16 October 1436	*Wills and Inventories, part 1*, Surtees Society 2 (1835), p. 85
died	*1436*	*GEC VI, p. 195*

MORPETH NO. 3

History

mentioned	1310, 1343	King, p. 351

NESBIT IN GLENDALE

Owners

Thomas Grey		
in	1415	Bates, p. 18

NETHERWITTON

History

mentioned	1415	King, p. 338

NEWCASTLE (ON TYNE)

Owners

Crown during entire period		
on	6 April 1308	*CCR 1307–1313*, p. 29

Constables

Robert de Haunton		
to	16 October 1274	*CFR 1272–1307*, p. 30

John de Lithegraynes		
from	16 October 1274	*CFR 1272–1307*, p. 30
to	25 October 1278	*CFR 1272–1307*, p. 103
Walter de Camhou, kn.		
from	25 October 1278	*CFR 1272–1307*, p. 103
to	15 November 1281	*CFR 1272–1307*, p. 156
Thomas de Dyveleston		
from	15 November 1281	*CFR 1272–1307*, p. 156
William de Felton		
to	8 October 1314	*CFR 1307–1319*, p. 220
Nicholas de Scot		
from	8 October 1314	*CFR 1307–1319*, p. 220
to	3 May 1315	*CFR 1307–1319*, p. 245
William Rydel		
from	3 May 1315	*CFR 1307–1319*, p. 245
Hugh de Audley of Stratton Audley, senior, P.P.		
from	15 July 1317	*CPR 1317–1321*, p. 2
to	3 August 1317	*CFR 1307–1319*, p. 337
William Rydel		
from	3 August 1317	*CFR 1307–1319*, p. 337
to	12 October 1319	*CFR 1319–1327*, p. 5
John de Fenwick		
from	12 October 1319	*CFR 1319–1327*, p. 5
Adam Swynborn		
from	16 October 1319	*CFR 1319–1327*, p. 261
John de Fenwick		
to	3 July 1323	*CFR 1319–1327*, p. 217
Gilbert de Boroughdon		
from	3 July 1323	*CFR 1319–1327*, p. 217
to	19 February 1325	*CFR 1319–1327*, p. 332
John de Fenwick		
from	19 February 1325	*CFR 1319–1327*, p. 332
to	29 June 1327	*CFR 1327–1337*, p. 51
John de L'isle of Wodeburn		
from	29 June 1327	*CFR 1327–1337*, p. 51
John de Lilleburn		
to	30 June 1328	*CFR 1327–1337*, p. 94
Robert de Hornclyf		
from	30 June 1328	*CFR 1327–1337*, p. 94
to	13 August 1328	*CFR 1327–1337*, p. 101
John de Lilleburn		
from	13 August 1328	*CFR 1327–1337*, p. 101
to	5 December 1330	*CFR 1327–1337*, p. 199
Robert de Hornclyf		
from	5 December 1330	*CFR 1327–1337*, p. 199
John de Lilleburn		
to	8 October 1331	*CFR 1327–1337*, p. 275
William de Tynedale		
from	8 October 1331	*CFR 1327–1337*, p. 275
to	14 December 1332	*CFR 1327–1337*, p. 338

Roger Mauduyt		
from	14 December 1332	*CFR 1327–1337*, p. 338
to	15 June 1334	*CFR 1327–1337*, p. 406
Robert Darreys		
from	15 June 1334	*CFR 1327–1337*, p. 406
to	29 June 1339	*CFR 1337–1347*, p. 129
John de Lilleburn		
from	29 June 1339	*CFR 1337–1347*, p. 129
to	6 July 1339	*CFR 1337–1347*, p. 135
Gilbert de Boroughdon		
from	6 July 1339	*CFR 1337–1347*, p. 135
to	8 March 1341	*CFR 1337–1347*, p. 214
William de Felton		
from	8 March 1341	*CFR 1337–1347*, p. 214
to	28 May 1343	*CFR 1337–1347*, p. 320
to	22 November 1343	*CFR 1337–1347*, p. 349
John de Strivelyn, P.P.		
from	28 May 1343	*CFR 1337–1347*, p. 320
to	10 February 1344	*CFR 1337–1347*, p. 349
William de Felton		
from	10 February 1344	*CFR 1337–1347*, p. 349
to	6 July 1344	*CFR 1337–1347*, p. 357
Robert de Fenwick		
from	6 July 1344	*CFR 1337–1347*, p. 357
to	9 April 1345	*CFR 1337–1347*, p. 420
Robert Bertram		
from	9 April 1345	*CFR 1337–1347*, p. 420
Robert de Reymes		
from	5 May 1347	*CFR 1347–1356*, p. 23
to	4 June 1348	*CFR 1347–1356*, p. 83
John de Clifford		
from	4 June 1348	*CFR 1347–1356*, p. 83
to	29 April 1350	*CFR 1347–1356*, p. 213
John de Coupeland		
from	29 April 1350	*CFR 1347–1356*, p. 213
and from	22 October 1350	*CFR 1347–1356*, p. 262
Alan del Strothre		
from	10 November 1356	*CFR 1347–1356*, p. 19
and from	20 November 1357	*CFR 1356–1368*, p. 52
Henry de Strothre		
from	3 November 1358	*CFR 1356–1368*, p. 80
and from	1 October 1359	*CFR 1356–1368*, p. 102
John Heron		
from	21 November 1360	*CFR 1356–1368*, p. 121
Roger de Widdrington		
from	10 December 1361	*CFR 1356–1368*, p. 154
Richard de Horsley		
from	20 November 1362	*CFR 1356–1368*, p. 236
on	20 June 1363	*CCR 1360–1364*, p. 536
and from	20 November 1363	*CFR 1356–1368*, p. 268
to	28 January 1364	*CFR 1356–1368*, p. 280

Henry de Strother		
from	28 January 1364	*CFR 1356–1368*, p. 280
and from	16 November 1366	*CFR 1356–1368*, p. 328
Richard de Horsley		
from	27 November 1368	*CFR 1356–1368*, p. 392
and from	28 March 1370	*CFR 1369–1377*, p. 98
Robert de Umfraville		
from	5 November 1371	*CFR 1369–1377*, p. 146
Thomas Surteys		
from	12 December 1372	*CFR 1369–1377*, p. 190
John de Fenwick		
from	7 November 1373	*CFR 1369–1377*, p. 222
Bertram Monboucher		
from	12 December 1374	*CFR 1369–1377*, p. 272
Thomas de Hilderton		
from	4 October 1375	*CFR 1369–1377*, p. 297
Robert Umfraville		
from	26 October 1376	*CFR 1369–1377*, p. 369
to	26 November 1377	*CFR 1377–1383*, p. 34
Bertram Montboucher		
from	26 November 1377	*CFR 1377–1383*, p. 34
to	25 November 1378	*CFR 1377–1383*, p. 113
Thomas Surteys		
from	25 November 1378	*CFR 1377–1383*, p. 113
to	14 July 1379	*CFR 1377–1383*, p. 157
Alexander Surteys		
from	14 July 1379	*CFR 1377–1383*, p. 157
Bertram Montboucher		
from	5 November 1379	*CFR 1377–1383*, p. 171
John Heron, elder		
from	18 October 1380	*CFR 1377–1383*, p. 220
Bertram Montboucher		
from	3 December 1380	*CFR 1377–1383*, p. 220
Aymer de Athol		
from	6 December 1381	*CFR 1377–1383*, p. 270
to	3 November 1382	*CFR 1377–1383*, p. 327
Robert de Clifford		
from	3 November 1382	*CFR 1377–1383*, p. 327
John Heron		
from	1 December 1383	*CFR 1383–1391*, p. 7
Henry Percy, earl of Northumberland		
from	11 November 1385	*CFR 1383–1391*, p. 76
Betram son of Bertram Montbouche		
from	20 August 1388	*CFR 1383–1391*, p. 248
Thomas Umfraville		
from	1 December 1388	*CFR 1383–1391*, p. 248
Ralph de Eure		
from	15 November 1389	*CFR 1383–1391*, p. 306
John de Felton		
from	7 November 1390	*CFR 1383–1391*, p. 341
Henry Percy, earl of Northumberland		
from	21 October 1391	*CFR 1391–1399*, p. 7

John Stanley		
from	13 March 1394	*CPR 1391–1396*, p. 404
John Fenwick		
from	10 February 1399	*CFR 1391–1399*, p. 377
John Mosdale		
in	1401	Nthumb Petitions, pp. 176–177
on	25 December 1401	*CPR 1401–1405*, p. 36 (Keeper)
on	16 February 1402	*CPR 1401–1405*, p. 41 (Keeper)

Chaplains

Robert de Thyngden/Thynden		
on	11 February 1338	*CPR 1338–1340*, p. 8
to	12 February 1371	*CPR 1370–1374*, p. 47 (R.I.P.)
John de Clifford		
from	12 February 1371	*CPR 1370–1374*, p. 47

Gatekeepers

Nicholas de Ufton		
to	27 December 1350	*CPR 1350–1354*, p. 20 (R.I.P.)
William de Watford		
from	27 December 1350	*CPR 1350–1354*, p. 20
Thomas Rote		
for life from	3 June 1360	*CPR 1358–1361*, p. 372
for life from	1 December 1360	*CPR 1358–1361*, p. 509

Keeper of the Goal

Thomas Rote		
for life from	1 December 1360	*CPR 1358–1361*, p. 509
on	16 November 1364	*CCR 1364–1368*, p. 36

NEWLANDS IN WARENTON

Owners

John de Middleton		
licence to crenellate	22 July 1310	*CPR 1307–1313*, p. 272

NEWSTEAD NEAR BAMBOROUGH

Owners

Robert de Ogle		
in	1415	Bates, p. 18

NORHAM

Owners

Bishop of Durham		
restored	30 July 1314	*CPR 1313–1317*, p. 163
Crown		
temporary grant	23 Nov 1315	*CPR 1313–1317*, p. 396
Bishop of Durham		
void	11 October 1316	*CCR 1313–1318*, p. 369
on	11 October 1316	*CFR 1307–1319*, p. 305
restored	4 May 1317	*CPR 1313–1317*, p. 644
on	26 June 1323	*CCR 1318–1323*, p. 663
on	1 September 1325	*CCR 1323–1327*, p. 399
on	2 August 1326	*CPR 1324–1327*, p. 303

Bishop of Durham		
on	29 April 1326	*CCR 1323–1327*, p. 476
on	10 October 1331	*CCR 1330–1333*, p. 401
on	30 October 1340	*CCR 1339–1341*, p. 561
in	1415	Bates, p. 14
Royal Constables		
William Rydel		
to	14 August 1314	James Raine, ed., *Historical Papers and Letters from the Northern Registers*, Rolls Series 61 (1873), item CXLVI
Walter de Gosewyk		
on	11 October 1316	*CCR 1313–1318*, p. 369
temp	1316–1317	E.101/695/4
Robert de Hastang, P.P.		
to	20 January 1317	*CPR 1313–1317*, p. 616
John Darcy 'le cosyn'		
from	20 January 1317	*CPR 1313–1317*, p. 616
to	4 May 1317	*CPR 1313–1317*, p. 644
Thomas de Grey of Heton		
in	September 1322	Nthumb Petitions, p. 62
on	2 October 1323	*CCR 1323–1327*, p. 26
Thomas de Richmond		
on	20 February 1335	*CPR 1334–1338*, p. 78
Church Constables		
Robert de Clifford, kn., P.P.		
from	14 August 1314	James Raine, ed., *Historical Papers and Letters from the Northern Registers*, Rolls Series 61 (1873), item CXLVI
Robert de Manners		
on	28 July 1333	*CCR 1330–1333*, p. 68
on	30 October 1340	*CCR 1339–1341*, p. 561
in	1345	Dobson, p. 136
Nicholas de Dagworth, kn.		
to	20 July 1375	
John Heron, kn.		
from	20 July 1375	
confirmed	25 February 1381	*CPR 1381–1385*, p. 12
Sir Gerard Heron		
in	1386	Dobson, p. 136
Sir Robert Ogle		
in	1403	Dobson, p. 137
Ogle family		
to	1450	Dobson, p. 137

OGLE

Owners		
Robert de Ogle		
license to crenellate	11 May 1341	*CChR 1341–1417*, p. 4; Bates, p. 9
Robert de Ogle		
to	May 1362	*IPM XI*, no. 397 (R.I.P.)
to	23 May 1364	*IPM XII*, no. 205 (R.I.P.)

Robert de Ogle, grandson of above		
from	May 1362	*IPM XI*, no. 397
to	1 Nov 1409	*IPM XIX*, no. 734 (R.I.P.)
Robert de Ogle, son of above		
from	1 Nov 1409	*IPM XIX*, no. 734
in	1415	Bates, p. 14

OTTERBURN

Owners		
Thomas de Umfraville		
dead by	28 September 1403	*IMisc VII*, no. 233
Gilbert de Umfraville, son of above		
under age	28 September 1403	*IMisc VII*, no. 233
in	1415	Bates, p. 18
Robert de Umfraville		
from	1421	Bates, p. 18
Wardships		
Minority of Gilbert de Umfraville, 1391–1411		
Henry Percy		
forfeited by	28 September 1403	*IMisc VII*, no. 233
Keepers		
Peter de Stokhalgh for Percy		
on	28 September 1403	*IMisc VII*, no. 233

PONTELAND (VICARS PELE)

History		
mentioned	1415	King, p. 340
Owners		
The Vicar		
in	1415	Bates, p. 19

PONTELAND NO. 2

History		
taken by Scots	1388	King, p. 340
Owners		
Sir Aymer de Athol		
in	1386	Bates, p. 12

PRESTON BY ALNWICK

History		
mentioned	1415	King, p. 340
unroofed	1499	King, p. 340
mentioned	1570	King, p. 340
Owners		
Robert Harbottle		
in	1415	Bates, p. 16
to	1419	Bates, p. 195 (R.I.P.)

PRUDHOE

History

built	early C12	King, p. 340
siege	1173, 1174	King, p. 340
modified	C13 and early C14	King, p. 340
siege	1405	King, p. 340
ruinous	1596	King, p. 340

Owners

Gilbert de Umfraville, earl of Angus, P.P.		
from	1244	Bates, p. 201
to	13 October 1307	*IPM V*, no. 14 (R.I.P.)
Robert de Umfraville, earl of Angus, son of above, P.P.		
from	13 October 1307	*IPM V*, no. 14
to	12 April 1325	*IPM VI*, no. 607 (R.I.P.)
Gilbert de Umfraville, earl of Angus, son of above, P.P.		
from	12 April 1325	*IPM VI*, no. 607
to	6 January 1381	*IPM XV*, no. 434 (R.I.P.)
Maud, widow of Gilbert de Umfraville.		
on	10 February 1381	*CCR 1377–1381*, p. 430 (Jointure)
Maud, wife of Henry earl of Northumberland		
from	c.1381	Bates, p. 203
dead by	1 April 1398	*CCR 1396–1399*, p. 255
to	18 December 1398	*IPM XVII*, no. 1246 (R.I.P.)
Henry Percy		
from	1 April 1398	*CCR 1396–1399*, p. 255
not by	27 June 1405	*CPR 1405–1408*, p. 40
John, duke of Bedford, son of Henry IV		
from	27 June 1405	*CPR 1405–1408*, p. 40
on	1415	Bates, p. 15
Henry Percy, earl of Northumberland		
judgement in favour	5 July 1416	*IMisc VII*, no. 527
finally regained	1441	Bates, p. 204

Constables

Robert L'isle		
from	25 December 1403	Bates, p. 203
David Trollop		
from	15 June 1405	Bates, p. 203
John Skipton		
to	15 June 1405	*CPR 1405–1408*, p. 70
David Trollop		
from	15 June 1405	*CPR 1405–1408*, p. 70

Private Constables

John Skipton		
to	15 June 1405	Bates, p. 203

Wardships

Minority of Gilbert de Umfraville, earl of Angus (1325–1331)

Roger Mauduyt		
on	3 September 1325	*CCR 1323–1327*, p. 399
to	11 February 1327	*CFR 1327–1337*, p. 12

Gilbert de Boroughdon		
from	11 February 1327	*CFR 1327–1337*, p. 12
to	3 September 1327	*CPR 1327–1330*, p. 160
Maurice de Berkeley		
from	3 September 1327	*CPR 1327–1330*, p. 160

SCREMERSTON

Owners

John Swinhoe		
in	1415	Bates, p. 17

SEATON DELAVAL

Owners

William de Whitchester, kn.		
from	1402	Bates, p. 14
to	1410	Bates, p. 14 (R.I.P.)

SEGHILL

Owners

William Delaval		
in	1415	Bates, p. 16

SEWINGSHIELDS

Owners

Robert de Ogle		
on	1415	Bates, p. 15

SHAWDEN

Owners

Thomas Lilleburn		
in	1415	Bates, p. 15

SHILBOTTLE

Owners

Henry Percy		
not by	27 June 1405	*CPR 1405–1408*, p. 40
John, duke of Bedford, son of Henry IV		
from	27 June 1405	*CPR 1405–1408*, p. 40
on	1415	Bates, p. 19

SHORTFLATT

Owners

Robert de Reymes		
licence to crenellate	5 April 1305	*CPR 1301–1307*, p. 328
Robert de Reymes		
in	1415	Bates, p. 16

SIMONBURN

Owners

William Heron		
in	1415	Bates, p. 18

STAMFORDHAM

Owners

The Vicar		
in	1415	Bates, p. 18

STANTON

Owners

John Corbet		
in	1415	Bates, p. 16

STAWARD

Owners

Hugh de Louthre		
to	26 April 1326	*CPR 1324–1327*, p. 261
Queen Philippa		
from	1337	Bates, p. 10

Constables

Thomas de Featherstonehaugh		
from	26 April 1326	*CPR 1324–1327*, p. 261
John Darcy 'le Cosyn'		
for life from	25 April 1329	*CPR 1327–1330*, p. 385
Edmund de Langley, future duke of York		
for life from	23 April 1373	*CPR 1370–1374*, p. 288
Hexham Priory		
from	1386	Bates, p. 11

SWINBURNE, WEST

Owners

Roger de Widdrington		
license to crenellate	10 May 1346	*CPR 1345–1348*, p. 88
John de Widdrington		
in	1415	Bates, p. 14

TARSETT

Owners

John Comyn		
licence to crenellate	5 December 1267	Bates, p. 8

THIRWALL

Owners

Roland de Thirwall		
in	1415	Bates, p. 15

THROPTON

Owners

William Green		
in	1415	Bates, p. 17

TREWIT, NETHER

Owners

Hugo Galon		
in	1415	Bates, p. 17

TROUGHEND

Owners

William Buticom		
in	1415	Bates, p. 18

TWEEDMOUTH

History

tower built	1209	King, p. 355
destroyed	1209	King, p. 355
mentioned	1385	King, p. 355
not mentioned	1415	King, p. 355
mentioned	1541	King, p. 355

TWIZEL

Owners

John Heron		
in	1415	Bates, p. 14

TYNEMOUTH

Owners

Tynemouth Priory		
licence to crenellate	5 September 1296	*CPR 1292–1301*, p. 197; Bates, p. 8
in	1415	Bates, p. 13

WALLINGTON

Owners

William Strother		
in	1415	Bates, p. 16

WARK ON TWEED

Owners

Robert de Ros		
from	7 May 1274	*CCR 1272–1279*, p. 83
Robert de Ros of Wark, P.P.		
died	*1295/6*	*GEC XI, p. 121*
not by	2 December 1301	*CChR 1300–1326*, p. 23
William de Ros of Helmsley, P.P.		
from	1296	

Crown for defence of the border		
on	13 October 1300	*CPR 1292–1301*, p. 538
William de Ros of Helmsley, son of above P.P.		
to	25 September 1317	*CPR 1321–1324*, p. 212
Crown		
from	25 September 1317	*CPR 1321–1324*, p. 212
confirmed	22 August 1322	*CPR 1321–1324*, p. 212
William de Montague, earl of Salisbury		
from	2 August 1333 (and heirs)	
confirmed	7 June 1335	*CPR 1334–1338*, p. 162
to	30 January 1344	*IPM VIII*, no. 532 (R.I.P.)
John de Montague, ynr., son of above, P.P.		
from	17 June 1344	*CCR 1343–1346*, p. 319
to	25 February 1390	*IPM XVI*, no. 871
John Montague, kn., son of above		
from	25 February 1390	*IPM XVI*, no. 871
to	12 February 1397	*CPR 1396–1399*, p. 73
Ralph Neville, earl of Westmorland, enfeofed by Montague		
from	12 February 1397	*CPR 1396–1399*, p. 73
to	17 September 1398	*CPR 1396–1399*, p. 410
Thomas Grey, kn., of Heton		
from	17 September 1398	*CPR 1396–1399*, p. 410
Joan, widow of Thomas Gray, kn.		
from	5 December 1402	*CCR 1399–1402*, p. 11
on	30 November 1402	*CPR 1401–1405*, p. 182
Thomas Grey of Heton and Wark		
on	1415	Bates, p. 14

Constables

Thomas le Pestour of Langeton		
on	24 August 1300	*CChW 1244–1326*, p. 113
David de Langeton		
from	1 February 1320	*CFR 1319–1327*, p. 15
Roger Mauduyt		
to	20 May 1328	*CFR 1327–1337*, p. 97
William de Roos of Helmsley , P.P.		
from	20 May 1328	*CFR 1327–1337*, p. 97
Robert Ogle		
to	1419	Bates, p. 342

WARK IN TYNDALE

Owners

Thomas Grey		
in	1415	Bates, p. 18

WARKWORTH

Owners

Robert fitz Roger of Clavering, P.P.		
to	29 April 1310	*IPM V*, no. 219 (R.I.P.)

John de Clavering, son of above, P.P.		
from	29 April 1310	*IPM V*, no. 219
reversion granted to king	20 February 1327	*CPR 1327–1330*, p. 15
for life on	1 March 1328	*CPR 1327–1330*, p. 243
to	18 January 1332	Bates, p. 93
Henry Percy		
granted reversion	2 March 1328	Bates, p. 93
from	18 January 1332	Bates, p. 93
to	26 February 1352	*IPM X*, no. 43 (R.I.P.)
Henry Percy, son of above		
to	18 May 1368	*IPM XII*, no. 242 (R.I.P.)
Henry Percy, son of above		
from	18 May 1368	*IPM XII*, no. 242
to	6 August 1400	*CPR 1399–1401*, p. 358
Thomas Percy, earl of Westmorland		
from	6 August 1400	*CPR 1399–1401*, p. 358
on	27 June 1405	*CPR 1405–1408*, p. 40
Crown		
from	1 July 1405	Bates, p. 107
to	14 April 1416	Bates, p. 107
Henry Percy, earl of Northumberland, grandson of two above		
from	14 April 1416	Bates, p. 107
in	1415	Bates, p. 14

Constables

Robert Darreys, possibly private		
in	1322	Bates, p. 93
Ralph Neville of Raby, P.P.		
on	15 September 1322	*CPR 1321–1324*, p. 205
William Heron, lord Say		
from	7 September 1403	Bates, p. 102
Robert Umfraville		
in	May 1406	Bates, p. 109 (Captain)

Subconstables

John Hardyng for Robert Umfraville		
from	May 1406	Bates, p. 109

Private Constables

William de Toggesdene		
in	1297	Bates, p. 91
John Cresswell		
to	7 September 1403	Bates, p. 102
John de Middleham		
to	1 July 1405	Bates, p. 107

Chaplains

John de Crayk		
on	12 December 1334	Percy Chartulary, p. 301

WEETSLADE

History

mentioned	1415	King, p. 355

WHITFIELD

Owners		
Matthew Whitfeld		
in	1415	Bates, p. 19

WHITLEY NEAR TYNEMOUTH

Owners		
Gilbert de Whitley		
licence to crenellate	9 April 1345	*CPR 1343–1345*, p. 446
Priory of Tynemouth		
in	1415	Bates, p. 16

WHITTINGHAM

Owner		
William de Heron		
in	1415	Bates, p. 17

WHITTON NEAR ROTHBURY

Owners		
The Rector		
in	1415	Bates, p. 18

WIDDRINGTON

Owners		
Gerard de Widdrington		
licence to crenellate	10 September 1341	*CPR 1340–1343*, p. 289
John de Widdrington		
on	1415	Bates, p. 19

Nottinghamshire

GREASLEY

Owners

Nicholas de Cauntelo, P.P.		
licence to crenellate	5 April 1340	*CPR 1338–1340*, p. 449
died	*31 July 1355*	*GEC III, p. 112*
Nicholas de Cauntelo		
on	10 March 1366	*CPR 1364–1367*, p. 281
to	21 February 1371	*IPM XIII*, no. 97 (R.I.P.)
William de Cauntelo, brother of above		
from	21 February 1371	*IPM XIII*, no. 97
to	31 March 1375	*IPM XIV*, no. 108 (R.I.P.)
William la Zouche of Harringworth, uncle of above, kn., P.P.		
from	31 March 1375	*IPM XIV*, no. 108
to	23 April 1382	*IPM XV*, no. 641 (R.I.P.)
William la Zouche of Harringworth, kn., and Agnes, son of above		
from	23 April 1382	*IPM XV*, no. 641
to	13 May 1396	*IPM XVII*, no. 717 (R.I.P.)
not by	4 July 1396	*CCR 1396–1399*, p. 4 (R.I.P.)
William la Zouche, son of above		
from	13 May 1396	*IPM XVII*, no. 717
granted away	21 November 1396	*CCR 1396–1399*, p. 66
dead by	13 February 1416	*CPR 1413–1416*, p. 260
Thomas lord Berkeley, Thomas la Warre and Robert Isham		
from	13 February 1416	*CPR 1413–1416*, p. 260

LOWDHAM

History

in use	to c.1400	King, p. 380

NEWARK

Owners

Bishop of Lincoln		
on	13 April 1149	*Registrum Antiquissimum of the Cathedral Church of Lincoln, vol. I*, Lincoln Record Society, 27 (1931), no. 250
not by	2 November 1317	*CPR 1317–1321*, p. 45
Crown		
on	2 November 1317	*CPR 1317–1321*, p. 45
Henry Burghersh, bishop of Lincoln		
restored	27 March 1324	*CCR 1324–1327*, p. 85
John Buckingham, bishop of Lincoln		
on	28 March 1382	*CPR 1381–1385*, p. 143
Henry Beaufort, bishop of Lincoln		
on	26 September 1402	*CPR 1401–1405*, p. 122

Constables during voidances

Robert de Pirpount for Crown		
from	2 November 1317	*CPR 1317–1321*, p. 45
Douenald de Mar		
on	30 January 1322	*CPR 1321–1324*, p. 53
to	27 March 1324	*CCR 1323–1327*, p. 86
on	20 February 1325	*CCR 1323–1327*, p. 260

Constables for the Church

Henry Beek (Possibly for the King?)		
on	30 April 1354	*CCR 1354–1360*, p. 72

NOTTINGHAM

Owners

Crown		
on	6 April 1308	*CCR 1307–1313*, p. 29
Crown – Queen Anne		
for life from	16 November 1382	*CCR 1381–1385*, p. 192
on	26 May 1390	*CPR 1388–1392*, p. 252
Crown – Queen Joan		
from	4 June 1403	*CPR 1401–1405*, p. 234
on	2 November 1406	

Constables

Walter Grey, archbishop of York		
on	6 February 1272	*CLibR 1267–1272*, no. 1793
Robert de Tibotet		
from	3 January 1274	*CFR 1272–1307*, p. 39
Richard Tibotet		
from	3 December 1274	*CPR 1272–1281*, p. 73
Robert de Tibotet		
on	4 February 1275	*CCR 1272–1279*, p. 146
on	10 June 1280	*CFR 1272–1307*, p. 129
Gervase de Clifton		
on	16 July 1283	*CPR 1281–1292*, p. 70
Robert de Tibotet		
on	22 April 1287	*CCR 1279–1288*, p. 447
on	24 January 1292	*CCR 1288–1296*, p. 215
Richard le Clerk		
on	4 January 1296	*CPR 1292–1301*, p. 9
Robert de Tibotet		
on	31 August 1297	*CPR 1292–1301*, p. 59
to	7 July 1298	*CPR 1292–1301*, p. 344 (R.I.P.)
Robert de Clifford, P.P.		
from	7 July 1298	*CFR 1272–1307*, p. 401
to	12 March 1308	*CFR 1307–1319*, p. 17
John de Segrave, P.P.		
from	12 March 1308	*CFR 1307–1319*, p. 17
for life from	6 February 1310	*CPR 1307–1313*, p. 206 (elder)
to	1 October 1310	*CFR 1307–1319*, p. 73
Piers Gaveston		
from	1 October 1310	*CFR 1307–1319*, p. 73
on	11 December 1310	*CPR 1307–1313*, p. 315 (For life)

John de la Beche		
from	10 December 1311	*CFR 1307–1319*, p. 118 (Just Castle)
to	3 April 1312	*CFR 1307–1319*, p. 130 (Just Castle)
Peter Gaveston		
from	3 April 1312	*CFR 1307–1319*, p. 130 (Just Castle)
Ralph de Crophull		
to	14 July 1312	*CFR 1307–1319*, p. 138
John de la Beche, with Nottingham and Derbyshire		
from	14 July 1312	*CFR 1307–1319*, p. 138
to	4 September 1312	*CFR 1307–1319*, p. 145 (Just castle)
John de Segrave, P.P.		
from	4 September 1312	*CFR 1307–1319*, p. 145 (Just castle)
for life from	1 November 1317	*CFR 1307–1319*, p. 344
on	13 February 1322	*CCR 1318–1323*, p. 418
Henry de Faucomberge		
from	4 October 1325	*CFR 1319–1327*, p. 362
to	14 December 1325	*CFR 1319–1327*, p. 370
Richard de Grey of Codnor, P.P.		
from	14 December 1325	*CFR 1319–1327*, p. 370
and from	13 May 1327	*CFR 1327–1337*, p. 42
to	26 October 1330	*CPR 1330–1334*, p. 18
William de Eland		
from	26 October 1330	*CPR 1330–1334*, p. 18 (King's yeoman)
on	4 November 1342	*CPR 1340–1343*, p. 532
John Darcy, the father, P.P.		
on	29 May 1344	*CPR 1343–1345*, p. 258
to	16 June 1347	*CPR 1345–1348*, p. 337 (R.I.P.)
Stephen Romylowe, king's yeoman		
from	16 June 1347	*CPR 1345–1348*, p. 333
on	11 February 1370	*Issue Rolls*, p. 438
Collard Daubrichecourt		
on	12 July 1373	*CPR 1370–1374*, p. 325
Nicholas Daubrichecourt		
for life from	9 October 1376	*CPR 1374–1377*, p. 349
on	30 June 1377	*CCR 1377–1381*, p. 7
John de Burley, kn.		
for life from	28 October 1377	*CPR 1377–1381*, p. 34
to	23 November 1381	*CPR 1381–1385*, p. 60
William de Neville		
from	23 November 1381	*CPR 1381–1385*, p. 60 (Just castle)
on	15 February 1388	*CPR 1385–1389*, p. 394
John Golafre, kn.		
on	26 September 1392	*CCR 1392–1396*, p. 18
keeper for life from	25 June 1394	*CPR 1391–1396*, p. 449
to	21 December 1396	*CPR 1396–1399*, p. 147 (R.I.P.)
William de Arundel, kn.		
from	21 December 1396	*CPR 1396–1399*, p. 147
temp	1399	E.101/42/27
Thomas Rempston		
for life from	4 August 1400	*CPR 1399–1401*, p. 353
to	1 November 1406	*CPR 1405–1408*, p. 260 (R.I.P.)

Richard lord Grey of Codnor, P.P.		
from	1 November 1406	*CPR 1405–1408*, p. 260
for life from	2 November 1406 (For Queen Joan)	
on	21 March 1411	*CCR 1409–1413*, p. 148
on	28 June 1412	*CPR 1408–1413*, p. 370
Deputy Constables		
Robert de Morton		
on	12 July 1373	*CPR 1370–1374*, p. 325
John Knevyton		
temp	1399	E.101/42/27
Robert Harbottle		
temp	1399	E.101/42/27
Chaplain		
William de Byrlay		
from	8 December 1302	*CPR 1301–1307*, p. 98
Roger de Sheffield		
from	1 November 1307	*CPR 1307–1313*, p. 11
Surveyors of works		
William le Coper		
from	14 February 1329	*CPR 1327–1330*, p. 360
Robert de Beskewood		
from	14 February 1329	*CPR 1327–1330*, p. 360
Goaler		
Owin Martyn		
from	10 May 1421	*CPR 1416–1422*, p. 342
Porter, Gaoler and Warrener		
John Wolfreymer		
for life from	11 July 1394	*CPR 1391–1396*, p. 471
Hans Wolfreymer		
not by	27 November 1398	*CPR 1396–1399*, p. 465
John Donne of Wharton		
from	27 November 1398	*CPR 1396–1399*, p. 465
Clerk of the Works		
William Dionys, clerk		
on	1 October 1399	*CPR 1399–1401*, p. 58

Oxfordshire

Inactive Licenses

CHISELHAMPTON for Richard de Luches		
	26 July 1318	*CPR 1317–1321*, p. 194
DRATTON for Robert de Ardern		
	25 January 1329	*CPR 1327–1330*, p. 357
KERSINGTON for William de Montague		
	26 September 1317	*CPR 1317–1321*, p. 29
WYKHAM for Robert de Ardern		
	2 May 1330	*CPR 1327–1330*, p. 515

BAMPTON (HAM COURT)

Owners

Aymer de Valence, earl of Pembroke		
licence to crenellate	3 May 1315	*CPR 1313–1317*, p. 278

BANBURY

Owners

Bishops of Lincoln		
on	13 April 1149	*Registrum Antiquissimum of the Cathedral Church of Lincoln, vol. I,* Lincoln Record Society, 27 (1931), no. 250
to	3 January 1322	*CPR 1321–1324*, p. 46
before	26 April 1322	*CFR 1319–1327*, p. 124
restored	27 March 1324	*CCR 1323–1327*, p. 86
on	28 June 1334	*CPR 1330–1334*, p. 580
on	16 September 1398	*IMisc VI*, no. 392

Church Constables

Thomas Chaucer		
on	3 March 1411	*Register of Bishop Philip Repingdon*, Lincoln Record Society, 57 (1963), p. 208
on	10 January 1412	*ibid.* p.243

Constables while in Royal hands

Robert de Ardern		
from	3 January 1322	*CPR 1321–1324*, p. 46
on	26 February 1322	*CCR 1318–1323*, p. 426
Robert de Stoke		
to	26 April 1322	*CFR 1319–1327*, p. 124
Robert de Ardern		
from	26 April 1322	*CFR 1319–1327*, p. 124
on	18 April 1323	*CCR 1318–1323*, p. 641
to	27 March 1324	*CCR 1323–1327*, p. 86

BROUGHTON

Owners

John de Broughton, kn.		
built	c.1300's	*VCH vol. 9*, p. 89
died	1315	*VCH vol. 9*, p. 89
John de Broughton, son of above.		
of age	1327	*VCH vol. 9*, p. 89
alive	1346	*VCH vol. 9*, p. 89
Thomas de Broughton, kn., son of above.		
in	1356	*VCH vol. 9*, p. 89
dead before	1377	*VCH vol. 9*, p. 89
William Wykeham, bishop of Winchester, purchased from heiresses of above		
bought by	1377	*VCH vol. 9*, p. 89
Thomas Wykeham, esq., son of a niece of above		
by	1402	*VCH vol. 9*, p. 89
licence to crenellate	19 March 1406	*CPR 1405–1408*, p. 161
died	1443	*VCH vol. 9*, p. 89

DEDDINGTON

Owners

Henry de Dive		
to	17 October 1277	*IPM II*, no. 234 (R.I.P.)
John de Dive, son of above		
from	17 October 1277	*IPM II*, no. 234
minor in	1281	*VCH vol.2*, p. 90
to	18 December 1310	*IPM V*, no. 268 (R.I.P.)
Henry de Dive, son of above		
from	18 December 1310	*IPM V*, no. 268
Wardens and canons of the free chapel of Windsor		
on	26 June 1393	*CChR 1341–1417*, p. 337

OXFORD

Constables

Henry de Shotbroc		
from	19 October 1274	*CFR 1272–1307*, p. 33
to	5 November 1278	*CFR 1272–1307*, p. 104
Alan son of Roald		
from	5 November 1278	*CFR 1272–1307*, p. 104
James Cox		
to	9 May 1281	*CFR 1272–1307*, p. 146
John de Thedmers		
from	9 May 1281	*CFR 1272–1307*, p. 146
to	1 July 1285	*CPR 1281–1292*, p. 183
Ralph de Berners		
from	1 July 1285	*CPR 1281–1292*, p. 183
Amauri de St. Amand, P.P.		
from	18 March 1301	*CFR 1272–1307*, p. 439
Nicholas de Spershete		
from	19 February 1305	*CFR 1272–1307*, p. 508

Richard Damory, P.P.		
from	28 September 1311	*CFR 1307–1319*, p. 103
to	25 October 1311	*CFR 1307–1319*, p. 119
Thomas Danvers		
from	25 October 1311	*CFR 1307–1319*, p. 119
to	12 November 1311	*CCR 1307–1313*, p. 386
Richard Damory, P.P.		
from	12 November 1311	*CCR 1307–1313*, p. 386
to	24 February 1321	*CCR 1318–1323*, p. 290
Sheriff of Oxford		
from	24 February 1321	*CCR 1318–1323*, p. 290
John de Brompton		
to	20 May 1322	*CFR 1319–1327*, p. 130
Drew de Barentyn		
from	20 May 1322	*CFR 1319–1327*, p. 130
to	8 February 1327	*CFR 1327–1337*, p. 17
John de Brompton		
from	8 February 1327	*CFR 1327–1337*, p. 17
to	8 November 1328	*CFR 1327–1337*, p. 109
John de Buklonde		
from	8 November 1328	*CFR 1327–1337*, p. 109
to	2 January 1330	*CFR 1327–1337*, p. 158
Philip de la Beche		
with county from	2 January 1330	*CFR 1327–1337*, p. 158
to	5 December 1330	*CFR 1327–1337*, p. 199
Richard de Coleshull		
from	5 December 1330	*CFR 1327–1337*, p. 199
to	7 August 1332	*CFR 1327–1337*, p. 322
John de Brompton		
from	7 August 1332	*CFR 1327–1337*, p. 322
to	26 October 1333	*CFR 1327–1337*, p. 377
Richard de Abberbury		
from	26 October 1333	*CFR 1327–1337*, p. 377
to	18 December 1333	*CFR 1327–1337*, p. 381 (R.I.P.)
John de Leukenore		
from	18 December 1333	*CFR 1327–1337*, p. 381
to	20 December 1333	*CFR 1327–1337*, p. 381
William de Spersholt		
from	20 December 1333	*CFR 1327–1337*, p. 381
to	17 June 1335	*CFR 1327–1337*, p. 448
John de Alveton		
from	17 June 1335	*CFR 1327–1337*, p. 448
to	8 October 1340	*CFR 1337–1347*, p. 192
Edmund de Malyns		
from	8 October 1340	*CFR 1337–1347*, p. 192
to	10 November 1341	*CFR 1337–1347*, p. 247
John de Aulton		
from	10 November 1341	*CFR 1337–1347*, p. 247
to	19 November 1341	*CFR 1337–1347*, p. 250
Robert fitz Elys		
from	19 November 1341	*CFR 1337–1347*, p. 250
to	4 November 1342	*CFR 1337–1347*, p. 300

Thomas de Alveton		
from	4 November 1342	*CFR 1337–1347*, p. 300
John de Alveton		
from	22 November 1343	*CFR 1337–1347*, p. 349
to	11 November 1347	*CFR 1337–1347*, p. 57
John de Laundeles		
from	11 November 1347	*CFR 1347–1356*, p. 57
to	6 November 1352	*CFR 1347–1356*, p. 349
John de Alveton		
from	6 November 1352	*CFR 1347–1356*, p. 349
Richard de Williamescote		
from	10 November 1354	*CFR 1347–1356*, p. 409
Thomas de Besiles		
from	26 March 1355	*CFR 1347–1356*, p. 419
John de Noers		
from	1 April 1355	*CFR 1347–1356*, p. 419
John Laundels		
from	28 November 1355	*CFR 1347–1356*, p. 444
and from	20 November 1357	*CFR 1356–1368*, p. 52
Thomas Barentyn		
from	13 November 1358	*CFR 1356–1368*, p. 80
John Laundels		
from	21 November 1358	*CFR 1356–1368*, p. 80
and from	1 October 1359	*CFR 1356–1368*, p. 103
Roger de Elmerigg		
from	21 November 1360	*CFR 1356–1368*, p. 122
Roger de Coteford		
from	20 November 1362	*CFR 1356–1368*, p. 236
and from	20 November 1363	*CFR 1356–1368*, p. 268
John de Trillowe		
from	15 July 1365	*CFR 1356–1368*, p. 305
Roger de Elmerigg		
from	17 November 1365	*CFR 1356–1368*, p. 316
Roger de Coteford		
from	27 November 1368	*CFR 1356–1368*, p. 392
to	5 November 1369	*CFR 1369–1377*, p. 36
Thomas de la Mare		
from	5 November 1369	*CFR 1369–1377*, p. 36
and from	28 March 1370	*CFR 1369–1377*, p. 98
Gilbert Wace		
from	5 November 1371	*CFR 1369–1377*, p. 146
Roger de Elmerigg		
from	12 December 1372	*CFR 1369–1377*, p. 190
John James		
from	7 November 1373	*CFR 1369–1377*, p. 221
Gilbert Wace		
from	12 December 1374	*CFR 1369–1377*, p. 271
Reynold de Malyns		
from	4 October 1375	*CFR 1369–1377*, p. 297
John Rothewell		
from	26 October 1376	*CFR 1369–1377*, p. 369
and from	22 June 1377	*CFR 1377–1383*, p. 2

Edmund de Stonore		
from	26 November 1377	*CFR 1377–1383*, p. 34
Thomas Barentyn		
from	25 November 1378	*CFR 1377–1383*, p. 113
Gilbert Wace		
from	5 November 1379	*CFR 1377–1383*, p. 171
John James		
from	18 October 1380	*CFR 1377–1383*, p. 220
Richard Bruns of Harwell		
from	1 November 1381	*CFR 1377–1383*, p. 269
Thomas Barentyn		
from	24 November 1382	*CFR 1377–1383*, p. 327
John Holcote		
from	1 November 1383	*CFR 1383–1391*, p. 7
Robert Bullok		
from	11 November 1385	*CFR 1383–1391*, p. 76
to	16 October 1385	*CFR 1383–1391*, p. 107
John Holcote		
from	16 October 1385	*CFR 1383–1391*, p. 107
to	20 July 1386	*CFR 1383–1391*, p. 148
William Golofre		
from	20 July 1386	*CFR 1383–1391*, p. 148
Thomas Barentyn		
from	18 November 1386	*CFR 1383–1391*, p. 152
Gilbert Wace		
from	18 November 1387	*CFR 1383–1391*, p. 208
Thomas de la Poile		
from	1 December 1388	*CFR 1383–1391*, p. 249
William atte Wode		
from	15 November 1389	*CFR 1383–1391*, p. 306
Hugh Wolf		
from	7 November 1390	*CFR 1383–1391*, p. 341
Robert Bullok		
from	21 October 1391	*CFR 1391–1399*, p. 7
William Wilcotes		
from	18 October 1392	*CFR 1391–1399*, p. 56
Thomas Faryndon		
from	7 November 1393	*CFR 1391–1399*, p. 95
Thomas Barentyn		
from	11 November 1394	*CFR 1391–1399*, p. 132
Edmund Spersholt		
from	9 November 1395	*CFR 1391–1399*, p. 166
William atte Wode		
from	1 December 1396	*CFR 1391–1399*, p. 197
to	3 November 1397	*CFR 1391–1399*, p. 240
John Golafre		
from	3 November 1397	*CFR 1391–1399*, p. 240
John Willicotes		
from	8 November 1401	*CFR 1399–1405*, p. 143
Robert Corbet		
to	23 November 1407	*CFR 1405–1413*, p. 87

John Willicotes		
from	23 November 1407	*CFR 1405–1413*, p. 87
Robert Andrewe		
to	23 November 1419	*CFR 1405–1413*, p. 296
John Willecotes		
from	23 November 1419	*CFR 1405–1413*, p. 296

Porters and Gaolkeepers

Andrew de Wauburgh		
from	3 October 1340	*CPR 1340–1343*, p. 39

ROTHERSFIELD GREYS

Owners

John de Grey of Rothersfield, P.P.		
license to crenellate	22 February 1348	*CPR 1348–1350*, p. 36
died	*1 September 1359*	*GEC VI, p. 145*
John de Grey of Rothersfield, son of above, P.P.		
inherited	*1 September 1359*	*GEC VI, p. 147*
died	*4 June 1375*	*GEC VI, p. 147*

SHIRBOURN

Owners

Warin L'isle		
licence to crenellate	5 March 1377	*CPR 1374–1377*, p. 434

WATLINGTON

Owners

Nicholas de la Beche, kn.		
licence to crenellate	3 March 1338	*CPR 1338–1340*, p. 24

Pembroke

BENTON

History

built	late C13	King, p. 391
mentioned	temp. Elizabeth I	King, p. 391

CAREW

Tenant in Chief

John de Hastings		
on	5 June 1362	*IPM XI*, no. 300

Owners

John de Carew		
to	5 June 1362	*IPM XI*, no. 300 (R.I.P.)
Leonard de Carew, his son		
from	5 June 1362	*IPM XI*, no. 300

CASTLE MORRIS

History

mentioned	1326	King, p. 398

CILGERRAN

Owners

William Cauntelo		
not by	1 May 1273	*CPR 1272–1281*, p. 9
George de Cauntelo		
from	1 May 1273	*CPR 1272–1281*, p. 9
to	28 October 1273	*CFR 1272–1307*, p. 12 (R.I.P.)
John de Hastings, son of Joan de Hastings, sister of above		
from	28 October 1273	*CFR 1272–1307*, p. 12
to	30 September 1307	*CCR 1307–1313*, p. 2
William de Hastings		
from	30 September 1307	*CCR 1307–1313*, p. 2
John de Hastings, snr., P. P,		
to	15 March 1309	*CPR 1307–1313*, p. 108
John de Hastings, jnr., son of above, P.P.		
from	15 March 1309	*CPR 1307–1313*, p. 108
to	27 January 1325	*IPM VI*, no. 612 (R.I.P.)
Laurence de Hastings, son of above		
heir on	27 January 1325	*IPM VI*, no. 612
Juliana, widow of John de Hastings		
dower	23 September 1325	*CCR 1323–1327*, p. 404
John Hastings, earl of Pembroke		
on	20 February 1369	*CPR 1367–1370*, p. 223
to	16 April 1375	*IPM XIV*, no. 148 (R.I.P.)

John de Hastings, son of John de Hastings earl of Pembroke		
from	16 April 1375	*IPM XIV*, no. 148
to	30 December 1389	*IPM XVI*, no. 889 (R.I.P.)
Reynold, Lord Grey of Ruthin, P.P.		
from	30 December 1389	*IPM XVI*, no. 889
Francis de Courte, kn.		
from	30 October 1403	*CPR 1401–1405*, p. 315 (Tail male)
on	6 January 1406	*CPR 1405–1408*, p. 111
Humphrey, duke of Gloucester		
from	20 July 1413	*CPR 1413–1416*, p. 170
to	1 July 1418	*CPR 1416–1422*, p. 129 temporary grant to clear debts

Constables

John Beaufitz		
for life from	1 June 1389	
Richard Chelmeswyk, king's esquire		
for life from	12 February 1390	*CPR 1388–1392*, p. 189
John Golafre, kn.		
for life from	16 September 1390	*CPR 1388–1392*, p. 302
John Beaufitz		
for life from	17 February 1397	*CPR 1396–1399*, p. 72
William Beauchamp		
for life from	29 November 1399	*CPR 1399–1401*, p. 140 (Custody)

Wardships

Minority of John de Hastings, 1273–1283

Henry de Bray		
from	28 October 1273	*CFR 1272–1307*, p. 12
William de Valence		
from	12 May 1275	*CPR 1272–1281*, p. 87
in	1275	C.47/2/2/1

Minority of Laurence, son and heir of John de Hastings, 1325–1341

Roger Mortimer, earl of March		
from	29 July 1330	*CPR 1327–1330*, p. 546

Minority of John, son of John de Hastings Earl of Pembroke, 1375–1389

Thomas del Castell		
from	16 July 1375	*CPR 1374–1377*, p. 127 (Steward)
Philip Gyby		
on	2 May 1377	*CCR 1374–1377*, p. 508
Walter Mille		
from	2 July 1377	*CPR 1377–1381*, p. 4
from	9 March 1378	*CFR 1377–1383*, p. 80
William Beauchamp		
from	9 March 1378	*IMisc III*, no. 375
on	11 October 1386	*CPR 1385–1389*, p. 222

HAVERFORD WEST

Owners

Humphrey de Bohun, earl of Hereford and Essex		
not by	15 September 1274	*CPR 1272–1281*, p. 56 (R.I.P.)

Humphrey de Bohun, earl of Hereford and Essex		
from	15 September 1274	*CPR 1272–1281*, p. 56
to	1289	*HKW II*, p. 670
Queen Eleanor of Castile		
from	1289	*HKW II*, p. 670
to	12 January 1291	*CFR 1272–1307*, p. 287
Prince Edward		
from	7 February 1301	*CChR 1300–1326*, p. 6
from	7 February 1301	*CPR 1292–1301*, p. 576
Mary de St. Pol, countess of Pembroke		
released rights	13 March 1327	*CCR 1327–1330*, p. 109
Crown		
released to	13 March 1327	*CCR 1327–1330*, p. 109
Queen Isabella		
from	20 November 1331	*CPR 1330–1334*, p. 225
to	22 August 1358	*IPM X*, no. 447 (R.I.P.)
dead by	15 July 1359	*CPR 1358–1361*, p. 533
Edward Prince of Wales		
from	22 August 1358	*IPM X*, no. 447
from	15 July 1359	*CPR 1358–1361*, p. 533
on	5 October 1367	

Constables

Robert de Bures (for Queen Eleanor)		
to	12 January 1291	*CFR 1272–1307*, p. 287
Walter de Pederton		
from	12 January 1291	*CFR 1272–1307*, p. 287
to	3 January 1295	*CFR 1272–1307*, p. 368
Hugh de Cressingham		
from	3 January 1295	*CFR 1272–1307*, p. 368
to	21 September 1297	*CFR 1272–1307*, p. 391 (R.I.P.)
Walter de Pederton		
from	21 September 1297	*CFR 1272–1307*, p. 391
Walter Hakelute		
to	7 February 1301	*CChR 1300–1326*, p. 6
to	7 February 1301	*CPR 1292–1301*, p. 576
Hugh de Paunton		
from	12 August 1308	*CFR 1307–1319*, p. 28
to	15 November 1308	*CPR 1307–1313*, p. 145
Aymer de Valence, earl of Pembroke		
for life from	15 November 1308	*CPR 1307–1313*, p. 145
to	26 June 1324	*IPM VI*, no. 518 (R.I.P.)
Richard fitz Simon, after death of Aymer de Valence		
from	26 February 1325	*CFR 1319–1327*, p. 332
to	30 January 1326	*CFR 1319–1327*, p. 374
Robert de Penres		
from	30 January 1326	*CFR 1319–1327*, p. 374
on	26 June 1326	*CCR 1323–1327*, p. 484
Mary, widow of Aymer de Valence		
surrendered by	13 March 1327	*CPR 1327–1330*, p. 37
Guy de Brian, king's yeoman		
from	4 January 1331	*CFR 1327–1337*, p. 216
to	20 November 1331	*CPR 1330–1334*, p. 225

Robert de Penres		
on	6 February 1332	*CCR 1330–1333*, p. 428
Thomas de Felton, kn.		
for life from	5 October 1367	
confirmed	8 February 1381	*CPR 1377–1381*, p. 604
to?	20 August 1385	*CPR 1385–1389*, p. 8 (R.I.P.)
John de Clanvowe, king's bachelor		
for life from	5 May 1381	*CPR 1377–1385*, p. 627
to	9 June 1392	*CPR 1391–1396*, p. 210 (R.I.P.)
Thomas Percy		
for life from	9 June 1392	*CPR 1391–1396*, p. 210

Receiver and Approver

Thomas More		
from	2 July 1377	*CFR 1377–1383*, p. 1

HAYSCASTLE

History

mentioned	1326 (name)	King, p. 393

LLAWHADEN

Owners

Bishops of St. Davids		
temp	entire period	R.R. Davies, *Lordship and society in the March of Wales, 1282–1400*, Oxford, 1978, p. 39
on	8 September 1403	*CCR 1402–1405*, p. 111; *CACW*, XLIII.109

MAENCLOCHOG

Owners

John de Roche, kn.		
to	26 June 1376	*IPM XIV*, no. 279 (R.I.P.)
John de Roche, son of above		
from	26 June 1376	*IPM XIV*, no. 279

MANOBIER

Owners

William de Windsor, kn., P.P.		
to	15 September 1384	*IPM XVI*, no. 172 (R.I.P.)
Taken into King's hands by Richard Wyryot		
from	14 December 1384	*CFR 1383–1391*, p. 87
John de Hastings, son of earl of Pembroke		
inherited	*1375*	
under age	15 May 1386	*CPR 1385–1389*, p. 146
Elizabeth, countess of Huntingdon		
on	22 January 1402	*CCR 1399–1402*, p. 504
John Cornwall, kn.		
on	8 September 1403	*CCR 1402–1405*, p. 111

Constables

Elizabeth, countess of Huntingdon

for life from	22 January 1402	
confirmed	18 February 1402	*CPR 1401–1405*, p. 44

NARBERTH (ARBERTH)

Owners

Roger Mortimer, earl of March

to	26 November 1330	*IPM X*, no. 188 (R.I.P.)

Roger Mortimer, earl of March

on	31 August 1359	*CCR 1354–1360*, p. 641
dead by	3 July 1360	*CCR 1360–1364*, p. 46

Philipa, widow of Roger Mortimer

on	3 July 1360	*CCR 1360–1364*, p. 46
to	5 January 1382	*IPM XV*, no. 565 (R.I.P.)

Roger Mortimer, earl of March

from	5 January 1382	*IPM XV*, no. 565
enfeofed away	8 July 1397	*CPR 1396–1399*, p. 256

Edmund Mortimer, brother of above

from	8 July 1397	*CPR 1396–1399*, p. 256 (Tail Male)
forfeited by	24 April 1404	*CPR 1401–1405*, p. 384

Constables

Henry, bishop of St. Davids

from	15 January 1331	
confirmed	20 October 1339	*CPR 1338–1340*, p. 322

Thomas Carrewe

temp	1404	E.101/43/23
for life from	24 April 1404	*CPR 1401–1405*, p. 384
on	12 August 1405	*CPR 1405–1408*, p. 35

Wardships

Minority of Roger Mortimer, earl of March, 1381–1395

Simon de Burley, king's knight

from	25 September 1382	*CFR 1377–1383*, p. 320

William Jouet

from	16 December 1382	*CPR 1381–1385*, p. 65

Thomas de Beauchamp, earl of Warwick, Roger Mortimer, earl of March, John lord Neville and Henry Percy, earl of Northumberland

from	16 December 1383	*CFR 1383–1391*, p. 22

Minority of Edmund Mortimer, earl of March, 1398–1412

John Holland, earl of Huntingdon, duke of Exeter

from	11 August 1398	*CPR 1396–1399*, pp. 408, 514

Henry Percy, earl of Northumberland

from	2 March 1400	*CFR 1399–1405*, p. 50

NEWPORT (TREFDRAETH) (IN CAMOIS)

Owners

John Peverel, for life from Nicholas fitz Martin (R.I.P.)

to	22 March 1282	*IPM II*, no. 440

John Peverel, for life from William Martyn, grandson of Nicholas above

from	22 March 1282	*IPM II*, no. 440

William Martyn, P.P.		
to	8 October 1324	*IPM VI*, no. 563 (R.I.P.)
William son of William Martyn, P.P.		
from	8 October 1324	*IPM VI*, no. 563
to	4 April 1326	*IPM VI*, no. 710 (R.I.P.)
James de Audley of Heighley, P.P., son of Nicholas de Audley and Joan, sister of above		
on	10 May 1363	*CPR 1361–1364*, p. 331
given to below	16 June 1374	*CPR 1370–1374*, p. 454
Nicholas de Audley of Heighley, kn., son of above, P.P.		
from	16 June 1374	*CPR 1370–1374*, p. 454
to	22 July 1391	*IPM XVI*, no. 1064 (R.I.P.) (With Elizabeth)
Elizabeth, widow of Nicholas de Audley, kn.		
from	22 July 1391	*IPM XVI*, no. 1064 (Jointure)
to	18 November 1400	*IPM XVIII*, no. 484 (R.I.P.)
Half to John Tuchet, lord Audley, P.P.		
to	19 December 1409	*IPM XIX*, no. 594 (R.I.P.)
Half to James Tuchet, lord Audley, P.P., son of above		
from	19 December 1409	*IPM XIX*, no. 594
Half to Margaret Hillary		
to	24 April 1411	*IPM XIX*, no. 880 (R.I.P.)
Half to James Tuchet, lord Audley, P.P. above, her cousin		
from	24 April 1411	*IPM XIX*, no. 880
James Tuchet, lord Audley, entire castle, P.P.		
entire castle from	24 April 1411	*IPM XIX*, no. 880
died	*23 September 1459*	*GEC I, p. 341*

PEMBROKE

Owners

Joan de Valence, countess of Pembroke		
to	20 September 1307	*IPM V*, no. 56 (R.I.P.)
Aymer de Valence, earl of Pembroke, son of above		
from	20 September 1307	*IPM V*, no. 56
to	26 June 1324	*IPM VI*, no. 518 (R.I.P.)
Laurence de Hastings, earl of Pembroke		
pourparty done	15 May 1322	*CCR 1323–1327*, p. 359
to	28 August 1348	*IPM IX*, no. 118 (R.I.P.)
John de Hastings, earl of Pembroke, son of above		
from	28 August 1348	*IPM IX*, no. 118
to	16 April 1375	*IPM XIV*, no. 148 (R.I.P.)
John de Hastings, son of above		
from	16 April 1375	*IPM XIV*, no. 148
to	30 December 1389	*IPM XVI*, no. 889 (R.I.P.)
Reynold lord Grey of Ruthin, P.P.		
from	30 December 1389	*IPM XVI*, no. 889
Francis de Courte, kn.		
from	30 October 1403	*CPR 1401–1405*, p. 315 (tail male)
on	6 January 1406	*CPR 1405–1408*, p. 111
Humphrey, duke of Gloucester		
from	20 July 1413	*CPR 1413–1416*, p. 170
to	1 July 1418	*CPR 1416–1422*, p. 129 temporary grant to clear debts

Constables

Richard fitz Simon, after death of Aymer de Valencia

from	26 February 1325	*CFR 1319–1327*, p. 332

William de Beauchamp

on	10 March 1378	*CCR 1377–1381*, p. 69

Margaret, countess of Norfolk

on	3 June 1388	*CPR 1385–1389*, p. 415

John Golafre, king's knight

for life from	28 July 1390	*CPR 1389–1392*, p. 297
for life from	16 September 1390	*CPR 1389–1392*, p. 302

William le Scrope, earl of Wiltshire

for life from	28 November 1396	*CPR 1396–1399*, p. 36
for life	28 November 1396	*CCR 1396–1399*, p. 27

Thomas Roche, esq.

for life from	29 November 1399	*CPR 1399–1401*, p. 117
for life from	5 November 1399	*CPR 1399–1401*, p. 145

William de Beauchamp

for life from	29 November 1399	*CPR 1399–1401*, p. 140 (Custody)

Francis Courte

on	26 March 1404	*CCR 1402–1405*, p. 329

Wardships

minority of Laurence de Hastings, 1325–1341

Roger Mortimer, earl of March

from	29 July 1330	*CPR 1327–1330*, p. 546

Elizabeth de Burgo

from	16 November 1331	*CFR 1327–1337*, p. 286
from	23 October 1339	*CCR 1338–1340*, p. 209

minority of John de Hastings, earl of Pembroke, 1348–1368

Thomas de Clopton

to	24 January 1349	*CPR 1348–1350*, p. 252

Richard Talbot, kn., elder

from	24 January 1349	*CPR 1348–1350*, p. 252
confirmed	27 January 1349	*CPR 1348–1350*, p. 252

John Hakelut and Agnes his wife, widow of Laurence de Hastings

from	12 November 1351	*CFR 1347–1356*, p. 317

minority of John, son of John Hastings Earl of Pembroke, 1375–1389

Thomas del Castell

from	16 July 1375	*CPR 1374–1377*, p. 127

William de Beauchamp

from	9 March 1378	*CFR 1377–1383*, p. 80
on	11 October 1386	*CPR 1385–1389*, p. 222

Deputy Wardships

John Gybon

temp.	William de Beauchamp (1378)	

Receiver and Approver

Thomas More

from	2 July 1377	*CFR 1377–1383*, p. 1

Garrison provided by

Degarius Seys, kn. and John Joce, kn.

on	2 July 1377	*CPR 1377–1381*, p. 6

PICTON

History

built	late C13 or early C14	King, p. 396
mentioned	1377	King, p. 396
siege	1405	King, p. 396
siege	temp. Civil War	King, p. 396

ROCH

History

built	pre C13	King, p. 396
mentioned as deserted	temp. Henry VI	King, p. 396

TENBY

Owners

Aymer de Valence, earl of Pembroke		
to	26 June 1324	*IPM VI*, no. 518 (R.I.P.)
Laurence de Hastings, earl of Pembroke		
pourparty done	15 May 1322	*CCR 1323–1327*, p. 359
to	28 August 1348	*IPM IX*, no. 118 (R.I.P.)
John Hastings earl of Pembroke, son of above		
from	28 August 1348	*IPM IX*, no. 118
to	16 April 1375	*IPM XIV*, no. 148 (R.I.P.)
John de Hastings, son of John de Hastings, earl of Pembroke		
from	16 April 1375	*IPM XIV*, no. 148
to	30 December 1389	*IPM XVI*, no. 889 (R.I.P.)
Reynold lord Grey of Ruthin, P.P.		
from	30 December 1389	*IPM XVI*, no. 889
William Beauchamp, lord of Abergavenny, P.P.		
from	12 October 1400	*CPR 1401–1405*, p. 54
on	21 March 1402	*CPR 1401–1405*, p. 54
Francis de Courte, kn.		
from	30 October 1403	*CPR 1401–1405*, p. 315 (tail male)
on	6 January 1406	*CPR 1405–1408*, p. 111
Humphrey, duke of Gloucester, temporary grant to clear debts		
from	20 July 1413	*CPR 1413–1416*, p. 170
to	1 July 1418	*CPR 1416–1422*, p. 129

Constables

Richard fitz Simon, after death of Aymer de Valencia		
from	26 February 1325	*CFR 1319–1327*, p. 332
Thomas Hamme		
for life from	2 January 1390	*CPR 1388–1392*, p. 171
William Beauchamp		
for life from	29 November 1399	*CPR 1399–1401*, p. 140 (Custody)
John Stephen, esq.		
for life from	12 October 1400	
confirmed	21 March 1402	*CPR 1401–1405*, p. 54

Private Constables

William Redhefd for Hastings		
from	17 January 1348	
confirmed	7 November 1348	*CPR 1345–1348*, p. 200
on	28 December 1348	*CCR 1346–1349*, p. 577
Roger Abraham for Hastings		
confirmed	24 February 1376	*CPR 1374–1377*, p. 247
John Stephen, esq.		
for life from	12 October 1400	
confirmed	21 March 1402	*CPR 1401–1405*, p. 54

Wardships

Minority of Laurence, son and heir of John de Hastings, 1325–1341

Roger Mortimer, earl of March		
from	29 July 1330	*CPR 1327–1330*, p. 546
Elizabeth de Burgo		
from	16 November 1331	*CFR 1327–1337*, p. 286
from	23 October 1339	*CCR 1339–1341*, p. 209

minority of John de Hastings, earl of Pembroke, 1348–1368

Thomas de Clopton		
to	24 January 1349	*CPR 1348–1350*, p. 252
Richard Talbot, kn., elder		
from	24 January 1349	*CPR 1348–1350*, p. 252
confirmed	27 January 1349	*CPR 1348–1350*, p. 252
John Hakelut and Agnes his wife, widow of Laurence de Hastings		
from	12 November 1351	*CFR 1347–1356*, p. 317

minority of John, son and heir of John de Hastings, earl of Pembroke, 1375–1389

Thomas del Castell		
from	16 July 1375	*CPR 1374–1377*, p. 127
William de Beauchamp		
from	9 March 1378	*IMisc III*, no. 375

Receiver and Approver

Thomas More		
from	2 July 1377	*CFR 1377–1383*, p. 1

UPTON

History

built	mid or late C13	King, p. 397

WALWYN'S CASTLE

Owners

Guy de Brian		
from	1307	*RCH*, p. 403
to	17 June 1347	*IPM IX*, no. 333 (R.I.P.)
Guy de Brian, P.P., son of above		
from	17 June 1347	*IPM IX*, no. 333
on	4 February 1378	*CCR 1377–1381*, p. 122

WOLF'S CASTLE

History

mentioned	1229	King, p. 398
in use	1326	King, p. 398

Radnor

ABEREDW

Owners

Thomas Beauchamp, earl of Warwick		
not by	24 November 1397	*IMisc VI*, no. 228

BLEDDFA

History

mentioned	1195	King, p. 406
siege	1262	King, p. 406
abandoned by	1304	King, p. 406

BOUGHROOD (BOSKERET)

Owners

Elizabeth de Penbrugge		
to	29 June 1309	*IPM vol. V*, no. 165
John de Penbrugge, kn.		
from	29 June 1309	*IPM vol. V*, no,165
Elizabeth, widow of John de Penbrugge.		
to	23 August 1400	*IPM XVIII*, no. 58
Alice, sister of John de Penbrugge.		
from	23 August 1400	*IPM XVIII*, no. 58

CEFNLLYS (KEVENETHES)

Owners

Roger Mortimer of Wigmore		
on	22 July 1273 or 1274	*CACW*, XIX.35
in	1280	Morris, p. 147
Edmund Mortimer of Wigmore, P.P.		
to	25 July 1304	*IPM IV*, no. 235 (R.I.P.)
Roger Mortimer, earl of March, son of above		
from	25 July 1304	*IPM IV*, no. 235
on	24 June 1316	*CPR 1313–1317*, p. 491
confiscated before	23 January 1322	*CFR 1319–1327*, p. 91
Edmund de Woodstock, earl of Kent, brother of Edward II		
from	30 March 1322	*CCR 1318–1323*, p. 442
Edmund Mortimer of Wigmore, P.P. son of Roger, earl of March		
from	12 October 1331	*CCR 1330–1333*, p. 345
to	21 January 1332	*IPM VII*, no. 387 (R.I.P.)
Roger Mortimer, earl of March, son of above		
heir on	21 January 1332	*IPM VII*, no. 387
Elizabeth, widow of Edmund Mortimer		
to	8 June 1356	*IPM X*, no. 291 (R.I.P.)
not by	4 July 1356	*CCR 1354–1360*, p. 271 (R.I.P.)

Roger Mortimer, earl of March, as two above
from 8 June 1356 *IPM X*,. no. 291
to 26 February 1360 *IPM X*, no. 640 (R.I.P.)
Philippa, widow of Roger Mortimer, above
from 22 November 1360 *CCR 1360–1364*, p. 81
Roger Mortimer, earl of March
a minor on 13 May 1382 *CPR 1381–1385*, p. 117
to 20 July 1398 *IPM XVII*, no. 1206 (R.I.P.)
Edmund Mortimer, son of above
from 20 July 1398 *IPM XVII*, no. 1206

Constables
Griffin ap Rees
from 23 January 1322 *CFR 1319–1327*, p. 91
to 23 January 1322 *CFR 1319–1327*, p. 91
Walter le Gras
from 23 January 1322 *CFR 1319–1327*, p. 91
on 23 January 1322 *CCR 1318–1323*, p. 415
Robert de Harle
to 4 February 1331 *CFR 1327–1337*, p. 230
Thomas de Cloune
from 4 February 1331 *CFR 1327–1337*, p. 230

Wardships
Minority of Roger Mortimer, earl of March, 1381–1395
Thomas Idefen
from 13 May 1382 *CPR 1381–1385*, p. 117
on 2 October 1383 *CCR 1381–1385*, p. 321 (Ydefen)
Thomas de Beauchamp, earl of Warwick, Roger Mortimer, earl of March, John lord Neville and Henry Percy, earl of Northumberland
from 16 December 1383 *CFR 1383–1391*, p. 22
Minority of Edmund Mortimer, earl of March, 1398–1412
John Holland, earl of Huntingdon, duke of Exeter
from 11 August 1398 *CPR 1396–1399*, pp. 408, 514
Henry Percy, earl of Northumberland
from 2 March 1400 *CFR 1399–1405*, p. 50
Hugh Burnell, kn.
from 24 November 1401 *CPR 1401–1405*, p. 22
from 9 March 1402 *CFR 1399–1405*, p. 155
Richard Grey of Codnor
from 8 December 1407 *CPR 1405–1408*, p. 293

CLYRO

Owners
Thomas de Beauchamp, earl of Warwick
not by 24 November 1397 *IMisc VI*, no. 228

COLWYN

Owners
Robert de Tony, P.P.
to 28 November 1309 *IPM V*, no. 198 (R.I.P.)

Alice de Leybourne, sister of above
from | 28 November 1309 | *IPM V*, no. 98
Guy de Beauchamp, earl of Warwick, husband of above
to | 16 August 1315 | *IPM V*, no. 615 (R.I.P.)
Thomas de Beauchamp, earl of Warwick, son of above
from | 16 August 1315 | *IPM V*, no. 615
William la Zouche, Mortimer, P.P.
to | 1 March 1337 | *IPM VIII*, no. 112 *(R.I.P.)*
Thomas de Beauchamp, earl of Warwick, as above
from | 1 March 1337 | *IPM VIII*, no. 112
Thomas Beauchamp, earl of Warwick
not by | 24 November 1397 | *IMisc VI*, no. 228

CYMARAN

History

rebuilt	1144	King, p. 407
rebuilt	1179	King, p. 407
rebuilt	1195	King, p. 407
siege	1215,1262	King, p. 407
abandoned	by 1316	King, p. 407

GLASBURY

Owners

Roger Mortimer, earl of March
on | 22 February 1398 | *CCR 1396–1399*, p. 278

Wardships

Minority of Roger Mortimer, earl of March, 1381–1395

Thomas de Beauchamp, earl of Warwick, Roger Mortimer, earl of March, John lord Neville and Henry Percy, earl of Northumberland
from | 16 December 1383 | *CFR 1383–1391*, p. 22

KNIGHTON

Owners

Edmund Mortimer of Wigmore
to | 1304 | R.R.Davies, *Lordship and society in the March of Wales, 1282–1400*, Oxford, 1978, p. 42 n.
Margaret de Fiennes, widow of Edmund Mortimer
from | 1304 | *ibid.*
to | 1334 | *ibid.* (R.I.P.)

KNUCKLAS

Owners

Edmund Mortimer of Wigmore, P.P.
to | 25 July 1304 | *IPM IV*, no. 235 (R.I.P.)
Roger Mortimer of Wigmore, son of above
heir on | 25 July 1304 | *IPM IV*, no. 235
Margaret de Fiennes, widow of Edmund Mortimer
on | 24 June 1316 | *CPR 1313–1317*, p. 491

Roger Mortimer, earl of March		
not by	12 October 1331	*CCR 1330–1333*, p. 350
Edmund Mortimer of Wigmore, P.P., son of earl of March		
from	12 October 1331	*CCR 1330–1333*, p. 350
Roger Mortimer, earl of March, son of above		
under age	6 September 1341	*CFR 1337–1347*, p. 239
Edmund Mortimer, earl of March		
heir	*26 February 1360*	*IPM X, no. 640*
granted away	24 November 1374	*CPR 1374–1377*, p. 37
to	27 December 1381	*IPM XV*, no. 556 (R.I.P.)
Roger Mortimer, earl of March, son of above		
from	27 December 1381	*IPM XV*, no. 556

Wardship

minority of Roger Mortimer, earl of March, 1332–1342

William de Bohun, earl of Northampton, and Elizabeth, his wife, widow of Edmund Mortimer		
from	6 September 1341	*CFR 1337–1347*, p. 239

Minority of Roger Mortimer, earl of March, 1381–1395

Thomas de Beauchamp, earl of Warwick, Roger Mortimer, earl of March, John lord Neville and Henry Percy, earl of Northumberland		
from	16 December 1383	*CFR 1383–1391*, p. 22

NEW RADNOR

Owners

Roger Mortimer of Wigmore		
in	1280	Morris, p. 147
Maud Mortimer		
to	23 March 1301	*IPM IV*, no. 41
Edmund Mortimer, of Wigmore, P.P. , son of above		
from	23 March 1301	*IPM IV*, no. 41
to	25 July 1304	*IPM IV*, no. 235 (R.I.P.)
Roger Mortimer, earl of March, son of above		
from	25 July 1304	*IPM IV*, no. 235
Margaret de Fiennes, widow of Edmund Mortimer		
on	24 June 1316	*CPR 1313–1317*, p. 491
from	9 February 1322	*CCR 1318–1323*, p. 422
on	20 April 1326	*CPR 1324–1327*, p. 258
Edmund Mortimer of Wigmore, P.P., son of Roger earl of March		
from	12 October 1331	*CCR 1330–1333*, p. 350
Roger Mortimer, earl of March		
on	2 November 1341	*CCR 1339–1341*, p. 341
to	26 February 1360	*IPM X*, no. 640 (R.I.P.)
Edmund Mortimer, earl of March and Ulster, son of above		
from	26 February 1360	*IPM X*, no. 640
to	27 December 1381	*IPM XV*, no. 561 (R.I.P.)
Roger Mortimer, earl of March, son of above		
from	27 December 1381	*IPM XV*, no. 561
Edmund Mortimer, earl of March		
on	28 January 1405	*CPR 1401–1405*, p. 483
on	October 1405	*IPM XIX*, no. 49

Constables

Humphrey de Littlebury		
on	9 February 1322	*CCR 1318–1323*, p. 419
to	21 March 1323	*CPR 1321–1324*, p. 266
John Greyndor, kn.		
from	24 September 1402	*CPR 1401–1405*, p. 120
on	17 May 1403	*CCR 1401–1405*, p. 69

Private Constables

John Danyel		
from	3 January 1326	*CPR 1324–1327*, p. 206
from	20 April 1326	*CPR 1324–1327*, p. 258

Wardships

minority of heir of Roger Mortimer the elder

Roger Springehoese		
from	29 October 1282	*CPR 1281–1292*, p. 39

minority of Roger Mortimer, earl of March, 1332–1342

Hugh Tyrel		
from	27 February 1334	*CFR 1327–1337*, p. 389
on	13 September 1342	E.101/20/8 m.1
Roger Mortimer, earl of March		
from	2 November 1341	*CFR 1337–1347*, p. 246

minority of Edmund Mortimer, earl of March, 1360–1373

John Chirbury, king's archer		
from	7 February 1361	*CPR 1361–1364*, p. 9

Minority of Edmund Mortimer, earl of March, 1398–1412

John Holland, earl of Huntingdon, duke of Exeter		
from	11 August 1398	*CPR 1396–1399*, pp. 408, 514
Henry Percy, earl of Northumberland		
from	2 March 1400	*CFR 1399–1405*, p. 50
Richard Grey of Codnor		
from	28 January 1405	*CPR 1401–1405*, p. 483

PAINSCASTLE

Tenant in Chief

Beauchamp earls of Warwick		
on	1 March 1337	*IPM VIII*, no. 112 (R.I.P.)

Owners

Robert de Tony, P.P.		
to	28 November 1309	*IPM V*, no. 198 (R.I.P.)
Alice de Leybourne, his sister		
from	28 November 1309	*IPM V*, no. 198
Guy de Beauchamp, earl of Warwick, husband of above		
to	16 August 1315	*IPM V*, no. 615 (R.I.P.)
Thomas de Beauchamp, son of above		
heir from	16 August 1315	*IPM V*, no. 615 (?)
William la Zouche, Mortimer, P.P. via Alice de Tony, his wife		
to	1 March 1337	*IPM VIII*, no. 112 (R.I.P.)
Thomas de Beauchamp, earl of Warwick		
jointured	24 April 1344	*CPR 1343–1345*, p. 251
to	13 November 1369	*IPM XII*, no. 326 (R.I.P.)

Thomas de Beauchamp, earl of Warwick, son of above		
from	13 November 1369	*IPM XII*, no. 326
from	7 February 1370	*CCR 1369–1374*, p. 123
not by	24 November 1397	*IMisc VI*, no. 228
William le Scrope, earl of Wiltshire		
from	29/30 September 1397	*CPR 1396–1399*, pp. 196, 269 (tail male)
Thomas de Beauchamp, earl of Warwick		
to	8 April 1401	*IPM XVIII*, no. 506 (R.I.P.)
Richard de Beauchamp, son of above		
from	8 April 1401	*IPM XVIII*, no. 506

Constables

Robert de Hilton, esq.		
on	5 February 1398	*CPR 1396–1399*, p. 285

Wardships

Minority of Richard Beauchamp, earl of Warwick (1401–1403)

Thomas de Aldebury, William de Beauchamp of Abergavenny and John Owdeby, clerk		
from	12 May 1401	*CFR 1399–1405*, p. 135

PRESTEIGNE

History

mentioned	1244	King, p. 411
siege	1262	King, p. 411
mentioned	1337	King, p. 411

RHAYADER

Owners

Edmund Mortimer of Wigmore, P.P.		
to	25 July 1304	*IPM IV*, no. 235 (R.I.P.)
Roger Mortimer, earl of March, son of above		
heir on	25 July 1304	*IPM IV*, no. 235
Margaret de Fiennes, widow of Edmund Mortimer		
on	24 June 1316	*CPR 1313–1317*, p. 491
Edmund Mortimer of Wigmore, son of above, P.P.		
from	12 October 1331	*CCR 1330–1333*, p. 350

STAPLETON

Owners

Brian de Cornwall, kn.		
to	17 January 1400	*IPM XVIII*, no. 61 (R.I.P.)
Richard de Cornwall, brother of above.		
from	17 January 1400	*IPM XVIII*, no. 61

TINBOETH

Owners

Roger Mortimer of Wigmore		
on	1280	Morris, p. 147
Edmund Mortimer of Wigmore, P.P.		
to	25 July 1304	*IPM IV*, no. 235 (R.I.P.)

Roger Mortimer, earl of March, son of above		
heir on	25 July 1304	*IPM IV*, no. 235
confiscated before	23 January 1322	*CFR 1319–1327*, p. 91
Edmund de Woodstock, earl of Kent, brother of Edward II		
from	30 March 1322	*CChR 1300–1326*, p. 442
Edmund Mortimer of Wigmore, son of above, P.P.		
from	12 October 1331	*CCR 1330–1333*, p. 345
on	7 December 1332	*CCR 1330–1333*, p. 515

Constables

Griffin ap Rees		
from	23 January 1322	*CFR 1319–1327*, p. 91
to	23 January 1322	*CFR 1319–1327*, p. 91
Walter le Gras		
from	23 January 1322	*CFR 1319–1327*, p. 91
on	23 January 1322	*CCR 1318–1323*, p. 415

Rutland

Unknown Licenses

LYDYNGTON for Henry Burghersh, bishop of Lincoln

	16 November 1336	*CPR 1334–1338*, p. 330

BURLEY (ALSTOE)

Owners

Roger Burley		
not by	6 April 1401	*CPR 1401–1405*, p. 86
John Burley, son of above		
on	6 April 1401	*CPR 1401–1405*, p. 86

Wardship
minority of John Burley

Richard Arundel, kn. and Alice.		
from	6 April 1401	*CPR 1401–1405*, p. 86

OAKHAM

Owners

Richard, earl of Cornwall		
in	1262	*Rottuli Ricardi Gravesend*, ed. F.N.Davies, Lincoln Record Society, 20 (1922), p. 101
Edmund, earl of Cornwall		
to	1298	*IPM III*, no. 604 (R.I.P.)
The King, his heir		
from	1298	*IPM III*, no. 604
Margaret, widow of Edmund, earl of Cornwall		
dower	12 February 1310	*CCR 1307–1313*, p. 426
Margaret, countess of Cornwall, widow of Gaveston		
from	20 September 1312	*CPR 1307–1313*, p. 497
on	20 December 1316	*CPR 1313–1317*, p. 576
before	23 July 1318	*CCR 1318–1323*, p. 3
Hugh de Audley, earl of Gloucester, husband of above		
by	23 July 1318	*CCR 1318–1323*, p. 3
temporarily royal	6 March 1327	*CPR 1327–1330*, p. 30
restored	6 March 1327	*CPR 1327–1330*, p. 30
forfeited	16 January 1329	*CFR 1327–1337*, p. 116
restored	6 February 1329	*CCR 1327–1330*, p. 434
on	26 January 1341	*CPR 1340–1343*, p. 118
Margaret, countess of Cornwall, wife of Hugh de Audley, earl of Gloucester		
from	20 July 1319	
on	12 January 1331	*CPR 1330–1334*, p. 49
to	15 April 1343	*IPM VIII*, no. 382 (R.I.P.)
Hugh de Audley, earl of Gloucester		
to	11 November 1347	*IPM IX*, no. 56 (R.I.P.)

William de Bohun, earl of Northampton		
from	11 November 1347	*IPM IX*, no. 56
to	16 September 1360	*IPM X*, no. 639 (R.I.P.)
Humphrey de Bohun, earl of Hereford and Essex, son of above		
from	16 September 1360	*IPM X*, no. 639
on	6 May 1363	*CCR 1360–1364*, p. 482
Thomas, duke of Gloucester		
granted reversion	8 August 1394	*CPR 1391–1396*, p. 504
Edward, duke of Aumarle, future duke of York		
on	12 December 1390	*CPR 1388–1392*, p. 354
from	15 September 1398	*CPR 1296–1399*, p. 415 (Tail Male)
confirmed	20 February 1400	*CPR 1399–1401*, p. 204
William Burghchier and Anne his wife daughter of Thomas, duke of Gloucester		
from	1 December 1414	*CCR 1413–1419*, p. 160

Reversions

William de Bohun		
on	20 June 1338	*CPR 1338–1340*, p. 100

Constables while Royal

Gilbert de Holm		
from	12 July 1318	*CFR 1307–1319*, p. 367
to	8 May 1321	*CFR 1319–1327*, p. 55
John de Whitlebury		
from	8 May 1321	*CFR 1319–1327*, p. 55
to	24 May 1321	*CFR 1319–1327*, p. 58
Ivo de Aldeburgh		
from	24 May 1321	*CFR 1319–1327*, p. 58
to	4 July 1322	*CPR 1321–1324*, p. 144
Edmund de Woodstock, earl of Kent		
from	4 July 1322	*CPR 1321–1324*, p. 144
John de Whitlebury		
to	17 August 1326	*CFR 1319–1327*, p. 405
William Howard		
from	17 August 1326	*CFR 1319–1327*, p. 405
Edmund de Woodstock, earl of Kent		
to	19 April 1327	*CCR 1327–1330*, p. 76
Robert de Stangrave		
from	19 April 1327	*CCR 1327–1330*, p. 76
to	22 April 1327	*CCR 1327–1330*, p. 76
Hugh and Margaret de Audley		
from	22 April 1327	*CCR 1327–1330*, p. 76
William de Whappelade, king's yeoman		
from	11 February 1373	*CPR 1370–1374*, p. 246
Simon Warde		
on	12 June 1372	*CCR 1369–1374*, p. 503
from	26 July 1373	*CFR 1369–1377*, p. 217
William de Whappelade, king's yeoman		
from	5 December 1373	*CPR 1370–1374*, p. 371
Simon Warde		
on	8 April 1374	*CCR 1374–1377*, p. 40
William de Whappelade		
to	3 November 1377	*CPR 1374–1377*, p. 373

John Rukwyk		
from	3 November 1377	*CPR 1374–1377*, p. 373
on	1 December 1376	*CCR 1374–1377*, p. 411
Ralph Porter of Eltham		
from	24 October 1382	*CPR 1381–1385*, p. 180
Robert Vere, earl of Oxford		
for life from	27 July 1385	*CPR 1385–1389*, pp. 7, 69
on	9 May 1386	*CCR 1385–1389*, p. 147
forfeited by	23 April 1388	*IMisc IV*, no. 391
Edward, duke of York		
on	12 May 1390	*CPR 1388–1392*, p. 251
on	26 November 1403	*CPR 1401–1405*, p. 323
Richard Reyle		
on	17 October 1405	*CPR 1405–1408*, p. 83 (Keeper)
Edward, duke of York		
for life from	22 March 1410	
on	9 June 1412	*CPR 1408–1413*, p. 413
for life from	20 June 1412	
to	1 December 1414	*CPR 1413–1416*, p. 269
William Burghchier and Anne his wifeGloucester		
from	1 December 1414	*CPR 1413–1416*, p. 269

Deputy Constables

Thomas de Wympton (for John de Whitlebury)		
on	24 May 1321	*CFR 1319–1327*, p. 58

Receiver

William Flore of Okham		
from	22 June 1377	*CFR 1377–1383*, p. 6

Gatekeeper and Gaoler

Thomas Ednesouere		
for life from	22 February 1412	*CPR 1408–1413*, p. 404

Gatekeeper

Richard Rayle		
for life from	30 October 1399	*CPR 1399–1401*, p. 95
to	22 February 1411	
Thomas Ednesouere		
from	22 February 1411	

Chaplains of the Free Chapel

Richard		
to	1262	*Rottuli Ricardi Gravesend*, ed. Lincoln Record Society, 20 (1922), p. 101
William		
from	1262	*ibid.*

Shropshire

Unknown Licenses

ACTON BURNELL to Robert Burnel, bishop of Bath and Wells		
on	28 January 1284	*CPR 1281–1292*, p. 110
HOUSE IN SHREWSBURY for John de Cherleton		
on	14 September 1325	*CPR 1324–1327*, p. 178
WHITCHURCH for Fulk le Strange of Blackmere		
on	14 July 1322	*CPR 1321–1324*, p. 175

ADDERLY

History

built	C13	King, p. 420

ALBERBURY

Owners

Fulk fitz Waryn		
temp	early 13th cty.	*VCH, vol. 8*, p. 196
in use	17th cty.	*VCH, vol. 8*, p. 196
modified	19th cty.	*VCH, vol. 8*, p. 196

APLEY

Owners

Alan de Charlton		
licence to crenellate	10 July 1327	*CPR 1327–1330*, p. 145

BISHOP'S CASTLE

Owners

Bishops of Hereford		
void	20 January 1322	*CPR 1321–1324*, p. 51
restored on	6 February 1322	*CPR 1321–1324*, p. 53
void	4 December 1360	*CPR 1358–1361*, p. 499
void	31 May 1361	*CCR 1360–1364*, p. 192

Constables while void

Thomas de Hastang		
from	20 January 1322	*CPR 1321–1324*, p. 51
to	6 February 1322	*CPR 1321–1324*, p. 53
John atte Wode, king's yeoman		
on	10 January 1360	*CPR 1358–1361*, p. 511
from	4 December 1360	*CPR 1358–1361*, p. 499
to	3 January 1361	*CPR 1358–1361*, p. 508
Henry de Molyneux, king's yeoman		
from	3 January 1361	*CPR 1358–1361*, p. 508
John atte Wode		
on	31 May 1361	*CCR 1360–1364*, p. 192

John Brigge		
temp	1403–1404	E.101/43/28

BRIDGNORTH

Owner

Crown		
from	1102	*HKW II*, p. 57
on	30 January 1342	*IMisc I*, no. 1795 (Town owns outer Bailiwick)

Constables

Hugh Mortimer		
to	23 January 1272	*CFR 1272–1307*, p. 2 (R.I.P.)
Ralph Mortimer		
from	23 January 1272	*CFR 1272–1307*, p. 2
Robert de Trillek		
to	27 October 1274	*CFR 1272–1307*, p. 33
Bevis de Knovill		
from	27 October 1274	*CFR 1272–1307*, p. 33
to	5 November 1278	*CFR 1272–1307*, p. 104
Roger Springehoese		
from	5 November 1278	*CFR 1272–1307*, p. 104
Edmund de Mauley		
from	29 September 1311	*CFR 1307–1319*, p. 103
Hugh de Audley of Stratton Audley, senior, P.P.		
to	15 December 1311	*CFR 1307–1319*, p. 120
Hugh de Croft		
from	15 December 1311	*CFR 1307–1319*, p. 120
to	28 January 1312	*CFR 1307–1319*, p. 124
Hugh de Audley of Stratton Audley, senior, P.P.		
from	28 January 1312	*CFR 1307–1319*, p. 124
to	24 October 1314	*CFR 1307–1319*, p. 220
Roger de Cheigny		
from	24 October 1314	*CFR 1307–1319*, p. 220
to	4 December 1314	*CFR 1307–1319*, p. 221
William de Mere		
from	4 December 1314	*CFR 1307–1319*, p. 221
to	2 March 1315	*CFR 1307–1319*, p. 234
Roger de Cheigny		
from	2 March 1315	*CFR 1307–1319*, p. 234
to	1 September 1315	*CFR 1307–1319*, p. 258
Ralph de Crophull		
from	1 September 1315	*CFR 1307–1319*, p. 258
Roger de Cheigny		
to	27 September 1316	*CFR 1307–1319*, p. 301
Roger Tromewyn		
from	27 September 1316	*CFR 1307–1319*, p. 301
to	1 March 1318	*CFR 1307–1319*, p. 354
Peter de Lymesy		
from	1 March 1318	*CFR 1307–1319*, p. 354
Roger Tromewyn		
to	29 November 1318	*CFR 1307–1319*, p. 381

Robert de Grendon, P.P.		
from	29 November 1318	*CFR 1307–1319*, p. 381
to	1 January 1322	*CFR 1319–1327*, p. 85
John de Swynnerton		
from	1 January 1322	*CFR 1319–1327*, p. 85
to	26 November 1322	*CFR 1319–1327*, p. 183
Henry de Bisshebury		
from	26 November 1322	*CFR 1319–1327*, p. 183
William de Ercelewe		
to	4 February 1327	*CFR 1319–1327*, p. 16
Henry de Bisshebury		
from	4 February 1327	*CFR 1327–1337*, p. 16
to	27 June 1327	*CFR 1327–1337*, p. 51
John de Hinkley		
from	27 June 1327	*CFR 1327–1337*, p. 51
Roger Chaundos, P.P.		
to	20 August 1329	*CFR 1327–1337*, p. 146
John de Cheilmerssh		
from	20 August 1329	*CFR 1327–1337*, p. 146
Roger Mortimer and heirs granted reversion of constableship		
on	20 August 1359	*CPR 1358–1361*, p. 267
Leo de Perton		
for life from	1 January 1341	*CPR 1340–1343*, p. 85
to	15 December 1370	*CPR 1367–1370*, p. 341
John de Beauchamp, of Holt and Kidderminster, king's esquire, P.P.		
from	15 December 1370	*CPR 1367–1370*, p. 341
vacated	12 August 1375	
on	28 September 1375	*CCR 1374–1377*, p. 160
Hugh Burnell, P.P.		
for life from	16 May 1387	*CPR 1385–1389*, p. 292
on	29 May 1388	*CPR 1385–1389*, p. 407

BROMPTON AND RHISTON (BROMPTON HALL)

Owners

Brian de Brompton		
to	28 December 1295	*IPM III*, no. 291 (R.I.P.)

CALLOWHILL

History

mentioned	1274–8	King, p. 433

CAUS

Owners

Peter Corbet, P.P.		
on	5 May 1286	*IPM II*, no. 606
to	10 August 1300	*IPM III*, no. 600 (R.I.P.)
Peter Corbet, son of above, P.P.		
from	10 August 1300	*IPM III*, no. 600
jointured	14 March 1315	*CPR 1313–1317*, p. 266
died	*1321/2*	

Beatrice, widow of Peter Corbet of Caux		
dead by	1 September 1347	*CFR 1347–1356*, p. 44
Ralph, earl Stafford		
on	1 March 1351	*CPR 1350–1354*, p. 67
to	August 1372	*IPM XIII*, 210 (R.I.P.)
Hugh, earl of Stafford, son of above		
from	August 1372	*IPM XIII*, no. 210
to	16 October 1386	*IPM XVI*, no. 452 (R.I.P.)
Thomas, earl of Stafford		
from	16 October 1386	*IPM XVI*, no. 452
to	4 July 1392	*IPM XVII*, no. 215 (R.I.P.)
William, brother of Thomas earl of Stafford, brother of above		
from	4 July 1392	*IPM XVII*, no. 215
to	6 April 1395	*IPM XVII*, no. 1260 (R.I.P.)
Edmund, earl of Stafford		
from	6 April 1395	*IPM XVII*, no. 1260
to	21 July 1403	*IPM XVIII*, no. 825 (R.I.P.)
Humphrey, son of above		
from	21 July 1403	*IPM XVIII*, no. 825
Queen Joan		
from	24 January 1404	*CPR 1401–1405*, p. 347
in	January 1405	*CACW*, XLIII.65

Wardships

Minority of Thomas, earl of Stafford (1386–1389)

Thomas de Beauchamp, earl of Warwick and William Beauchamp and John lord Neville		
from	25 February 1387	*CFR 1383–1391*, p. 173

Minority of William, Brother of Thomas earl of Stafford (1392–1395)

Thomas Woodstock, duke of Gloucester		
from	24 July 1392	*CFR 1391–1399*, p. 54

Minority of Edmund, earl of Stafford (1395–1399)

Thomas Woodstock, duke of Gloucester		
to	23 July 1397	*CFR 1391–1399*, p. 219
Edward, earl of Rutland		
from	23 July 1397	*CFR 1391–1399*, p. 219

Minority of Humphrey, son of Edmund de Stafford (1403–)

William Bromshull		
from	21 July 1403	*IPM XVIII*, no. 825
on	29 November 1403	*IPM XVIII*, no. 825
John Prendregest		
on	27 February 1404	*CCR 1402–1405*, p. 249

Keepers while in Royal hands

John de Cherleton and John le Strange		
from	1 September 1347	*CFR 1347–1356*, p. 44
William Bromshull		
in	January 1405	*CACW*, XLIII.65

Chaplains

Hugh Bergan		
on	17 August 1302	*CPR 1301–1307*, p. 55

CHENEY LONGVILLE

Owners

Sir Hugh Cheney		
licence to crenellate	1 September 1394	*CPR 1391–1396*, p. 500
dead by	*5 August 1404*	*CPR 1401–1405, p. 414*

CHESWARDINE

Tenant in Chief

Fulk le Strange		
to	16 October 1330	*IPM vol. VII*, no. 280

Owner

John le Strange of Cheswardine, held for life from below		
to	16 October 1330	*IPM vol. VII*, no. 280 (R.I.P.)
Fulk le Strange		
from	16 October 1330	*IPM vol. VII*, no. 280

CHIRBURY

Constables

Philip de Middleton		
inquiry into terms	16 December 1336	Fryde, no. 887

CLUN

Owners

Richard, earl of Arundel		
to	15 January 1302	*IPM IV*, no. 90 (R.I.P.)
Edmund, earl of Arundel, son of above		
from	15 January 1302	*IPM IV*, no. 90
before	13 September 1327	*CPR 1324–1327*, p. 328
Roger Mortimer		
from	13 September 1327	*CPR 1324–1327*, p. 328
from	13 September 1327	*CChR 1327–1341*, p. 55
Richard earl of Arundel		
away and back	24 June 1345	*CPR 1343–1345*, p. 487
foot of fine	2 November 1354	*Feet of fines relating to Wiltshire* Wiltshire Record Society 29 (1973), no. 421
Richard, earl of Arundel		
on	19 November 1386	*IMisc IV*, no. 234
Thomas le Despenser		
dead by	6 April 1405	*CPR 1405–1408*, p. 4
Richard le Despenser		
under age on	6 April 1405	*CPR 1405–1408*, p. 4

Wardship of Richard le Despenser, 1400–

Edward, duke of York		
from	17 May 1403	*CPR 1401–1405*, p. 235
Queen Joan		
from	6 April 1405	*CPR 1405–1408*, p. 4

Constables
Thomas Hoorde
not by | 21 November 1397 | *IMisc VI*, no. 234
Robert Menell
on | 21 November 1397 | *IMisc VI*, no. 234
Edward, earl of Rutland, future duke of York
for life from | 28 September 1397 | *CPR 1396–1399*, p. 205

CORFHAM

Owners

John Giffard of Brimpsfield, P.P., from Maud Longspey, his wife		
to	5 June 1299	*IPM III*, no. 544 (R.I.P.)
to	23 October 1299	*CFR 1272–1307*, p. 421 (R.I.P.)
Eleanor Giffard, daughter of above		
from	23 October 1299	*CFR 1272–1307*, p. 421
Fulk le Strange of Blackmere, P.P., from his wife Eleanor Giffard		
to	23 January 1323	*IPM VI*, no. 516 (R.I.P.)
John le Strange of Blackmere, P.P., son of above		
from	23 January 1323	*IPM VI*, no. 516
died	*21 July 1349*	*GEC XII (I), p. 343*
Fulk le Strange of Blackmere		
inherited	*21 July 1349*	*GEC XII (I), p. 343*
to	22 August 1349	*IPM IX*, no. 224 (R.I.P.)
John le Strange of Blackmere, P.P., brother of above		
from	22 August 1349	*IPM IX*, no. 224
died	*12 May 1361*	*GEC XII (I), p. 344*

DAWLEY (DALILEY)

Owners

William de Morton		
licence to crenellate	17 November 1316	*CPR 1313–1317*, p. 566
Richard earl of Arundel		
forfeited by	21 March 1398	*CFR 1391–1399*, p. 253

Constables

William le Scrope, earl of Wiltshire		
for 20 years from	21 March 1398	*CFR 1391–1399*, p. 253
Adam de Peshale, kn.		
for life from	24 April 1399	*CPR 1396–1399*, p. 540

ELLESMERE

Owners

Hamon le Strange		
from	1267	*HKW II*, p. 646
Ebulo le Strange, P.P. and Alice de Lacy his wife		
from	16 February 1331	*CChR 1327–1341*, p. 213
to	17 September 1335	*IPM II*, no. 681 (R.I.P.)
Alice de Lacy		
from	17 September 1335	*IPM II*, no. 681
on	9 October 1335	*CCR 1333–1337*, p. 444 (Prob)

Roger le Strange of Knockin, P.P.		
from	17 September 1335	*IPM VII*, no. 716
to	29 July 1349	*IPM IX*, no. 290 (R.I.P.)
Roger le Strange of Knockin, son of above, P.P.		
from	29 July 1349	*IPM IX*, no. 290
died	*23 August 1382*	*GEC XII(I), p. 354*
John le Strange of Knockin, son of above, P.P.		
inherited	23 August *1382*	*GEC XII(I), p. 354*
died	*28 July 1397*	*GEC XII(I), p. 354*
Richard le Strange of Knockin, son of above, P.P.		
inherited	*28 July 1397*	*GEC XII(I), p. 355*
died	*9 August 1449*	*GEC XII(I), p. 355*

Constable

Bevis de Knovill		
from	10 December 1274	*CFR 1272–1307*, p. 39
Roger le Strange of Ellesmere, P.P.		
for life from	24 November 1275	*CPR 1272–1281*, p. 125
John de Felton		
from	8 September 1320	*CFR 1319–1327*, p. 32
to	19 June 1321	*CFR 1319–1327*, p. 61
Oliver de Ingham, P. P, kn.		
from	19 June 1321	*CFR 1319–1327*, p. 61
Thomas de Hastang		
to	19 December 1330	*CFR 1327–1337*, p. 215
John de Reppes		
from	19 December 1330	*CFR 1327–1337*, p. 215
Joan, widow of Roger le Strange		
1/3 from	24 September 1349	*CCR 1349–1354*, p. 111

HODNET

Owners

Henry, duke of Lancaster		
dead by	16 July 1361	*CFR 1356–1368*, p. 165
Maud, his daughter		
from	16 July 1361	*CFR 1356–1368*, p. 165

HOLGATE

Owners

Robert Burnell, bishop of Bath and Wells, private property		
on	1285	*CCR 1279–1288*, p. 367
to	26 October 1292	*IPM III*, no. 65 (R.I.P.)
Philip Burnell, brother of above		
from	26 October 1292	*IPM III*, no. 65
a minor	8 May 1301	*CPR 1292–1301*, p. 594
Edward Burnell, P.P.		
to	1 September 1315	*IPM V*, no. 611 (R.I.P.)
Maud, his sister		
from	1 September 1315	*IPM V*, no. 611
Nicholas Burnell, kn., P.P.		
succeeded	*1348*	*GEC II, p. 435*
to	19 January 1383	*IPM XV*, no. 726 (R.I.P.)

Hugh Burnell, kn., son of above, P.P.		
from	19 January 1383	*IPM XV*, no. 726
died	*27* November *1420*	*GEC II, p. 435*

HOPTON

History

keep	Norman	Pevsner, p. 153
modified	C14	King, p. 425

KNOCKIN

Tenant in Chief

Richard, earl of Arundel		
on	23 August 1382	*IPM XV*, no. 843

Owners

Hame le Strange		
before	7 July 1311	*IPM V*, no. 264
John le Strange of Knockin, acquired from above		
to	6 February 1311	*IPM V*, no. 264
Iseult, widow of above, in jointure		
from	7 July 1311	*IPM V*, no. 264
on	20 January 1322	*CPR 1321–1324*, p. 50
Robert le Strange, kn.		
to	23 August 1382	*IPM XV*, no. 843 (R.I.P.)
Alina, widow of above.		
from	23 August 1382	*IPM XV*, no. 843 (Jointure)
John le Strange of Knockin, P.P.		
from	23 August 1382	*IPM XV*, no. 843
to	August 1397	*IPM XVII*, no. 1100 (R.I.P.)
Maud, widow of John son of Roger le Strange		
from	August 1397	*IPM XVII*, no. 1100
to	20 September 1400	*IPM XVIII*, no. 943
Richard le Strange, P. P , son of above		
from	20 September 1400	*IPM XVIII*, no. 943

LEA

History

built	C14	King, p. 426
siege	1645	King, p. 426

LUDLOW

Tenants in Cheif

Sir Geoffrey de Genevill, father of Peter below		
on	8 June 1292	*IPM III*, no. 43

Owners

Peter de Genevill		
to	8 June 1292	*IPM III*, no. 43 (R.I.P.)
Roger Mortimer of Wigmore		
to	23 January 1322	*CFR 1319–1327*, p. 93
Confiscated by Ralph de Botiller		
on	23 January 1322	*CFR 1319–1327*, p. 93

Roger Mortimer, earl of March		
to	12 January 1331	*CCR 1330–1333*, p. 111
Joan, wife of Roger Mortimer		
acknowledged	6 December 1330	*IMisc II*, no. 1117
livery on	12 January 1331	*CCR 1330–1333*, p. 111
to	19 October 1356	*IPM X*, no. 307 (R.I.P.)
Roger Mortimer, earl of March		
from	19 October 1356	*IPM* X, no. 307
Edmund Mortimer, earl of March and Ulster		
heir	*25 February 1360*	*IPM X, no. 640*
granted away	24 November 1379	*CPR 1377–1381*, p. 37
to	27 December 1381	*IPM XV*, no. 556 (R.I.P.)
Roger Mortimer, son of above		
from	27 December 1381	*IPM XV*, no. 556
John de Hastings and Philippa his wife, daughter of the earl of March		
for 8 years from	24 February 1388	*CCR 1385–1389*, p. 472
Edmund Mortimer, earl of March		
under age on	26 August 1404	*CPR 1401–1405*, p. 472

Constables

Ralph de Botiller		
on	23 January 1322	*CCR 1318–1323*, p. 415
on	1 November 1322	*CPR 1321–1324*, p. 215
John de Barewe		
to	10 October 1324	*CFR 1319–1327*, p. 306
John Inge		
from	10 October 1324	*CFR 1319–1327*, p. 306

Wardships

Minority of Roger Mortimer, earl of March, 1381–1395

Thomas de Beauchamp, earl of Warwick, Roger Mortimer, earl of March, John lord Neville and Henry Percy, earl of Northumberland		
from	16 December 1383	*CFR 1383–1391*, p. 22

minority Edmund Mortimer, earl of March, 1398–1412

Edward, duke of York		
from	11 August 1398	*CPR 1396–1399*, p. 408
Henry Percy, earl of Northumberland		
from	2 March 1400	*CFR 1399–1405*, p. 50
John de Lovel, kn.		
for three months from	31 July 1402	*CPR 1401–1405*, p. 140
Thomas Beaufort, kn.		
from	21 August 1402	*CPR 1401–1405*, p. 140
Hugh Cheyne, kn.		
from	6 June 1403	*CPR 1401–1405*, p. 237
dead by	5 August 1404	*CPR 1401–1405*, p. 414
Roger Acton, king's esq.		
from	5 August 1404	*CPR 1401–1405*, p. 414
from	26 August 1404	*CPR 1401–1405*, p. 407
exiled and outlawed by	12 February 1408	*CPR 1405–1408*, p. 394
John Brigge (Captain)		
from	12 February 1408	*CPR 1405–1408*, p. 394

MEOLO BRACE

History

mentioned	1273	King, p. 434

MYDDLE

Owners

John le Strange of Myddle		
on	1 April 1308	*CPR 1307–1313*, p. 62

OSWESTRY

Owners

Richard, earl of Arundel		
on	8 August 1282	*CPR 1281–1292*, p. 32
to	15 January 1302	*IPM IV*, no. 90 (R.I.P.)
Edmund, earl of Arundel, son of above		
from	15 January 1302	*IPM IV*, no. 90
before	13 September 1327	*CPR 1324–1327*, p. 328
Roger Mortimer		
from	13 September 1327	*CPR 1324–1327*, p. 328
from	13 September 1327	*CChR 1327–1341*, p. 55
Richard earl of Arundel		
away and back	24 June 1345	*CPR 1343–1345*, p. 487
foot of fine	2 November 1354	*Feet of fines relating to Wiltshire* Wiltshire Record Society 29 (1973), no. 421
Richard, earl of Arundel		
on	19 November 1386	*IMisc IV*, no. 367

Constable

Robert de Legh, kn.		
for life from	4 October 1397	*CPR 1396–1399*, p. 204

Wardships

minority of Richard fitzAlan, earl of Arundel, –1288

John son of Aer		
to	7 December 1272	*CFR 1272–1307*, p. 2
John de Oxendon		
from	7 December 1272	*CFR 1272–1307*, p. 2
Adam de Montgomery		
to	10 December 1274	*CFR 1272–1307*, p. 38
Bevis de Knovil		
from	10 December 1274	*CFR 1272–1307*, p. 38
to	17 July 1277	*CPR 1272–1281*, p. 223
Roger le Strange of Ellesmere, P.P.		
from	17 July 1277	*CPR 1272–1281*, p. 223
to	28 April 1279	*CPR 1272–1281*, p. 309
Isabella Mortimer		
from	28 April 1279	*CPR 1272–1281*, p. 309
Isabella, widow of John son of Alan		
on/from?	14 November 1280	*CPR 1272–1281*, p. 404
Roger Springehoese		
to	8 August 1282	*CPR 1272–1281*, p. 32

Edmund Mortimer		
from	8 August 1282	*CPR 1272–1281*, p. 32
Chaplains		
Adam de Chetewynd		
to	28 December 1282	*CPR 1272–1281*, p. 53 (R.I.P.)
Richard de Bishopston		
from	28 December 1282	*CPR 1272–1281*, p. 53

PONTESBURY

History		
ringwork	12th cty.	*VCH vol. 1*, p. 252
tower added	c.1200	*VCH vol. 1*, p. 252
destroyed by fire	c.1300	*VCH vol. 1*, p. 252

REDCASTLE

Tenant in Chief		
heirs of Richard de Betteleye		
on	28 August 1299	*IPM III*, no. 536
Owner		
William de Audley of Heighley		
to	25 December 1282	*IPM II*, no. 476 (R.I.P.)
Nicholas de Audley of Heighley, brother of above		
from	25 December 1282	*IPM II*, no. 476
to	28 August 1299	*IPM III*, no. 536 (R.I.P.)
Thomas de Audley of Heighley, son of above		
from	28 August 1299	*IPM III*, no. 536
to	16 January 1308	*IPM V*, no. 62 (R.I.P.)
Nicholas de Audley of Heighley, brother of above, P.P.		
from	16 January 1308	*IPM V*, no. 62
to	6 December 1316	*IPM VI*, no. 56 (R.I.P.)
James de Audley of Heighley, kn., son of above, P.P.		
from	6 December 1316	*IPM VI*, no. 56
on	17 September 1352	*CPR 1350–1354*, p. 341
to	1 April 1386	*IPM XVI*, no. 195 (R.I.P.)
Nicholas de Audley of Heighley, kn., son of above, P.P.		
from	1 April 1386	*IPM XVI*, no. 195
to	22 July 1391	*IPM XVI*, no. 1065 (R.I.P.)
Elizabeth, widow of Nicholas de Audley, kn. (R.I.P.)		
from	25 November 1391	*CCR 1389–1392*, p. 513
to	18 November 1400	*IPM XVIII*, no. 483 (R.I.P.)
1/3 to Fulk fitz Waryn		
to	31 October 1407	*IPM XVIII*, no. 431 (R.I.P.)
1/3 to Fulk fitz Waryn, son of above		
from	31 October 1407	*IPM XVIII*, no. 431
1/9 to Anne, widow of Fulk fitz Waryn (From Fulk's third)		
from	15 February 1408	*IPM XVIII*, no. 483 (Dower)
1/2 (1/3?) to John Tuchet, lord Audley, P.P.		
to	19 December 1409	*IPM XIX*, no. 599 (R.I.P.)
1/2 (1/3?)to James Tuchet, lord Audley, son of above, P.P.		
from	19 December 1409	*IPM XIX*, no. 599

1/3 to Margaret Hillary		
to	24 April 1411	*IPM XIX*, no. 879
1/3 to James Tuchet, lord Audley, her cousin, P.P.		
from	24 April 1411	*IPM XIX*, no. 879
Nicholas de Audley		
dead by	28 May 1413	*CPR 1413–1416*, p. 76
Crown		
on	28 May 1413	*CPR 1413–1416*, p. 76

Wardship

minority of James de Audley, 1316–1334

John de Felton		
from	18 January 1322	*CFR 1319–1327*, p. 89 (Custody)
on	16 February 1322	*CCR 1318–1323*, p. 524 (Custody)
Roger Corbet		
to	11 May 1324	*CFR 1319–1327*, p. 275 (Custody)
Ralph de Camoys, P.P.		
from	11 May 1324	*CFR 1319–1327*, p. 275 (Custody)

minority of John Tuchet, lord Audley, 1391–1392

John Delves and William Walsall		
from	3 September 1391	*CFR 1391–1399*, p. 11

RUYTON OF THE ELEVEN TOWNS

Owners

Edmund fitzAlan, earl of Arundel		
built by	early 14th century	Pevsner, p. 238

SHRAWARDINE

Owners

Richard, earl of Arundel		
to	15 January 1302	*IPM IV*, no. 90 (R.I.P.)
Edmund, earl of Arundel, son of above		
from	15 January 1302	*IPM IV*, no. 90
before	13 September 1327	*CPR 1324–1327*, p. 328
Roger Mortimer		
from	13 September 1327	*CPR 1324–1327*, p. 328
from	13 September 1327	*CChR 1327–1341*, p. 55
Richard, earl of Arundel		
away and back	24 June 1345	*CPR 1343–1345*, p. 487
foot of fine	1 November 1354	*Feet of fines relating to Wiltshire* Wiltshire Record Society 29 (1973), no. 421
Richard, earl of Arundel		
on	19 November 1386	*IMisc IV*, no. 367
Thomas, earl of Arundel		
on	25 July 1407	*CPR 1405–1408*, p. 342
Arundel		
on	17 June 1422	*CFR 1416–1422*, p. 436

Constables

Thomas Beston		
for life from	9 October 1397	*CPR 1396–1399*, p. 212

SHREWSBURY

Constables

Hugh Mortimer		
to	23 January 1272	*CFR 1272–1307*, p. 2 (R.I.P.)
Ralph Mortimer		
from	23 January 1272	*CFR 1272–1307*, p. 2
Robert de Trillek		
to	27 October 1274	*CFR 1272–1307*, p. 33
Bevis de Knovill		
from	27 October 1274	*CFR 1272–1307*, p. 33
to	5 November 1278	*CFR 1272–1307*, p. 104
Roger Springehoese		
from	5 November 1278	*CFR 1272–1307*, p. 104
Robert Corbet		
on	12 October 1289	*CCR 1288–1296*, p. 22
Hugh de Audley of Stratton Audley, senior, P.P.		
to	15 December 1311	*CFR 1307–1319*, p. 120
Hugh de Croft		
from	15 December 1311	*CFR 1307–1319*, p. 120
Hugh de Audley of Stratton Audley, senior, P.P.		
from	28 January 1312	*CFR 1307–1319*, p. 124
to	24 October 1314	*CFR 1307–1319*, p. 220
Roger de Cheigny		
from	24 October 1314	*CFR 1307–1319*, p. 220
to	4 December 1314	*CFR 1307–1319*, p. 221
William de Mere		
from	4 December 1314	*CFR 1307–1319*, p. 221
to	2 March 1315	*CFR 1307–1319*, p. 234
Roger de Cheigny		
from	2 March 1315	*CFR 1307–1319*, p. 234
to	1 September 1315	*CFR 1307–1319*, p. 258
Ralph de Crophull		
from	1 September 1315	*CFR 1307–1319*, p. 258
Roger de Cheigny		
to	27 September 1316	*CFR 1307–1319*, p. 301
Roger Tromewyn		
from	27 September 1316	*CFR 1307–1319*, p. 301
to	1 March 1318	*CFR 1307–1319*, p. 354
Peter de Lymesy		
from	1 March 1318	*CFR 1307–1319*, p. 354
Roger Tromewyn		
to	29 November 1318	*CFR 1307–1319*, p. 381
Robert de Grendon, P.P.		
from	29 November 1318	*CFR 1307–1319*, p. 381
to	1 January 1322	*CFR 1319–1327*, p. 85
John de Swynnerton		
from	1 January 1322	*CFR 1319–1327*, p. 85
to	26 November 1322	*CFR 1319–1327*, p. 183
Henry de Bisshebury		
from	26 November 1322	*CFR 1319–1327*, p. 183
to	13 January 1326	*CFR 1319–1327*, p. 373

William de Ercalewe		
from	13 January 1326	*CFR 1319–1327*, p. 373
to	4 February 1327	*CFR 1327–1337*, p. 16
Henry de Bisshebury		
from	4 February 1327	*CFR 1327–1337*, p. 16
to	27 June 1327	*CFR 1327–1337*, p. 51
John de Hinkley		
from	27 June 1327	*CFR 1327–1337*, p. 51
to	22 February 1330	*CFR 1327–1337*, p. 163
Henry de Bisshebury		
from	22 February 1330	*CFR 1327–1337*, p. 163
to	20 March 1330	*CFR 1327–1337*, p. 167
John de Hinkley		
from	20 March 1330	*CFR 1327–1337*, p. 167
to	5 December 1330	*CFR 1327–1337*, p. 199
Henry de Bisshebury		
from	5 December 1330	*CFR 1327–1337*, p. 199
Richard de Peshale		
to	23 February 1335	*CFR 1327–1337*, p. 432
John de Hinkley		
from	23 February 1335	*CFR 1327–1337*, p. 432
to	26 March 1335	*CFR 1327–1337*, p. 474
Simon de Rugley		
from	26 March 1335	*CFR 1327–1337*, p. 474
to	28 June 1338	*CFR 1337–1347*, p. 85
Richard de Peshale		
from	28 June 1338	*CFR 1337–1347*, p. 85
to	30 July 1339	*CFR 1337–1347*, p. 139
Simon de Rugley		
from	30 July 1339	*CFR 1337–1347*, p. 139
John de Hethey, king's yeoman		
for life from	17 November 1339	*CPR 1338–1340*, p. 335
Simon de Rugley		
and from	6 April 1340	*CFR 1337–1347*, p. 168
to	8 January 1341	*CFR 1337–1347*, p. 200
Adam de Peshale		
from	8 January 1341	*CFR 1337–1347*, p. 200
John de Hethey		
for life on	10 August 1341	*CCR 1341–1343*, p. 188
dead by	22 May 1342	*CPR 1340–1343*, p. 430
John de Windsor		
for life from	22 May 1342	*CPR 1340–1343*, p. 430
to	27 December 1365	*CFR 1356–1368*, p. 321 (R.I.P.)
Hugh Cheyne		
for life from	27 December 1365	*CFR 1356–1368*, p. 321
on	8 October 1378	*CCR 1377–1381*, p. 160
John Byketon		
on	May 1389	
on	22 June 1389	*CCR 1389–1392*, p. 63
Hugh Cheyne		
on	16 June 1390	*CPR 1388–1392*, p. 255

Thomas Hinkley, esq.		
for life from	4 November 1399	*CPR 1399–1401*, p. 60
to	1 August 1402	*CPR 1401–1405*, p. 116 (R.I.P.)
John Acton		
for life from	1 August 1402	*CPR 1401–1405*, p. 116
Nicholas Gerard, esq.		
for life from	8 November 1407	*CPR 1405–1408*, p. 379
to	15 February 1413	*CPR 1408–1413*, p. 466
Urian Seinpiere		
for life from	15 February 1413	*CPR 1408–1413*, p. 466
confirmed	1 July 1413	*CPR 1413–1416*, p. 56

Chaplains

Robert de Cottingham		
from	18 October 1295	*CPR 1292–1301*, p. 154
Geoffrey de Hakenesse		
on	21 July 1313	*CPR 1313–1317*, p. 2
on	15 October 1313	*CPR 1313–1317*, p. 28
William de Chaylou		
to	30 March 1329	*CPR 1327–1330*, p. 380
Walter de London		
from	30 March 1329	*CPR 1327–1330*, p. 380
to	27 May 1330	*CPR 1327–1330*, p. 528
John de la Chaumbre		
from	27 May 1330	*CPR 1327–1330*, p. 528
Adam de Overton		
from	24 October 1330	*CPR 1330–1334*, p. 13
Ralph Repynton		
to	4 February 1402	*CPR 1401–1405*, p. 53
John Repynton, brother of above		
from	4 February 1402	*CPR 1401–1405*, p. 53

Gatekeeper and Goaler

Gilbert de Brompton		
from	18 October 1335	*CPR 1334–1338*, p. 171

STOKESAY

Owners

Laurence de Ludlow, son of a clothier		
licence to crenellate	19 October 1291	*CPR 1281–1291*, p. 450

TONG

Owners

Fulk de Pembrugge, kn.		
licence to crenellate	24 July 1381	*CPR 1381–1385*, p. 31

WATTLESBOROUGH

Owners

Robert Corbet of Moreton Corbet		
in	1255	*VCH vol. 8*, p. 107
to	1300 (R.I.P.)	*VCH vol. 8*, p. 107

Thomas Corbet, son of above		
from	1300	*VCH vol. 8*, p. 107
to	1310 (R.I.P.)	*VCH vol. 8*, p. 107
Robert Corbet, son of above		
underage	1310	*VCH vol. 8*, p. 107
Robert Corbet, and Elizabeth his wife		
temp.	1366	*VCH vol. 8*, p. 107
to	1375 (R.I.P.)	*VCH vol. 8*, p. 107
Elizabeth, widow of above		
from	1375	*VCH vol. 8*, p. 107
to	1379 (R.I.P.)	*VCH vol. 8*, p. 107
Fulk Corbet		
from	1379	*VCH vol. 8*, p. 107
to	1382	*VCH vol. 8*, p. 107
Fulk Mawddy (?), son of Elizabeth, da. and heir of Fulk above and John Mawddy		
temp.	1403	*VCH vol. 8*, p. 107
to	1414 (R.I.P.)	*VCH vol. 8*, p. 107
Elizabeth, sister of above, wife of Hugh Burgh		
from	1414	*VCH vol. 8*, p. 107
John Burgh, kn., son of above		
underage	1429	*VCH vol. 8*, p. 107
underage	1431	*VCH vol. 8*, p. 107
to	1471 (R.I.P.)	*VCH vol. 8*, p. 107

WEM

Owners

Ralph le Botiler		
to	3 July 1281	*IPM II*, no. 390 (R.I.P.)
Gawaune le Botiler		
to	21 March 1290	*IPM II*, no. 773 (R.I.P.)
Maud, lady of Wem		
to	14 June 1290	*IPM II*, no. 774 (R.I.P.)
William le Botiler, P.P. brother of Gawaune		
from	14 June 1290	*IPM II*, no. 774
died	*1334*	*GEC II, p. 232*
William le Botiler of Wem, son of above		
inherited	*1334*	*GEC II, p. 232*
died	*1361*	*GEC II, p. 232*
William le Botiler of Wem, P.P. son of above		
inherited	*1361*	*GEC II, p. 232*
died	*1369*	*GEC II, p. 232*

WHITTINGTON

Owners

Fulk fitz Waryn, P.P.		
restored	8 December 1330	*CCR 1330–1333*, p. 76
died	*June 1336*	*GEC V, p. 497*
Fulk fitz Waryn, son of above		
to	25 July 1349	*IPM IX*, no. 177 (R.I.P.)

Fulk fitz Waryn, son of above		
from	25 July 1349	*IPM IX*, no. 177
to	12 February 1374	*IPM XIV*, no. 82 (R.I.P.)
Fulk fitz Waryn, son of above		
from	12 February 1374	*IPM XIV*, no. 82
to	8 August 1391	*IPM XVI*, no. 31 (R.I.P.)
Fulk fitz Waryn, son of above		
from	8 August 1391	*IPM XVI*, no. 31
to	31 October 1407	*IPM XIX*, no. 431 (R.I.P.)
Fulk fitz Waryn, son of above		
from	31 October 1407	*IPM XIX*, no. 431
1/3 to Anne, widow of Fulk fitz Waryn		
from	15 February 1408	*IPM XIX*, no. 483 (Dower)

Constables

Warin de Rugge		
from	27 April 1330	*CFR 1327–1337*, p. 188
to	8 December 1330	*CCR 1330–1333*, p. 76

Wardship

Minority of Fulk fitz Waryn, 1349–1361

William fitz Waryn		
from	4 May 1350	*CFR 1347–1356*, p. 236

Minority of Fulk, son of Fulk fitz Waryn

Alice Perrers		
to	Forfeiture	*IPM XV*, no. 765
James de Audley of Heighley		
from	26 March 1378	*CFR 1377–1383*, p. 85
lately	20 August 1378	*CCR 1377–1381*, p. 152
John Wykes		
from	12 May 1378	*CFR 1377–1383*, p. 89
James de Audley of Heighley		
from	7 November 1378	*CFR 1377–1383*, p. 110

Minority of Fulk fitz Waryn, 1391–1407

John Devereux of Maugne		
from	17 February 1392	*CFR 1391–1399*, p. 38
Thomas de Percy		
from	17 March 1393	*CFR 1391–1399*, p. 76
Ives fitz Waryn		
from	12 February 1394	*CFR 1391–1399*, p. 111
on	1 October 1404	*CCR 1402–1405*, p. 387

WROCKWARDINE (CHARLETON)

Owners

John de Cherleton of Powis, P.P.		
license to crenellate	17 November 1316	*CPR 1313–1317*, p. 566
died	*1353*	*GEC III, p. 160*
John de Cherleton of Powis, son of above, P.P.		
inherited	*1353*	*GEC III, p. 160*
died	*1360*	*GEC III, p. 160*
John de Cherleton of Powis, son of above, P.P.		
inherited	*1360*	*GEC III, p. 161*
died	*13 July 1374*	*GEC III, p. 161*

John de Cherleton of Powis, son of above, kn., P.P.		
inherited	*13 July 1374*	*GEC III, p. 161*
to	19 October 1401	*IPM XVIII*, no. 650 (R.I.P.)
Edward de Cherleton, kn., brother of above, P.P.		
from	19 October 1401	*IPM XVIII*, no. 650
on	26 November 1401	*CPR 1401–1405*, p. 21
to garrison for 3 months	23 July 1402	*CPR 1401–1405*, p. 139
died	*14 March 1421*	*GEC III, p. 161*

Somerset

Unknown Licenses

TORVESTON for Adam le Bret		
	22 June 1316	*CPR 1313–1317*, p. 480
YERDLYNGTON for Simon de Montague, P.P.		
	20 October 1313	*CPR 1313–1317*, p. 31

BRIDGEWATER

Reversion

Roger Mortimer of Wigmore		
to	30 June 1316	*CPR 1313–1317*, p. 491
Edmund Mortimer, of Wigmore, son of above, P.P.		
from	30 June 1316	*CPR 1313–1317*, p. 491

Owners

Roger Mortimer of Wigmore		
to	5 November 1282	*IPM II*, no. 446 (R.I.P.)
Matilda, widow of Roger Mortimer		
from	10 January 1283	*CCR 1279–1288*, p. 200
William Mortimer		
to	30 June 1297	*IPM III*, no. 407 (R.I.P.)
to	14 November 1297	*CPR 1292–1301*, p. 73 (R.I.P.)
Maud Mortimer, his mother		
from	30 June 1297	*IPM III*, no. 407
to	23 March 1301	*IPM IV*, no. 41
Edmund Mortimer of Wigmore, son of above, P.P.		
from	23 March 1301	*IPM IV*, no. 41
to	25 July 1304	*IPM IV*, no. 235 (R.I.P.)
Margaret de Fiennes, widow of Edmund Mortimer		
from	25 July 1304	*IPM IV*, no. 235 (Jointly)
on	30 June 1316	*CPR 1313–1317*, p. 491
Crown		
on	29 October 1322	*IMisc II*, no. 617
Margaret de Fiennes, widow of Edmund Mortimer, snr., above		
to	21 February 1334	*IPM VII*, no. 577
Elizabeth, widow of Edmund Mortimer, jnr. (d.1331)		
from	21 February 1334	*IPM VII*, no. 577
from	13 July 1334	*CCR 1333–1337*, p. 237
Roger Mortimer, earl of March		
to	26 February 1360	*IPM X*, no. 640 (R.I.P.)
Edmund Mortimer, son of above		
heir on	26 February 1360	*IPM X*, no. 640
Philippa, widow of Roger Mortimer		
to	5 January 1382	*IPM XV*, no. 564 (R.I.P.)
Roger Mortimer, earl of March		
from	5 January 1382	*IPM XV*, no. 564
to	20 July 1398	*IPM XVII*, no. 1195 (R.I.P.)

Eleanor, widow of Roger Mortimer		
from	16 March 1399	*CCR 1396–1399*, p. 451
dead by	6 October 1405	*IPM XIX*, no. 47

Constables

John de Lortye and John de Say		
from	15 January 1322	*CFR 1319–1327*, p. 94
to	28 December 1322	*CPR 1321–1324*, p. 230
John de Beauchamp of Somerset, P.P.		
from	1 December 1322	*CFR 1319–1327*, p. 189
to	19 August 1325	*CFR 1319–1327*, p. 358
Simon de Furneux		
from	19 August 1325	*CFR 1319–1327*, p. 358
William de Weylond		
to	12 October 1326	*CFR 1319–1327*, p. 419
John de Say and Simon de Furneux		
from	12 October 1326	*CFR 1319–1327*, p. 419

Wardships

Minority of Roger Mortimer, earl of March, 1381–1395

Philip Holgoyt		
from	16 December 1382	*CPR 1381–1385*, p. 65
Thomas de Beauchamp, earl of Warwick, Roger Mortimer, earl of March, John lord Neville and Henry Percy, earl of Northumberland		
from	16 December 1383	*CFR 1383–1391*, p. 22

minority Edmund Mortimer, earl of March, 1398–1412

Edward, duke of York		
from	11 August 1398	*CPR 1396–1399*, p. 408
Henry Percy, earl of Northumberland		
from	2 March 1400	*CFR 1399–1405*, p. 50

DUNSTER

Owners

John de Mohun		
to	14 July 1279	*IPM II*, no. 306 (R.I.P.)
dead by	7 January 1281	*CPR 1281–1292*, p. 8
John de Mohun, son of above, P.P.		
from	14 July 1279	*IPM II*, no. 306
dead by	14 December 1330	*CCR 1330–1333*, p. 96
Sibyl, widow of above		
livery	14 December 1330	*CCR 1330–1333*, p. 96
John de Mohun, P.P.		
from	23 June 1346	*CPR 1345–1348*, p. 126
to	14 September 1376	*IPM XIV*, no. 322 (R.I.P.)
Joan, widow of John Mohun, kn.		
to	4 October 1404	*IPM XVIII*, no. 1133 (R.I.P.)
dead by	26 February 1406	*IMisc VII*, no. 327
Heirs: Elizabeth, Philippa, Richard		
on	4 October 1404	*IPM XVIII*, no. 1133
Hugh Luterell, kn., from Joan, lady de Bohun		
from	17 February 1405	*CFR 1399–1405*, p. 302

Wardships		
minority of John de Mohun, 1271–1291		
Ralph de Sandwich		
to	27 May 1280	*CPR 1272–1281*, p. 374
Francis Accursii		
from	27 May 1280	*CPR 1272–1281*, p. 374
John de Vescy		
from	7 January 1281	*CPR 1281–1292*, p. 8
Constables		
Patrick Everard		
on	16 May 1385	*CPR 1381–1385*, p. 599

FARLEIGH HUNGERFORD

Owners		
Sir Thomas de Hungerford		
pardon for crenellating	26 November 1383	*CPR 1381–1385*, p. 340

HARPTREE

Owners		
Olive de Gournay		
to	12 May 1296	*IPM III*, no. 337 (R.I.P.)
Elizabeth, her daughter		
from	12 May 1296	*IPM III*, no. 337
Thomas de Gournay		
paying for l. to cren.	22 July 1343	*IPM VIII*, no. 434
to	22 July 1343	*IPM VIII*, no. 434 (R.I.P.)
John de Gournay, son of above		
under age	22 July 1343	*IPM VIII*, no. 434

NUNNEY

Owners		
John de la Mare		
licence to crenellate	28 November 1373	*CPR 1370–1374*, p. 367

STOGURSEY

Owners		
Robert Walraund		
dead by	1301	*IPM IV*, no. 457
John Walrand, son of above		
an idiot	12 May 1301	*IPM IV*, no. 457
mad by	8 May 1308	*CCR 1307–1313*, p. 33
Constables		
Ralph de Sandwich		
to	26 June 1278	*CPR 1272–1281*, p. 272
Amisius de Sabaudia		
from	26 June 1278	*CPR 1272–1281*, p. 272
on	10 August 1278	*CCR 1272–1279*, p. 472

Wardships
Madness of John Walrand

Robert Fitz Payn, P.P.		
from	8 May 1308	*CCR 1307–1313*, p. 33

TAUNTON

Owners

Bishop of Winchester		
on	29 January 1269	*CLibR 1267–1272*, no. 579
void	30 December 1279	*CPR 1272–1281*, p. 365
on	8 November 1280	*CPR 1272–1281*, p. 403 (void?)
void	6 August 1323	*CCR 1323–1327*, p. 132
on	10 March 1327	*CPR 1327–1330*, p. 81
void	20 December 1345	*CPR 1345–1348*, p. 19

Constables

Adam Draycote for Bishop of Winchester		
before	10 March 1327	*CPR 1327–1330*, p. 81

Wardships

Nicholas de Clere, King's Clerk		
from	3 March 1280	*CPR 1272–1281*, p. 365
William Beaufou		
from	20 December 1345	*CPR 1345–1348*, p. 19

WELLS (BISHOPS PALACE)

History

fortified	mid C14	King, p. 445

Staffordshire

Unknown Licenses

BERKMONDESCOTE for Roger Hillary		
	13 February 1345	*CPR 1343–1345*, p. 438
BRUGHTON for Hugh de Whytemor		
	10 August 1299	*CPR 1292–1301*, p. 139
CHEBSEY for John de Hastanges		
	1 August 1309	*CPR 1307–1313*, p. 178
MADLEE for Ralph, Baron Stafford		
	6 February 1348	*CPR 1348–1350*, p. 13
SWYNNERTON for Roger de Swynnerton, P.P.		
	6 October 1315	*CPR 1313–1317*, p. 356

ALTON (ALVETON)

Owners

Theobald de Verdon, P.P.		
to	28 August 1309	*IPM V*, no. 187 (R.I.P.)
Theobald de Verdon II, P.P. , son of above		
from	28 August 1309	*IPM V*, no. 187
to	30 July 1316	*IPM VI*, no. 54 (R.I.P.)
Thomas de Furnivall, P.P. and Joan his wife, da. of above		
livery	16 October 1328	*CCR 1327–1330*, p. 328
to	16 October 1339	*IPM VIII*, no. 243 (R.I.P.)
Thomas de Furnivall, son of above, P.P.		
from	16 October 1339	*IPM VIII*, no. 243
to	21 April 1365	*IPM XII*, no. 29 (R.I.P.)
William de Furnivall, P.P. , brother of above		
from	21 April 1365	*IPM XII*, no. 29
died	*12 April 1383*	*GEC V, p. 587*
Thomas de Neville, kn., through Joan, his wife, da. of above		
to	14 March 1407	*IPM XIX*, no. 245
John Talbot, through Maud his wife, daughter of above		
from	14 March 1407	*IPM XIX*, no. 245

Wardship of Theobald de Verdon

Roger Damory		
from	24 January 1317	*CFR 1307–1319*, p. 316

Constables

Thomas de Furnivall, P.P. (Before Livery)		
from	10 February 1328	*CFR 1327–1337*, p. 79

CAVERSWALL

Owners

William de Caverswell		
licence to crenellate	7 November 1275	*CPR 1272–1281*, p. 109

CHARTLEY

Owners

Thomas de Ferrers		
before	26 July 1276	*CPR 1272–1281*, p. 156
Edmund, earl of Lancaster, king's brother		
from	26 July 1276	*CPR 1272–1281*, p. 156

Constables

Roger le Strange of Ellesmere, P.P.		
to	6 May 1273	*CPR 1272–1281*, p 9
Richard de Clifford		
from	6 May 1273	*CPR 1272–1281*, p. 9
Bogo de Knovill		
to	26 July 1276	*CPR 1272–1281*, p. 156

DUDLEY

Owners

Roger de Somery		
to	26 August 1273	*IPM II*, no. 16
Roger de Somery		
from	26 August 1273	*IPM II*, no. 16 (age 18)
to	11 October 1291	*IPM II*, no. 813 (R.I.P.)
John de Somery, son of above, P.P.		
from	11 October 1291	*IPM II*, no. 813
to	24 August 1322	*IPM VI*, no. 428 (R.I.P.)
John de Sutton (son of Richard de Sutton) and Margaret his wife, eldest sister of J. de Somery		
from	26 November 1322	*CFR 1318–1323*, p. 188
Hugh le Despenser, yng., P.P.		
from	12 October 1326	CCR *1323–1327*, p. 510
to	15 December 1326	CCR *1333–1337*, p. 141
John de Sutton (son of Richard de Sutton) and Margaret his wife, eldest sister of J. de Somery		
from	29 March 1327	*CCR 1327–1330*, p. 63
on	12 April 1327	*CPR 1327–1330*, p. 97
John de Sutton of Dudley		
away and back	28 May 1340	*CPR 1338–1340*, p. 530
to	22 November 1359	*IPM X*, no. 516 (R.I.P.)
Isabel, widow of John de Sutton (R.I.P.)		
from	22 November 1359	*IPM X*, no. 516 (Jointure)
to	10 April 1397	*IPM XVIII*, no. 431
John de Sutton, her great grandson		
from	10 April 1397	*IPM XVIII*, no. 431
to	3 September 1406	*IPM XIX*, no. 208
John de Sutton, son of above		
from	3 September 1406	*IPM XIX*, no. 208

Notes

Release by John de Sutton to Hugh le Despenser, yng.		
on	12 October 1326	*CCR 1323–1327*, p. 510

Constables

William de Bermucham		
from	15 December 1326	*CFR 1324–1327*, p. 428
to	9 April 1327	*CCR 1333–1337*, p. 141

Henry de Bisshebury		
from	6 March 1327	*CMR*, no. 111
to	9 April 1327	*CCR 1327–1330*, p. 63

ECCLESHALL

Owners

See of Lichfield and Coventry		
on	1 November 1317	*CCR 1313–1318*, p. 505
on	16 November 1321	*CFR 1319–1327*, p. 77
restored to	12 April 1322	*CPR 1321–1324*, p. 96
See of Chester		
on	6 May 1330	*CPR 1327–1330*, p. 522
See of Lichfield and Coventry		
void	2 June 1359	*CPR 1358–1361*, p. 213
void	12 July 1359	*IMisc III*, no. 348
void	12 August 1359	*CCR 1354–1360*, p. 588

Wardships

Roger de Swynnerton		
from	16 November 1321	*CFR 1319–1327*, p. 77
to	12 April 1322	*CPR 1321–1324*, p. 96
Richard de Hampton, king's yeoman		
from	2 June 1359	*CPR 1358–1361*, p. 213
on	12 August 1359	*CCR 1354–1360*, p. 588
Peter de la Hay		
from	14 October 1385	*CPR 1385–1389*, p. 23

Private Constables

Gilbert de Cottesmor		
not by	12 July 1359	*IMisc III*, no. 348

HEIGHLEY

Tenant in chief

Theobald de Verdon		
on	22 April 1276	*IPM II*, no. 196
on	25 December 1282	*IPM II*, no. 576
William de Betteleye		
on	28 August 1299	*IPM III*, no. 536

Owners

Henry de Audley of Heighley		
to	22 April 1276	*IPM II*, no. 196 (R.I.P.)
William de Audley of Heighley, brother of above		
from	22 April 1276	*IPM II*, no. 196
to	25 December 1282	*IPM II*, no. 476 (R.I.P.)
Nicholas de Audley of Heighley, brother of above		
from	25 December 1282	*IPM II*, no. 476
to	28 August 1299	*IPM III*, no. 536 (R.I.P.)
Thomas de Audley of Heighley, son of above		
from	28 August 1299	*IPM III*, no. 536
to	16 January 1308	*IPM V*, no. 62 (R.I.P.)

Nicholas de Audley of Heighley, brother of above, P.P.		
from	16 January 1308	*IPM V*, no. 62
to	6 December 1316	*IPM VI*, no. 56
James de Audley of Heighley, son of above, P.P.		
from	6 December 1316	*IPM VI*, no. 56
to	1 April 1386	*IPM XVI*, no. 194 (R.I.P.)
Nicholas de Audley of Heighley, son of above, P.P.		
from	1 April 1386	*IPM XVI*, no. 194
to	22 July 1391	*IPM XVI*, nos. 428, 1065
John Tuchet, lord Audley, P.P.		
from	20 May 1392	*CCR 1389–1392*, p. 467
Fulk fitz Waryn claims one third of the castle		
to	31 October 1407	*IPM XIX*, no. 434

Wardships

During minority of James Audley, 1316–1334

Roger Corbet of Tassele		
from	16 January 1322	*CFR 1319–1327*, p. 89
on	16 February 1322	*CCR 1318–1323*, p. 523
William Martyn		
from	10 December 1322	*CFR 1319–1327*, p. 190
to	5 November 1324	*CFR 1319–1327*, p. 312 (R.I.P.)
Ralph de Camoys		
from	5 November 1324	*CFR 1319–1327*, p. 312

NEWCASTLE UNDER LYME

Owners

Edmund, earl of Lancaster		
on	6 February 1292	*CPR 1281–1292*, p. 477
not by	3 July 1297	*IPM III*, no. 423 (R.I.P.)
Alice de Lacy		
on	10 July 1322	*CCR 1318–1323*, p. 578
Henry, duke of Lancaster		
in	March 1356	Somerville, p. 362
to	23 March 1361	*IPM XI*, no. 118 (R.I.P.)
dead by	16 July 1361	*CFR 1356–1368*, p. 165
Maud, his daughter		
from	16 July 1361	*CFR 1356–1368*, p. 165
to	14 May 1362	
Leased to Sir Godfrey Foljaumbe		
for life from	20 May 1362	*CPR 1361–1364*, p. 202
John of Gaunt, duke of Lancaster		
on	2 January 1381	*JGR 1379–1383*, no. 970
on	3 January 1381	*JGR 1379–1383*, no. 449

Private Constables

John de Rocheford		
in	March 1356	Somerville, p. 362

Porter

Thomas de Hanselape		
for life from	2 January 1381	*JGR 1379–1383*, no. 970
on	3 January 1381	*JGR 1379–1383*, no. 449

STAFFORD

Owners

Ralph, earl of Stafford		
licence to crenellate	6 February 1348	*CPR 1348–1340*, p. 13
to	August 1372	*IPM XIII*, no. 210 (R.I.P.)
Hugh, earl of Stafford, son of above		
from	August 1372	*IPM XIII*, no. 210
to	16 October 1386	*IPM XVI*, no. 453 (R.I.P.)
Thomas, earl of Stafford		
from	16 October 1386	*IPM XVI*, no. 453
to	4 July 1392	*IPM XVII*, no. 214 (R.I.P.)
William, brother of Thomas earl of Stafford		
from	4 July 1392	*IPM XVII*, no. 214
to	6 April 1395	*IPM XVII*, no. 1261 (R.I.P.)
Edmund, earl of Stafford, brother of above		
from	6 April 1395	*IPM XVII*, no. 1261
to	21 July 1403	*IPM XVIII*, no. 829 (R.I.P.)
Humphrey, son of above		
from	21 July 1403	*IPM XVIII*, no. 829
Queen Joan		
from	24 January 1404	*CPR 1401–1405*, p. 347

Constables

Ralph Basset, P.P.		
from	1 November 1317	*CFR 1307–1319*, p. 344

Wardships

Minority of Thomas, earl of Stafford (1386–1389)

Thomas de Beauchamp, earl of Warwick and William Beauchamp and John lord Neville		
from	25 February 1387	*CFR 1383–1391*, p. 173

Minority of William, Brother of Thomas earl of Stafford (1392–1395)

William Walsall		
from	19 July 1392	*CPR 1391–1396*, p. 124
Thomas Woodstock, duke of Gloucester		
from	24 July 1392	*CFR 1391–1399*, p. 54

Minority of Edmund, earl of Stafford (1392–1399)

Thomas Woodstock, duke of Gloucester		
to	23 July 1397	*CFR 1391–1399*, p. 219
Edward, earl of Rutland, future duke of York		
from	23 July 1397	*CFR 1391–1399*, p. 219

TAMWORTH

Owners

Philip Marmion		
on	19 June 1275	*CPR 1272–1281*, p. 120
to	5 December 1291	*IPM II*, no. 29 (R.I.P.)
Joan de Moreteyn, daughter of above		
to	3 January 1295	*CFR 1272–1307*, p. 368
to	13 August 1295	*IPM III*, no. 279 (R.I.P.)
Alexander de Freville (From his wife Joan)		
from	3 January 1295	*CFR 1272–1307*, p. 368
to	18 March 1328	*IPM VII*, no. 134 (R.I.P.)

Joan de Freville, widow of Alexander		
from	18 March 1328	*IPM VII*, no. 134 (Jointure)
to	27 October 1339	*IPM VIII*, no. 210 (R.I.P.)
Baldwin de Freville, kn., son of above		
from	27 October 1339	*IPM VIII*, no. 210
to	4 November 1343	*IPM VIII*, no. 445 (R.I.P.)
Baldwin de Freville, son of above		
from	4 November 1343	*IPM VIII*, no. 445
to	23 March 1375	*IPM XIV*, no. 136 (R.I.P.)
Baldwin de Freville, kn., son of above		
from	23 March 1375	*IPM XIV*, no. 136
to	30 December 1387	*IPM XVI*, no. 578
Baldwin de Freville, kn., son of above		
from	30 December 1387	*IPM XVI*, no. 578
to	4 October 1400	*IPM XVIII*, no. 422 (R.I.P.)
Baldwin, son of above		
from	4 October 1400	*IPM XVIII*, no. 422 (Age 5)

Wardships

minority of Baldwin, son of Baldwin de Freville, 1387–1389

Thomas Grene		
from	8 May 1388	*CFR 1383–1391*, p. 227

TUTBURY

Owners

Robert de Ferrers		
in	13 November 1278	*CCR 1272–1279*, p. 486
Edmund, earl of Lancaster		
on	5 May 1277	*CPR 1272–1281*, p. 202
on	13 November 1278	*CCR 1272–1279*, p. 486
not by	3 July 1297	*IPM III*, no. 423 (R.I.P.)
Confiscated from Lancaster		
before	12 March 1322	*CFR 1319–1327*, p. 106
John of Eltham to hold after Edward II's death		
from	9 July 1322	*CChR 1319–1327*, p. 448
Thomas, earl of Lancaster		
writ	5 February 1327	*IPM VII*, no. 82
Henry, earl of Lancaster		
heir on	5 February 1327	*IPM VII*, no. 82
on	23 April 1327	*CCR 1327–1330*, p. 78
Henry, duke of Lancaster		
on	16 March 1361	*CPR 1358–1361*, p. 575
John of Gaunt, earl of Lancaster		
from	1361	DL.27/242
from	18 November 1361	*CPR 1361–1364*, p. 118
on	23 July 1381	*JGR 1379–1383*, no. 569
Henry Bolingbroke, future Henry IV		
on	18 October 1388	*CPR 1396–1399*, p. 547

Constables

Ralph Basset of Drayton		
from	12 March 1322	*CFR 1319–1327*, p. 106
to	24 March 1322	*CFR 1319–1327*, p. 118

Roger Beler		
from	24 March 1322	*CFR 1319–1327*, p. 118
to	4 July 1323	*CFR 1319–1327*, p. 220
John de Leke		
from	4 July 1323	*CFR 1319–1327*, p. 220
accounting	13 March 1327	*CMR*, no. 77
Henry, earl of Lancaster		
from	7 December 1326	*CFR 1319–1327*, p. 424
Walter Blount, kn.		
confirmed	26 April 1399	*CPR 1396–1399*, p. 547
on	21 January 1400	*CPR 1399–1401*, p. 330 (For life)
Private Constables		
Philip de Barrington		
in	1313–1314	Somerville, p. 352
to	1322	Somerville, p. 352
Walter Blount, kn.		
for life from	8 January 1373	*JGR 1372–1376*, no. 606
from	18 October 1388	*CPR 1396–1399*, p. 547
Porter		
John de Haytefeld		
from	22 July 1381	*JGR 1379–1383*, no. 987
on	23 July 1381	*JGR 1379–1383*, no. 569
Chaplain		
John de Tamworth		
dead by	19 February 1380	*JGR 1379–1383*, no. 239

TYRLEY

History		
mentioned	1281 as incomplete	King, p. 452

Suffolk

Unknown Licenses

HERKESTEDE for Nicholas Bonde		
	12 April 1335	*CPR 1334–1338*, p. 96
HUNTYNGFELD for Michael de la Pole, elder		
	27 April 1385	*CPR 1381–1385*, p. 555
LE PONDE at HADDELEGH for Helming Leget		
	1 March 1371	*CPR 1370–1374*, p. 54
SMALBRIGG in ST MARY BURES for Richard Waldegrave		
	10 May 1384	*CPR 1381–1385*, p. 410
STERNEFELD for Michael de la Pole, elder		
	27 April 1385	*CPR 1381–1385*, p. 555

BUNGAY

Owners

Roger le Bygod, earl of Norfolk and Marshal		
license	20 April 1294	*CPR 1292–1301*, p. 68
to	6 December 1306	*IPM IV*, no. 434 (R.I.P.)
Crown, as has no heir		
from	6 December 1306	*IPM IV*, no. 434
Alice, widow of Roger le Bygod, as part of dower portion		
from	20 February 1307	*CFR 1272–1307*, p. 551
Thomas of Brotherton, earl of Norfolk		
on	24 October 1317	*CCR 1313–1318*, p. 504
Edward de Montague, P.P.		
to	14 July 1361	*IPM XI*, no. 140 (R.I.P.)
Joan, his da., and William de Ufford, her husband		
from	14 July 1361	*IPM XI*, no. 140
William de Ufford, earl of Suffolk		
to	15 February 1382	*IPM XV*, no. 605 (R.I.P.)
Margaret Marshal, countess of Norfolk, da. of Thomas of Brotherton		
from	15 February 1382	*IPM XV*, no. 605

CLARE

Owners

Gilbert de Clare		
to	14 December 1295	*IPM III*, no. 371 (R.I.P.)
Joan, widow of Gilbert Clare		
to	1 May 1307	*IPM IV*, no. 435 (R.I.P.)
Gilbert de Clare, son of above		
from	1 May 1307	*IPM IV*, no. 435
to	10 July 1314	*IPM V*, no. 538 (R.I.P.)
Roger Damory, P.P., husband of Elizabeth, third daughter of above		
from	15 November 1317	*IPM VI*, no. 129
Elizabeth de Burgo		
to	4 November 1360	*IPM X*, no. 637 (R.I.P.)

John Bardolf, P.P., from Elizabeth da. of above,		
from	4 November 1360	*IPM X*, no. 637
Lionel, duke of Clarence		
to	17 October 1368	*IPM XII*, no. 332 (R.I.P.)
Philippa, da. of above		
from	17 October 1368	*IPM XII*, no. 332
Edmund Mortimer, earl of March and Ulster		
to	27 December 1381	*IPM XV*, no. 555 (R.I.P.)
Roger Mortimer, earl of March, son of above		
from	27 December 1381	*IPM XV*. no. 555
under age	21 January 1381	*CPR*, p. 88
to	20 July 1398	*IPM XVII*, no. 1191 (R.I.P.)
Edmund Mortimer, earl of March, son of above		
from	20 July 1398	*IPM XVII*, no. 1191
on	16 October 1414	*CPR 1413–1416*, p. 291

Constables

John de Haustede, P.P.		
from	19 November 1321	*CFR 1319–1327*, p. 79
to	13 May 1322	*CFR 1319–1327*, p. 129
Robert de Bures		
from	13 May 1322	*CFR 1319–1327*, p. 129
on	25 August 1322	*CCR 1318–1323*, p. 592
William Aylemer		
on	12 July 1371	*CPR 1370–1374*, p. 173
on	20 October 1373	*CPR 1370–1374*, p. 400

Private Constables

John de Toucester		
temp	1273–1274	Denholm–Young, p. 42

Wardships

Minority of Roger Mortimer, earl of March, 1381–1395

Adam Ramsey		
from	21 January 1381	*CPR 1381–1385*, p. 88
Thomas de Beauchamp, earl of Warwick, Roger Mortimer, earl of March, John lord Neville and Henry Percy, earl of Northumberland		
from	16 December 1383	*CFR 1383–1391*, p. 22

minority Edmund Mortimer, earl of March, 1398–1412

Edward, duke of York		
from	11 August 1398	*CPR 1396–1399*, p. 408
Henry Percy, earl of Northumberland		
from	2 March 1400	*CFR 1399–1405*, p. 50
Thomas Swynburn, kn.		
from	27 November 1401	*CPR 1401–1405*, p. 16
Elmyng Leget, esq.		
from	30 July 1403	*CPR 1401–1405*, p. 258
Thomas Erpyngham, kn.		
from	12 November 1403	*CFR 1401–1405*, p. 233
Henry, Prince of Wales		
from	15 June 1409	*CFR 1408–1413*, p. 151

EYE

Owners

Margaret, widow of Edmund, earl of Cornwall		
dower	12 February 1301	*CCR 1296–1302*, p. 426
Margaret, countess of Cornwall		
on	20 December 1316	*CPR 1313–1317*, p. 576
with Audley	13 May 1317	*CPR 1313–1317*, p. 664
before	23 July 1318	*CCR 1318–1323*, p. 3
Hugh de Audley, earl of Gloucester, husband of above		
by	23 July 1318	*CCR 1318–1323*, p. 3
to	20 July 1319	*CFR 1319–1327*, p. 2
Royal		
from	20 July 1319	*CFR 1319–1327*, p. 2
Queen Isabella		
from	6 November 1319	*CPR 1317–1321*, p. 400
on	12 April 1330	*CPR 1327–1330*, p. 512
John de Eltham		
from	1 December 1330	*CPR 1330–1334*, p. 51
from	4 December 1330	*CChR 1327–1341*, p. 198
Robert de Ufford, earl of Suffolk		
from	26 March 1337	*CCR 1337–1339*, p. 60
on	1 August 1348	*CPR 1348–1350*, p. 137
to	4 November 1369	*IPM XII*, no. 424 (R.I.P.)
William de Ufford, earl of Suffolk, son of above		
from	4 November 1369	*IPM XII*, no. 424
to	15 February 1382	*IPM XV*, no. 606 (R.I.P.)
Crown		
probably from	15 February 1382	*IPM XV*, no. 606
Queen Anne		
for life from	24 May 1382	*CPR 1381–1385*, p. 125
on	5 January 1391	*CPR 1366–1392*, p. 359
Michael de la Pole, earl of Suffolk (d.1389)		
forfeited before	5 January 1391	*CPR 1388–1392*, p. 359
dead by	12 July 1398	*CCR 1396–1399*, p. 318
Michael de la Pole, earl of Suffolk, son of above)		
from	12 July 1398	*CCR 1396–1399*, p. 318
on	27 January 1405	*IMisc VII*, no. 316
dead by	1 March 1416	*CCR 1413–1419*, p. 263
Elizabeth, widow of above		
from	1 March 1416	*CCR 1413–1419*, p. 263

Constables

Roger de Morwode		
from	28 November 1312	*CFR 1307–1319*, p. 152
Gilbert de Risheton		
from	18 September 1313	*CFR 1307–1319*, p. 179
to	20 December 1316	*CPR 1313–1317*, p. 578 (Ryston)
Nicholas de Fayrford		
from	6 July 1318	*CFR 1307–1319*, p. 365
Aymer de Boteville		
from	16 October 1318	*CPR 1317–1321*, p. 218

John Stillego		
on	12 April 1330	*CPR 1327–1330*, p. 512
on	12 December 1332	*CPR 1330–1334*, p. 378
Walter Fakoun		
to	1 December 1330	*CPR 1330–1334*, p. 51
Bartholomew de Burghersh, snr., P.P. and William de Cusancia		
to	26 March 1337	*CCR 1337–1339*, p. 60
Robert Bucton, esq.		
for life from	29 September 1394	*CPR 1391–1396*, p. 495

Wardships

After the death of Michael de la Pole (1415–1416)

Robert Bolton and William Phelyp and Thomas Erpyngham		
from	8 December 1415	*CPR 1413–1416*, p. 383
to	1 February 1416	*CCR 1413–1419*, p. 263

FRAMLINGHAM

Owners

Roger le Bygod, earl of Norfolk and Marshal		
to	6 December 1306	*IPM IV*, no. 434 (R.I.P.)
Crown, as has no heir		
from	6 December 1305	*IPM IV*, no. 434
Thomas Brotherton, earl of Norfolk		
from	12 May 1338	*CPR 1338–1340*, p. 61 (And heirs)
Mary, countess of Norfolk		
from	16 December 1338	*CCR 1337–1339*, p. 582
to	9 June 1362	*IPM XI*, no. 397 (R.I.P.)
William de Ufford, earl of Suffolk husband of Joan, second heir		
from	1 August 1362	*CFR 1356–1368*, p. 218
from	12 February 1363	*CCR 1360–1364*, p. 444
to	15 February 1382	*IPM XV*, no. 605 (R.I.P.)
Margaret Marshal, duchess of Norfolk, da. of Thomas de Brotherton, earl of Norfolk		
from	15 February 1382	*IPM XV*, no. 605
to	24 March 1399	*IPM XVII*, no. 258 (R.I.P.)
Thomas de Mowbray, earl Marshal, great grandson of above		
from	24 March 1399	*IPM XVII*, no. 258 (Age 14)
Elizabeth, widow of Thomas duke of Norfolk		
livery	10 July 1400	*CCR 1399–1402*, p. 165
to	5 December 1400	*CPR 1399–1401*, p. 392
Thomas de Mowbray, earl Marshal, as two above		
from	5 December 1400	*CPR 1399–1401*, p. 392 (Under age)
to	4 June 1405	*IPM XVIII*, no. 310 (R.I.P.)
forfeited by	12 June 1405	*CPR 1405–1408*, p. 26
Crown		
on	6 October 1405	*CPR 1405–1408*, p. 86
John de Mowbray, brother of above		
from	4 June 1405	*IPM XVIII*, no. 310

Constables

John de Thord		
to	18 March 1308	*CFR 1307–1319*, p. 19

Walter de Muncy, P.P.		
from	18 March 1308	*CFR 1307–1319*, p. 19
dead by	*29 September 1308*	*GEC IX, p. 427*
John de Thorpe		
to	1 October 1311	*CFR 1307–1319*, p. 103
John Botetourt, P.P.		
from	1 October 1311	*CFR 1307–1319*, p. 103
Simon Felbrigg, kn.		
from	4 April 1399	
confirmed	19 June 1399	*CPR 1396–1399*, p. 580
Thomas Erpyngham, kn.		
for life from	12 November 1399	*CPR 1399–1401*, p. 93
on	25 March 1401	*CCR 1399–1402*, p. 334 (Farmer or occupier)
John Lancaster		
on	6 October 1405	*CPR 1405–1408*, p. 86

Private Constables

William atte Lee		
from	10 May 1382	
confirmed	24 August 1384	*CPR 1381–1385*, p. 456

Constables while in Crown hands after forfeiture of Thomas de Mowbray, earl Marshal

Henry Prince of Wales		
from	12 June 1405	*CPR 1405–1408*, p. 26

Wardships

Minority of Thomas de Mowbray, earl Marshal, 1399–1405

Thomas Erpyngham		
for life from	12 November 1399	*CPR 1399–1401*, p. 93
on	1 January 1402	*CPR 1401–1405*, p. 47

Farmers

Thomas Erpyngham, king's knight		
on	25 March 1401	*CPR 1399–1401*, p. 474

METTINGHAM

Tenant in Chief

John de Lynne, Clerk		
on	21 June 1366	*IPM XII*, no. 27

Owners

John de Norwich		
licence to crenellate	21 August 1343	*CPR 1343–1345*, p. 106
died	*15 August 1362*	*GEC IX, p. 763*
not by	30 August 1362	*CCR 1360–1364*, p. 355
Margery, widow of above		
by	21 June 1366	*IPM XII*, no. 27 (R.I.P.)
John de Norwich, kn., grandson of above		
from	21 June 1366	*IPM XII*, no. 27
to	December 1373	*IPM XIV*, no. 43 (R.I.P.)
Katherine de Brews, his heir and kinswoman		
from	December 1373	*IPM XIV*, no. 43

The chantry of John de Norwich at Norton Soupecers		
from	6 August 1387	*CPR 1385–1389*, p. 344

ORFORD

Owners

Queen Eleanor of Castile		
from	22 October 1275	*CCR 1272–1279*, p. 192
Robert de Ufford		
to	9 September 1298	*IPM III*, no. 469 (R.I.P.)
Robert de Ufford, P.P. son of above		
from	9 September 1298	*IPM III*, no. 469
died	*9 September 1316*	*GEC XII (ii), p. 150*
John de Sturmy		
on	20 April 1327	*CMR*, no. 45
not by	18 January 1331	*CPR 1330–1334*, p. 41
Robert de Ufford, earl of Suffolk		
from	1 May 1330	*CPR 1327–1330*, p. 522
and from	21 March 1336	*CFR 1327–1337*. p. 475
to	4 November 1369	*IPM XII*, no. 424 (R.I.P.)
William de Ufford, earl of Suffolk, son of above		
from	4 November 1369	*IPM XII*, no. 424
to	15 February 1382	*IPM XV*, no. 606 (R.I.P.)
Michael de la Pole, earl of Suffolk		
on	14 June 1382	*CCR 1381–1385*, p. 65
'held'	May/June 1388	*IMisc V*, no. 56
Countess of Suffolk		
on	20 September 1395	*CPR 1391–1396*, p. 659
Michael de la Pole, earl of Suffolk		
on	23 February 1400	*CCR 1399–1402*, p. 49
on	24 November 1403	*CPR 1401–1405*, p. 331
dead by	1 February 1416	*CCR 1413–1419*, p. 263
Elizabeth, widow of above		
from	1 February 1416	*CCR 1413–1419*, p. 263
Robert de Willoughby, P.P.		
from	16 November 1416	*CFR 1413–1422*, p. 180

Constables

Hugh de Digneton		
from	3 March 1274	*CPR 1272–1281*, p. 44
to	15 May 1275	*CPR 1272–1281*, p. 89
Robert de Ufford		
from	15 May 1275	*CPR 1272–1281*, p. 89
to	17 May 1276	*CPR 1272–1281*, p. 141
Richard de Holebrok		
from	17 May 1276	*CPR 1272–1281*, p. 141
to	27 June 1280	*CPR 1272–1281*, p. 384
Robert de Ufford		
from	27 June 1280	*CPR 1272–1281*, p. 384
for life from	28 December 1280	*CPR 1272–1281*, p. 421
Roger le Bygod, earl of Norfolk		
for life from	4 October 1304	*CPR 1301–1307*, p. 261
for life from	4 October 1304	*CCR 1302–1307*, p. 177

Nicholas de Segrave of Barton Segrave, P.P.		
to	7 October 1315	*CFR 1307–1319*, p. 262
William de Cleidon		
from	7 October 1315	*CFR 1307–1319*, p. 262
John de Sturmy		
from	2 August 1317	*CFR 1307–1319*, p. 337
and from	1 August 1318	*CFR 1307–1319*, p. 371

Wardships

After the death of Michael de la Pole (1415–1416)

Robert Bolton and William Phelyp and Thomas Erpyngham		
from	8 December 1415	*CPR 1413–1416*, p. 383
to	1 February 1416	*CCR 1413–1419*, p. 263

WINGFIELD

Owners

Michael de la Pole, elder		
licence to crenellate	27 April 1385	*CPR 1381–1385*, p. 555

Surrey

BETCHWORTH

Owners

John de Arundel, kn., P.P.		
licence to crenellate	26 July 1379	*CPR 1377–1381*, p. 380

FARNHAM

Owners

Owned by bishops of Winchester for entire period		
on	29 January 1269	*CLibR 1267–1272*, no. 579
void	6 August 1323	*CCR 1323–1327*, p. 132
on	5 January 1369	*CCR 1369–1374*, p. 502

GUILDFORD

Owners

Crown – Queen Eleanor of Provence		
from	1272	*HKW II*, p. 658
to	1291	*HKW II*, p. 658
Crown – Queen Margaret		
from	10 September 1299	*CPR 1292–1301*, p. 451
to	1317	*HKW II*, p. 658
Crown – Queen Isabella		
from	1327	*HKW II* p. 658
to	1330	*HKW II* p. 658

Constables

Oliver de Burdegala, king's yeoman		
on	25 September 1318	*CCR 1318–1323*, p. 11
from	13 January 1331	*CFR 1327–1337*, p. 219
John de Brocas		
for life from	20 November 1335	*CFR 1327–1337*, p. 464
Hugh Bouscy, with Surrey and Sussex		
to	3 January 1342	*CFR 1337–1347*, p. 256
Andrew Peverel, with Surrey and Sussex		
from	3 January 1342	*CFR 1337–1347*, p. 256
John de Brocas		
on	28 June 1359	*CPR 1358–1361*, p. 235 (Keeper)
Andrew de Sakevill, sheriff of Surrey and Sussex		
from	25 September 1367	*CPR 1367–1370*, p. 15
Robert Echyngham		
on	16 April 1391	*CPR 1388–1392*, p. 389 (Unwilling)

REIGATE

Owners

John de Warenne, earl of Surrey		
on	26 November 1302	*CCR 1302–1307*, p. 1
died	*1304*	
John de Warenne, earl of Surrey		
to king and back	1 July 1316	*CPR 1313–1317*, p. 483
to	30 June 1347	*IPM IX*, no. 54 (R.I.P.)
dead by	6 July 1347	*CFR 1347–1356*, p. 39
Joan de Bar, widow of above		
jointure	24 August 1347	*CCR 1346–1349*, p. 314
Richard, earl of Arundel		
granted reversion	12 December 1346	*CPR 1345–1348*, p. 221
on	12 April 1366	*CPR 1364–1367*, p. 237
died	*1376*	
Richard, earl of Arundel, son of above		
on	19 November 1386	*IMisc IV*, no. 367
to	1397	L.D. Duls, *Richard II in the Early Chronicles*, The Hague, 1975, p. 73
Seized by King		
on	14 July 1397	*CFR 1391–1399*, p. 219
John de Holland, earl of Huntingdon, duke of Exeter		
from	15 January 1399	*CPR 1396–1399*, p. 467 (Tail male)

Constables while in Kings hands

William de Arundel		
from	13 July 1397	*CCR 1396–1399*, p. 138
for life from	7 October 1397	*CPR 1396–1399*, p. 207 (+Porter)
on	20 May 1398	*CPR 1396–1399*, p. 354
John Fethere of Reigate, gentilman		
on	April/May 1415	*IMisc VII*, no. 566

STERBOROUGH

Owners

Reynold de Cobham of Sterborough, P. P.		
licence to crenellate	18 October 1341	*CPR 1340–1343*, p. 304
died	*5 October 1361*	*GEC III, p. 353*
Reynold de Cobham, Lord Sterborough, P.P.		
inherited	*5 October 1361*	*GEC III, p. 353*
seisen	*5 February 1370*	*GEC III, p. 353*
on	18 June 1404	*CCR 1405–1409*, p. 469

Sussex

Unknown Licenses

BATTLE ABBEY for the Abbot		
	9 June 1338	*CPR 1338–1340*, p. 92
BURNE for Matthias de Monte Martini		
	24 April 1307	*CPR 1301–1307*, p. 522
DACHESHAM for Thomas Tregoz, P.P.		
	30 September 1329	*CPR 1327–1330*, p. 495
LA MOTE for Edmund de Passeleye		
	10 December 1318	*CPR 1317–1321*, p. 255
PERCHYNG for Robert de Ardern		
	25 January 1329	*CPR 1327–1330*, p. 357
PETTEWORTH for Henry Percy		
	4 October 1308	*CPR 1307–1313*, p. 144

AMBERLEY

Owners

Bishop of Chichester		
licence to crenellate	10 December 1377	*CPR 1377–1381*, p. 76

ARUNDEL

Owners

Richard fitz Alan, earl of Arundel		
on	2 June 1285	*CPR 1281–1292*, p. 169
to	15 January 1302	*IPM IV*, no. 90 (R.I.P.)
Edmund, earl of Arundel, son of above		
from	15 January 1302	*IPM IV*, no. 90
before	26 Feb. 1327	*CPR 1324–1327*, p. 332
Edmund de Woodstock, earl of Kent		
from	27 February 1327	*CChR 1300–1326*, p. 4
from	26 Feb. 1327	*CPR 1324–1327*, p. 332
forfeited by	20 March 1330	*CCR 1330–1333*, p. 14
dead by	20 December 1330	*IPM VII*, no. 300 (R.I.P.)
Queen Isabella		
for life from	3 April 1330	*CPR 1327–1330*, p. 519
Richard, earl of Arundel		
from	16 October 1331	*CPR 1330–1334*, p. 194
foot of fine	2 November 1354	*Feet of fines relating to Wiltshire* Wiltshire Record Society 29 (1973), no. 421
Richard, earl of Arundel		
on	9 July 1381	*CPR 1381–1385*, p. 73
forfeited by	24 October 1397	*IMisc VI*, no. 369
Seized by King		
on	13 July 1397	*CFR 1391–1399*, p. 219

John de Holland, duke of Exeter		
from	28 September 1397	*CPR 1396–1399*, p. 360 (Tail Male)

Constables

Robert de Aguillon		
on	8 September 1272	*CLibR 1267–1272*, no. 2079
to	28 October 1274	*CFR 1272–1307*, p. 33
William de Hevere		
from	28 October 1274	*CFR 1272–1307*, p. 33
to	7 November 1275	*CFR 1272–1307*, p. 57
John de Wauton		
from	7 November 1275	*CFR 1272–1307*, p. 57
to	13 December 1276	*CFR 1272–1307*, p. 70
Ralph de Sandwich		
from	13 December 1276	*CFR 1272–1307*, p. 70
Henry de Novo Burgo / Heuburg		
on	29 July 1278	*CCR 1272–1279*, p. 470
to	25 March 1279	*CFR 1272–1307*, p. 109 (R.I.P.)
Emeric de Cancellis		
from	25 March 1279	*CFR 1272–1307*, p. 109
Edmund de Woodstock, earl of Kent		
on	2 December 1326	*CCR 1323–1327*, p. 622

Constable while in King's hands

Robert de Aguillon		
on	8 September 1272	*CLibR 1267–1272*, no. 2079
Roger atte Assh		
from	16 March 1330	*CFR 1327–1337*, p. 166
on	8 December 1330	*CCR 1330–1333*, p. 80
John de Holland, duke of Exeter		
from	13 July 1397	*CFR 1391–1399*, p. 219
on	29 September 1397	*CCR 1396–1399*, p. 159
John Assheburnham		
on	30 August 1403	*CPR 1401–1405*, p. 286

Wardships

minority of Richard fitzAlan, earl of Arundel, –1288

Henry de Novo Burgo		
from	29 July 1278	*CPR 1272–1281*, p. 275
Emeric de Cancellis		
from	25 March 1279	*CPR 1272–1281*, p. 306
to	27 May 1280	*CPR 1272–1281*, p. 374
Isabella widow of John fitzAlan, lord of Arundel		
from	27 May 1280	*CPR 1272–1281*, p. 374
Isabella Mortimer		
to	8 August 1282	*CPR 1281–1292*, p. 32
Edmund Mortimer		
from	8 August 1282	*CPR 1281–1282*, p. 32
Isabella Mortimer		
to	2 June 1285	*CPR 1281–1292*, p. 169
Robert Burnel. bishop of Bath and Wells		
from	2 June 1285	*CPR 1281–1292*, p. 169

BODIAM

Owners

Edward Dalyngrugge		
licence to crenellate	21 October 1385	*CPR 1385–1389*, p. 42
John Dalyngrugge, kn.		
granted away	25 January 1396	*CCR 1392–1396*, p. 499
on	3 May 1398	*CPR 1396–1399*, p. 341

BRAMBER

Owners

William de Brewose, kn., P.P.		
on	21 March 1291	*CCR 1281–1292*, p. 195
to crown for life	5 September 1324	*CPR 1324–1327*, p. 21
Crown		
by	5 September 1324	*CPR 1324–1327*, p. 21
John de Mowbray of Axholme, P.P. through his wife Aline, eldest da. of William de Brewose		
to	4 October 1361	*IPM XI*, no. 144 (R.I.P.)
John de Mowbray of Axholme, P.P. son of above		
from	4 October 1361	*IPM XI*, no. 144
to	17 June 1368	*IPM XII*, no. 397 (R.I.P.)
John de Mowbray of Axholme, , earl of Nottingham		
from	17 June 1368	*IPM XII*, no. 397
died	*1383*	
Thomas de Mowbray, duke of Norfolk		
on	16 September 1398	*IMisc VI*, no. 390
to	22 September 1399	*IPM XVII*, no. 288
Thomas de Mowbray, earl Marshall, son of above		
from	22 September 1399	*IPM XVII*, no. 288
to	4 June 1405	*IPM XVIII*, no. 300 (R.I.P.)
forfeited by	11 June 1405	*CPR 1405–1408*, p. 26
John de Mowbray, brother of above		
from	4 June 1405	*IPM XVIII*, no. 300

Wardships

Minority of John Mowbray of Axholme, earl of Nottingham, 1368–1383

Henry Percy, earl of Northumberland		
on	5 November 1378	*CPR 1377–1381*, p. 293

Minority of Thomas de Mowbray, earl Marshal (1399–1405)

Thomas Tutbury		
from	1 November 1399	*CFR 1399–1405*, p. 29
Richard Burgh, John de Lancaster, John Lewes, Richard fitz Nicholl, John Rome, John Staverton, Thomas Burham		
from	10 May 1403	*CFR 1399–1405*, p. 209

After death of Thomas de Mowbray, earl Marshal

John Dalyngrugge		
from	11 June 1405	*CPR 1405–1408*, p. 26
dead by	6 October 1408	*CPR 1408–1413*, p. 3
Richard fitz Nichol		
from	6 October 1408	*CPR 1408–1413*, p. 3

Minority of John, brother of Thomas de Mowbray, earl Marshal

Nicholas Ledewichh, Richard Steresacre and John Wilcotes		
from	12 March 1410	*CFR 1405–1413*, p. 200

Constables for the Mowbrays

John de Derby		
from	20 February 1362	
confirmed	28 April 1369	*CPR 1367–1370*, p. 240
on	8 October 1371	*CCR 1369–1374*, p. 253
Richard fitz Nichol		
temp	1404	*CPR 1408–1413*, p. 3

HASTINGS

Constables

William de Dover		
to	8 April 1301	*CFR 1272–1307*, p. 440
Stephen Sprot		
from	8 April 1301	*CFR 1272–1307*, p. 440
on	9 April 1301	*CCR 1296–1302*, p. 442
Richard de Elsefeld		
from	2 November 1312	*CFR 1307–1319*, p. 152
to	10 August 1325	*CFR 1319–1327*, p. 357
Robert de Holden		
from	10 August 1325	*CFR 1319–1327*, p. 357
William de Percy		
from	6 July 1339	*CPR 1337–1347*, p. 271

Chapel

Edmund de London		
on	15 September 1321	*CPR 1321–1324*, p. 24

LEWES

Owners

John de Warenne, earl of Surrey		
to king and back	1 July 1316	*CPR 1313–1317*, p. 483
to	30 June 1347	*IPM IX*, no. 54 (R.I.P.)
dead by	6 July 1347	*CFR 1347–1356*, p. 39
Richard earl of Arundel		
granted reversion	12 December 1346	*CPR 1345–1348*, p. 221
from	30 June 1347	*IPM IX*, no. 54
Joan de Bars, widow of Warenne		
jointure	24 August 1347	*CCR 1346–1349*, p. 314
Richard, earl of Arundel		
on	23 January 1366	*CPR 1364–1367*, p. 198 (Granted out..)
on	12 April 1366	*CPR 1364–1367*, p. 237 (..and back)
Richard, earl of Arundel, son of above		
on	9 July 1381	*CPR 1381–1385*, p. 73
on	19 November 1386	*IMisc IV*, no. 367
Thomas de Mowbray, earl Marshal, earl of Nottingham		
from	28 September 1397	*CPR 1396–1399*, p. 220 (Tail Male)
John Holland, earl of Huntingdon, duke of Exeter		
tail male from	23 September 1398	*CPR 1396–1399*, pp. 421, 458

Constables

Thomas de Mowbray, earl of Nottingham		
from	26 July 1397	*CPR 1396–1399*, p. 175
to	28 September 1397	*CPR 1396–1399*, p. 220

PEVENSEY

Owners

Queen Margaret		
from	10 September 1299	
confirmed	19 March 1310	*CPR 1307–1313*, p. 216
Queen Isabella		
on	20 April 1327	*CMR*, no. 49
Queen Philippa		
on	12 March 1339	*CPR 1338–1340*, p. 208
on	19 July 1364	*CPR 1364–1367*, p. 9
John of Gaunt, duke of Lancaster		
from	25 June 1372	W. Hardy, *Charters of the Duchy of Lancaster*, London, 1845, p. 28
on	6 October 1395	Somerville p. 380
Katherine, widow of John of Gaunt		
from	9 March 1398	*CCR 1396–1399*, p. 365
from	9 March 1399	*CPR 1396–1399*, p. 516

Constables

Walter de Berstan		
to	8 June 1294	*CFR 1272–1307*, p. 339
to	8 June 1294	*CPR 1292–1301*, p. 71
William de Leybourne, P.P.		
from	8 June 1294	*CFR 1272–1307*, p. 339
from	8 June 1294	*CPR 1292–1301*, p. 71
Robert de Kendal		
to	13 August 1312	*CPR 1307–1313*, p. 485
Robert de Sapy		
from	27 July 1312	*CFR 1307–1319*, p. 141
for life from	3 October 1319	*CFR 1319–1327*, p. 5
on	3 July 1336	*CCR 1333–1337*, p. 601
Henry Romyn (For Queen)		
from	12 March 1339	*CPR 1338–1340*, p. 208
John de Saham, queen's yeoman, (For Queen)		
from	25 August 1351	
confirmed	10 January 1352	*CPR 1350–1354*, p. 195
Nicholas de Lovaigne		
for life from	19 July 1364	*CPR 1364–1367*, p. 9 (For Queen)
on	26 June 1372	*CPR 1370–1374*, p. 183
Roger Newent		
on	15 July 1396	*CPR 1396–1399*, p. 14
John Pelham		
on	7 October 1405	*CCR 1405–1409*, p. 2
on	27 May 1422	*CCR 1419–1422*, p. 242

Private Constables

Nicholas Loveyne		
to	3 December 1372	*JGR 1372–1376*, no. 1110

John de Colpeper, esq.		
from	3 December 1372	*JGR 1372–1376*, no. 1110
on	21 May 1379	Somerville p. 380
not by	22 June 1380	*JGR 1379–1383*, no. 1099
William Batesford		
from	22 June 1380	*JGR 1379–1383*, no. 1099
John de Colpeper		
for life from	3 December 1381	*JGR 1379–1383*, no. 1106
Roger Newent		
on	8 July 1389	
John Pelham		
on	6 October 1395	Somerville p. 380

Guards

William de Fyenes and William de Batteston		
on	22 June 1381	*CPR 1381–1385*, p. 72

Porter

John de Winchester		
for life from	13 August 1372	*JGR 1372–1376*, no. 452

SEDGEWICK

Owners

John le Savage		
to	1272	G.C.E. Dudley, and C.J. Robinson, *A History of the Castles, Mansions and Manors of West Sussex* London, 1879, p. 5
William de Brewose II, peaceful exchange with above		
from	1272	*ibid.*
died	1290	*ibid.*
William de Brewose III		
from	1290	*ibid.*
to	1326	*ibid.*
Brawose family		
to	Sixteenth Century	*ibid.*

Warwickshire

Unknown Licenses

LANGELE for Edmund de Bereford, king's clerk		
	7 October 1327	*CPR 1327–1330*, p. 179

ASTLEY

History

licensed	1266	King, p. 480

ASTON CANTLOW

History

mentioned	1274	King, p. 481

BAGINTON

Owners

Sir William Bagot		
in	1398	King, p. 487, n.4

BEAUDESERT

Tenant in Chief

William de Beauchamp, earl of Warwick		
on	11 May 1296	*IPM III*, no. 364
Thomas de Beauchamp, earl of Warwick		
foot of fine	20 October 1361	*Feet of fines relating to Wiltshire*, Wiltshire Record Society 29 (1973), no. 495
to	13 November 1369	*IPM XII*, no. 326 (R.I.P.)
Thomas de Beauchamp, son of above		
from	13 November 1369	*IPM XII*, no. 326

Owners

John de Montfort, P.P.		
to	11 May 1296	*IPM III*, no. 364 (From Beauchamp)
John de Montfort, son of above, P.P.		
from	11 May 1296	*IPM III*, no. 364
died	*24 June 1314*	*GEC IX, p. 128*
Walter de Langeton, bishop of Coventry and Lichfield		
license to cren.	16 September 1306	*CPR 1301–1307*, p. 462
Thomas de Beauchamp, earl of Warwick		
on	29 July 1361	*CPR 1361–1364*, p. 48

Peter de Montfort, P.P., son of John de Montfort above		
from	1350	
for life on	20 October 1361	*Feet of fines relating to Wiltshire*, Wiltshire Record Society 29 (1973), no. 495
on	13 November 1369	*IPM XII*, no. 326 (For life)
died	*24 January 1369/70*	*GEC IX, p. 128*
Baldwin de Freville, kn.,		
to	23 March 1375	*IPM XIV*, no. 136 (R.I.P.)
Baldwin de Freville, son of above		
from	23 March 1375	*IPM XIV*, no. 136
William Beauchamp, lord of Abergavenny, P.P.		
for life to	8 May 1411	*IPM XIX*, no. 846 (JB)
Richard de Beauchamp, earl of Warwick		
on	7 June 1412	*IMisc VII*, no. 434

BRANDON

T. in C.

Guy de Beauchamp, earl of Warwick		
on	28 August 1309	*IPM V*, no. 187

Owners

Theobald de Verdon, P.P.		
to	28 August 1309	*IPM V*, no. 187 (R.I.P.)
Theobald de Verdon, P.P. son of above		
from	28 August 1309	*IPM V*, no. 187

CALUDON

Owners

John de Segrave elder, P.P.		
licence to crenellate	2 February 1305	*CPR 1301–1307*, p. 314
Stephen de Segrave, son of above		
to	12 December 1325	*IPM VI*, no. 700 (R.I.P.)
John de Segrave, son of above		
from	12 December 1325	*IPM VI*, no. 700

CASTLE BROMWICH

History

modified	C14	King, p. 482

FILLONGLEY

Owners

John de Hastings, P.P.		
licence to crenellate	2 February 1301	*CPR 1292–1301*, p. 564
died	*1313*	*GEC I, p. 23*
John de Hastings, son of above, P.P.		
inherited	*1313*	*GEC I, p. 23*
to	27 January 1325	*IPM VI*, no. 612 (R.I.P.)
Laurence de Hastings, son of above		
heir on	27 January 1325	*IPM VI*, no. 612

Juliana, widow of John de Hastings		
dower	23 September 1325	*CCR 1323–1327*, p. 404

Minority of Laurence, son and heir of John de Hastings, 1325–1341

Roger Mortimer, earl of March		
from	29 July 1330	*CPR 1327–1330*, p. 546

KENILWORTH

Owners

Edmund, earl of Lancaster		
not by	3 July 1297	*IPM III*, no. 423 (R.I.P.)
Thomas, earl of Lancaster		
confiscated	12 March 1322	*CFR 1319–1327*, p. 107
writ	5 February 1327	*IPM VII*, no. 82
Henry, earl of Lancaster		
heir of	5 February 1327	*IPM VII.*, no. 82
Henry, duke of Lancaster		
on	18 September 1359	*CPR 1358–1361*, p. 264
to	23 March 1361	*IPM XI*, no. 118 (R.I.P.)
dead by	16 July 1361	*CFR 1356–1368*, p. 164
John of Gaunt, duke of Lancaster		
from	16 July 1361	*CFR 1356–1368*, p. 164
on	8 July 1391	*CPR 1388–1392*, p. 449

King's Stewards

John de Somery and Ralph Basset of Drayton		
from	12 March 1322	*CFR 1319–1327*, p. 107
Humphrey de Walden and Richard de Ikene		
from	8 March 1324	*CFR 1319–1327*, p. 259
Richard de Wynferthyng and Richard de Ikene		
from	20 August 1324	*CFR 1319–1327*, p. 295

Constable

Randolf Charun		
from	16 March 1322	*CFR 1319–1327*, p. 109
to	23 January 1323	*CPR 1321–1324*, p. 240
John de Hastings, P.P.		
to Easter from	23 January 1323	*CPR 1321–1324*, p. 240 (Keeper)
Randolf Charun		
to	11 March 1324	*CFR 1319–1327*, p. 259
Odo de Stoke		
from	11 March 1324	*CFR 1319–1327*, p. 259
on	12 February 1326	*CPR 1324–1327*, p. 241 (Eudo)

Private Constables

Richard de Wandeshaf		
before	26 November 1281	Somerville, p. 347
Nicholas de Eyton		
on	October 1298	J.R. Maddicott, *Thomas of Lancaster*, Oxford, 1970, p. 340
Walter de Bath		
from	October 1298	Maddicott, p. 340
Edmund de Wasteneys		
in	September 1307	Maddicott, p. 340

Ralph de Schepeye		
in	1313/14	Somerville, p. 350
Hugh Cuilly		
before	August 1322	Maddicott, p. 340
John Deyncourt (for Lancaster)		
on	11 January 1380	*JGR 1379–1383*, no. 208 (Esq.)
on	8 July 1391	*CPR 1388–1392*, p. 449

Lieutenant

John Herley		
on	18 April 1383	*JGR 1379–1383*, no. 880

Keeper of outlying woods

Rande de Tynneslowe		
on	11 February 1382	*JGR 1379–1383*, no. 668
on	18 April 1383	*JGR 1379–1383*, no. 880

Surveyor of works

John Herley		
on	4 December 1380	*JGR 1379–1383*, no. 1083
on	11 Fen 1382	*JGR 1379–1383*, no. 668
William Hales		
from	4 February 1382	*JGR 1379–1383*, no. 1110

KINGSBURY

History

built	C14	King, p. 483

MAXSTOKE

Tenants in Chief

John Dodyngselles, kn.		
to	4 December 1403	*IPM XVIII*, no. 902 (R.I.P.)
Edward, son of above.		
from	4 December 1403	*IPM XVIII*, no. 902

Owners

William de Clinton		
licence to crenellate	12 February 1345	*CPR 1343–1345*, p. 444
John de Clinton, nephew of above, P.P.		
from	12 February 1345	*CPR 1343–1345*, p. 444
to	6 September 1398	*IPM XVII*, no. 1140 (R.I.P.)
William de Clinton, grandson of two above, P.P.		
heir	6 September 1398	*IPM XVII*, no. 1140
holds reversion	4 December 1403	*IPM XVIII*, no. 902
Elizabeth, widow of three above, wife of John Russell		
on	12 February 1399	*CCR 1396–1399*, p. 433
on	4 December 1403	*IPM XVIII*, no. 902 (R.I.P.)

Notes

Broken into by Alex Ferour, Monday after close of Easter 30 Edw III (1356), pardoned 24 October 1357

CPR 1354–1358, p. 651

RAGLEY

Owners

John Rous		
licence to crenellate	8 December 1381	*CPR 1381–1385*, p. 64

WARWICK

Owners

William de Beauchamp, earl of Warwick		
to	12 June 1298	*IPM III*, no. 477 (R.I.P.)
Guy de Beauchamp, earl of Warwick, son of above		
from	12 June 1298	*IPM III*, no. 477
to	16 August 1315	*IPM V*, no. 615 (R.I.P.)
Thomas de Beauchamp, earl of Warwick, son of above		
from	16 August 1315	*IPM V*, no. 615
to	13 November 1369	*IPM XII*, no. 326 (R.I.P.)
Thomas de Beauchamp, earl of Warwick, son of above		
from	13 November 1369	*IPM XII*, no. 326
on	10 May 1393	*CCR 1392–1396*, p. 64
Thomas Holland, earl of Kent		
from	28 September 1397	*CPR 1396–1399*, p. 200 (Fee simple)
from	28 September 1397	*CPR 1396–1399*, p. 215 (Tail Male)
Thomas de Beauchamp, earl of Warwick		
to	8 April 1401	*IPM XVIII*, no. 509
Richard de Beauchamp, son of above		
from	8 April 1401	*IPM XVIII*, no. 509

In wardship for Beauchamps

Minority of Thomas de Beauchamp (1315–1335)

Walter de Beauchamp		
on	10 June 1317	*CPR 1313–1317*, p. 664
to	9 June 1321	*CFR 1319–1327*, p. 61
William de Sutton		
from	9 June 1321	*CFR 1319–1327*, p. 61
John Pecche		
from	6 November 1321	*CFR 1319–1327*, p. 76
on	23 July 1326	*CCR 1323–1327*, p. 592
Thomas le Blount		
from	25 July 1326	*CFR 1319–1327*, p. 403
to	18 October 1326	*CFR 1319–1327*, p. 421
Peter de Montfort		
from	18 October 1326	*CFR 1319–1327*, p. 421

Minority of Richard Beauchamp, earl of Warwick (aged 19 in 1401)

Thomas de Aldebury and William Beauchamp of Abergavenny and John Owdeby		
from	12 May 1401	*CFR 1399–1405*, p. 135

Constables

John de Clinton		
from	3 August 1397	*CPR 1396–1399*, p. 176

Under Constable

William de Sniton		
on	4 March 1322	*CCR 1318–1323*, p. 520

WEOLEY

Owners

Roger de Somery		
licence to crenellate	1264	King, p. 485
John Buttetourt, kn.		
to	4 April 1386	*IPM XVI*, no. 205
Hugh Burnell, kn. and Joyce his wife, daughter of above?		
from	4 Aprill 386	*IPM XVI*, no. 205
away and back	22 May 1386	*CPR 1385–1389*, p. 149
Joyce, wife of Hugh Burnell, kn.		
to	1 January 1407	*IPM XIX*, no. 264 (R.I.P.)
Hugh Burnell, above, kn., husband of Joyce, P.P.		
from	1 January 1407	*IPM XIX*, no. 264
livery	10 May 1407	*CCR 1405–1409*, p. 204

Westmorland

APPLEBY

Owners

Roger de Clifford, kn.		
on	3 January 1280	*IMisc I*, no. 1207
Isabel de Clifford, d. and heir of Robert de Veteri Ponti		
to	14 May 1292	*IPM III*, no. 70 (R.I.P.)
Robert de Clifford, son of above, P.P.		
from	14 May 1292	*IPM III*, no. 70
to	28 July 1314	*IPM V*, no. 533 (R.I.P.)
Roger de Clifford, son of above, P.P.		
from	28 July 1314	*IPM V*, no. 533
forfeited	8 February 1322	*CFR 1319–1327*, p. 94
Robert de Clifford, brother of above, P.P.		
restored	12 February 1327	*IPM VII*, no. 77
to	20 May 1344	*IPM VIII*, no. 531 (R.I.P.)
Robert de Clifford, son of above		
heir on	20 May 1344	*IPM VIII*, no. 531
died	*1345*	*GEC III, p. 292*
Roger de Clifford, kn., brother of above, P.P.		
inherited	*1345*	*GEC III, p. 292*
to	13 July 1389	*IPM XVI*, no. 836 (R.I.P.)
Thomas de Clifford, kn., son of above, P.P.		
from	13 July 1389	*IPM XVI*, no. 836
to	4 October 1391	*IPM XVI*, no. 13
John lord Clifford, son of above, P.P.		
from	4 October 1391	*IPM XVI*, no. 13
died	*13 March 1421/2*	*GEC III, p. 293*
Thomas de Clifford, son of above, P.P.		
inherited	*13 March 1421/2*	*GEC III, p. 293*
of age	*c.1435*	*GEC III, p. 293*
died	*22 May 1455*	*GEC III, p. 293*

Private Constables

Geoffrey de Melkengthorp		
on	3 January 1280	*IMisc I*, no. 1207

Constables while in Royal hands

Walter de Stirkeland		
from	31 October 1322	*CFR 1319–1327*, p. 182
to	30 December 1322	*CFR 1319–1327*, p. 193
Anthony de Lucy, P.P.		
from	30 December 1322	*CFR 1319–1327*, p. 193
to	3 July 1323	*CFR 1319–1327*, p. 218
Patrick de Colewenn		
from	3 July 1323	*CFR 1319–1327*, p. 218
Henry de Wardecop		
to	22 May 1324	*CFR 1319–1327*, p. 278

Henry de Threlkeld		
from	22 May 1324	*CFR 1319–1327*, p. 278

Wardships
minority of Roger de Clifford, 1345–1355

William de Langwathby		
from	17 March 1345	*CFR 1337–1347*, p. 412

ASBY

History

built	C14	King, p. 490

ASKHAM HALL

Owners

Owned by Sanfords		
from	1375	*RCH*, p. 21

BEETHAM NO. 2 (HAZELSLACK TOWER)

History

built	C14	King, p. 490

BEWLEY

Owners

Bishops of Carlisle		
temp	Period	*RCH*, p. 43

BROUGH (BURGH UNDER STAYNESMORE)

Owners

Roger de Leybourne		
to	21 February 1284	*IPM II*, no. 525 (R.I.P.)
Idonea, widow of above		
from	21 February 1284	*IPM II*, no. 525
Robert de Clifford, P.P.		
to	28 July 1314	*IPM V*, no. 533 (R.I.P.)
Matilda or Maud, widow of above		
from	27 September 1314	*CCR 1313–1318*, p. 117
to	24 May 1327	*IPM VII*, no. 52 (R.I.P.)
Robert de Clifford III, P.P.		
from	24 May 1327	*IPM VII*, no. 52
to	20 May 1344	*IPM VIII*, no. 531 (R.I.P.)
Robert de Clifford, son of above		
heir on	20 May 1344	*IPM VIII*, no. 531
died	*1345*	*GEC III, p. 292*
Isabel, widow of Robert Clifford III		
to	25 July 1362	*CPR 1361–1364*, p. 312
Roger de Clifford, kn., her son, P.P.		
to	13 July 1389	*IPM XVI*, no. 836 (R.I.P.)
Thomas de Clifford, kn., son of above, P.P.		
from	13 July 1389	*IPM XVI*, no. 836
to	4 October 1391	*IPM XVI*, no. 13

Elizabeth, mother of John de Clifford, widow of Thomas		
from	20 December 1392	*CCR 1392–1396*, p. 97
on	7 May 1415	*CPR 1413–1416*, p. 320 (BURGH)
Constables		
Sir Ralph fitz William, P.P.		
to	27 September 1314	*CCR 1313–1318*, p. 117
Private Constable for the Cliffords		
Robert de Clitheroe (from context)		
on	3 August 1316	*CCR 1313–1318*, p. 356
Adam Correy	(from source)	
to	1 February 1390	*CPR 1388–1392*, p. 254
John de Crakanthorpe (from source)		
from	1 February 1390	*CPR 1388–1392*, p. 254
on	8 June 1390	*CPR 1388–1392*, p. 254

BROUGHAM

Owners		
Robert de Clifford, P.P.		
licence to crenellate	1309	*CChW 1244–1326*, p. 291
to	28 July 1314	*IPM V*, no. 533 (R.I.P.)
Roger de Clifford, P.P. son of above		
from	28 July 1314	*IPM V*, no. 533
forfeited	8 February 1322	*CFR 1319–1327*, p. 94
Robert de Clifford, brother of above, P.P.		
from	12 February 1327	*IPM VII*, no. 77
to	20 May 1344	*IPM VIII*, no. 531 (R.I.P.)
Robert de Clifford		
heir on	20 May 1344	*IPM VIII*, no. 531
died	*1345*	*GEC III, p. 292*
Roger de Clifford, kn., P.P.		
inherited	*1345*	*GEC III, p. 292*
to	13 July 1389	*IPM XVI*, no. 836 (R.I.P.)
Thomas de Clifford, kn., son of above		
from	13 July 1389	*IPM XVI*, no. 836
reversion to	4 October 1391	*IPM XVI*, no. 13
Maud, widow of Roger Clifford, kn.		
on	4 October 1391	*IPM XVI*, no. 13
to	28 February 1403	*IPM XVIII*, no. 779 (R.I.P.)
John de Clifford, her grandson, P.P.		
from	28 February 1403	*IPM XVIII*, no. 779
died	*13 March 1421/2*	*GEC III, p. 293*

HARTLEY (HARCLA)

Tenant in Chief		
Clifford family		
on	4 October 1353	*CPR 1350–1354*, p. 493
Owners		
Thomas de Musgrave, P.P.		
licence to crenellate	4 October 1353	*CPR 1350–1354*, p. 493

HOWGILL

History

built	C14	King, p. 492

KENDAL

Owners

Peter de Bruce		
dead by	16 December 1272	*CCR 1272–1279*, p. 4
Robert de Ros of Wark		
from	16 December 1272	*CCR 1272–1279*, p. 4
to	20 April 1274	*IPM II*, no. 70 (R.I.P.)
Margaret, his wife, daughter of Peter de Bruce		
from	20 April 1274	*IPM II*, no. 70
to	20 August 1297	*CPR 1292–1301*, p. 304
William de Ros of Kendal, her son		
from	20 August 1297	*CPR 1292–1301*, p. 304
to	12 March 1310	*IPM V*, no. 218 (R.I.P.)
Thomas de Ros of Kendal		
from	12 March 1310	*IPM V*, no. 218
to	1391	J.F.Curwen, 'Kendal Castle', *C.and W.A.and A.S.* New Series, 8 (1909), pp. 84–5
William de Parr, husband of Elizabeth, granddaughter of above		
from	1391	Curwen, pp. 84–5
to	1405	Curwen, pp. 84–5
John de Par, son of above		
from	1405	Curwen, pp. 84–5
to	1408	Curwen, pp. 84–5
Agnes, widow of above		
from	13 January 1409	*IPM XIX*, no. 667 (One tower)
Thomas del Par, son of John and Agnes above		
from	1408	Curwen, pp. 84–5
to	1464	Curwen, pp. 84–5

KENTMERE

History

built	C14	King, p. 492

LAMMERSIDE

History

built	C14	King, p. 493
Late C14 peel tower, probably part of larger building		*RCH* p. 240

PENDRAGON

Owners

Roger de Leybourne		
to	21 February 1284	*IPM II*, no. 525 (R.I.P.)
Idonea, widow of above		
from	21 February 1284	*IPM II*, no. 525

Robert de Clifford, P.P.		
licence to crenellate	1309	*CChW 1244–1326*, p. 291
to	28 July 1314	*IPM V*, no. 533 (R.I.P.)
Roger de Clifford, son of above, P.P.		
from	28 July 1314	*IPM V*, no. 533
forfeited	8 February 1322	*CFR 1319–1327*, p. 94
Robert de Clifford, brother of above, P.P.		
from	12 February 1327	*IPM VII*, no. 77
died	*20 May 1344*	*GEC III, p. 291*
Roger de Clifford, kn., P.P.		
inherited	*1345*	*GEC III, p. 292*
to	13 July 1389	*IPM XVI*, no. 836 (R.I.P.)
Thomas de Clifford, kn. (R.I.P.), son of above, P.P.		
from	13 July 1389	*IPM XVI*, no. 836
to	1392 (R.I.P.)	
John de Clifford, son of above, P.P.		
from	4 October 1391	*IPM XVII*, no. 22 (1/3 held by his grandmother)
died	*13 March 1421/2*	*GEC III, p. 293*

Constables while in Royal hands

Anthony de Lucy, P.P.		
to	8 July 1323	*CFR 1319–1327*, p. 221
Thomas de Synythwayt		
from	8 July 1323	*CFR 1319–1327*, p. 221
to	20 May 1324	*CFR 1319–1327*, p. 278
Robert de Welle		
from	20 May 1324	*CFR 1319–1327*, p. 278

SIZERGH

Owners

Strickland family		
from	C13	*RCH*, p. 106
to	C17 (At least)	*RCH*, p. 106

STRICKLAND ROGER

Owners

Burnesheads then Bellinghams		
temp	period	*RCH*, p. 223

Wiltshire

Unknown Licenses

FALLARDESTON for Nicholas Benton		
	10 October 1376	*CPR 1374–1377*, p. 353

CASTLE COMBS

History

prob.	C12	King, p. 498
derelict	1478	King, p. 498

CASTLE EATON

Owners

Nicholas de Seymour		
licence to crenellate	28 May 1311	*CPR 1307–1313*, p. 361

DEVIZES

Owners

Crown		
from	1157	*HKW II*, p. 626
Queen Margaret		
from	1299	*HKW II*, p. 627
from	10 September 1299	*CPR 1292–1301*, p. 451
confirmed	19 March 1310	*CPR 1307–1313*, p. 216
Queen Isabella		
from	5 March 1318	*CPR 1317–1321*, p. 115
on	20 April 1327	*CMR*, no. 51
Queen Philippa		
from	1 January 1331	*CPR 1330–1334*, p. 55
on	2 October 1350	*CPR 1348–1350*, p. 571
Queen Anne		
on	4 May 1372	
for life from	16 November 1382	*CCR 1381–1385*, p. 192
'held'	27 January 1405	*IMisc VII*, no. 315
Queen Joan		
from	1 June 1405	*CCR 1402–1405*, p. 455
to	1437	*HKW II*, p. 628
Crown		
to	16th Century	*HKW II*, p. 628

Constables

Philip Basset		
on	6 January 1270	*CLibR 1267–1272*, no. 960
on	15 October 1270	*CLibR 1267–1272*, no. 1239
John de Havering, P.P.		
to	8 December 1275	*CPR 1272–1281*, p. 127

Ralph de Sandwich		
from	8 December 1275	*CPR 1272–1281*, p. 127
Walter Lillebon		
on	29 February 1276	*CCR 1272–1279*, p. 273
Walter L'isle		
on	14 October 1278	*Wiltshire Goal Delivery and Trailbaston Trials, 1275–1306*, Wiltshire Record Society, 33 (1977), no. 135
Ralph de Sandwich		
to	17 May 1287	*CFR 1272–1307*, p. 236
Matthew son of John (kn.)		
for life from	18 March 1287	*CPR 1281–1282*, p. 270
on	18 July 1290	*CPR 1282–1292*, p. 95
John Bluet		
to	12 March 1308	*CPR 1307–1313*, p. 51
Hugh le Despenser		
from	12 March 1308	*CPR 1307–1313*, p. 51
to	2 December 1308	*CPR 1307–1313*, p. 96
Robert Lewer		
from	5 December 1321	*CPR 1321–1324*, p. 40
Gilbert de Berewyk		
from	14 December 1330	*CFR 1327–1337*, p. 214
Roger de Beauchamp, P.P.		
for life from	25 October 1340	*CPR 1340–1343*, p. 115
on	16 March 1379	*CCR 1377–1381*, p. 179
before	30 January 1380	*CFR 1377–1383*, p. 182
Nicholas de Sharnesfeld, kn.		
for life from	30 January 1380	*CFR 1377–1383*, p. 182
to	28 November 1381	*CPR 1381–1385*, p. 62
John Lovel, kn., P.P.		
for life from	28 November 1381	*CPR 1381–1385*, p. 62
temp	Queen Anne	
Deputies		
John Flavel		
on	29 December 1287	*IMisc I*, no. 1450
Gatekeepers		
Robert		
on	20 July 1364	*CPR 1364–1367*, p. 8
Porters		
Robert Ranger		
on	4 November 1364	*CPR 1364–1367*, p. 39
Walter Hightr		
from	4 May 1372	
on	22 October 1372	*CPR 1370–1374*, p. 207
Janitor		
John Hotte		
from	18 February 1410	*CPR 1408–1413*, p. 19

LUDGERSHALL

Owners

Queen Eleanor of Provence		
from	1272	*HKW II*, p. 731
to	1291	*HKW II*, p. 731
Mary, sister of Edward II, a nun		
from	1317	*HKW II*, p. 731
to	1332	*HKW II*, p. 731

MARLBOROUGH

Owners

Queen Eleanor of Provence		
on	23 August 1273	*CPR 1272–1281*, p. 27
on	14 July 1290	*CPR 1281–1292*, p. 374
dead by	12 March 1308	*CPR 1307–1313*, p. 51
Queen Margaret		
from	10 September 1299	*CPR 1292–1301*, p. 451
confirmed	19 March 1310	*CPR 1307–1313*, p. 216
Queen Isabella		
from	5 March 1318	*CPR 1317–1321*, p. 115
on	20 April 1327	*CMR*, no. 51
Queen Philippa		
from	1 January 1331	*CPR 1330–1334*, p. 55
on	6 November 1376	*CPR 1377–1381*, p. 182
Humphrey Hungerford and his heirs		
from	1 December 1403	*CPR 1401–1405*, p. 320

Constables

Roger de Cheyne		
on	20 February 1270	*CLibR 1267–1272*, no. 1005
on	28 December 1270	*CLibR 1267–1272*, no. 1333
Roger Mortimer of Wigmore		
on	2 January 1272	*CLibR 1267–1272*, no. 1755
to	17 September 1273	*CCR 1272–1279*, p. 31
John de Bradenham		
not by	3 June 1290	*CPR 1281–1292*, p. 84
Eustace de Hache, P.P.		
on	29 March 1299	*CCR 1296–1302*, p. 237
on	24 January 1302	*CCR 1296–132*, p. 510
John Abel		
to	12 March 1308	*CPR 1307–1313*, p. 51
Hugh le Despenser, elder, P.P., for Edward II		
from	12 March 1308	*Ancient Deeds vol. III*, A.4815
to	2 December 1308	*CPR 1307–1313*, p. 96
William de Rammeshill		
on	11 February 1313	*Ancient Deeds vol. I*, C.64
Hugh le Despenser, elder, P.P.		
from	2 May 1321	*CPR 1317–1321*, p. 578
Oliver de Ingham, P.P., kn.		
from	5 December 1321	*CPR 1321–1324*, p. 40

William de Rammeshill		
on	15 February 1325	*CCR 1323–1327*, p. 257
on	17 May 1327	*Ancient Deeds vol. I*, C.192
Isabel de Hastings		
from	19 February 1326	*CPR 1324–1327*, p. 243
William de Rammeshill		
from	14 December 1330	*CFR 1327–1337*, p. 215
Robert Russell		
on	8 April 1345	*Ancient Deeds vol. I*, C.659
on	12 July 1349	*Ancient Deeds vol. I*, C.394
Thomas de Hungerford		
on	20 October 1359	*CPR 1358–1361*, p. 303 (For Queen)
on	8 February 1360	*CPR 1361–1364*, p. 6 (For King)
Nicholas de Tamworth, knight		
for ten years from	20 March 1370	*CFR 1369–1377*, p. 68
Roger de Beauchamp, P.P.		
from	6 November 1376	*CFR 1369–1377*, p. 369
confirmed	4 March 1378	*CPR 1377–1381*, p. 182
before	28 May 1380	*CFR 1377–1381*, p. 200
Robert Power		
for 9 years from	28 May 1380	*CFR 1377–1381*, p. 200
John de Roches, king's knight		
for life from	28 March 1382	*CPR 1381–1385*, p. 107
on	20 April 1382	*CCR 1381–1385*, p. 53
William Hasthorpe, knight, to start after Power finishs		
grant	7 August 1386	*CPR 1385–1389*, p. 197
John de Roches, king's knight		
on	3 November 1388	*Ancient Deeds vol. I*, C.30
on	17 May 1391	*Ancient Deeds vol. I*, C.340
William le Scrope, king's knight, future earl of Wiltshire		
for life from	2 July 1393	*CPR 1391–1396*, p. 309
on	4 December 1397	*Ancient Deeds vol. I*, C.2590
Walter de Hungerford, king's knight		
for life from	2 November 1399	*CPR 1399–1401*, p. 62

Porters

Richard Bentele		
for life from	9 March 1400	*CPR 1399–1401*, p. 256

Farmers

Nicholas de Tamworth, kn.		
not by	18 February 1382	*CPR 1381–1385*, p. 133

MERE

Owners

Edmund, earl of Cornwall		
to	1298	*IPM III*, no. 604 (R.I.P.)
The King, his heir		
from	1298	*IPM III*, no. 605
Queen Margaret		
from	20 February 1303	*CPR 1301–1307*, p. 118
confirmed	19 March 1310	*CPR 1307–1313*, p. 217
died	1318	

Queen Isabella		
from	5 March 1318	*CPR 1317–1321*, p. 115
on	20 April 1327	*CMR*, no. 51
John of Eltham, earl of Cornwall		
from	10 October 1331	*CChR 1327–1341*, p. 233
died	1337	
Edward, the Black Prince		
to	16 November 1347	*BPR I*, p. 147
Queen Isabella		
from	16 November 1347	*BPR I*, p. 147
to	22 August 1359	*CCR 1354–1360*, p. 599 (R.I.P.)
Edward, prince of Wales		
from	22 August 1358	*IPM X*, no. 447
on	1 October 1365	*CPR 1364–1367*, p. 186
on	17 March 1376	

Constables

Richard de Chuseldem		
on	4 February 1303	*CPR 1301–1307*, p. 113
on	12 March 1308	*CPR 1307–1313*, p. 52
John de Mere		
from	14 December 1330	*CFR 1327–1337*, p. 214
William de Cusancia		
to	10 March 1337	*CPR 1334–1338*, p. 441
John de Mere		
for life from	9 March 1337	*CFR 1337–1347*, p. 6
on	28 September 1337	*CPR 1334–1338*, p. 529
dead by	13 July 1358	*CPR 1358–1361*, p. 82
Reginald Rede		
for life from	17 March 1376	
confirmed	18 May 1384	*CPR 1381–1385*, p. 403
Ives fitz Waryn		
for life from	26 August 1381	*CPR 1381–1385*, p. 37
Reginald Rede		
to	8 March 1386	*CPR 1385–1389*, pp. 109, 159 and 194
William Stourton		
for life from	8 March 1386	*CPR 1385–1389*, pp. 109, 159 and 194
temp	1397–1399	E.101/547/8
Henry, prince of Wales		
on	1 July 1400	*CPR 1399–1401*, p. 309

Private Constables for the Black Prince

Sir John de Mere		
on	16 November 1347	*BPR I*, p. 148
Hervey Hewe, yeoman of the prince's scullery		
from	19 October 1361	*BPR IV*, p. 396
Walter del Hay, yeoman of the prince's spicery		
for life from	24 May 1364	*BPR IV*, p. 528

OLD SARUM

Constables

Robert de Glaston		
on	18 November 1267	*CLibR 1267–1272*, no. 24 (20l./year)
William Dun		
on	12 December 1269	*CLibR 1267–1272*, no. 943
on	3 February 1270	*CLibR 1267–1272*, no. 988
Hildebrand de London		
to	2 April 1281	*CFR 1272–1307*, p. 145 (R.I.P.)
John de Wotton		
from	2 April 1281	*CFR 1272–1307*, p. 145
Andrew de Grymstede		
to	12 March 1308	*CFR 1307–1319*, p. 17
Alexander Cheveroyl		
from	12 March 1308	*CFR 1307–1319*, p. 17
John Mauduyt		
to	1 December 1311	*CFR 1307–1319*, p. 119
Adam Walraunt		
from	1 December 1311	*CFR 1307–1319*, p. 119
to	4 May 1313	*CFR 1307–1319*, p. 170
John de Kyngeston		
from	4 May 1313	*CFR 1307–1319*, p. 170
to	16 November 1314	*CFR 1307–1319*, p. 221
John de Holte		
from	16 November 1314	*CFR 1307–1319*, p. 221
to	28 April 1315	*CFR 1307–1319*, p. 245
Philip de la Beche		
with county from	28 April 1315	*CFR 1307–1319*, p. 245
to	15 May 1318	*CFR 1307–1319*, p. 360
Adam Walerand		
from	15 May 1318	*CFR 1307–1319*, p. 360
to	29 November 1318	*CFR 1307–1319*, p. 383
Walter de Rysum		
from	29 November 1318	*CFR 1307–1319*, p. 383
to	19 February 1320	*CFR 1319–1327*, p. 15
Philip de la Beche		
with county from	19 February 1320	*CFR 1319–1327*, p. 15
to	8 October 1321	*CFR 1319–1327*, p. 72
John de Tycheborne /Ticheburn		
from	8 October 1321	*CFR 1319–1327*, p. 72
to	20 May 1322	*CFR 1319–1327*, p. 130
Adam Waleraund		
from	20 May 1322	*CFR 1319–1327*, p. 130
to	4 February 1327	*CFR 1327–1337*, p. 16
Philip de la Beche		
with county from	4 February 1327	*CFR 1327–1337*, p. 16
to	1 December 1329	*CFR 1327–1337*, p. 156
John Mauduyt		
from	1 December 1329	*CFR 1327–1337*, p. 156
to	5 December 1330	*CFR 1327–1337*, p. 199

Hildebrand de London		
from	5 December 1330	*CFR 1327–1337*, p. 199
to	3 May 1332	*CFR 1327–1337*, p. 311
John Mauduyt		
from	3 May 1332	*CFR 1327–1337*, p. 311
to	26 November 1333	*CFR 1327–1337*, p. 380
John de Ticheburn		
from	26 November 1333	*CFR 1327–1337*, p. 380
to	22 October 1334	*CFR 1327–1337*, p. 421
Gilbert de Berewyk		
from	22 October 1334	*CFR 1327–1337*, p. 421
to	12 October 1335	*CFR 1327–1337*, p. 460
Reynold de Pavely		
from	12 October 1335	*CFR 1327–1337*, p. 460
to	24 June 1336	*CFR 1327–1337*, p. 490
Gilbert de Berewyk		
from	24 June 1336	*CFR 1327–1337*, p. 490
to	14 August 1337	*CFR 1337–1347*, p. 27
Peter Doynel		
from	14 August 1337	*CFR 1337–1347*, p. 27
to	20 February 1338	*CFR 1337–1347*, p. 67
John Mauduyt		
from	20 February 1338	*CFR 1337–1347*, p. 67
to	12 March 1338	*CFR 1337–1347*, p. 70
Peter Doynel		
from	12 March 1338	*CFR 1337–1347*, p. 70
to	23 April 1338	*CFR 1337–1347*, p. 74
John Mauduyt		
from	23 April 1338	*CFR 1337–1347*, p. 74
Thomas de Seymor		
to	15 January 1341	*CFR 1337–1347*, p. 200
John de la Ryvere		
from	15 January 1341	*CFR 1337–1347*, p. 200
Thomas de St. Mauro		
to	15 December 1341	*CFR 1337–1347*, p. 250
John Mauduyt		
from	15 December 1341	*CFR 1337–1347*, p. 250
to	4 November 1344	*CFR 1337–1347*, p. 397
John de Roches		
from	4 November 1344	*CFR 1337–1347*, p. 397
to	21 April 1347	*CFR 1347–1356*, p. 22
Thomas de St. Mauro		
from	21 April 1347	*CFR 1347–1356*, p. 22
to	25 April 1347	*CFR 1347–1356*, p. 27
or to	11 November 1347	*CFR 1347–1356*, p. 57
Andrew de Sakevill		
from	25 April 1347	*CFR 1347–1356*, p. 27
Robert Russell		
from	11 November 1347	*CFR 1347–1356*, p. 57
and from	30 September 1348	*CFR 1347–1356*, p. 83

Thomas de la Ryvere		
from	16 October 1351	*CFR 1347–1356*, p. 307
and from	17 January 1354	*CFR 1347–1356*, p. 388
John Everard		
from	10 November 1354	*CFR 1347–1356*, p. 409
Thomas de Hungerford		
from	24 November 1355	*CFR 1347–1356*, p. 444
and from	1 October 1359	*CFR 1356–1368*, p. 103
Henry Sturmy		
from	21 November 1360	*CFR 1356–1368*, p. 121
and from	17 November 1365	*CFR 1356–1368*, p. 315
Walter Haywood		
from	16 November 1366	*CFR 1356–1368*, p. 328
and from	28 March 1370	*CFR 1369–1377*, p. 98
William de Workton		
from	5 November 1371	*CFR 1369–1377*, p. 146
Henry de Sturmy		
from	12 December 1372	*CFR 1369–1377*, p. 189
John Pauntesey		
from	7 November 1373	*CFR 1369–1377*, p. 221
John de la Mare		
from	12 December 1374	*CFR 1369–1377*, p. 271
Hugh Cheyne		
from	4 October 1375	*CFR 1369–1377*, p. 297
Ralph Cheyne		
from	26 October 1376	*CFR 1369–1377*, p. 369
and from	22 June 1377	*CFR 1377–1383*, p. 3
Peter de Cusance		
from	26 November 1377	*CFR 1377–1383*, p. 34
William de Worfton		
from	25 November 1378	*CFR 1377–1383*, p. 113
Ralph de Norton		
from	5 November 1379	*CFR 1377–1383*, p. 171
Laurence de St. Martin		
from	18 October 1380	*CFR 1377–1383*, p. 220
Hugh Cheyne		
with county from	6 May 1381	*CFR 1377–1383*, p. 220
to	13 October 1381	*CFR 1377–1383*, p. 269
Nicholas de Wodehull		
with county from	13 October 1381	*CFR 1377–1383*, p. 269
Richard Becket, king's esquire		
for life from	7 August 1382	*CCR 1381–1385*, p. 158
Nicholas Glastonbury		
for life from	6 October 1402	*CPR 1401–1405*, p. 171
to	20 May 1409	*CPR 1408–1413*, p. 94
William Malbirthorpe		
from	22 May 1409	*CPR 1408–1413*, p. 94
Nicholas Glastonbury		
for life from	26 November 1409	*CPR 1408–1413*, p. 165

Chaplain

Walter de Ludgershall		
to	24 May 1290	*CPR 1281–1292*, p. 81 (R.I.P.)

Michael Turpyn of Wodeford		
from	24 May 1290	*CPR 1281–1292*, p. 81

TROWBRIDGE

Reversions

William de Montague, earl of Salisbury		
from	16 March 1337	*CPR 1334–1338*, p. 426

Owners

John de Warenne, earl of Surrey		
on	16 March 1337	*CPR 1334–1338*, p. 426
for life on	6 December 1355	*BPR II*, p. 91
Joan, widow of Warenne, in dower		
not by	20 December 1361	*CCR 1360–1364*, p. 220
William de Montague, earl of Salisbury		
by	20 December 1361	*CCR 1360–1364*, p. 220
in	1363	
John of Gaunt, duke of Lancaster and Blanche, his wife		
jointured	2 November 1366	*Feet of fines relating to Wiltshire* Wiltshire Record Society 29 (1973), no. 548

WARDOUR

Owners

John 5th Lord Lovel, P.P.		
licence to crenellate	27 February 1393	*CPR 1391–1396*, p. 261
died	*10 September 1408*	*GEC VIII, p. 219*
John Lovel, son of above, P.P.		
inherited	*10 September 1408*	*GEC VIII, p. 219*
died	*19 October 1414*	*GEC VIII, p. 221*
William Lovel, son of above, P.P.		
inherited	*19 October 1414*	*GEC VIII, p. 221*
of age	*c.1418*	*GEC VIII, p. 221*
died	*13 June 1455*	*GEC VIII, p. 221*

Worcestershire

Unknown Licenses

DORMESTON for Sir John Russell		
	12 February 1388	*CPR 1385–1389*, p. 446
EVESHAM ABBEY for Abbot and Convent		
	15 March 1336	*CPR 1334–1338*, p. 230
WODEMANTON for John de Wysham		
	26 November 1332	*CPR 1330–1334*, p. 242

ELMLEY

Owners

William de Beauchamp, earl of Warwick		
to	12 June 1298	*IPM III*, no. 477 (R.I.P.)
Guy de Beauchamp, earl of Warwick, son of above		
from	12 June 1298	*IPM III*, no. 477
to	16 August 1315	*IPM V*, no. 615 (R.I.P.)
Thomas de Beauchamp, earl of Warwick, son of above		
from	16 August 1315	*IPM V*, no. 615
on	1 December 1315	*CFR 1307–1319*, p. 265
Hugh le Despenser		
from	2 August 1317	*CFR 1307–1319*, p. 336
wardship	18 March 1318	*CPR 1317–1321*, p. 123
Thomas de Beauchamp, earl of Warwick		
on	28 August 1369	*CCR 1369–1374*, p. 108
on	13 November 1387	*IMisc IV*, no. 302
Seized by King		
on	20 July 1397	*CFR 1391–1399*, p. 219
Thomas le Despenser, earl of Gloucester and Constance		
from	28 September 1397	*CPR 1396–1399*, p. 219 (Tail Male)
Thomas de Beauchamp, earl of Warwick		
to	8 April 1401	*IPM XVIII*, no. 502
Richard de Beauchamp, son of above		
from	8 April 1401	*IPM XVIII*, no. 502
Margaret, widow of Thomas de Beauchamp		
on	27 June 1401	*CCR 1399–1401*, p. 363 (Dower)
to	22 January 1407	*IPM XIX*, no. 282 (R.I.P.)
Richard de Beauchamp, earl of Warwick		
livery	1 March 1406	*CCR 1405–1409*, p. 183
from	22 January 1407	*IPM XIX*, no. 282

Constables while in King's hands

Thomas lord le Despenser		
from	20 July 1397	*CFR 1391–1399*, p. 219
to	28 September 1397	*CPR 1396–1399*, p. 219

Wardships

Minority of Thomas Beauchamp, earl of Warwick (1315–1335)

Hugh le Despenser, snr.		
from	2 August 1317	*CFR 1307–1319*, p. 336
on	18 March 1318	*CPR 1317–1321*, p. 123

Minority of Richard Beauchamp, earl of Warwick (1401–1403)

Thomas de Aldebury, William de Beauchamp of Abergavenny and John Owdeby		
from	12 May 1401	*CFR 1399–1405*, p. 135

Warden of the chapel

William de Wellesbourne		
on	14 February 1312	*Ancient Deeds vol. I*, B.803

HANLEY

Owners

Crown		
by	7 November 1273	*CPR 1272–1281*, p. 14
Gilbert de Clare		
to	10 July 1314	*IPM V*, no. 538 (R.I.P.)
Matilda, widow of above		
from	1314	*HKW II*, p. 667
Hugh Despenser, yng.		
from	November 1317	*HKW II*, p. 667
to	May 1321	*HKW II*, p. 667
Crown		
from	May 1321	*HKW II*, p. 667
to	1322	*HKW II*, p. 667
Hugh Despenser, yng		
from	1322	*HKW II*, p. 667
to	1326	*HKW II*, p. 667
Queen Isabella		
for life from	10 February 1330	*CPR 1327–1330*, p. 500
to	12 July 1330	*CChR 1327–1341*, p. 178
Roger Mortimer, earl of March		
for life from	12 July 1330	*CChR 1327–1341*, p. 178
Eleanor, widow of Hugh Despenser		
to	9 July 1337	*IPM VIII*, no. 132 (R.I.P.)
Hugh de Despenser, son of above, P.P.		
from	9 July 1337	*IPM VIII*, no. 132
to	8 February 1349	*IPM IX*, no. 428 (R.I.P.)
Elizabeth, widow of Hugh Despenser		
from	8 February 1349	*IPM IX*, no. 428
to	30 May 1359	*IPM X*, no. 523 (R.I.P.) (Dower)
Edward le Despenser, kn., P.P.		
from	30 May 1359	*IPM X*, no. 523
to	12 November 1375	*IPM XIV*, no. 209 (R.I.P.)
Thomas le Despenser, son of above		
heir on	12 November 1375	*IPM XIV*, no. 209
Elizabeth, widow of two above		
from	22 February 1376	*CCR 1374–1377*, p. 305
on	6 February 1400	*CCR 1399–1402*, p. 54

Richard Beauchamp of Abergavenny, P.P., through Isabel his wife		
on	1 September 1414	*IMisc VII*, no. 489

Constables

Hugh le Despenser, yng., P.P.		
to	21 May 1321	CPR *1317–1321*, p. 585
Malcolm Musard and William Payn		
from	21 May 1321	CPR *1317–1321*, p. 585
Alexander de Lilleford		
on	11 October 1326	*CPR 1324–1327*, p. 331
Thomas de Hanley		
to	20 June 1327	*CFR 1327–1337*, p. 49
Robert de Bracy		
from	20 June 1327	*CFR 1327–1337*, p. 49
Thomas de Blount		
from	17 August 1327	*CPR 1327–1330*, p. 145
Richard de Haukeslowe		
from	19 December 1330	*CFR 1327–1337*, p. 215

HARTLEBURY

Owners

Walter de Cauntelo, bishop of Worcester		
began building	1255	Pevsner, p. 190
Bishop Giffard of Worcester		
license to crenellate	1268	Pevsner, p. 190

STRENSHAM

Owners

Sir John Russell		
licence to crenellate	12 February 1388	*CPR 1385–1389*, p. 446

WORCESTER

Owners

William de Beauchamp, earl of Warwick		
to	12 June 1298	*IPM III*, no. 477 (R.I.P.)
Guy de Beauchamp, earl of Warwick, son of above		
from	12 June 1298	*IPM III*, no. 477
to	16 August 1315	*IPM V*, no. 615 (R.I.P.)
Thomas de Beauchamp, earl of Warwick, son of above		
from	16 August 1315	*IPM V*, no. 615
on	1 December 1315	*CFR 1307–1319*, p. 265
Hugh le Despenser		
from	2 August 1317	*CFR 1307–1319*, p. 336
wardship	18 March 1318	*CPR 1317–1321*, p. 123
Thomas de Beauchamp, earl of Warwick		
on	29 July 1361	*CPR 1361–1364*, p. 48
to	13 November 1369	*IPM XII*, no. 326 (R.I.P.)
Thomas de Beauchamp, earl of Warwick, son of above		
from	13 November 1369	*IPM XII*, no. 326
to	8 April 1401	*IPM XVIII*, no. 502

Richard de Beauchamp, earl of Warwick, son of above

from	8 April 1401	*IPM XVIII*, no. 502

Wardships

Minority of Thomas Beauchamp, earl of Warwick (1315–1335)

Hugh le Despenser, snr.

from	2 August 1317	*CFR 1307–1318*, p. 336
on	18 March 1318	*CPR 1317–1321*, p. 123

Minority of Richard Beauchamp, earl of Warwick (1401–1403)

Thomas de Aldebury and William Beauchamp of Abergavenny and John Owdeby

from	12 May 1401	*CFR 1399–1405*, p. 135

Yorkshire

Unknown Licenses

A HOUSE IN THE CATHEDERAL CLOSE, YORK for John de Cadamo		
	21 August 1298	*CPR 1292–1301*, p. 358
BURTON CONSTABLE for Geoffrey le Scrope		
	8 June 1338	*CPR 1338–1340*, p. 94
CLIFTON–UPON–YORE for Geoffrey le Scrope		
	25 September 1317	*CPR 1317–1321*, p. 26
HERSSEWELL IN SPALDINGMOOR for Gerard Salvayn		
	20 October 1303	*CPR 1301–1307*, p. 160
LERMITAGE IN TANFELD for John Marmion		
	24 September 1314	*CPR 1313–1317*, p. 177
MONKETON ON THE MOOR and KEXBY BY STAYNFORDBRIDGE for Thomas Ughtred		
	25 February 1342	*CPR 1340–1343*, p. 388
SCULCOATES for John de Grey of Rothersfield		
	2 February 1348	*CPR 1348–1350*, p. 36
SPOFFORD for Henry Percy		
	4 October 1308	*CPR 1307–1313*, p. 144
BOULTON and SUTTON for Robert de Percy		
	22 February 1293	*CPR 1292–1301*, p. 6
WALTON for Thomas de Burgh		
	28 February 1334	*CPR 1330–1334*, p. 519
WHETELE for John de Sandal, king's clerk		
	2 April 1311	*CPR 1307–1313*, p. 340
WILTON IN PYKERYNGLITH for John de Heslarton		
	3 February 1335	*CPR 1334–1338*, p. 88
WEST TANFELD for Maud, widow of John de Marmion		
	18 November 1348	*CPR 1348–1350*, p. 210

ALMONSBURY

Owners

de Lacy earls of Lincoln		
to	1310	J.K. Walter, 'Almondbury in Feudal Times', *Yorkshire Arch. Journal* 2 (1873), p. 7
Earls and dukes of Lancaster		
from	1310	*ibid.*
Crown		
from	1399	*ibid.*

ARMLEY

History

mentioned	1300 as place	King, p. 529

AYTON

Owners

Ralph de Eure		
built by	c.1400	D.G.Hunt, 'Medieval Britain in 1961', *Medieval Archaeology*, 6–7 (1962–3), p. 336

Architect

John Lewyn	c.1400	*ibid.*

BOLTON

Owners

Sir Richard le Scrope, P.P.		
licence to crenellate	4 July 1379	*CPR 1377–1381*, p. 369
died	*30 May 1403*	*GEC XI, p. 539*
Roger le Scrope, son of above, P.P.		
from	*30 May 1403*	*GEC XI, p. 541*
died	*3 December 1403*	*GEC XI, p. 541*
Richard le Scrope, son of above		
from	*3 December 1403*	*GEC XI, p. 542*
died	*29 August 1420*	*GEC XI, p. 542*
Henry le Scrope, son of above, P.P.		
from	*29 August 1420*	*GEC XI, p. 543*
died	*14 January 1458/9*	*GEC XI, p. 543*

Wardships

minority of Henry le Scrope of Bolton, 1420–1439

Richard Neville		
from	19 September 1420	*CPR 1416–1422*, p. 333
on	5 September 1421	*CPR 1416–1422*, p. 208

BOWES

Owners

Peter de Sabaudia		
to	15 May 1280	*IPM II*, no. 381 (R.I.P.)
John de Brittany, earl of Richmond		
to	17 October 1285	*IPM II*, no. 579 (R.I.P.)
Alice, his granddaughter		
from	17 October 1285	*IPM II*, no. 579
John duke of Brittany		
to	15 October 1306	*CChR 1300–1326*, p. 69 (R.I.P.)
John, duke of Brittany and earl of Richmond		
from	15 October 1306	*CChR 1300–1326*, p. 69
to	5 May 1331	*CPR 1330–1334*, p. 150
Mary de St. Pol, countess of Pembroke		
from	5 May 1331	*CPR 1330–1334*, p. 150
on	16 May 1341	*IPM VIII*, no. 335 (From Balliolo)
John of Brittany earl of Richmond		
to	16 May 1341	*IPM VIII*, no. 335 (R.I.P.) (Possibly)
Queen Anne		
to	3 November 1388	*CPR 1385–1389*, p. 13

Henry Fitz Hugh, leased for twelve years

from	3 November 1388	*CPR 1385–1389*, p. 13
confirmed	23 March 1391	*CPR 1388–1392*, p. 393
to	1394	

Thomas Arundel, archbishop of York, Edward, earl of Rutland and John Waltham, bishop of Salisbury

from	1394	*CPR 1396–1399*, p. 11

Ralph de Neville, earl of Westmorland, granted by above for 12 years

from	1394	*CPR 1396–1399*, p. 11
on	11 July 1396	*CPR 1396–1399*, p. 11

Constables

Guichard de Charrun, kn.

on	15 May 1280	*IPM II*, no. 381

William de Felton

3 years from	21 February 1326	*CFR 1319–1327*, p. 377
on	24 February 1326	*CPR 1324–1327*, p. 244

Private Constables

John Nowel

on	18 May 1322	*CPR 1321–1324*, p. 157

BRADFORD

History

built	14th cty.	King, p. 514

BURTON–IN–LONSDALE

History

mentioned	1130	King, p. 515
abandoned	1173?	King, p. 515

Constable while in Royal hands

Henry de Malton

from	24 March 1322	*CFR 1318–1327*, p. 118

CASTLETON

Owners

Peter de Bruce, son of above

from	1240	*VCH North Riding vol. II*, p. 336
to	1272	*VCH North Riding vol. II*, p. 336

Marmaduke de Thweng through Lucy, his wife, sister of above

from	1272	*VCH North Riding vol. II*, p. 336

Lucy, granddaughter of above

underage	1285	*VCH North Riding vol. II*, p. 336

William, son of William Latimer, husband of above

by	1295	*VCH North Riding vol. II*, p. 336
received manor	February 1311	*VCH North Riding vol. II*, p. 336
died	March 1327	*VCH North Riding vol. II*, p. 336

William Latimer, son of above

from	March 1327	*VCH North Riding vol. II*, p. 336
to	1335	*VCH North Riding vol. II*, p. 336 (R.I.P.)

William Latimer, son of above		
from	1335	*VCH North Riding vol. II*, p. 336
to	1381	*VCH North Riding vol. II*, p. 336 (R.I.P.)
Elizabeth, widow of John lord Neville of Raby		
from	1381	*VCH North Riding vol. II*, p. 336
died	1396	*VCH North Riding vol. II*, p. 336
Robert lord Willoughby de Eresby, her second husband		
to	1396	*VCH North Riding vol. II*, p. 336
John Neville, lord Latimer, probable builder of successor castle at Danby		
from	1396	*VCH North Riding vol. II*, p. 336

CAWOOD

Owners

Archbishop Neville		
rebuild by	1391	*VCH vol. II*, p. 48

CONISBOROUGH

Owners

John de Warenne, earl of Surrey		
to king and back	1 July 1316	*CPR 1313–1317*, pp. 483, 485
to	1 January 1319	*CPR 1317–1321*, p. 264
Thomas, earl of Lancaster		
from	1 January 1319	*CPR 1317–1321*, p. 264
writ	5 February 1327	*IPM VII*, no. 82
Henry, earl of Lancaster, brother of above		
heir on	5 February 1327	*IPM VII*, no. 82
John de Warenne, earl of Surrey		
requests its return	1318–1322	*CAPW*, p. 293
on	2 March 1328	*Ancient Deeds vol. I*, A.351
to	30 June 1347	*IPM IX*, no. 54 (R.I.P.)
Edmund de Langley, duke of York		
gift from the King	6 August 1347	*CChR 1341–1417*, p. 63
to	1 August 1402	*IPM XVIII*, no. 641 (R.I.P.)
Edward, duke of York, son of above		
from	1 August 1402	*IPM XVIII*, no. 641

Constables

Frank de Bresnes		
on	23 October 1240	*CLibR 1267–1272*, no. 2279
Adam le Bloy and Peter de St. John		
to	19 March 1322	*CFR 1319–1327*, p. 112
Simon de Wodeham		
from	19 March 1322	*CFR 1319–1327*, p. 112
to	24 March 1322	*CFR 1319–1327*, p. 117
Thomas Deyvill		
from	24 March 1322	*CFR 1319–1327*, p. 117
Simon de Wodeham		
to	8 November 1322	*CFR 1319–1327*, p. 185
Roger de Flete, king's yeoman		
from	8 November 1322	*CFR 1319–1327*, p. 185
to	16 April 1324	*CFR 1319–1327*, p. 275

Richard de Mosele		
from	16 April 1324	*CFR 1319–1327*, p. 275
to	4 November 1324	*CFR 1319–1327*, p. 313
Roger de Flete		
from	4 November 1324	*CFR 1319–1327*, p. 313
to	7 December 1324	*CFR 1319–1327*, p. 322
Richard de Mosele		
from	7 December 1324	*CFR 1319–1327*, p. 322
on	16 July 1334	*C.C.R 1333–1337*, p. 241 (Moseley)
William de Montague		
on	14 February 1339	*CPR 1338–1340*, p. 203 (For life)
Walter Whithors, yeoman		
for life from	10 July 1347	*CPR 1345–1348*, p. 545
Thomas Neville, Lord Furnivall, kn.		
from	21 March 1405	*CFR 1399–1405*, p. 307
Edmund fitz William		
from	23 May 1410	
on	1 December 1415	*CPR 1413–1416*, p. 377

Wardships
minority of Edmund de Langley, duke of York

Queen Philippa		
from	4 July 1348	*CPR 1348–1350*, p. 164

COTTINGHAM

Owners

William de Stuteville		
licence to crenellate	1201	King, p. 516
Thomas Wake, P.P.		
licence to crenellate	6 March 1327	*CPR 1327–1330*, p. 31

CRAYKE

Owners

Bishops of Durham		
temp	entire period	W.M. I'Anson, 'The Castle of the North Riding', *Yorkshire Archaeological Journal*, 22 (1913), p. 343

CROPTON

Owners

Joan de Stuteville		
to	6 April 1276	W. Brown, *Yorkshire Inquisitions of the reign of Henry III and Edward I, vol. I*, Yorkshire Archaeological and Topographical Association Record Series, 12 (1891), p. 170
Baldwin Wake		
from	6 April 1276	Brown, p. 170

DANBY

Owners

John Neville, lord Latimer, probable builder, P.P.		
inherited site	1396	*VCH North Riding vol. II*, p. 336
died	1430	*VCH North Riding vol. II*, p. 336

ELSLACK

Owners

Godfrey Dawtrey		
licence to crenellate	24 November 1318	*CPR 1317–1321*, p. 242

FLAMBOROUGH

Owners

Marmaduke Constable		
licence to crenellate	24 May 1351	*CPR 1350–1354*, p. 75
licence to crenellate	11 February 1352	*CPR 1350–1354*, p. 225

GILLING EAST

Owners

Etton family		
temp.	entire period	J.Bilson, 'Gilling Castle', *Yorkshire Archaeological Journal*, 19 (1907), pp. 106–192

HAREWOOD

Owners

William de Aldeburgh, P.P.		
licence to crenellate	27 December 1366	*CPR 1364–1367*, p. 355
dead by	*1388*	*GEC I, p. 101*
William de Aldeburgh of Harewood, son of above		
from	*1388*	*GEC I, p. 101*
dead by	*1391*	

HAVERAH PARK

Owners

Crown		
from	1316	*HKW II*, p. 671
on	14 April 1358	*CPR 1358–1361*, p. 30
to	1372	*HKW II*, p. 673
John of Gaunt		
from	1372	*HKW II*, p. 673
to	1399	*HKW II*, p. 673
Crown		
from	1399	*HKW II*, p. 673

Constables

John de Newsum		
in	1333	*HKW II*, p. 672
to	15 November 1335	*CPR 1334–1338*, p. 176 (R.I.P.)

Edmund de Tidemerssh		
from	15 November 1335	*CPR 1334–1338*, p. 176
to	22 September 1343	*CPR 1343–1345*, p. 121
Roger de Normanvill		
from	22 September 1343	*CPR 1343–1345*, p. 121
to	25 February 1350	*CPR 1348–1350*, p. 477
John de Barton		
from	25 February 1350	*CPR 1350–1354*, p. 477
to	14 April 1358	*CPR 1358–1361*, p. 30
Thomas del Bothe, king's yeoman		
from	14 April 1358	*CPR 1358–1361*, p. 30
for life from	20 August 1360	*CPR 1358–1361*, p. 455
to	29 April 1369	*CPR 1367–1370*, p. 240 (R.I.P.)
Peter de Routhe, king's Yeoman		
for life from	29 April 1369	*CPR 1367–1370*, p. 240

HAZLEWOOD

Owners

William le Vavasour, P.P.		
licence to crenellate	28 August 1290	*CPR 1281–1292*, p. 383
died	*22 March 1312/3*	*GEC XII (ii), p. 232*
Walter le Vavasour, son of above		
inherited	*22 March 1312/3*	*GEC XII (ii), p. 232*
died	*7 December 1315*	*GEC XII (ii), p. 232*

HELMSLEY

Owners

Robert de Ros of Belvoir		
to	4 June 1285	*IPM II*, no. 580 (R.I.P.)
William de Ros, son of above, P.P.		
from	4 June 1285	*IPM II*, no. 580
William de Ros of Helmsley, P.P.		
away and back	10 September 1326	*CPR 1324–1327*, p. 320
to	16 February 1343	*IPM VIII*, no. 474 (R.I.P.)
William de Ros, son of above, P.P.		
heir on	16 February 1343	*IPM VIII*, no. 474
to	29 September 1352	*IPM X*, no. 45 (R.I.P.)
Thomas de Ros of Helmsley, kn., brother of above		
from	29 September 1352	*IPM X*, no. 45
to	21 May 1383	*IPM XVI*, no. 49
Beatrice, widow of above		
livery	24 October 1384	*C.C.R 1381–1385*, p. 487 (Jointure)
John de Ros of Helmsley, P.P.		
away and back	30 May 1386	*CPR 1385–1389*, p. 127
Richard de Burley		
on	4 November 1385	*CPR 1385–1389*, p. 57
John de Ros of Helmsley, kn., P.P.		
to	6 August 1394	*IPM XVII*, no. 414 (R.I.P.)
William de Ros, kn., Brother of above		
from	6 August 1394	*IPM XVII*, no. 414
died	*1 September 1414*	*GEC XI, p. 102*

John de Ros, kn., son of above		
from	*1 September 1414*	*GEC XI, p. 102*
not by	22 November 1421	*CPR 1416–1422*, p. 187
Margaret, widow of above		
from	22 November 1421	*CPR 1416–1422*, p. 187 (Dower)

Wardships

Minority of William de Ros (1343–1349)

Ralph de Bevyll		
from	15 May 1343	*CFR 1337–1343*, p. 330

Minority of Thomas de Ros (1353–1359)

Robert de Flaynburn		
from	20 January 1353	*CFR 1350–1354*, p. 352
Roger Mortimer, earl of March		
from	15 July 1355	*CPR 1354–1358*, p. 271
to	8 November 1356	*CPR 1354–1358*, p. 475

Minority of John de Ros (1414–1419)

Thomas Beaufort, earl of Dorset, duke of Exeter.		
from	22 September 1414	*CPR 1413–1416*, p. 234
to	8 July 1419	*CPR 1416–1422*, p. 263

Porter

John de la More		
for life on	16 February 1343	*IPM VIII*, no. 474

HOOD

Owners

John de Eyvill		
licence to crenellate	1264	King, p. 518

HORNBY

Owners

William St. Quintin		
temp.	after 1332	*VCH North Riding vol. I*, p. 315
John St. Quintin, son of above		*VCH North Riding vol. I*, p. 315
alive on	28 November 1386	*CPR 1385–1389*, p. 263
Anthony St. Quintin, son of above, probable builder		
died	end 14th cty.	*VCH North Riding vol. I*, p. 315
Margarat, da. of above and John Conyers		*VCH North Riding vol. I*, p. 315
Christopher Conyers, son of above		
temp	*1422–1429*	*VCH North Riding vol. I*, p. 315

KILLERBY

Owners

Brian Fitz Alan, P.P.		
licence to crenellate	20 September 1291	*CPR 1281–1292*, p. 445

KILTON

Tenant in Chief

Henry Percy		
on	22 April 1344	*IPM VIII*, no. 525

Henry Percy		
on	6 June 1374	*IPM XIV*, no. 58
on	31 December 1374	*IPM XIV*, no. 76

Owners

Robert de Thweng		
to	22 April 1344	*IPM VIII*, no. 525 (R.I.P.)
Thomas de Thweng, brother of above		
from	22 April 1344	*IPM VIII*, no. 525
to	May? 1374	*IPM XIV*, no. 58 (R.I.P.) Four potential heirs
Robert de Lumley		
to	31 December 1374	*IPM XIV*, no. 76 (R.I.P.)
Ralph de Lumley, brother of above, P.P.		
from	31 December 1374	*IPM XIV*, no. 76
Thomas de Lumley, son of above		
to	31 May 1400	*IPM XVIII*, no. 955 (R.I.P.)
John, brother of above		
from	31 May 1400	*IPM XVIII*, no. 955
Ralph de Lumley		
forfeited by	11 January 1400	*IMisc. VII*, no. 54
forfeited by	27 February (1 Henry IV?)	*IMisc. VII*, no. 57

Private Constables

John de Mowbray, esq.		
from	temp Ralph de Lomley	
still alive	11 January 1400	*IMisc. VII*, no. 54

Royal Constables

John de Beaufort, earl of Somerset		
from	22 January 1400	*CPR 1399–1401*, p. 173
William de Lambeton		
on	27 February (1 Henry IV?)	*IMisc. VII*, no. 57

KIRKBY FLEETHAM

Owners

Henry le Scrope		
licence to crenellate	20 September 1314	*CPR 1313–1317*, p. 175

KIRKBY MOORSIDE

Owners

Stuteville family		
temp	13th cty.	King, p. 520
Neville family, when not fortified		
temp	16th cty	King, p. 520

KIRKBY SIGSTON

Owners

John de Siggeston		
licence to crenellate	10 February 1336	*CPR 1334–1338*, p. 221

KNARESBOROUGH

Owners

Edmund, earl of Cornwall		
to	1298	*IPM III*, no. 605 (R.I.P.)
The King, his heir		
from	1298	*IPM III*, no. 605
Piers Gaveston		
from	5 August 1309	*CChR 1300–1326*, p. 131
to	26 July 1309	*CCR 1307–1313*, p. 225
from	5 August 1309	*CCR 1307–1313*, p. 225
Thomas of Lancaster		
to	3 November 1317	*CCR 1313–1318*, p. 575
Queen Isabella		
on	10 March 1327	*CCR 1327–1330*, p. 124
on	20 April 1327	*CMR*, no. 33
Queen Philippa		
from	1 January 1331	*CPR 1330–1334*, p. 55
to	25 December 1369	*IPM XII*, no. 434 (R.I.P.)
Crown		
from	25 December 1369	*IPM XII*, no. 434
John of Gaunt		
from	25 June 1372	W. Hardy, *Charters of the Duchy of Lancaster*, London, 1845, p. 28
from	25 June 1372	*JGR 1372–1376*, no. 13
on	20 July 1377	*CPR 1377–1381*, p. 294
Katherine, widow of John of Gaunt		
from	9 March 1398	*C.C.R 1396–1399*, p. 365
from	9 March 1399	*CPR 1396–1399*, p. 516

Constables

Miles de Stapleton, P.P.		
on	11 July 1302	*CCR 1302–1307*, p. 535
on	26 March 1307	*CPR 1301–1307*, p. 508
Piers Gaveston		
for life from	7 June 1308	*CPR 1307–1313*, p. 78
William de Vaus		
from	10 December 1311	*CFR 1307–1319*, p. 119
William de Vallibus		
from	26 June 1312	*CFR 1307–1319*, p. 136
to	5 January 1315	*CFR 1307–1319*, p. 224 (R.I.P.)
Roger Damory, P.P.		
from	5 January 1315	*CFR 1307–1319*, p. 224
on	25 September 1316	*CCR 1313–1318*, p. 365
William de Ros of Helmsley, P.P. and John de Mowbray, P.P.		
to	28 January 1318	*CFR 1307–1319*, p. 351
Nicholas de Grey		
from	28 January 1318	*CFR 1307–1319*, p. 351
to	4 March 1318	*CFR 1307–1319*, p. 255
Roger Damory, P.P.		
from	4 March 1318	*CFR 1307–1319*, p. 355
to	27 May 1318	*CFR 1307–1319*, p. 362

John de Wysham		
from	27 May 1318	*CFR 1307–1319*, p. 362
to	2 February 1319	*CPR 1317–1321*, p. 269
Edmund de Woodstock, earl of Kent		
from	2 February 1319	*CPR 1317–1321*, p. 269
to	6 November 1319	*CFR 1319–1327*, p. 11
John de Wysham		
from	6 November 1319	*CFR 1319–1327*, p. 11
on	22 November 1322	*CCR 1318–1323*, p. 611
accounting	30 September 1326	*CMR*, no. 23
John de Wauton		
from	6 March 1325	*CPR 1324–1327*, p. 106
Queen Isabella		
on	3 March 1328	*CFR 1327–1337*, p. 249
John de Wauton		
from	3 December 1330	*CFR 1327–1337*, p. 201
William fitz Waryn		
on	7 October 1332	*CPR 1330–1334*, p. 344
on	16 February 1338	E.101/20/19 m.1
William de Nessefeld (for queen)		
for life from	30 September 1351	*CPR 1350–1354*, p. 152
to	5 January 1356	*CPR 1354–1358*, p. 561
Thomas de Alberton, yeoman of queen's son (For queen)		
for life from	5 January 1356	*CPR 1354–1358*, p. 561
confirmed	20 May 1357	*CPR 1354–1358*, p. 561
William Gamdon, king's servant		
from	10 September 1370	*CPR 1370–1374*, p. 4
John de Marmion		
for life from	20 July 1377	*CPR 1377–1381*, p. 294
confirmed	12 January 1379	*CPR 1377–1381*, p. 294
Robert Rocle		
on	27 June 1396	*C.C.R 1396–1399*, p. 2 (Keeper)
Private Constables		
William Gamdon, king's servant		
confirmed	25 June 1372	*JGR 1372–1376*, no. 13
from	11 August 1372	*JGR 1372–1376*, no. 272
Wardship until inherited by Henry Bolingbroke		
William le Scrope, earl of Wiltshire		
from	2 April 1399	*CPR 1396–1399*, p. 502
Sub–constables		
William de Burbrigge		
dead by	6 March 1325	*CPR 1324–1327*, p. 106
Henry du Boys		
on	6 March 1338	E.101/20/19 m.3
on	7 July 1338	E.101/21/19 m.4
Robert Dowbyggynge		
on	27 June 1396	*CCR 1396–1399*, p. 2 (Lieutenant)

MALTON (THE LODGE)

History

destroyed	1322	King, p. 521

Constables

John de Mowbray, P.P.		
on	30 September 1317	*CPR 1317–1321*, p. 28

Notes

Being held by 'ill–disposed people', preventing new constable from taking over. Order to Sheriff of York to retake it

	30 September 1317	*CPR 1317–1321*, p. 28

MIDDLEHAM

Tenant in chief

lord of Richmond Castle		
on	17 October 1388	*IPM XVI*, no. 739

Owners

Ralph de Neville of Raby, P.P.		
on	20 July 1357	*CPR 1354–1358*, p. 586
to	5 August 1367	*IPM XII*, no. 160 (R.I.P.)
John Neville of Raby, son of above		
from	5 August 1367	*IPM XII*, no. 160
to	17 October 1388	*IPM XVI*, no. 739
Ralph Neville, earl of Westmorland, son of above		
from	17 October 1388	*IPM XVI*, no. 739

MULGRAVE

Owners

Peter de Mauley III, P.P.		
to	25 August 1309	*IPM V*, no. 199
Peter de Mauley IV, P.P. , son of above		
from	25 August 1309	*IPM V*, no. 199
on	13 February 1327	*CPR 1327–1330*, p. 15
died	*May 1348*	*GEC VIII, p. 560*
Peter de Mauley, V, P.P., son of above		
to	18 January 1356	*IPM X*, no. 252 (R.I.P.)
Margaret, widow of above		
from	18 January 1356	*IPM X*, no. 252 (Jointure)
to	8 August 1382	*IPM XV*, no. 818 (R.I.P.)
Peter de Mauley VI, P.P., son of both above		
from	8 August 1382	*IPM XV*, no. 818
to	20 March 1383	*IPM XV*, no. 815 (R.I.P.)
Peter de Mauley, VIII, grandson of above, P.P.		
under age	8 December 1383	*CPR*, p. 358
from	20 March 1383	*IPM XV*, no. 815
died	*6 September 1415*	*GEC VIII, p. 569*
Maud, widow of Peter Mauley, kn.		
from	27 November 1415	*CPR 1413–1416*, p. 248

NORTHALLERTON NO. 2

Owners		
Bishops of Durham		
temp.	entire period	W.M.I'Anson, 'The Castles of the North Riding', *Yorkshire Archaeological Journal*, 22 (1913), p. 368

PICKERING

Owners		
Edmund, earl of Lancaster		
from	temp. Henry III	
on	6 February 1292	*CPR 1292–1301*, p. 477
not by	3 July 1297	*IPM III*, no. 324 (R.I.P.)
Thomas earl of Lancaster		
confiscated before	13 March 1322	*CFR 1319–1327*, p. 105
writ	5 February 1327	*IPM VII*, no. 82
Henry, earl of Lancaster		
heir on	5 February 1327	*IPM VII*, no. 82
on	23 April 1327	*C.C.R 1327–1330*, p. 78
Henry, duke of Lancaster		
on	13 November 1352	*C.C.R 1327–1330*, p. 567
to	23 March 1361	*IPM XI*, no. 118 (R.I.P.)
dead by	16 July 1361	*CFR 1356–1368*, p. 164
John of Gaunt, duke of Lancaster		
from	16 July 1361	*CFR 1356–1368*, p. 164
on	8 March 1393	*CPR 1396–1399*, p. 500
not by	12 December 1393	*CPR 1396–1399*, p. 500
Henry Bolingbroke, future Henry IV		
by	12 December 1393	*CPR 1396–1399*, p. 500
Constables		
Thomas de Ughtred, P.P.		
from	13 March 1322	*CFR 1319–1327*, p. 105
to	8 November 1322	*CFR 1319–1327*, p. 187
John de Kyluyngton		
from	8 November 1322	*CFR 1319–1327*, p. 187
and from	16 April 1324	*CFR 1319–1327*, p. 272
Henry, earl of Lancaster		
from	7 December 1326	*CFR 1319–1327*, p. 424
David de Rouclyf, kn.		
confirmed	2 April 1399	*CPR 1396–1399*, p. 500
William le Scrope, earl of Wiltshire		
from	20 March 1399	*CFR 1391–1399*, p. 295
David de Rouclyf		
on	2 June 1403	*CCR 1402–1405*, p. 5
Stewards		
Henry Percy		
from	12 March 1322	*CFR 1319–1327*, p. 106

Private Constables

David de Rouclyf, kn.		
for life from	8 March 1393	CPR *1396–1399*, p. 500
confirmed	12 December 1393	CPR *1396–1399*, p. 500

PONTEFACT

Owners

Henry de Lacy, earl of Lincoln		
on	28 December 1292	*CChR 1257–1300*, p. 427 (fee tail)
to	6 February 1311	*IPM V*, no. 279 (R.I.P.)
Thomas, earl of Lancaster and Alice de Lacy his wife, daughter. of above		
from	6 February 1311	*IPM V*, no. 279
forfeited before	13 March 1322	*CFR 1319–1327*, p. 105
writ	5 February 1327	*IPM VII*, no. 82
Henry of Lancaster, brother of above		
heir on	5 February 1327	*IPM VII*, no. 82
Queen Isabella		
on	20 April 1327	*CMR*, no. 33
to	10 February 1330	*CPR 1327–1330*, p. 500
Queen Philippa		
from	12 February 1330	*CPR 1327–1330*, p. 500
on	12 June 1338	*CPR 1338–1340*, p. 92
not by	18 November 1348	*CPR 1345–1348*, p. 217
Henry, duke of Lancaster		
restored to	20 November 1348	*CFR 1347–1356*, p. 102
to	23 March 1361	*IPM XI*, no. 118 (R.I.P.)
John of Gaunt, duke of Lancaster		
from	16 July 1361	*CFR 1356–1368*, p. 164
on	17 June 1381	*JGR 1379–1383*, no. 551

Private Constables

Oliver de Stanefeld		
in	September 1296	*Two Compoti of the Lancashire and Cheshire Manors of Henry de Lacy, earl of Lincoln*, Chetham Society, 112 (1884), p. 147

Constables

Prior of St. Oswalds		
from	16 November 1292	*CPR 1281–1292*, p. 511
William le Vavasour, P.P.		
to	27 May 1311	*CPR 1307–1313*, p. 346 (Keeper)
Simon de Driby		
from	13 March 1322	*CFR 1319–1327*, p. 105
to	24 March 1322	*CFR 1319–1327*, p. 118
Thomas Deyvill		
from	24 March 1322	*CFR 1319–1327*, p. 118
on	18 November 1323	*CCR 1323–1327*, p. 146
William Grammary and Thomas Devill		
to	3 July 1323	*CPR 1321–1324*, p. 306

Richard de Mosele		
from	3 July 1323	*CPR 1321–1324*, p. 306
to	16 April 1324	*CFR 1319–1327*, p. 272
on	21 April 1324	*CCR 1323–1327*, p. 93
Thomas Deyvill		
from	16 April 1324	*CFR 1319–1327*, p. 272
to	3 January 1326	*CPR 1324–1327*, p. 205
Simon Warde, P.P.		
from	3 January 1326	*CPR 1324–1327*, p. 205
Thomas Deyvill		
on	20 February 1326	*CCR 1323–1327*, p. 455
on	13 February 1327	*CCR 1327–1330*, p. 69
Edward, duke of Aumale		
from	20 March 1399	*CFR 1391–1399*, p. 297
Robert Waterton		
on	28 July 1405	*CPR 1405–1408*, p. 74
on	21 November 1415	*CPR 1413–1416*, p. 237

Private Constables

Oliver de Stanefeld		
on	20 April 1306	*CCR 1302–1307*, p. 375 (For Lacy)
Ralph de Beeston		
in	March 1322	J.R.Maddicott, *Thomas of Lancaster*, Oxford, 1970, p. 339
Robert de Bosevill for Queen Isabella		
on	8 March 1328	*CPR 1327–1330*, p. 248
on	28 July 1338	*CPR 1338–1340*, p. 139

Maker of Bows, springalls, crossbows and cannons

Robert Walys		
for life from	15 November 1399	*CPR 1399–1401*, p. 100

Notes

Duke's chapel moved here		
from	17 June 1381	*JGR 1379–1383*, no. 551

RAVENSWORTH

Owners

Fitz Hugh family		
temp	entire period	P. T.Ryder, 'Ravensworth Castle, North Yorkshire', *Yorkshire Archaeological Society* 51 (1979), p. 81
Henry fitz Hugh, kn., P.P.		
to	29 August 1386	*IPM XVI*, no. 396 (R.I.P.)
Henry fitz Hugh, son of above, P.P.		
from	29 August 1386	*IPM XVI*, no. 396
from	6 November 1386	*CPR 1385–1389*, p. 182

RICHMOND

Owners

John de Brittany, earl of Richmond		
in	c.*1281–1286*	*Yorkshire Deeds vol. V*, C.T.Clay, YorkshireArchaeological Society Records Series, 69 (1926), no. 329
to	17 October 1285	*IPM II*, no. 579 (R.I.P.)
Alice, his granddaughter		
from	17 October 1285	*IPM II*, no. 579
John, duke of Brittany		
to	15 October 1306	*CChR 1300–1326*, p. 69 (R.I.P.)
John of Brittany, earl of Richmond		
from	15 October 1306	*CChR 1300–1326*, p. 69
to	2 August 1310	*CPR 1307–1313*, p. 275
Arthur, duke of Brittany, brother of above		
from	2 August 1310	*CPR 1307–1313*, p. 275
John of Brittany, earl of Richmond		
on	1 January 1328	*CPR 1327–1330*, p. 197
to	5 May 1331	*CPR 1327–1330*, p. 150
Mary de St. Pol, countess of Pembroke		
from	5 May 1331	*CPR 1327–1330*, p. 150
John III, duke of Brittany, earl of Richmond		
from	4 July 1334	*CPR 1330–1334*, p. 235
to	16 May 1341	*IPM VIII*, no. 335 (R.I.P.)
His children		
on	25 May 1341	*CPR 1340–1343*, p. 197
John of Gaunt, earl of Richmond, duke of Lancaster		
on	20 November 1342	*CPR 1340–1343*, p. 569
to	25 June 1372	*JGR 1372–1376*, no. 13
John, duke of Brittany, count of Montfort		
from	20 July 1372	*CPR 1370–1374*, p. 183
from	20 July 1372	*CChR 1341–1417*, p. 224
Queen Anne		
before	14 December 1391	*CPR 1391–1396*, p. 13
not by	10 July 1394	*CPR 1391–1396*, p. 469 (R.I.P.)
to	3 November 1388	*CPR 1388–1392*, p. 13
Henry fitz Hugh, leased for twelve years		
from	3 November 1388	*CPR 1388–1392*, p. 13
to	death of Queen Anne	
Thomas Arundel, bishop of York, Edward, earl of Rutland and John Waltam, bishop of Salisbury		
from	death of Queen Anne	
John, duke of Brittany and earl of Montfort		
on	14 December 1391	*CPR 1388–1392*, p. 13
Ralph de Neville, earl of Westmorland, granted by above for 12 years		
from	death of Queen Anne	
on	11 July 1396	*CPR 1396–1399*, p. 13
Edward, duke of Aumale		
on	22 January 1398	*CPR 1396–1399*, p. 350
Joan, sister of John earl of Richmond duke of Brittany, widow of Ralph de Neville, earl of Westmorland		
for life from	20 October 1399	*CPR 1399–1401*, p. 24
on	25 January 1406	*IPM XIX*, no. 137

Constables

William de Felton		
3 years from	21 February 1326	*CFR 1319–1327*, p. 377
on	24 February 1326	*CPR 1324–1327*, p. 244
Robert de Bincestre		
on	8 December 1326	*CPR 1324–1327*, p. 342
Roger de Quassington		
on	24 April 1338	*CPR 1338–1340*, p. 29
Peter de Richmond		
to	25 May 1341	*CPR 1340–1343*, p. 197
Thomas de Metham		
from	25 May 1341	*CPR 1340–1343*, p. 197
Walter de Urswyk		
on	30 August 1394	*CPR 1391–1396*, p. 499 (Kn.)
John Parker, esq.		
granted reversion	30 August 1394	*CPR 1391–1396*, p. 499
John Littelbury		
reversion for life	5 April 1395	*CPR 1391–1396*, p. 563
for life from	25 July 1395	
confirmed	26 July 1395	*CPR 1391–1396*, p. 612
Joan, widow of Ralph Basset of Drayton; Anthony Ricz; Nicholas Alderwych		
custody from	28 April 1398	*CPR 1396–1399*, p. 350
William Newesom		
from	12 August 1399	*CPR 1399–1401*, p. 546
confirmed	26 August 1401	*CPR 1399–1401*, p. 546

Private Constables

Roger de Quassington (from context)		
on	24 April 1338	*CPR 1338–1340*, p. 29
Walter de Urswyk, duke's esquire		
for life from	20 May 1362	*CPR 1367–1370*, p. 77
to	25 June 1372	*JGR 1372–1376*, no. 13
William le Scrope, earl of Wiltshire		
for life from	22 January 1398	
confirmed	23 February 1398	*CPR 1396–1399*, p. 317

Wardships
for minority of John of Gaunt

Queen Philippa		
from	20 November 1342	*CPR 1340–1343*, p. 569

SANDAL

Owners

John de Warenne, earl of Surrey		
to king and back	1 July 1316	*CPR 1313–1317*, pp. 483, 485
to	1 January 1319	*CPR 1317–1321*, p. 264
Thomas earl of Lancaster		
from	1 January 1319	*CPR 1317–1321*, p. 264
before	19 March 1322	*CFR 1321–1324*, p. 112
writ	5 February 1327	*IPM VII*, no. 82
Henry earl of Lancaster, brother of above		
heir on	5 February 1327	*IPM VII*, no. 82

John de Warenne, earl of Surrey		
requests its return	1318–1322	*CAPW*, p. 293
to	30 June 1347	*IPM IX*, no. 54 (R.I.P.)
Edmund de Langley, duke of York		
gift from the King	6 August 1347	*CChR 1341–1417*, p. 63
to	1 August 1402	*IPM XVIII*, no. 641
Edward, earl of Rutland, duke of York, son of above		
from	1 August 1402	*IPM XVIII*, no. 641
Henry le Scrope		
on	15 May 1413	*CPR 1413–1416*, p. 65
Joan, widow of Edmund, duke of York		
from	28 November 1415	*CPR 1413–1416*, p. 245

Constables while in Royal hands

Frank de Bresnes		
on	23 October 1240	*CLibR 1267–1272*, no. 2279
William de la Beche		
from	19 March 1322	*CFR 1319–1327*, p. 112
to	24 March 1322	*CFR 1319–1327*, p. 118
Thomas Deyvill		
from	24 March 1322	*CFR 1319–1327*, p. 118
to	16 April 1324	*CFR 1319–1327*, p. 275
Laurence de Castellay		
on	3 March 1324	*CCR 1323–1327*, p. 71
Richard de Mosele		
on	20 May 1324	*CCR 1323–1327*, p. 104 (Musele)
on	16 July 1334	*CCR 1333–1337*, p. 241
William de Montague		
on	14 February 1339	*CPR 1338–1340*, p. 203 (For life)
Peter de Routhe		
for life from	17 July 1348	*CPR 1348–1340*, p. 121

Private Constables

John Bosevill of Chete		
for life from	10 September 1368	*CPR 1367–1370*, p. 390
confirmed	22 April 1370	*CPR 1367–1370*, p. 390

Sieges

Attacked by John Boteler, John de Neuwerk and others (successfully)		
before	15 May 1413	*CPR 1413–1416*, p. 65

Wardships

minority of Edmund Langley, duke of York

Queen Philippa		
from	4 July 1348	*CPR 1348–1350*, p. 164

SCARBOROUGH

Owners

Crown		
on	6 April 1308	*CCR 1307–1313*, p. 29

Superior Custody

Henry Percy, P.P.		
from	1 October 1311	*CPR 1307–1313*, p. 391
to	20 February 1312	*CPR 1307–1313*, p. 429

Robert de Felton, P.P.		
from	20 February 1312	*CPR 1307–1313*, p. 429
Constables		
William de Percy		
to	7 November 1274	*CFR 1272–1307*, p. 35
mention	27 May 1275	*CCR 1272–1279*, p. 177
John de Vescy		
from	7 November 1274	*CFR 1272–1307*, p. 35
to	13 December 1276	*CFR 1272–1307*, p. 76
Robert de Neville		
from	13 December 1276	*CFR 1272–1307*, p. 76
John de Vescy		
on	27 March 1278	*IMisc I*, no. 1131
to	22 August 1289	*CPR 1281–1292*, p. 320
William de Vescy, P.P.		
from	22 August 1289	*CFR 1272–1307*, p. 264
to	2 June 1292	*CPR 1281–1292*, p. 492
John Sampson		
from	2 June 1292	*CPR 1281–1292*, p. 492
to	3 October 1297	*CFR 1272–1307*, p. 391
Ralph fitz William, P.P.		
from	3 October 1297	*CFR 1272–1307*, p. 391
to	23 February 1301	*CPR 1292–1301*, p. 575
John Sampson		
for life from	23 February 1301	*CPR 1292–1301*, p. 575
on	20 October 1305	*CCR 1302–1307*, p. 295
Henry Percy, P.P.		
from	16 March 1308	*CFR 1307–1319*, p. 18
right to dwell here	13 May 1308	*CPR 1307–1313*, p. 68
John Sampson		
on	17 March 1308	*CCR 1307–1313*, p. 25
on	1 October 1311	*CPR 1307–1313*, p. 391
Henry Percy, P.P.		
to	6 March 1312	*CFR 1307–1319*, p. 127
Robert de Felton, P.P.		
from	6 March 1312	*CFR 1307–1319*, p. 127
to	13 March 1312	*CFR 1307–1319*, p. 128
Piers Gaveston		
from	13 March 1312	*CFR 1307–1319*, p. 128
on	4 April 1312	*CPR 1307–1313*, p. 454
Taillifer de Tillio, king's yeoman		
from	26 June 1312	*CPR 1307–1313*, p. 466
on	1 January 1313	*CFR 1307–1319*, p. 160
John de Rolleston		
on	23 May 1313	*CCR 1307–1313*, p. 533
on	9 March 1314	*CPR 1313–1317*, p. 141 (Keeper)
Taillifer de Tillio		
to	26 September 1317	*CPR 1317–1321*, p. 29
John de Mowbray, P.P.		
from	26 September 1317	*CPR 1317–1321*, p. 29

Giles de Beauchamp		
from	15 January 1319	*CFR 1307–1319*, p. 393
to	16 November 1321	*CFR 1319–1327*, p. 78
Thomas de Ughtred, P.P.		
from	16 November 1321	*CFR 1319–1327*, p. 78
to	25 December 1321	*CFR 1319–1327*, p. 82
Henry Percy		
from	25 December 1321	*CFR 1319–1327*, p. 82
to	30 March 1324	*CFR 1319–1327*, p. 264
William Barde and Robert Wawayn		
from	30 March 1324	*CFR 1319–1327*, p. 264
to	19 September 1324	*CFR 1319–1327*, p. 305
Alexander de Bergh and Robert Wawayn		
from	19 September 1324	*CFR 1319–1327*, p. 305
to	26 November 1325	*CPR 1324–1327*, p. 192
Eleanor de Percy		
from	26 November 1325	*CPR 1324–1327*, p. 192
to	13 August 1328	*CFR 1327–1337*, p. 101 (R.I.P.)
Henry Percy		
from	13 August 1328	*CFR 1327–1337*, p. 313
on	16 February 1342	*IMisc II*, no. 1805
Richard Tempest		
temp	1347–1358	E.101/25/34
not by	1 December 1376	*CPR 1374–1377*, p. 398 (R.I.P.)
Ingram de Umfraville		
for life from	1 December 1376	*CPR 1374–1377*, p. 398
on	15 February 1380	*CFR 1377–1383*, p. 180
dead by	1382	E.101/38/6
Ralph Standyssh		
from	14 August 1381	*CPR 1381–1385*, p. 32
on	10 February 1382	*CFR 1377–1383*, p. 284
John de St. Quentin, kn.		
for life from	26 October 1382	*CPR 1381–1385*, p. 212
on	28 November 1386	*CPR 1385–1389*, p. 263
forfeited by	5 February 1393	*CPR 1391–1396*, p. 193
John Mosdale		
for life from	5 February 1393	*CPR 1391–1396*, p. 193
on	16 February 1402	*CPR 1401–1405*, p. 41

Deputy

Philip de Hambury		
on	14 July 1335	*CCR 1333–1337*, p. 426 (Supplies place)
on	8 December 1336	*CCR 1333–1337*, p. 639

King's Stewards

Humphrey de Walden		
from	26 April 1320	*CFR 1319–1327*, p. 20
Humphrey de Walden and Richard de Ikene		
from	8 March 1324	*CFR 1319–1327*, p. 259
Richard de Wynferthyng and Richard de Ikene		
from	20 August 1324	*CFR 1319–1327*, p. 295

SHEFFIELD

Owners

Thomas de Furnivall the elder, P.P.		
livery	*5 June 1291*	*GEC V, p. 581*
to	18 April 1332	*IPM VII*, no. 470 (R.I.P.)
Thomas de Furnivall, son of above, P.P.		
from	18 April 1332	*IPM VII*, no. 470
on	2 March 1343	*Feet of Fines for the county of York, 1327–1377*, Yorkshire Archaeology Society Records Series, 42 (1910), case 274, file 116, no 5
died	*October 1339*	*GEC V, p. 583*
Thomas de Furnivall, son of above, P.P.		
jointured	26 November 1343	*CPR 1343–1345*, p. 150
on	18 February 1362	*CPR 1408–1413*, p. 168
died	*21 April 1365*	*GEC V, p. 585*
William de Furnivall, P.P.		
inherited	*21 April 1365*	*GEC V, p. 585*
to	12 April 1383	*IPM XV*, no. 784 (R.I.P.)
Joan, daughter. of above, wife of Thomas de Neville		
from	12 April 1383	*IPM XV*, no. 784
Thomas de Neville, kn.		
on	25 January 1406	*IPM XIX*, no. 137
to	14 March 1407	*IPM XIX*, no. 245
John Talbot, through Maud his wife, daughter of above		
from	14 March 1407	*IPM XIX*, no. 245

SHERIFF HUTTON

Owners

John de Neville of Raby		
licence to crenellate	26 April 1382	*CPR 1381–1385*, p. 108
Ralph de Neville, earl of Westmorland		
on	18 October 1424	*Wills and Inventories, part 1*, Surtees Society 2 (1835), p. 73

SKELTON

Owners

Peter de Bruce		
dead by	14 December 1272	*CCR 1272–1279*, p. 3
Walter de Faucomberge, P.P. via Agnes, his wife, sister of above		
from	14 December 1272	*CCR 1272–1279*, p. 3
to	6 November 1304	*IPM IV*, no. 215 (R.I.P.)
Walter de Faucomberge, P.P.		
from	6 November 1304	*IPM IV*, no. 215
to	2 January 1319	*IPM VI*, no. 185 (R.I.P.)
John de Faucomberge, son of above		
from	2 January 1319	*IPM VI*, no. 185
to	18 September 1349	*IPM IX*, no. 198 (R.I.P.)
Walter de Faucomberge, son of above, P.P.		
from	18 September 1349	*IPM IX*, no. 198
to	September 1362	*IPM XI*, no. 330 (R.I.P.)

Thomas Faucomberge, son of above		
from	September 1362	*IPM XI*, no. 330
on	3 December 1366	*CPR 1364–1367*, p. 339
granted away	November 1366	*CCR 1364–1368*, p. 307
Thomas Faucomberge		
mad on	17 August 1403	*CPR 1401–1405*, p. 255
to	9 September 1407	*IPM XIX*, no. 386 (R.I.P.)
Joan, daughter of above		
from	9 September 1407	*IPM XIX*, no. 386
William Neville and Joan, his wife, above		
from	28 May 1422	*CCR 1419–1422*, p. 242

Wardships

During Madness of Thomas Faucomberge

Robert and John Conyers, brothers		
from	17 August 1403	*CPR 1401–1405*, p. 255

Minority of Joan, daughter of Thomas Faucomberge

Ralph de Neville, earl of Westmoreland		
from	2 March 1408	*CFR 1408–1413*, p. 103

SKIPSEA

Owners

William de la Pole		
before	18 July 1340	*CPR 1340–1343*, p. 89
Isabel, king's daughter		
on	13 November 1363	*CPR 1361–1364*, p. 497
Thomas, duke of Gloucester		
from	30 May 1395	*IMisc VI*, no. 348
Edward, earl of Rutland		
from	28 September 1397	*CPR 1396–1399*, p. 281 (Tail Male)
Thomas de Lancaster, king's son		
granted away	5 September 1407	*CPR 1405–1408*, p. 362

SKIPTON (IN CRAVEN)

Owners

Isabella de Forz, countess of Aumale		
temp	*1267–1269*	Denholm–Young, p. 39
Queen Eleanor of Provence		
from	23 January 1286	*CPR 1281–1292*, p. 218
died	1291	
Crown		
on	4 June 1307	*IPM IV*, no. 424
on	6 April 1308	*CCR 1307–1313*, p. 29
Piers Gaveston		
from	7 June 1308	*CChR 1300–1326*, p. 111
to	5 August 1309	*CCR 1307–1313*, p. 225
Robert de Clifford, P.P.		
on	5 August 1310	*CPR 1307–1313*, p. 273 (and Heirs)
to	20 October 1311	*CPR 1307–1313*, p. 395
from	13 November 1311	*CCR 1307–1313*, p. 386
to	28 July 1314	*IPM V*, no. 533 (R.I.P.)

Roger de Clifford, son of above, P.P.		
from	28 July 1314	*IPM V*, no. 533
under age	21 November 1317	*CPR 1317–1321*, p. 55
on	16 July 1318	*CFR 1307–1319*, p. 370
forfeited	8 February 1322	*CFR 1319–1327*, p. 94
Robert de Clifford, brother of above, P.P.		
from	12 February 1327	*IPM VII*, no. 77
to	20 May 1344	*IPM VIII*, no. 531 (R.I.P.)
Isabel, widow of above.		
from	20 May 1344	*IPM VIII*, no. 531 (Jointure)
to	25 July 1362	*IPM XI*, no. 312 (R.I.P.)
Roger de Clifford, kn., her son, P.P.		
from	25 July 1362	*IPM XI*, no. 312
to	13 July 1389	*IPM XVI*, no. 833 (R.I.P.)
Thomas de Clifford, kn., son of above, P.P.		
from	13 July 1389	*IPM XVI*, no. 833
to	4 October 1391	*IPM XVII*, no. 22 (1/3 held by his mother)
John lord of Clifford, son of above, P.P.		
from	4 October 1391	*IPM XVII*, no. 22 (1/3 held by his grandmother)
on	7 May 1415	*CPR 1413–1416*, p. 320
died	*13 March 1421/2*	*GEC III, p. 293*
Wardships		
Minority of Robert de Clifford (1315–1318)		
Bartholomew de Badelesmere		
to	2 November 1317	*CPR 1317–1321*, p. 45
John de Rithre		
from	2 November 1317	*CPR 1317–1321*, p. 45
on	6 July 1318	*CCR 1318–1323*, p. 5
not by	2 August 1318	*CCR 1318–1323*, p. 6
Private Constables		
John Sampson		
temp	1267–1269	Denholm–Young
Constables		
John de Crokesle		
on	11 August 1293	*CCR 1288–1296*, p. 298
John de St. John		
for life from	26 September 1300	*CPR 1292–1301*, p. 537
dead by	20 October 1303	*CPR 1301–1307*, p. 160
Richard Oysel (Skipton in Craven)		
on	8 March 1303	*CCR 1302–1307*, p. 17
to	18 August 1307	*CPR 1307–1313*, p. 1
Henry de Lacy, earl of Lincoln		
from	18 August 1307	*CPR 1307–1313*, p. 1
on	28 October 1307	*IMisc II*, no. 23
Gerard Salvayn		
on	10 August 1308	*CCR 1307–1313*, p. 74
Henry de Lacy, earl of Lincoln		
from	14 September 1309	*CFR 1307–1319*, p. 49
to	8 June 1310	*CCR 1307–1313*, p. 213

Robert de Clifford, P.P.		
for life from	19 March 1310	*CPR 1307–1313*, p. 220
to	20 October 1311	*CPR 1307–1313*, p. 395
Robert de Wodehous, King's Clerk		
from	20 October 1311	*CPR 1307–1313*, p. 395

Constables while forfeited 1322–1327

Henry de Malton		
from	24 March 1322	*CFR 1319–1327*, p. 118
to	13 September 1322	*CFR 1319–1327*, p. 177
John de Rythre		
from	13 September 1322	*CFR 1319–1327*, p. 177
on	15 May 1326	*CPR 1324–1327*, p. 267
Geoffrey le Scrope		
3 Years from	21 July 1326	*CFR 1319–1327*, p. 400
Henry Percy		
from	11 February 1327	*CFR 1327–1337*, p. 7

Private Constables

Nicholas Grandorge, for Cliffords		
to	8 May 1389	*CPR 1388–1392*, p. 408
Gilbert Dautre, for Cliffords		
from	8 May 1389	*CPR 1388–1392*, p. 408
confirmed	20 April 1391	*CPR 1388–1392*, p. 408

SLINGSBY

Owners

Ralph de Hastings		
licence to crenellate	28 January 1344	*CPR 1343–1345*, p. 190
Ralph de Hastings, kn. (Held of Thomas son of Duke of Norfolk)		
to	27 October 1397	*IPM XVII*, no. 540 (R.I.P.)
Richard de Hastings, kn, son of above, held from same		
from	27 October 1397	*IPM XVII*, no. 540
Maud, widow of Ralph de Hastings		
livery	15 October 1401	*CCR 1399–1402*, p. 428 (Jointure)

SWINE (BRANDSHOLME)

Tenant in Chief

Robert de Hilton		
on	5 May 1356	*IPM X*, no. 311
Maud, widow of Robert de Hilton		
on	5 October 1363	*IPM XI*, no. 531
Thomas, duke of Clarence		
on	27 November 1415	*CPR 1413–1416*, pp. 249–50

Owners

John de Sutton, P.P.		
pardon for crenellating	4 February 1352	*CPR 1350–1354*, p. 218
to	5 May 1356	*IPM X*, no. 311
Alina de Sutton, widow of above, in jointure		
from	5 May 1356	*IPM XI*, no. 531
to	5 October 1363	*IPM XI*, no. 531 (R.I.P.)

Thomas de Sutton, brother of John de Sutton above		
from	5 October 1363	*IPM XI*, no. 531
Constance, wife of Peter de Mauley VI (R.I.P.)		
to	9 June 1401	*IPM XVIII*, no. 419
Peter de Mauley VIII		
from	9 June 1401	*IPM XVIII*, no. 419
livery	23 June 1401	*C.C.R 1399–1402*, p. 370
5 people		
from	27 November 1415	*CPR 1413–1416*, pp. 249–50

TICKHILL

Owners

Queen Eleanor of Castile		
on	10 June 1280	*CPR 1272–1281*, p. 380
Constance de Bearn, daughter of Gaston viscount Bearn		
not by	24 August 1299	*CPR 1292–1301*, p. 433
Amaneuus de le Bret		
from	24 August 1299	*CPR 1292–1301*, p. 433 (and heirs)
Crown		
on	6 April 1308	*CCR 1307–1313*, p. 29
Queen Isabella		
on	20 April 1327	*CMR*, no. 33
on	18 December 1328	*CPR 1327–1330*, p. 344
Queen Philippa		
from	1 January 1331	*CPR 1330–1334*, p. 55
to	25 December 1369	*IPM XII*, no. 434 (R.I.P.)
Crown		
from	25 December 1369	*IPM XII*, no. 434
John of Gaunt, duke of Lancaster		
from	25 June 1372	*CPR 1377–1381*, p.24
on	11 February 1397	*CPR 1396–1399*, p. 76
Katherine, widow of above		
from	9 March 1399	*CPR 1396–1399*, p. 516
on	25 January 1401	*CPR 1399–1401*, p. 408

Constables

Michael de Weston		
from	25 August 1273	*CFR 1272–1307*, p. 10
Geoffrey de Sandiacre		
from	6 October 1273	*CPR 1272–1281*, p. 30
to	3 May 1274	*CPR 1272–1281*, p. 49
Constance de Bearn, widow of Henry de Alemannia		
from	3 May 1274	*CPR 1272–1281*, p. 49
Master Reymund de Nolmeriis		
on	5 February 1275	*CPR 1272–1281*, p. 78
to	12 November 1276	*CFR 1272–1307*, p. 75
Nicholas de Stapelton		
from	12 November 1276	*CFR 1272–1307*, p. 75
to	11 March 1279	*CPR 1272–1281*, p. 305
Constance, widow of Henry de Alemannia		
from	11 March 1279	*CPR 1272–1281*, p. 305
on	15 April 1279	*CChW*, p. 5

Constance de Bearn		
for life on	20 January 1283	*CPR 1281–1292*, p. 54
Amaneuus de le Bret		
on	23 August 1301	*CCR 1296–1302*, p. 464
to	30 October 1304	*CFR 1272–1307*, p. 499
John de Doncaster		
from	30 October 1304	*CFR 1272–1307*, p. 499
on	6 November 1304	*CCR 1302–1307*, p. 188
Constance de Bearn		
on	15 October 1305	*CCR 1302–1307*, p. 294
John de Staynton		
on	20 March 1312	*CCR 1307–1313*, p. 453
to	27 June 1312	*CPR 1307–1313*, p. 464
Vitalis de Saurnak, king's yeoman		
from	27 June 1312	*CPR 1307–1313*, p. 464
William de Aune		
from	17 July 1312	*CFR 1307–1319*, p. 139
on	1 June 1315	*CPR 1313–1317*, p. 327
John de Cromwell, P.P.		
from	25 December 1317	*CPR 1317–1321*, p. 64
William de Aune		
on	13 February 1322	*CCR 1318–1323*, p. 418
on	15 December 1324	*CCR 1323–1327*, p. 243
Simon de Bereford		
on	18 December 1328	*CPR 1327–1330*, p. 344
rebeled by	22 December 1331	*CPR 1330–1334*, p. 34
John Byk		
from	3 December 1330	*CFR 1327–1337*, p. 201
on	8 January 1331	*CCR 1330–1333*, p. 108
William Fraunk		
on	3 May 1336	*CPR 1334–1338*, p. 291
on	10 July 1344	*CPR 1343–1345*, p. 331
Thomas de Haukeston		
on	19 November 1346	*CPR 1345–1348*, p. 211
on	26 September 1351	*CPR 1350–1354*, p. 177
Richard Charles, yeoman, for the queen		
from	18 November 1358	*CPR 1358–1361*, p. 290
for queen from	18 March 1361	*JGR 1372–1376*, no. 23
confirmed by king	27 March 1361	*JGR 1372–1376*, no. 23
to	1 August 1372	*JGR 1372–1376*, no. 57
John Noble		
on	10 February 1362	*CPR 1361–1364*, p. 207
John atte Wode		
confirmed	25 June 1372	*JGR 1372–1376*, no. 13
from	12 August 1372	*JGR 1372–1376*, no. 261
Sir Walter Irsewyk		
on	18 June 1381	*JGR 1379–1383*, no. 535
William Crishill		
on	16 May 1398	*CCR 1396–1399*, p. 264

Keepers

Hugh de Totehill		
on	16 June 1347	*CFR 1347–1356*, p. 22

King's Stewards

Master William Miremonte
on 12 November 1279 *CPR 1272–1281*, p. 350
Humphrey de Walden
from 26 April 1320 *CFR 1319–1327*, p. 20
Humphrey de Walden and Richard de Ikene
from 8 March 1324 *CFR 1319–1327*, p. 259
Richard de Wynferthyng and Richard de Ikene
from 20 August 1324 *CFR 1319–1327*, p. 295

Chaplains

John Clarel
to 11 May 1295 *CPR 1292–1301*, p. 135 (R.I.P.)
Boniface de Saluciis
from 11 May 1295 *CPR 1292–1301*, p. 135

Notes

The Duchess of Brittany was kidnapped from here by Warmer de Giston and her men and taken to the honour of Pontefract
28 November 1347 *CPR 1345–1348*, p. 468

Garrisons

20 men at arms and archers
on 18 June 1381 *JGR 1379–1383*, no. 535

UPSALL

Owners

Scrope family
from c.1327 King, p. 529 (n.109)

WAKEFIELD

Constables

Roger de Flete
to 16 April 1324 *CFR 1319–1327*, p. 275
Richard de Modele
from 16 April 1324 *CFR 1319–1327*, p. 275

WHORLTON

Tenant in Chief

Archbishop of Canterbury
on 5 March 1356 *IPM X*, no. 310

Owners

John Darcy, the son, kn., P.P.
to 5 March 1356 *IPM X*, no. 310 (R.I.P.)
John Darcy, son of above, died underage
from 5 March 1356 *IPM X*, no. 310
Elizabeth, widow of Peter de Mauley VI
to 9 July 1368 *IPM XII*, no. 240 (R.I.P.)
Philip Darcy, P.P. son of John Darcy above and Elizabeth
from 9 July 1368 *IPM XII*, no. 240
died 24 April 1399 GEC IV, p. 63

John Darcy, son of above, P.P.		
inherited	*24 April 1399*	*GEC IV, p. 63*
died	*9 December 1411*	*GEC IV, p. 63*
Philip Darcy, son of above		
from	*1411*	*GEC IV, p. 63*
underage	*1413*	*GEC IV, p. 63*

WRESSLE

Owners

Percys		
from	1380–1390	J. Bilson, 'Proceedings in 1912, Wressle Castle', *Yorkshire Archaeological Journal*, 22 (1913), p. 182
Henry Percy, earl of Northumberland		
forfeited by	10 August 1405	*CPR 1405–1408*, p. 46
Ralph Neville, earl of Westmorland		
on	27 June 1405	*CPR 1405–1408*, p. 40
Queen Joan		
from	10 August 1405	Jacob, p. 63

Constables

Robert Badthorpe, esq.		
for life from	8 August 1403	*CPR 1401–1405*, p. 247
Queen Joan		
for life from	10 September 1403	*CPR 1401–1405*, p. 259
for life from	10 August 1405	*CPR 1401–1405*, p. 46

WILTON–IN–CLEVELAND (BISHOP'S WILTON)

Owners

Ralph de Bulmer, P.P.		
licence to crenellate	12 May 1330	*CPR 1327–1330*, p. 519
Ralph Bulmer, kn.		
to	24 April 1406	*IPM XIX*, no. 107 (R.I.P.)
Ralph Bulmer,		
age 23+ on	April 1406	*IPM XIX*, no. 107
to	5 August 1406	*IPM XIX*, no. 107 (R.I.P.)
Ralph Bulmer		
heir, age 3 on	August 1406	*IPM XIX*, no. 107
Agnes, widow of Ralph Bulmer, kn.,		
from	8 November 1406	*CCR 1405–1409*, p. 164 (Jointure)

YORK (CLIFFORDS TOWER)

Constables

Roger le Strange of Ellesmere, P.P.		
on	12 July 1273	*CFR 1272–1307*, p. 8
to	18 October 1274	*CFR 1272–1307*, p. 31
Alexander de Kirton		
from	18 October 1274	*CFR 1272–1307*, p. 31
to	25 October 1278	*CFR 1272–1307*, p. 103

Ranulf de Dacre		
from	25 October 1278	*CFR 1272–1307*, p. 103
to	29 May 1280	*CFR 1272–1307*, p. 127
John de Lithegraynes		
from	29 May 1280	*CFR 1272–1307*, p. 127
and from	15 November 1280	*CPR 1272–1281*, p. 404
John de Eure		
to	5 March 1311	*CFR 1307–1319*, p. 86
Gerard Salvayn		
to	1 October 1314	*CFR 1307–1319*, p. 212
John Malebys		
from	1 October 1314	*CFR 1307–1319*, p. 212
to	24 May 1315	*CFR 1307–1319*, p. 249
Nicholas de Meinill, P.P.		
from	24 May 1315	*CFR 1307–1319*, p. 249
to	20 October 1315	*CFR 1307–1319*, p. 261
Simon Warde, P.P.		
from	20 October 1315	*CFR 1307–1319*, p. 261
to	21 January 1317	*CFR 1307–1319*, p. 316
Nicholas de Grey		
from	21 January 1317	*CFR 1307–1319*, p. 316
to	15 May 1318	*CFR 1307–1319*, p. 360
Simon Warde, P.P.		
from	15 May 1318	*CFR 1307–1319*, p. 360
to	29 November 1318	*CFR 1307–1319*, p. 382
Robert de Rithre		
from	29 November 1318	*CFR 1307–1319*, p. 382
to	19 December 1318	*CFR 1307–1310*, p. 387
Simon Warde, P.P.		
from	19 December 1318	*CFR 1307–1319*, p. 387
to	15 June 1323	*CFR 1319–1327*, p. 213
Roger de Somervill		
from	15 June 1323	*CFR 1319–1327*, p. 213
after	9 November 1324	*CFR 1319–1327*, p. 317
to	26 February 1325	*CFR 1319–1327*, p. 332
Henry de Faucomberge		
from	26 February 1325	*CFR 1319–1327*, p. 332
Roger de Somervill		
to	4 February 1327	*CFR 1327–1337*, p. 15
Henry de Faucomberge		
from	4 February 1327	*CFR 1327–1337*, p. 15
to	30 September 1327	*CFR 1327–1337*, p. 64
John Darcy le Neveu, the son, P.P.		
from	30 September 1327	*CFR 1327–1337*, p. 64
to	16 August 1328	*CFR 1327–1337*, p. 101
Henry de Faucomberge		
from	16 August 1328	*CFR 1327–1337*, p. 101
to	5 December 1330	*CFR 1327–1337*, p. 199
Ralph de Bulmer, P.P.		
from	5 December 1330	*CFR 1327–1337*, p. 199
to	3 June 1332	*CFR 1327–1337*, p. 315

Peter de Saltmerssh		
from	3 June 1332	*CFR 1327–1337*, p. 315
Gerard Salvayn		
for life from	22 October 1334	*CPR 1334–1338*, p. 36
Peter de Saltmerssh		
to	27 January 1335	*CFR 1327–1337*, p. 430
Peter de Middleton		
from	27 January 1335	*CFR 1327–1337*, p. 430
to	3 November 1335	*CFR 1327–1337*, p. 462 (R.I.P.)
Thomas de Rokeby		
from	3 November 1335	*CFR 1327–1337*, p. 462
to	24 March 1337	*CFR 1327–1337*, p. 9
Ralph de Hastings		
from	24 March 1337	*CFR 1337–1347*, p. 9
to	18 February 1340	*CFR 1337–1347*, p. 159
or to	10 April 1340	*CFR 1337–1347*, p. 169
John Moryn		
from	18 February 1340	*CFR 1337–1347*, p. 159
or from	10 April 1340	*CFR 1337–1347*, p. 169
to	26 April 1340	*CFR 1337–1347*, p. 172 (R.I.P.)
Ralph de Hastings		
from	26 April 1340	*CFR 1337–1347*, p. 172
to	1 October 1340	*CFR 1337–1347*, p. 195
John de Eland		
from	1 October 1340	*CFR 1337–1347*, p. 195
to	19 November 1341	*CFR 1337–1347*, p. 250
John Faucomberge, P.P.		
from	19 November 1341	*CFR 1337–1347*, p. 250
to	7 October 1342	*CFR 1337–1347*, p. 300
Thomas de Rokeby		
from	7 October 1342	*CFR 1337–1347*, p. 300
to	25 July 1349	*CFR 1347–1356*, p. 131
or to	25 August 1349	*CFR 1347–1356*, p. 131
William Playce		
from	25 July 1349	*CFR 1347–1356*, p. 131
Brian de Thornhull		
from	25 August 1349	*CFR 1347–1356*, p. 131
Gerard Salvayn		
from	24 October 1349	*CFR 1347–1356*, p. 171
to	22 October 1350	*CFR 1347–1356*, p. 227
William de Plumpton		
from	22 October 1350	*CFR 1347–1356*, p. 227
to	17 October 1351	*CFR 1347–1356*, p. 307
Peter de Nuttle		
from	17 October 1351	*CFR 1347–1356*, p. 307
and from	3 October 1352	*CFR 1347–1356*, p. 349
Miles de Stapelton of Hathelseye		
from	22 November 1352	*CFR 1347–1356*, p. 349
to	16 September 1353	*CFR 1347–1356*, p. 388
Peter de Nuttle		
from	16 September 1353	*CFR 1347–1356*, p. 388
to	10 November 1354	*CFR 1347–1356*, p. 409

Miles de Stapelton of Hathelseye		
from	10 November 1354	*CFR 1347–1356*, p. 409
to	10 March 1356	*CFR 1347–1356*, p. 19
Peter de Nuttle		
from	10 March 1356	*CFR 1347–1356*, p. 19
to	30 September 1359	*CFR 1356–1368*, p. 102
Thomas de Musgrave, P.P.		
from	30 September 1359	*CFR 1356–1368*, p. 102
Marmaduke Constable		
from	21 November 1360	*CFR 1356–1368*, p. 122
to	20 November 1362	*CFR 1356–1368*, p. 236
Thomas de Musgrave, P.P.		
from	20 November 1362	*CFR 1356–1368*, p. 236
and from	10 November 1364	*CFR 1356–1368*, p. 283
Marmaduke Constable		
from	13 May 1366	*CFR 1356–1368*, p. 328
John Chaumon		
from	14 December 1367	*CFR 1356–1368*, p. 359
William de Aton, P.P.		
from	27 November 1368	*CFR 1356–1368*, p. 392
to	28 March 1370	*CFR 1369–1377*, p. 98
John Bygod		
from	28 March 1370	*CFR 1369–1377*, p. 98
Robert de Ros of Ingmanthorp		
from	5 November 1371	*CFR 1369–1377*, p. 146
William de Aton, P.P.		
from	12 December 1372	*CFR 1369–1377*, p. 190
John Bygot		
from	7 November 1373	*CFR 1369–1377*, p. 222
William Percehay		
from	12 December 1374	*CFR 1369–1377*, p. 272
William Melton		
from	4 October 1375	*CFR 1369–1377*, p. 297
Ralph de Hastings		
from	26 October 1376	*CFR 1369–1377*, p. 369
and from	22 June 1377	*CFR 1377–1383*, p. 3
John Constable of Halsham, kn.		
from	26 November 1377	*CFR 1377–1383*, p. 34
Robert Neville of Hornby		
from	7 November 1378	*CFR 1377–1383*, p. 113
to	5 November 1379	*CFR 1377–1383*, p. 170
William Melton		
from	5 November 1379	*CFR 1377–1383*, p. 170
John Sayvill		
from	3 March 1380	*CFR 1377–1383*, p. 171
to	18 October 1380	*CFR 1377–1383*, p. 220
Ralph de Hastings		
from	18 October 1380	*CFR 1377–1383*, p. 220
William de Ergum		
from	6 December 1381	*CFR 1377–1383*, p. 270
John Sayvill		
from	24 November 1382	*CFR 1377–1383*, p. 327

Robert de Hilton		
from	1 November 1383	*CFR 1383–1391*, p. 7
to	11 November 1385	*CFR 1383–1391*, p. 76
Gerard de Usflete		
from	11 November 1385	*CFR 1383–1391*, p. 76
Robert Constable of Flamborough		
from	20 October 1385	*CFR 1383–1391*, p. 107
to	18 November 1386	*CFR 1383–1391*, p. 152
Robert de Hilton		
from	18 November 1386	*CFR 1383–1391*, p. 152
to	18 November 1387	*CFR 1383–1391*, p. 208
John Sayvill		
from	18 November 1387	*CFR 1383–1391*, p. 208
John Gobard		
from	1 December 1388	*CFR 1383–1391*, p. 248
James de Pickering		
from	15 November 1389	*CFR 1383–1391*, p. 306
to	7 November 1390	*CFR 1383–1391*, p. 341
William Melton		
from	7 November 1390	*CFR 1383–1391*, p. 341
to	21 October 1391	*CFR 1391–1399*, p. 7
Ralph de Eure		
from	21 October 1391	*CFR 1391–1399*, p. 7
John Depeden		
from	18 October 1392	*CFR 1391–1399*, p. 56
James Pickering		
from	7 November 1393	*CFR 1391–1399*, p. 95
Robert Constable of Flamborough		
from	11 November 1394	*CFR 1391–1399*, p. 132
Ralph de Eure		
from	9 November 1395	*CFR 1391–1399*, p. 166
Robert Neville of Hornby		
from	1 December 1396	*CFR 1391–1399*, p. 197
James de Pickering		
from	3 November 1397	*CFR 1391–1399*, p. 240
William Dronsfeld, kn.		
from	8 November 1401	*CFR 1399–1405*, p. 143
Edmund Stanford		
to	10 December 1411	*CFR 1405–1413*, p. 221
Thomas de Rokeby		
from	10 December 1411	*CFR 1405–1413*, p. 221
to	3 November 1412	*CFR 1405–1413*, p. 249
John Etton		
from	3 November 1412	*CFR 1405–1413*, p. 249
from	21 March 1413	*CFR 1413–1422*, p. 5
to	6 November 1413	*CFR 1413–1422*, p. 41
William Harington, P.P.	(probably not taken up)	
from	6 November 1413	*CFR 1413–1422*, p. 41
Thomas Brounflete		
from	12 November 1414	*CFR 1413–1422*, p. 83
to	1 December 1415	*CFR 1413–1422*, p. 129

Richard Redeman		
from	1 December 1415	*CFR 1413–1422*, p. 129
to	30 November 1416	*CFR 1413–1422*, p. 177
Edmund Hastings		
from	30 November 1416	*CFR 1413–1422*, p. 177
to	10 November 1417	*CFR 1413–1422*, p. 215
Robert de Hilton		
from	10 November 1417	*CFR 1413–1422*, p. 215
to	4 November 1418	*CFR 1413–1422*, p. 261
John Bygod		
from	4 November 1418	*CFR 1413–1422*, p. 261
Thomas Brounflete		
to	16 November 1420	*CFR 1413–1422*, p. 358
Alnath Maweleverer		
from	16 November 1420	*CFR 1413–1422*, p. 358
in	2 April 1422	*York Memoranda Book, I (1376–1419)*, Surtees Society, 120 (1912), p. 203
Gatekeeper		
John		
in	1300	*Select Cases in the Exchequer of Pleas*, Selden Society, 48 (1931), case 231
Henry Miles		
from	16 November 1420	*CFR 1413–1422*, p. 358
Porter		
Richard Sutton		
dead by	20 February 1392	*CPR 1391–1396*, p. 33
Simon de Elvyngton		
for life from	20 February 1392	*CPR 1391–1396*, p. 33
Gaoler		
William de Tyryngton		
for life from	October 1377	*CPR 1377–1381*, p. 27
Gaoler, keeper and Porter		
Henry Maunsell, esq.		
for life from	February 1400	*CPR 1399–1401*, p. 192
vacated	1402	
to	12 May 1402	*CPR 1401–1405*, p. 92
William de Hoton		
from	12 May 1402	*CPR 1401–1405*, p. 92 (Vacated)
John Manfeld		
for life from	6 June 1413	*CPR 1413–1416*, p. 39
John de Leventhorpe		
from	27 March 1411	
confirmed	4 May 1414	*CPR 1413–1416*, p. 289

Bibliography

Manuscript Sources

PUBLIC RECORD OFFICE, LONDON

Chancery

C.47 Chancery Miscellanea

C.49 Parliament and Council

C.60 Fine Rolls

C.62 Liberate Rolls

C.76 Treaty Rolls

C.258 Chancery Files: *Certiorari (corpus cum causa)*

Exchequer

E.36 Treasury of Receipt, Books

E.101 King's Remembrancer, Accounts Various

E.156 Original Letters Patent

E.372 Lord Treasurer's Remembrancer, Pipe Rolls

E.403 Exchequer of Receipt, Issue Rolls

E.404 Ex. of R., Warrants for Issues; Wardrobe Debentures

Duchy of Lancaster

DL.27 Duchy of Lancaster: Deeds

Palatinate of Lancaster

PL.1 Palatine of Lancaster: Chancery: Patent Rolls

Special Collections

SC.1 Ancient Correspondence

BRITISH LIBRARY, LONDON

Additional Manuscripts

Cotton Manuscripts

Stowe Manuscripts

NORTHALLERTON RECORD OFFICE

ZBO 1 Scrope of Bolton Manuscripts

JOHN RYLANDS LIBRARY, MANCHESTER

Latin MS 240

Printed Primary Sources

1341 Royal Inquest in Lincolnshire, ed. B.W. McLane, Lincoln Record Society, 78 (1987)

Abstract of Feet of Fines relating to Wiltshire for the Reign of Edward III, ed. C.R. Elrington, Wiltshire Record Society, 29 (1973)

Accounts of the Constables of Bristol Castle, ed. M. Sharp, Bristol Record Society, 34 (1982)

Bishop Langley's Register vol. 4, ed. R.L. Storey, Surtees Society, 170 (1955)

Calendar of Ancient Correspondence concerning Wales, ed. J.G. Edwards, Cardiff, 1935

Calendar of Ancient Petitions Relating to Wales, ed. W. Rees, Glamorgan, 1975

Calendar of Chancery Warrants, 1244–1326, London, 1927

Calendar of Close Rolls, 31 vols., London, 1892–1938

Calendar of Documents relating to Scotland, ed. J. Bain, 4 vols., 1881–1888

Calendar of Fine Rolls, 14 vols., London, 1911–1962

Calendar of Inquisitions Post Mortem, vols. 2–20, London, 1906–1995

Calendar of Inquisitions Miscellaneous, Chancery, vols. 1–7, London, 1916–1968

Calendar of Liberate Rolls 1267–1272, London, 1964

Calendar of Memoranda Rolls (Exchequer). Michaelmas 1326–Michaelmas 1327, London, 1968

Calendar of Patent Rolls, 31 vols., London, 1891–1971

'Calendar of Welsh Rolls, 1277–1294' in *Calendar of various Chancery Rolls*, London, 1912, pp. 157–382

Calendarium Rotularum Patentium in Turri Londinensi, London, 1802

Catalogue of Ancient Deeds, vols. 1–6, London, 1890–1915

Charters of the Duchy of Lancaster, ed. W. Hardy, London, 1845

Chronicle of Adam Usk, 1377–1421, ed. C. Given-Wilson, Oxford, 1997

Chronicle of Bury St. Edmunds, 1212–1301, ed. and trans. A. Gransden, London, 1964

Chronicle of Lanercost, 1272–1346, trans. H. Maxwell, Glasgow, 1913

Chronicles of the Reign of Edward I and Edward II, vol. 1, Annales Londonienses and Annales Paulini, ed. W. Stubbs, Rolls Series, 76 (1882)

Chronicon de Lanercost, 1201–1346, ed. J. Stevenson, Edinburgh, 1839

Coucher Book of Furness Abbey, part 1, ed. J.C. Atkinson, Chetham Society, New Series, 9 (1886)

Descriptive Catalogue of Derbyshire Charters, compiled I.H. Jeayes, London, 1906

Fœdera, conventiones, litteræ, ed. T. Rymer, revised edition by A. Clarke, F. Holbrooke and J. Coley, 4 vols. in 7 parts, Record Commission, 1816–69

Feet of Fines for the county of York, 1327–1377, W.P. Baildon, Yorkshire Archaeology Society Records Series, 42 (1910)

Feet of Fines for the county of York from 1300 to 1314, ed. M. Roper, Yorkshire Archaeology Society Records Series, 127 (1963)

Gesta Stephani, ed. K.R. Potter and R.H.C. Davis, Oxford, 1976

Great Roll of the Pipe for the Twentieth Year of the Reign of King Henry the Second, 1173–1174, Pipe Roll Society, 21 (1896)
Hemingby's Register, ed. H.M. Chew, Wiltshire Record Society, 18 (1962)
Historical Papers and Letters from the Northern Registers, ed. J. Raine, Rolls Series, 61 (1873)
Household Accounts from Medieval England, C.M. Woolgar, 2 vols., Oxford, 1992–1993
Issue Roll of Thomas de Brantingham, ed. F. Devon, London, 1835
John of Gaunt's Register, 1372–1376, ed. S. Armitage-Smith, Camden Society, 3rd series, 20 (1911) and 21 (1911)
John of Gaunt's Register, 1379–1383, ed. E.C. Lodge and R. Somerville, Camden Society, 3rd series, 56 (1937) and 57 (1938)
List of Welsh Entries in the Memoranda Rolls 1282–1343, N. Fryde, Cardiff, 1974
Ministers' Accounts of the Earldom of Cornwall, ed. L.M. Midgley, Surtees Society, 3rd Series, 66 (1942) and 68 (1945)
Northumberland Petitions, ed. C.M. Fraser, Surtees Society, 176 (1966)
Northumbrian Pleas from De Banco Rolls 1–19, ed. A.H. Thompson, Surtees Society, 158 (1943)
Percy Chartulary, ed. M.T. Martin, Surtees Society, 117 (1909)
Plea Rolls of the County Palatine of Lancaster, Roll 1, ed. Colonel J. Parker, Chetham Society, New Series, 87 (1928)
Records of Anthony Bek, Bp. and Patriarch, 1283–1311, ed. C.M. Fraser, Surtees Society, 162 (1953)
Records of some Sessions of the Peace in Lincolnshire, 1360–75, ed. R. Sillem, Lincoln Record Society, 30 (1933)
Register of Bishop Philip Repingdon, 1405–1419, vol. 1, ed. M. Archer, Lincoln Record Society, 57 (1963)
Register of Bishop Philip Repingdon, 1405–1419, vol. 2, ed. M. Archer, Lincoln Record Society, 58 (1963)
Register of Edward, the Black Prince, part I: 1346–1348, London, 1930
Register of Edward, the Black Prince, part II: Duchy of Cornwall 1351–1365, London, 1931
Register of Edward, the Black Prince, part III: Palatinate of Chester 1351–1365, London, 1932
Register of Edward, the Black Prince, part IV: England 1351–1365, London, 1933
Register of John Chandler, Dean of Salisbury 1404–1417, ed. T.C.B. Timmins, Wiltshire Record Society, 39 (1984)
Registrum Antiquissimum of the Cathedral Church of Lincoln, vol. I, ed. C.W. Foster, Lincoln Record Society, 27 (1931)
Registrum Antiquissimum of the Cathedral Church of Lincoln, vol. II, ed. C.W. Foster, Lincoln Record Society, 28 (1933)
Registrum Antiquissimum of the Cathedral Church of Lincoln, vol. III, ed. C.W. Foster, Lincoln Record Society, 29 (1935)

Registrum Epistolarum J. Peckham Arch. Cant., ed. C.T. Martin, Rolls Series, 77 (1885)

Rolls and Register of Bishop Oliver Sutton, 1280–1299, vol. 1: Archdeaconry of Lincoln, ed. R. Hill, Lincoln Record Society, 39 (1942)

Rottuli Ricardi Gravesend, ed. F.N. Davis, Lincoln Record Society, 20 (1922)

Rotuli Litterarum Patentium in Turri Londinensi, vol. 1, part 1, London, 1835

Rotuli Scotiae, vol. 1, ed. D. Macpherson et al., Record Commssion, 1814

State Trials of the Reign of Edward the First, 1289–1293, ed. T.F. Tout and H. Johnstone, Camden Society, 3rd Series, 9 (1906)

'Scalacronica' of Sir Thomas Gray, trans. H. Maxwell, Glasgow, 1907

Select Cases in the Court of King's Bench under Richard II, Henry IV and Henry V, vol. 7, ed. G.O. Sayles, Selden Society, 88 (1971)

Select Cases in the Exchequer of Pleas, ed. H. Jenkinson and B. Formoy, Selden Society, 48 (1931)

Treaty Rolls volume II 1337–1339, ed. J. Ferguson, London, 1972

Two Compoti of the Lancashire and Cheshire Manors of Henry de Lacy, earl of Lincoln, trans. Rev. P.A. Lyons, Chetham Society, 112 (1884)

Wardrobe Book of William de Norwell, 12 July 1338 to 27 May 1340, ed. M. Lyon, B. Lyon, H.S. Lucas and J. de Sturler, Brussels, 1983

Wills and Inventories, part 1, Surtees Society, 2 (1835)

Wiltshire Gaol Delivery and Trailbaston Trials, 1275–1306, ed. R.B. Pugh, Wiltshire Record Society, 33 (1977)

York Memoranda Book, I (1376–1419), ed. M. Sellers, Surtees Society, 120 (1912)

Yorkshire Deeds vol. 5, C.T. Clay, Yorkshire Archaeological Society, Records Series, 69 (1926)

Yorkshire Inquisitions of the reign of Henry III and Edward I, vol. 1, ed. W. Brown, Yorkshire Archaeological & Topographical Association Record Series, 12 (1891)

Secondary Sources

Aberth, J., *Criminal Churchmen in the age of Edward III, the Case of Bishop Thomas de Lisle*, Pennsylvania, 1996

Alban, J.R., 'English Coastal Defence: some Fourteenth-Century Modifications within the System', in R.A. Griffiths, ed., *Patronage, The Crown and the Provinces*, Gloucester, 1981, pp. 57–78

Allmand, C., *Henry V*, London, 1992

Aston, M., *Thomas Arundel, A Study of Church Life in the Reign of Richard II*, Oxford, 1967

Austin, D., 'Barnard Castle co. Durham, 2nd Interim Report: Excavations in the Town Ward 1974–6', *Journal of the British Archaeological Association*, 132 (1979), pp. 50–72

Austin, D., 'Barnard Castle co. Durham, 2nd Interim Report: Excavations in the Inner Ward, 1976–8: The Later Medieval Period', *Journal of the British Archaeological Association*, 133 (1980), pp. 74–85

Ayton, A., 'William de Thweyt, esquire, Deputy constable of Corfe Castle in the 1340s', *Somerset and Dorset Notes and Queries*, 32 (1989), pp. 731–738

Ayton, A., 'The Robin Hood Legend in the Fourteenth Century', *Nottingham Medieval Studies*, 34 (1992), pp. 136–147

Ayton, A., 'English Armies in the Fourteenth Century', in *Arms, Armies and Fortifications in the Hundred Years War*, Anne Curry and Michael Wolfe (eds.), Woodbridge, 1994, pp. 21–38

Ayton, A., *Knights and Warhorses*, Woodbridge, 1994

Ayton, A., 'Edward III and the English Aristocracy at the beginning of the Hundred Years War', in M. Strickland (ed.), *Armies, Chivalry and Warfare in Medieval Britain and France*, Stamford, 1998

Barber, R., *Edward, Prince of Wales and Aquitaine*, London, 1978

Bates, C.J., 'The Barony and Castle of Langley', *Arch. Aeliana*, New Series, 10 (1885), pp. 38–56

Bates, C.J., 'The Border Holds of Northumberland, vol. 1', *Archaeologia Aeliana*, 14 (1891)

Bean, J.W., *The Decline of English Feudalism, 1215–1540*, Manchester and New York, 1968

Bilson, J., 'Gilling Castle', *Yorkshire Archaeological Journal*, 19 (1907), pp. 106–92

Bilson, J., 'Proceedings in 1912, Wressle Castle', *Yorkshire Archaeological Journal*, 22 (1913), pp. 182–93

Brown, R.A. and Colvin, H.M., *The History of the King's Works volume II: The Middle Ages (Part 2)*, London, 1963

Brown, R.A., 'A List of Castles, 1154–1216', *English Historical Review*, 74 (1959), pp. 249–280

Brown, R.A., *English Castles*, London, 1976

Bond, E.A., 'Notices of the last days of Isabella, Queen of Edward the Second, drawn from an account of the Expenses of her Household', *Archaeologica*, 34 (1853), pp. 453–469

Bond, S., 'The Medieval Constables of Windsor Castle', *English Historical Review*, 323 (1967), pp. 225–249

Burley, S.J., 'The Provisioning of Calais, 1347–1365', unpublished M.A. thesis, Leeds, 1951

Butler, L., 'Dolforwyn Castle, Montgomery, Powis', *Arch. Cambrensis*, 144 (1995), pp. 133–203

Carpenter, C., 'The Fifteenth-Century English Gentry and their Estates', in M. Jones, ed., *Gentry and Nobility in late Medieval Europe*, Gloucester, 1986

Carpenter, C., 'Gentry and Community in Medieval England', *Journal of British Studies*, 33 (1994), pp. 340–380

Clay, J.W., *The Extinct and Dormant Peerages of the Northern Counties of England*, London, 1913

The Complete Peerage, ed. Cokayne, G.E., revised by V. Gibbs, H.A. Doubleday, and H.A. Walden, 12 vols. in 13, London, 1910–1957

Coss, P., *The Knight in Medieval England, 1000–1400*, Stroud, 1993

Coulson, C., 'Structural Symbolism in Medieval Castle Architecture', *Journal of the British Archaeological Association*, 132 (1979), pp. 73–90

Coulson, C., 'Some Analysis of the Castle of Bodiam', *Medieval Knighthood IV*, Woodbridge, 1992, pp. 51–108

Coulson, C., 'Freedom to Crenellate by Licence: An Historiographical Revision', *Nottingham Medieval Studies*, 38 (1994), pp. 86–137

Coulson, C., 'Community and Fortress – Politics in France in the Lull Before the Hundred Years War in English Perspective', *Nottingham Medieval Studies*, 15 (1996), pp. 80–18

Coulson, C., 'Valois Powers over Fortresses on the Eve of the Hundred Years War', in M. Strickland, ed., *Armies, Chivalry and Warfare in Medieval Britain and France*, Stamford, 1998

Curwen, J.F., 'Kendal Castle', *C.& W.A.& A.S.*, New Series, 8 (1909), pp. 84–94

Davies, J.C., 'The Despenser war in Glamorgan', *Transactions of the Royal Historical Society*, 3rd series, 9 (1915), pp. 21–64

Davies, R.R., *Lordship and society in the March of Wales, 1282–1400*, Oxford, 1978

Davies, R.R., *The Revolt of Owain Glyn Dwr*, Oxford, 1995

Denholm-Young, N., *Seignoral Administration in England*, London, 1937, reprinted 1963

Dixon, P. and Marshall, P., 'The Great Tower in the Twelfth Century: The Case of Norham', *The Archaeological Journal*, 150 (1993), pp. 410–32

Dobson, B., 'The Church of Durham and the Scottish borders, 1378–88', in A. Goodman, and A. Tuck, eds., *War and Border Societies in the Middle Ages*, London, 1992

Dudley, G.C.E. and Robinson, C.J., *A History of the Castles, Mansions and Manors of West Sussex*, London, 1879

Duls, L.D., *Richard II in the Early Chronicles*, The Hague, 1975

Emery, A., *Greater Medieval Houses of England and Wales, 1300–1500, vol. I: Northern England*, Cambridge, 1996

Emery, A., *Greater Medieval Houses of England and Wales, 1300–1500, vol. II: East Anglia, Central England and Wales*, Cambridge, 1999

Fairclough, G., 'Edlingham Castle, Northumberland', *Transactions of the Ancient Monuments Society*, New Series, 28, pp. 40–60

Fairclough, G., 'Edlingham Castle: the military and domestic development of a Northumbrian Manor: Excavations 1978–80: Interim Report', *Château-Gaillard*, 9–10 (1982), pp. 373–387

Faull, M.L. and Moorhouse, A., *West Yorkshire: An Archaeological Survey to AD 1500*, 3 vols., Wakefield, 1981

Fry, P.S., *Castles of Britain and Ireland*, Newton Abbot, 1996
Fryde, E.B., *Peasants and Landlords in Later Medieval England, c.1380–c.1525*, Stroud and New York, 1996
Fügedi, Erik, 'Castles and Society in Medieval Hungary (1000–1437)', in *Studia Historica, Academiae Sientiarium Hungaricae*, 187 (1986)
Gibson, J., 'Featherston Castle', *Arch. Ael.*, 4th series, 2 (1926), pp. 125–131
Given-Wilson, C., *The Royal Household and the King's Affinity*, New Haven and London, 1986
Given-Wilson, C. 'Wealth and Credit, Public and Private, the earls of Arundel 1306–1397', *EHR*, 106 (1991), pp. 1–26
Given-Wilson, C. 'Richard II and the Lancastrian inheritance', *EHR*, 109 (1994), pp. 553–71
Goodman, A., *The Loyal Conspiracy*, London, 1971
Goodman, A., *John of Gaunt: The Exercise of Princely Power in Fourteenth-Century Europe*, Harlow, 1992
Goodman, A. and Tuck, A., eds., *War and Border Societies in the Middle Ages*, London, 1992
Goodman, A., 'The Defence of Northumberland; a Preliminary Survey', in M. Strickland, ed., *Armies, Chivalry and Warfare in Medieval Britain and France*, Stamford, 1998, pp. 161–172
Griffiths, R.A., *The Principality of Wales in the Later Middle Ages: The Structure and Personnel of Government, I. South Wales, 1277–1536*, Cardiff, 1972
Haines, R.M., *The Church and Politics in Fourteenth Century England – the career of Adam Orleton c.1275–1345*, Cambridge, 1978
Hajdu, R., 'Castles, Castellans and the structure of politics in Poiteur, 1152–1272', *Journal of Medieval Studies*, 4 (1978), pp. 27–53
Hamilton, J.S., *Piers Gaveston, Earl of Cornwall 1307–12*, Detroit, 1988
Harris, G.L., *King, Parliament and Public Finance in Medieval England to 1369*, Oxford, 1975
Hatcher, J., *Rural Economy and Society in the Duchy of Cornwall, 1300–1500*, Cambridge, 1973
Hewitt, H.J., 'Mediaeval Cheshire', *Chetham Society*, New Series, 88 (1929)
Hewitt, H.J., *The Organisation of War under Edward III, 1338–1362*, Manchester, 1966
Hislop, M.J.B., 'John of Gaunt's building works at Dunstanburgh Castle', *Archaeologia Aeliana*, 5th series, 23 (1995), pp. 139–144
Hislop, M.J.B., 'Lumley Castle, its Antecedents and its Architect', *Archaeologia Aeliana*, 5th series, 24 (1996), pp. 93–98
History of Northumberland, vol. 11, Vickers, K.H., ed., London and Newcastle, 1922
Howell, M., 'Notes and Documents: The Resources of Eleanor of Provence as Queen Consort', *EHR*, 102 (1987), pp. 372–393
Hunnisett, R.F., 'The Reliability of Inquisitions as Historical Evidence', in D.A. Bullough and R.L. Storey, eds., *The Study of Medieval Records*, Oxford, 1971

Hunter Blair, C.H., 'Mitford Castle', *Arch. Aeliana*, 4th series, 14 (1937), pp. 74–94
Hunter Blair, C.H., 'The Early Castles of Northumberland'. *Arch. Aeliana*, 4th series, 22 (1944), p. 116–170
Hurst, D.G., 'Medieval Britain in 1961', *Medieval Archaeology*, 6–7 (1962–3), pp. 336–337
Hutchinson, W., *The History of the County Palatine of Durham, vol. 3*, Durham, 1823
I'Anson, W.M., 'Kilton Castle', *Yorkshire Archaeological Journal*, 22 (1913), pp. 55–125
I'Anson, W.M., 'The Castles of the North Riding', *Yorkshire Archaeological Journal*, 22 (1913), pp. 303–399
I'Anson, W.W., 'Helmsley Castle', *Yorkshire Archaeological Journal*, 24 (1917), pp. 325–368
Jones, M., ed., *Gentry and Nobility in late Medieval Europe*, Gloucester, 1986
Kenyon, J.R., *Castles, town defences, and artillery fortifications in Britain and Ireland: a bibliography*, vol. 3, London, 1990
Kenyon, J.R., *Medieval Fortifications*, London, 1990
King, D.J.C., *Castellarium Anglicanum*, 2 vols., New York, 1983
Labarge, M.W., *A Baronial Household of the Thirteenth Century*, Trowbridge, 1965
Lewis, S., *A Topographical Dictionary of England*, 4 vols., London, 1862
Lyon, B., *A Constitutional and Legal History of Medieval England*, New York, 1960
Maddicott, J.R., *Thomas of Lancaster, 1307–1322*, Oxford, 1970
May, T., 'The Cobham Family in the Administration of England, 1200–1300', *Archaeologia Cantiana*, 132 (1967), pp. 1–31
Meisel, J., *Barons of the Welsh Frontier: The Corbet, Pantulf, and Fitz Warin Families, 1066–1272*, Lincoln and London, 1944
Menache, S., 'Isabella of France, queen of England – a reconsideration', *Journal of Medieval History*, 10 (1984), pp. 107–124
Mertes, K., *The English Noble Household 1250–1600, Good Governance and Politic Rule*, Oxford, 1988
Morgan, D.A.L., 'The Individual Style of the English Gentlemen', in M. Jones, ed., *Gentry and Nobility in late Medieval Europe*, Gloucester, 1986, pp. 15–35
Morley, B., 'Hylton Castle', *The Archaeological Journal*, 133 (1976), pp. 118–134
Morris, J.E., *The Welsh Wars of Edward I*, Oxford, 1901
Morris, J.E., 'Cumberland and Westmorland Military Levies in the time of Edward I and Edward II', *Transactions of the C.&W.A.&A.S.*, New Series, 111 (1903), pp. 307–327
Morris, W.A., *The Medieval English Sheriff to 1300*, Manchester, 1927
National Register of Archives report 12614 – Records of the earls of Arundel at Arundel Castle

National Register of Archives report 21647 – Berkeley Castle Lists
Newman, J., *The Buildings of England – North East and East Kent*, Harmondsworth, 1976
Newman, J., *The Buildings of England – West Kent and the Weald*, Harmondsworth ,1976
Ormerod, G., *History of the County Palatine and City of Chester*, 2nd edition, London, 1882
Painter, S., *Studies in the history of the English Feudal Barony*, Baltimore, 1943
Palmer, R.C., *The County Court*, Princeton, 1982
Parker, J., 'Some notes on the lords of Harewood Castles', *Yorkshire Archaeological Journal*, 22 (1912), pp. 150–158
Parsons, J.C., *The Court and Household of Eleanor of Castile in 1290*, Toronto, 1977
Parsons, J.C., *Eleanor of Castile, Queen and Society in Thirteenth-Century England*, London, 1994
Patourel, J. le, *The Moated Sites of Yorkshire*, London, 1973
Penn, S.A.C., 'A hidden workforce: building workers in 14th century Bristol', *Transactions of the Bristol and Gloucestershire Archaeological Society*, 109 (1991), pp. 171–178
Pevsner, N., *The Buildings of England – Cambridge*, Harmondsworth, 1954
Pevsner, N., *The Buildings of England – Cornwall (South)*, Harmondsworth, 1952
Pevsner, N., *The Buildings of England – Cumberland*, Harmondsworth, 1967
Pevsner, N., *The Buildings of England – Durham*, London, 1953
Pevsner, N., *The Buildings of England – Shropshire*, Harmondsworth, 1958
Pevsner, N., *The Buildings of England – Worcestershire*, Harmondsworth, 1968
Pevsner, N. and Hubbard, E., *The Buildings of England – Cheshire*, Harmondsworth, 1971
Pevsner, N. and Lloyd, D., *The Buildings of England – Hampshire and the Isle of Wight*, Harmondsworth, 1973
Pevsner, N., Nairn, I., and Cherry, B., *The Buildings of England – Surrey*, Harmondsworth, 1970
Pevsner, N. and Radcliffe, E., *The Buildings of England – Suffolk*, Harmondsworth, 1974
Phillips, J.R.S., *Aymer de Valence, Earl of Pembroke 1307–1324: Baronial Politics in the Reign of Edward II*, Oxford, 1972
Platt, C., *The Castle in Medieval England and Wales*, London, 1981
Pounds, N.J.G., *The Medieval Castle in England and Wales, A Social and Political History*, Cambridge, 1990
Prestwich, M., *The Three Edwards, War and State in England 1272–1377*, London, 1980
Prestwich, M., 'English castles in the reign of Edward II', *Journal of Medieval History*, 8 (1982), pp. 159–178
Prestwich, M., *Edward I*, London, 1988

Prestwich, M., *Armies and Warfare in the Middle Ages: The English Experience*, London, 1996
PRO Lists and Indexes, vol. 9: List of Sheriffs for England and Wales, London, 1898
PRO Lists and Indexes, vol. 15: Ancient Correspondence, Kraus Edition, New York, 1968
Pugh, T.B., ed., *Glamorgan County History, vol. 3: The Middle Ages*, Cardiff, 1971
Raimes, A.L., 'Shortflatt Tower and its owners', *Archaeological Aeliana*, 4th series, 32 (1954), pp. 126–159
Robertson, W.A.S., 'Coulyng Castle', *Archaeologia Cantiana*, 11 (1877), pp. 128–144
Roskell, J.S., Clark, L. and Rawcliffe, C., *The History of Parliament: The House of Commons 1386–1421*, 4 vols., Far Thrupp, 1993
Royal Commission on Historical Monuments: Dorset
Royal Commission on Historical Monuments: Glamorgan
Royal Commission on Historical Monuments: Hereford
Royal Commission on Historical Monuments: Hertfordshire
Royal Commission on Historical Monuments: Huntingdon
Royal Commission on Historical Monuments: Pembroke
Royal Commission on Historical Monuments: Westmorland
Ryder, P.F., 'Ravensworth Castle, North Yorkshire', *Yorkshire Archaeological Journal*, 51 (1979), pp. 81–100
Ryder, P.F. and Coleman, S., 'Paull Holme Tower', *The East Riding Archaeological Society*, 7 (1983), p. 85
Saul, N., 'The Despensers and the downfall of Edward II', *EHR*, 99 (1984), pp. 1–33
Saul, N., *Scenes from Provincial Life, Knightly Families in Sussex 1280–1400*, Oxford, 1986
Saul, N., 'Conflict and Crisis in English Local Society', in J. Taylor and W. Childs, eds. *Politics and Crisis in fourteenth-century England*, Gloucester, 1990
Saunders, A.D. and Pugh, R.B. *Old Wardour Castle (Wiltshire)*, London, 1968
Shenton, Caroline, 'The English Court and the Restoration of Royal Prestige, 1327–1345', Oxford D.Phil. thesis, 1995
Sherbourne, J., 'The Defence of the Realm and the Impeachment of Michael de la Pole in 1386', in J. Taylor, and W. Childs, *Politics and Crisis in fourteenth-century England*, Gloucester, 1990, pp. 97–116
Simpson, W.D., 'Dunstanburgh Castle', *Archaeologia Aeliana*, 4th series, 16 (1939), pp. 31–42
Simpson, W.D., 'Further note on Dunstanburgh Castle', *Archaeologia Aeliana*, 4th series, 27 (1949), pp. 1–28
Smith, B., 'A County Community in Early Fourteenth Century Ireland: The case of Louth', *EHR*, 103 (1993), pp. 561–88

Smith, D.M., *Guide to Bishop's Registers of England and Wales*, London, 1981

Somerville, R., *Duchy of Lancaster: Vol. 1, 1265–1603*, London, 1953

Spurgeon, C.J., 'St. Donat's Castle – A recent revised interpretation by the R.C.A.H.M. Wales', *The Archaeological Journal*, 150 (1993), pp. 498–502

Stenton, F.M., *The First Century of English Feudalism, 1066–1166*, Oxford, 1932

Stratford, J., *The Bedford Inventories*, London, 1993

Summerson, H., 'Responses to War: Carlisle and the West March in the late fourteenth century', in A. Goodman, and A. Tuck, eds., *War and Border Societies in the Middle Ages*, London, 1992

Sylvester, D., *A History of Cheshire*, Henley on Thames, 1971

Thompson, M.W., 'An alert in 1318 to the constable of Bolingbrook Castle, Lincs', *Medieval Archaeology*, 9 (1965), pp. 167–168

Thompson, M.W., *The Decline of the Castle*, Cambridge, 1987

Thompson, M.W., *The Rise of the Castle*, Cambridge, 1990

Timbs, J. and Gunn, A., *Abbeys, Castles and Ancient Halls of England and Wales*, 3 vols., London, 1872

Tout, T.F., *The Place of the Reign of Edward II in English History*, Manchester, 1914

Tuck, A., *Richard II and the English Nobility*, London, 1973

Tuck, A., 'The Percies and the Community of Northumberland in the late fourteenth century', in A. Goodman and A. Tuck, eds., *War and Border societies in the middle ages*, London, 1992, pp. 178–195

Turvey, R.K., 'The Marcher Shire of Pembroke and the Glyndwr rebellion', *Welsh History Review*, 15 (1990), pp. 151–168

Vale, M.G.A., 'Seigneurial fortification and Private War in late Medieval Gascony', in M. Jones, ed., *Gentry and Nobility in late Medieval Europe*, Gloucester, 1986, pp.133–58

Verduyn, A., 'The Politics of Law and Order during the Early Years of Edward III', *EHR*, 108 (1993), pp. 842–867

Verey, D., *The Buildings of England – Gloucestershire 1: The Cotswolds*, Harmondsworth, 1970

Verey, D., *The Buildings of England – Gloucestershire 2: Vale and forest of Dean*, Harmondsworth, 1970

Victoria County History of the counties of England: Cambridge, vol. 2

Victoria County History of the counties of England: Cumberland, vol. 2

Victoria County History of the counties of England: Lancashire, vol. 3

Victoria County History of the counties of England: Lancashire, vol. 4

Victoria County History of the counties of England: Lancashire, vol. 8

Victoria County History of the counties of England: Northamptonshire, vol. 2

Victoria County History of the counties of England: Northamptonshire, vol. 4

Victoria County History of the counties of England: Oxfordshire, vol. 2

Victoria County History of the counties of England: Oxfordshire, vol. 9

Victoria County History of the counties of England: Yorkshire, vol. 2

Victoria County History of the counties of England: Yorkshire, North Riding, vol. 2
Walker, J.K., 'Almondbury in Feudal Times', *Yorkshire Arch. Journal*, 2 (1873), pp. 1–34
Ward, J.C., *English Noblewomen in the Later Middle Ages*, London, 1992
Ward, J.C., *Women of the English Nobility and Gentry 1066–1500*, Manchester, 1995
Waugh, S.L., *The Lordship of England, Royal Wardships and Marriages in English Society and Politics, 1217–1327*, Princeton, 1988
Wood, M.E., 'The Bishop's Palace, Wells', *Archaeological Journal*, 107 (1950), pp. 108–110
Wood, M., *The English Mediaeval House*, London, 1965
Woolgar, C.M., *The Great Household in Late Medieval England*, London, 1999

Castle Index

Person Index

Subject Index